Financial support for editing this volume has been provided by a special grant from the National Historical Publications Commission to the Wyoming Historical and Geological Society, Wilkes-Barre, Pennsylvania.

Timothy Pickering (1745-1828), by Charles B. J. F. de St. Memin, reproduced by permission of the Museum of Fine Arts, Boston, Frederick Brown Fund.

Sheldon Reynolds Memorial F

The
Susquehannah Coi
Papers

VOLUME IX: 1787-1788

EDITED BY

ROBERT J. TAYLOR

PUBLISHED FOR

Wyoming Historical & Geological Society

WILKES-BARRE, PA.

Cornell University Press

ITHACA and LONDON

TABLE OF CONTENTS

LIST OF DOCUMENTS

xii

APPENDIX

ILLUSTRATIONS

INTRODUCTION

The years 1787 and 1788 saw the Connecticut settlers along the Susquehanna River become more sharply divided than ever into two hostile factions. The clash of Yankee "intruders" and Pennamite "outsiders" gave way to a more personal, more ugly struggle between leaders at Wyoming, each seeking to win the minds and active support of the settlers. And the settlers got many an opportunity to declare themselves, for there were oaths and other testimonies of loyalty to support or refuse, petitions to sign or ignore.

In 1786, William Hooker Smith had tried to oppose the leadership of John Franklin, but he was overmatched and easily driven out. In 1787 and 1788, Franklin's opponent became Timothy Pickering, a far different sort of man—intelligent, articulate, fair-minded, and influential in Philadelphia. That Franklin's supporters resorted to such low tricks as terrifying Pickering's wife and holding Pickering himself hostage suggests the measure of their desperation.

Although a New England man, Pickering came as an outsider, for he was no member of the Susquehannah Company; but he was determined to put himself on the same footing with the Connecticut claimants by holding lands at Wyoming under a Connecticut title. Thus he sought to demonstrate his faith in the state's willingness to deal justly at last with those who had built their homes on land once claimed as part of Connecticut. Pickering came to Wilkes-Barre as clerk of the several courts to be established for the newly created Luzerne County, and he came with the special mission of persuading the settlers to participate in elections for state and county officers. Participation meant formally swearing allegiance to the state and giving up the extralegal arrangements that had in one form or another served for local government ever since Connecticut's authority had been denied at Trenton in 1782. More particularly, accepting Pickering's lead meant rejecting the rulings of the local committee of the Susquehannah Company and its spokesman, John Franklin. The inducement that Pickering offered was the real possibility of state confirmation of titles to lands in the seventeen towns, where most of the Connecticut people had congregated.

Confirmation is the theme of these years. The General Assembly passed, amended, and finally suspended a confirming law; it also approved for publication a substitute measure. Pickering himself spent long hours choosing for a proposed bill the exact language that would satisfy the reasonable hopes of those who had faced every adversity at Wyoming, but that would deny encouragement to mere adventurers. Always there was the pressure from disappointed Pennsylvania claimants to ease and from Company adherents to resist. The maneuvering took place against the background of Shays' Rebellion in Massachusetts; more than one observer believed that missteps could bring rebellion in Luzerne or make that county into a natural refuge for Shaysites. The cry went up that frustrated Company men intended to separate the county from Pennsylvania as a nucleus for a new state, to be called Westmoreland. As a result John Franklin landed in jail on charges of high treason, and Timothy Pickering was kept chained in the woods for days, his life threatened if harm came to Franklin. Like Massachusetts, Pennsylvania sought help from the Continental Congress to deal with her internal disturbances. But the charges against Franklin eventually came to nought, and Pickering grew bitter over the vacillations of the state.

II

Pickering arrived in Wilkes-Barre on January 8 to begin the work of persuading the Connecticut claimants to accept their status as residents of a Pennsylvania county and to elect a representative, a councilor, and commissioners, as well as candidates for coroner and sheriff. Staying at the home of Mathias Hollenback, he welcomed visits from a number of the leaders of the Connecticut people. He also drafted and sent to key men in outlying areas a long letter which set forth rational arguments for the acceptance of Pennsylvania law.[1] He traveled to settlements near Wilkes-Barre to meet with the people informally and in specially called meetings. He eased their fears, answered patiently and carefully all their questions. As he went from house to house, Pickering found a warm-hearted curiosity about himself and his mission, an interest that was returned. Pickering happily noted in his journal the signs of industry he found and the kindnesses he was offered.

From the people he learned of their concern that acceptance

---

[1] No. 3.

of the new status would permit Pennamites to clog the county courts with suits of ejectment. They were apprehensive, too, that holding a Connecticut title would not qualify one for freemanship and that Connecticut people would be helpless in the hands of Pennamite voters. Almost as bad, they feared that confirmation of titles would mean heavy back taxes to pay. Several claimed that the decision at Trenton had been corrupt and would be set aside, but Pickering was satisfied that this was a vain hope, that any recognition of Connecticut titles would have to come from Pennsylvania's General Assembly. He made it plain from the start that although he was certain from his conversations with government officeholders in Philadelphia that confirmation of land titles would be forthcoming, any hope that the entire Susquehannah Company purchase would be confirmed was a foolish one. He took comfort in the apparent willingness of most settlers to seek no more than a legal title for their own farms, and he scored with many listeners when he announced that he himself would hold no land at Wyoming except under a Connecticut title, which he planned to purchase.[2]

Since his appeals to the people were persuasive with many, the election took place on February 1 without serious incidents, over two hundred men going to the polls. By a larger majority than that of any other successful candidate, John Franklin was chosen as the county's representative in the General Assembly.[3] In deciding thus to be a part of Pennsylvania, those voting ignored the advice that came from partisans in Connecticut. William Judd had written to Zebulon Butler that acceptance of Pennsylvania law would put their lands "all at Hazard," and he held out the prospect of four hundred new men who could be sent on in the spring to fill up the purchase and augment the strength of the Connecticut people. In his view the central government was "upon its last Leggs and you may stand an Equal chance with the rest of mankind if you are firm Steady and United."[4] Timothy Hosmer also wrote from Connecticut to say that whichever way Shays' Rebellion went, the people on the Susquehanna would benefit. If the Massachusetts regulators lost, they would probably seek refuge among the Connecticut settlers; if they won, the feeble central government would collapse and the ensuing monarchy would annihilate state lines. Hosmer declared that the change would mean "a Tryal before majesty which I had rather Submit to Tho. it were a Nero or a Caligula Than to the Land Jobing Jockying State of Pennsylva-

[2] No. 18, pp. 33-37, 45-49.   [3] No. 13.   [4] No. 4.

nia." [5] Hosmer and Judd, as well as Franklin and others, were newly named commissioners of the Susquehannah Company, empowered to determine land titles in accordance with the records of the Company. To the later disgust of Judd, Zebulon Butler read Judd's letter to a public meeting in Wilkes-Barre.[6]

A fews days after the election some of the Connecticut settlers with the help of Pickering drew up a petition asking the General Assembly for confirmation of their lands. What they asked for was the original seventeen towns, the township of Athens, and certain "detached lots capable of cultivation between the townships"—all assigned to individuals before the Trenton decree. The names of only one hundred and thirty signers have come down to us, the list lacking the names of such prominent settlers as Zebulon Butler, Obadiah Gore, and Nathan Denison, although these men, according to Pickering, helped to draft the petition. Also notably absent from the list of signers are the names of partisans of John Franklin.[7]

Soon after Pickering returned to Philadelphia on February 8, John Franklin returned to Wyoming from Connecticut, bearing the latest resolves of the Susquehannah Company. The political atmosphere at Wyoming began to change almost at once. According to Dr. Joseph Sprague, supporters of Franklin set about burning copies of the petition being circulated; and while some were resentful of such behavior, many seemed to be undergoing a change of heart.[8] Franklin wrote to the Speaker of the General Assembly to explain that he could not attend the session because he had only just returned home after an absence of two months.[9] But according to Sprague and William Hooker Smith,[10] the extremists at Wyoming had deliberately voted for Franklin in the knowledge that he would not serve and had expected that Nathan Denison, who was elected councilor, would not be able to serve. Their accusations may be correct, but Franklin's total vote shows that he got the support of many moderates as well as extremists. For most of the Wyoming settlers, he was their trusted leader.

Franklin's refusal to take his seat made political difficulties for the backers of the petition, for his absence dramatized the opposition of some to the petition and to the jurisdiction of Pennsylvania. Denison, in pleading to have Franklin come to Philadelphia, showed himself to be unaware of a plot by Franklin's partisans to undermine Pickering's work. Denison sought

[5] No. 14.   [6] No. 18, p. 50.
[7] Nos. 16 and 18, entry for February 5.   [8] No. 22.   [9] No. 26.
[10] No. 23.

to explain to the Assembly why many had not signed the petition, and he worked with the Assembly committee, as did Pickering, to get as favorable a report as possible.[11] Their task was not an easy one. The irritation of Assembly members with the apparent bad faith of the Connecticut settlers colored the tone of the report. For example, the committee noted that John Franklin and John Jenkins, as duly accredited agents of the settlers, had months before promised that when claims were made they would be individual ones, not the collectively made one of the petition. The committee also expressed its resentment of the recent resolve of the Susquehannah Company, which provided for land distribution as though the government of Pennsylvania did not even exist. Nevertheless, the committee, conceding the petition was a sign of submission, however unsatisfying, recommended confirmation of titles to land settled by Connecticut people and compensation to disappointed Pennsylvania claimants.[12] Its report won acceptance.

The actual drafting of a confirming law provoked a debate over the constitutional rights of the Assembly and of the Supreme Executive Council. George Clymer, a leading Republican, moved that the Assembly choose the three men to act as commissioners for examining land claims, leaving to the Council only the right to fill vacancies in the commission. The passage of the motion caused seventeen Assembly members, virtually all of them Constitutionalists, to enter a formal dissent, claiming this method of appointment violated the Constitution.[13] In the Council where the appointing power supposedly belonged, the Constitutionalists had the majority which they lacked in the Assembly.

The Confirming Act itself, passed March 28, 1787, recognized the right of Connecticut people and their heirs to lots "occupied or acquired" by actual settlers and assigned to them prior to the Trenton decree. To establish their titles settlers had to present their claims to the commissioners within eight months of the passage of the law. Named commissioners were Peter Muhlenberg, Timothy Pickering, and Joseph Montgomery. Those Pennsylvania claimants who would be deprived of lands by operation of the law were to have compensation in the form of equivalent grants of land elsewhere.[14]

Not unnaturally, Pickering was pleased with the Confirming Act, which he asserted went beyond the expectations of Con-

---

[11] Nos. 29 and 30.   [12] No. 31.   [13] Nos. 37 and 39.
[14] No. 38.

necticut delegates to the Continental Congress, and which he affirmed would satisfy "all indeed who had any right to expect a confirmation of their titles." [15] But he underestimated the opposition. Two tests of the settlers' loyalty to Pennsylvania and to the state's proposed solution of the Connecticut claims lay ahead: the elections for justice of the peace in each of the three judicial districts of the county and the reception that would be given to the work of the commissioners of the Susquehannah Company.

Elections for justices had not been held in February, probably for sound tactical reasons. That is, it had seemed best not to choose judicial officers until after the Assembly had clarified what would be done about land titles.[16] Originally Pickering and Zebulon Butler had set election day as April 19, but only in the third district did the election actually take place on that day. In the first district, which included Wilkes-Barre, Christopher Hurlbut, who was judge of the election for that district, had delayed posting the notice, probably deliberately, causing Pickering, who had returned to Wilkes-Barre about April 12, and Butler to order postponement until April 26.[17]

While these maneuvers were going on, a bombastic address to the settlers, written by William Judd, arrived at Wyoming. Reminding them of past sufferings and promising that "hundreds and hundreds of your Company friends are preparing to emigrate to you," Judd cautioned the Connecticut claimants against accepting Pennsylvania law before their property was secured and warned them that Pickering was an "artful man and made use of (being of New-England extract) to deceive" them.[18] In the second district, on April 19, John Franklin harangued the voters at Forty Fort, apparently in Pickering's presence; and while most of what he said was directed against the Confirming Act, he did charge that the whole election could be easily invalidated if a vote were accepted from someone who was not deemed a freeholder.[19] An attempt to hold the election in the second district as scheduled emboldened the extremists twice to carry off James Sutton, judge of the election. When fighting broke out, the election was postponed until May 3.[20] Meanwhile those supporting

[15] Nos. 41 and 46.

[16] In 1790 in rebutting testimony offered before an Assembly committee, Pickering asserted that elections for justices were postponed "till y* confirming law sh⁴ pass"; M. H. S., Pickering Papers, LVIII, 225, in Vol. X. See also the reason given in Pickering's journal; no. 18, entry for January 28. [17] Nos. 47 and 48. [18] No. 49. [19] No. 52. [20] No. 71.

Pickering mounted a campaign to get signatures on a statement favoring an election of justices.[21] Increasingly, the settlers were pressured to take a stand publicly with either Pickering or Franklin.

All the time that the two factions were testing each other on the elections issue, the Susquehannah Company commissioners had been meeting at intervals to determine land titles according to Company records. Because these meetings had begun before the Assembly had had time to respond to the settlers' petition by passing a confirming law, Pickering had condemned the commissioners for their impatience and bad faith; but even some of Pickering's supporters thought it prudent to work with the Company's commissioners. As their secretary, they had chosen Lord Butler, who had recently received the highest number of votes as candidate for sheriff. His father, Zebulon, who acted with Pickering in setting county election dates, sat as one of their number. The first case the commissioners heard was brought by Mathias Hollenback, at whose home Pickering had lived. Obviously there was more impatience at Wyoming than Pickering dreamed of.[22]

But the successful holding of the election in the first district and the arrival of Lord Butler's commission as sheriff caused the two Butler men to stop their activities in behalf of the Company. Their wavering and the prospective disaffection of other prominent men led Franklin on April 29 to write gloomily to Joseph Hamilton of New York about self-seeking and ingratitude.[23] Apparently it was time to consolidate the opposition to Pickering and Pennsylvania, for within a few days eighty men had signed a statement naming Franklin as their agent to appear before Congress, the Connecticut General Assembly, and the Susquehannah Company in an effort to get the Trenton decision reversed or to get a new trial for determining the private right of soil. Virtually none of these signers had earlier put their names to the petition asking Pennsylvania to confirm rights to lands.[24]

In a petition to the Connecticut General Assembly dated May 10, Franklin, speaking for the settlers, asked Connecticut to urge Congress "to direct a Revision" of the Trenton decree.[25] Accepting at face value the various charges of fraud in connection with the Trenton trial made by the Franklin petition, the lower house asserted that the long-disputed territory was in fact part of Connecticut and called for an accommodation between Connect-

---

[21] No. 55.   [22] Nos. 68 and 41.   [23] No. 65.   [24] No. 69.
[25] No. 75.

icut and Pennsylvania either through Congress or directly; but the upper house firmly refused to reopen the whole question.[26] The Pennsylvania Council, perhaps because of Pickering's urging, had forwarded a copy of the Confirming Act to Connecticut, as had Connecticut's delegates in Congress.[27] Undoubtedly the provisions of this law seemed sufficient to many Connecticut leaders who had long wanted to wash their hands of a troublesome problem. Subsequently Jeremiah Wadsworth wrote to Pickering to assure him that the Connecticut legislature would never fall in with Franklin's scheme.[28] A meeting of the Susquehannah Company commissioners in Hartford, on May 14, however, authorized Franklin to act as the Company's agent before Congress to try to get the private right of soil settled, but no appeal was made. Franklin was also authorized to act alone in any business that would benefit the Company.[29]

If all was not going well for Franklin, Pickering, too, had cause for disappointment. Although he was pleased to announce the peaceable opening of the Luzerne County courts in May, implementation of the Confirming Act lagged alarmingly. He and the other commissioners who were to review the claims of the Connecticut settlers were not able even to get to Wyoming until May 28, the very day their work was to have begun (Pickering had returned to Philadelphia on May 9).[30] Once there, they found themselves confronted with a petition calling for the removal of one of their number, Joseph Montgomery, on the grounds that he had been hostile to the Connecticut people in the past.[31] Montgomery's resignation from this post was accepted by the Council on May 31. Actually this was the second resignation; Peter Muhlenberg had resigned on May 17. The man who took his place, Daniel Hiester, resigned on July 19.[32] Obviously these resignations caused delays in the commission's getting down to work and bred a suspicion among the Connecticut people that state leaders still had no real intention of doing them justice. Pickering, who had staked a good deal on the Confirming Act, worried over the news from his business partner, Samuel Hodgdon, that the resignations of Muhlenberg and Hiester were a delaying tactic to hold up operation of the law until the Pennsylvania General Assembly could meet once again and reconsider it.[33] The Council had already received remonstrances against the Confirming Act, and September would bring to the Assembly a

---

[26] No. 80.   [27] Nos. 38 and 50.   [28] No. 81.   [29] No. 76.
[30] Nos. 74 and 79.   [31] No. 78.   [32] No. 38, note 2.
[33] Nos. 90 and 91.

spate of such protests.[34] As it was, the state's commissioners were not able to start their work until after the middle of August, nearly three months after the date originally set. Even then Pickering had to send personal pleas to hurry on William Montgomery and arrange for his prompt swearing in as a substitute for Hiester.[35]

With the state's commission apparently dragging its feet, it was the easier for Franklin's party to keep alive the illusion that the country could be filled up with new settlements of half-share men.[36] The whole of the original Susquehannah Company purchase, he promised, would then have to be handed over to those who had worked and suffered for so long in its behalf. Functioning as a lone commissioner for the Company, Franklin authorized the taking up of land at "Hamilton," fifty miles west of Athens, and the commissioners proclaimed their intention to look into land titles in Newport.[37] In the area of Athens, Franklin and Jenkins kept busy surveying and selling off half-share rights at bargain rates, an activity that Pickering denounced as common cheating of deluded purchasers.[38] Franklin kept in close touch with Joseph Hamilton of Hudson, New York, one of the recently named commissioners of the Company, and one committed to sending onto the Company lands hundreds of settlers to fill up the purchase. Associated with Hamilton were Caleb Benton, Col. John McKinstry, and others.

In September, Hamilton felt the need to shore up what he sensed was the wavering resolution of John Franklin in opposing Pennsylvania law. He and his backers were growing weary of Franklin's willingness to tolerate the presence of the state's commissioners, who were implementing the Confirming Act, side by side with the Company's own commissioners. Franklin for his part believed the Hamilton group was growing discouraged, that it was holding back, but Hamilton explained that what was needed was solid evidence that Franklin and his supporters stood ready to use armed force to protect their lands from Pennsylvania: "no righteous wheel will move until you move and that in such manner as to make the world know you are in earnest, they all think you are jesting." [39]

---

[34] Nos. 35, 77, and 84.   [35] Nos. 95 and 96.

[36] It will be recalled that half-share men were those able-bodied males who had been encouraged by the Susquehannah Company to go to Pennsylvania to settle on the purchase in return for a half-share in the Company provided they remained three years. See Vol. VIII, no. 141.

[37] Nos. 86, 94, and 119.   [38] No. 118.   [39] Nos. 111, 112, and 113.

In Pickering's opinion Franklin did not dare risk force against the state's commissioners, for he knew well the settlers' great desire to have their work proceed. The state's commissioners began their work on August 21; and according to court testimony given in 1795 by Griffith Evans, secretary to the commission, "we had more than we could do—generally every day." To expedite matters the commissioners admitted and recorded all claims offered, postponing decision on their validity so as to bring in as many claims as possible.[40] Among those willing to submit to the commission's decision were Eliphalet Dyer, one of the Susquehannah Company's original members and one of its most faithful supporters, and Ebenezer Gray, son of the Company's long-serving secretary, Samuel Gray. Roger Sherman, who had performed many services for the Company in the past, wrote to Zebulon Butler expressing his hope that the Connecticut settlers would abide by the commission's rulings.[41]

Still, rumors persistently circulated that the work of the commissioners would be impeded, that they would be driven from the settlements. Pickering laughed at the stories and chafed his supporters for their credulity, but this was his public stance. At night he kept arms by his bed.[42] Franklin, however, chose a less direct path to his goal. He began a campaign against commissioner William Montgomery in the expectation that his resignation or recall could be achieved, just as an earlier protest had secured Joseph Montgomery's resignation. One hundred and forty-three Franklin partisans remonstrated against Montgomery's holding an office for which he was unsuitable by reason of his hostility to the Connecticut claims. The answer of the commissioners, temperate and to the point, emphasized that Montgomery's views of four years ago on the legality of Connecticut titles had no relevance now that the Confirming Act was operative. Their answer was drafted by Pickering; the remonstrance had been drafted by Franklin.[43]

Moderate and rational in their public statements, Pickering and the commissioners were quietly laying their plans to end Franklin's threatening maneuvers by having him jailed on serious charges. In what Pickering believed to be an excess of zeal, the county grand jury had already found two counts against Franklin for assault and battery and for theft of grain. Pickering saw here only a gesture that proved there were some in Wyoming

---

[40] No. 99 and Rawle's notes on the testimony of Evans in *Van Horne's Lessee* vs. *Dorrance*; Lackawanna Hist. Soc., Wilcox MSS., envelope 33.
[41] Nos. 98, 116, and 117.   [42] No. 99.   [43] Nos. 121 and 122.

whom Franklin could not intimidate.[44] But the commissioners had a trump card they could play. At the end of August they had received a warrant from the state for Franklin's arrest on the grounds that he perniciously and seditiously denied Pennsylvania's jurisdiction and encouraged resistance to government. The commissioners were given full discretion whether to use or suppress the warrant.[45]

Meanwhile evidence began to accumulate that Franklin was involved in even darker designs—no less than treason. On September 25 the state issued a public proclamation offering rewards for the apprehension of Franklin, John Jenkins, Zerah Beach, and John McKinstry.[46] Under a new state warrant charging misprision of treason, a small party led by Col. John Craig, which had been sent quietly to Wyoming, arrested John Franklin on October 2. Pickering secreted these men in his home and assisted them in subduing Franklin when he was seized.[47]

III

The charge of treason had its basis partly in recurrent stories that Franklin in association with several New Yorkers was planning to carve out of the Susquehannah purchase and lands in New York a separate state. This charge was not new in 1787; it had been originally made the preceding year, when Franklin was supposedly scheming to the same end with that notable separatist, Ethan Allen.[48] The question remains whether in Pennsylvania a movement analagous to those of Kentucky and the state of Franklin against Virginia and North Carolina was in the making.[49]

The earliest hint in 1787 that the Franklin faction sought some form of independence is found in a semiliterate letter from Dr. Joseph Sprague to Pickering, dated February 20. Sprague's

---

[44] No. 107.   [45] No. 101.   [46] No. 128.

[47] The state warrant has not been found; the charge of misprision of treason was changed to high treason after the commissioners were driven from Wyoming; no. 163. See also nos. 126, 128, note 3, and nos. 139, 142, and 150. For Pickering's part in Franklin's capture, see Pickering's petition of March 2, 1790, in Vol. X.

[48] See Vol. VIII, Introduction, pp. xxxvi-xxxvii.

[49] For an interpretation of the new state movement that differs markedly from that given here, see Julian P. Boyd, "Attempts to Form New States in New York and Pennsylvania, 1786-96," New York State Historical Association, *Quarterly Journal,* XII, 257-70 (July, 1931). I am much indebted to this article for information about speculative schemes in New York in this period.

letter was a gloss upon a letter from Dr. Timothy Hosmer to John Paul Schott, brought by Franklin into the settlements with other letters and papers upon his return to Wyoming from Connecticut. Where Hosmer had predicted, as has been mentioned, that the failure of Massachusetts to suppress the Shaysites would mean general anarchy, a disappearance of the central government, and a dissolving of state lines, Sprague construed his assertions to mean that the Wyoming settlers would have "the Sam Chanc for Indepandecy as any Body of men."[50] Independence, in short, would be possible in the general collapse of all government.

The first specific mention, in 1787, of Franklin's design to erect an independent state comes in a letter of August 9 from Pickering to Hodgdon, based on information supplied by Obadiah Gore. According to one gullible talebearer from New York, Franklin, in returning from Connecticut to Wyoming down the Susquehanna River, was boasting as he went through New York State that he had a commission from Connecticut's governor to erect a separate state in those parts. Pickering assumed that the center of activity of Franklin's partisans would be at Newtown, near the present-day site of Elmira, which he expected would be a refuge when Luzerne County would no longer tolerate their presence.[51]

The more particular scheme of independent statehood which would involve lands in both New York and Pennsylvania was first described in an anonymous letter sent to the Pennsylvania Council in mid-August. Pickering, informed either by the Council or relying upon local sources of information, confirmed the story in letters to Hodgdon.[52] But the plot now took on a more ominous twist, for allegedly the conspirators were seeking the aid of Great Britain in erecting their separate state. Franklin's involvement in such a plot was eventually assumed because he had connections with men like Caleb Benton, known to be active with other New Yorkers in the Lessee Company, a land company seeking separate statehood to get full title to lands illegally leased in western New York from Indians. It is worth noting, however, that the warrant of August 31 for Franklin's arrest, which was sent to the state's commissioners to be used at their discretion, did not mention separate statehood or treason. The Council's informant had apparently said nothing that incriminated Franklin directly.

[50] No. 22. Pickering did hear some young men speak out for independence a few weeks earlier; see no. 18, entry for January 26.
[51] No. 92.   [52] Nos. 97, 99, and 100.

Incrimination presumably came with two depositions taken before Obadiah Gore. One by Tunes Dolsan gave wholly hearsay testimony that Franklin's party intended to form a separate state; the other, by Thomas Wigton, described the plans of the plotters as armed resistance to the laws of Pennsylvania.[53] Although Ethan Allen was supposedly to be sent for, Wigton made no specific mention of separate statehood, and in contrast to Dolsan, most of what Wigton testified to, he claimed to have heard directly. Pickering sent these depositions to the Council, which in turn sent them on to Gov. George Clinton of New York. The Council urged the governor's cooperation and warned that the people gathered at Tioga (Athens) would probably receive reinforcements from Shays' disappointed followers.[54] Yet when Pickering wrote to Benjamin Rush on September 13, while he mentioned the gathering of Franklin and others at Tioga at the end of August, he did not even hint of their supposed plans for separate statehood or their possibly treasonable involvement in the New York separatist movement. Pickering charged them with selling off lands to which they had no right, an activity that had been going on openly for weeks.[55]

The state's proclamation for the arrest of Franklin, Zerah Beach, John McKinstry, and John Jenkins, given out on September 25, relied for its facts mainly on the testimony of Thomas Wigton. Wigton cited a notice signed by Franklin which has not been found, and which may have mentioned a separate state, although Wigton did not so describe it. John Shepard much later testified that it called upon people to choose a local committee to regulate town affairs.[56] Such local committees were quite in keeping with Company practice and did not, in the eyes of Connecticut settlers, imply separation, although Pennsylvania officials naturally looked upon them as a sign of independency. Franklin, as one ready to resort to armed force against the state, unwittingly completed the evidence against himself when he sent a written order to the half-share men to assemble with arms and oppose the militia of the "Pennsylvania Loyalists."[57] The state later offered this order as evidence when it indicted Franklin in 1788 for attempting to form a separate government.

Sometime in September, 1787, those in and around Tioga who still would not accept the Confirming Act signed an agreement that later came to be called the "Combination." It was meant formally to justify their conduct and to put on an equal footing

---

[53] Nos. 105 and 109.   [54] Nos. 106 and 125.   [55] No. 118.
[56] No. 320.   [57] No. 113.

the claims of actual settlers and those of absentee claimants associated with the settlers. The signers of the Combination argued, as of old, that the Company's right to the whole purchase was a valid one and that only a specially constituted court set up by Congress could legally rule on the validity of the title to the purchase. They solemnly asserted that they would claim no lands "under any other Title but that of the Susquehannah Company" and promised to defend their possessions "against all invaders." Here, then, was their justification for armed resistance. At the head of the list of sixty-seven signatures stood the names of McKinstry, Beach, and Benjamin Allen, all of them speculators and none of them residents.[58]

Talk of Franklin's plotting with others for separate statehood increased when letters to him from Joseph Hamilton were seized from messenger Asa Starkwather after Franklin himself had been arrested on October 2. In a letter of October 4, Pickering refers to Franklin's plan for a separate state as "pretty clearly seen & generally known"; and Hodgdon, writing from Philadelphia and describing the elation felt at Franklin's arrest, remarked that Franklin's "Plan for Independancy seems to lay heaviest against him." [59]   But John Swift, leader of those who drove Pickering and the other commissioners out of Wyoming after Franklin's arrest, wrote Pickering that "Upon my honour the Notion of Independancy was not in our heads, Neither was it (to my knowledge) Franklins object, at the time he was taken." [60] Swift tried to excuse the armed uprising he had led as the fruit of sudden passion and concern over Franklin's fate; the rioters disbursed the next day without having done harm to anyone, more than frightening Mrs. Pickering by threatening to carry her off to Tioga. Zebulon Butler and other responsible leaders requested of President Benjamin Franklin that the state's commissioners who had fled be sent back, and assured him that there was no danger, that cooperation would be forthcoming from every side.[61]

Pickering, no timid man, was all for going back to Wyoming even before troops could be sent to protect the commissioners. Once assured of the safety of his family, he saw no reason to delay his return, but those closest to him at Wyoming and in Philadelphia cautioned him to wait.[62]   In November, while he was still in Philadelphia, the Luzerne County voters chose him as their delegate to the Pennsylvania convention for ratifying the Constitution of the United States. In the words of Obadiah Gore

---

[58] No. 135.   [59] Nos. 136 and 139.   [60] Nos. 141 and 143.
[61] No. 144.   [62] Nos. 162 and 164.

to Pickering, "as Mr. Wm Stewart & Some Others were making an Interest among the opposers to Government [, their example] put us on the plan of runing one person only in our ticket and by that means you had it by a Great majority." [63]

Apparently there was no simple correlation between the position which one took upon the laws of Pennsylvania and that which one took upon the Constitution. Although Ebenezer Bowman, Pickering's assistant at Wyoming, wanted to keep from Wyoming settlers the knowledge that anyone at all opposed the Constitution (for fear that the settlers' habitual opposition to government would determine their attitude on the Constitution), he, too, admitted that Pickering, a known supporter of the Constitution, won election by a large majority. [64] Personalities rather than issues prevailed; many probably voted for Pickering out of sorrow for the treatment he had received. No one in the settlements seems to have associated a stronger central government with possible increased capacity of Pennsylvania or any other state to enforce the law within its borders.

Biding his time at Philadelphia, Pickering remained wholly unconvinced that an independent state was not the aim of the rioters, and in a letter to John Swift he ticked off the things that had been done, said, and written which he felt admitted of no other interpretation. The concerted plans for armed resistance made no sense otherwise. In his view, "All the writings of Hamilton, Judd & others clearly prove it, to those who have not been blinded by the lies & artifices of the leading conspirators." [65] But can one reasonably infer from the letters of Joseph Hamilton and Caleb Benton to John Franklin a design to erect an independent state?

Obviously absentee speculators were encouraging Franklin and his supporters forcibly to prevent the confirmation of titles to lands under Pennsylvania law; William Judd's address to the Wyoming settlers was no less clear in its intent than the letters of Hamilton and Benton. But none of the captured documents still extant refers to a separate state even by implication. [66] All that is said can be understood as a determination to obtain the whole

---

[63] No. 175.   [64] No. 177.

[65] No. 149. In writing to George Clymer, Pickering said that lands in New York combined with the Susquehannah purchase "were *probably* intended to form a New State"; no. 170, italics supplied.

[66] Pickering's interpretation of William Judd's address to the Wyoming inhabitants is typical of the disposition to read intention of separate statehood into the words of opponents; no. 170, especially note 12. As noted below, however, we do not now have all the documents mentioned by correspondents.

of the Susquehannah Company purchase either through wearying the state into that concession or through eventual legal action.[67] Staving off confirmation of titles in the seventeen towns, even by force, was crucial if the speculators were ever to attain their larger objective.

Granted resort to force was desperately foolish and fore-doomed to failure, but meanwhile the state's commissioners had halted their work, and sales of land rights outside the seventeen towns to those gullible enough to buy could go on. Men like Hamilton and Benton readily sold lands for which they could not guarantee a legal title. If it be suggested that conspirators might for their own safety be wary of putting in writing plans for separate statehood, it can be answered that they showed no re-luctance to commit to paper proposals for armed resistance to the state, treason enough for any man. When the Council for-warded on to New York Hamilton's and Benton's letters to Franklin, that state quickly ordered the arrest of the New Yorkers.

The most damning charge that separate statehood was actually planned is the allegation that the plotters had drafted a con-stitution and proposed a name for the new state—Westmoreland. The earliest mention of the constitution appears in a letter of November 12 from Obadiah Gore to Pickering. Gore declared that two Company men, Thomas Dyer and Ebenezer Gray, told him that the scheme for independence originated with Judd, Hamilton, and others and was unknown to the Company's com-mittee at Windham. Before leaving for Wyoming, Dyer and Gray had visited Judd and found him highly wrought up, for not only had Franklin and Hamilton been arrested, but Judd "had but little before Sent on a Constitution for the Government of that people together with a number of letters attending which he Concluded had fell into the hands of Government and he feared would prove fatal to Franklin as he had not viewed them." [68] The reference can only be to the seizure of papers from Asa Starkwather. Among the documents he carried was the Com-bination, already mentioned. Conceivably this could have been the "constitution" to which Judd had referred. No constitution

---

[67] Pickering believed that the Trenton decree had settled not only juris-diction over the disputed land but the private right of soil as well so far as law goes; nos. 181, 277, and 327. The Trenton judges had, in fact, denied that they could rule on the private right of soil and the Wyoming settlers had made one unsuccessful attempt to persuade Congress to authorize a trial for such a determination.

[68] No. 175. See also Judd's deposition of September 5, 1793, in Vol. X.

has ever been found, although many have searched for it.[69] In any case, it is well to remember that Gore is quoting two men, recalling Judd's words of a number of days or even weeks before. Gore, moreover, wished to ingratiate himself with Pickering, although he had connections with the speculators opening up lands to the west of Tioga.[70] In a sense he had a foot in both camps.

A few days after Gore wrote to Pickering, the latter wrote to his brother and told the story of the constitution. Pickering said the proposed new state was to be called Westmoreland. Probably his information came from Mathias Hollenback, whose letter to John Nicholson giving the name of the new state was carried to Philadelphia with Gore's letter.[71] Hollenback mentions an intercepted letter which named Judd as the author of the constitution and gave the new state's name; unfortunately this letter has not been found. That Judd was one of the prime movers in the statehood movement was confirmed in Pickering's mind by information supplied by John Allen of Plymouth, although Allen's account of his conversation with Judd was not recorded until more than a year after it had taken place, and there was an obvious discrepancy in it.[72]

The only other mention of independence at about this time occurs in a letter from Samuel Gordon of November 24, 1787. He recounted the indiscreet remarks of an emissary of "McKinstry Beach Levingston's & Co's," who asserted their willingness even to seek the help of the British to establish themselves independently.[73] Pickering seems not to have been clear in his own mind whether the new state plans were linked up with the conspiracy in New York and involved the British, or whether Westmoreland was a wholly separate enterprise; but in any case, he feared that any such scheme would attract the disaffected everywhere, especially those who had suffered defeat in Shays' Rebellion.[74]

---

[69] Charles Miner in a conversation with one Captain Richards was told that William Judd had shown a draft of the constitution to Richards, and that it had been drawn up by Oliver Wolcott. "I well remember it commenced like the Declaration of Independence, by setting forth a series of wrongs, or the declaration of rights, justifying the deed, and then came the organization, &c." *History of Wyoming in a Series of Letters to His Son* (Philadelphia, 1845), 412 n. The Combination begins with grievances and continues with this phrasing: "Therefore we hearby jointly and Severally pledge our Honors & all our properties Real and Personal," etc. See also the discussion in Oscar J. Harvey and Ernest G. Smith, *A History of Wilkes-Barré* (Wilkes-Barre, 1927), III, 1616-20.
[70] Nos. 112 and 65.   [71] Nos. 181 and 178.   [72] No. 284.
[73] No. 187.   [74] No. 170.

The question of independence and a constitution came to the fore again late in the fall of 1788, when John Franklin was at long last formally indicted. The presentment of the grand jury held that Franklin and others had on September 29, 1787, tried to erect an independent government within the commonwealth. The evidence was Franklin's signed order, already mentioned, to the half-share men to assemble in arms to oppose the militia.[75] Two depositions taken in this period, clearly of the most hearsay sort, lend support to the charge, but they were apparently not introduced as evidence. That of John Shepard describes the storing of gunpowder and the design to establish committee government in Athens. Shepard heard men in an adjacent room reading something, which from remarks he heard later, he took to be the constitution for a new state, which Capt. Benjamin Allen of Rhode Island said would be established "if the country was not otherwise obtained." Support from Rhode Island and Vermont, the deponent was told, could be counted upon.[76] The deposition of John J. AcModer was taken well after Franklin's indictment, probably for use at his trial, which, as it turned out, was never held. AcModer had earlier worked actively on the side of the New York speculators and the Franklin party, but he came to be pretty generally distrusted as one given to boasting and lying. In his deposition, AcModer explicitly declared that every one of his former associates not only talked the language of armed resistance to Pennsylvania but avowed an intention to establish a separate state which would run as far north as the British lines.[77]

Yet apart from AcModer, who deserted the cause of the Susquehannah Company, not a single participant in the alleged conspiracy to form a separate state admitted in any letter or other document which has been found that separate statehood was an objective, even an objective if all other means of securing the entire purchase failed. Despite repeated mention of it, no draft constitution has come to light.

Moreover, two additional facts need emphasis. When Attorney General William Bradford was trying to build the case against Franklin for presentment to the grand jury in 1788, he examined letters written by Franklin to Joseph Hamilton which were seized when Hamilton was arrested. These letters have not survived, and perhaps with good reason, for Bradford decided that they had nothing of an incriminating nature in them.[78] The sole document mentioned in the grand jury's indictment is the

---

[75] No. 319.   [76] No. 320.   [77] No. 326.   [78] No. 317.

order to assemble under arms signed by John Franklin, colonel commandant. Further, Zerah Beach resorted to the newspapers to deny formally that separate statehood was sought. As one of the leaders of the Susquehannah Company, he was, of course, a biased witness; yet he admitted without reluctance that he and fellow members of the Company stood ready to defend their land "against all invaders" and to refuse all titles except those from the Company itself. His words repeat the language of the Combination, which Beach included verbatim in his signed newspaper article. In the eyes of Pennsylvania, of course, his words were seditious. Beach went on. Far from wishing a dissolution of the federal union, the members of the Company, he asserted, testified to their respect for Congress and national law by their willingness to resort to Congress for a trial to determine the private right of soil. As the Company saw it, Pennsylvania as an interested party could not settle private land titles. As a practical matter, Beach estimated that only one-third of the Connecticut claimants would have their titles confirmed under Pennsylvania's Confirming Act.[79]

The immediate occasion of his article was Pennsylvania's expressed willingness to use troops in 1787 to bring all of Luzerne County into obedience. In fact, the state had even appealed to Congress for men, so serious did the situation seem, but absenteeism in that body prevented action on Pennsylvania's request.[80] State militia on short-term enlistments went to Luzerne instead, where they found the inhabitants remarkably calm and offering no resistance to government. Indeed, even before the arrival of the militia, the county had been able peaceably to hold elections for military and civil officers.

Reviewing all the charges relating to the plans for a separate state, one would, I believe, be justified in saying that satisfactory positive evidence for such a conspiracy among members of the Susquehannah Company is lacking. The sources do indicate that the record is not complete so that reservation of final judgment is called for. On the other hand, the evidence is full and clear that members of the Company were willing to oppose Pennsylvania and the Confirming Act with arms. While vindictiveness undoubtedly animated some of the accusers of Franklin and his party, most were probably genuinely confused about

---

[79] No. 171.
[80] Nos. 167 and 173. President Benjamin Franklin was also unable to get from the Assembly authorization for a permanent force at Wyoming. See the debate on this question; no. 180.

the aims of the Company so far as statehood goes. To some, separation seemed a logical sequel to armed resistance. To others, particularly those holding office under Pennsylvania or strongly partisan toward the state, resort to rule by local committees of the Company could only signify a desire for independence. Finally, it was plausible to see a connection between rushing to fill up the Susquehannah Company purchase by enticing onto the land hundreds of new settlers and conspiring for statehood in New York. Some of the men involved, like Joseph Hamilton and Caleb Benton, were busy at both, and these men corresponded frequently with John Franklin.

IV

For actual settlers in the Wyoming Valley, the immediate importance of statehood schemes and of forcible opposition to the Confirming Act was that securing legal titles to lands would be delayed, and worse, that a disillusioned General Assembly, yielding to Pennamite pressure, might modify the act or repeal it altogether. These fears were justified. Pennamite opposition to the Confirming Act had stiffened during the spring and summer of 1787, and in the fall the Assembly became the locus of contending interests. Petitions complaining about injustice had their day, motions and countermotions sparked debates, proposed amendments and their substitutes burdened the committee system. Positive decision supported by consensus remained beyond reach.

The third session of the Eleventh General Assembly, meeting in September, 1787, received petitions from several hundred inhabitants of Northampton and Northumberland counties, claimants to lands in Luzerne, asking that the Confirming Act be repealed. Other petitions begged that a different mode of compensation, preferably state certificates, be made to Pennamite claimants whose lands would be confirmed to Connecticut settlers.[81] Even among some of those in the Assembly, who had voted the preceding March for the Confirming Act, doubts had arisen over the terms of the law. Thomas Fitzsimons, for example, speaking for a number of others, explained to Pickering that "Original settlers, & their Legal Representatives were all that were intended to be provided for."[82] The language of the act was ambiguous, for it referred to lands "occupied or acquired," encouraging the interpretation that lands assigned but not actually settled could be confirmed to Connecticut claimants.

---

[81] No. 127.   [82] No. 123.

Since the session of the Assembly ran only through September 29, too brief a period to permit resolution of so contested an issue, action on the law was left to the new Assembly elected in October.

In the first session of that Assembly a seven-man committee, to which had been referred the Council's message on disturbances at Wyoming and various Pennamite petitions, made a series of reports designed to supplement the Confirming Act. In response to these reports the Assembly resolved to exact new oaths of allegiance from the freemen of Luzerne County, to offer more generous terms for compensation to Pennamite claimants, and to extend the original time limits of the Confirming Act.[83] William Findley, prominent member of the Constitutionalist faction, moved from the floor a further amendment that would have restricted the law's application to those Connecticut claimants actually settled on the land before the decree at Trenton, and would have limited the size of the tracts for each to three hundred acres.[84] While Findley's motion obtained a majority vote, neither it nor the other resolutions became part of the law; final enactment was never achieved.

The proposal to restrict the benefits of the law to actual settlers, however, caused Pickering serious concern, for it eliminated from consideration those who had been unable to occupy their assigned lands because their location would have exposed settlers to danger during the war. Furthermore, the three-hundred-acre limit ignored the way townships had actually been divided among settlers, taking account neither of multiple grants in various locations, nor of the lands reserved for public use. Yet the state's commissioners had already given heed to these peculiarities in their decisions on titles.[85] About this time Pickering drafted an amendment to the Confirming Act that reflected the wishes of the established Connecticut settlers in recognizing their right to lands in certain "detached places, capable of cultivation between the townships" (called "pitches") and to lands assigned to settlers, but because of danger never actually occupied by them. Pickering did, however, accept the three-hundred-acre limitation that Findley had proposed.[86] There is no record that the Assembly ever considered Pickering's proposal. Pickering spoke out for two reasons: he saw the Confirming Act justly applied as the only hope for bringing peace to Wyoming, and critics had impugned his motives for helping the settlers to frame

---

[83] Nos. 170, note 22, and 180.   [84] Nos. 182 and 183.   [85] No. 184.
[86] No. 189.

their petition and the Assembly committee to draft the original law.

Pickering's opposition to Findley's amendment obtained backing from a number of Pennsylvania landholders, who later organized themselves into an association.[87] As large speculators, with whom Pickering associated in several deals, they had interests in the area of the Susquehannah Company purchase and elsewhere, but they did not seek home plots in the seventeen towns. With the passing years they had come to understand that total opposition to the Connecticut claimants was not a paying proposition. A peaceful solution that would satisfy Connecticut settlers would be in the speculators' interest, for stable settlements would raise the value of their holdings. The petitions against the Confirming Act came not from them but from inhabitants of counties bordering Luzerne, many of whom hoped to claim farms from which they had been driven, and whom the speculators now saw as indecent troublemakers.[88] The large landholders' association succeeded in coaxing from the Assembly a substantial grant toward defraying the costs of a road that would run to Athens and thus encourage settlement in that area. Wyoming settlers saw this road as "a Landjobbers accommodation without advantage to the Public," although the landholders spelled out at some length the general benefits that would accrue to the state.[89]

Doubtless some of Pickering's anger with Franklin and others who were scheming at Athens was owing to the threat he saw to his investments in that quarter, but his speculations there do not necessarily throw doubt upon the sincerity of his desire for justice for the Connecticut claimants. He did not hide the fact of his speculations from Wyoming people, although the charge was made that he did. As he pointed out, he would have gained in no way at Wyoming by the defeat of Findley's amendment.[90] The lands he had purchased under a Connecticut title would not have increased in size. In drafting the settlers' petition and in laboring over the wording of a confirming law, Pickering adopted what seemed to him a reasonable solution to an often bloody dispute that had dragged on for years. He sensed correctly the temper of the Assembly and the longings of a majority

---

[87] No. 185.

[88] *Cf.* Thomas Fitzsimons' characterization: "Nothing Can Exceed the Virulence & Indecency of Some of the Pennsylvania Land owners, but to men so disposed Little Regard will be paid"; no. 123.

[89] Nos. 239 and 205.   [90] Nos. 134 and 184.

at Wyoming. Ultimate failure cannot be charged to his account.

Two days after he had proposed an amendment to the Confirming Act, Findley offered another and more sweeping one, the effect of which would have been quite the opposite of the first one. On November 24, he proposed confirmation of lands not only to those who had actually settled upon them before the Trenton decree, but to all those who had settled since that decree within the eighteen towns. How much land would be confirmed to each he left open, but by using the term *half-share,* he would have recognized the rights of those men brought onto the purchase beginning in 1785, when the Susquehannah Company had decided to crowd in new settlers as a way of maintaining its claim in defiance of the state of Pennsylvania. Even some of the long-time settlers at Wyoming detested the half-share men, who allegedly seized rights already claimed by the helpless widows and children of men who had lost their lives in the Revolution.[91] Moreover, by stipulating *eighteen* towns Findley was recognizing Athens, where many half-share men were securing rights that threatened the speculative interests of Pickering and those with whom he was associated. After debate Findley's second proposed amendment failed by a decisive vote.[92] Although Findley gave as his reason for introducing this amendment the desire to make unnecessary the establishment of a permanent force at Wyoming, his offering of two such conflicting motions gives support to George Clymer's accusation that the Constitutionalists were seeking above all else to embarrass the Republicans (who had a strong majority in the Assembly) by pursuing measures that would make Luzerne County more restless than ever.[93]

Findley also seconded a motion offered by Richard Peters, which would have made possible compensation to Pennamites in state certificates instead of in lands to be granted from the state's holdings.[94] While to many, such a measure seemed fair, its practicality was dubious, for the state had already overcommitted itself in terms of foreseeable income. The Peters motion never came to a vote. The proliferation of proposed amendments to the Confirming Act in the fall session of the Assembly finally led James McLene, another Constitutionalist, to attempt to bring about suspension of the law altogether; but his motion failed.[95]

---

[91] No. 156. Yet many of the old settlers held half-share rights as well as their full ones. According to Pickering, John Franklin had encouraged old settlers to take up half-shares so that he would win their support for confirmation of the whole purchase; nos. 268 and 285.
[92] No. 186.   [93] Nos. 183 and 209.   [94] No. 186.   [95] No. 188.

The session ended without final action on any of the proposed changes.

The interim between the first and second session of the Twelfth General Assembly of 1787-1788 saw public pleas for compensation to Pennamites in money in preference to certificates or land, and even for the outright repeal of the Confirming Act.[96] Actually, Pennsylvania claimants differed sharply over the form of compensation they preferred, and the Assembly considered every alternative.[97] The confusion of proposals once again prevented any solution. To simplify the voting, George Clymer tried to get confirmation of titles to Connecticut people separated from compensation to Pennamites, but the Assembly rejected that way around the impasse.[98] When McLene came forward this time with his proposal to suspend the Confirming Act, he was successful. The preamble to the resolution as passed set forth two reasons for suspension: the violence directed against the state's commissioners and the ambiguities in the law itself. Virtually all the votes against suspending the Confirming Act came from the eastern counties, where the land speculators who wanted to keep Luzerne County quiet were concentrated.[99]

Between the time of the first reading of the McLene resolution and final passage on March 29, 1788, the Assembly gave favorable consideration to two other proposals. One, also introduced by McLene, authorized the Council to ascertain the exact quantity and value of lands within the seventeen towns that were claimed through a Pennsylvania title so that compensation could be more adequately determined.[100] The other, presented by Samuel Maclay, offered a new confirming law, designed to eliminate the ambiguities of the original one and to make the Connecticut settlers pay the costs of confirmation.

Maclay's measure, which was approved for public consideration, confirmed to the actual settlers before the Trenton decree the seventeen towns, the individual holdings within them to be determined "in any way, which they may judge most convenient to them." To secure valid titles the Connecticut claimants in each of the towns would have to elect a prospective patentee, who would act as trustee for the inhabitants of the town. The Council would then direct the Land Office to issue a warrant to each of the seventeen patentees, and after the Surveyor General by a resurvey had confirmed the original bounds of each of the towns, a patent would be issued in trust. This procedure meant that the

---

[96] Nos. 196 and 198.   [97] Nos. 208 and 209.   [98] Nos. 209 and 212.
[99] Nos. 214, 215, 216, and 220.   [100] No. 219.

state would be spared the expense of the commissioners' having to scrutinize individual claims, and the Connecticut settlers would be left to devise their own method for equitable division of the lands in each town and the settlement of conflicting claims.[101] This new proposal, of course, ignored the eighteenth town, Athens, and ignored also claims to lands, called pitches, that lay between the towns. Thus it was not fully responsive to the Connecticut settlers' original petition. Like the original confirming law, it did not at all satisfy, of course, those who demanded confirmation of the entire Susquehannah Company purchase.

Tench Coxe, one of those engaged in land speculation in association with Pickering, was not hopeful that this new confirming law would survive the final step necessary for enactment. He urged Pickering to gather, from those with claims in the pitches, petitions "signifying their desire to remove off the pitches & take their Share in the Townships, and some declaration of those in & out of the 17 Townships that they would be disposed to relinquish all pretensions *without* the Townships, if the lands *within* the Townships should be given them."[102] Here, neatly put, was the prescription of the typical large land speculator; for the sake of peace, write off the seventeen towns and move people around until the boundaries of the Connecticut settlements were clear and tidy. It was a solution that would appeal to a mapmaker, but it took little account of people who had toiled to cultivate a farm. Life along the Susquehanna River was hard; Pickering had been struck from the first by the poverty of the settlements. Conflict with the Pennamites and natural disasters had kept herds of livestock low, and poor roads kept from market such surplus grain as was produced. A barter economy made opening a store an unpromising venture, Pickering confided to Hodgdon, even though the demand for goods was great.[103] To Pickering's credit, he did not forget what their own farms meant to the families who had struggled to make the land bear, many of whom more than once had had to begin all over again.

Knowing the people at Wyoming as he did, Pickering offered a different version of Maclay's new confirming act. Pickering's draft, drawn up in September, 1788, would have confirmed titles upon proper proof to such lots within the seventeen towns as had been actually settled before the Trenton decree, and also to those occupied lots within pitches but outside the townships. Rights to those lots assigned but not occupied because they were too ex-

---

[101] Nos. 217 and 218.   [102] No. 221.   [103] Nos. 92 and 100.

posed to danger could have also been proved before commissioners, but confirmation of their titles would have been left to the discretion of the Assembly. Within the townships whole, not partial, tracts held under Pennsylvania titles but not overlapping Connecticut claims could have been vested in Pennsylvania claimants. Pickering kept Maclay's device of the single patentee for each township, but each would have been trustee for only those parts of the township which the commissioners had designated as proved to individuals.[104] Thus Pickering, in clearing up ambiguities in the original law, would have kept more closely to the wishes of the people as expressed in their petition of February, 1787. Only with respect to the exposed lands did he weaken the position he had taken in November, 1787.

The third session of the Twelfth General Assembly, meeting from September 2 to October 4, 1788, found itself unable to make any headway on the confirming act. It heard petitions for and against Maclay's bill, but the complexity of the issues left insufficient time for action other than to recommend the law to the early and serious consideration of the succeeding Assembly.[105] In the Thirteenth Assembly a large committee was named to consider disturbances at Wyoming, and some days later it was ordered by the chamber to report a bill if it thought necessary. On November 19, the committee reported a bill to confirm titles to the Connecticut claimants, but what its provisions were is not known.[106] Samuel Hodgdon wrote Pickering[107] that as near as he could find out, the proposed bill offered to the Connecticut claimants, who were actual settlers before the Trenton decree, equivalent grants in the old and new purchases, bought by the state from the Indians in 1786 or 1784. When George Clymer sought a second reading of the committee's bill, James McLene successfully moved postponement of consideration, effectively killing any action in 1788. It was just as well. If the bill did indeed offer equivalent grants elsewhere in the state, it would only have antagonized the Connecticut settlers and discredited the state's good faith. Long ago the Connecticut people had made it plain that they were contending not for lands but for homes. They disdained compensation in the state's wild regions.

V

The suspension of the Confirming Act and the uncertainties associated with Maclay's measure could only encourage the extremists at Wyoming. As weeks passed with John Franklin still

---

[104] No. 310.   [105] No. 311.   [106] *Ibid.*, note 3.   [107] No. 324.

in jail and no talk of when he would get his right to trial, hot-heads in the Connecticut settlements schemed to take direct action.

In February, 1788, Franklin had applied to the Assembly to be admitted to bail; but although the committee to which his petition was referred had reported favorably upon it, the Assembly refused his request.[108] Then the Supreme Court judges looked into his plight and ruled that despite his being charged with treason, he could be released on £2000 bail. Departing from normal practice, the judges permitted the bail to be made up of small sums from as many freeholders at Wyoming as necessary. Ten men entering into recognizances for the amounts between £100 and £400 made up the total; yet Franklin remained in jail.[109] Council members kept him there on the grounds that his bail was insufficient. Reportedly, one irate Council member declared that the whole pack at Wyoming was together not worth £2000.[110] Eighteenth-century jails were miserable places at best, and much of the time Franklin had been kept so closely confined his health was threatened. Even the governor of Connecticut had written to protest the severity of the state's treatment of him.[111] When, despite the sureties, he continued to languish in jail, anger began to grow.

Of course some at Wyoming saw the effort at bail as a dodge employed merely to free Franklin so that he could concert opposition to the state.[112] According to Pickering, even Zebulon Butler, a former associate of Franklin's, believed his release would have been a dangerous move.[113] But many at Wyoming saw the refusal of bail as deliberate persecution of the leader of the Connecticut settlements and thought they detected behind the refusal the influence of Pickering, Franklin's challenger for leadership. When Franklin's supporters struck, Pickering could claim no surprise, for he had received ample warning of a plot to kidnap him and hold him hostage for Franklin's safety and release. Four days before Pickering was actually taken, Andrew Ellicott had told him of the plan to seize him.[114]

On the night of June 26, 1788, fifteen young men, all but two of them painted like Indians, entered Pickering's home, forced him from his bed, and took him off.[115] Their plans were well

---

[108] No. 201, note 4.   [109] No. 225.
[110] No. 307. That it was Council members who were keeping Franklin in jail is confirmed by Samuel Hodgdon, but for this particular outburst we have only John Franklin's word.   [111] No. 201.   [112] No. 229.
[113] No. 233.   [114] No. 245.   [115] No. 271.

known to and abetted by some of their fathers. The abductors kept Pickering bound a good part of the time and moved him from place to place in the woods every two or three days, but they allowed him to write to his wife. The list of things that he requested her to send is instructive, suggesting a man determined to make the best of his situation—to keep his clothes in good repair and his mind calm with the reading of Dr. Price's sermons.

Like a good New Englander, Pickering improved his idle hours by learning from his captors the lore of pig breeding, the art of plowing corn with a team of oxen, a means for making a coffee substitute, and the Vermonters' methods of clearing and planting new lands. He observed the flora around him, discovering wintergreen and speculating whether ginseng could be grown in the shade of his orchard trees.[116] Obviously his captors were not vicious; and although they exchanged shots with the militia, which came after them, their determination wavered before the realities and their consciences. On July 15, they released Pickering. Then, there began the long task of gathering depositions and rounding up the guilty. The depositions are more interesting for the clues they give to daily life and diet and for their revelations about Wyoming personalities than for their rehearsal of the tedious facts of the kidnapping. The number of gallons of whiskey deemed essential for the small party in the woods is awesome.[117]

Pickering parted on good terms with his abductors. He promised to forgive them for the personal injury they had done him if they would obey the laws of Pennsylvania in the future. For their part they agreed to help the law officers serve writs against their members and against others; and if they failed to keep their word, Pickering was to be free to bring suit against them for damages. Their petition to the Council to obtain forgiveness for their public offense explained their conduct as arising from their erroneous belief that at a time when Franklin's life was endangered by his confinement, Pickering had written to oppose granting bail to him.[118] The young men also tried to get Pickering to intercede for them with the Council, but Pickering refused unless they would furnish him with the names of the men who had organized the plot and who acted as advisers. After a day's consideration, the young men rejected his stipulation. Pickering, however, did forward their petition to the Council and did convey the information that if Franklin were admitted to bail Franklin probably would leave the settlements.[119]

---

[116] No. 253.   [117] No. 260.   [118] Nos. 254 and 255.   [119] No. 258.

The Council, of course, as soon as it had been notified of Pickering's capture, had taken steps to secure his release. Believing that his kidnapping was probably part of the larger conspiracy that had long been under way in New York, the Council had written immediately to the government of that state to assure cooperation, and it had instructed the Pennsylvania delegation in Congress to find out whether aid could be furnished by the Continental troops then being moved to duty on the western frontier.[120] When they had assembled at Easton, it would have been easy to detach some for duty in Wyoming. Congress did in fact agree to help Pennsylvania if employment of the troops would take no longer than two weeks; but since it voted after Pickering's release and the quieting of the county, Pennsylvania never made use of the troops.[121]

For a time Pickering himself believed that the New York conspirators had plotted his capture, but no hard evidence supports such an explanation. Later Pickering blamed simply the half-share men, and more particularly, John Jenkins.[122] Samuel Hodgdon wondered whether one David Perkins, who had carried messages to Philadelphia for Pickering, had also carried information about the kidnapping to John Franklin, whom he had visited in jail. Perkins had been recommended to Pickering by John Jenkins. Or perhaps, said Hodgdon, Franklin had given the plan to Perkins to carry back to Jenkins and others.[123] Franklin, of course, denied having any foreknowledge of the scheme, and nothing in the depositions implicates him directly.[124] These leave the impression that some of the older, diehard Franklin supporters urged their sons into the harebrained scheme, and that all of them soon regretted their folly. When one of the young men turned state's evidence, rewards offered by the Council spurred the hunting down of his fellows.

The episode had the effect of uniting many of the settlers temporarily at least behind Pickering.[125] Nothing so solidifies a

---

[120] Nos. 256 and 257.   [121] Nos. 265 and 266.

[122] Nos. 258 and 277. Several depositions indicate that men like John McKinstry were kept informed and approved of the kidnapping, but initiative, planning, and carrying out of the plot seem to have been the work of Franklin's partisans among the settlers; nos. 260, 269, 280, and 297.

[123] No. 287.   [124] No. 312.

[125] Pickering at first did not sense any change, his failure to do so being perhaps the natural result of his sense of outrage right after his release. Later he felt that the episode had had the good effect of strengthening the will of the better affected settlers; nos. 268, 285, and 289. Zebulon Butler was much more optimistic, but the mood of each man, of course, reflected the purposes each sought to accomplish; no. 272.

community as righteous action against an outrageous violation of common decency. The snatching of an officer of government from his bed to keep him chained in the woods for nearly a month and the pressure applied to reluctant settlers to support the enterprise affronted Wyoming sensibilities; even the guilty parties finally came to sense the horror of their action. Righteousness begets suspicions, however, and some thought that John Paul Schott and Zebulon Butler were tainted.[126] The craggy honesty of poor, slow-thinking Colonel Butler is touchingly apparent in his letter to Nathan Denison requesting that testimony taken against himself be made public.[127] Quicker minds made use of the aging and respected leader, but humble integrity shines through his painfully composed letters. Schott managed before a military court to get himself cleared of charges of insufficient zeal in the pursuit of Pickering's captors.[128]

Pickering kept free of pettiness, but his strict New England sense of duty caused him to bend every effort toward insuring the full punishment of the kidnappers and guarding the future security of the county. One of his firmest convictions was that much of Pennsylvania's past trouble with the Connecticut settlers originated in changeable and confusing state policies that alternated between the extremes of unjust force and excessive leniency. Disappointment quickly turned into anger when he learned that the Supreme Court judges had, out of expediency, ruled that his kidnappers would be tried only for riot, not for high treason.[129] The failure of the state to plan for a permanent military force among the settlements alarmed him, for he did not delude himself that the quick sympathy expressed for him and his family would transform itself into lasting submission to Pennsylvania law and rejection of Franklin's leadership. Pickering believed that at bottom the old settlers' attraction to Franklin was bound up with devotion to their own interests; Franklin was their hope amidst their despair at ever getting confirmation of their titles from an indecisive government. Credulous and deeply suspicious by turns, they were a means to power that Franklin could manipulate for the Company's benefit.[130]

In a bitter letter to the Council, Pickering declared that the state was letting him down, that he had risked much in going to Wyoming and now the state was not furnishing the backing he needed or standing by its expressed intention to confirm lands to Connecticut settlers; but his black mood did not last.[131] In

---

[126] No. 305.   [127] No. 267.   [128] No. 251.
[129] Nos. 277, 282, and 289.   [130] Nos. 268 and 285.   [131] No. 268.

September, 1788, the county grand jury returned indictments against his captors.[132]   Having the men indicted by the jury, allowing bail to be set for those deserving it, and then transferring the cases to the Supreme Court for trial was the course recommended to test the disposition of the county to uphold the laws.[133] The county passed the test, and Pickering was soon at work drafting amendments to the Confirming Act, already mentioned, which would treat his neighbors fairly.

John Franklin, the man for whose benefit Pickering had been kidnapped, was fearful that the deed would prejudice his cause. In September, 1788, he again petitioned the Assembly to be released on bail, and again he was unsuccessful.[134]   He wrote to Samuel Huntington, governor of Connecticut, detailing his fears.   In a letter to President Benjamin Franklin, Huntington declared that since the Wyoming settlers were once under Connecticut's care, "Government have always thought themselves under some kind of obligation to take notice of their complaints and distresses"; and he reminded Pennsylvania's president of "the powerful connection, which the settlers there have with a numerous class of Citizens in this State in both ties of interest and consanguinity, and the disagreeable consequences of wounding an old fracture when apparently healed." [135]   Huntington was uneasy not only about the treatment of John Franklin but about the suspension of the Confirming Act as well.   The Council in reply could only breathe its hope that the Assembly would deal justly with the settlers.   As for Franklin, it added, he was shortly coming to trial; his confinement meanwhile was essential for the tranquility of Luzerne County.[136]

Indicted with others in November, Franklin pleaded his unreadiness for trial.   Pickering was happy enough to see him packed off again to jail in Philadelphia.[137]   If for the moment the county seemed quiet, it was the quiet of exhaustion from the weeks of turmoil and the bitterness of neighbor testifying against neighbor.   Pickering had prevailed, for the machinery of county government was working; but no one knew better than he that the future rested with the Assembly.   Failure to provide adequately for confirmation of the claims of the Connecticut settlers would only bring renewed trouble.

---

[132] No. 299.   [133] No. 296.   [134] No. 307.   [135] No. 312.
[136] No. 315.   [137] No. 321.

Documents
1787-1788

Susquehannah Company Papers

[1] William Hooker Smith and Others to Timothy Pickering.[1]

Sir,

we have Ever Since The Trentown Desision Judg⁴ our Selves To be within The Boundaries of The Charter of Pensylvania. we Have Taken an oath of Fidelety To The State, we have bin Recognis⁴ in Conformety To The Laws.[2] we are Convinsed That Goverment has Granted To The Settlers at wioming Every Thing which we have asked, That was Resonable, Namly To make Us Sitesons, and freeholders, & Lastly To make Us into a New County.[3] There Is but one Thing wanting To make us happy Subiects, That Is an Introduction & Istablishment of The Laws of honnor, & fidelety To The State of Pensylvania & are Redy To Pay obedience when Ever Called Uppon. we wish Sir, To assure You of our Joy In your approch To us, with the Laws & Directions from Goverment, by you Directed, To Us.[4] we are Sincearly Ready To Conform, & as friends To Goverment are humbly and at your Service
wioming Jan. 9ᵗʰ 1786 [1787] [5]

> Wᵐ Hooker Smith
> Abrahᵐ Westbrook
> By his order—
> Samuel Hover

---

[1] [1] M. H. S., Pickering Papers, LVII, 85, in Smith's hand and signed by him and Hover.

[2] The three men were among those who took advantage of the amnesty act in April, 1786; *Susquehannah Company Papers,* VIII, no. 208.

[3] Luzerne County was established by act of the Assembly on September 25, 1786; *ibid.,* no. 183, note 4.

[4] Pickering's letter to the three men has not been found. They had shown themselves for some time to be friendly to the Pennsylvania government and opposed to the faction in Wyoming led by John Franklin. For their most recent expression of loyalty, see *ibid.,* no. 267.

[5] Smith inadvertently wrote 1786 for 1787. This letter was handed to Pickering by Smith and Hover; no. 18 *post,* entry for January 9.

[2] Notice of Wyoming Election.[1]

NOTIFICATION.

Whereas by an Act of the General Assembly of the Commonwealth of *Pennsylvania,* passed on the twenty-fifth Day of *September* last, the northern Part of the County of *Northumberland* was erected into a separate County, by the Name of *Luzerne;* and a Representative, Councillor, and other Officers were to have been chosen on the Day of the General Election, in *October* last; but the Electors where prevented from assembly, by an extraordinary Flood, and no Elections were made. And whereas the General Assembly, by a Supplement to that Act, passed on the Time for making the said Elections,[2] and have accordingly appointed the same to be held on the first Day of *February* next.

Now, in pursuance of the Powers vested in us by the said supplementary Act,

NOTICE IS HEREBY GIVEN,

To the Electors of the said County of Luzerne,

To assemble on the said first Day of *February* next, at the House of *Zebulon Butler,* in *Wilkesborough,* in the same County, then there to elect one Representative to serve in the General Assembly, one Councillor, two fit Persons for Sheriffs, two fit Persons for Coroners, and three Commissioners; and also three Inspectors of the said Elections.

Given under our[3] hands, at *Wilkesborough* aforesaid, the tenth[4] Day of January, 1787.

Timothy Pickering
Zebⁿ Butler [5]

Philadelphia: Printed by Thomas Bradford.

---

[2] [1] M. H. S., Pickering Papers, LVII, 86, a printed handbill.

[2] The original act establishing Luzerne County inadvertently omitted mention of the holding of preliminary elections for the choosing of inspectors of elections, who would in turn choose judges to supervise the balloting for a representative and county officials. The omission was corrected and an election day for February 1 was set in a supplementary act passed December 27, 1786; James T. Mitchell and Henry Flanders (comps.), *The Statutes at Large of Pennsylvania from 1682 to 1801* (Harrisburg, 1896-1915), XII, 300-03 and 339-43.

[3] The word *our* and the "s" on *hand* are written in.

[4] The word *tenth* is written in.

[5] The two names are signatures. The supplementary act (see note 2 above) designated Pickering, Butler, and John Franklin to give notifica-

[3] Timothy Pickering to Simon Spaulding and Others.[1]

Wilkesborough Jan[r] 10, 1787.

Sir,

Herewith you will receive a copy of an act of the General Assembly of Pennsylvania, passed on the 27th of December last, to enable the inhabitants of the county of Luzerne to meet on the first day of February next, to elect a representative, councillor, and other officers;[2] and I also inclose notifications, signed by Col° Butler and me, agreeably to that act.[3] I take the liberty of writing this letter, to prevent or remove any misconceptions of the tendency or consequences of that act.

I find some are apprehensive that the choosing of county officers will at once absolutely subject the inhabitants of the county to the laws of Pennsylvania, that ejectments will immediately be brought to dispossess them of their lands and, in a word, that they shall be hardly and unjustly used.

As to the first article, nothing can be more evident than that the election of officers will make no difference in the circumstances of the people, in respect to any obligation to submit to the laws of Pennsylvania; for all of them are within the state, and a great proportion of them have already taken the oath of allegiance; and if their residence and their oaths do not, in their apprehension, bind them to submit unconditionally to the laws, surely the bare giving in of their votes for a representative & other officers will not do it.

It is very true, when the courts shall be opened in the county, ejectments may be brought, *as the laws now stand:* but if the people would at this time think themselves warranted in opposing any process in the law, will they not think and act in the same manner, after the courts shall be opened, until equitable measures shall be taken for the security of their property?

In the third place, I will venture to affirm and I would stake my life and reputation upon it that the government of Pennsyl-

---

tion to the voters, to administer oaths, and to set a date for the election of justices of the peace; but the powers of all three could be exercised by one or more of them. Franklin was absent in Connecticut until February and would not have cooperated in holding elections in any case.

[3] [1] M. H. S., Pickering Papers, LVII, 87, in Pickering's hand.

[2] See no. 2, *ante,* note 2.

[3] No. 2, *ante.*

vania have no inclination to treat the people here either hardly or unjustly. I have reason to know the sentiments of government, because I have conversed with many leading members in the council & assembly and find them unanimously disposed to attend to the equitable claims of the inhabitants of this county, and to do them all possible justice.

Let us admit, for a moment, that the government of Pennsylvania were really hostile to this settlement, and disposed to crush it: What ought you more to wish for, than to have agents at court who would give you the earliest notice of every thing intended to disturb your peace? And what agents can be so useful as a councillor & representative who would know every *secret* as well as *public* transaction of the Council & Assembly? And (which deserves some consideration[)] these agents would be maintained at the expense of your *enemies* as the wages of councillors and assemblymen are paid out of the public treasury.

But I cannot admit that you have any enemies either in the Council or Assembly: On the contrary, they both manifest the most equitable and friendly disposition towards you: expecting, however, that you, on your parts, will manifest the like equity and moderation.

You are sensible, sir, that when a quarrel subsists between two individuals, the most likely way to bring it to a happy issue, is for the parties to come together calmly to discuss the matter in dispute. For whilst their jealousies or resentments keep them from seeing each other the quarrel cannot but continue. Just such, sir, will be the unhappy situation of this county, unless they now close with the offers of government, affording them a fresh opportunity of choosing persons to represent them in the council and assembly. Your councillor & representative would immediately enter on such negotiations with government, and propose such plans for settling their fatal dispute, as I doubt not would end agreeably to the wishes of the people. If I know these wishes, they are, that they may continue in possession & quietly enjoy those lands which they or their fathers settled & improved, for which they have suffered innumerable hardships, & many of them death itself, and on which the survivours depend for the support of themselves and families. These wishes, I may venture to say, will be gratified: for all the members of government whom I have heard speak of it (& I have heard many) say, that such original possessors, their heirs and assigns, ought not to be disturbed in their possessions. Hence I conclude that some equitable plan will be devised, that shall put all such lands out of dispute; & in furthering such measures, your own councillor & representative may render the most essential services. In the choice of them permit me to express my sincere wishes that your votes may be given for those persons who (in the language of the constitution) "are most noted for wisdom and virtue."

Much more might be added: but I have already drawn this letter to a great length: and as the electors will have an opportunity to make further enquiries on these and all other interesting points, when they assemble at Wilkesborough, I forbear to enlarge.

As 'tis my desire to give the most candid information to the people, I request you to communicate this letter to your neighbours and others within your reach, as they are too distant for me personally to converse with them before the day of election. In the mean time I remain, sir, Y^r most obedient servant

T. P.

P. S. There will be some inhabitants in your neighbourhood, but on the opposite side of the river, whom the bearer cannot see: Col° Butler joins me in requesting that you would be so good as to send some of the notifications over to them, and give them all necessary information on the subject. The Assembly is adjourned to the 20th of February; and so early a day as the first, was appointed for the election, that you might have the advantage of being represented in that session.

[Four copies addressed]
To Captain Simon Spaulding, New-Sheshekin.
Mr Rosewell Franklin, Wysocks.
Col° Nathan Dennison, Wyalusing,
Mr Zebulon Massey, Tunkhanock.

[4] William Judd to Zebulon Butler.[1]

Farmington Jan^r 11th 1786 [1787]

Sir

I was disappointed when I found my Letter directed to you relateing to the Susq^h Meeting failed of being sent forward from Hudson.[2]

[4] [1] Wyoming Historical and Geological Society, Butler Papers, in Judd's hand; M. H. S., Pickering Papers, LVII, 89, a copy in Pickering's hand. Judd inadvertently dated his letter 1786 instead of 1787.

[2] The meeting was held on December 26 and 27; *Susquehannah Company Papers*, VIII, no. 268. Hudson, New York, was the home of Joseph Hamilton, who had come to the fore as one of the leaders of the Company; see *ibid.*, Index.

At our last Meeting at Hartford we have made many New regulations. I have not the Copy & must beg leave to refer you to Col° Franklin, who will be at Wyoming soon and hath the Copies at Large. a Court of Commissioners is appointed with plenary powers to act and Transact all matters in the power of the Company to do of which Number among others are Col° Butler Col° Denison O Gore Esqʳ Col° Franklin Majʳ Jenkins Capᵗ Schotts & others. One thing we are alarmed about here and that is, it is said Col° Pickering is Coming among you to hold an Election, should that be the Case unless you Contrive some way to Avoid his request you are Compleatly saddled with the Laws of Pensylvania and your property all at Hazard.³ there are so many Inconsistances in the Two Acts of the legislature⁴ it appeares to me you may Easily play him off for the present. if you want assistance we have a fair prospect of Augmenting your force next spring at Least 400 that may be relyed upon, the Susqʰ Cause gains friends day by Day & your Intollerable suffering hath made you many friends in the Country. and public policy seems to be in your favour. the federal Government is upon its last Leggs and you may stand an Equal Chance with the rest of mankind if you are firm Steady and United, preperation is made to fill up all the Granted Towns & to settle a man upon all the rights that are now Destitute of a Settler. the Commissioners are Authorised to Survey to any man that Joins you from one to two Hundred acres of Land & Charge it to the Accᵗ of any proprietor that has no man upon his Right in the Settlement. Be not desponding but play the Man as heretofore; providence helps them that help themselves. please to make my compliments to Mʳˢ Butler and all my Acquaintance in the Country.⁵ I am sir Your humble servant.

Wᵐ Judd.

---

³ *Cf.* Pickering's handling of this apparently prevalent fear; no. 3, *ante.*

⁴ Judd is probably referring to the act of September 25, 1786, which established Luzerne County, and the supplementary act of December 27, which by providing for elections, remedied a defect in the earlier act.

⁵ Butler read Judd's letter before a meeting in Wilkes-Barre at which Pickering sought to answer local objections to the forthcoming election; no. 18, *post,* p. 50.

[5] Timothy Pickering to Samuel Hodgdon.[1]

Wyoming Jan^r 12. 1787.

Dr Sir

I arrived here last Monday morning. Franklin is still in Connecticut. Col° Butler has joined me to hold the elections, and the notifications are gone forth.[2] I have conversed with a considerable number of the people, & have reason to think that when they have all heard a just account of things, there will be a clear majority for the election. Yesterday I conversed with Jenkins: He has formed an opinion on the subject—he is interested in its being right—has probably long supposed it well founded—and I do not expect to convince him. Franklin is looked for back, & will join Jenkins with all his force. These two persons have kept the people under their controul: but I believe the time is come when they will assert their freedom, and venture to contradict those leaders. I have been received by all with perfect civility.

I forgot to bring with me the act of assembly passed last September for erecting this district into a county.[3] I shall want it—pray find it, if possible before the day of election, which is the 1st of February. Please also to look into the Journals of Congress for 1782 (Autumn) and find the proceedings, or report, of the federal Court held at Trenton, relative to the Connecticut claim, & let Mr Rea make out a copy for me.[4] Look also into the articles of Confederation (which you will find in my volume of the Constitutions of the states, & in the 2^d vol. of the laws of Penn^a) and let Rea transcribe the articles or article, which respects the holding of federal courts for deciding on the property of land, as well as *jurisdiction* between states.[5] They make a distinction here—& say the decree at Trenton only determined the *jurisdiction,* & not the *right of soil.* These two copies and the law before mentioned would be very useful to me before and at the election. I brought with me the laws for regulating the elections of Justices of the peace; but as these elections will be held in three districts, so I should have three copies of the laws. The first of the laws to regulate such elections was passed on the

---

[5] [1] P. H. M. C., Div. of Arch. and MSS., Record Group 27, Series: Exec. Corr., 1777-90, in Pickering's hand.
  [2] No. 2, *ante.*   [3] See no. 1, *ante,* note 3.
  [4] See Vol. VII, no. 128.   [5] Article IX of the Confederation.

31st of March 1784; and the law to alter and amend that, passed
on the 4th day of March 1786. Bradford can furnish you with
the two sets, and the sheets containing these particular laws may
be cut out & sent me. But I am most anxious to receive the law
for erecting this county, and the copies above mentioned. Of
these I could wish you to send me duplicates, one by the way of
Easton, and one by Hallers tavern, near the Wind-Gap. You
will probably find persons at Geisse's tavern (next door to Caspar Singers) market street, who will be coming to Haller's. I
wish you to wait on Mr Wilson, and request him to write me in
regard to the distinction before mentioned, of *jurisdiction* and
right of soil.[6] I remember the Connecticut Delegates made an
application to Congress for another court, to try the right of
soil; but did not obtain it: I wish to know why: they say here
that Mr Wilson prevented it.[7] For my own part, I think the
distinction groundless; and that the Court gave the *jurisdiction*
to Penn^a on the very principle that the *soil* belonged to this state.
But I w^d be happy to receive information on the subject from
Mr Wilson; and the sooner the better: for it enters into every
conversation I have with opponents. I remain dear sir affectionately yours,

T. Pickering

P. S. Tell Mrs P. that I am in perfect health.
† The Vermont Goliah [8] has not been here, as our good neighbour
pretended: I scarcely believe that he had heard so.

[6] William Hooker Smith to Zebulon Butler.[1]

Dear Sir,
    The people in This Neibourhood are fully Convins'd of Corn^l
Pickerings Friendship, & from His Reports are Not onely Sattisfyed of The mild Disposion of Goverment Towards us, but
also That They will, If Sutably applyd To, Confirm To Us
Settlers & Inhabetants our Improvements. You once had The
Leade of This Settlement, Then all Things went well, but of Late
we have bin wandering without a head.[2] (I mean The Settlers).

---

    [6] See no. 8, *post*.   [7] See Vol. VIII, Introduction, pp. xxvii-xxviii.
    [8] Ethan Allen; see *ibid.*, pp. xxxvi-xxxvii.
[6] [1] Wyoming Historical and Geological Society, Butler Papers, in
Smith's hand.
    [2] *Cf*. Vol. VIII, no. 159.

I hope The Time Is Near when we Shall becom an orderly Regular People. Nothing in my opinion will make us happy Subjects, but a Steady & firm attachment to Goverment, & Introduction & Istablishment of The Laws of Pensylvania & I Sincearly wish That you may Spend The Remander of your Days In Peace & affluance, & In order To Do honnor To you, In the Close of Life, I am Determined To Give for you at The Election my Vote & Influance for Counsiler, as will The People in General In This Neibourhood. I am in hops as The Riding Is So Good, to Receve a Visit from you & Spouse, Mʳ Baly and wife, If So Pray Invite Corn¹ Pickring To Rid with you. Der Sir after my Best wishes for you & yours I am your Humble Servᵗ

Wᵐ Hooker Smith

Jacobs Plains
Jan : 15ᵗʰ 1787.
Corn¹ Butler

P. S. Doctʳ Hooker Smith offeres him Selfe as a Candidate for Sherrif. I wish Corn¹ Denisson assembleman.

[7] Extract of a Letter from Tioga.[1]

Tioga Janʳ 22, 1787.

"Dear Sir,

For fear that the extremity of weather should prevent our attending the election, I send you these lines to inform you that the greater part of the people are agreed to take the law, though some are much against it & threaten to come down & drive gen¹ Pickering away; but I think their hearts will fail them.* I wish to get Mʳ Gore in Assemblyman if possible [2] and if you'll make interest that way we will give all our interest for the other officers as you think most advisable &c. I have had a private hint that there is about 30 persons intends to act desperate on the election

[7] [1] M. H. S., Pickering Papers, LVII, 90, a copy in Pickering's hand. There is no clue to sender or recipient.
    * there is 5 or 6 talks of going from here to join them. The way to prevent mischief is to guard against it in time &c."
    [2] Obadiah Gore had long been a leader in Wyoming but in recent months he had been overshadowed by John Franklin and John Jenkins. He led a group that sought land in New York; see *Susquehannah Company Papers*, VII, nos. 142 and 205. On Gore see also no. 112, *post*, note 4.

9

day to disturb it if possible but let 30 or 40 good men bring their arms over and that will prevent any such attempt."

Endorsed: Extract of a letter from Tioga dated Jan' 22. 1787. Election.

[8] James Wilson to Timothy Pickering.[1]

Dear Sir

I have been favoured with the perusal of your letter of the 12th inst to Col° Hodgdon,[2] in which you request me to write to you "in regard to the distinction of *jurisdiction* and *right of soil*," which, you say, is made at Wyoiming where it is alleged that the former *only* was determined, and *not* the latter, in the federal court that was held at Trenton. The most satisfactory answer that can be given on this subject is in the terms of the judgement of that court (see Journals of Congress of January 1783, page 83 & 84) "We are unanimously of opinion that the State of Connecticut has no right to the lands in controversy. We are also unanimously of opinion that the Jurisdiction and right of pre-emption of all the territory lying within the charter Boundary of Pennsylvania, and now claimed by the State of Connecticut, do of right belong to the State of Pennsylvania."[3] From this judgement and the States of the cases on which it is founded, it appears 1st That Connecticut had no right to the lands. 2d That Connecticut, and consequently those claiming under her, had no right even to a pre-emption from the Indians of their "native right" to the said lands (See the State of the Claim of of Connecticut Journ: Cong: January 1783. p: 74.)[4] for that the pre-emption *of right* belong to the State of Pennsylvania. As between the States therefore, the right of pre-emption of the soil is, as well as the right of jurisdiction, decided against Connecticut, and in favour of Pennsylvania.

There was indeed a question left open under the ninth article

---

[8] [1] M. H. S., Pickering Papers, LVII, 91-92, in Wilson's hand. A long endorsement in Pickering's hand gives the inclusive dates of the Trenton trial and lists the names of the five judges who signed the decree.

[2] Samuel Hodgdon was a business partner of Pickering's. His letter to Hodgdon has not been found.

[3] *Susquehannah Company Papers*, VII, no. 128, pp. 245-46; Worthington C. Ford *et al.* (eds.), *Journals of the Continental Congress* (Washington, 1905-37), XXIV, 31-32. The original decision did not use the phrase "right of" before "pre-emption."

[4] Vol. VII, no. 128, p. 166; Ford *et al., Journals*, XXIV, 23.

of Confederation, by the Court at Trenton; but that respected only the "*private* right of Soil claimed under Titles from the State of Pennsylvania and Connecticut respectively" (See Journal page 61.) [5] The mode of determining that question is provided for by that article, in favour of those who are within its description.

The reason why the Delegates of Connecticut did not succeed in their application for another Court was (as far as I recollect, not having the resolutions of Congress on that point before me) that their application did not specify the requisite descriptions, and was too vague and undeterminate both with regard to Lands and Claimants.[6]

You will now be able to detect and expose the artifice by which things so materially distinct have been industriously blended together.[7]

I wish you every success in the important business in which you are engaged; and am, with much truth and Esteem, dear Sir, Your Obedient humble Servant

James Wilson

Phil* January 26, 1787.

[9] William Hooker Smith and Others to Zebulon Butler and Timothy Pickering.[1]

Jacobs Plains Jan: 29th 1787.

Gentlemen

Wee the UnderSigners Receive Grat Sattisfaction When we viue Coronal Butlers Conduct Towards Coronal Pickring, & his

---

[5] In refusing to call the Wyoming settlers to appear before the court, as Connecticut agents had requested, the Trenton judges cited their commission under Article IX of the Articles of Confederation, which they said limited them to a determination of jurisdiction only between the two states. The judges more explicitly distinguished the issue of right of soil when they wrote to John Dickinson right after the trial was over to explain that their decision applied only to jurisdiction and not to private right of soil; Vol. VII, no. 129.

[6] Wilson is correct; see Vol. VIII, no. 155.

[7] See the Appendix, no. 327, *post*, for Pickering's conclusions about the private right of soil.

[9] [1] M. H. S., Pickering Papers, LVII, 94, in Smith's hand and signed by thirty-seven in a single column, Smith's name heading the list. Obviously this statement was offered in response to the notification of elections sent out by Pickering and Butler; no. 2, *ante*.

11

atachment To The Requirements of Goverment, which is manefest In his Zeale In Calling The people Together In the Several Destricts, in order That Coronal Pickring may Publish his mission from Goverment, also To Colect The minds of the People in Regard To The Election. we wish for a full Declaration from Coronal Butler on The Day of The Election, Previous Thareto. we are fully Sensable That we Cannot be happy without a Regular Establishment of Laws. we are absolutly Convinsed of The mild Disposition of Goverment. we are also further Sattisfyed That Goverment will Do for us all That is Resonable. Thare is one Thing onely which will quiet us after our Excaptance & Istablishment of The Laws of Pensylvania, That Is To Confirm To us our Posessions & Improvements, which we Think we have an Equetable write Too. we Give Up Every Idea from any other quorter, we have No Doupt but when Goverment in Thare, Grate wisdom, Come to Consider our Early Setlings Under the Countenance & Protection of A Sister State, our amazeing Sufferings, & Loss of Blood, as a frontear & Barer to Pensylvania, but That Goverment will adopt Sum mode, or way of accomedation & Settlement betwixt Us The Connectticut Settlers & other Clamants. we are The most of Us Under the Sollom Tye of Phydelety, & have bin Recognized in Conformety To The Laws of Pensylvania.[2] Gentlemen, you may be well assured That we Think it our Duty to Come Into The Election, & That wee will Extraordenaries Excepted attend on The Election, at The Day Place appointed, & be Redy To Give our Votes.

Corn¹ Zeblon Butler & Timothy Pickring Esqʳ

Wᵐ Hooker Smith	William Stark
Abraham Westbrook	his
Samuel Hover	Temothy X Perce
John Staples	Mark
his	Silas Smith
John X Rozecrance	William Stark Juʳ
mark	Silas Jackson
Casper Elsler	Jonathan Smith
Richard Westbrook	James Westbrook
Leonard Westbrook	William Jackson
Cornelius Cortright	Henry Buck
Daniel Holly	Charles W. Adams
	Nathen Draper

---

[2] Of the thirty-seven signers, fifteen had complied with the act of December 24, 1785, according to two extant lists; *Susquehannah Company Papers,* VIII, nos. 200 and 208.

his	Daniel Gore
Jacob X Osstkemp (?)	John Prouty
mark	Edward Prouty
Increase Billins	William Smith
Gorge Cuper	James Smith
Abner Tuttle	Martin Smith
Jonathan Davis	Henry Tuttle
John Hover	Ephraim Lewis
John Trusdale	
Isacc Vanorman	

[10] William Hooker Smith and Others to Timothy Pickering and Zebulon Butler.[1]

Dear Gentlemen

we from Jacobs Plains offer ourSelves as Gards To you on The The Day of Election. we wish To Receive Directions from you as To our Particular Conduct. we shall Com all Down In a Body & Keep Together unless otherways advised by you. we Intend To Presarve Decancy Regularety & order however, we will Submit To Your Direction. we on That Day shall be at your Service.

Wm Hooker Smith
Samuel Hover
Abraham   Westbrook

Jacobs Plains Jan : 30th 1787
Corⁿ Butler & Timothy Pickring Esqr

[11] Oaths of Allegiance before Timothy Pickering and Others.[1]

I   swear that I renounce & refuse all allegiance to George the third King of Great Britain his heirs & successors; & that I will be faithful & bear true allegiance to the Commonwealth of Pennsylvania, as a free and independent state; and that I will not at any time do or cause to be done any matter or thing that will be prejudicial or injurious to the freedom & independence

---

[10] [1] M. H. S., Pickering Papers, LVII, 96, in Smith's hand and signed by the three men. For Pickering's response, see no. 18, *post,* p. 56.
[11] [1] M. H. S., Pickering Papers, LVII, 97-103 and 106A-113, signed by each individually, but see note 2.

thereof; & I do further swear that I never have, since the declaration of the independence of the United States of America, voluntarily joined, aided, assisted or abetted the king of Great Britain, his Generals fleets or armies, or their adherents (knowing them to be such) whilst employed against the said United States or either of them.

Names	Occupations	Places of Abode	Time when taken
1. Nicholas Brink	Husbandman	3 miles below Shawney	Jany 13. 1787.
2. Gilbert Van Gorden	ditto	ditto	ditto
3. Leonard Westbrook	ditto	Wilkesboro'	Jany 13.
4. John Staples [2]	ditto	ditto	19th
5. John Hollenback	Yeoman	Wilkesborough	Jany 22. 1787.
6. Daniel Holly	Brewer	ditto	ditto
7. James Westbrook	Husbandman	ditto	ditto
The mark of 8. Jacob X Ossencup	husbandman	ditto	Jany 30. 1787.
9. Henry Buck	Physician	Wilkesborough	Jany 31. 1787.
10. John Squire	Husbandman	Exeter	Jany 31. 1787.
The mark of 11. Peter X Roberts	ditto	ditto	ditto
12. Simon Spalding	Gentleman	Sheshecanock	Feby 1. 1787
13. Mathias Hollenback	ditto	Wilkesborough	ditto
14. timothy perce	Husbandman	Pittstown	ditto
15. William Stark, Ju	husbandman	ditto	ditto
The mark of 16. Increase X Billings	yeoman	ditto	ditto
17. Jonathan Davis	yeoman	ditto	ditto
18. Jonathan Smith	Cooper	Wilkesboro'	ditto
19. William Smith	husbandman	ditto	ditto
20. Caleb Newman	Yeoman	Tunkhannock	ditto
21. William Jackson	Cooper	Wilkesboro'	ditto
22. Leonard Lott	husbandman	Tunkhannock	ditto
The mark of 23. Benjamin B Brink	hunter	Wilkesborough	ditto
24. John Inman	blacksmith	Hanover	ditto
The mark of 25. George X Charles	husbandman	Waupollopy	ditto
26. Elisha Cortwright	Yeoman	Waupollopy	ditto
27. John Pottman	Yeoman	ditto	ditto
28. Henry McCormick	Husbandman	Kingston	ditto

[2] The first four names are actually listed separately under the following designation in Pickering's hand: "Names of Inhabitants of the County of Luzerne who took the oath of Allegiance to the State of Pennsylvania, before Timothy Pickering." The names of Brink and Van Gorden do not appear to be signatures. In the same hand, probably Pickering's, follow the names of Westbrook and Staples without being numbered. These are crossed out. The Westbrook and Staples names then follow as numbers 3 and 4 and appear to be bona fide signatures.

Names	Occupations	Places of Abode	Time when taken
29. Thomas Gibson	husbandman	Wilkesborough	ditto
30. Elisa Decker	husbandman	Hanover	ditto
31. Abraham Lane	Husbandman	Hanover	ditto
32. And^w Decker	Husbandman	hanover	February 1. 1787.
33. Jno Hagemen	Shopkeeper	Wilkesborough	Feby 1. 1787.
The mark of			
34. James X Brown	yeoman	Pittstown	ditto
35. James Brown j^r	husbandman	ditto	ditto
36. John Budd	yeoman	ditto	ditto
37. Gideon Osterhout	yeoman	Tunkhanock	ditto
38. Elias decker	husbandman	Hanover	ditto
The mark of			
39. Daniel D Sherrard	husbandman	Waupollopy	ditto
40. John Johnson	husbandman	Hanover	ditto
41. jedediah Stephens Jr.	husbandman	Kingston	ditto
42. Robert Coeley	ditto	ditto	ditto
43. William Jacways	Husbandman	Exeter	ditto
44. Thomas Gardner	husbandman	Exeter	ditto
45. Joseph Leonard	ditto	Pittstown	d^o
46. Enos Tubbs	ditto	Tunkhannock	d^o
47. jeremiah Blanchard	Yeoman	Pittstown	d^o
48. Chester Bingham	husbandman	Ulster (Wyalusing)	d^o
49. Henry Birney	ditto	Kingston	d^o
50. Ambrose Gaylor	yeoman	d^o	d^o
51. John Lutsee	husbandman	Wilkesboro	d^o
52. Eleazar Blackman	d^o	d^o	d^o
53. Nehemiah Crofoot	d^o	Hanover	d^o
54. Edward Inman	d^o	Wilkesboro'	d^o
55. Ebenezer Enos	d^o	Kingston	d^o
56. Elisha Blackmin jun	d^o	Wilkesboro	d^o
57. Ira Manvill	Sadler	Kingston	d^o
58. Martin Dudley	husbandman	Wilkesborough	Feby 1. 1787.
59. William Hyde	d^o	d^o	d^o
60. James Millage	d^o	d^o	d^o
61. Henry Decker	Shoemaker	Kingston	d^o
62. Jehoiada Johnston	husbandman	Wilkesborough	d^o
63. Abraham Smith	d^o	d^o	d^o
64. Elisha Blackman	d^o	d^o	d^o
65. Joseph Hageman	d^o	d^o	d^o
66. Nathan Northrup	Carpenter	Hanover	d^o
67. Wall^d [?] Spencer	husbandman	d^o	d^o
68. Jonothon Fris^e	d^o	d^o	d^o
69. James Lassly	d^o	Hanover	d^o
70. Daniel Sulvan	Labourer	Kingston	d^o
71. Stephe Sticland	Cordwainer	Wilkesborough	d^o
72. justin Gaylord j^r	blacksmith	Kingston	
73. Jonathan Newman	ditto	Pittstown	d^o
74. David McCormick	husbandman	Kingston	d^o

15

Names	Occupations	Places of Abode	Time when taken
75. George Crooms	ditto	Wilkesborough	d°
76. Roger Searles	cordwainer	Pittstown	d°
77. Nehemuh Northrup	millwright	Hanover	d°
78. Sam^{el} Ayres	carpenter	Plymouth	d°
79. Stephen Burvilt	husbandman	Hanover	d°
80. Abram Addonis	ditto	ditto	d°
81. Jeremiah Baker	cordwainer	Plymouth	d°
82. Gilbert Carpenter	carpenter	Kingston	
83. Joshua Vanfleet	husbandman	Wilkesborough	d°
84. Zeb^n Marcy	ditto	Putnam	d°
85. Oliver Bennet	d°	Hanover	d°
86. James Esland	d°	Plymouth	d°
87. Joab Enos	d°	Kingston	d°
88. Josiah Rogers	d°	Plymouth	d°
89. Gideon Church	d°	Kingston	d°
90. Benjamin Carpenter	joiner	ditto	d°
91. Benjamin Cary	husbandman	Wilkesborough	Feby 1. 1787.
92. samuel Miller	d°	d°	d°
93. Benjamin Crawford	Cooper	Kingston	d°
94. Stephen Jenkins	husbandman	Exeter	d°
95. William Baker	ditto	Plymouth	d°
96. John King	d°	Kingston	d°
97. Elnathan Cory	cordwainer	ditto	d°
98. John Davison	husbandman	Pittstown	d°
99. Thomas Drake	ditto	Kingston	d°
100. Isaiah Howell	joiner	d°	d°
101. Barnabas Cary	husbandman	Pittstown	d°
102. Thomas Joslon	Carpenter	Exeter	d°
103. Josiah Kellogg	husbandman	Plymouth	d°
104. Isaac Bennet	ditto	Newport	d°
The mark of 105. Lebeus X tubs	ditto d°	Exeter d°	d° d°
106. Stephen Harding	d°	Hanover	d°
107. Edward spencerd	d°	Pittstown	d°
108. Samuel meddagh	d°	Kingston	d°
109. John Woolley	d°	Pittstown	d°
110. Elijah silbee	Carpenter	Wilkesborough	d°
111. Joseph Kilborn	cordwainer	Plymouth	d°
112. Thomas Thorp	husbandman	Kingston	d°
113. John Montany	Tailor	Wilkesborough	Feby 1. 1787.
114. John Kennedy			
The mark of 115. Nathan X Jones			ditto
The mark of 116. Daniel X Gridley	husbandman	Wilkesboro'	d°
117. Daniel Roberts	d°	d°	d°
118. Lebeus Hammond	d°	Exeter	d°
Mark of 119. Samuel X Daly	husbandman	Exeter	Feby 1. 1787
120. Stephen Gardner	d°	Pittstown	d°
121. Adam Dilley	d°	Wilkesboro'	d°
122. Abraham vantilbury	d°	Plymouth	d°

16

Names	Occupations	Places of Abode	Time when taken
123. Richard Hallsted	d°	Pittstown	d°
124. Joseph Dewey	d°	Waupollopy	d°
Mark of			
125. David O Dale	d°	Exeter	d°
126. Thadbury Cowl	d°	Tioga	d°
127. Edward Edgerton	labourer,	Wilkesboro'	d°
128. John Dickson	husbandman	Pittstown	d°
mark			
129. Ebenezer X Ellis's			
jun.	husbandman	Wilkesboro'	d°
130. Moses Depui	d°	Kingston	d°
131. John Durkee	ditto	Wilkesboro'	d°
132. James Whitney	labourer	Wilkesboro'	d°
mark of			
133. Robert X Alexander	weaver	Kingston	d°
The mark of			
134. Nicholas X Depue			
135. William Simrell	husbandman	Providence	d°
mark of			
136. Eben' X Ellis sen'	husbandman	Hanover	d°
137. Eleazer Miller	husbandman	Wilkesborough	d°
138. Abel yarington	Ferryman	ditto	d°
139. Elijah Oakley	Husbandman	Putnam	d°
140. Jeremiah Shaw [3]	husbandman	Ulster	d°

[12] List of Election Officials for Luzerne County.[1]

A list of the Names of the Judges, Inspectors & Clerks chosen and appointed at the Election holden at the House of Col° Butler at Wilkesborough in the County of Luzerne on the first day of February 1787.

Judges

Obadiah Gore. Sworn

James Sutton   Affirmed

Christopher Hurlbutt   Sworn

---

[3] An endorsement in Pickering's hand lists the total as 141, including "2 sworn before Col° Butler" and "3 British deserters, two of them Germans."

Additional men who took the oath in February were Lawrence Myers, William Dorton, Caspar Elster, John Platner, Abraham Pyke, and William Schaff.

An alphabetical arrangement of the names made by Pickering has an endorsement claiming that 146 men took the oath.

[12] [1] M. H. S., Pickering Papers, LVII, 115.

Inspectors

Simon Spalding   Sworn
John Swift   Sworn
John Hurlbutt   Sworn

Clarks

Elisha Satterlee   Sworn
Lord Butler   Sworn
John Hyde   Sworn

Certify⁴ Per.

✓ Obad^h Gore   ⎫ Judges
Christopher Hurlbut ⎬   of
James Suttons   ⎭ Elextion

[13] Votes Cast in Luzerne County Election.[1]

Representative

John Franklin   one hundred and forty five [2]
✓ Obadiah Gore,   fifty four
Nath^n Denison   Seventeen
Zebulon Butler   three
Christopher Hurlbut   one
Jn° Paul Shott   one
James Suttons   one.

Councellors

Nathan Denison   Ninety Seven
Matthew Hollenback   forty Seven
Jn° Paul Shott   forty Seven
Zebulon Butler   twenty three [3]
John Jenkins   two.
✓ Oba^d Gore   one.
John Franklin   one

[13] [1] M. H. S., Pickering Papers, LVII, 116-19. The election of those with the highest number of votes was duly certified to the authorities by judges Obadiah Gore, Christopher Hurlbut, and James Sutton; *ibid.*, 120-22.

[2] Franklin's popularity is obvious; only Lord Butler, Zebulon's son, got a higher total vote.

[3] The small vote for Butler here and for representative is some measure of his declining influence among the Wyoming settlers, although perhaps his unwillingness to hold office was a factor as well.

18

Commissioners

Jonah Rogers   one hundred and five
Christopher Hurlbut   one hundred and three
Nat[h] Kingsley   one hundred.
Simon Spolding   Seventy Nine
Abel Pearce   Sixty four
Abraham Westbrook   twenty Six
Sam[ll] Hover,   twenty Six
Nat[hn] Carey   twenty
Jabez Fish   five
✓ Daniel Gore   Eleven
Asa Bennett   four
John Swift   two
✓ oba[d] Gore   two
John Hurlbut   two
James Sutton   two
Robert M[c]Dowel   one
✓ Benj[a] Bailey   one
Silas Smith   one
John Rosecrants   one
John Jinkins   one
John Hide   one
John Phillips   one.
Jonathan Woodworth   one
✓ Abel yarrington   one
Benj[a] Cairey   one.
Thomas Neill   one
John Hallenback   one
Zebulon Butler   one
Benjamin Carpenter   one
Ebenezer Massy   one
Jn[o] Paul Shott   one
Richard Halsted   one

Coroners

Nathan Cary   one hundred and Seven
John Dorrance   Ninety Six
Abel Yarrington   Sixty three ✓
Benj[a] Bailey   thirty five ✓
Jn[o] Paul Shott   thirty Seven
Tho[s] Niell   twenty four
John Swift   fourteen
Abel Pierce   Six

Daniel Gore   Six
John Inman   three
Christopher Hurlbut   three
Mason Fitch Alden   two
Abraham Westbrook.   one
Phineas Nash.   one
Elisha Satterly   one.
Jabez Fitch   one
Jonathan Smith   one
John Phillips   one
Silas Smith   one
Tho⁸ Harding   one
Obadiah Gore   one
John Kenady   one

Sheriffs

Lord Butler   one Hundred and Seventy
Mason Fitch Alden   one Hundred and thirty Eight
William Hooker Smith   fifty five [4]
Thomas Martin   thirteen
Lawrance Myers   thirteen
John Swift   twelve
Cornelius Cortwright   five
Benjamin Jenkins   three
Leonard Westbrook   two
Simon Spolding   two
Daniel Gore   two
Abraham Westbrook   two
John Hide   two
John Inman   three
James Westbrook   one
William Jackson   one
John Hurlbut   one
Christopher Hurlbut   one
Benjamin Bailey   one
John Trusdale   one
Jonathan Rosson   one
John Hollenback   one.

---

[4] Some measure of Smith's influence is reflected in this vote. He had declared there were fifty men at Jacob's Plains alone, some thirty-six of whom had signed a loyal statement with him. Apparently his influence did not carry far beyond his own neighborhood. Smith actively sought the office of sheriff.

Jonathan Smith one
Leonard Lott one
Abel Yarrington one
Benjamin Smith one
John Jinkins one
Daniel Hawley one
Nathan Cary one

[14] Timothy Hosmer to John Paul Schott.[1]

Farmington Feby 2^d 1787

Sir

The News of this Country Col. Franklin will be able to Communicate to you. The Tumults in the State of Masachusets have Grown to a Serious War. The Insurgents (or as they Call themselves Regulators) are in arms upwards of Two Thousands Strong.[2] Genl Lincoln is in Pursuit of them with Four Thousand Troops but hath not yet overtook them so as to Come to any Action. The war is Carried on by the Three West County* Vz Worchestor Hampshire & Berkshire, it is a very Inflamatory disordor and Catches accross the State Line. Many of our People feel the Influence of the Disease and are Waiting the Event of this Present Expedition. If the Regulators are Successful I Think it Probable that the New England States will be Generally thrown into Confusion. will it not be Advantageous to the Susquehannah Settlement, let the event Go which way it will. If Government succeeds those opposers must look for some other Place to make their Residence and I have no doubt but numbers of them will flee to your Goodly Country: If they Fail (the Governmental Troops) we Shall be Flung into a State of Anarchy, from which a new form of Government must Grow, from the Feebleness of the present Foederal Government, it is not likely it will be attempted but a Monarchical of some kind will it is most probable Grow out of it. If so we have all the reason to draw this Conclusion That the holders of the Lands will have

---

[14] [1] M. H. S., Pickering Papers, LVII, 123, marked "copy" and in an unknown hand. Hosmer, who was a military surgeon during the Revolution, had been recently chosen as a commissioner of the Susquehannah Company; *Record of Service of Connecticut Men in the War of the Revolution* (Hartford, 1889), p. 374, and *Susquehannah Company Papers,* VIII, no. 268.

[2] The reference, of course, is to Shays' Rebellion.

it secured to them after the Revolution for undoubtedly there will be an anihilation of State lines under a one Headed Government. That we shall not have to Quarell with a State but have a Tryal before Majesty which I had rather Submit to Tho. it were a Nero or Caligula Than to the Land Jobing Jockying State of Pennsylvania.

We have Just received Information that Col. Pickering is at Wyoming & That the Inhabitants are warned to attend an Election to begin yesterday. will your people allow themselves to be Gull⁴ out of their Estates by receiving the Laws of that State which you have had so much Experience of; the moment you submit to their law you relinquish all your property in that Country, and must Expect to hold your Estates by no other Tenure than that of Tenn[ants.] For Gods Sake and your own Honour & Intrest Oppose it in every Stage. let no Glare of Honour or Specious Flattery of a Smooth Tongue induce you to Submit for you will find yourself as unhappily Situated as Insult and Poverty can make you. My Compliments to Mʳˢ Shott and your Good Family, should have been very happy to have seen you with us at our meeting ³ the doings of which Col Franklin will be able to Communicate to you by which you will find we are attentive to the Genˡ Interest of the Settlers & Company. Let me hint before I Close that the State will I believe Take up the Matter and apply to Congress for to set aside the Trenton Decree which will undoubtedly be complyd with. My best wishes attend you & yours. Stand fast by the Connecticut Claim and you undoubtedly will be secure in your Property in Peace. I am Sir your Friend and Humble Servᵗ

Timᵒʸ Hosmer

[15] John Van Campen to Timothy Pickering.¹

Larns 3ᵗʰ February 1787

Sir

I waited here this Day Expecting to See you on your Return from wioming to Philadelphia. I was happy to be inforᵐ of your business at that place but am unhappy to be informd Last Evening of Riots and tumults the Day of your Election. our Laws and Constitution, Says all Elections shall be free and voluntary. that has not [been] the Case at wioming as my informr [told]

³ Of December 26 and 27; Vol. VIII, no. 268.
[15] ¹ M. H. S., Pickering Papers, LVII, 125, in Van Campen's hand.

me many Citizens Exspected to Enjoy [the] Liberty of freemen. Some had their [heads] broke, others made their Escape, This Evening I am informd by men of [Candor?] and [Pepirtration?] [?] those Electors informd them they mean to abide by the Laws untill actions were brought. if that should be the Case where will Liberty and freedom Land. I would [be] Exceeding happy to see you at my House. I am Sir your very Humble Srv^t

NB Exspect to be in Philadelphia soon   John Van Campen

Endorsed : rec^d at Learned's the 8th

[16] Petition of Luzerne County Inhabitants to the Pennsylvania General Assembly.[1]

The Address and Petition of the Inhabitants of the county of Luzerne, to the Honourable The General Assembly of the Representatives of the Freemen of Pennsylvania.

May it please the Assembly to accept our grateful acknowledgements for their attention to our requests, in erecting this district into a seperate county, and giving us an opportunity of choosing civil officers, and of being represented in the Assembly and in the Supreme Executive Council. We are happy in the prospect now opened, of our receiving and enjoying the blessings of regular and constitutional government. Nothing will then be wanting to remove every cause of jealousy and complaint, but the confirmation of the titles to our lands.

These lands have been the source of such disorders, such losses, and such sufferings, that we have reason to deplore the fatal day when we and our fathers first set foot upon this hostile ground. But here we now are, an indigent and distressed people. A people whose substance often acquired, has often been destroyed. Even what our various enemies at any time left us, or allowed us respite to procure, has repeatedly been overwhelmed & ruined, or swept away, by destructive floods. So that we are now more wretched, and are enduring greater hardships, than at the first moment of our migration hither.

Pardon us that we have glanced upon our sufferings : we would not wound the ear of humanity with a detail of miseries

---

[16] [1] M. H. S., Pickering Papers, LVII, 127-29, a copy in Pickering's hand. Pickering drew up the petition in agreement with the settlers; no. 18, *post,* entries for February 3 and 5.

23

that are past: particularly we would not describe those which were above all others the most insupportable; those which were inflicted by men who appeared in the light of subjects of Pennsylvania, and consequently of fellow citizens. But the justice of the State has held those transactions up [to] public censure; and with this reparation we will be content. Those outrages we have not forgotten; we *cannot yet forget them;* for at this hour we are experiencing distresses which spring from that very source: But we will endeavour to *forgive* them. Some among ourselves have not been favored less; and it may be essential to the peace of the county that all past offences be buried in oblivion. Some of us have large claims for injuries received but we are willing to sacrifice them on the altar of peace. We wish not to open afresh those wounds which now are healing: and therefore express our hope, that it may consist with the wisdom of the Assembly to pass an act of oblivion and indemnity, as well for private trespasses as public wrongs.

It is our earnest desire to ground our petition on the basis of reason and equity: but our all is at stake: for, seperate from our lands, we have no property worth naming: and under the operation of such an interest—an interest dear to us as our lives —perhaps we may ask more than reason and equity can grant. We wish not to offend: and if any part of our request should appear amiss, we pray for the indulgent consideration of the Honourable Assembly, that such impropriety may not prejudice those equitable rights to which we shall be thought entitled.

In the event of things, our lands have cost us dear indeed. Their price has been paid (too dearly paid) in the blood of our fathers, husbands, sons, and brothers! And now, of the hard labour of seventeen years, no fruits remain! In such unhappy circumstances, shall we be thought unreasonable, if we ask a free and gratuitous confirmation of our titles to those lands? We hope not.

The lands we refer to, are those which are comprehended in the annexed list of townships,[2] and a few detached lots capable

---

[2] A copy of the list in the Pickering Papers (LVII, 129-30) briefly describes the boundaries of eighteen towns, but only seventeen names are given. A second list, with briefer descriptions, omits the name of Athens. Fifteen towns are described as bordering on the Susquehanna River. All towns except Athens are said to have been laid out before the Trenton decree. On Athens, see no. 18, *post,* entry for February 6. The towns in alphabetical order are Athens, Bedford, Claverack, Exeter, Hanover, Huntington, Kingston, Newport, Northmoreland, Pittstown, Plymouth, Providence, Putnam, Salem, Springfield, Ulster, and Wilkes-Barre. According

of cultivation between the townships, which under the Authority of Connecticut were laid out and settled prior to the decree of the federal court at Trenton. These townships are generally squares of five miles, & severally divided into fifty three farm-lots, of three hundred acres each; of which one was appropriated to the use of the first settled minister, in fee, one for a parsonage, and one for the support of a school; and the remaining fifty were allotted to such persons as settled upon or purchased them. The farm-lots in all the towns were not actually occupied prior to the settlement of jurisdiction between the states of Pennsylvania and Connecticut: but in some of the towns the distinct families were twice as numerous as the farm-lots; and many such families, who had rights in other towns, were prevented from making actual settlements, thro' fear of destruction from the Indians, during the late war. The farm-lots so laid out and occupied, or which had been assigned to persons living within the settlement, and who during the war could not with safety commence their improvements, comprehend all the lands, the titles to which we pray the General Assembly to confirm.

[We hope that equity and just policy may warrant a gratuitous confirmation of those farm lots: but if not, then we pray we may be enabled to hold them on reasonable terms of payment: that to save the delays, perplexities and expense which must attend a State enquiry into the comparative value of those farm-lots, one general price may be fixed for each hundred acres; and that the county commissioners, with the township assessors hereafter to be chosen, may be impowered and required to meet together to make a valuation of the said farm-lots & fix the quota to be paid for each. But in making such payment—if required—we do most earnestly entreat for the indulgence of the Honourable Assembly, that we may be enabled to do it by small annual installments. For at present we have no money, nor the means of raising any, unless we sell a few cattle we are possessed of (and which are essentially necessary for the cultivation of our lands, & food [for] our families)—or the lands themselves.] [3]

Without entering into farther details, which must appear tedious, we here rest our cause; committing it to the wisdom, the

to the endorsement the list was compiled from information supplied by Obadiah Gore, Captain Spaulding, James Sutton, and Nathan Denison. *Cf.* the list in *Susquehannah Company Papers,* I, note on Maps (after the Table of Contents).

[3] The paragraph in brackets is crossed out. Its deletion came at the request of some of the settlers who did not want to raise the question of paying for the lands; no. 18, *post,* entry for February 5, evening.

equity, & the kindness of the General Assembly: and with all possible respect beg leave to subscribe our names.[4]
County of Luzerne February 5. 1787.

Vicheson Morey
Zebulon Cady
Isaac Addems
Daniel Earl
Elisha Drake
Benjamin Jones j
Juston Jones
Benjamin Jones
Ebenezer Stephens
David Daley
Joseph Leonard
Benjamin Smith
Thomas Stoddard
Jeremiah Osterhart
William Hall
Thomas Harding
Elisha Harding
Richard Holsted
Elija Silsbury
Abraham Trait
Joseph Harding
Daniel Cambel
Edward Prouty
John Roberts
John Phillips
Amos Egilston
Cornel Hopper
David Michel
Thomas Gardner
Caleb Bates
Ebenezer Morey
John Scott

Enos Tubbs
John Marcy
Gideon Osterhart
Math° Goodspeed
Abner Beach
Alexander Beach
Caleb Newman
Peletiah W. Osterhart
Sephti[h] Earls
Ely Newman
Nathan Draper
Henry Tutle
Daniel Holley
Richard Westbrook
Leonard Westbrook
Cornelius Cortwright
James Westbrook
John Prouty
John Hover
John Cortrecht
Thomas Read
John Rosencranz
Samuel Midough
Abraham Hardin
John Kennedy
Casper Elster
William Stark
Timothy Pierce
William Stark
William Smith
Jonathin Smith
Martin Smith

[4] Names are not given in Pickering's copy. The 130 names here given are taken from a nineteenth century copy of a certified copy of the original petition; Amer. Phil. Soc., Documents relative to the Wyoming or Connecticut Controversy, I, 221-26.

This petition was read in the General Assembly on March 6 and referred to a committee composed of George Clymer, Gerardus Wynkoop, Adam Hubley, Robert Brown, and William Findley. Its report was read on March 10 and again on March 17; see no. 31, *post*.

James Scott
Joseph Rider
Seth Carey
Barnabas Carey
Richard Halstad Jun'
Francis Phillips
John Dickson
Job Tripp
Daniel Taylor
Preserved Taylor
Thomas Picket
James Brown sen'
William Griffith
Leonard Lott
Joel Newman
Joseph Arthur
Ephraim Sanford
Asahel Therton
Isaac Trip
Stephen Gardner
Isaih Halsted
Jeremiah Blanchard
Amos Harding
Isaac Irvin
James Brown Jr.
John Budd
William Jackson
Abner Tutle
John Staples
James Rosurory
Ephraim Lewis
Zeb' Marcy

John Tindal
W'" Hooker Smith
Samuel S Muir
Abraham Westbrook
Daniel Gore
James Smith
Jos' Sprague Jun'
Samuel Miller
John Davison
Samuel Miller Jr.
Daniel Cambell
William Miller
Sarah Lee
Henry Decker
Bezer Robards
John Squire Jr.
Abijah Patterson
Samuel Gore
Benjamin Brinck
Jacob Ausencop
Increase Billings
Increase Billings Jr.
George Cooper
Chareack Westbrook
Jonathan Rosson
Ransler Billings
James Armstrong
Jonathan Davis
William Hurlbut
Pelich Comstut
John Woodley

[17] The Rev. Jacob Johnson to Timothy Pickering.[1]

Sir

I am fully perswaded the Lands in controversy appertain both in Law Equity & Justice to the State of Connecticut and Proprietors who hold under that State

[17] [1] M. H. S., Pickering Papers, LVII, 131-32, in Johnson's hand but not signed. Johnson probably gave this letter directly to Pickering.

Nevertheless for the Sake of ending the unhappy controversy in Peace & Love I am rather inclind to come to a Division of the Lands agreable to the President or Example set us by King David very Simular to the present Case

The King gave all the Lands appertaining to the House of Saul to Mephebosheth. Afterwards the King gave away The Same Lands & even the whole to Ziba upon which a Controversy arose betwxt Mephibosheth & Ziba who was heir in Law to the forsaid Lands Seing a grant was equally made to both. The King ends the controversy by ordering a Division to each one as fellow Commoners in Law to Said Lands. This medium of ending the Controversy I have proposed Some time ago agreeable to the Divideing Lines drawn by Congress [2] betwixt the East & West branches of susquehanna Setting off the East branch to Connecticut Proprietors & the west to Pensylvania. This medium of compromisement I would still propose & urge agreable not only to the Royal Example above But also a late Settlement of Massachusets & New York.[3]

If it should be objected that the Decree at Trenton was Definitive And gave the Right of Jurisdiction & pre-empton to the State of Pensylvania consequently the Proprietors of the State of Connecticut have no right to a Division.

Answ' That Decree at Trenton was either Inclusive of the Right of Connecticut in common with that of Pensylvania or Exclusive. If inclusive then we have a Right of Division even by that Decree, or if supposd by the Objector, To be exclusive, we nevertheless have a Right in Law to plead the most favourable construction wherfore tuurn the Tables which way-soever the Objector pleases we have still a Right in Law to an equitable Division. And on this Bassis we Rest the whole matter. Do therefore Petition and plead only for Law Equity & Justice to be done us. If it should be farther objected that to make a Division of so considerable a Tract of Country to so few & inconsiderable company of Proprietors would be too much. Is it too much to pay for the Price of so much blood spilt & Treasure left on this hostile & unhappy ground who-where Is the man in all Pensylvania would give such a price, I am sure If it was to do again I would not purchase it at so dear a Rate.

But what great thing is it: Seperate the Lands of worth from those of wast & worthless, what have the Proprieters now

---

[2] Johnson has reference to a resolution of Congress in 1775; *Susquehannah Company Papers,* VI, nos. 240 and 241.

[3] See *ibid.,* VIII, no. 93, note 4.

on the ground but a moderate farm to be sure if we take in their Posterity with them.

If it be objected That the state of Pensylvania can't give away Lands that are the Property of Governor Pen or the Land-holder under Him Answr we want no such Gift But only what we have a Right to in Law equity & Justice. we dont come to the Assembly to begg a Gift but to protect & defend us in the enjoyment of our own.

Should it be Said we are now a County & Have or may have benefit of Common Law, what need we more. Be it so. As the present State of things are This will not prevent Hostilities vexations Law suits Tumults & Confusions among us. But I submit the Cause to the supreme Arbiter of the universe and wisdom of the Assembly of the state of Pensylvania. You will please Sir to enforce the Reason Law & equity of divideing these controverted Lands as above proposed. And you will in so doing be an Advocate in the Suffering Cause of Right & Oblige Yours &c

Endorsed: Rec⁴ Mʳ Johnson's letter, rec⁴ of him Febʸ 7, 1787.

[18] Journal of Timothy Pickering's Visit to Wyoming.¹

Wednesday Janʸ 3ᵈ at 12 o'clock, set out from philadelphia, with S. Wheeler, & went that night to his house, 20 miles.

Janʸ 4ᵗʰ proceeded for Bethlehem: but being informed at Shultz's tavern that the Creek Tohicken, & the Branch were too high to be forded, I went another road, to the left, for Quakertown; & there was advised to take another left hand road, which passed by Cooper's tavern (6 miles from Quakertown) where I lodged. Both these roads, it was said, made as short a way to Bethlehem, as that usually travelled: but they are not so good: from Coopers, in particular, the land is very stony.

Janʸ 5ᵗʰ (Friday) Rode to Bethlehem, & breakfasted; then proceeded to Haller's tavern, near the Wind gap. Here I found M. Holleback.

Janʸ 6. Left Hallers, & proceeded 16 miles (to Learnar's) on our way to Wyoming.

[18] ¹ M. H. S., Pickering Papers, LVII, 39-84, in Pickering's hand.

29

[2] [2] *Jany 7th* (Sunday)   proceeded 12 miles to Tobyhanna Creek.   Just on the other side lives one *Luce,* who formerly (about 16 years ago), agreed with Mr Allen (Andrew) for a tract of 250 acres of land at Lackawanack Creek, to pay £80. p. 100 acres, after 8 years quiet possession : but Luce says he never had 3 years quiet possession.   in the 3^d year he was driven off by the New England people ; & then he went to live on Juniata.   About 3 years ago the Pennsylvania settlers were notified to return & take possession ; which he did ; but was again obliged by the N. E. people to remove, leaving a large quantity of grain on the ground.   He then went into the hut which he now lives in, & which he found ready built, by Tobyhanna Creek. He here supplies travellers with *rum* & *victuals:* but has neither *grain* nor *hay.*   (Luce says he was the first occupant of the land he claims at Lackawannack.)

Tobyhanna, at the present fording place [3] has steep banks, and a muddy bottom.   At this time, the water was up half way my horse's sides.   Tis about 3 rods wide.

From Tobyhanna we went forward to Kelly's (formerly Bullocks tavern) 17 or 18 miles, & 7 from Wyoming.   Here our horses got a little bog hay ; & it being near dark, & the road very bad, I concluded to stay at Kelly's till the next morning.   Holleback & Oehmig went on to Wyoming.   About 7 miles from Tobyhanna we crossed the *Lehi,* where it is about 4 rods wide & was nearly as deep (with a rocky bottom) as Tobyhanna. Bear Creek is about 2 rods wide, has a very rocky bottom, [4] is rapid, was now about 3 feet deep, & lies about 8 miles from the Lehi.   From Bear Creek to Kelly's is about 2 miles.   So the whole distance from Learnar's to Wioming is about 36 miles, to which add 16 (the distance from Hallers to Learnar's) & 68 (the distance from Phila^a to Hallers) & you have 120 miles for the whole distance from Phila^a to Wyoming.

36
16
52
68
120

About   miles from Learnar's you enter the Great Swamp.   There after passing   miles of higher ground, you enter that part of the swamp which is called the *Shades of Death;* and   miles farther, you enter Bear Swamp which is also a *branch* of the Great Swamp.

The swamps are filled chiefly with white pines & hemlock : but there is a mixture of proper spruce,   beach, maple, black [5] birch & wild cherry tree.   The high grounds between the swamps are but moderate risings, tho' pretty rocky.   And it seems that but few parts (not exceeding 2 miles, if added together) of the swamps are miry ; the other parts are rocky.

---

[2] Numbers in brackets indicate page numbers of the journal.

Jany 8. Left Kelly's before sun-rise, and came to Wyoming to breakfast. 3 miles from Kelly's I crossed *Laurel-Run,* in one hour's riding. The road along the run excessively rocky, & for several rods the run has got into the road, & gullied it 3 and four feet deep. In one mile more I reached the top of the mountain, by a very easy ascent. Here I had a view of the Susquehanna, & the flats on each side. Wyoming seemed just at hand; Yet was 3 miles distant. It cost me half an hour to descend the mountain, part of the way pretty steep. The rest of the ground to Wyoming consists of several ranges [6] of very moderate, swelling hills, with low grounds, fit for meadows between them. Thro' one of these low parts (which is called a swamp) runs a small creek, which running about a mile below the town lots of Wilkesborough turns & runs up near to the lower end of ye town lots into the Susquehanna

The mountain, is exceedingly barren; bearing only bushes and a few oaks and pines of small growth. All the high grounds, indeed, from this to the Blue Mountain, appeared alike barren.

AT WYOMING. *Jany 8.* In conversing with Jn° Holleback on the articles of *rum* & *whiskey,* he informed me that he was in the practice of distilling whiskey, when grain was plenty: that he used to sell one [7] gallon of whiskey for 2 bushels of rye, which two bushels would make at least 4 gallons; and his wood cost him nothing but the cutting and halling: ☞ for every body cuts wood where he pleases on the un-inclosed grounds; and none are inclosed but the *flats.* Rye whiskey (he says) is preferred, because more fiery than whiskey made of wheat, which is soft and mild; tho' rye produces rather the most liquor.

WHISKEY. To 1½ bushel of chopped (or course ground) rye, add 8 quarts of malt made of rye, for a mash, and so much water as will fill a hogshead. To the whole add so much good yeast as the heat or coldness of the weather requires, to produce a proper fermentation. The mash having been duly fermented, is put into the cooper and distilled.

[8] *Jany 8.* EVENING Col° Butler & Capt. Schott called to see me on the subject of the proposed elections. I had given Col° Butler a copy of the law & of the printed notifications,[3] in the forenoon. He thought it prudent to advise the *Committee* of the matter, before the notifications should be issued; and was to consult Capt. Schott, who is one of the Com^{tee} Capt. Schott now

---

[3] No. 2, *ante.*

confirmed the necessity of this measure. He said the Com^tee were appointed to watch over the settlements, to prevent any measures being taken which might be injurious to their rights: that the people had suffered so much, & had so often been amused with proposals which in the end they had found deceitful, they had become extremely jealous; and would therefore hardly enter into any measure not previously [9] approved by their committee. At the same time he added, "That he did not doubt the people would readily come into the election," or words to that effect, by which I understood him to mean, "that they would elect a representative, councillor, &c." As Mr Franklin, one of the Com^tee, was absent [4] (in Connecticut) & probably might not return in time to sign the notifications with Col° Butler & me, I closed with his & capt. Schott's proposal; & accordingly furnished them with copies of the act & notifications which they undertake to send to Mr Jenkins at Lackawanack & Mr Hurlbut at Nantikoke (the only two others of the Com^tee now in the settlement) to meet us at Wyoming to-morrow evening, to converse on the matter of the elections.

In the forenoon, on my presenting [10] the act to Col° Butler, he hesitated about joining in the conducting of the election; because he had uniformly declined all offices, & had determined not to accept of any. But I reminded him of his having acted as moderator at the meetings of the inhabitants; and that the business committed to him, Franklin & me, by the act, was of a nature exactly similar to that of a moderator; & therefore I hoped he would consent to act. He admitted the likeness of the two cases; and as he made no farther objection, I conclude he intends to join in executing the business committed to us by the law.

Jany 9th In the Afternoon, Dr Smith & capt. Hover (from Jacob's Plains) called on me, to converse on the subject of the elections, & to get copies of the act, to show to their neighbours, who were anxious to see it. I gave each of them a copy of the act, & of the printed notifications. The Doctor said their settlement, to the amount of 50 men [11] (two or 3 excepted) were for receiving the laws.[5] After some conversation, the Doctor handed me a paper (directed to me) signed by him for himself, & for Abraham Westbrook, and by Samuel Hover.[6] In this paper they say they entered into recognizance, in conformity to the law, and

---

[4] Franklin was attending a meeting of the Susquehannah Company; *Susquehannah Company Papers,* VIII, no. 268.
[5] *Cf.* no. 9, *ante.*   [6] No. 1, *ante.*

took the oath of fidelity to the state of Pennsylvania, that they hold themselves bound by their oaths, & are ready to pay obedience when called upon; they also profess their joy at my coming with the laws. The Doctor said if I could name a day when I would be at his house, he would give notice to his neighbours at Jacob's Plains to assemble, that they might make enquiries & receive information, relative to the public concerns of the settlement.

[12] EVENING *Jan*ʸ *9.* Saw Mʳ Hurlbut at Col° Butler's. After a conversation on the Wioming affairs, I asked him what was his opinion on the subject of the proposed election. He answered, that he was in doubt what would be best. He expressed his apprehension of more difficulties arising from the suits already commenced in N°umberland County, than from any other provision in the laws. The people of that county were unfriendly to the Wioming people, and the same justice could not be expected from them as from juries of their neighbours.

In answer, I observed, That the clause in the act, authorizing the further prosecution of suits already commenced in N°umberlᵈ county, to judgement & execution, was a common provision, inserted in all the laws for erecting New-Counties; and in that, as well as other clauses of the act, the different and peculiar circumstances of this people were not adverted to; that it appeared to me probable, that on a proper representation [13] of this matter to the legislature, relief wᵈ be granted, so that all the inhabitants of Wyoming might be put on precisely the same footing in respect to suits at law; and that in this and all other points of grievance relief might be expected more speedily & effectually, thro' the agency of their own representatives in Council & Assembly, than in any other way.

*Jan*ʸ *11*ᵗʰ This morning I despatched James Whitney with copies of the act, and notifications signed by Col° Butler & me (Mʳ Franklin not being in the County) to deliver and post up thro' the whole settlement from Lackawanack to Tioga, on both sides of the river, I also wrote four letters (all of the same tenor) addressed to Zebulon Massey at Tunkhanock, Col° Nathan Dennison at Wyalusing [14] Rosewell Franklin at Wysocks, and Capt. Simon Spaulding at New-Sheshekin.[7] The intention of the letter was to obviate the objections which might arise against the election, & which I had heard mentioned at Wilkesborough, and

---

[7] No. 3, *ante.*

33

to state some of the advantages which would result from their making the elections. Those gentlemen were named to me by Col° Butler & Capt. Schott, as suitable persons so to be addressed, for the information of themselves and neighbours, to whom I desired them to communicate the letters. Butler & Schott entirely approved of the contents of the letters.

AFTERNOON   Major Jenkins from Exeter, old Mr Thos Bennet from Abraham's Plains, Major McCormick from Kingston, Capt. John Swift from Shawnee, Mr Martin from Nantikoke, and divers others, came to my lodgings, to speak & hear in relation [15] to the proposed elections.

Major Jenkins's first objection was to the oath of allegiance, which was that prescribed for the tories. [On my first arrival I was informed that Mr Franklin (who rec^d a draught of the bill the evening before he set off for Connecticut) at some stage on his way to Connecticut, wrote back to (Jenkins I think) to prevent the election being held before his return, telling him that it would be destruction to the people, and that the oath of allegiance prescribed to be taken was the *tory oath*.] [8]   This I removed, by giving the history of that act, for want of which a large body of valuable citizens had been excluded from the rights of freemen; and that without it, all the freemen in the county of Luzerne who had been residents within the state during the operation of former laws, & omitted taking the oath of allegiance, would be in like manner excluded. These with other observations appeared to give satisfaction on this head. [16] I then entered at large on the subject, pointing out the advantages which would doubtless flow from an admission of the laws of election, and assuring the company of the friendly disposition of government towards this settlement; and seeing the principal members of government had individually said that the actual possession of the settlers and their fathers and grantors, on which improvements had been made prior to the decree of Trenton, ought to be confirmed to the present owners. I could not entertain a doubt but that government would devise an equitable plan for such confirmation: That the difficulty lay in the interfering claims under Pennsylvania; for as many of the claimants had legal titles under Pennsylvania, & had paid valuable considerations for their lands, at the same time

---

⁸ Franklin's letter has not been found, but *cf.* no. 4, *ante*. The brackets are Pickering's. For revision of the test laws see Robert L. Brunhouse, *The Counter-Revolution in Pennsylvania, 1776-1790* (Harrisburg, 1942), 179-81.

34

that Government should give relief to the New England settlers, the like regard to justice and equity would oblige it to provide for a reasonable compensation to those claimants [17] whose lands sh^d be confirmed to the present actual possessors. That I would undertake to say that Government would confirm such lands as a gift to the people here: but if some consideration was to be paid for them, I believed it would be a moderate one; and that if the sums so paid should be inadequate to the just demands of the Penn^a Claimants, then Government, I trusted, would supply the deficiencies, by grants of waste lands elsewhere.

Jenkins said He did not believe Government had any friendly designs towards the settlers, but only meant to deceive them; and that as soon as the laws should be introduced, ejectments would be brought, & they should be stripped of their lands. That an honourable member of Council told him (at Philadelphia) that the lands were honestly theirs, by the laws of God and nature but the laws of Pennsylvania would take them from them. If (said he) the Assembly [18] really meant to do us justice, why do they not confirm our lands to us, in the first place? I answered That if the people still kept up their jealousies, if they could place no confidence in the state, there remained no chance of bringing the dispute to an amicable conclusion. That because Government had done wrong in times past, it did not follow, that they must continue to injure them; that the transactions he referred to had been since reprobated by all persons in & out of government; and that if any judgement could be formed by the public acts & private declarations of the members of government, the Council & Assembly had certainly the most friendly dispositions towards them, & would assuredly pay a due regard to their equitable claims.

I asked him what were the lands of which he demanded a confirmation? whether the old possessions which I had described, or all the lands contained in the Susquehanna purchase? [9] He said [19] that the purchase of the Indians was a good one;

---

[9] Pickering was here touching a basic problem in the dispute. The faction in Wyoming led by Franklin had gone on record as favoring confirmation by Pennsylvania of the whole of the original purchase from the Indians. In Congress, William Samuel Johnson, acting as agent of the Susquehannah Company, had hinted that proprietors would get compensation outside Pennsylvania in Connecticut's Western Reserve; thus he had made a distinction between shareholders in the Company and actual settlers in Wyoming, a distinction long made by Pennsylvania and rejected by extremist leaders like Franklin and Jenkins; see Vol. VIII, Introduction, pp. xxix-xxxiii.

and that he had as good a right to go & settle 20 or 30 miles west of the Susquehanna, as on his own particular farm, being one of the Susquehanna company: but that for his own part in particular he only wanted the confirmation of 600 acres of land; for that he considered himself as much entitled to the lands he had taken up since the decree at Trenton, as to those of wh. he was before possessed.

I told him, in plain terms, that if they persisted to claim the whole Susquehanna purchase, they would hazard the loss of all their lands, that Government would never yield to such demands, or to any thing beyond their actual possessions prior to the Trenton decree: that the great body of land contained in this county was too valuable to lie any longer vacant, on account of this dispute; [20] and that as government were united in their dispositions to confirm the equitable rights of the people, so they were equally united in their determination to oppose their other claims; and if these were persisted in, forcible measures would be adopted, to put an end to them; & if Pennsylvania once armed for the purpose, every man of common sense must see the folly of opposing.

As he laid much stress on the Susquehanna purchase, I gave the history of the Indian Deed, as it was unravelled before the court at Trenton, and related to me by Mr Wilson & Mr Sergeant: [10] But Jenkins professed to disbelieve them.

After two hours conversation, and more points being started, the company rose to go, it being near dark. I am to visit [21] Jenkins at his house (at Exeter) & several other persons, on the other side of the river, agreeable to their invitations; when the subject is to be again discussed.

EVENING I am informed that the company in general think it will be proper to hold the election, and that this is now the prevailing sentiment, so far as the minds of the people have been discovered.

FRIDAY *Jany 12.* A man living a mile below Holleback's called to ask for a copy of the act, to satisfy himself whether there was any foundation for what was reported down where he lives, viz. that if they accepted the laws, *they w^d have to pay 12 years back taxes.* I gave him the act, and assured him he [22] might make himself perfectly easy on that head, as no such thing was thought

---

[10] James Wilson and Jonathan D. Sergeant had been two of Pennsylvania's agents at the Trenton trial.

of; and that I was satisfied that not a penny of back taxes w⁴ be demanded of them; adding, that the opposers must be put to hard shifts to support their cause, when they propagated such groundless stories for that purpose.

FORENOON I went up to Jacobs Plains, to Dʳ Smith's. He immediately sent out to collect his neighbours. Capt. Gore and others (about 10 in all) presently assembled. I related the substance of what had passed the day before between Jenkins & me, and added what other observations occurred; and they all appeared satisfied, & thanked me for the trouble I had taken to give them information.

[23] Dʳ Smith had asked me (on the 9ᵗʰ) who were to be deemed freeholders, to vote for Justices of the peace? for "that when Patterson & the rest of them were here, they admitted only a few to vote, who had Pennsylvania titles.["] He renewed the subject now, and desired me to mention my opinion to his neighbours.

I then repeated what I had said to the Doctor. That for the purposes of the ensuing election of justices, all persons holding lands in fee under the Connecticut grants, must be deemed to be freeholders; that they certainly were & w⁴ continue such until better titles were shown; and that without this construction of the act, it would be a nullity.

(Sent 2 letters to Mʳ Hodgdon, requesting copies of the laws for electing Justices of the peace, a copy of the act erecting yᵉ county of Luzerne, and of the decree of the Court at Trenton.)

[24] SATURDAY *Janʸ 13*. Nicholas Brink, Gilbert Van Gorden & Leonard Westbrook called on me. The two former live about 3 miles below the Shawney Plains; the latter at Jacob's Plains. Brink lives on a lot surveyed for Dʳ Ewing, containing about 170 or 180 acres, of which above half is hilly or mountainous. If the Pennᵃ titles were confirmed, Brink was to give the Dʳ *a guinea an acre,* which however Brink thought a very high price. He has lived in the settlement about 6 years; but was warned (by written order of Franklin) to move off by the 20th of December, or abide the consequence. Capt. Swift of Shawney was to take some of his men & see this order carried into execution. But he had not yet been disturbed; & he then asked my advice whether to move or not. I advised him by all means to remain on the ground; and told him I w⁴ speak to Capt. Swift on the subject.

Van Gorden bought 150 acres of John Van Campen, about 15

years ago, on Shawney plain & mountain, less than half is [25] on the plain, at 20/ p^r acre. He said that if he, and others in the same situation, should not have their lands restored to them, at least they should have their monies refunded, with interest.

These three men took the oath of allegiance.

EVENING Col° Butler & Capt. Schott came to see me. In speaking of the election, they gave their opinion That if Franklin returned, and with any extraordinary encouragement from the Susquehanna Company, he would make every effort to prevent an election, even to the bringing men in arms: but that if open force were not used, the election would take place.

They said that Ethan Allen was one of the Com^tee of the Susquehanna Comp^y & that he would doubtless be with Franklin at the meeting at Hartford, & probably come with him to Wioming, together with one Beach,[11] another of that Com^tee. I had before supposed that Allen would be at Hartford & that it was likely he would be here at the Election; tho' I did not know he was of ye Com^tee

[26] SUNDAY, *Jany 14th*. There lives at Wilkesborough an old gentleman named Johnson,[12] who was formerly minister to the people here, who at this place had erected a church, which was burnt by Butler & his Indians in 1778. Mr Johnson still preaches to the people in private houses here & in all the neighbouring settlements on both sides of the river. This day he preaches at Shawnee. He is said to be very constant in performing divine service on Sundays: but receives nothing for it from the people, except now & then a trifling present of a few bushels of grain.

Neither are there any school-houses: tho' here and there the people have employed a temporary school-master.

EVENING. At Capt. Schotts with Col° Butler: learnt from them that the people were consulting about the candidates for offices; & several are applying for votes: wh has a favourable aspect.

[27] MONDAY *Jany 15th*. On friday we had a severe frost, after a snow on Wednesday. Saturday was cold, but the air growing milder. Sunday a very pleasant day. Last night it began to thaw sensibly, & rained. This morning the rain continues, the air very warm.

---

[11] Zerah Beach; see Vol. VIII, Index.
[12] Reverend Jacob W. Johnson; see Vol. V, Index.

AFTERNOON Crossed the river to Kingston, with Col° Butler & Capt. Schott, & went to Mr Law^ce Myers's. He, with his brother & another young man (all from Maryland) keep a small store of goods, wet & dry. Myers was formerly a lieut. in Schotts company, and deputy sheriff to Col° Antis, Sheriff of Northumberland. He is now a candidate for the Sheriff's office.

Here we were informed That it was evidently the mind of most of the inhabitants of Kingston, that we should hold the election.

About a dozen of the inhabitants happening to come in, & among them [28] a Mr Enos, I was drawn into a conversation on the subject of the elections, in which I mentioned the principal reasons which sh^d induce the people to adopt the measure; which appeared to be satisfactory. Mr Enos has not long resided in the settlement, but holds a Connecticut right. He appear'd to be a man of good sense, and pretty well informed.

TUESDAY *Jany 16.* Crossed the river this day with Col° Butler, & Capt. Schott, to go to visit Major Jenkins at Exeter. On our way we stopped at old Thomas Bennet's, at Abraham's plains, who pressing us to dine with him, we agreed to return from Jenkin's by 3 oclock, for that purpose. About 2 miles beyond Bennets we met Jenkins coming to Wilkesborough, on business. He said if he had known that we were coming, he w^d have staid at home. We parted, went to a Mr Smiths, and then returned to Bennets.

[29] I have seen more industry at Mr Bennets than at all other places in the county. The old man was near his house, with another hand, breaking flax; and when we entered the house, we found his wife & two daughters spinning. The room, too, was hung round with cloathing, chiefly of their own spinning, and hanks of linen yarn, like the Low-Dutch houses in Jersey. The old man put on a brown linen coat, waiscoat & breeches, of their own fabric, save the weaving which is well executed in the settlement. His wife said that since their sheep had been destroyed, they were obliged to content themselves with linen garments; & the old man said that use rendered him comfortable in them. They dined us well & hospitably.

EVENING Returning by the way of Myer's, we stopped a few minutes, finding Mr Jenkins there. Lord Butler (the [30] Colonel's son) was with us. He is a candidate for the Sheriff's office, & got engaged with Jenkins; so capt. Schott & I off on foot for the ferry, leaving Col° Butler, who staid till his son had done conversing with Jenkins. The Col° now informs me, that tho' Jenkins has all-along declared his determination not to join in the election, yet that he heard him speaking with another man about proper characters for officers, for the purpose of fixing the tickets. He says also, that entering into conversation with Jenkins, & repeating some of the reasons why an election sh[d] be held, he discovered less opposition than formerly; particularly when he mentioned my opinion that all persons holding Connecticut titles for their lands were to be deemed freeholders, in voting for Justices of the peace, it seemed to give great satisfaction. Butler says he also told him that the design of my [31] visit to him to-day was for the purpose of having a conversation with him. On which Jenkins replied, that if he had known that, he w[d] have turned back when he met us: that he w[d] therefore come to see me at Wilkesborough, the latter end of this week. This looks well: and I begin to think that Jenkins is convinced it will be best to hold the elections, on the principles I have advanced: but as he has warmly & firmly opposed, decency requires that he lets himself down gently & by degrees, & after repeated conversations with me & others who are in favour of the measure; on which he may at length acknowledge that there is reason for changing his opinion & conduct.

I suppose this afternoon at Wilkesborough, he had some communications with W[m] Slocum, another [32] warm opposer, who spent an hour with me on Monday evening, alone, & who, at first, said, whatever others might be willing to do, he should hold fast his *general* claim to the Susquehanna lands, as well as his *particular possession*. Nevertheless, before we parted, he appeared to be satisfied with the expectation of the people's holding their original farms, actually settled & improved before the decree at Trenton: for I in plain terms told him that nothing more w[d] be granted by the Assembly of Penn[a] but that I had no doubt so much w[d] be yielded, & on easy terms of payment, if any payment sh[d] be demanded. Just as he was going I drank to him; & when he rec[d] the bowl, he prefaced his drinking with "Here's wishing that you & other good men may bring about an amicable settlement."

[33] WEDNESDAY *Jan[y] 17*. Went this day to Nantikoke & Newport. At Nantikoke we (Col° Butler & capt. Schott were with me) called on M[r] Hurlbut, the Com[tee] man. We conversed but little on public matters: however, Hurlbut concluded with saying,

"That it was and had been his opinion, that the election should be held."

At Newport (about 9 miles from Wilkesboro') we stopped at Mr Alden's, a son of Major Alden.   Here we found a Mrs Jameson, an elderly woman of agreeable manners, and a good understanding.   She was clad as it might be expected an industrious, prudent woman would be; and I find her family has uniformly exhibited examples of industry.   She was curteous, & pressed us to call and take a bed at her house.   She remarked that I must be [34] tired of staying so much at Wilkesborough, & urged me to spend a day at her house.   I told her that perhaps by this time twelvemonths I might bring my wife to see her, and that I sh^d take pleasure in doing it.   Just at this time she understood I was a New-England-man.   This gave her much pleasure; and she thought well of the state, that they had commissioned a Yankee on this business.   She is a native of Ireland, & came when a child, with her parents to Boston, & resided some little time at Londonderry, whence they removed to Connecticut, where she had spent the greater part of her life.

Major Alden had notice from his son that we were at his house: so the old man & his wife came thither.   He bid me welcome.   Pretty soon he began to speak on the subject of the election: expressed some doubts: [35] and made some objections; but these were grounded on mistakes, & so easily removed. He prefaced his objections with saying "That he wished not to be overjealous & suspicious; *for that jealousy & suspicion were the inseperable companions of little minds."*   We dined at his sons; and the time being too short to go far into the subject of election & its consequences, the old gentleman said he would come up to see me at Wilkesborough.   "I am pleased (said he) to find it easy to converse with you; I did not know but they had sent a man whom we could not speak to."

Alden's son told me there was a large body of bog oar near them, wh. had been tried & found of a good quality.   He said also that about a mile from his house there was plenty of good mountain oar.   A mill stream ran near his house, where works might be erected.

[36] THURSDAY *Jany 18.*   MORNING   A Mr Kilburn (a carpenter of Wilkesboro') called to converse with me, & I think went away satisfied of the propriety of holding the election.   He appeared to have thought that Connecticut & the Susquehanna Comp^y had a good title to this land, that the decree at Trenton determined

41

nothing but the jurisdiction, and that the right of soil stood on its original foundation. This led me to express my mind fully on the subject. He said he had been told by persons whom he thought men of veracity, that Dr Johnson, as well as Col° Dyer, said publicly, that the Federal Court had been bribed to give their decree in fav^r of Penn^a. I answered That I was persuaded Dr Johnson's good sense & [37] prudence would have prevented him from ever making any such declarations *on a mere suspicion;* and if there had been any *evidence* of it, certainly it w^d have been a good & sufficient ground for demanding another trial; but as this had never been urged, it was doubtless a false report; because no *gentleman* would hazard such a declaration *on a mere suspicion.*

I observed further That whatever party lost a cause in court or on an arbitration, it was extremely common to complain of corruption or partiality in the court, or jury, or arbitrators: that I believed the present complaints of the Trenton decision spring only from a like disappointment; and that such stories were diligently propagated by a few [38] busy members of the Susquehanna Company (of which I believed 49 in 50 totally abandoned the cause) for the purpose of keeping up the quarrel, from a hope to reap something in the event of it. That if they could rouse the people here to acts of desperation, in opposing the authority of Penn^a they hoped the state might at length grow weary of the contest, & give up the lands.

After a long conversation, he retired, thanking me for the information I had given him; & saying *that he had hardly expected to be indulged in the freedom he had taken to request such a conversation.* I assured him it gave me pleasure that he had called.

[39] FORENOON Went with Jn° Holleback across the river to see Capt. Swift, at Shawanee. Swift gave us a narrative of some parts of the contest between the Yankees & Pennamites, since the decree of Trenton. He particularly mentioned the conduct of Armstrong & Boyd.[13] The Yankeys had agreed, before their arrival, to lay down their arms, at the instance of some Pennsylvania agents; & accordingly grounded them by J. Hollebacks. This was on condition that the troops in the fort also surrendered *their* arms to these agents; but the latter refused so the agents advised the people to resume their arms, & go to their

---

[13] John Armstrong, Jr. and John Boyd; see Vol. VIII, Index. The episode described involving these two men occurred in August, 1784.

42

homes, & to defend themselves, if molested by the troops. They retired accordingly.

After this, Armstrong & Boyd arrived, with the militia. The former (particularly) desired the people to testify their submission to government, by surrendering their arms. [40] The people said that they had once done it, to the other agents, or commissioners. Armstrong said that he wished to be able to give personal evidence of their submission; he and Boyd at the same time declaring upon their honour That no advantage should be taken of their delivering up their arms. The people were jealous of a deception: however, at length, 'Squires Mead & Martin pledging their honour also that no advantage sh⁴ be taken, the people (reluctantly) laid down their arms, to the number of 60 or 70 rifles & muskets. As soon as their arms were grounded & they by order had marched from them, a platoon of the militia took possession of them, & immediately began to dispute about the disposition of them. The arms were thus given up to *private plunder*. Previous to the surrender, the militia had been formed into a sort of square; and now the Yankies were inclosed, [41] & marched as prisoners, with a platoon in front & rear, & two ranks, marching by files, on each flank. It was not enough to trepan them by this dishonourable artifice: to add *insult* to *treachery*, Armstrong ordered the drums & fifes to strike up *Yanky Doodle*.

As soon as they arrived at the fort, near 30 of them were immediately confined as prisoners; being pinioned, & their hands, besides, tied behind them; and in this condition they were ordered to lay down in the barn where they were lodged, & the sentries had orders to kill instantly any man who should attempt to get up.

At one period of the contest, after the people had been driven from the settlement, four persons only for some time kept the adjacent woods, & harrassed the pennamites. These were Capt. Swift, Capt. Satterly, Phineas Stevens & Waterman Baldwin. At this time Charles Stewart came into Wyoming; and finding [42] what daring attempts were made by those four men (& fearing probably that the people might return & collect to them) sent capt. Sims to them, with an offer of a *hundred half joes* if they would leave the country. One (or more) was for receiving the money, & then still keeping their ground, in order to retaliate, by this deception, in part, for the treachery which had been practised by Armstrong: but Swift would not consent to do it, he rejected the proposal, despising the very idea of such deceit. They kept their ground accordingly, & the people soon collected

43

to them in numbers. Soon afterwards, the violent & extravagant conduct of the Pennamites engaged the notice of Government. Many of them were indicted, and the whole retired from the settlement.

In this struggle a few were killed & wounded on each side.

[43] EVENING. We returned to Wilkesborough. Matt. Holleback had been to Kingston, at a meeting of the people there. About 50 had assembled. Mr Jenkins was present, & warmly opposed the election; urging his former reasons; & again absurdly declaring that the law for erecting the county of Luzerne was unconstitutional: for that when the bill was reading for the last time, after it had been published for consideration, Col° Antis (member from N°umberland) objected to the boundary line on the west side of the river, & proposed that instead of running a west course from the mouth of Nescopeck, it sh^d run a northwest course: That this motion was agreed to, & the law altered, which *therefore* was *unconstitutional.* He had mentioned this a week before at my lodgings, in presence of the people met there, & I had answered, I supposed satisfactorily, as he ceased to object. But I learn from all quarters that he [44] is a wilful, obstinate man. I told him that bills were published for consideration, for the very purpose of discovering errors, & defects, that they might be corrected & supplied at the last reading, when they were to be passed into laws. But besides, in the present instance, he was totally mistaken in the fact: for that the alteration of the boundary lines he mentioned was made by the *supplementary* law. But he persisted in asserting that it was done by the first law, in the manner he stated. I told him I had not the first law with me: but that it could not be presumed that the legislature, with the first law before them, would insert a clause in the supplement, stating an error in the boundary line, & then declaring the alteration, if this very thing had been done by the first law; [45] or, in other words, that they would not recite an error in fact which had no existence. But he would not give up the matter, that the boundary was altered by the original law; and I did not chuse longer to contend against a palpable absurdity.

FRIDAY *Jany 19.* Went this day with Col° Butler & Mr Bailey to dine with Dr Smith, at Jacob's Plains. We agreed to go to Lachawanock on Monday, to meet the inhabitants there by noon; & Dr Smith undertook to give them notice, that they might assemble. The D^r said that Mr Finn, the Baptist minister who lives there, had also expressed a desire to converse with me.

Wrote to Capt. Swift, that if I were informed when the people sh⁴ meet at Shawwanee, I w⁴ attend them, if there were no objection to it.

[46] SATURDAY *Jan*ʸ *20*. Dined to-day with Capt. Schott.

In the morning wrote to Mʳˢ P. desiring her to ask Mʳ Hodgdon to send me copies of the petition of Pennᵃ & Connecticut, or either of those states, to Congress, to appoint a federal court,¹⁴ & of the order of Congress thereon; ¹⁵ that I may know what were the points submitted to the court; as tis pretended that they went out of their way, in judging of the right of soil as well as of the jurisdiction.

Took a walk along the bank of the river, beginning at the bend, & going down as far as Button-Wood island. The bank along the bend is in a ruinous condition, tumbling in & washing away at every thaw after frost, & at every fresh. The earth is extremely tender, & without [47] any gravel or stones for perhaps 10 or 12 feet in depth. Many acres have already washed away since the N. England people settled here. There is not a tree or bush along the bend, for upwards of a half a mile. I see no chance of preserving the lots along that bank from destruction, unless the bank should be formed into a gentle slope, & seeded with some deep-rooting & strong swarded grass; and this would be a work more laborious & expensive than will probably be undertaken for many years to come. After turning the point, the bank downwards seemed pretty secure, both grass, trees & bushes growing on it; tho' here & there was a breach which, if repaired soon, the bank may be saved with little difficulty.

[48] SUNDAY *Jan*ʸ *21*. No preaching at Wilkesborough.

MONDAY *Jan*ʸ *22*. Went to Lachawanock (Pittstown) to meet the people there, pursuant to notification. It was a snowy day, which probably occasioned a thinner meeting than otherwise there w⁴ have been: However, there was nearly a room-full, I judge about 25. Mʳ Finn was not present.

After the act relative to the election had been read, I desired the company to make every objection which occurred to them.

1. Objection. Some mentioned their fears of being [49] obliged to pay back taxes ever since the decree at Trenton

---

¹⁴ The petition came from Pennsylvania; Vol. VII, no. 74.
¹⁵ *Ibid.*, no. 80.

A. This probably was a groundless fear. When their distresses and inability to pay even present taxes sh^d be properly represented to the Assembly, by their own representative, there was little doubt of their being exempted from all back taxes. But with respect to future taxes, altho' their present unhappy condition might justly entitle them to an exemption for a year to come, and the Assembly might feel disposed to grant it, yet as that would give umbrage for discontent among all the people on the other frontiers of the state, they w^d probably be called on for taxes: but then those w^d be proportioned to their ability. As they had neither houses nor [50] barns of any value, & but very small stocks of cattle, their taxes must necessarily be extremely small. And even these w^d perhaps be more than counterbalanced by the grants of the Assembly for opening roads & other public purposes. The Assembly had already granted £300. which is to be applied for the purpose of opening a good road to Philadelphia, which must be the great market for the produce of this county; and perhaps a farther sum may be granted to continue that road from Wilkesborough to Tioga.

2. Objection. There are named in the act Zebulon Butler & John Franklin. Col° Butler was well known to have held a commission in the Continental army: why is he (and we thro' him) treated with so little respect that his title is not given him as well as to Col° Pickering?

A. By Col° Butler, That the Assembly of Pennsylvania did not practise given titles unless to their own officers; that Col° Pickering had just been [51] commissioned by the government, & therefore it was proper to give him his title.

3. Objection. Pennsylvania has used us ill and deceived us: we are afraid they mean to deceive us again.

4. Objection. If We receive the laws, writs of ejectment will immediately be brought, & the people turned out of their possessions.

Answers. Such as I have repeatedly given in other companies of the people. I also proceeded to observe That if they thought the government now meant to deceive them, & consequently that a majority of the rulers were wicked & unprincipled men, it was not possible for government to do anything wh. c^d gain their confidence. If the Assembly were to pass a law to confirm their lands to them; yet if composed of wicked men, they [52] c^d repeal the law, as soon as the people had submitted & suffered the laws to take their course; This reduced the company to a dilemma; & they then saw the necessity of beginning at some one time to place a confidence in Government.

☞ One of the people present asked me if I should come to live here; I answered yes, of necessity, if the laws were introduced. If that were known (said he) it would give the people more confidence in what you say; for some are jealous that you are sent here to draw them into a snare. I then added That I sh^d not only live here, but I sh^d want some land to raise provisions for the support of my family, because it w^d be a good while before my offices w^d yield anything of consequence; and therefore I w^d now purchase enough for a farm; [53] if I could get it at the rate at which it was selling under the Connecticut title; and I w^d purchase nothing but a Connecticut title: for I had such a confidence in the good disposition of government to do what was equitable to this settlement, that I was willing to take my chance with the people of obtaining a confirmation of that title on reasonable terms. The same person then replied, This being known, it w^d give great satisfaction to the people: for if you should deceive them, you will then be in their power to take revenge: Another person then remarked, But how easy will it be for the pennamites to reimburse to Col^o P. any monies he shall now pay for Connecticut titles; and he may purchase for the purpose of drawing us into his measures, & yet run no hazard at all. I then declared That I w^d pledge my honour & my life, that [54] while the people of the settlement held only under the Connecticut title I w^d hold by the same & by no other. That I had a wife & 5 children with whom I sh^d move to Wilkesborough; which I certainly sh^d never dare to do if I now meant to deceive them. That I must of necessity move hither, because the laws could not be carried into execution, without the exercise of the offices wh. I held; and in order to exercise them I must be here. But I added, That tho' I was willing to take my chance with them, by purchasing connecticut titles at the rates at which they were selling, provided they proceeded in the election; yet if the people should refuse to hold the election, I would not then give six pence an acre for their best lands: for if after the State had at their request erected them into a county and given them an opportunity of electing their own officers, by which they would enjoy every right & privilege enjoyed by [55] the other freemen of Penn^a, if after all this they sh^d refuse to receive the laws, I had no reason to expect that the state w^d ever make another offer *in peace:* Arms would then *compel* submission to government.

5. Objection. Penn^a c^d not raise an army to come against us. The people would not fight for the sake of the Land-Jobbers. And if three thousand men were to come against us, we need not fear; for 100 boys raised in this settlement would stand a 1000 of such troops as w^d come against us. Or if they did break up the settlement, 100 boys whom he (the objector) could muster, w^d keep 3000 men in perpetual alarm &c &c.

A. (what is too obvious to relate: and that Penn^a had as good riflemen in her 5 frontier counties as any in this settlement however valiant, &c &c)

[56] TUESDAY *Jany 23^d*. Proposed to Col° Butler & Capt Schott the expediency of holding meetings in the towns of Wilkes-borough, Nantikoke Kingston (with Exeter) & Shawanee, for the purpose of giving the people true information; as many idle & false stories were propagated to deceive them. For the meeting at Lachawanock had evidently a good effect, the warmest opposers going away satisfied, & the wavering being confirmed. They agreed; and Col° Butler issued notifications to all those towns.

WEDNESDAY *Jany 24th*. Mr Samuel Allen came over from Kingston this afternoon, to converse with me. He informed of the proceedings of the meeting at Forty-Fort,[16] before noticed page 43. Jenkins warmly opposed the [57] election; and said *it was in his power to stop it* but sh^d not do it if a majority appeared in favour of it.

Mr Allen mentioned the Trenton decree & the manner in which it was obtained, as the matter had been reported to him: So I went into a long detail on the constitution of that court, showing how fairly it had been formed, & the absolute necessity of its being constituted with such powers as it had exercised. If in fact only 3 members out of 5 agreed in the decree, it was immaterial.[17] &c &c. I also explained the affair of the Indian deed. He appeared to be perfectly satisfied. He mentioned a new thing. I had only heard before that *the Judges were bribed:* it was now said that Col° Dyer (the most zealous agent on behalf of Connecticut, & one deeply interested in the Susquehannah Company) was also bribed by Pennsylvania, to betray the cause of Connecticut & of the Company.

---

[16] Forty-Fort was in Kingston.

[17] The Trenton decision was announced as unanimous, but among Connecticut people the belief persisted that two of the judges were in fact opposed to the decision reached.

[58] THURSDAY *Jany 25th.* The inhabitants of Wilkesborough assembled: upwards of 50 men were present, including a few from Kingston, &c.

They were desired to ask any questions relative to the election, where any doubt remained in their minds as to the expediency of holding it.

The grand point insisted on was the confirmation of the title to their particular farms: if this were granted, they sh^d be satisfied: and not one man appeared desirous of supporting the Susquehannah Comp^y in their claims. The few who intimated that they had general interests in those claims expressed a willingness to relinquish them if their particular farms could be confirmed to them. But they feared an adoption of the laws w^d strip them [59] of their possessions.

I asked if the inhabitants of this settlement were entitled to superiour privileges above all the other citizens of Penn^a? Nobody answered. I observed That if titles to land were disputed elsewhere in Penn^a the parties resorted to the laws & trials by juries for decisions; & that they had no other remedy. That the same laws were now tendered to them; and that by receiving them they would then enjoy equal rights & privileges with the first citizens of the state. That the trials of their titles must be by juries of their neighbours, that they could not be held out of the county, and that if there were appeals, to the supreme court, yet that court must sit in the county, and the juries of that court must be composed of inhabitants of the county. And thus they w^d enjoy the constitution & every right of freemen in Penn^a. And could they complain because *greater* privileges were not granted them, than any other citizens enjoyed?

[60] Mr Cary said They were not able to defend their rights in courts of law: They had been stripped of their moveable property by Patterson & others acting by authority from Penn^a & now had not wherewith to fee lawyers & bear other charges of lawsuits.

I then said That I had been reasoning on the ground of mere law, & showed they if they pleased they might now enjoy all the rights of the freemen of Penn^a. But that I wished to put them on a better footing, on account of their distresses occasioned by the general destruction of the settlement by the Indians, by 'Squire Patterson & his assistants, and by the two sweeping floods.[18] These losses & sufferings (particularly those occasioned

---

[18] For Alexander Patterson, see Vol. VII, Index. Severe floods occurred in Wyoming in March, 1784 and October, 1786.

by Patterson & others pretending to act under the authority of the state) had excited a general sympathy, and people now said they ought not to be driven from their actual possessions, such as they held & improved [61] prior to the decree at Trenton: That on this equitable ground there was a fair prospect of their succeeding to obtain the confirmation of their farms; and that this claim would be more effectually supported by their own representatives in the council & Assembly than in any other way whatever. That if they refused to go into the election, and yet were to petition for their farms, it would be an insult to the Assembly. For the plain language of such conduct w⁴ be, That tho' they had petitioned for a seperate county, & it had been granted, tho' they had prayed to be authorized to elect their officers agreeably to the Constitution & the laws, & promised to support such officers in the full administration of the laws, and this also was granted: yet that they suspected a majority of the Assembly were bad men & they could not trust them, or receive the laws, untill their land sh⁴ be confirmed. I added That [62] this was probably the last peaceable offer the Assembly would make them: & that if they refused it, the next step w⁴ be to raise & send a body of troops to *compel* them to submit to the laws: that all who sh⁴ resist the government w⁴ be deemed rebels, & be punished as such. That they themselves acknowledged Penn^a had the right of jurisdiction, that jurisdiction was the right of making and executing laws, and that resistance in arms w⁴ of course be rebellion.

Col° Butler read Major Judd's letter.[19] Judd says "if they held the election, they w⁴ be compleatly *saddled* with the laws of Penn^a.["] On this an old man (Mr Hide) wittily remarked "That he was more afraid of the *halter* than the *saddle*."

Much more was said; for the conversation lasted about 2 hours. The general disposition appeared in favour of the election.

[63] THURSDAY EVENING *Jany 25.* Parson Johnson was at the meeting to-day. He told Col° Butler That he could answer all my questions. &c. I proposed to the Col° to go & see him this evening. We did so. He immediately began on the subject. I found him possessed of all the prejudices of the warm abettors of the Susquehanna Comp^y claim, & in full belief of all the falsehoods & misrepresentations which have been industriously raised & propagated to support it, and of some absurdities peculiar to himself.

---

[19] No. 4, *ante.*

He believed the charter of Connec[t] was better than that of Penn[a]. That the Indian deed was a good one. That the original produced at Trenton was not the fair one, & was only kept by the Comp[y] but not intended to be used. That after receiving that of the Indians, the Comp[y] got another, in a fuller assembly of the Indians, & this was perfectly fair. That this had been sent to England. That it had been [64] returned, & fell into the hands of the Pennsylvanians, who kept it & would not produce it at the federal court, & that they still had it: [20] That the great men of Penn[a] & among them the great M[r] Wilson, acknowledged that these lands belonged to the Con[t] people, by the laws of God & nature; but that the laws of Penn[a] would take them from them: that laws contrary to the laws of God & Nature were not to be obeyed. That the Court a[t] Trenton had no right to decide any thing but the *jurisdiction.* That the Controversy was between the two *states,* that the Susquehanna Comp[y] had never submitted their right of soil to the decision of that court, & that Conn[t] could not do it, for they had given it away to the Comp[y]. That tho' the decree said the right of preemption was in Penn[a] yet as M[r] Penn had so long neglected to purchase of the Indians, the Susquehanna Comp[y] had a right to step in & purchase. That the Trenton Court was an [65] unconstitutional court, that in that article the Confederation was unconstitutional, that the Court ought to have consisted of a majority of 13, judges, one from each state, that it was a defect in the articles which he with others early observed; that the court being unconstitutional their decree was illegal & void. That Col[o] Brearly was an unlawful judge, for he had given his opinion long before That Conn[t] had no title to the land in dispute: That when questioned on that point by Col[o] Dyer, he denied his having given such opinion, or did not remember it, and that if he had given such an opinion, *he had now changed his mind; upon which Col[o] Dyer consented to his sitting as one of the judges.* (I suppose M[r] Johnston & others who tell this story of Col[o] Brearly, understood that he finally gave his opinion against Connecticut.)

I answered all these objections: but the old gentleman w[d] believe no fact [66] however plain or probable, if it contradicted his former belief; nor in argument abide by any consequence resulting from any proposition he had before admitted; and at last, when hard pinched, and all farther evasion failed, he crowned all with this remarkable declaration, *"you are of one opinion & I am*

---

[20] Zebulon Butler first made this charge; see Vol. VII, no. 160.

of another. I am fixed, and shall never change till the day of Christ comes to judgement."

FRIDAY *Jany 26.* Went with Col° Butler to attend a meeting of the people of Nantikoke. Full 50 were assembled. I met with more opposition than at any meeting elsewhere; but it arose chiefly from a few rash young men. Old Mr Alden also spoke; and tho' he repeated the sentiment, "That Jealousy & suspicion were the [67] inseperable companions of little minds & therefore to be guarded against;" yet in spite of plain facts & conclusive reasoning he persisted in his jealousy & suspicion, that because Penn^a had injured & oppressed them, in the case of Patterson, Armstrong & Boyd, therefore the state w^d persevere in their oppression & that the law I brought to hold the election, was only a snare to catch them; and he concluded with an expression in the spirit of Parson Johnson, That his opinion was fixed.

☞ Perhaps the most difficult characters to reason with are the young & the old; the former are too sanguine & rash, the latter think that "years teach wisdom"; & having long entertained their prejudices, it is next to impossible to eradicate them.

Mr Harvey & Northrup, both men in years, were also opposers. Harvey has lately returned from Hartford [68] where he saw some members of the Susquehannah Comp^y & got his ears filled with fine stories, not only of the undoubted maintenance of their most extensive claims of land, but of independence itself.[21] The whole Susquehanna purchase he said was their honest due. Harvey brought to the settlement this report, "That if there had been present at the meeting of the Susque^h C° at Hartford in December, only *one* person from Wyoming, they w^d have made a declaration of independence." One Center also from Hartford, made the same report, to Col° Butler & others.

I asked the company whether they were ripe for independence, & desired it? Yes! answered three or four of the *young* men. No where else has this been *avowed;* and this I suppose the mere effect of rashness & ignorance, not of a preconcerted plan. I am fully [69] satisfied that not one man in fifty entertains the idea; indeed it appears that the design is rather intended to be kept concealed from the body of the people; and tho' Dr Hamilton's letter (clearly enough expressing it) [22] had been made

---

[21] There had been some talk of making the Susquehannah Company lands and part of New York into a separate state; see Vol. VIII, Introduction, pp. xxxvi-xxxvii.

[22] *Ibid.,* no. 182. But Hamilton's letter does not clearly call for a separate state. He does mention a forthcoming visit by Ethan Allen to Wyoming; this fact was probably the source of the inference drawn.

public by D[r] Smith;[23] yet Franklin pretended that it had no such meaning, & put such glosses upon it as blinded the people. But Major Judd's letter brought by Harvey confirms the point;[24] and there is other corroborating evidence. On every occasion therefore I make known to the people the crafty but wicked & ruinous designs of their few leaders.

After a long conversation, & answering a variety of questions, Harvey & others declared, that tho' they had jealousies of the state, yet they believed that *I* had no intention to deceive them.

[70] Notwithstanding the opposition I met with at Nantikoke, yet it appeared to me that, on the close of the debate, many minds were soothed & satisfied, & that there will be a majority for the election. M[r] Hurlbut (the Com[tee] man) who lives there, & is well acquainted with the people, confirms this opinion. ☞ He is a sensible, discreet man, & as fit as any man I have met with for a *justice of the peace* in his district.

On our return Col° Butler told me that Major Jenkins had lodged at Nantikoke (at young Alden's) the night before, & had visited a number of houses. This accounts for the opposition. He had been down there to prepare them for the meeting. He is an obstinate man with but little discernment, and only makes bold and ill-bred assertions, without argument. Old M[r] Stanbury speaking of Jenkin's father, said "he had more sense than honesty." But as [71] to the son, I think he has as little of one as the other.

SATURDAY *Jan[y] 27.* Went with Butler & Schott to Forty-Fort, to attend a meeting of the Kingston & Exeter people. It was a large meeting, probably of 60 or more. And tho Jenkins gave sundry striking proofs of his ill manners, ignorance, absurdity, folly and obstinacy, yet upon the whole, it was a meeting (as Friends say) "very solid & satisfactory, and many hearts were tendered," and satisfied, which before had been either wavering, or opposed to the election. All of them (even Jenkins) disavowed any intention of independence.[25]

[72] EVENING On our return we stopped at Myer's. There was a M[r] Bingham there from Sheshekin earnestly speaking on

[23] *Ibid.,* no. 199, notes 5 and 6.   [24] See note 19, above.
[25] The speech attributed to Jenkins and printed in *P. A.,* 2nd ser., XVIII, 666-67, is probably apocryphal. According to Oscar J. Harvey and Ernest G. Smith, *A History of Wilkes-Barré* (Wilkes-Barre, 1927), III, 1550 n, it was furnished by Steuben Jenkins. It hardly fits the mood of Jenkins as described by Pickering.

the election. He had been present at the latter part of the meeting. After listening a little while, I discovered him to be a man of exceeding good sense, & therefore took some pleasure in conversing with him & explaining the motives to & consequences of the election; and the evident designs of the junto of the Susque^h Comp^y. He admitted the reasons to be conclusive. He asked (as the only difficulty resting on his mind) in case of trial of the Connecticut title, whether after a verdict of a Jury in the County, at the Supreme Court, there could not be an appeal to a court of Chancery, or other court, *out* of the county? I answered That I believed not. That trials of titles to land were regulated by the Common Law, which required [73] them to be in the county where the lands lay. That there was a High Court of errors & appeals in Penn^a but I did not know its powers. That there was a difference between trials of *personal,* or transitory, & *real* actions: that the former might be tried in any county; but that in every court, even on the last appeal, I had no doubt that the latter must be had in the county where the lands lay.

Several persons were present listening most attentively to our discourse; and I am persuaded it will be of no small use.

SUNDAY *Jany 28th* No public worship at Wilkesboro'. This morning Mr Bailey informs, That Parson Johnson has *changed* his mind; & thinks it will be best to hold the election!!! (See page 66.)

[74] Sunday Evening. Stephen Jenkins is down from Exeter: says he has been pressing his brother, major Jenkins, to cease opposing the election; has brought a note from him to Capt. Schott, in these words

(I forgot to take a copy. The substance was this. That if the election of Justices c^d be postponed till after the ensuing session of the Assembly, he would not oppose the holding the election of a representative &c. but on the contrary use all his influence in favour of it.)

Capt. Schott asked me what was my determination relative to the election of Justices. I answered, That I could ease Major Jenkins's mind on that head; for I had concluded not [75] to appoint the time of meeting until after the other election was over; and then meant to consult some of the principal gentlemen of each district as to the time and places in the districts most convenient to the freeholders for holding the elections. This

54

captain Schott is to write to Major Jenkins. This conversion, or yielding of Jenkins is a wonderful event: but I give him little credit for it: he sees the tide is turning (or rather turned) and makes a virtue of necessity.

MONDAY *Jan* 29. Met the people of Shawanee (Plymouth) this afternoon. It was in a snow storm; which with the shortness of the notice, occasioned a thin meeting, about 20 persons present. [76] Mr Nash began the debate. His first declaration was, "That the Assembly w^d do justice, & give the land to those who ought to have it." After he had made his speech, I repeated his own words (as above) & remarked, if it was so, there was nothing to dispute about. But then I found him unwilling to trust to the justice of the assembly, until the titles to their lands sh^d be confirmed. On one hand they admit that they cannot support their titles in a court of law; and yet continually dwell on the *justice* of their titles. But they speak of the laws of *Pennsylvania* as singularly unjust; and in a manner which shows that they believe the laws of any other state would *secure* & confirm their titles. Pains have been [77] taken to diffuse this erroneous opinion among the people. Major Jenkins is always repeating it. The councillor mentioned page 17, it seems was M^r McLean.[26] If he made the declaration there noted (That the lands honestly belonged to the people here, by the laws of God & Nature; but that the laws of *Pennsylvania* would take them from them) it was a very imprudent as well as absurd one. The laws of God (if distinguished from the laws of Nature) must be found in the bible: but that book is not introduced into courts in deciding questions of property. The laws of Nature may perhaps be intended to mean *the principles of Natural Justice:* But property & titles to land are objects of the *positive* laws of *Society,* and have existence among men living in a state of nature; except [78] so long as actual occupancy shall continue. The question in dispute, then, must be decided by the positive regulations of the Society within which the contested territory lies. In respect to the *general* title, the United States form that Society; and the *general* title being determined, the *particular* titles must be established in the particular society within whose jurisdiction the lands lay; & this is Pennsylvania; and if, taken on *strictly legal* ground, the Connecticut titles cannot be defended, they must regret it as a *misfortune,* & not magnify it into a *grievance.* But on *equitable*

---

[26] James McLene.

ground, I have admitted not only the possibility, but the *probability* of supporting their claims; and on this idea the people seem generally [79] to acquiesce in the measure of holding an election.

The Meeting at Plymouth was not satisfactory; it bore some resemblance to that at Nantikoke; and yet I have reason to think the few active opposers will not have much influence.

TUESDAY *Jany 30*. Rec^d from Mr A. Westbrook a paper signed by him, Dr Smith and others of Jacob's Plains professing their attachment to Government; [27] also a note from the Doctor & Mr Westbrook & Capt. Hover, offering (for themselves & the electors of Jacob's plains) to be a guard to Col° Butler & me at the election, if any violence should be attempted. [28] I advised with Col° Butler; & we concluded it best that no person sh^d appear in arms; which answer I del^d to Dr Smith.

[80] WEDNESDAY *Jany 31*. I learn from various quarters that the considerate people at Nantikoke are uneasy that I there met with a reception so defective in decency & respect; but I made light of it; because a want of decency was manifested only by a few young men, who wanted consideration, & who I believed, had been inflamed by Major Jenkins.

Old Harvey's opposition is easily accounted for. He has not (at least on the valuable part of Shawanee plains in his possession) *even* a *Connecticut* title. The whole was some years ago taken in execution, and appraised, agreeably to the Connecticut laws, to satisfy a large debt he owed to Joseph Fry of Middletown; & the moment Penn^a law can operate he must hall up stakes & depart.

[81] THURSDAY *Feby 1. Morning*. I hear of no opposition intended to the election.

Evening. The Election has gone on with great quiet & regularity, A *private* fray happened in the forenoon, between two of A. Westbrooks sons and some others: but it seems they had got in liquor: and as soon as Mr Westbrook discovered them, he parted the disputants, & sent his sons home; telling them "That if they wanted to fight, they might do it to-morrow: & not on the day of election."

There were also two men, pennamites, up from Wapollopy, whom some of the warm Yankees got scent of, and immediately sought for. They [82] were found at Jn° Hollebacks; and got a

---

[27] No. 9, *ante*.   [28] No. 10, *ante*.

56

severe beating. It was said These two men had been active under Patterson in driving the Connecticut people out of the settlement. I find their names were George Charles & Jn° Pottman. They, with one Cortwright, had been with me in the morning, & taken the oath of allegiance. Cortwright said he had heard threatenings had been given out, That if they attempted to vote, they w⁴ be ill-used; and asked my advice what they had best do. I did not hesitate to recommend to them to avoid the election if they found such threats had been uttered; that if they were lovers of peace, they had better retire, than hazard a disturbance of the election. Cortwright answered [83] That he w⁴ rather retire than do that. In this sentiment I thought both Charles & Pottman acquiesced. Cortwright accordingly went off, and escaped unhurt: but the others loitered, and were beaten. It was said Cortwright had been remarkably cruel in his treatment of the settlers, at the general driving.

No other disturbance happened; except a private quarrel arising about the manner of paying for some liquor

141 persons have taken the oath of allegiance, to qualify themselves as electors. 130 of them took the oath this day, & received Certificates therof.

The poll was closed between nine and ten o'clock and at ½ past 2 in the morning the Inspectors and Judges had [84] gone thro' the examination of the lists of electors, votes & tally papers, & made a public declaration of the names of the persons elected; many Electors being present, & waiting to know the issue.

The persons elected are

                                                              Votes

John Franklin, Representative 145
Nathan Dennison, Councillor 97
Lord Butler   ⎱ 170
Mason F. Alden ⎰ Sheriffs
                 138
Nathan Cary ⎱ 107
Jn° Dorrance ⎰ Coroners
                96
Jonah Rogers   ⎤ 105
Christ' Hurlbut ⎬Commissioners 103
Nathan Kingsly ⎦ 100

[85] FRIDAY *Feby 2^d*. The Judges of election have returned to me the names of the persons elected; and delivered me a box

57

sealed agreeably to law, & containing the votes,[29] lists of electors and tally papers; there being no Justice of the peace to receive it.

I consulted them, Capt. Spaulding an Inspector, and Col° Butler on the time & places which w^d be most convenient for the meetings of the freeholders to elect Justices of the peace. It is concluded that this election be held on the same day, viz. Thursday April 19th, in all the districts. The meeting [86] for the 1st district to be at Col° Butlers House in Wilkesbarré: for the 2^d at Forty-Fort, in Kingston: for the 3^d at Capt. Spaldings, in Ulster (Sheshequemink). The 3 Judges consent to preside at the elections; viz. Christopher Hurlbut for the 1st district, James Sutton for the 2^d district and Obadiah Gore for the 3^d district. N. B. 2 Copies of the laws directing the mode of election of Justices must be sent up, one for Mr Hurlbut & one for Mr Sutton. Mr Gore takes the copy I have here.

SATURDAY *Feby 3^d* Agreed with O. Gore, Ja^s Sutton, capt. Spalding &c on the heads of a petition to the Assembly, which I am to draw up.[30]

[87] SUNDAY *Feb^y* 4th No meeting at Wilkesbarre. prepared the petition to the Genl Assembly.

MONDAY *Feb^y* 5th. Col° Dennison, Col° Butler, Mr O. Gore, and Capt. Spalding considered & approved of the petition, as I had drawn it. It prays the Assembly gratuitously to confirm the Connecticut titles to all farm-lots in towns laid out, or in detached places between any towns, and which had been either occupied by, or assigned to persons *living within the settlement,* prior to the decree at Trenton. Or if equity & just policy will not authorize the Assembly to give such gratuitous confirmation, then that the people may hold them on reasonable terms of payment, and that the payments might be made easy, by small annual installments.

EVENING The clause about *payment* for the lands objected to by some people, who are pleased with the rest of the petition: so for the sake of unanimity, and of making some advance towards an accommodation, t^t clause is struck out.

[88] TUESDAY, *Feb^y* 6. At the instance of 'Squire Gore, & Col° Dennison, the town of *Athens* (Tioga) was added to the list of

---

[29] No. 13, *ante.*   [30] No. 16, *ante.*

58

the 17 towns before enumerated as settled (more or less) prior to y° Trenton decree: but Athens was expressly mentioned to have been settled *since;* tho' that a number of farm-lots there had been assigned to persons who had been Wyoming settlers prior to the decree. This mention was made of Athens, by way of soothing its inhabitants; the Gentlemen saying, They w⁴ rather that the Assembly threw it out than they. Col° Butler took the list, & is to annex it to one copy of the petition.

WEDNESDAY *Feb* 7. Col° Butler informed me that it was not Jn° Franklin who had hurt his knee & stopped at Seely's on the Delaware (as reported on Sunday) but another Franklin, brother of Rosewell Franklin.

[89] THURSDAY *Feb* 8. Left Wilkesbarre this morning between 9 and 10 o'clock, in company with Christ° Hurlbut. Col° Butler & M. Hollenback went with us as far as Bullocks (7 miles) We pursued our Journey 18 miles to Luce's at Tobyhannah; and then 12 miles to Learneds, where we lodged; arriving between 9 & 10 in the evening. A snow storm the whole day.

FRIDAY Feb 9. Rode 16 miles to Hallers tavern, & breakfasted, past 11 o'clock. At ½ after One set out for Nazareth, 7 miles, baited, & then went forward to Bethlehem, where I arrived at 6 in the evening, 10 miles from Nazareth.

Saturday 10th. Left Bethlehem before Sun-rise; and reached Philadelphia a little past nine in the Evening, 53 miles. These distances make Wilkesbarre 123 miles from Philadelphia

37
33
53
———
123

[90] The Federal Court appointed to hear the controversy between Connecticut & Pennsylvania, opened at Trenton Nov. 12 1782; and made their decree on the 30th of December, in favour of Pennsylvania. The decree was declared to be unanimous, and was signed

Wᵐ Whipple
Welcome Arnold
Wᵐ C. Houston
Cyrus Griffin
David Brearly

[19] Expense Account of Timothy Pickering.[1]

The State of Pennsylvania
To Timothy Pickering ....D[r]

For executing the duties required of him by an Act of the General Assembly passed on the 27th Dec[r] 1786, for notifying and holding elections in the county of Luzerne in which services he was employed from January 3[d] to Feb[y] 10th 1787, including the time in going and returning, 39 days at 17/6	£34. 2.0
For Cash paid James Whitney, express, to carry & distribute notifications	1.10.
d° paid Matthew Hollenback at Wilkesbarré for stationary	.10
d° paid M[r] Sill for boxes for the Votes	5.3
	£36. 7.9
Thomas Bradford's bill for printing notifications, copies of the laws &c	4.11.3
	£40.19.0 [2]

Endorsed: Account of Expences at Wyoming, January & Feby 1787

[20] Hugh Williamson to William Samuel Johnson.[1]

Edenton 14th Feb[y] 1787

Dear sir

I frequently hear with Pleasure that you continue at New York to represent your State in Congress. I heartily wish that every state in the Union would shun that yearly or half yearly shifting of Helm'smen and that they were equally attentive with

---

[19] [1] M. H. S., Pickering Papers, LVII, 133, in Pickering's hand.

[2] Itemization of his expenses shows a board bill from John Hollenback which includes thirty-eight bowls of "tody" during the thirty days he spent in Wyoming.

[20] [1] C. H. S., William Samuel Johnson Papers, IV, 39, in Williamson's hand. A postscript is omitted. On Williamson see *Susquehannah Company Papers*, VIII, no. 95, note 1.

Connecticut to keep Gentlemen at the Helm whose abilities aided by Experience might give them a Claim to full confidence. In such Case the Union might not be quite so inattentive to congressional Recommendations. I hope you have heard with Pleasure that our Counties who formed what was called the state of Franklin are returned to the Government of this State. If measures equally lenient had been adopted and that too at an early Hour with dissedents from other States I think that our Union needed not have been disgraced as it now is by imperium in imperio. By the way I am extremely sorry that the generous measure adopted by Congress of giving Connecticut Lands nearly of the Extent of a State have not hitherto had the salutary Effect of terminating an actual Rebellion in the Center of Pennsylvania.[2] It is greatly to be lamented that the Interest of a few individuals who have some concern in the Lands on Susquehannah should be the means of fomenting discord and distracting a large & respectable State. I fear that your countryman Dyer finds it much more easy to promote Discord than you and twenty other good men find it to restore Peace.[3] It is very unfortunate that the Opinions of a Gentleman who is otherwise honest and a good Citizen should be so strangely perverted by a few Acres of Land as to promote or encourage Sedition & hazard treasons the Sheding of blood the loss of national Honor and Subversion of Government.

When I hear of the convulsed State of government in Rhode Island and from the Effects of Paper Mony and the Rebellions in Massachusets, from, as I suspect, similar Causes viz. Too strong a Desire to contract Debts and too weak a desire to pay them, I observe with great Pleasure that the Honor of Connecticut is

---

[2] Williamson, like many others, had expected that Connecticut's Western Reserve would be used to compensate members of the Susquehannah Company for loss of their lands in Pennsylvania, but none of the measures adopted by the state made provision for them, despite Johnson's optimism (see note 3).

[3] Extant documents do not suggest that Eliphalet Dyer was directly responsible for the turmoil in Wyoming. He was, of course, a member of long-standing in the Company, but the minutes of meetings in 1785 and 1786 do not list him among those on important committees.

In his answer, dated March 31, 1787 William Samuel Johnson commented: "The obstacles to Peace in Pen^a will I trust be soon removd. This Legisl^e have before them a very liberal L. & when these Act^l Sett^s are once quieted Conn^t I believe will take prop^r Meas^s with all the rest that are concerned"; C. H. S., William Samuel Johnson Papers, IV, 40; Edmund C. Burnett (ed.), *Letters of Members of the Continental Congress* (Washington, 1921-36), VIII, 568.

hitherto unwounded by public attempts to defraud Creditors by the forms or Law or contrary to the forms of Law. Many attempts I hear have been made by southern gentlemen to fit the mode of taking up Lands in the Western Country to the appetite of Land Speculators, hitherto without Success. I have the Honor to be with great Regard Dear sir Your most obed[t] Serv[t]

Hu Williamson

[21] William Hooker Smith and Others to Zebulon Butler.[1]

Dear Sir,

We beheld with Pleasure, The apointment of Goverment of you one of The Directtors & manageers of The Election.[2] Your approbation, attention, & Zeale in the affare, Gave Infanite Pleasure Not onely To us The Signers but To The people at Large. How Redely Did The people, in The Several Destricts attend on you & Coron[l] Pickring, at Times before The Election, at your Request as Soon as The people ware Convinsed of your aprobation of The Election, with what alaccrety Did They attend without the Least hesetation, & the whole Conducted without the Least opposition. We further Expect That you Corn[l] Denisson, Corn[l] Pickring obad[a] Gore, Capt[a] Spalding & a Number of others who are heads of The People, Did Recomend a Number of Petitions In order That Thay should be offered To The People for Thare Signing, To Send by our Representetives, To The assembly.[3] One of Said Petitions was handed To Doct[r] Smith by Corn[l] Denisson, in order That he Smith Should Send The petition first To Lacawana, & after Thay at Lacawana had signed, That The said Petition Should be Returned To said Smith, in order That It should be offerred, To The People on Jacobs Plains, for There Signing & then Log[d] with said Smith for him To Give To The Representatives when They Should Go To Philadalph[a]. The Petition has bin forwarded To Lacawana & Delivered To Ebinezer Mercy Esq[r] who applyd To The People Particularly who Did ananamisly Sign. The Petition was also Sent To Capows by Esq[r] Mercy for The people There To Sign, if Thay approved, with Promis To Return The Petition To Mercy after Thare

---

[21] [1] Wyoming Historical and Geological Society, Butler Papers, in Smith's hand.
[2] See no. 2, *ante*, note 5.   [3] No. 55, *post*.

Perusal. The Said Petition has Not bin Returned, but Sum men from That quorter have Brought The s⁴ Petition Into your Neibourhood, & Thare In Publick Company Did Burn & Distroy The Said Petition, which we Think Is In Contempt Not onely of The Signers & Leading men In This Settlement, but also in Contempt of Goverment. we Expect That our Representatives must Soon Set out for Phyladelp⁴. Pray Sir, advise us what To Do, Shall we Draw an other, (as we have a Coppy) & Recomend it for Signing or Shall we let all Rest whare it Is & Do No more. We must Humbly Rely on you for advice In This Crittecal Matter. Dear Sir, we are with affection, & Dependance, at your Service.

Wm Hooker Smith
Samuel Hover
Abraham Westbrook
Lodwick Updick
Perregreen Pickle ⁴

Jacobs Plains, Feb 18ᵗʰ 1787.
Corn¹ Butler

Substance good enough but (modestly speaking) Shillingly perform⁴ This Letter, Is it not?⁵

[22] Dr. Joseph Sprague to Timothy Pickering.¹

The face of pubelick afarers alter and chang as ofen as the wather and when the moust pleseing prospact of Acomadation and Uniting of this County in Law and goverment with the State witch a fuw Days ago by your unwared Diligence and panes had put in the most Likely way of uniting this County into the Policetecla Famely of this State witch thing has ben presued by goverment for this Number of years without the sines of Susess till your Inflence head broght about to all aperence the greates Chang and fares porspect of a hapy union of this County with this State then Ever head Apereed Sence the Tirel of Trent town and I wish that I Cold teel you that afares were in as good away as

⁴ Probably the last signature is fictitious.
⁵ This note is in a different handwriting, suggesting that the letter fell into hostile hands.
[22] ¹ M. H. S., Pickering Papers, LVII, 136, in Sprague's hand.

when you laft this place but by the Chang of masters the Poletick of this place in mutch oltered and a new Tune is Sange hear, and I am afread that Every thing will go rong. Mr Frankelin has Came hom and I am afraid that his Inflence will undo all that you have don. he has Broght in a number of Laters from m[r] Judd and others of his Asoceates from Newengland to gather with the Resolves of the Sisquehannah meeting [2] the Copey of witch I wold have Tranmeted to you but I Expect that Conal Danson will give you them when he Coms to Town but as he is a New Convart and a vary modes man I Dont know but he may omet it. I will give you the general Porport of them (wat Inflence thes polictak writers will have over the pepel a Cant Say. they Deret the pepels by all meenes not to Exept the Law of Pensilvevania as thay hed bater put them Salves under Brittan or the gratis Tiront then Pencilvenia how [who] has So ofen abused and Deceved them[)]. thay are Excited to Pasavere in thar Obstence from this polectek princebals that Feaderal Govement will Sun be Desolve to Gather with the Intornal Palascy of the States and that Taretoraeel Lines will be of now Veletley whin the States are all Thoron into a State of Anearcey and thay will then have the Sam Chanc for Indepandecy as any other Body of men. it Semes that these princebals are Bilt on the facttion now in Boston State for Say thay if the moob Suceeds the Consequenc will be the disalution of Feaderel goverment if not then 2000 of them Insugents will Take Aselum in your Butefull Country and will anable you to seport your Salvs aganst the power and arms of Pensilvania [3] (the Sisquehannah Commisioners are ogmented to the Number of 19 and all the Power and agensey of the hole Company are Invest in them to act and Trantact all Bness for and in behalf of the Company to Locate form Towns and Devide this Taretory of Country to form Centers and Detarming Titels of Land[)]. one of thare Resolves I have here trancribed to you Vis Resolve that aney three of Said Commissioners to-gather with thar Secretary Shall be a quorum to Trancesact aney of the Biness aforesaid that the Expence of Locating Survires and Detarming all maters aforesaid Shall be payed by Persons in whose faver Such Location &C. Shall be mad and Down and that Said Cort of Commissioners Shall in now Instance Excat or Receed Exorbetent fees that anney 5 of S[d] Commissioners with thar Secretary Shall be a Cort with powers to hear and finely to Detarming all Contervases betwen actual Occupants Respecting the Titles of Lands and to aword

---

[2] *Susquehannah Company Papers*, VIII, no. 268.   [3] *Cf.* no. 14, *ante.*

Equeteble Costs in the usual form of Triel at Law, this Power to Determine whenever a form of Intarnel Goverment Shall be Established in that Country &c &c. S^r you may Eseely See that the princebal are Independence and Exsest in a few ambishus and unpalict men who had the power of Inflence of this poore Deluded pepel and if posebal will be thare Ruine. the partistion [4] that the pepel war asining and was Sined by a grate Number of the Inhabatance but it is fall a Sacarafise to Franklin and his asassciates and by them wos Cometed to the flams but is has Cossed Sum [Perets?] of Resentment. thare is another on the Carpet and will Com Down by Cornol Danson. For I am not abel to tetarming wat the Consequence of this will be nor how it will End but I hope that the frinds of goverment will Exart them Selve in this Cretecail moments and I am Confident that Goverment will So far as thay ar abele protact all thar good Sitizens hear in our Dangeres Setewation. Connol Danson will be at Counsal and that is all the hopes I have as he is the only Shet Anker that we have to Depend on. Rember S^r I wos Taling you in our Convasation that if the Franklin party Jined in the Electtion that thay Elect one that wold not Sarve So that thay wold be in the Same Case after the alecttion as thay was before they Thought that Cornol Danson wos a going out of the State and wold not. But Thank God he Coms to Consell witch will be Conterey to the Intenchon of Franklin Party and I am in Grat hope that he will be the meens of Estableshing Sivel Goverment fully in this County. Sir I wold have Wrote more prtickelrs but Conol Danson will be abel to Inform you in Every Pertickelers. I wos in hopes to have had one owers or two Conversation with you on other Topects before you went hom but you was so Bese I head Now oprtunity but I Shall be in this Sitey Next munth and will present you a queit map of the Northen part of this County. if you are Disposed to Secure any Lands in that part I Can help you to the knoleg of Sevrel Track of the first Rate in that Country and Comodasly Sitewated with Som thousen acours in a Trak that is unpropriated. So this from your most abedent and Humbel servnt
Wilkbary Febuwary 20 day 1787   Joseph Sprague
To Timothy Pickron Esqr

NB Sence Franklin has Come in Every thing is turned up Sid down and Every Instrement is yused to Preswed the pepel not to Comply and Seport goverment. Every mathod is Tring to prevent Cornol Danson from Coming to Consell. to make a long

---

[4] No. 16, *ante.*

Story a Short one the Divel is to pay and the Sucomstance of this place is goeing wose and wost and I am afraid twil Ind in the Totol Dessilation of this Setelment. Doctr Smith is Vey Active and Exurtes him Silf to the Atumost. he has Gat the Pratistion Sined the Seventh time by the Jecob plenes and Lackewon and up the River to the N° 120, these Siners Sem to Stand to thar Intearety but Nanticock Shany King Town and part of wilkbery I beleve will apostintise. 22 day.

NB I Cold most have wished that that Portison had not ben So Universal but had Asks of goverment for the pratisiners only and not fer the Setelement in general as a great part of the Inhabetance So mutch Dispute it and Excalame aganst it that thay Desares no Banefet from it. Sir Excuse me fer writing on Craps of paper for thar is non to be gat hear.

[23] William Hooker Smith to Timothy Pickering.[1]

Sir

After you Left us The weales all Stop[d]. It Is True Thare was Coppies of The petition & Loged at Corn[l] Butlers & Thare Thay Lay Untill about The 16th when Corn[l] Denisson Came Down. The Coppy which Esq[r] Gore Took up The River was Distroyd in Contempt however an other was Drawn & Signed which Corn[l] Denisson has if you Remember. I Took a Coppey which was Designed for Lacawaney & Jacobs Plains. I Sent it To Esq[r] Marcy & M[r] Carey at Lackawaney who are Good men. Thay offerred it To The people & all Signed To whom it was offerred Except one man. Marcy Sent it to Capows for The perusal of The people Thare. it was mostly Liked & Signed by Several & Sent back by Two men To Deliver To marcy which marcy Intended To Convey To me In order To have it offered To The people in This Neibourhood. The Two men which had The petition in Trust To Deliver To marcy Carryed it first To Wilkesbury Then To Shaney & finally To Kingstown in order To Shew it To Sum of Those Disafected To Goverment which was Don & at Last Sum of Those Disafected sort of folkes Colected at Kingstown & made Derision of The petition & fixt To It a Number of Fictious Names, yours for one with a Slure To

[23] [1] M. H. S., Pickering Papers, LVII, 138, in Smith's hand. This letter was carried to Philadelphia by the newly elected councilor, Nathan Denison.

it & finally Comited it To the Flames Denouncing Cursings against The promoters The Signers & all That Favored it.[2] Coron[1] Franklin Came to Capows whilest The petition was Thare; after Reading it was in a Grate Rage and Declared That he had Reather See Human Blood Run as Deep over The Land as The waters Did Last fall in The Great flood Than to have Seen So many Signers To That Petetion. Franklin was present at The Conflagration at Kings Town. you was pleasd To See a fue men Joyn In The Election. That was Thare pollecy in order That we should Not be Repesented. Denisson They Expected wold Not or Could Not Go & franklin Should Not. you must be Convinced That That party Can Do what Thay Please at a General meating. The moderate Good Sort of People are Discorag[d] & but few appear but The opesite party appear To a man. Thare was but about 130 Electors. we have more Than Duble That Number if Thay wold appear. Dear Sir how must The Good Regular well Disposd feal when Thay See a Certain man Distinguish[d] by Goverment at The head of The Election Chosen to Represent us a man who has Declared his avoudness To The State. as To his Practices & Designes you by This Time are aquainted. Sesquehannah Proprators have had meeting of Late. I Send you Thare Resolves.[3] here is News arived from The Eastward That The mob Party Increassis & are Likely To Carrey Thare points & That Thare will be a General Revolution as well in This State as others & I fear Unless This Poor Distres[d] almost Distracted people are made Easey in Thare Improvements it will Begin hear. Corn[l] Butler has Rec[d] from Mag[r] Jugd[d] by Franklin a Sever Repremand for Incorageing The Election.[4] Corn[l] Denisson has favoured Us with a petition which was Sent To Tuncannock & Signed by a Number Thare. This has bin at Lacawana & Signed by a Number Thare. I Rec[d] The Petition from Lacawane yesterday & Called The people In This Neibourhood Together which Signed it To a man. we have To This petition 120 Signers. The people in This Neibourhood are To a man in favour of Goverment. This is Thursday 21[t] of Fab. This moment Came home from Wilkesbury whare I Delivered The above petition To Corn[l] Danisson. he appears Discorag[d]. If he Comes he will Set out Next Day after Tomorrow. I fear Thare Is No Distinct Provision made in The Petition for Those who have Through the war Strugled on These fruntears who have No Lands aloted To Them In The Towns if The Towns are Granted. Provision I hope will be made for such To be Supply[d]

---

[2] See also no. 21, ante.
[3] *Susquehannah Company Papers*, VIII, no. 268.   [4] No. 4, ante.

out of The Loots in These Towns which were aloted To men abraud who nevour Settled Them or have Dun The Least in Defence of The Cuntrey. what The Settlers Desire is That Those who have lived hear before The war & Through The war & have Sufferred Through The whole Should have Lands Granted & further if a Committe should be appointed by Goverment To Discribe Those Intitled & if Such as has bin Enemyes To Goverment Should be appointed Those That are friends will have No Lands hear. Sir I am with Esteame your most obe* Humble Sarv*

Wm Hooker Smith

Jacobs Plains Wioming Fab. 21ᵈ 1787

[24] Benjamin Franklin to the Pennsylvania General Assembly.[1]

The Council met.

PHILADELPHIA, Friday, February 23d, 1787.

The following draft of a message to the General Assembly, was read and approved, vizt:

A Message from the President and the Supreme Executive Council to the General Assembly.

GENTLEMEN :—During your recess an election has been held for the county of Luzerne. While this event affords a proof of the wisdom of your measures, we must acknowledge that Mr. Pickering, a Commissioner for holding the election, was instrumental in its accomplishment, by exposing the many false and artful representations which had been made by the people opposed to the authority of Government.

We think it our duty again to recommend to your Honorable house the receiving the funded certificates of the State for the arrearages due on lands, located or warranted before the year 1776; it appears to us a measure just, and so reasonable that it will be highly beneficial and give General satisfaction. Many of the citizens who are in arrear have suffered by the calamities of the war, and cannot settle at the Land Office unless their certificates are received in payment. If this indulgence is not granted they will be obliged to give part of their lands to speculators to have it patented, or endeavour to evade payment.

---

[24] [1] *Pa. C. R.*, XV, 167-68.

We are convinced it will be of advantage to the State to lower the price of land within the late Indian purchase,[2] only eight warrants have been taken out for lands there these six months past. * * *

Benjamin Franklin.

[25] Christopher Hurlbut to Timothy Pickering.[1]

Sir. I Should not act a fair Part if after declining to Sign the Petition I Should decline Giving my reasons. The petition begins with Seting forth our Sufferings from the Indians also those inflicted by fellow-Citizens and by destroying floods. Those things may operate upon the Passions of men but not on their Reason, which I think it more Necessary to work in our favour. I think it highly Reasonable that we Should hold these Lands, because we were here During the Indian war and many blows we bore that if we had not been here would most likely been struck on the Interior Parts of the State, we were no Cost to the State and finally our most Cruel Persecutors were officers of Government and their tools and if we had nothing Else to Plead in Vindication of our title but to have reparation Made for our Damages and Sufferings I think it would be Less expence to the State to Give us the Lands than to Make good the damages. To Petition for an Act of Oblivion will silence that Plea. Further the Petition Includes no person but Such as were Actual Setlers here before the decree at trenton as entitled to the benefit of a Grant. That would Enclude me. But it would be Ungenerous to Exclude the Major Part of our Inhabitants by our own act. If the Assembly think no others but actual Setlers before the Trenton Decree Intitled, we Cannot help it. If we ask for all, we are not to be blamed if only half obtain. It is my earnest wish to have Peace Established and in order to obtain that would do nothing to Give Occasion of offence. I am Sir your Friend and Very Hum. Servant.

Christopher Hurlbut.

Febr⁷ 23, 1787. Timothy Pickering Esq⁷
Philadelphia

---

² The reference is to land purchased from the Indians in 1784. See *Susquehannah Company Papers*, VIII, no. 88, note 6.
[25] ¹ M. H. S., Pickering Papers, LVII, 140, in Hurlbut's hand. This letter was carried to Philadelphia by Nathan Denison. For Pickering's answer, see no. 47, *post*.

[26] John Franklin to the Speaker of the Pennsylvania General Assembly.[1]

Wilkbarre, County of Luzerne Feb[r] 24, 1787

Sir

Having the honour of being elected the first and only Representative for the county of Luzerne, I feel myself sensibly indebted to my Constituents for the honour conferr'd on me, and under the greatest obligation to represent them in your Hon[ble] House, should I be so happy as to be admitted a seat as a Member of such an Honourable Body, this being the first opportunity this settlement have ever had of a Legal Representation since we commenced citizens of this opulent State. It is my earnest and sincere hope (and I trust well founded) that those unhappy and ruinous disputes that have long subsisted in this settlement will now subside, that Peace and Tranquillity will prevail, shall feel myself happy if I can be Instrumental in promoting such just measures as shall be for the Peace Happiness and Welfare of my Constituents, and consequently terminate in the Weal and Prosperity of this State at large, at the same time have to regret that my own domestic affairs are [such] that it is not in my power to attend as early as I would otherwise wish, having just returned to this settlement after two months absence therefrom. was not apprized of my appointment in time that I could possibly attend at the first meeting of this Sessions. would therefore pray the indulgent consideration of your Hon[ble] House that the aforesaid reasons may apologize my absence which will be gratefully acknowledged by your Hon[rs] most obe[t] and humble Servant signed

John Franklin.

[27] William Judd to Zebulon Butler.[1]

Farmington Feb[r] 26th 1787

Dear Sir

We are alarmed at the news of your Countrys submiting to the state of Pennsylvania before you are quieted in the Lands. we do not intend to Loose you. So, greate exertions are makeing

---

[26] [1] M. H. S., Pickering Papers, LVII, 143, a copy in an unknown hand.
[27] [1] Wyoming Historical and Geological Society, Butler Papers, in Judd's hand.

by the Company to fill the Country with Inhabitants and our prospects are fair however. Ingratitude is a base fault, your friends are disappointed and feel a Glow of resentment.

The barer M' Roswell Wells is determined to make a settlement in your Country if he finds due encouragement. he is a Gentleman of Education & good reputation. permit me to recommend him to your Attention. I am sir Your most Obed' Humble servant

Col° Butler. Wm Judd

[28] Nathan Denison to Zebulon Butler.[1]

Philadelphia the 5th of march 1787.

Sir

I hear inclose a letter to Colon^l Franklin and let him no that his attendence at the assembled is absolutely nessasery as it may be of Servies to the Settlers. our Enemies in the assembley Say he will not attend [2] Which if he does not may prejudus the minds of Some of the members against us. I Wold request you to use your influence to have him Come to the assembley Which if he Declines Will make us appear like a faithles People as Some of the People hear have us to be.

At Present the members of assembley and Counsel Sem to be Disposed to Do us Justis and Sem to be determin to take up the matter Wheather the Petition is laid in or not and as there Was Such an opposesion to the Petition in our Settlement and it Equally Conserns those that did not Signe as Well as those that Did I thing [think] it Will give the most Sattisfaction to the People to Let it Come before the house in Some other Way by representing the Diferent Clases of People both Settlers & Proprietors. so far as I Can Discribe these Difrent Situations I Expect Soon to have the matter Laid before the assembley.[3] What Will be Don in our favour time Will bring forth.

Pleas to give my Complement to all inquiring frins and Except the Same your Self from your frind and very humbl Servent Colonel Zebulon Butler Nathan Denison

PS I think it Will be of importenc for Col^n Franklin to Come to the assembley and answer to his name if no more as it will Stop the mouths of those Who Wish to have him not Come.

---

[28] [1] Wyoming Historical and Geological Society, Butler Papers, in Denison's hand.
[2] *Cf.* no. 26, *ante.*   [3] See no. 29, *post.*

[29] Nathan Denison to the Speaker of the Pennsylvania General Assembly.[1]

Philadelphia March 5, 1787.

Sir,

I have the honour to enclose a petition from sundry inhabitants of the county of Luzerne,[2] praying for a confirmation of their titles to certain lands in that county, which thro' the medium of the Susquehanna Company, were derived from the Colony and State of Connecticut. As that petition has not been generally signed,[3] I think it a duty which I owe to my constituents, and a matter of information proper to be laid before the General Assembly, to mention the other classes of people in the county, who claim under titles in like manner, derived from Connecticut. These are,

1. Actual settlers, prior to the decree of the federal court at Trenton, who, or those whom they represent, were proprietors in the Susquehanna purchase, but to whom particular rights have never been assigned, or only on the West Branch of the Susquehanna, of which they were divested.

2. Actual settlers prior to that decree, but to whom rights have since been assigned.

3. Actual settlers who were and are proprietors, but who amidst their various distresses, sold their old rights, and have, now no interest but as general proprietors in the Susquehanna purchase.

4. New-Comers, now actual settlers, who since that decree have had rights assigned them.

The several farms, or rights, which are the subjects of these claims, generally contain 300 acres.

If it shall please the assembly to appoint a Committee on this business, which in behalf of my constituents I pray may be done, I shall be happy to attend them, to communicate all the information on the subject of which I am possessed. I have the honour to be with great respect, Sir, your most humble servant.

Nathan Denison

---

[29] [1] P. H. M. C., Div. of Arch. and MSS., John Franklin Papers, in an unknown hand but signed by Denison; M. H. S., Pickering Papers, LVII, 146, a draft in Pickering's hand.
[2] No. 16, *ante*.   [3] *Cf.* nos. 23 and 25, *ante*.

[30] [Nathan Denison to Zebulon Butler?].[1]

Philadelphia the 9th of March 1787

Sir

I here With transmit to you a Coppy of a letter which I Sent to the Speeker of the assemley [2] With the Petitions Which Was Signed by our Settlers Was Emediatly taken up by the house a Compittee appointed after the Second reading of the petition, to take the matter in to Consideration and make report there on to the assembley the foregoing Was Done on the 6th instant,[3] on the 7th Colon[1] Pickering and my Self Was Caled on to Wate on the Committee at 4 oClock and acordingly meet them at the time appointed Who are as foloweth (viz) Mr Finley of Westmoreland County Mr G Climer of Philedelphia Mr Robat Brown of Northamton Mr Hubley of Lankestor and Mr A. Wenkoop of Bucks County and give them an account of the Situation of the Settlement and advanst Som argements Why We Shold have the title of our land absoutely Confairmed to us free gratis. I must Say that Col[n] Pickering is very active and holds up Every reasonable argament in favour of our title and Spears no Pains to bring the matter to a reasonable [se]ttlement. What the avent Will be I Cannot say but things he[re] [se]em to have a fair prospect and I make no Doubt but that the [Ass]embley Design to do that Which Will be Judged Just and [Re]asonable [i]n the Eyes of the World, but Wheather it Will be Sattisfactory [fragment ends].

[31] General Assembly Committee Report on the Petition from Luzerne Inhabitants.[1]

The report of the committee on the petition from a number of inhabitants of the county of *Luzerne,* read March 10th, was read the second time, and in part adopted, as follows, *viz.*

---

[30] [1] Wilkes College Library, McClintock Papers, a fragment in Denison's hand. Brackets are used to indicate parts of words supplied where the ms. is damaged.

[2] No. 29, *ante.*

[3] *Minutes of the Second Session of the Eleventh General Assembly,* 136 (microfilm copy).

[31] [1] *Minutes of the Second Session of the Eleventh General Assembly,* 162-63, dated March 17, 1787 (microfilm copy). The report was read the first time on March 10; *ibid.,* 141. The copy of the committee's report in M. H. S., Pickering Papers, LVII, 147, omits mention of the committee named to bring in a bill and the motion by Morris.

The committee on the petition from the inhabitants of the county of *Luzerne,* called *Connecticut* claimants, report,

That conceiving it of importance to the subject, they enter upon their report by first stating to the House, that during the former session, and in conference between a committee of the House and the agents of the *Connecticut* claimants, *John Franklin* and *Jenkins,*[2] the agents, were explicitly told, that every case would be considered specially, and that no claims, unless urged in behalf of individuals, and for particular occupancies, would be received. The agents, admitting the propriety of this restrictive mode, doubted not of a conformity to it on the part of their constituents, when next they should make application to the House: But the present petition, on the contrary, advances claims collectively, and is made for entire and extensive districts. From this circumstance, the House might well wave any present deliberations on the subject of the claims; but in consideration of the peace of the county of *Luzerne,* as well as to testify our satisfaction at the submission at length paid to the laws by the petitioners, the committee recommend to the House, notwithstanding, to proceed to establish the principles on which they will quiet the possessions and occupancies of the petitioners, and others of that county in the like predicament; and also those on which they will make compensation to such proprietors under titles from this state, as may in consequence be deprived of their lands.

The committee, in connection with the subject, refer the House to a printed paper accompanying this report, dated at *Hartford,* in *Connecticut, December* 26th, 1786, signed *Joel Barlow,* as worthy of their animadversion. This paper, purporting to be the resolutions of the *Susquehanna* Company,[3] revives their pretended title to a large territory within this state, including in it the lands of the *Connecticut* settlers, directs a mode of distribution, and intimates a design of erecting it into a government, independent of the authority of this state.

Upon the whole matter, the committee recommend to the House the following resolutions:

Resolved, That such of the people called *Connecticut* claimants, their heirs or assigns, as were the actual possessors or occupants of lands within the county of *Luzerne* at or before the

---

[2] Franklin and John Jenkins as duly accredited agents had appeared before the Assembly in September, 1786; for Jenkin's account of their activities, see *Susquehannah Company Papers,* VIII, no. 250.

[3] *Ibid.,* no. 268.

date of the decree at *Trenton,* be quieted and confirmed in their several possessions and occupancies.

That compensation in lands, equivalent in the value, be made therefor to proprietors under the rights of this state.

That commissioners be appointed to carry the foregoing resolutions into execution.

Ordered, That Mr. G.[eorge] *Clymer* Mr. [Gerardus] *Wynkoop* and Mr. [Adam] *Hubley* be a committee, to bring in a bill conformably to the foregoing resolution.[4]

Whereupon, On motion of Mr. [Robert] *Morris,* seconded by Mr. [Robert] *Whitehill,*

Ordered, That the residue of the said report be postponed.

[32] William Judd to Zebulon Butler.[1]

Farmington March 19th 1787

Sir

I am excedingly mortified at the thought you Could be so base as to show my Letter written to you in the Confidence of a friend to Col° Pickering and suffer him to have the Possession of it for his purposes.[2] it was hastely written the Messenger waiting and not calculated for the Inspection of any but friends. I hope you have not suffered him to take it away or to take Copies from it. if you have shall be further disappointed and induced to beleive worse of you than I wish. I always have stood your friend and verily believed I might rank myself among that Class of Men you regarded. our Common Interest I thought had also Cemented a reciprocal friendship. I never treated you with reserve but freely communicated my sentaments to you upon all Matters of Business and fondly supposed I might rely upon your Confidence, but it seems I am mistaken, and am hapy to find it out tho late, shall in future be Cautious who I trust with my Secreets. if you have any of my Letters on hand will thank you to Inclose them to me or burn them for no One Can know what

---

[4] The bill was brought before the Assembly on March 20 and on March 21, it was read a second time, debated, and ordered printed for public consideration; *Minutes,* 170, 172. See no. 38, *post.* According to Pickering's later account to his son, Pickering made the draft of the bill for the committee; Pickering Papers, XXXVIII, 241.

[32] [1] Wyoming Historical and Geological Society, Butler Papers, in Judd's hand.

[2] No. 4, *ante.* It will be recalled that this letter was read by Butler before a meeting in Wilkes-Barre.

Use may be made of them. I feel a resentment I little expected
to have occasion to feel towards My old friend Butler. it gives
me pain to Loose a friend, but perhaps it may be gain to others.
the delicacy of the subject prevents me being very Lengthy. I
have long thought if the Settlers were fully quieted in all their
Claims it would be well for them but to see them precipitated
into a measure without any sure prospect of Confirmation gives
me pain.[3] if you proceed you must trust the Clemency of the
State and what you are to Expect should suppose your past Ex-
periance would easily shew you. I am sir Your once devoted
friend & very humble servant

Col° Butler   Wm Judd

Endorsed: Major Judds Scolding Litter 1787

[33] Timothy Pickering to Aaron Cleveland.[1]

Mr Aaron Cleveland.

Philadelphia Mar. 20th 1787.

Sir,

Having been appointed to some public offices in the County
of Luzerne, in this State (which county comprehends the Wyoming lands) I was authorized by the General Assembly, in conjunction with Col° Butler and Mr Franklin, to hold an election
there. Franklin was absent: but Col° Butler joined me, and with
much labour and difficulty we persuaded the people to elect a
Councillor, Representative &c. The Councillor (Col° Dennison[)] has taken his seat in Council: but Mr Franklin has staid
at home, dissatisfied (as I am well informed) at their having
been an election; and he may probably continue his opposition
to the measures pursuing by government for giving peace to that
unhappy Country: However, I am disposed to believe that peace
is not far distant: for I think those measures will give general
satisfaction. I shall in consequence move up to that Country,
with my family. When there last winter I was informed that
you owned a town-lot in Wilksbarré, and that you would probably be willing to sell it: if so, and you will inform me of the
terms, or authorize any freind of yours here to sell it and we
agree as to the price, I will purchase it. I observed a clump of

---

[3] In the Pickering Papers this sentence appears almost verbatim on a
small sheet with this note: "N. B. The above is nearly in the words of
—— —— in his letter dated March 19, 1787, to —— ——." It is endorsed:
"Extract from a letter dated March 19, 1787 to Col° B——."

[33] [1] M. H. S., Pickering Papers, V, 397-98, a copy in a clerk's hand.

76

young apple trees on the plain, which, it was said, were in your lot. As they are exposed to the cattle, and, may not probably be wanted for the lot on which they stand, I shall be greatly obliged if you will give me leave to remove them: what they are worth I shall be willing to pay. You may perhaps recollect me: I think I once saw you at Salem (Massachusetts) where I then lived. I beleive it was at your relation's, Mrs Higginson's. On the ground of that connection, I will ask your freindship, to assist me in bargaining for one half the right in Wilksbarré which belonged to Col° Durkee, and which was sold, by his son John, to Capt Spalding and (as I am informed) Mr Jedediah Hide of Norwich. When at Wyoming I bought Spalding's half. (vizt half the meadow lot, half a five acre lot, and half the back lot) for sixty five pounds Pennsylvania currency. Capt Spalding told me that Mr Hide desired him to let him know when he sold, because the whole lot together he supposed, would sell better than in halves. When I purchased of Spalding it was in expectation that I could purchase Mr Hides half. I now beg the favour of you to see Mr Hide and in my behalf to treat with him for his interest aforementioned. I shall write to Mr Hide (but I am not certain whether I am right in his christian name) [2] and as I am a stranger to him, beg leave to refer him to you for farther information: I am to pay Capt Spalding one half his money the 15th Sep^t next, and the other half on the first of May 1788. If Mr Hide does not apply to you, I beg you will see him as soon as you can with convenience. Please to direct to me at Philadelphia. If I should be gone, Mr Samuel Hodgdon my freind, will act in my behalf. I expect shortly to go to Wyoming, to bring forward an election of Justices of the Peace. I am Sir Your Most Ob^t serv^t.

T. P.

[34] Timothy Pickering to Jedidiah Hyde.[1]

Philadelphia March 20th 1787.

Mr Jedidiah Hide
Sir
    When I was at Wyoming, in February last, I purchased of Capt Spalding half of the meadow lot, back lot, and of a five

---

[2] No. 34, *post.* Hyde's first name was Peleg; see Cleveland's answer, no. 42, *post.*
[34] [1] M. H. S., Pickering Papers, V, 397, a copy in a clerk's hand. Hyde's first name, however, was Peleg.

acre lot, which were the late Col° Durkee's. He told me that the other half of those lots belonged to you, and that you was desirous of selling it; and for this purpose desired him to advise you when he sold, that the whole might go together. I intended to make you an offer of the same price I gave him; this was sixty-five pounds Pennsylvania Currency, or 173 ⅓ dollars, payable one half on the 15ᵗʰ Sepᵗ next, and the other half on the first of May 1788. However, if different periods of payment would suit you better, we should not differ on that account. There appears to be a prospect of peace to that unhappy country, and if the laws of Pennsylvania are submitted to, I shall go there to live, to excercise some civil offices to which I am appointed.

You perhaps might have been willing to have taken less than I agreed to give Captain Spalding: but I supposed you would like to know what that was; and therefore I have candidly told you; as well as of the prospect of the Wyoming quarrel without which settlement, indeed, the lands there would be of little value. I am a stranger to you, and therefore request you to apply to Mʳ Aaron Cleveland, whom I have requested to treat with you on the subject. Or, if you have a freind in this City, you can authorize him to act for you in this matter. I am Sir, Your most hble serv.

Timothy Pickering

[35] Protest against the Confirming Act.[1]

To the Honorable MEMBERS of the ASSEMBLY of the State of PENNSYLVANIA.

Gentlemen,

I hear that you have made it the order of the day for to-morrow to take up a bill you have published but 4 or 5 days ago, about giving the lands belonging to a number of citizens of this State to the settlers of Wioming.[2] The subject is certainly of a very delicate nature, and requires more mature deliberation.

When a legislative body finds itself under the necessity of invading private property, the necessity should be very apparent indeed, to justify their proceedings. The interested views and conversations of a few individuals should not be considered as the sense of the public, in a matter of such magnitude. Time

[35] [1] *Pennsylvania Packet,* March 28, 1787. A prefatory note from the printer states that lack of space kept the letter from being printed the preceding day.
[2] No. 38, *post.*

should be given to the State, to express their sense of such an unusual stretch of legislative power, as the circumstances very rarely occur, which could justify such a procedure: at least, the owners of the lands should have time to meet and agree upon some representation to you, on so important a subject: but to publish a bill in one week, and enact it into a law in the beginning of the next, to invade the private property of your constituents, when it is not practicable for the owners to consult together upon the subject, will, I am afraid, appear to be only an insult to them, and a palpable evasion of the constitution. The consequences of such a step must appear alarming to every citizen, and dangerous to their property.

It is easy for an Assembly to insert plausible arguments, for laying hold of the private property of an individual, whom they may be pleased to represent as dangerous to the liberties of the State, while he is allowed to possess the whole of his property, and then fondly imagine that they would be justified in confiscating or dividing it among their friends. Does it not set aside our courts of justice, or render them perfectly trifling? They are the sole judges of private property, and have a right to determine whether your constitutional power extends to the making of such a law, and therefore of disallowing such a law, as appears to them to have been made without competent authority, or to be subversive of the fundamental rights of the citizens.

But why would you hurry your judges into such disagreeable circumstances as these, when you can easily prevent them by appointing commissioners on the part of the State, to purchase the lands from the owners, or their agents, at an equitable price, before you bestow them on others?

When a State is obliged to dispossess a citizen of his property it is always done with the utmost deliberation, and then a generous price is always given, which either will, or ought to satisfy the owner, and justify the legislature in the eyes of the State at large, and without this the precedent is dangerous and alarming.

26 March, 1787   A CITIZEN.

[36] Timothy Pickering to John Pickering.[1]

Philaˢ March 27, 1787.

Dear Brother,

I have so far accomplished a business of great moment, as to bring the Wyoming people to consent to receive the laws of

[36] [1] M. H. S., Pickering Papers, XL, 199-200, in Pickering's hand. An incomplete copy is in *ibid.,* V, 404.

Pennsylvania, provided their old possessions could be confirmed to them; and this day the General Assembly have agreed to a law for quieting them on the principles I held out to the people;[2] so peace & good government will be introduced into a settlement with which Penn[a] has been contending these seventeen or eighteen years. The result of this measure will oblige me to go to Wyoming (now called the county of Luzerne) in a few days, with the law confirming their titles, acquired prior to the decree of the federal court at Trenton, in Dec[r] 1782, by which the claim of Connecticut to the lands in question (and other lands within the charter bounds of Pennsylvania) was rejected. I thus consider myself as fixed for the remainder of my life in this state; and here I should wish to concenter my interest. I would sell not only my lot in Brown's (or Fitch's) farm but the residue of my lands, provided it should be agreeable to you to take them; and this the happy recovery of your health I hope will enable you to do. I am the more induced to make this proposal now, because I have bargained for several parcels of land at Wyoming, containing in the whole about seven hundred acres, for which I shall have to pay about five hundred dollars, in the course of five months, and nearly five hundred more in a year.[3] This will make it convenient to me to receive part of the money for my lands in Salem, as early as may be; for some of my first payments will be due by the last of June next. For this reason I should wish the lot in Fitch's farm were sold to him immediately, and the money sent to me (or in my absence to my partner M[r] Samuel Hodgdon) at Philadelphia. I owe sister Gooll by a note for the house furniture I purchased [of] her. If it should be agreeable to you to take my lands, then I should desire you to assume the debt to sister Gooll at the amount of the principal and interest at the time you assume it. I request your answer on this subject as early as may be.

Some of my law books will be useful to me. Such as you do not want yourself I should wish to have shipped to me by the first vessel from Salem. Such as I shall not wish to retain I can readily sell here. Blackstone and Burn in particular will be useful to you, and I shall not want them, as I have a late edition of Blackstone, & intend to get the latest of Burn. Cokes Institute 3 Vol[s] & Bacon's Abridgement 5 Vols. I sh[d] wish to receive, if you have not sold them.[4]

---

[2] No. 38, *post.* The actual date of final passage was March 28, not March 27.   [3] See nos. 33 and 34, *ante.*

[4] Sir William Blackstone, *Commentaries on the Laws of England* (1st American ed., Philadelphia 1771); Richard Burn, *The Justice of the Peace*

I am a little at a loss what to say about my son John : I wish
to have him with me; & his mother is very desirous of his coming home : However, I will let the matter rest, until I return
from Wyoming, which will be the beginning of May.

Present my love to all under your roof, & believe me, dear
brother, most affectionately yours

Tim. Pickering

Endorsed : T. P. March 27, 1787

[37] Debate on the Confirming Act.[1]

The bill, entitled *"An Act for ascertaining and confirming
to certain persons, called* Connecticut *claimants, the lands by
them claimed within the county of* Luzerne, *and for other purposes therein mentioned,"* was read the third time : And in debating the following paragraph, *viz.*

Sect. 3. And whereas it will be necessary to institute a summary mode of ascertaining and establishing the right of each
claimant, Be it further enacted by the authority aforesaid, That
the Supreme Executive Council shall appoint three judicious persons to be commissioners, to repair to the county of
Luzerne [2] ***

It was moved by Mr. *G. Clymer,* seconded by Mr. *D. Clymer,*

To strike out the words *"the Supreme Executive Council shall
appoint three prudent and judicious persons to be commissioners,
to"* and in lieu thereof to insert," *be, and
they are hereby appointed commissioners, for the purposes herein
after expressed and declared; and that in case of the death, absence, or refusal to serve, of any or all of the said commissioners,
the Supreme Executive Council are hereby authorized and required to supply the vacancy or vacancies occasioned thereby, by
other new appointment or appointments."*

"Sect. 4. *And be it further enacted by the authority aforesaid, That the said commissioners shall"*

And on the question,—*"Will the House adopt the amendment*

---

and Parish Officer (15th ed., London, 1785) ; Edward Coke, *The First Part
of the Institutes of the Laws of England,* 3 vols. (London, various years) ;
Matthew Bacon, *A New Abridgement of the Law* (London, various years).
[37] [1] *Minutes of the Second Session of the Eleventh General Assembly,*
185-86, dated March 27, 1787 (microfilm copy).

[2] The passage here omitted is included in section 4 of the act as amended
(no. 38, *post*) except that the final wording required the commissioners to
begin action within two months, not eight months.
* * *

proposed?"—the Yeas and Nays were called by Mr. *Findley* and Mr. *Whitehill,* and were as follows, *viz.*[3]

So it was determined in the affirmative.

It was then, on motion, *Ordered,* That the further consideration of the said clause, as amended, be postponed, and that tomorrow be assigned to elect commissioners for the purposes contained in the foregoing paragraph, and that the nomination continue until that day.[4]

[38] The Confirming Act.[1]

An act for ascertaining and confirming to certain Persons called Connecticut claimants, the Lands by them claimed within the County of Luzerne, and for other purposes therein mentioned.

SECTION 1. *Whereas,* an unhappy dispute for many years subsisted between the province and State of Pennsylvania on one part, and the Colony and State of Connecticut on the other part, relative to certain lands within the charter boundary of Pennsylvania, but which were claimed by Connecticut, as falling within the limits of her charter, which dispute was finally terminated by the decree of the Court of Commissioners at Trenton, on the thirtieth day of December, one thousand seven hundred and eighty-two, in the mode prescribed by the articles of Confederation of the United States, by which decree the question between the two States was decided in favour of Pennsylvania; *And whereas,* before the termination of the said claim of Connecticut, a number of its inhabitants with their associates settled upon and improved divers tracts of land lying on or near to the Northeast branch of the river Susquehanna, and the waters thereof, and now within the County of Luzerne; *And whereas,* parts of the same lands have been claimed under titles derived from the late proprietaries of Pennsylvania, and these interfering claims have occasioned much contention, Expense and bloodshed, and this assembly being desirous of putting an end to those evils by con-

---

[3] Thirty-six voted *yea;* twenty-three voted *nay.* See no. 39, *post.*

[4] The record gives no further debate or mention of men nominated for the post of commissioner.

[38] [1] *P. A.,* 2nd ser., XVIII, 660-64; *Pennsylvania Packet,* April 12, 1787. On April 13, Connecticut's delegates to Congress sent a copy of the act to Gov. Samuel Huntington; C. H. S., William Samuel Johnson Papers, IV, 41. See no. 66, *post.*

firming such of the Connecticut claims as were acquired by actual settlers prior to the termination of the said dispute, agreeably to the petition of a number of the said settlers, and by granting a just compensation to the Pennsylvania claimants; *And whereas,* the lands aforesaid, claimed by the Connecticut settlers have been usually assigned to them in rights, or lots, of about three hundred acres each, which rights, or lots, have either been entire or in two or more divisions; therefore,

SECTION 2. *Be it enacted, and it is hereby enacted, by the Representatives of the Freemen of the Commonwealth of Pennsylvania in General Assembly met, and by the authority of the same,* That all the said rights, or lots, now lying within the County of Luzerne, which were occupied or acquired by Connecticut claimants, who were actually settlers there at or before the termination of the claim of the State of Connecticut, by the decree aforesaid, and which rights, or lots, were particularly assigned to the said settlers prior to the said decree, agreeably to the regulations then in force among them, be and they are hereby confirmed to them and their heirs and assigns; *Provided,* that all the claimants whose lots are hereby confirmed, shall, by themselves, guardians, or other lawful agents, within eight months next after the passing of this act, prefer to the Commissioners hereinafter mentioned their respective claims to the lots aforesaid, therein stating the grounds of their claims and sufficiently describing the lots claimed, so that the same may be made known and ascertained, and support the same by reasonable proofs.

SECTION 3. *And whereas,* it will be necessary to institute a summary mode of ascertaining and establishing the right of each claimant, Be it further enacted by the authority aforesaid, that Peter Muhlenberg, Timothy Pickering and Joseph Montgomery, Esquires,[2] be and are hereby appointed Commissioners for the purposes hereinafter expressed and declared; and in case of death, absence or refusal to serve, of any or all of the said Commissioners, the Supreme Executive Council are hereby authorized and required to supply the vacancy or vacancies occasioned thereby by other new appointment or appointments.

SECTION 4. And be it further enacted by the authority

---

[2] See nos. 37, *ante* and 39, *post.*

Muhlenberg, whose resignation was accepted by the Council on May 17, was replaced by Daniel Hiester; *Pa. C. R.,* XV, 214, 217. Hiester resigned on July 19 and was replaced by William Montgomery on July 23; *ibid.,* 237, 245, 248. Joseph Montgomery, who was permitted to resign on May 31, was replaced on June 1 by Stephen Balliet; *ibid.,* 221.

aforesaid, That the said Commissioners shall repair to the County of Luzerne within two months, next after the passing of this act, and at such place within the same county and at such time as the said Commissioners shall appoint to meet together, for the purpose of receiving and examining the claims of all persons to the lots intended by this act to be confirmed, and the said Commissioners are hereby empowered to adjourn their meeting from time to time, and to such places within the said county, as they shall judge best for the proper and speedy Execution of their Commission; and that all persons interested in the said lots may be duly notified to make and support their claims thereto, within the time prescribed by this act; the said Commissioners shall cause it to be published in one or more of the newspapers printed in Pennsylvania and Connecticut, with an advertisement subjoined, Expressing the time and place proposed for their first meeting, and copies of this Act, and of the said advertisement, shall also be posted up at sundry places within the said county, for the information of the inhabitants. And the Examination of the said claims shall be by witnesses, on their oaths or affirmations (which the said Commissioners are severally empowered to administer), and such other Evidence as shall be produced to the said Commissioners, or which they can obtain. And of such claims as shall be supported by evidence satisfactory to the said Commissioners, or any two of them, there shall be made a fair entry, in which the lots so claimed shall be described, and in such a manner that the same may be clearly known and ascertained. *Provided,* that where two or more claims of Connecticut claimants to the same lot shall be presented, and it shall appear to the said Commissioners by satisfactory evidence that the same lot ought to be confirmed, agreeably to the meaning of this Act, they shall make a fair entry thereof as aforesaid, and if the several claimants agree to submit their claims to the determination of the said Commissioners, they shall proceed to hear and determine the same accordingly, but if they do not thus agree, either of the claimants may prosecute his claim in the proper court of law, as in ordinary cases of contested titles.

SECTION 5. And be it further enacted by the authority aforesaid, That the said Commissioners be, and are hereby authorized to appoint a surveyor or surveyors to survey all the lots aforesaid of the Connecticut claimants, and the surveys thereof shall be returned to the said Commissioners for their information and assistance in prosecuting their enquiries and Examinations; the surveys of such of the said lots, the claims to which shall be admitted by the said Commissioners, shall by them be afterwards returned, together with their book of entries describing the same, to the Supreme Executive Council, who shall cause patents to be issued for their confirmation, and each patent shall comprehend all the parcels of land which are to be confirmed to the same claimants or joint claimants to whom by the return of the Commissioners aforesaid, the same shall be found to belong, and for each patent there shall be paid to the Secretary of the Council the sum of twenty shillings. And the said surveyors shall appoint proper persons for their chain carriers and markers, and the surveyors, chain carriers and markers shall severally be sworn or affirmed before a Justice of the Peace, or one of the said Commissioners, faithfully to perform their respective duties; and they shall be allowed a reasonable compensation for their services, to be fixed by the said Commissioners, and paid by the claimants aforesaid, whose claims to the lands so surveyed shall be admitted as aforesaid, and upon whom the same shall be apportioned by the said Commissioners in the manner they shall judge most equitable.

SECTION 6. And be it further enacted by the authority aforesaid, That each of the said Commissioners, before he acts under his commission, shall take an oath or affirmation before one of the Members of the Supreme Executive Council or a Judge of the Supreme Court, diligently to proceed in the business of his commission, and well and truly to hear and determine upon all claims and questions which shall come before him, in pursuance of this Act, without favour, affection or hope of reward.

SECTION 7. And be it further enacted by the authority aforesaid, That the said Commissioners be and they are hereby authorized to appoint a suitable person for a clerk, who shall before them be sworn or affirmed, faithfully to register all the proceedings of the said Commissioners, in pursuance of this Act.

SECTION 8. And be it further enacted by the authority aforesaid, That there be allowed and paid out of the public treasury to each of the said Commissioners Twenty shillings per day, and to the said Clerk Fifteen shillings per day, for each day they shall be employed in performing the duties required of them by this Act.

SECTION 9. *And whereas,* the late Proprietaries and divers other persons have heretofore acquired titles to parcels of the lands aforesaid, agreeably to the laws and usages of Pennsylvania, and who will be deprived thereof by the operation of this Act, and as justice requires that compensation be made for the lands of which they shall thus be divested, and as the State is possessed of other lands in which an equivalent may be rendered to the claimants under Pennsylvania, and as it will be necessary that their claims should be ascertained by a proper examination, Be it therefore enacted by the authority aforesaid, That all persons having such claims to lands which will be affected by the operation of this Act, shall be and they are hereby required, by themselves, guardians or other lawful agents, within twelve months from the passing of this Act, to present the same to the Board of Property, therein clearly describing those lands, and stating the grounds of their claims, and also adducing the proper proofs, not only of their titles, but of the situations, qualities and values of the lands so claimed, to enable the Board to judge of the validity of their claims, and of the quantities of vacant lands proper to be granted as equivalents.

And for every claim which shall be admitted by said Board, as duly supported, the equivalent by them allowed, may be taken either in the old or new purchase,[3] at the option of the claimant; and warrants and patents and all other acts of the public offices relating thereto, shall be performed free of Expense. The said Board shall also allow such a quantity of vacant land to be added to such equivalent as shall in their judgement be equal to the expences which must necessarily be incurred in locating and surveying the same. And that the Board of Property [4] may in every case obtain satisfactory evidence of the quality and value of the land, which shall be claimed as aforesaid, under the proprietary title, they may require the Commissioners aforesaid, during their sitting in the said County of Luzerne, to make the necessary enquiries by the oaths or affirmations of lawful witnesses to ascertain those points; and it shall be the duty of the said Commissioners to enquire and report accordingly.

Signed by order of the House,

THOMAS MIFFLIN, *Speaker.*

Enacted into a law at Philadelphia, on Wednesday, the twenty-eighth day of March, in the year of our Lord one thousand seven hundred and eighty-seven.

PETER ZACHARY LLOYD,
Clerk of the General Assembly.

---

[3] That is, within the lands purchased from the Indians in 1768 or in 1784.

[4] The Board of Property had been set up several years earlier to deal with conflicting land claims. Its membership included the president or vice president of the Council, one other Council member, the secretary of the Land Office, the Receiver-General, and the Surveyor-General; Norman B. Wilkinson, "Land Policy and Speculation in Pennsylvania, 1779-1800" (unpub. Ph.D. dissertation, Univ. of Pennsylvania, 1958), pp. 24-25 (microfilm copy).

[39] Dissent to the Confirming Act.[1]

DISSENTIENT *to the appointment, by this House, of the Commissioners, who are to ascertain the claims of the settlers under* Connecticut, *within the county of* Luzerne

1st. BECAUSE it is expressly declared in the 20th section of the constitution of this state, that "the President and Council are to expedite the execution of such measures as shall be resolved on by the General Assembly;" and we consider the nominating of the Commissioners in this case by the General Assembly as a similar violation of the constitution with that of the appointing Commissioners by act of legislature to execute the act for guarding and defending the navigation of the *Delaware,* enacted the 9th of *April,* 1782, which hath been denounced against, as an infringement of the constitution, by the Council of Censors.

2d. Because the appointment of officers, whether occasional or permanent, is in its nature an executive business, and as such, in a government like ours, where the legislative authority is severed from the executive, belongs exclusively to the President and Council; an idea which is decidedly supported by the first part of the twentieth article of the frame of government, and which accords with the writings of the best authors or republican governments, who declare that the liberty of the citizens depends on the separation of these powers.

Robert Whitehill,   John McDowell,
Thomas Kennedy,   John Flenniken,
David Mitchell,   James Allison,
Robert Brown,   Theophilus Philips,
David Davis,   John Gilchreest,
Samuel Dale,   Abraham Smith,
William Findley,   Alexander Wright,
Robert Clark,   John Piper.[2]
Joseph Heister,

---

[39] [1] *Minutes of the Second Session of the Eleventh General Assembly,* 197-98, probable date March 29, 1787 (microfilm copy).

[2] Although there are only seventeen signers of this statement, twenty-three members of the Assembly had opposed appointment of the first commissioners by that body. Later it was said that planned resignations were designed to delay operation of the law; see nos. 90 and 91, *post.*

Of the seventeen signers, fifteen are identifiable as Constitutionalists. In the Assembly the Republicans had a narrow majority, but Constitutionalists dominated in the Council; Brunhouse, *Counter-Revolution in Pennsylvania,* 193 and *passim.*

[40] Notice of Meeting of Wyoming Commissioners.[1]

Philadelphia, April 2d, 1787.

IN PURSUANCE OF THE FOREGOING ACT of the General Assembly of Pennsylvania,[2] we hereby give Public Notice. That the Commissioners thereby appointed, will meet at the house of Col. Zebulon Butler, in Wilkes-borough (otherwise called Wilkes-barre) in the county of Luzerne, on Monday the twenty eighth day of May next, to receive and examine the Connecticut Claims to Lands in that county, and to perform the other duties required of them by the said act.

PETER MUHLENBERG,
TIMOTHY PICKERING, } Commissioners.[3]

[41] Timothy Pickering to Zebulon Butler.[1]

Philadelphia April 2, 1787.

Dear Sir,

I think it a little extraordinary that some people at Wyoming should not have patience enough to wait for the result of the late sessions of Assembly of Pennsylvania, before they proceeded to execute the unwarrantable resolves of the Susquehanna Company.[2] Such precipitation, however, serves to confirm the opinion, that certain characters, notwithstanding all pretences to the contrary do not desire peace with this state on any reasonable

[40] [1] M. H. S., Pickering Papers, LVII, 152, clipping from a newspaper, probably the *Pennsylvania Packet* of April 12, 1787.

[2] No. 38, *ante.*

[3] The third commissioner, Joseph Montgomery, was not in Philadelphia at the time. He lived in Harrisburg; Harvey-Smith, *Wilkes-Barré*, III, 1562.

[41] [1] Wyoming Historical and Geological Society, Butler Papers, in Pickering's hand; M. H. S., Pickering Papers, LVII, 153, a draft.

[2] Pickering has reference to the resolves passed in December, 1786; *Susquehannah Company Papers*, VIII, no. 268. He found them "unwarrantable" because the Company appointed commissioners to determine claims and to allocate lands to new settlers. The commissioners began their work on March 1, and ironically, Butler participated in their court; no. 68, *post.*

terms. 'Tis nevertheless a satisfaction, to the real lovers of peace. to reflect, that a great majority of the settlement are disposed to accept of such terms as Pennsylvania has granted. They are terms which give entire satisfaction to the Connecticut gentlemen in town with whom I have conversed, and go to the full extent of what the Connecticut Delegates in Congress expected or desired; or rather, I believe, beyond their expectations.[3]

All the lands prayed for in the petition are *confirmed*—and *freely, without price*. But to give a regular title it was necessary that they should be surveyed & patented; and the expences for these articles are put upon a footing entirely new, on purpose to ease the people; and still further to favour them, the Committee of the House consented to have all the parcels of land belonging to the same person, included in one patent. Whereas usually, for each seperate piece of land, a seperate patent is to be paid for.

The surveying expence will be extremely light. Three Commissioners are appointed to receve and examine the claims of the Connecticut Claimants, and report to Council such as are supported by reasonable proofs, on which patents are to issue. But for further particulars, I must refer you to Dr Smith, who has a copy of the bill; but which was altered in several parts (as I have noted upon it) before it was passed into a law.

I trust the prudent part of the settlement will have Spirit enough to maintain their own rights, and pay no regard to the extravagant claims or wild impracticable schemes of men who have not the true interest of the settlement at heart.

The Insurgents in Massachusets are entirely quelled, and General Lincoln, Mr Phillips president of the Senate, & Mr Otis a member of the Assembly, are gone into the Western counties to determine who of the rebels shall be pardoned without trial;[4] while the Supreme Court are sitting to try some of the most atrocious offenders for their treason. Inclosed is a News-Paper of this day, in which you will find some articles of importance. I am with much esteem dear Sir y^r h'ble servant

Timothy Pickering

---

[3] The following words are crossed out in the draft: "for I am informed that they make the same distinction which I made, viz. between actual occupants prior to the decree of Trenton."

The Connecticut delegates attending at this time were William Samuel Johnson and Stephen Mix Mitchell. For the distinction made between actual settlers and proprietors of the Company, see *ibid.*, Introduction.

[4] Benjamin Lincoln, Samuel Phillips, Jr., and Samuel Otis were the members of the pardon commission; Marion L. Starkey, *A Little Rebellion* (New York, 1955), 96.

[42] Aaron Cleveland to Timothy Pickering.[1]

Norwich Ap[r] 3, 1787

Sir,

Yours of the 20th Inst I have recv'd.[2] had previously ben inform'd of your visit to Wioming and of the Election in consiquence. am Sorry to hear that Co[lo] Franklin was not acquiessent enough to take his Seat in Assembly he being in my opinion posses'd of Such knowledge and abilities as would have render'd him very Servicable in that capasity to the Wioming Settlement, but he doubtless has his reasons for nonattendance which for ought I know may be well founded.[3] I am not compotent to judge at present. Col° Dennisson you inform me has taken his Seat. he is a good Character but [I a]m no judge of his Abilities as I am but little [ac]quanted with him but I hope he will honor his appointment. you are pleased to observe as your oppinion that peace is not far distant from that Settlement. I wish it may eventually prove so, but there are many and complicated dificulties to Settle and jaring interests to be attended to, which needs the utmost attention of your wisest polititions. you mention your design of removing to Wioming, good characters are much wanted there and I hope you will not fail to prosicute your design. you propose buying my House lot, but as I Should aske much higher for it than what you gave Col° Butler for his, 'tis needless perhaps to mention A price, indeed S[r] I intend Settling there myself and your going before hand will be an additional motive. at any rate I must value my lot the higher for it. respecting the apple Trees, if M[r] Benj. Bailey who has the care of the Lot does not git it fenced this spring agreable to my directions, you may have the Trees agreeing with him on the terms for I know it is high time they were transplanted but Should the lot be fenced this Spring I have directed M[r] Bailey to Set the Trees in the rear of the Lot, but in this case Should there be any to spare you may have them ag[reeing] with him as above mentioned. agreeable to [damaged] I have consulted M[r] Peleg Hyde (not Jedidiah) respecting your proposal of buying his land.[4] he is by no means inclin'd to sell, but Says he always intended to have Spaldings part whenever he Sold and that Spalding had promissed it to him.

---

[42] [1] M. H. S., Pickering Papers, LVII, 154, in an unknown hand but signed by Cleveland. For Cleveland see *Susquehannah Company Papers*, VIII, no. 249.

[2] No. 33, *ante.*   [3] See no. 26, *ante.*   [4] No. 34, *ante.*

he intends to be at Wioming this Summer when and where you will probably See him. as you mention S[r] I have Some knowlidge of you but was more acquanted with your brother John. my friends as well as yours live at Salem. I hope before many years to be happy in your acquantance at Wioming, mean while am ready with cheerfulness to serve you in anything within my power. I am Sir your very Humble Servant

Aaron Cleveland

[43] Benjamin Franklin to Lord Butler.[1]

In Council, Philad[a] April 4, 1787

Sir,

With this you will receive a Number of printed Copies of an Act of Assembly lately passed, respecting the Settlers from Connecticut in your County.[2] The Spirit of Condescension and Good-Will of the Legislature towards those Settlers, manifested by this Act, in attending so readily to their Petitions, and in giving them so fair an Opportunity of establishing their Claims and quieting their Possessions for themselves and their Posterity, will we are persuaded have its proper Effect on the prudent and reasonable Majority, who can set a just Value on the Blessings of Peace and Good Government; and we hope therefore that the Endeavours of a few restless Individuals, if such should remain, who may expect to find their own private and separate Advantage in public Troubles, will not have any Effect in disturbing this Commencement of Harmony, which in its Completion will secure to the Inhabitants not only the Lands that have been in question, but all the additional Advantage of our excellent Constitution, and the Protection of one of the principal States in the Union. You will observe the Directions of the Act in making it publick; and you may assure the People that the good Disposition of Council towards them is not inferior to that which has been manifested by the General Assembly. I am, Sir, Your humble Servant,

B. Franklin, Presid[t]

To Lord Butler, Esquire, High Sheriff of the County of Luzerne [3]

[43] [1] Wilkes College Library, Wilkes-Barre, Pennsylvania, Gilbert S. McClintock Papers, signed by Franklin; M. H. S., Pickering Papers, LVII, 157-57A, a copy.

[2] No. 38, *ante.*

[3] Actually Lord Butler was not commissioned sheriff until April 7; *Pa. C. R.*, XV, 193. He took his oath of office before Pickering on April 18; M. H. S., Pickering Papers, LVII, 160.

[44] Timothy Pickering to Peter Muhlenberg.[1]

Philadelphia, April 5, 1787.

Dear Sir,

The Assembly having granted £150 for the purpose of opening a road from the mouth of Nescopeck Creek to the Lehigh (a distance of about three & twenty miles,) [2] two persons will undertake to perform the work, if that sum can be appropriated to that use. They proposed getting an additional sum by subscription, to be called for if the public grant proved inadequate. But this seemed a beginning at the wrong end; and after a full consideration of the matter, I proposed the following plan of proceedure viz.

That application should be made to Council to appoint Evan Owen a commissioner to explore, survey, & mark the best route for the road,[3] and that Jacob Weiss should contract to open it, so as to render it fit for the passing of Waggons carrying a ton weight.

This proposal I made on this principle: That persons deeply interested in having the shortest and best road cut, would be the fittest to be employed to execute the work.

Mr. Owen is an intelligent man, and (I find on enquiry) a man in whom the public may repose great confidence. He owns a tract of land opposite the mouth of Nescopeck, which he has laid out into lots for a town, and has no *intermediate* interest. He, therefore pursuing his own interest will seek the shortest & best route; and is so solicitous to have the work done, that he has consented to undertake the trust; and as the public grant will probably be insufficient for opening a good road, he will perform the duty of *Commissioner & Surveyor, gratis;* the public only furnishing, out of the £150 granted, provisions and paying the hands necessary to be employed as chain carriers and markers, this service of his to come in place of the sum he would otherwise *subscribe* to the work.

---

[44] [1] *P. A.*, XI, 133-34.

[2] Such a road had been recommended by Stephen Balliet in March, 1787; *ibid.*, 131. Balliet had estimated the cost at £200 or £250. On March 29 a bill was passed; *Minutes of the Second Session of the Eleventh General Assembly*, 192 (microfilm copy).

[3] On April 12, the Council appointed Owen a commissioner for the purpose, paraphrasing Pickering's language; *Pa.* C. R., XV, 195. A detailed description of the road and the Council's acceptance of it are given in *ibid.*, 230-32.

Mr. Weiss has an interest near the *hither* end of the proposed road, and is equally anxious to have it opened. He will contract to do it, for the remainder of the £150, trusting to obtain by subscriptions what shall be requisite to complete the road, if that remainder should be insufficient.

Mr. Owen will *explore* & *Survey* the road, & return a plan of it to Council, by the last of this month; and if the Council approve of it, Mr. Weiss will open it without delay; and he thinks he can complete it by midsummer; provided he can begin to work early in May and is furnished with a part of the money to lay in provisions &c.

I confess that I cannot conceive of a more eligibe mode of executing this business; and I hope it may be agreeable to Council. 'Tis an object of great importance. At present the only way in which any necessary goods can be transported to the county of Luzerne, is by land from Philadelphia to Middletown 98 miles, or to Harrisburg upwards of a hundred miles; and then by boats up the Susquehannah about 120 miles to Wyoming. This circuitous route is so expensive as to forbid the attempt to bring any produce form Wyoming to this city.

I trust this matter will appear to you deserving of the immediate attention of Council; and that the necessity of the measure, and the ease and certainty with which, in the the way above proposed, it may be executed, will be motives sufficient to induce Council to adopt it if it be *possible* to furnish the *money,* and I hope the circumstances of this case may warrant an extraordinary exertion.

I feel the greater solicitude on this subject, because I fear a direct road to Wyoming, (for which the Assembly granted £300) cannot soon be opened.[4] The sum being double what is granted for the other road, cannot so conveniently be spared; and perhaps it will be proper to have another examination of the country before the route is fixed. When last at Wyoming I had good information that a road might be opened from thence to this city, without ascending or descending a single mountain; and that the part of it which would cross the Great Swamp would be easly made good; and yet that the distance would not probably exceed 110 or 115 miles.

I wished to have conversed with you on this business, & called this evening at your house; but you were not at home. If I could learn the opinion of Council upon it, before I set off for

---

[4] Balliet had laid out a road from Wyoming to the Lehigh water gap; see *Susquehannah Company Papers,* VIII, no. 246.

Wyoming, it would give me great pleasure & therefore I pray you to introduce it tomorrow morning. I am respectfully sir, your most obedt. Servt.

T. Pickering.

[45] Timothy Pickering to Peter Muhlenberg.[1]

Philadelphia April 7, 1787.

Dear Sir,

Since I saw you this afternoon, I have consulted with Col° Denison on the subject of a road to Wyoming, and we are clearly of opinion that it will not be expedient to open one until the country is farther explored. We have such information as to induce us to believe that a road may be cut from the Water Gap of Lehigh to Wilkesbarre, without ascending or descending a single mountain; there being very practicable gaps in all the mountains which intervene; and the taking the advantage of those gaps, it appears to us, will not materially increase the length of the road; or whatever that increase may be the greater facility of making & travelling the road, will more than counterbalance the greater length. On Mr Balliots route [2] several bad mountains appear; & he passes them by many *detours,* or zigzag directions; and the making in such places a tolerable waggon-road will occasion a great expense; and tis an expense which will never have an end; for such steep roads are generally in bad condition; because every great rain will destroy what much labour has effected; and however well repaired, still the toil of horses & cattle in passing them is severe and perpetual. Whereas a road thro' a swamp or morass, when once well made, will last an age, and is passed with loaded teams with perfect ease. But what is called the Great Swamp is generally *hard ground;* and all the miry parts on the present route, (being what is called Sullivan's road) which is by no means deemed an eligible one, would not together exceed two miles. This is the opinion of a man who has passed it a hundred times. Can it admit of a question which is most expedient—to make a two or four mile road over a mountain, & be subject to toil up & down it forever, or in the first instance to make a cause-way of two miles long? We therefore hope that no more money may be expended on the

[45] [1] Haverford College Library, Haverford, Pa., Charles Roberts Collection, in Pickering's hand; *P. A.,* XI, 135-36.

[2] See no. 44, *ante,* note 3.

road marked by Mr Balliot, until, on a farther examination, it shall appear that none better can be found. When we are at Wyoming, we will endeavour to get farther information, and, if possible, to engage proper persons to explore a new route. On my return from thence I will give you whatever information we shall obtain.

Our solicitude on this subject arises from our sense of the importance of choosing the *best* route; because when once chosen & much money shall have been expended upon it, it will not be easy to alter it: a permanent improvement of such consequence, it would seem, should not be begun without a *thorough* examination.

In the mean time, it would be a matter of regret, if so fair an opportunity as that suggested in my former letter,[3] of making the road to Nescopeck, could not be embraced. I am, dear Sir, your most obed^t servant

T. Pickering.

General Muhlenberg.

[46] Timothy Pickering to Obadiah Gore.[1]

Wilkesbarre [2] Ap^l 12. 1787.

Dear Sir

I have the pleasure to inclose you half a dozen copies of the law of Penn^a confirming to the Connecticut Claimants the rights they acquired before the Trenton decree, agreeably to the petition of the people.[3] This act I trust will satisfy a great majority of the people—all indeed who had any right to expect a confirmation of their titles. I am happy to find that you have advertised the election of Justices: the same laudable motives will impel you to go thro' with the business, in spite of all opposition. Mr Hurlbut, to my surprize, has not notified the election.[4] I shall see, or write to him, today; and I presume he will yet put up notifications: if he declines it, Col^o Butler & I shall appoint some other person to preside at the election: *for we are determined to have an election.*

[3] *Ibid.*
[46] [1] M. H. S., Pickering Papers, LVII, 164, a draft in Pickering's hand.
[2] "Wilkesbarre" was substituted for "Phila^a." [3] No. 38, *ante.*
[4] Hurlbut and Gore were judges of elections in the First and Third Districts respectively. Election day was April 19.

I shall send you some blank certificates for the oath of allegiance & perhaps some other papers by Col° Dennison who intends to proceed for Wyalusing to-morrow. I am sir y^r very h'ble serv^t.

T. P.

P. S. Hint at an association if he apprehends any forceable opposition to the election.

[47] Timothy Pickering to Christopher Hurlbut.[1]

Wilkesbarre April 12, 1787.

Sir

I received your letter by Col° Denison expressing your reasons for not signing the petition to the General Assembly.[2] Since my arrival here I have been informed that you have thought it inexpedient to post up notifications for holding the election for Justices of ye Peace:[3] I am sorry for the omission, as it will occasion delay. I have brought with me the law confirming the lands to the Connec^t claimants, agreeably to the petition, and now inclose you a copy.[4] This confirmation I trust will give you satisfaction, and remove all scruples about holding the election. It is necessary however that I should know your determination immediately; that if you decline the office (which I shall regret) another may be appointed in your stead. Be pleased to favour me with answer. I am sir y^r most obed. serv^t

T. P.

Mr Christ° Hurlbut

---

[47] [1] M. H. S., Pickering Papers, LVII, 165-66, a draft in Pickering's hand.

[2] No. 25, *ante.*

[3] The sentences that follow are interlined and substituted for the following, which was lined out: "I have not heard of any satisfactory reasons for the omission. I should be glad if it be agreeable to you to hear from you on this subject; or rather to see you, if you should be coming to Wilkesbarre to morrow; for by to morrow evening I wish to know with certainty from you whether you are willing to exercise the powers granted you relative to the election, or not; that if you decline the execution of the office another may be appointed in your stead, without more delay.

[4] No. 38, *ante.*

[48] [Timothy Pickering and Zebulon Butler] to Christopher Hurlbut.[1]

To M[r] Christ[o] Hurlbut.

As notifications of the time & place for the meeting of the Freeholders of the first district in the County of Luzerne to elect Justices of the Peace, have not yet been posted up;[2] and it will now be proper to fix on a more distant day than that before appointed, in order that the freeholders may be duly notified: We hereby appoint Thursday the twenty sixth day of April instant for the day of the said election; and you will be pleased accordingly to notify the freeholders of the said district, to meet on that day at 12 o'clock, at the house of Col[o] Zeb[n] Butler in Wilkesbarre in said county, to elect four justices of the peace for the said district; and in this matter you will observe the directions heretofore given you on this subject.

Given under our hands at Wilkesbarre on the 13th day of Ap[1] 1787

[49] William Judd's Address to the Settlers at Wyoming.[1]

AN ADDRESS

To The Settlers at Wyoming under the Connecticut Claim.

Gentlemen,

IMPRESSED with the distresses through which you have passed— the intolerable sufferings you have sustained in the settlement of a new country distant from other inhabited parts of the country— the depredations you have experienced from a savage enemy— the relentless cruelty of opposing claimants, aided by the power

---

[48] [1] M. H. S., Pickering Papers, LVII, 166-67, a draft in Pickering's hand.

[2] See no. 47, *ante.* On April 15, Hurlbut wrote Pickering, telling him that he had posted notifications of the election in various places; Pickering Papers, LVII, 168.

[49] [1] M. H. S., Pickering Papers, LVII, 167, a broadside. Endorsed "Major Judd's Address to the Inhabitants of Wyoming—brought into the Settlement about the 13th of April 1787."

of a potent state, together with the dangers you appear surrounded with, from the insinuating craft of a junto, soiled and disappointed in their stratagems to dispossess you by force of a country the fair inheritance of your fathers, purchased, settled and defended by your prowess, through a long, cruel and bloody war, a territory enriched by the blood of your fathers, brothers and sons and still reaking with the mangled carcases and blood of your dearest friends, whose scattered bones are still whitening in the sun, promiscuously dispersed from your borders on the south, to the falls of Niagara on the north, the sad remembrance will force a tear of compassion, from the manly bosom of every virtuous inhabitant of that so long devoted country.

My dear friends, I have shared with you in some of the enumerated distresses, and in all my heart hath bled for your misfortunes, suffer me for a moment to point you to what you have been—still are—and the prospects still within your reach.

You were once the free citizens of a free country, justly entitled to all the blessings resulting from a free and equal government, established in a country the purchase of your ancestors, and transmitted to you, unclogged by the shackles of rents or tythes or any other engine of despotism, a fair inheritance, which your personal valour hath defended with much applause.

And now you are become powerful—have braved the dangers with which you have been surrounded—put to silence the tongue of slander, and established yourselves beyond the reach of those that sought your ruin, aided by your numerous friends in Connecticut, whose exertions have ever sustained you while tottering beneath the power and stratagem of Pennsylvania—have fostered you in their bosoms—generously parted with their property for mutual advantage, and are daily furnishing you additional strength, in men and means, all calculated to sustain you against the impotence of that gasconading power that hath sought your ruin—disappointed in her primary design to destroy by force, is now with the smoothe artifice of court flattery leading you, as unsuspecting victims, to the vortex of irremedilous destruction and horror.

I am next to point you to the prospects fully within your reach, and which, if you fail of obtaining, the fault must be your own.

Your country is fertile, pleasantly situated and healthful— your numbers are an over match for your opponents—considering your local situation, your strength is daily increasing, and without doubt will be augmented three-fold in the course of the present year, unless prevented by your internal divisions—the eyes of the eastern states are upon your country—hundreds and hundreds of your Company friends are preparing to emigrate to you—men of property and ability are sending out their sons, and many calculating to remove with their families and effects into your country—the deathful languor you so much fear is dissipating—your cause hath new and powerful advocates, arising in one part and another—many heretofore cool are incensed and determined to support you—preparations are making to disannul the infamous decree of Trenton—our Assembly, already sufficiently alarmed, will be petitioned—Congress will be applied to in full confidence that the end will be joyous and happy—where then are your present fears conjured from? unless the guilty dreams of the apostates prompt them to mislead you, hoping the specious delusion may cover their dark designs from the eye of truth, till you are sunk beyond the power of humanity to relieve you.

The day brightens upon you, all is sunshine without, every thing around contributes for your support, and nothing from within deserves the name of danger, arouse then, my friends, prove yourselves capable of enduring to the last, when the fair possession, your deserts have gained, will be established in safety and peace, and, if supported by the government of any state in the union, you may become an important branch of a national government, that hastens upon us with uncommon strides.

Can you, my friends, forget the malicious spirit with which you have been persecuted? Do you not remember the administration of Moore and Patterson [2]—the cruel and faithless conduct of Boyd and Armstrong? [3] Do not the deep wrought fears occasioned by handcuffs and fetters still remain upon your hands and feet? Hath the filthy stench of prison dungeons quite escaped your remembrance? Are your late feebled limbs and dreary countenances, lank faces and tattered carcases, the effects of long confinement, wholly forgotten by you? Are the dismal apprehensions of an ignominious death with which many of you, my dear friends, were threatened by the then implacable enemy, all strangers to your apprehensions? Are the miserable sufferings of your old men, your wives and children driven through the wilderness by the hand of cruelty (dishonourable to savage barbarity) all overlooked? Where are your herds, your flocks, your furniture and clothing of which you were mercilessly despoiled by an inhuman banditti, palmed upon your country by

[2] See *Susquehannah Company Papers*, VII, Index.
[3] See *ibid.*, VIII, Index.

government to destroy you? Where is the evidence of a prompt and ready disposition on the part of Pennsylvania to restore your plundered property, and reimburse your losses, sustained by their troops and taken from you by the command of their leaders, with an avowed design to impoverish and thereby disable you from holding and enjoying the fruits of your purchase and labour?

From what quarter are you assured of the favour of that government that is gaping to receive you? Where is your title to your lands under that state? What ground of security have you that shall be permitted to inhabit your country one moment after you submit to that government? Have you not petitioned with humility? Have you been answered with a graceful smile? or have your petitions been treated with disrespect and totally unanswered?

Are not all those lands granted by Pennsylvania to their subjects? How then can they grant them to you? If they do grant them,[4] of what avail is a second grant of the same lands, unless they will go further and declare, by a legislative act, that our Indian Purchase is valid, and on that ground confirm the settlement under that purchase?[5] Here you rest, but short of this you will be forever insecure. And provided you submit to the government of that state before you obtain security for your property, all prospects of property are at an end, and you may depend you will be ejected from your land, so soon as the shackles of that government are so fast riveted upon you that you cannot shake them off.

As a friend to the settlement and from my knowledge and experience of the duplicity of that government a few of you seem to wish—I thought it my duty solemnly to warn you to be cautious and not to leap before you look and clearly see your way lest you repent your folly when too late—if after all my admonitions you will destroy yourselves, I shall be acquitted and the folly will be chargeable to your own account. Col. Pickering is an artful man and made use of (being of New-England extract) to deceive you—he is interested under Pennsylvania—beware of this disguise. Let me entreat you to be wise and stedfast, look to

[4] This clause and the earlier statement that Wyoming petitions had not been answered suggest that the address was written in ignorance of the Confirming Act passed on March 28.

[5] Judd was one of those who vehemently opposed the distinction being made between actual settlers and proprietors of the Company. He wanted outright confirmation of the whole original purchase from the Indians. See *ibid.*, Introduction.

Col. Franklin, he hath been and is still your friend, his ability and integrity you may rest secure upon. I am, gentlemen, Your devoted friend And very humble servant,

WILLIAM JUDD.

PRINTED IN HUDSON, BY
ASHBEL STODDARD

[50] Benjamin Franklin to [Samuel Huntington].[1]

Philad[a] April 14. 1787

Sir,

I have the honour of transmitting herewith to your Excellency, an Act of our Legislature, entitled, *An Act for ascertaining and confirming to certain Persons called Connecticut Claimants, the Lands by them claimed within the County of Luzerne; and for other Purposes therein mentioned.*

Our Government has by this Act manifested its Regard for Peace and good Neighbourhood; and we have no doubt but that yours will show the same amicable Disposition, by discouraging any Attempt, if such should be made by any Inhabitants of your State, to revive and continue the Animosities that have heretofore been attended with such mischievous Consequences. With great Respect I have the honour to be Sir, Your Excellency's most obedient & most humble Servant

B Franklin
Presid[t]

His Excellency the Governor
of the State of Connecticut

[51] Obadiah Gore to Timothy Pickering.[1]

Sheshequin April 17th 1787

D[r] S[r], I received yours by the hand of M[r] More Together with the acts of assembly[2] and am happy in the Prospect before us of

[50] [1] L. C., Franklin Papers, 2nd ser., VIII, fols. 1768-69, a press copy. I am indebted to Leonard W. Labaree, editor of *The Papers of Benjamin Franklin,* for telling me the location of this letter.
[51] [1] M. H. S., Pickering Papers, LVII, 170, in Gore's hand.
[2] No. 46, *ante.*

haveing those unhappy Disputes (which have So long Subsisted in these parts) Terminated. I think the foundation is So wisely and Equitably laid as will Likely make a permanent and lasting peace. I was Determined to proceed to the holding of the Election had I not heard from the assembly and I believe there would not been no Great opposition in this Destrict altho I had one of the petitions burnt that I brought up from Wyoming [3] and one of my notifications for Election pulled Down but they were both done or procured to be Done by a Certain Character from below, the particulars I will Give you the first ti[me] I see you. I have Dispersed these new acts into the Different parts of the Destrict for the Information of the people but have not yet heard an objection made by a Single person. but the principle Opposition to the Elections I believe will be in the Two Lower Destricts for as the Great Goddess Diana is in Danger of being Set at nought and the unjust Gains cease perhaps there will be some faint struggles but I believe nothing of any Great Consequence [4] I am S[r], your Hum[ble] Serv[t]

Obad[h] Gore

[52] Timothy Pickering's Notes on John Franklin's Speech at Forty Fort.[1]

1. Wishes to remain here peaceably.
2. One Foremost in petitioning had sold his Connecticut rights.
3. Denison said the intentin of the petition was to get all the lots in the 18 towns confirmed. Denison w[d] not otherwise agree to it.
4. No lots yet confirmed; but intended to be confirmed.
5. Defending the country & [suffering?].
6. Lost lands on West Branch & Fishing Creek.
7. Moved locations since the decree as soon as possible.
8. No Court or Jury—but 3 gentlemen appointed for the purpose to examine the Claims.
9. Depend on the Gentlemen's being satisfied.
10. Federal Court ought to determine the title to the lands.

---

[3] See no. 23, *ante.*

[4] Also on this day Gore wrote to Pickering applying for the post of secretary to the commissioners who would act under the Confirming Act; Pickering Papers, LVII, 169.

[52] [1] M. H. S., Pickering Papers, LVII, 173-76, in Pickering's hand.

Obadiah Gore (1744-1821), reproduced from Oscar J. Harvey, *A History of Wilkes-Barré*, II, 833.

11. Constitution of Penn^a requires Jury of y^e County
12. Commission appointed without Consent of the People;—Did they Consent to the Susquehana Com^y?[2]
13. T. P. has interest in the purchase—Sheshequem in opposition.
14. Montgomery[3]—experiences of him—Com^{rs} to effect a compromise in Feby 1783 solemnly plighted faith that ye people sh^d be protected. Long story about the proposals of those Com^{rs}—Their Conduct reprobated.
15. Supposes these lands given for satisfaction for losses sustained by the troops &c.
16. Montgomery likely to be president—Dear [Friends! ?]
17. W^d not wish for any opposition to the Laws—But thinks the lands sh^d be confirmed first.
18. Petition not the voice of the People of ye County.
19. Com^{tee} not consulted.
20. Petition calculated to deceive. Artful clause in the petition.
21. Majority of Com^{rs} opposed to the interest or claims of the people.
22. Settlers may be ejected.
23. Vote of one not a freeholder renders ye election unlawful.
[24. Do inspecters require ye deeds or other proof of Freehold?][4]
25. Col^o Dennison's letter to Assembly.[5]
26. His opinion that the people remain silent.
    No assurance that an acre is confirmed.
    More than ⅔^{ds} of ye people have not a foot.
    Have granted ye same lands to their Citizens quere if they can grant them again.
    Connecticut Claims to be carried before the board of property[6]—told by Gentleman learned in the law.
27. Bind themselves down by the law.
28. Right to a Continental trial—Connecticut alarmd.—Who are the authorities? Petition goes or will go to Congress Wait only for an agent from here—but we may do this when we please.
29. Acknowledgment of law—for Federal trial.

[2] This question is probably a comment of Pickering's own.

[3] Joseph Montgomery, one of the three commissioners under the Confirming Act. In February, 1783, he had been named with William Montgomery and Moses McClean as a commissioner to examine Connecticut claims. The report of the earlier commission had been very dissatisfying to the Connecticut settlers; Vol. VII, nos. 140 and 167.

[4] Probably Pickering's query.   [5] No. 29, *ante.*

[6] See no. 38, *ante,* note 4.

30. W^d not fling away life for the Proprietors—regards not his own property. W^d pain him to see others stripped.
31. What is in the petition granted.
32. Wish for an opportunity of applying to Assembly.
33. If the Com^rs confirm the lands—Amen.
34. But federal trial &c.
35. Law—& stripped of property.
36. Amiable settlement.[7]

Endorsed: Notes of Col. Franklin's Speech, Apr. 19, 1787.

[53] Obadiah Gore to Timothy Pickering.[1]

Tioga point April 20th 1787

D^r S^r

I am happy to Inform you that I Yesterday held the Election without any opposition.[2] I had for some time flattered my Self that there would be no difficulty attending the Election but the Evening of the 17th In^t Jn° Jenkins came up for the purpose of preventing if possible the Election being held. he made it his business to Call on all these he thot to Influence Desering them to meet him at the point. accordingly Sundry met him. and to his mortification he Could prevail with only six to Stand by him in opposing the Election (viz) Benj Gardner Joel Thomas Wm Jenkins,—Burble, Walter Watrous & Phin. Stevens. At the time of Election they all Came down Except Watrous and was at a Neighbouring house. and before I opened it I Desered Col° Denison & Capt Spalding to Go with me to them and Col° Denison Informed them particularly what was done at the assembly Together with the favourable Disposition of both Council &

---

[7] There follows a neater summation of some of Franklin's points, which is also described as notes on his speech at Forty Fort. This later summary repeats the substance and often the very wording of points 1, 5, 9, 10, 11, 12, 15, 17, 18, 19, 20, 22, 26, 28, 31, 33, but not in order. These are regrouped under eight points. Two additional Pickering comments occur, one in connection with Franklin's insistence that the claims should be left to the determination of a federal court: "Content—Apply for it—Whatever the event the Jurisdiction must remain in Pennsylvania." The other comment relates to Franklin's assertion that lands cannot be granted a second time: "Public good required it. He has presented petitions to the Assembly for the lands & now says &c."

[53] [1] M. H. S., Pickering Papers, LVII, 177, in Gore's hand.

[2] The election referred to was that of the Third District, where no postponement was necessary.

assembly and farther we told them that we Came to Descourse
them in a friendly manner and if they Could point out any better
and more safer way than to hold the Election We Should be Glad
to hear it. and finally talked them out. they had an Address
from Maj^r Judd.^{3} I desired them to Shew it and if agreable I
would read it publickly after which I waited a few minutes and
no person made any reply. I then proceeded in my business as
I said above without opposition. however this day Stevens appears Deserous to know if no way Can be proscribed for him to
make his peace. he has Descoursed Col° Denison largely on the
Subject and Says if he has been Wrong he wou^d Wish to be right
for the future and is Determined to retract from his former practices. the Col° has advised him to call on you S^r for advice in
the afair. however this I can say toward the Close of the Election he offered his vote as has taken the oath of fidelity. Inclosed
I send the proceedings of the Election.^{4} I am S^r your humb^{le}
Servt

Obad^h Gore

[54] James Smith to William Hooker Smith.^{1}

Tioga Point ap^r ye 20 1787
Honourd farther after my Duty to you I hop that This will foynd
you in health as it Leaves me. S^r the Motive of my Staying hear
So Long Was That When i Came hear Last Wednday morning i
found jinkins hear a Straining Ivery Nearve that Lay in his
Power to Brak up the Election. Several Came to me to git me
to joyn them and if would Head a party they Did not Dispute
But that the Election would go on. accordingly I agreed to head
a paty and Warnned a meeting that Evening. they amediately
went round And Notify all Such as they thought wold Come. we
musterd 32 in Number and agred to Stand By one a nother and
the Prinsibel part Met in the morning and went to the Election
altogether. the oppiset Party found that our Party Was So
Strong that they Gave up Without Making up any Disturbence
and then most of them to our Surprise fell in and voted With us.

---

^{3} No. 49, *ante.*

^{4} In the Third District Obadiah Gore, Elijah Buck, Nathan Kingsley,
and Joseph Kinney received the highest number of votes, from among whom
the Council would commission two justices; Pickering Papers, LVII, 212.
See no. 74, *post,* note 2.

[54] ^{1} M. H. S., Pickering Papers, LVII, 179-80, in James Smith's hand.

We Elected obediah gore Elijeth Buck Nathan kingsly and Joseph Keney. this from your Duetiful Son Jeames Smith

N. B Mr Woodworth Gives his Complements to Do^r Smith and Say that he hopes to Sea him in about a fortnite

[55] Declarations in Support of the Laws of Pennsylvania.[1]

WE WHOSE NAMES ARE HERETO SUBSCRIBED inhabitants of the County of Luzerne, do hereby declare that it is our sincere desire, that the Elections of Justices of the Peace for the said County may forwith take place; and that the Government and Laws of Pennslvania may immediately be submitted to, and have their free Operation in this County, as they have in every other County of the State.

COUNTY OF LUZERNE April 21th 1787

Wm Dorton	Zeb^n Butler	David Richards
Martin young	Abel Yarington	Nathan Waller
Robert Young	William Ross	Benjamin Cary
John Hollenback	John P. Schott	Charles Bingham
Joseph Kilborn	Jabez Fish	Rufus Bennet
Ase Bennet X	Jabez Sills	Ashbel Walter
Jn° Hagemen	John Downing	John Cary
Chis^t Oehmig	Stephen Stickland	Richard Dilley
Nathan Cary	Daniel Gridley	Elijah Bennet
Jonth Avery	Thomas Gibson	Mesheck Walker
Richard Price	Thomas Neill	Adam Man
Josiah Stanborough	Edward Edgerton	Stephen Holcom

[55] [1] M. H. S., Pickering Papers, LVII, 182-203A, signed. To save space, headings for each list of names have not been repeated. All were dated April 21, 1787.

The Pickering Papers contain drafts and clean copies of alternative statements, dated April, 1787. Both are longer and stronger in their sense of commitment. One mentions the Confirming Act, passed in response to the settlers' own petition, the awarding of jurisdiction to Pennsylvania by the Trenton decree, and the elections already held in which a councilor, representative, and other officials were chosen. The other statement would have bound signers to "solemnly associate and engage to assist and stand by each other" in support of the laws; Pickering Papers, LVII, 149, 151, 203B; neither statement was apparently used. The simpler language at the head of the following lists of names here given would obviously be less controversial.

Ebenezer Slocum
Jehoiada P. Johnson
Jacob Johnson Jur
Amos Bennet
Daniel Ross
Char' Bennet
jonathan Frisbey
Richard Dilley Jun
Cornales Gaile
Cofort Cary

Adam Dilley
George Crumb
William Veas
Guy Wells
Wm Young
Elisha Blackman
Ichabod Blackman
Eleazar Blackman
Elisha Blackman jr
Christopher Eliss

Asa Stevens
Daniel Roberts
Joseph Sprague
Banj' Bailey
Joseph Sprague jur
John Hyde
M. Hollenback
John Seelye
John Campbell
Nathan Abbott

Endorsed: Location N° 1   66 Wilkesbarre

Abraham Smith
umphrey raillighport
Hennery Teven
[Steven?]
Isaac Bennet
Elisha Bennet
olover X Bennet
(his / mark)
James X mullon
(his / mark)
James Lassly
Jac Whitcomb
Abraham Lane
Abijah Porter

[Updegraf?]
William Stewart
Isaac up the grave
Elijah Inman
John Carllinghouse
Edward Spencer

Aaron Hunt
John Johnson
Conrad X Loyes
(his / mark)
Elias Decker
Thomas Martin
Elisa decker

William Heberd
Andrew Decker
Richard Tromane
Elisha Decker [Jr?]
Benj^m Bidlack

James Stewart
Christopher Hurlbut
Alex^r Jameson
William Hyde
Joseph Hageman
John Ryon
Edward Inman

Endorsed: N° 1   34 Nantikoke

Wm Hooker Smith
Daniel Gore
John Stapels
Benj' Brown
James westbrook
John Kennedy
Increes Billings
George Cooper
William Jackson
enos brown ju
John Rezecrone
Abraham Van fleet
Stephen Prouty
Job Philups

Abraham Westbrook
William Hurbut
James Armstrong
William Stark
William Stark Junr
John Williams
Jonathan Rawson
Enos Brown
Richard Westbrook
Saml Hover
John Hover
Cornes Cortright
Wm Smith
Silas Smith

Jacob Ozencup
Danl Holley
Increase Billings
Jonathan Smith
Nathan Stark
Martin Smith
Isaiah Howell
Thomas Read
Edward Prowty
Isaac V^n Troman
Silv' Jacason
John Trusdel
Ben^m Trusdel

Endorsed: N° 1 41 Jacobs Plains

Jms Finn
Timothy Wood
John Philips
Abraham Harding
James Brown
John Budd
David Brown
James Brown Jun'
Elijah [?]
Hezekiah Dickson
Isaac Allen
Fraderick Fry
Abraham [Lucas ?]

Ebenezer Marcy
Barnabas Cary
Jonathan Newman
Timothy Pearce
John Cary
Casper Elster
Samuel Meadock
Joremiah Osterhout
William Hall
John scott
Amos Egelson
James Scott
Joseph Washburn

Jeremiah Blanchard
Jonathan Davis
Amos Harding
Henry harding
Thomas Pichet
Richard Hallsted
Samuel Miller
samuel Hallsted
Conrod Loots
Seth Cary
Caleb Bates
Richard Halsted Jun'
Joseph Halsted

Those that Chose Not to Sign the within written declaration Were

William Miller
Thomas Harding
David Morehouse

Marshal Dickson
Daniel Harding
John Dickson

Ishmael Bennet Jun'
Daniel Taylor

Endorsed: N° 2 [2] Lackawanock 39

Lord Butler
Abel Peirce
Henry M'Cormick
David M'Cormick
Rob' M'Dowl
Henry Decker
Noah Petibon
Joytis [Justis ?]
    Gaylord
Parshall Terry
John Gore
Benjamin Dorranc
justus Gaylor j'
Matthew teasdel
Andrew Bennet
Benjamin Smith

Timothy Jones
Titus Jones
Benagor Jones
Benjamin Crawford
Esrael Parshals
James Sutton
Thomas Bennet
Henry Tuttle
Richard Brockway
Jedediah Stephens
    jun'
John King Senior
Aaron Perkins
David Boyce
David Perkins
Isaac Cory

Asa Jackson
Philip Jackson
Elijah Rood
John Caray
Nathaniel Walker
John King
Ambros Jones
Ira Stephens
David Shoemake
Eleazer Gaylor
Peleck Comstock
Thomas Stoddard
John Coon
David Smith
Ebenz' Ennos
Jos'' Patrick

[2] This should be No. 1, for Lackawanock (modern Pittston) was in the
First District; see no. 58, *post.* Hurlbut, election judge for the First District, noted that he had put up a notice of the election at Abraham Harding's house; Hurlbut to Pickering, April 15, 1787, Pickering Papers, LVII, 168. Harding's name appears in the Lackawanock list.

Leban Blancher
Richard Vaughn
Jonathan Terry

Elnathan Cory
Samuel Finch

Benj[n] Carpenter
Gideon Churtch

Endorsed: N° 2   49 Kingston & Exeter [3]

Law[ce] Myers
Daniel Sullivan
Jeremiah Colman
Philip Myers
Hallet Gallup
Thomas Drake
Abr[m] Devens
Abr[m] Vangorden
Peregrine Jones
Samuel Allen
John montanye
Joseph montanye
Isaac X Parker (his mark)
John Griste
Nathan Hazen
Ebenezer Wyeth
Daniel Peirce

Ebez[r] Skinner
Joseph Hillman
Benjaman Dacker
John Dorrance
Zacharias hartsouf
Lewis Heartsouf
Jn° Voorhes
Samuel Landan
James Atheton Ju
Jonathan Carver
William wortman
Thomas alington
John Taylor
John Woolley
Ira Manvill
Joel Holcomb
Nathanel Evens

Sam[ll] X Wright (his mark)
Luke Evens
Jonas Williams
Phinehas Nash
William [Reyn-olds ?]
Daniel Ingersoll
Jacob Robards
Dan Robarts
Benoni [Taylor?]
Abraham Tilbury
James Earl
Thos Park
Amos Parks
Samuel Robarts
James Bidlack
Thomas P. Caler
Eliph[t] Richards

We Whose Names are heare unto Enext are of of Apinion that tis best for the Election of Justis to procede as soone as posable, if maters connot Rest.

John Swift
Jonah Rogers
Almerine Marshell
Josiah Rogers
Benjamin Robarts
Jonah Rogers jur
Samuel Ayres
Joseph Rogers
John Pierce

Eleshar Harvey
Benjaman Racer
Dan X Mittag [his] [mark?]
Thomas Brink
Matthis V. Loon
Nicholas V. Loon
Peter Chambery
James Cook

Pelatiah Pierce
Elisha Atherton
Hezekiah Robarts
Palmer Ransom
Timothy Hopkins
Abraham Dyke
Jacob Meeker
Amos Meeker
Jary Baker

[3] Actually, fifty-three signatures are included. This discrepancy comes from the fact that several names were added on the cover sheet after the count had been completed and that the original number of names was mis-counted.

Joseph Reynolds   James Nisbitt   Prince Alden
Bixbee Rogers   Nicholas Depue   old Mr Williams &
Elias Williams   Junr.   Sun
Stephen Doe   Joab Enos   Joshua Benett
Josiah Rogers jur   Moses Depui   Elesha Benett
                   John Bigelow   Benjaman Harvy
                   James Atherton

Endorsed: Shawnee N° 2 Names 87 [4]

Zebulon Marcy   Elisah Oakly   John Harding
Asahel Atherton   Caleb Newman   Nathl Goodspeed
Leonard Lord

Endorsed: District N° 1 Tunkhanunk

[56] Information Regarding the Designs of John Franklin.[1]

C. Thinks there will be no opposition to the election. has advised ——— not to oppose it, who says he will not, except by attempting to persuade the people not to elect or appear at the election. Thinks if there be an opposition, it will be *in arms;* and says that arms & amunition are deposited in convenient places for the purpose. That things are very different from the representation given him of them, before he came in. He was told the people were united. He finds they are not and that ——— is losing ground daily. 'Tis his opinion that if F. had the Athens lands confirmed, his opposition would cease.

Endorsed: Information of M^r C——— ——— by M^r ——— relative to Franklin's designs. April 22. 1787.

[57] Elijah Buck to Timothy Pickering.[1]

Tioga Apr^l 23^d 1787

Sir

As you are one of the Commissioners to Confairm or Disalow the Improvements Claim^d, by the Inhabitance of Wyoming and

---

[4] Ninety-three signatures appear, or ninety-four if one counts "and son." Again, the additional signatures were added to the cover sheet.
[56] [1] M. H. S., Pickering Papers, LVII, 204, in Pickering's hand. There is no clue to the identity of "C."
[57] [1] M. H. S., Pickering Papers, LVII, 205, in Buck's hand.

others up the Est branch of Susq^h &c. these are therefore to inform you of My Claim to three hundred acres of Land on the Mouth of Bowmans Crick which I purchised of the First Improveer who Lived Nine yers Peaseably on S^d place & had a Susq^h Right &c I wish your advise by way of My Honr^d parent who will be the Bearer hereoff, & Can give you further Information, &c. Sir, thinking My Exartions in defence of the Laws and Liberty* of this Commonwelth hes Merrited Every thing that is My Just Due, I Subscribe My Self your Frind and well wisher

Elijah Buck

N. B. M^r McClay has the Deed which Can be had at ani time when wanted. E. B.

[58] William Hooker Smith to Ebenezer Marcy and Barnabas Carey.[1]

Coppy of a Letter to Esqr Marcy & M^rCarey

Dear Gentlemen,

I was This Day in Town with Coron^l Pickrin, where I Saw a Number of assoceation Papers Designed for Each Town in This Derstrict.[2] The one for wilksbury had almost forty Signers before I Left The Town. Corn^l Pickrin had in my Pressence an opertunety To Send one To Mr Marcy at Tancannack.[3] he Desired me To write To you & Inclose one for Lackewana. I have one for This Neibourhood which will be Emediatly Signed by Every man. it Is Desired That Every man may have an oppertunety To Signe, who Desires To Live in The Countrey & Inioy The Privelidgeis of Cityzens & Protection of The Laws, weither a freeholder or Not—& it Is also Desired That Every man will Give Thare Bodely attendance on The Day of Election, weither free holder or Not, in Testemoney of Thare approbation. it Is also Desired That The Paper may be Signed & Returnd before The Day of Election To Coron^l Pickrin. I wish To See Sum of you as Soon as may be, It is also The Desire of The People on Jacobs Plains, That the Lacawana People will meet with Us at The House of M^r abraham Westbrook on The Election Day as Early as Posable, That we may attend To The biseness & have Time To Return. we & others at Wilksbury are Determened Not To Lissen To, or be put of by any Kind of Lockram Storeys,[4]

[58] [1] M. H. S., Pickering Papers, LVII, 207, in Smith's hand.

[2] See no. 55, *ante*. All the places mentioned here were in the First District for the purpose of electing justices of the peace.

[3] Probably Zebulon Marcy at Tunkhannock.   [4] That is, gibberish.

111

or Pleadings from any Persons whatsoever, but with Coolness, Deliberation, & firmness, To attend To The Bisness of The Day. i Think It Is Expedeant for Us To Róuse, if we Suffer a few, few in Deed, To Prevent The Election, we Shall becom odious, & a Lafing Stock To The world. Dear Gentlemen, I am with Esteam, your most obdᵗ Humble Servᵗ

Wᵐ Hooker Smith.

Jacobs Plains, April [23?] 1787.
P. S. Those That Refuse To Signe Return Thare Names.

[59] William Hooker Smith to Timothy Pickering.[1]

Der Sir,
Inclosd our assoation Paper, also a Coppy of a Letter which I Sent to Lacawana.[2] we are Amanemas [unanimous] in This Neiborhood. I hope That you will Not Lissen To any Intreags from Franklin or Jinkins, To put of The Election. How Ever, we Shall Submit To any Directions from you, & Coron¹ Butler. I Expect That you have Recd The accounts of The Election in The upper Destrict.[3] Dear Sir, I am with Grateest Esteem your most obdᵗ Humble Servᵗ

Wᵐ Hooker Smith

april 24ᵗʰ 1787

[60] Lawrence Myers to Timothy Pickering.[1]

Sir last Night a Gentleman Informed me that the opposite Party are to take you and Hurlbutt and Carry you both of to prevent the Election. Mʳ Thoday Cowl Came down from Sheshequin Informs me that Several men are prepairing their arms and are Coming to oppose the Election. Two of them were at the elec-

[59] ¹ M. H. S., Pickering Papers, LVII, 206, in Smith's hand.
    ² Nos. 55 and 58, ante.
    ³ That is, in the Third District, which had held its election on April 19; see nos. 53 and 54, ante.
[60] ¹ M. H. S., Pickering Papers, LVII, 208, in Myers' hand.

tion in kingston² and all of them belong to Tunkanick. I am
Sir in hast your Servᵗ.

Lawᵉ Myers
Wednesday morning³

[61] Timothy Pickering to John Hageman.¹

To Mʳ John Hageman of Wilkesbarre
By virtue of the power vested in us by an Act of the General
Assembly of Pennsylvania, passed on the twenty seventh day of
December last, to appoint one fit person in each district in the
county of Luzerne, to preside at a meeting of the freeholders of
the said district, to be held on Thursday the twenty sixth day of
April instant, at Noon, for the purpose of electing four Justices
of the Peace for the said district; we do hereby appoint you the
said John Hageman to preside at the said election, & to perform
all the duties required of you, thus appointed, by the said act,
and the laws for regulating the elections of Justices of the Peace,
excepting the notifying the said freeholders to assemble on said
26th instant, which hath been already done by Mʳ Christopher
Hurlbut, by us for that purpose appointed. Provided that if the
said Christopher shall attend & hold the said election, then you
will forbear to act upon this warrant, and return the same unexecuted to us. This precaution of appointing you to preside at
the said election being taken to frustrate the flagitous designs of
a few lawless men, by whom, (it is said) ² the said Christopher
is to be seized & carried away, to prevent an election of Justices
as aforesaid. Given under our hands at Wilkesbarre the twenty
fifth day of April 1787.

Timothy Pickering
Zebⁿ Butler

---

² Myers' reference to "the election in Kingston" is confusing, for the
election for the Second District had been postponed to May 3; no. 64, *post*.
Myers may have been referring to a local meeting held in Kingston on
April 19; Harvey-Smith, *Wilkes-Barré*, III, 1565.
³ The Wednesday before the election in the First District was April 25.
[61] ¹ M. H. S., Pickering Papers, LVII, 209, in Pickering's hand.
² See no. 60, *ante*.

[62] Oaths of Allegiance of Timothy Pickering and Others.[1]

I do swear that I will be faithful & bear true allegiance to the Commonwealth of Pennsylvania as a free and independent state; and that I will not at any time wilfully and knowingly do any act, matter or thing which will be prejudicial or injurious to the freedom and independence thereof.

County of Luzerne April 26, 1787

Timothy Pickering	Philadelphia	
Abraham Harding	Pittstown	yeoman
James Armstrong	d°	d°
Benjamin Brown	Wilkesbarre	d°
Nathan Draper	d°	d°
Thomas Read	d°	d°
John scott	Pittstown	d°
Edward Prouty	d°	d°
James Scot	d°	d°
Charles X Bennet's mark	d°	d°
mark of John X Rosecrantz	Wilkesbarre	d°
George Cooper	Pittstown	d°
Joseph Sprague	Wilkesbarre	Doctor
Nathanel Davenport	Hanover	Yeoman
Wᵐ Hooker Smith	Wilkesbarre	d°
adam Man	d°	d°
David Brown	Pittstown	d°
John Hyde	Wilkesbarre	d°
Nathan Waller	d°	d°
John Cary	d°	d°
William Heberd	Hanover	d°
Mark of Asa X Bennet	Wilkesbarre	d°
Samuel Finch	Kingston	yeoman
Robert MᶜDowel	d°	d°
Rufus Bennet	Wilkesbarre	d°
The mark of Cornelius X Gale	d°	d°
Jasper Taylor	ditto	Mason
Zacheus Mᶜgeringer	d°	Carpenter

[62] [1] M. H. S., Pickering Papers, LVII, 210, signed by each individually.

114

These may Certify that the above named persons did Voluntarily take and Subscribe the Above oath of Alligiance and Fidelity this twenty Sixth day of April 1787

before me Christopher Hurlbut.

Christopher Hurlbut Sworn to bear tru allegance & fidelity to the State before James Sutton

[63] Nathan Denison to Timothy Pickering.[1]

Wyelusing the 26[th] of April 1787.

Sir

I received your letter last Evening am glad to find that there is yet a prospect of Coming to an Election in that part of the County. after I left you at Doctr Smiths I called on Sundre people at Lackaw[a]nna and Concluded by What Was told me that the people Ware generaly for the Election. I then Expected opposision to the Election Wold be in this District.[2] after I found ginkins Was gon up to the point[3] I Was allmost Suer there Wold be Considerable Disturbance but at my arial [arrival] at the place of Election Was very agreeably Disappointed. I found the people had taken up the matter on general princaples. I must give it as my oppinion that there is not more then one fourth part of the people at the Election that are intitled to any land by the late act, tho for the Sake of peace they Come Cherfuly in to the Election in hops of giting land by petitioning the assembly. if the franklen party Continues to oppose the Election I make no Doubt but you Can have the gratest part of the people in this District to assist if it must be Carred by force. As to What Was Said between franklin and I before I Went to Philadelphia I Cannot pretend to no his hart but by his general Conduct. as to that the World may Judge for thim Selvs. I Shall not fail of being at Wyoming by the Election at Kingston.[4] your Hors is as Well taken Care of as our Circomstances Will permit and Will be Sent to you by a Safe hand if I do not Come my Self. I have the return of the Election for this District and Desire to Deliver them to you With my own hand. must refir you to Sq[r] gores Letter for information.[5] the bearer is Waiting. Am S[r] With Esteem and Respect your very Humbl Servt

Nathan Denison

[63] [1] M. H. S., Pickering Papers, LVII, 211, in Denison's hand.
[2] That is, the Third District.   [3] Tioga Point, or Athens.
[4] The election in the Second District had been postponed until May 3; no. 64, post.   [5] No. 53, ante.

115

[64] Timothy Pickering to Samuel Hodgdon.[1]

Wilkesbarre April 28, 1787.

Dear Sir,

M[r] Hollenback the Bearer will inform you of the particulars of the election held at this place last Thursday.[2] Franklin's career is at an end. I shall stay to be present at the election which is to be held next Thursday (May 3[d]) for the 2[d] district,[3] and by the 5th set out for Philadelphia. For several orders in his favour, & some advances, for lands purchased here, I am indebted to M[r] Hollenback One hundred & fifty nine dollars, (or £59.12.6) which he wants to pay in Philadelphia. If any debts due to us, or remittances, have been received, be pleased to pay him that sum : but if this should be inconvenient, then be pleased to assume the payment of that amount to such persons in Philadelphia as he shall request, so as to discharge him. M[r] Hollenback has been very obliging to me, and I wish perfectly to suit him in this payment. I remain dear sir yours affectionately

T. Pickering

P. S. Persons elected Justices for the 1st district, were Matthias Hollenback 45 votes, W[m] Hooker Smith 42, Christ[o] Hurlbut 39, Eben[r] Marcy 36.

Endorsed : Rec[d] 4th May.

[65] John Franklin to Joseph Hamilton.[1]

Wilkesbarre April 29th 1787.

D[r] Doctor,

You will receive this with my budget by M[r] Follet on his way to Windham. I hope Esq[r] Beach [2] will be here before I leave

---

[64] [1] M. H. S., Pickering Papers, LVII, 215-16, in Pickering's hand.

[2] Elected in the First District were Mathias Hollenback, William Hooker Smith, Christopher Hurlbut, and Ebenezer Marcy; *ibid.*, 212.

[3] Elected in the Second District were Benjamin Carpenter, James Nisbitt, Hezekiah Roberts, and John Dorrance; *ibid.*

For the names of those commissioned as justices in the three districts, see no. 74, *post*, note 2.

[65] [1] Amer. Phil. Soc., Documents Relative to the Wyoming or Connecticut Controversy, I, 219-20, a copy made in the nineteenth century.

[2] Zerah Beach of Amenia, New York, was one of the prominent members of the Susquehannah Company.

the settlement, which must be as early as the 9th of May. Pray, write as soon as possible, send your despatches that comprehend secrecy to Major Jenkins in case of my absence. I fear you have missed your politicks in putting too much trust on M[r] A. Mooder.[3] I believe him to be a friend to our cause but fear he will expose us by making too free with strangers. The address from Major Judd has fell into Pickerings hands.[4] I expect A. Mooder delivered one of them to some one who he supposed to be a friend, by which means it was convey to Pickering. M[r] Chapman is gone on to Tioga yesterday, he appears to be a gentleman of knowledge and capable of doing us Service, but I cannot put confidence in a stranger until I am fully acquainted with his character. We shall proceed with our Court of Directors. I expect that M[r] Wells or M[r] Starkweather will be appointed Secretary.[5] Col. Butler and Capt. Schotts have hitherto appeared willing to proceed though contrary to Pickerings advice; he endeavoured to prevent Col. Butler from proceeding some time since but to no purpose. how long Col. Butler will continue willing to act I cannot say, he was forward for the Election to take place. Capt Schott's appeared to be opposed to the election for some time, but finally fell in with it. at the election in this District he agreed to be run in the Ticket with M[r] Holenbacks and others for a Justice, but was much disappointed for the want of votes. he has since told me he shall proceed as one of the Commissioners. I believe he wishes us well but is too easily persuaded when he can discover a prospect of obtaining interest or honor. I fear you have put too much trust on Esq Gore. you may depend that he will sacrafice the company's interest to secure his own, he has not surveyed the Town of Franklin or Juddsbury.[6] I fear your settlers will be disappointed unless some other surveyor is provided. I hear M[r] Gore is about to move to Wilkesbarre immediately, expects to be Judge of the Court. I should had a greater esteem of him if he had laid aside Musk-rat Traps and assisted us in time of trouble. he is willing that Pennsylvania shall have the Town of Athens and cheat those of us who have been the salvation of this country, out of lands. Ingratitude, blacker than Hell! Perhaps he may curse the day he was born before he will accomplish his design in that respect. I am, Sir, your humb[le] Serv[t]

John Franklin

---

[3] John J. AcModer; see no. 89, *post*. [4] No. 49, *ante*.

[5] Starkwather became secretary to the Susquehannah Company commissioners when Lord Butler resigned; see no. 68, *post*.

[6] Proposed towns about fifty miles west of Athens along tributaries of the Tioga River; see no. 119, *post*.

To be communicated to Major Judd and others you may think proper by copy or otherwise, but I would wish this affair of Capt Shotts to be secret among yourselves as I would not wish to make him an enemy.

N. B. You will send these on by M' Follet if you think best. he can deliver them to Mess'' & Wolcott [7] or to Major Judd. he will stand in need of some expense money to help him to Windham. I was not able to furnish him with any.

[66] Timothy Pickering to Peter Muhlenberg.[1]

Wednesday Morning

Dear Sir

As you have particularly interested yourself in the affairs of Wyoming give me leave to suggest to you the expediency of the Council's writing to the Executive of Connecticut, inclosing a copy of the Act for quieting the claims of the Connecticut settlers,[2] and desiring that Government, by some public act, to express its approbation or satisfaction in the measure, and enjoining the people of that state to give no aid or countenance to persons who shall attempt to execute the late resolutions of the Susquehanna Company. But on farther reflection, perhaps it may not be expedient to hint an idea that any persons would be hardy enough to make the attempt. You will consider of this.

When the Council shall send their letter (if they adopt the measure here proposed) we can inclose the copy of the act and our advertisement to one of the Hartford printers.

Y'' affectionately
T. Pickering

[67] William Hooker Smith to Timothy Pickering.[1]

Dear Sir,

There is at my house [tod]ay [a] man from Lime in Connecticut who informs That there has bin a battle betwixt The

---

[7] Probably Oliver Wolcott, Jr., a member of the Company's commission.
[66] [1] Amer. Phil. Soc., Benjamin Franklin MSS., XLVIII, 68, in Pickering's hand. The probable date of this letter is April, 1787.
[2] No. 38, *ante.* A copy of the act was sent to Governor Huntington by Connecticut's delegates to Congress; see *ibid.*, note 1.
[67] [1] M. H. S., Pickering Papers, LVII, 217-18, in Smith's hand.

118

mob Party & Government at Springfield. The mob Kept The field. Thay had 15 Kild how many is Kild on The Side of Goverment he Does Not Know. Thay on The mob Side Give 30 hard dolors bounty & 40/ hard a month which Is Punctually Paid. Shay has Sent from Canady To inform The mob That he Expects Soon To Joyn Them with 8000 Solders.[2] I Think I fully Now Discover Franklins Sceam. I Send Inclosd a Letter for your Perusal That you may See what Parte he acted at The Election To The Northward.[3] I am very Uneasey Dear Sir, I am Sincerely at your Service.

W[m] Hooker Smith

May 1[t] 1787

[68] Proceedings of the Susquehannah Company Commissioners.[1]

Records of the Proceedings of the Court of Commissioners appointed & authorized [2] * * *

Pursuant to the afore Recited Resolves, the Commissioners met at the Dwelling house of Cap[t] John P. Shott in Wilksberry March 1st 1787. Present. Zebulon Butler John Franklin John Jinkins and John Paul Shott Commissioners, when they proceed on business respecting Appointing a Secretary for the purpose mentioned in s[d] Resolves. Lord Butler is appointed Secretary.

The Commissioners appoint a time and place for holding their first court agreeably to the afors[d] Resolves Viz at Cap[t] John P. Shott in Wilksberry on Tuesday the 6th Inst.

At a Court of Commissioners held at Cap[t] Shotts in Wilksberry March 6th 1787, Present Zebulon Butler John Franklin John Jinkins John P. Schott and Abel Pierce, Commissioners.

[2] These statements are the purest fiction. At no battle during Shays' Rebellion was there anything like fifteen killed. The last skirmish of any consequence took place in Stockbridge, where four were killed on February 26, 1787. In the attack on the Springfield arsenal in January, the Regulators lost four men also; Robert J. Taylor, *Western Massachusetts in the Revolution* (Providence, 1954), 160, 163.

[3] Not found, but he may be referring to no. 54, *ante,* in which Smith's son mentions Jenkin's activity, not Franklin's.

[68] [1] P. H. M. C., Div. of Arch. and MSS., John Franklin Papers, in Lord Butler's hand.

[2] Quoted but here omitted are the resolutions of the Susquehannah Company at its last meeting of December 26 and 27, 1786, concerning the powers of commissioners; Vol. VIII, no. 268.

Proceeded to hear a Complaint exhibited by Mathias Hollenback against Darkis Stewart that she Unjustly withholds a certain Lot of Land in Hanover Township. The parties appear to answer to the Complaint and the Defendant pleads for an Adjournment by reason of wanting Evidence present, therefore the Court considering the plan adjourns to the 26th Inst. at this place at 10 OClock in the forenoon.

Test Lord Butler Secret^y

Wilkesberry March 26th 1787.

At a Court of the Commissioners held this day at Capt Shotts by Adjournment, Proceeded to a Tryal between Mathias Hollenback & Dorcas Stewart.

Commissioners present Zebulon Butler, John Franklin, John Jinkins, John Paul Shott & Abel Pierce.

The Commissioners taking the Cause into their Deliberate Consideration, after hearing the parties & examining the evidences respecting the right of the parties to claim and hold the in lands in controversy, are unanimously of oppinion that the lot of Land N° 5 in the Town of Hanover claim'd to belong to the Heirs of Lazarus Stewart Junr Dec^d together with all the After Divisions in s^d Town belonging thereto, does of right belong to Mathias Hollenback agreeable to the Notes and Resolves of the Susquehannah Company, and that the s^d Hollenback has a right to take possession of & enjoy s^d Lands agreeably to said resited Resolves and that the s^d Dorcas Stewart pay cost of this Court.

At the same court of Commissioners. the Committee appointed to seze Thomas Wigdon's lot at Mashopin made their report. This court adjourns to Lord Butlers in Kingstown tomorrow morning at Nine OClock in the forenoon.

Test. Lord Butler Sect^y

March 27th 1787 This Court of Commissioners met agreeable to Adjournment & proseeded to hear the Dispute Subsisting between Thos Wigden and Martin Dudley. Adjourn to the House of Capt Shott in Wilksberry on Monday the 2^d of April 1787.

Test. Lord Butler Sect^y

April 2^d 1787 This court of Commissioners met agreeable to adjournment and proceed on the Tryal between Thos Wigden and Martin Dudley. Adjourn'd to the same place, the 12th Day of April at 1 OClock in the Afternoon Test Lord Butler Sect^y

April 12th 1787 The Court of Commissioners met agreeable to Adjournment & read the petition of Phinihas Nash setting fourth that he was admitted as a setler on James Ray's right and had encouragement of having a Right in Hanover which he has not

120

Obtain'd, prays relief. Ordered to be Rec^d and entered on file and that the Petitioner be recommended to apply to the Clark of Hanover for a list of the Proprietors and N° of Lots in s^d Hanover and lay the same before the Court at their Meeting, likewise read a petition from John Hyde setting forth that he was an Original setler and sufferer and had encouragement of having a Right on the West branch of which he was disappointed and praying Relief, as may be seen by the petition on file. The Commissioners taking the petitions into consideration are of oppinion that the petitioner be admitted as a setler and have liberty to lay out and survey two hundred acres on the unlocated lands in the Susquehannah purchase agreeable to the Resolves of the Susquehannah Company the 26th Decem^b 1786 and the same be confirmed accordingly,[3] likewise the Report of Committee appointed March 16th 1787 to lay out & Size to Thomas Wigdon his right of land on Mashopin Creek and laid before this Court the 26th of march last. Taken into Consideration is Approved of, The Commissioners are Unanimously of Oppinion that the right of Land at Mashoppin Creek containing one Hundred and fifty Acres described by the survey of John Jinkins Surveyor referenc thereto being had ought to be confirmed to the s^d Thos Wigdin and the same is hereby confirmed to him as part of his General right in the purchase entered on one half share wright and confirmed agreeably to the Resolves of the Susquehannah Company always reserving necessary Roads. And whereas Martin Dudley has erected a Saw mill on his supposed right by Virtue of the Grant of the Town of Whitehaven which s^d Mill appears to be on the lands of Thos Wigden, the Commissioners therefore order that the s^d Thos Wigden pay to s^d Martin Dudley for s^d Mill and the Appurtenances belonging thereunto forty one pounds, S^d Dudley to have the improvement of the Mills untill sufficient security is given, and any three of the Commissioners to determine the sufficientcy of the security, Dudley to have liberty to take all such board or Timber as shall be sawed at the time the security is given and that each party pay his equal proportion of Cost.[4] Bill of Cost twelve Dollars.

[3] Here is an example of the commissioners' being willing to establish new settlers within the original purchase even though Pennsylvania was committed by the Confirming Act to recognizing the rights of only those who had settled before the Trenton decree of 1782.

[4] On July 14, 1787, John Franklin gave Wigton a receipt for two dollars for the last tax on two rights in the Susquehannah Purchase and for six dollars as his share of the bill of costs in the suit between Wigton and Dudley. The original receipt in Franklin's hand as well as a copy in Pickering's hand is in M. H. S., Pickering Papers, LVII, 235.

Agreeably to their adjournment, the Court of Commiss[rs] was holden at the house of John Paul Schott in Wilksberry on tuesday May 1st 1787 Present John Franklin, John Jenkins & John Paul Schott, Commissioners. Lord Butler having resigned the office of Secretary, the Commissioners appoint Asa Starkwather their Secretary, And proceed to hear and take into consideration the petition of Abel Yarington, setting forth that he was possess'd of a right of land in Plymouth, which was afterwards granted & Confirmed to William Hurlbutt on condition that s[d] Yarington should have an equivalent in lands elsewhere within the Susq[h] Purchase; also showing that s[d] Yarington has already had an equal number of acres confirmed to him in the Township of Providence called Capous, but that he the s[d] Yarington considers that as not being an equivalent to his s[d] Right in Plymouth, and therefore prays a Grant of a sufficient number of acres to make him good in his original right in Plymouth. The Commissioners therefore resolved, That the s[d] Yarington have liberty to lay out two hundred acres in any of the unlocated lands within the Susq[h] purchase, to be laid out in such manner as not to discommode the laying out of other Lands adjoining thereto, which, together with what has been heretofore granted him, shall be considered as an equivalent to his right beforementioned in Plymouth. Adjourned to the 5th inst. at this place 4 o'clock P. M.[5]

Test Asa Starkwather Sec'ry.

[69] John Franklin's Power of Agency.[1]

Know all men by these presents, that we the subscribers do hereby ordain, constitute and appoint Our trusty friend John Franklin Esq[r] our Lawful Agent, to transact all matters of business for us in our name and stead, relative to the Settlement of the Susquehannah purchase, and to make application to the Honourable the Continental Congress, to the General Assembly of the State of Connecticut [2] and the Susq[h] Company for the purpose of bringing on a Revision of the Trial at Trenton, or a trial for the Right of

[5] This last entry is in the hand of Starkwather.
[69] [1] C. S. L., Susquehannah Settlers, I, 174 ab, signed by eighty men. Of the signers, only three had signed the petition of February (no. 16, *ante*) and twenty-seven had signed the earlier statements calling for an election and acceptance of the laws of Pennsylvania; no. 55, *ante*. Of the twenty-seven, eight were from Wilkes-Barre, twelve from Kingston and Exeter, two from Nanticoke, five from Shawnee, and none from Lackawannock or Jacobs Plains.
[2] No. 75, *post*.

Soil, included within the Limits of the aforesaid purchase. In
testimony whereof we have hereunto Set our hands this 2nd day
of May 1787

Gideon Church	And^w S Alden	Eb^n Slocum
Josh. Pattrick	Wm Jones	Elisha Blackman
Ira Stephens	Joseph Elliot	Ichadbod Blackman
J Avery Rathbun	Benjn Harvey	John Platner
Elijah Rood	Wm Ross	Stephen Wilcox
Jedidiah Stephens	William Jackays	Thos McCluer
David Smith	Fred^k Budd	Perigreen Garner
Nathaniel Walker	Jn° Jenkins	Thomas Brown
Edward Walker	Stephen Jenkins	Humphry Brown
Richard Brockway	Jed^h Stevens J^r	Moses Brown
Peleck Comstock	Wil^m Jenkins	Joseph Preston
Isaac Underwood	Mason F. Alden	Benjn Smith
Parshall Terry	Roswell Franklin	Ashbil Walter
John Coon	Nathan Nathrop	Lebbeus Tubbs
Oliver Bigelow	Joseph Jameson	Samuel Tubbs
Josiah Kellogg	Neh^m Nothrop	Chester Bingham
Elisha Satterlee	Benjamin Baily	John ONeil
Joel Holcomb	Wm Slocum	Reuben Jones
Jn° Manvil	Giles Slocum	Ed^w Spencer
Ab^m Pyke	Amos Parks	Wm Hybert
Sam^11 Ayres J^r	James Atherton	Richard Inman
Asa Bennet	John Clark	Isaac Tripp
Ishmael Bennet	Henry D. Tripp	James Atherton J^r
Ishmael Bennet J^r	Job Tripp	Aaron Hunt
Nathan Wade	Elisha Mathewson	Nathan Jones
Rufus Bennet	Benedick Satterlee	Thodey Cole
Joseph Rogers	Darius Park	

[70] Oaths of Allegiance of Nathan Denison and Others.[1]

I do swear that I will be faithful & bear true allegiance to the
Commonwealth of Pennsylvania, as a free and independent State;
and that I will not at any time wilfully and knowingly do any act
matter or thing which will be prejudicial or injurious to the freedom or independence thereof

Henry X Tuttle   kingston
  his · mark

Thomas Bennet   D°

Richard X Brockaway   D°
  his · mark

---

[70] [1] M. H. S., Pickering Papers, LVII, 218-19A, signed by each individually.

123

Nicholas X Lone mark	Shawney
Aaron Perkins	kingston
Andrew Bennet	Dº
Abram Nesbitt	Shawney
Abel Peirce	kingston
Parshall Terry	kingston
James Bidlack	Shawney
James atherton	kingston
Noah [Denison?]	kingston
James Wheaton Junʳ	Dº
Obadiah Scott	Huntington
Elisha Atherton	Kingston kingston
Thomas Reed [2]	Wilkesbarre
Hallot Gallup	kingston
Benj Carpenter [3]	kingston
Jnº Hageman [4]	Wilksberrey
Nathan Denison	Springfield
Philip Myers	Kingston
Isaac X Parker his ... mark	kingston

the two persons above Named and the twenty on the other Leaf was Sworn Before me

James Sutton

Endorsed: List of Persons who took the Oath of Allegiance before James Sutton May 3ᵈ 1787.

[71] Nathan Denison to Charles Biddle.[1]

County of Luzerne the 4ᵗʰ May 1787

Sir

After my arrivel at this place I found that Every unjust meas-

---

[2] Not to be confused with Thomas Read, also of Wilkes-Barre, who took the oath in April; no. 62, *ante*. The two signatures are clearly different.

[3] Benjamin Carpenter is also listed with those who took the oath in February; no. 11, *ante*, name no. 90. The two signatures look enough alike to have been written by the same man, but it is not clear why Carpenter would have taken the oath a second time.

[4] Not to be confused with John Hagemen, also of Wilkes-Barre, who took the oath in February; no. 11, *ante*, name no. 33. The two signatures are clearly different.

[71] [1] P. H. M. C., Div. of Arch. and MSS., Record Group 27, Series: Exec. Corr., 1777-90, in Denison's hand.

ure had been taken to imbitter the minds of the inhabitence against the Proceding of goverment towards them in short no Ston was lest unturnd by Some Carricktors to prevent our Coming to an Election tho the persons in the Second and third Districts that Ware appointed to Preside at the Elections had Putup there Wornings according to there appointment [2] I repaird to the place appointed for holding the Election in the third District Whear I Expected the gratest opposision but Was very agreeably Disappointed.

Contarary to my Expectation I found the Election almost to a man for Com[?]plying With the order of goverment, tho it is my oppinion that there is not more than one to four in the District that are intitled to any land by the late act of assembly yet for the Sake of peac and in hops of obtaining Lands by Petition the assembly they Chearfuly Came in to the Election, the Election in the Second District Was attempted on the Same Day.[3] after the Election had met at the place appointed the gratest part of the Day Was Spent in Debate on the Subject, the party in opposesion to the Election Did twise take and Cary off mr Sutton the person appointed to preside at the Election. When he was released the Second time Some bloos Ware Struck With Clubs on both Sids the Day being So far Spent that Col{n} Pickring W[ith] the advise of Col{n} Butler Was Disposed to appoint another Day for the Election, and Sr I am now very happy to inform your Self and the gentelm[en] members of Counsel, that We have Come to an Election through out the Count[y] without farther opposesion So that I am now in hops that We Shall be able to Suppor the authority of goverment Without farther Expence to the State. am Sr your most obedient and very Humble Servant

Nathan Denison

P S Wold Segest to Counsel Situation of the persons Elected for Justices in the third District mr Gore the person Highest in vote lives Within about Six miles of the north line of the County mr Buck the next highest in vote Lives Still further up the river nier the north Line of the County mr Kingsley the third person Elected livs about twenty-five miles Down the river below mr Gores So that if Kingsley Shold not be Commission{d}, the people that are in the Southard Parts of the District Will not have Les than fifty miles to travil to Do any business With a Justice.

---

[2] But see nos. 47 and 61, *ante.*

[3] That is, on April 19, the day originally set. The election in the Second District was finally postponed to May 3.

Kingley & Buck are Well affected to goverment and perhaps of Equil ability.[4]

[72] Samuel Huntington to Benjamin Franklin.[1]

Norwich May 5th 1787.

Sir

I am honoured with your Excellency' letter [2] of the 14th ult° with the Act of your Assembly to which it refers; which will be laid before the legislature of this State at their approaching Session, the Ensuing Week. I am persuaded they will be disposed to observe Such A line of Conduct, as Shall manifest a religious regard to Cultivate peace and good harmony, consonant to the principles of Justice. With Sentiments of the highest Respect; I have the Honour to be Your Ex'" Obedient, & humble Serv[t]

S. Huntington

[73] Timothy Pickering to Samuel Stroud.[1]

Learn's [2] May 7, 1787.

Sir,

I have the pleasure to inform you that the elections of Justices of the peace have finally been held in all the districts of the county of Luzerne, in perfect tranquility; and I consider the introduction of law and regular government as certain. This happy event will render an easy communication between that county and the lower parts of the State of great importance to both. The present route (which is called Sullivan's road) [3] will necessarily be continued,

---

[4] See nos. 53 ante, note 4 and 74, *post,* note 2.

[72] [1] M. H. S., Washburn Collection, 11.1.22.132, a copy in the hand of John Armstrong, Jr.

[2] No. 50, *ante.*

[73] [1] M. H. S., Pickering Papers, LVII, 220-21.

[2] Learn's is marked on the frontispiece map of *Susquehannah Company Papers,* VII, as "John Learns."

[3] Sullivan's Road went from Easton through the Wind Gap to modern Sciota, through Learn's, thence along the western edge of modern Monroe County across Tunkhannock and Tobyhanna creeks and the Lehigh River, through the Great Swamp and across the mountain to Wyoming; Harvey *Wilkes-Barré,* II, 1181-82.

whatever other communications shall be opened; and for some time will remain the only practicable one. I therefore feel a solicitude to have it so repaired as to render the passage of a waggon, moderately loaded, practicable & perfectly safe. I will candidly own this solicitude to be the greater, because I wish to move my family by this road to Wyoming, by the latter end of the present month; and for this reason I would contribute the more largely towards the expense. I now engage to pay ten pounds, on that account; and if the repairs should be so considerable that it should be judged proper that I should make a farther contribution, I will do it. It is also not improbable that I may engage some tradesmen at Philadelphia to go to settle at Wyoming; & I shall, in that case, endeavour to send them forward, so as to assist in this necessary work. I am now on my way to Philadelphia, where I beg you to send me an answer to this letter, with your opinion of what can & will be done on the subject of it, in the course of this month. Be pleased to direct to me in Front Street near Vine Street. I am sir Your humble serv^t

T. Pickering

[74] Timothy Pickering to Benjamin Franklin.[1]

Philadelphia May 10, 1787.

Sir,

I arrived here last evening, and now have the pleasure to inclose the returns of the elections of Justices of the Peace for the County of Luzerne.[2] The interruption of one of the intended elections by the violence of Franklin's party, I rather think an advantage to government. It has excited a spirit of firmness in supporting the measures of government, and of resentment against Franklin & his adherents. Agreeably to the desire of Council, communicated by the Secretary, I delivered to the Sheriff and Coroner of Luzerne their commissions, and administered to them the oaths of allegiance and of office. I also took the

---

[74] [1] M. H. S., Pickering Papers, LVII, 222, a copy in Pickering's hand.
  [2] A copy of these returns is in *ibid.*, 212. On May 11, the Council commissioned as justices the following: Mathias Hollenback and William Hooker Smith for the First District; Benjamin Carpenter and James Nisbitt, for the Second District; and Obadiah Gore and Nathan Kingsley for the Third District. *Pa. C. R.*, XV, 212.

Sheriffs bond; but by some mistake have left it with other papers, at Wilkesbarre. I will take care to send it to Council when I go thither again. I am &c.

T. P.

His Excellency the President of Pennsylvania In Council

[75] Petition of John Franklin to the Connecticut General Assembly.[1]

To the Honourable General Assembly of the State of Connecticut now seting at Hartford

The Memorial of John Franklin of Wyoming In behalf of himself and the rest of the Inhabitants settled upon the Waters of the Rivers Susqueh[a] & Delaware under the Title of the State of Connecticut humbly sheweth

That by the approbation of this State (then Colony) as Early as the Year 1754 a number of the Inhabitants of this State Made Bonafida Purchases of the Natives of a Large Tract of Land Extending from the River Delaware Westward about One Hundred & forty Miles including the whole breadth of the 42nd degree of Northern Latitude Lands fairly included in the Royal Grant made to the Plymouth Company in the year of our Lord *1620* & by Derivative grants Vested in the early Settlers of this State and confirmed to them by the Charter of King Charles the 2nd the year of our Lord 1662. That in the year 1755 a Considerable settlement was made upon the Waters of the Susqueh[a] by the said Purchasers which was soon Interupted by the then War between Great Brittain & France, but reasumed in the year 1769 & Continued down to the Year 1782 under the authority of this state during which time Towns were Established A County Erected & Civil Government duly administered under the authority of this State, that during that term many respectable Citizens of this State removed into that Country and Established themselves & families Contiguous to Each other (for better defence) upon small parcels of Land only Calculated for Immediate Support, and Located Other Lands as a future Dependence, but were prevented from Settleing thereon, by Means of the Late Warr, That their settlement was Cut off in the Year 1778 by the Savages aided by the arms of Great Brittain but soon regained by the Zeal

[75] [1] C. S. L., Susquehannah Settlers, I, 172a-b—173a-g, in an unknown hand.

128

and Prowess of those that escaped the Carnage in the first attempt of the Savages. That the Settlement by the Heavy Losses of Men & nearly all their property were reduced to Distress, great Numbers of Widows and Orphan Children were Left almost destitute of the Necessaries of Life & the families of about two Hundred Officers & Soldiers then in the Federal Army became almost helpless, and needy beyond discription, but were assisted by the then returned Inhabitants and releived by the Activity of that Country alone.

That the State of Pensylvania taking advantage of the debiltatated scituation of that Settlement and also by their agents haveing by meer Accident possessed themselves of the Indian Deed to the Purchasers and many other Important Papers Evidential of the Tittle of this State to the Lands aforesaid [2] Applyed to the Honourable the Congress of the United States for the Constituteing a federal Court for the Settlement of the Jurisdiction of the Country afores^d claimed by them In virtue of the grant to William Penn Esqr in the Year of Our Lord 1680, Eighteen Years after the Confirmation of the same Territory to this State by the Charter of King Charles the 2nd in the Year 1662.

That upon Notice of such Application it was Objected on the part of this State that part of the Deeds Evidences & papers necessary to be Used upon a Question of Tittle were then in great Brittain & Could not at that time be Obtained, the Warr preventing. that the State of Pensylvania Still Insisted upon a tryal said Objections Notwithstanding, at the same time s^d Agents Secretly held the very Papers and Evidence (we wanted) in their Hands, the same haveing been sent from Great Brittain in the year 1776 and falling into their Hands were by them most Injuriously kept from the Knowledge of this State and her Agents. And that the State of Pennsylvania had address sufficient to Induce the Honourable Congress to Compel this State to a tryal the aforesaid Objection Notwithstanding.

That Two of the Judges Named in the Commission to try the Question of Jurisdiction between this State and the State of Pennsylvania (and Particularly relyed upon by this State) by means of Sickness did not attend the tryal [3] and that a Decre Did

[2] It was a persistent belief among partisans of the Susquehannah Company that documents needed for Connecticut's case at Trenton had been returned from England and had fallen into the hands of James Wilson. The origin of this story can be traced to hearsay evidence passed on by Zebulon Butler; Vol. VII, no. 160.

[3] Thomas Nelson and Joseph Jones, both from Virginia; see *ibid.*, Introduction.

pass in the Month of Dece^r 1782 in favour of the State of Pennsylvania and Against this State by the Opinion of three Judges & against the Opinion of the other two Judges,[4] that in consequence thereof the Jurisdiction of the Country aforesaid fell to the State of Pennsylvania Whereupon the Settlers unable to Sustain the Expence of a Federal Court to Try the Right of Soil under their Purchase from the Indians and the grants from this State Solicited the Protection of their Persons & Confirmation of their Lands by the Legislature of s^d State of Pensylvania but were Amused with pretences of Justice untill that State had Established an Armed force in that Country under pretence of a Threatened Invasion from the Savages & then became Deaf to the Just claims of the Inhabitants and by their officers Civil & Milliterry there Established undertook and actually did Miserably Oppress abuse & Injure the s^d Inhabitants and at last by Fraud and Delusion disarmed them and then Drove all discription of Persons out of the Country That claimed Lands under this State. Roused at the affront offered to the Innocent Inhabitants many of their friends in this State and others Induced by their Pitiable scituation Joined[?] the Emigrants from the Contested Country and Return^d and after many sevear encounters Established themselves and in their turn drove the Adhearants of Pennsylvania therefrom since which time they have remained in peace and quiet, untill of Late the State of Pennsylvania in persuance of her former System hath Erected a New County in that Quarter of the Country [5] and passed an Act [6] pretending to quiet the Settlers upon report of Certain Commissioners Named in said Act different from what they have heretofore pretended they had any Authority to do, all the Lands haveing been Once granted by that State agreable to the Laws thereof and as they have said Veste[d] a tittle in the first Purchasers [7] and no Act or aftergrant Can Vest any Person or persons with a Legal Tittle to the same Lands which act by the Terms of it Excludes three fourths of the present settlers from any benefit and by that means they are Indeavouring to draw the Unwary under the Net of the Laws of that State & thereby have it in their power to dispossess all the afores^d Settlers by Writs

---

[4] Although the Trenton decree was announced a unanimous one, the belief persisted among some that two of the judges had really favored Connecticut and had been pressured into agreeing to a unanimous decision. The story first appeared in 1785 in an anonymous review of the trial in the *Connecticut Courant;* Vol. VIII, no. 94, note 17.

[5] September 25, 1786.   [6] Confirming Act, March 28, 1787.

[7] The reference is to the statement made by the commissioners sent to Wyoming in 1783; *ibid.*, VII, no. 149.

of Ejectments as soon as their government shall be sufficiently Established therein to denominate any opposition to that Government a Species of Rebellion and at One Stroke root out the whole of those Settlers.

That the Memoralists have suffered Every species of Cruelty in the power of Mortals to Conceive and have now no alternative but the Sword trusting the Event to Providence unless by the Intervention of this Honourable Assembly.

Whereupon the Memoralists humbly beg Leave to Suppose they are now able to prove beyond Contradiction that the aforesaid Deed and Evidences of Tittle were as truly in the Hands of the Agents of s^d State of Pennsylvania before that State Made their application to the Honourable the Congress of these States for the Establishment of s^d Federal Court and that they [8] Sicreted them untill after the afores^d Decree & now have them in their Power & Custody which was One very Influential Means of the failure on the Part of this State. whereby the Memorialists are subjected to a Thousand inconceivable distresses and their all Hazarded after the Important strugle to which they have Chearfully bourn their part.

The Memoralists beg Leave further to Observe that the Insult offered to the dignity of this State by the Agents of said State of Pennsylvania; will sufficiently Excite that Manly resentment Necessary to the Political Existance of Every sovereign State and Influence this Honourable assembly, to request Congress to direct a Revision of the afores^d Question of Jurisdiction and not tamely Submit to the Indignity so flagrantly manifest in A Sister State and in a Point that Involves the Interest of so many Individuals as well as the Honour and Dignity of this State or in some other way grant releife to the Memoralists.

That Means for Supporting the proposed Application and a Consequent tryal may be suggested Independant [from] any of the appropriation made by this State and without any New Tax and in a way Honourable and Safe to this State. And the Memoralists as in duty bound will ever Pray. Dated at Hartford the 10th day of May 1787

John Franklin [9]

Endorsed: John Franklin Memorial May 1787   Bill p 1 H N u H [10]

---

[8] The following words are here lined out: "held them in their own Hands without any Right thereto untill Long after s^d Decree."

[9] The signature is not Franklin's.

[10] For the action taken by the two houses, see no. 76, *post*.

131

[76] Commission of John Franklin.[1]

Whereas the Court of Commissioners for the Susquehannah company, at their meeting in Hartford [2] on the 14ᵗʰ day of May A D 1787, made the following Order viz "Ordered that Col° John Franklin be and he is hereby appointed an Agent on the part of the Susquehannah Company, for the purpose of prosecuting before the Congress of the United States, the petition of the settlers owners and claimers under said Company, for the establishing to said petitioners their private right of soil and property to the lands granted to said company by the late Colony of Connecticut; [3] and that said Colonel John Franklin have the power of substituting any person under him for the purposes aforesaid, and of transacting any other business for the benefit of said Company as he may judge necessary, and the Secretary of this Court is directed to grant to said Colº John Franklin a Commission for the purposes aforesaid," I do therefore in consequence of the powers vested in me by the order above recited, hereby authorize constitute and appoint, you the said Colº John Franklin to be the lawful Agent on the part of the Susquehannah Company for the purpose of appearing before the Congress of the United States, and prosecuting the petition referred to in the aforesaid order, and also to substitute any person under you for the purpose aforesaid and you are also hereby fully authorized to transact any business for the benefit of said Company as you may judge necessary. And I do hereby in behalf of the Susquehannah Company consent, agree, & determine that whatever you may legally do in the premisses shall be binding and conclusive to all concerned. In witness

---

[76] [1] P. H. M. C., Div. of Arch. and MSS., John Franklin Papers, in Barlow's hand. The list of notes is in Franklin's hand and obviously was intended to outline an argument on the validity of the Susquehannah Company's claim.

[2] Earlier the commissioners had met in the Wyoming settlement; no. 68, *ante.* Apparently the system was very flexible; only three commissioners out of twenty-one plus a secretary were sufficient to do all business except settle disputes among actual settlers. For disputes, the required quorum was five.

[3] The petition referred to may be that of November 11, 1783 (Vol. VII, no. 187), which was the basis for earlier efforts to obtain from Congress a trial to determine the private right of soil. No such later petition has been found. It would not have been that of September 22, 1785 (Vol. VIII, no. 156).

whereof I have hereunto set my hand & seal at Hartford this 17ᵗʰ day of May A D 1787

Joel Barlow Sec'y [4]

Bidwell to Griffin
Coppy of Griffins [5]
Commissioners
Bayard and others [6]
Gov Wolcotts opinion [7]
Lett from J Armstrong [8]
H Antis
Presdᵗ Reed to Colᵒ Butler [9]
from Govʳ Griswold [10]
L from B Franklin [11]
& l fr Comᵗᵉᵉ of Landholders [12]
    March 8 1785

[77] Resolutions, Remonstrance, and Circular Letter from the Town of Easton.[1]

Easton, Northampton County, May 21, 1787.

Inclosed are handed you for publication, the proceedings of a township meeting of the inhabitants of the town and township of Easton, on the subject of the late act of assembly, confirming to the people called Connecticut Claimants, their possessions in

---

[4] Barlow was himself a commissioner, appointed with others on December 27, 1786; Vol. VIII, no. 268.

[5] No letter of Barnabas Bidwell to Cyrus Griffin has been found, but he wrote in 1796 regarding the meaning of the Trenton trial decision. Griffin's answer, specifying that private rights of soil were a separate matter and not ruled upon in the decision, was printed in a broadside; M. H. S., Pickering Papers, LVIII, 350. Obviously, then, Franklin made his notes long after the date of his commission.

[6] Franklin here was referring to the commission sent by the Pennsylvania General Assembly to Wyoming in May, 1785. For the exchange of letters between the commission and the settlers see Vol. VIII, nos. 120-26 and 128.

[7] Probably Vol. I, no. 30.

[8] Probably Vol. VII, no. 42.

[9] Probably Vol. VIII, no. 92.

[10] Probably Vol. VIII, no. 222.

[11] Not identified.

[12] This letter from John Armstrong, Jr., whether sent to Sheriff Henry Antes or someone else, has not been identified.

[77] [1] *Pennsylvania Packet,* June 9, 1787. See no. 83, *post.*

the county of Luzerne [2]—together with a copy of the remonstrance agreed to be presented to the honorable the supreme executive council, and of the circular letter of the committee chosen at said meeting.

Several townships of this county have adopted the resolutions entered into at Easton; and as a part of the duty of the committee is to notify their fellow-citizens of the danger of so alarming a measure, they have thought it necessary to publish the inclosures, that the circulation of their opinions may be the more extensive.

At a meeting of the inhabitants of the town and township of Easton, in the county of Northampton, on the 7th of May, 1787, to take into consideration an act of the Assembly, passed on the 27th March, 1787, relative to the lands which are thereby taken from the original owners of them, and given to the claimants from Connecticut.

Doctor Andrew Ledlie [3] was placed in the chair, and the following resolutions unanimously agreed to:

RESOLVED,

1. That the great end of all government is to secure the citizens of the state in the inviolable possession of their inherent rights and privileges of freemen, and particularly of their lives, liberties, and property.

2. That the invaluable constitution of the state has made effectual provision for these, in the assurance which it gives, that no citizen shall be deprived of them but by a fair and impartial trial in open court, before a respectable jury of the vicinity.

3. That the act of Assembly passed the 27th of March last, depriving a great number of the citizens of their property in the county of Luzerne, without a trial by jury, is a direct and dangerous infringement of the constitution.

4. That the hasty manner of erecting the said law, was as unconstitutional as the matter of it, inasmuch as it was enacted within a week after the publication of the bill for consideration, and in the same session of the Assembly, before the persons whose property was affected by it, could possibly have any notice of so unusual an intention in the legislature, or any opportunity to consult together, and to express their sentiments concerning the general tendency of so alarming a measure, or the probable operation of so dangerous a precedent. This hasty proceeding, which de-

---

[2] No. 38, ante.

[3] Ledlie was a Pennsylvania land claimant; see Vol. IV, Index.

prives a number of citizens of their justly acquired property, without their consent, without law, or even without the form of a trial, is considered by us as a direct violation of our constitution; which has provided, that no bill shall be passed into a law, until it has been published for consideration at one session of the Assembly, and lain over to the next, excepting in cases of sudden necessity; which necessity certainly cannot be said to exist with respect to the disturbances at Wyoming, which have subsisted for more than seventeen years past.

5. That the compensation in the unlocated lands of the state proposed to the citizens, whose property the Assembly has secretly, hastily, and violently taken from them, is merely nominal, inadequate, and delusory, and such, as it is more than probable, not a single member of the house, who promoted the oppressive law, would be willing to take in exchange for his own property.

6. That had the compensation proposed, been more adequate than it is, yet it does not suit the circumstances of many of the injured citizens, to range through the woods in quest of lands that would be worth their acceptance from the state, or to employ men to do it for them. And the inexpressible distress to which this law has reduced others of them, has rendered all prospect of any compensation in the mode proposed by the law, absolutely impracticable, so that the oppressed citizens have just reason to complain of the wanton cruelty of the Assembly, in obliging them to sit down and mourn over their property, lost for ever, if the law should continue, without any other hope of compensation.

7. That the promoters of this law, were greatly deficient in their guardianship of the rights and property of their constituents, in offering to the plundered citizens, the vacant and unsettled lands of the state as a compensation, which they had no authority to bestow, because every citizen has a joint right in them, as a common fund for lessening the expences of government, and the taxes of the state, and their constituents have given them no authority to bestow their common property upon one class of citizens, to make way for a much more valuable present to a lawless banditti, who have intruded themselves into the state, in defiance of government and justice, and have held the property of its peaceable citizens by force of arms, murder, and violence, for more than seventeen years past.

8. That the citizens of this state, who pay such heavy taxes for the support of government, and have honestly bought and paid for their lands in the county of Luzerne, had a right to expect a legal protection in the quiet possession of their property, against

all invasion whatsoever; and it must be a species of oppression unknown in any free government, for our Assembly not only to withhold that protection, but also to take our property in a hasty and unconstitutional manner, and bestow it on the very invader.

9. That it is the duty of all the citizens of this Commonwealth, to unite together as one man, to oppose the execution of such an unconstitutional and oppressive law, which, from its dangerous precedent, sets all our property afloat, and renders every citizen insecure in his possessions, because a silent acquiescence in the execution, would be a virtual surrender of all their property into the hands of any assembly, which may be hardy enough to seize upon it, either for their own emolument, or the gratification of their friends.

10. That the attempt of Great Britain to subjugate America, and reduce the property of its inhabitants to their absolute disposal in parliament, was not a more outrageous violation of the rights of freemen, than the law in question; and if America was justifiable in resisting unto blood, the citizens of this state are bound by their mutual relation to each other, and their sacred regard to the rights and privileges of freemen to circulate among themselves, and present decent but spirited remonstrances against the oppression of such a law, and try every gentle and legal method of procuring the repeal of it, before they proceed to extremities in the defence of their common freedom.

11. That the promoters of this unconstitutional and oppressive law, have by this outrageous attempt upon the property of the good citizens of Pennsylvania, forfeited all right in the confidence of their fellow citizens, and deserve to be noted as tyrants who would enslave them, whenever they had an opportunity, and therefore, should be no further intrusted with any office, whether civil, military, or judicial, in the state of Pennsylvania.

12. That copies of these resolutions be speedily circulated through the different counties of the state, attended with circular letters, requesting the freemen of the Commonwealth, to express their sentiments upon the alarming measure lately adopted by our legislature, in decent, but decided, and spirited terms, and to transmit the same in proper and becoming addresses to council, to suspend the execution of the tyrannical law, until the next meeting of the Assembly for its total abrogation.

13. That until these remonstrances be answered to the satisfaction and relief of the injured citizens, that is, until protection is furnished by government, to all the people without exception, it

is the duty of the people to withhold the payment of those taxes, which are levied for the support of that government.

14. That David Waggoner, Henry Althouse, sen. and John Townes, be a committee for carrying the foregoing resolutions into effect, for corresponding with the other townships, and for drawing up instructions to the members in Assembly from Northampton county, expressive of the sense of the people.

ANDREW LEDLIE, Chairman.

To his Excellency the President and the honorable the Supreme Executive Council of the Commonwealth of Pennsylvania, The Remonstrance of the Subscribers, Inhabitants of the Town and Township of Easton, in the County of Northampton, Respectfully Sheweth,

THAT your remonstrants have seen, with the most lively apprehension, a very alarming attack made on the constitutional and sacred rights of the citizens of this commonwealth, by an act which was hurried through a few days of the late sessions of assembly, and passed the house on the 27th day of March, confirming to the people called Connecticut Claimants their possessions in the county of Luzerne, thereby depriving a number of good and faithful citizens of a property honestly acquired and amply paid for, without allowing them the smallest opportunity of being heard, either by their constitutional judges, a jury of the vicinage, or by any other jurisdiction whatever. And your remonstrants find, with the deepest concern, that a stretch of authority so arbitrary and excessive, is not even palliated by an offer of recompence to the injured, in any degree adequate to the injury.

That bearing in remembrance those principles which began and conducted these states successfully through the late glorious revolution, and conceiving it to be their indispensible duty as good citizens of this commonwealth, to express their indignation at an act as despotic as any which were the then objects of complaint and opposition. Your remonstrants have held a township meeting, to declare in a constitutional manner, their sentiments on the occasion. The proceedings and resolutions of this meeting are herewith transmitted to your honorable board.

It remains that we beg, in conformity with the spirit of the said resolutions, that your excellency and your honors will exercise the powers with which the constitution has invested you for valuable purposes, and which are the necessary appendages of

137

the executive authority of every government, by convening the legislature at as early a day as possible, for the reconsideration of the obnoxious act, and in the mean time suspend any further proceedings under the same. So salutary a measure, if timely adopted, your remonstrants have the warmest hopes will tend to quiet apprehensions which have been justly excited, and to renew that confidence which ought ever to subsist between the people and their representatives.

(Circular)

Gentlemen

WE take the liberty to inclose you the proceedings and resolutions of a meeting of the inhabitants of the town and township of Easton, assembled to take into consideration the late very unconstitutional act of the legislature with respect to lands in the county of Luzerne, the property of a number of our countrymen, which has been violently wrested from them and confirmed to the people called Connecticut Claimants. As one of the principal ends of government is the protection of property, and as this protection is expressly stipulated by our constitution, the inhabitants of this town have conceived themselves obliged to declare their sentiments on so daring an infringement of the sacred rights of the people of Pennsylvania—and also to warn their fellow-citizens of the impending danger.

The conduct of the assembly is universally interesting, the crisis is important, and no time should be lost in forming such firm and spirited resolutions as will prevent the loss of those invaluable privileges which we have so recently fought and bled for, and which are now encroached upon by our own representatives. The subscribers have been appointed a committee to correspond with the other townships of this county on the subject, in pursuance of their appointment, forward you the inclosed for your consideration.

We make no doubt, gentlemen, of your entire concurrence to our proceedings—and have the firmest confidence that the township of   will not be late in adopting measures evidently calculated for the general benefit of the commonwealth. We have the honor to be, with the most perfect esteem, Gentlemen, Your friends and fellow-citizens

To the inhabitants of the township of

[78] Remonstrance of Luzerne Inhabitants against Joseph Montgomery.[1]

His Excellencey the President, The Honourable the Supreme Executive Council of the Commonwealth of Pennsylvania. The remonstrance and Petition of the Inhabitants of the County of Luzerne: Humbly Sheweth:

That whereas the Honourable the General Assembly of this State by an Act, passed the 28th day of March appointed Joseph Montgomery Esq. one of the Commissioners for the purpose of enquiring into and ascertaining the claims of the Connecticut settlers in this County, and confirming the same to the said settlers according to the late Law in that case made and provided. And whereas we your petitioners consider our all as depending upon the decision of three Commissioners, we humbly conceive that a matter of such importance, demands that it be determined, by, not only men of knowledge and wisdom; but by unexceptionable Characters. Your petitioners therefore beg leave to remonstrate against the aforesaid Joseph Montgomery Esquire for the several manifestations of prejudice & Usurpation hereinafter mentioned.

That the partial proceedings of the board of Commissioners in this county in April 1783, (of which board the said J. Montgomery was then chairman) are too obvious not to be discerned by the meanest capacity.[2] That notwithstanding the Commissioners were instructed to pursue every just measure to bring about a reasonable compromise between the settlers & those claiming in opposition, and most solemnly pledged their own honour and the faith of the state, that an act should be past extending the advantages of civil government to the settlers authorizing & directing the choice of Justices of the peace &c. Yet, in violation of the trust reposed in them, and the sacred promise they had made to your petitioners, no reasonable compromise was proposed, but pledges were demanded for our good behaviour, and a total relinquishment of all claims to our lands, that we

---

[78] [1] M. H. S., Pickering Papers, LVII, 227-28, a copy in Pickering's hand. The probable date of this remonstrance is in May before the 28th, when the commissioners were to hold their first meeting.

[2] The exchange of letters in 1783 between the commissioners and representatives of the Wyoming settlers and of the Pennsylvania claimants is given in *Susquehannah Company Papers,* VII, nos. 147-54.

139

might thereby be entitled to the privileges of taking leases of our own improved lands for the term of one year, and that the said Montgomery averred to your petitioners that these offers were generous. That he the said Montgomery being afterwards appointed one of a Committee to make report on the report [3] of the aforesaid Commissioners reported [4] that he was fully satisfied with the laudable zeal & industry of said Commissioners & the generous offers they had made to the settlers at Wyoming. That altho' the General Assembly of this state resolved that after the afores[d] Com[rs] sh[d] make report to the Assembly an Act sh[d] be passed particularly directing the choice of Justices of the Peace, yet, in direct violation of the said resolve, the election of Justices was holden the 23[d] day of April 1783, by the direction of the Com[rs] previous to the report's being made,[5] & the inhabitants of this settlement were not notified of this election being composed principally of those that belonged out of the county, excepting a few who lived out of the state. That the partial proceedings of the aforesaid Joseph Montgomery, towards the settlers of Wyoming ought in the humble opinion of y[r] petitioners to be considered as a sufficient bar to his acting in the official character of a comm[r] in matters of such importance as they are appointed to decide.

We therefore pray the honourable Council to take the matter into your wise consideration & that the afores[d] Joseph Montgomery may not be permitted to act in the capacity of a Commissioner,[6] but that a new appointment may be of one from whose wisdom impartiality & integrity we may hope for a righteous petition. And y[r] petitioners as in duty bound will ever pray

[79] Timothy Pickering to Samuel Hodgdon.[1]

Wilkesbury May 29, 1787.

Dear Sir

It gives me pleasure to inform you That we have opened & held the first courts here this day in perfect tranquility.[2] Frank-

[3] *Ibid.*, no. 167.

[4] *Ibid.*, no. 168.

[5] See *ibid.*, no. 170, note 3.

[6] Montgomery's letter of resignation was accepted by the Council on May 31, 1787; *Pa. C. R.*, XV, 221.

[79] [1] M. H. S., Pickering Papers, LVII, 224, in Pickering's hand.

[2] On May 29, four attorneys were admitted to practice in Luzerne County courts; *ibid.*, 223.

lin is not in the Settlement.³ More lies have been told in my absence. the capital one was, That the People of Pennsylvania were generally dissatisfied with the law for confirming the Connecticut titles, & that it would be repealed. And this, it was said, prevented the coming of the Commissioners; for we did not arrive here till *near sunset* on the 28th, the *day appointed* for our meeting. And the people began to be alarmed. Our appearance however, has exposed these lies. I forgot to mention my having drawn on you for £20, in favour of Mʳ Erwin, who brought up my salt from Middletown when I was last here. He was to present the order in June when he shᵈ go to Philᵃ. Mʳ Rea may pay it out of such monies as will be in his hands. I wish you could get a market for our wines, or a good part of them, to relieve us in respect to money. Besides other considerations, I am satisfactorily informed of valuable unlocated lands in situations to be desired. I hope every thing in your last Journy corresponded with your wishes; and remain Affectionately yours

T. Pickering

[80] Resolution of the Connecticut General Assembly on the Petition of John Franklin.¹

(May 1787)

Upon the Memorial of John Franklin Esqʳ of Wyoming & others,² Inhabitants settled upon the Waters of the Rivers Susquehannah & Delaware under the Authority of this State

Shewing to this Assembly that at great hazard and Expence they purchased the native Right & planted themselves in the Country aforesᵈ under the tittle of this State, then & Still supposing the same fairly Included in the grant of King Charles the second to the then Colony of Connecticut, that they are materialy affected by the decree of the Federal Court Held at Trenton in the Months of November & December 1782 & that they have never been heard relative to their private right to the Lands by them settled, and that the Indian Deed under which they Claimed & other Material Evidences and Papers relative to the tittle of this State by Accident Came into the Hands of the Agents on the part of Pennsylvania antecedent to the aforesaid tryal and were by said Agents Injuriously suppressed & are Still holden by

---

³ Franklin was absent in Hartford appealing to the General Assembly and meeting with the commissioners of the Susquehannah Company.

[80] ¹ C. S. L., Susquehannah Settlers, I, 175a-d.

² No. 75, *ante.*

them or others Interested in the Lands in contest, and that they are lyable to be dispossessed of their Lands & Expeld the aforesaid Country under Colour of said decree of s^d Federal Court, praying for the Interposition of this State.

Resolved by this Assembly that the Aforesaid territory of Country is fairly included in the grants & Pattent to the Govenor and Company of this State then Colony [3] And that the said Settlers planted themselves in the aforesaid Country by the approbation of this State and Excercised Jurisdiction therein under the Authority of the Same and that Material Deeds Evidences and papers relative to the Tittle and Jurisdiction of the aforesaid Territory of Country were Injuriously suppressed and are Still detained by the Agents of Pennsylvania and that the same is a substantial ground for the seting aside and anuling said Decree, and that the Honour and dignity as well as Interest of this State is highly Concerned that due exertions be made [4] to accomidate the Contest between this State and the Common Wealth of Pennsylvania and the Claimants of private property in the aforesaid Country by an application to the Honourable the Congress of these United States or by [5] a private accomidations between the Contending States & private Claimants.

It is further resolved by this Assembly that the hon^{ble} William Samuel Johnson Roger Sherman & Oliver Elsworth Esquires or either two of them be and they are hereby fully authorised and Impowerd in behalf of this State and at the Request & Expence of the Stettlers under the Connecticut Claim to propose Terms of Accomidation to the Common Wealth of Pennsylvania relative to the Jurisdiction of s^d Country & of and Concerning the private right of Individuals & provided said Common Wealth grant a sure and permanent Tittle to a Certain Tract or Territory of Country upon the Easterly Branch of the River Susquehannah and that Branch of the Delaware Cald Lacawaxen [6] to the Settlers thereon sufficient to Cover their settlements & Locations & reasonably to accomidate s^d Settlers then the said William Saml Johnson Roger Sherman & Oliver Elsworth or any two of them

---

[3] In asserting that the Susquehannah Purchase was within the charter bounds of Connecticut, the General Assembly, of course, was rejecting the gentlemen's agreement reached with Pennsylvania a year earlier that the Trenton decree would be considered binding by Connecticut; see Vol. VIII, Introduction, pp. xxxiii-xxxiv.

[4] The following phrase is lined out: "on the Part of this State."

[5] The following phrase is lined out: "other more Eligible Measures."

[6] Members of the Delaware Company were to be included; for this company see Vol. I, Index.

be and they are hereby fully authorised on the part of this State & Such Settlers to release to the Common Wealth of Pennsylvania all other and further Claim of Jurisdiction and property to the Lands & Country in Contest between this State and the Common Wealth afores^d. And the said William Samuel Johnson Roger Sherman & Oliver Ellsworth be and they are hereby directed to act for and receive the s^d Indian Deed and other Documents Evidences & papers of any Person or persons that may be possessed thereof and the same transmit to & Lodge with the Secretary of this State, and that the further Consideration of said Memorial be refered to the Consideration of the General Assembly to be holden at New haven on the Second Thursday of Oct Next.
passed in the lower House

Test James Davenport Clerk.   Dissented to in the upper House
Test George Wyllys Secret^y

In the lower house the farther Consideration of the Memorial is on Reconsideration referd to the General Assembly to be holden in Oct next.   Jed Huntington Clerk

Dissented to in the upper House.^{7} Test George Wyllys Secret^y

[81] Jeremiah Wadsworth to Timothy Pickering.^{1}

Hartford June 10 1787
Dear Sir
Your letter ^{2} came here after Franklin had been recved before our Assembly, and part of his request granted in the lower House, but all was Negatived in the upper and his whole Scheme is fallen to the ground.   I am persuaded You will never be in-

---

^{7} This rejection by the upper house of the extreme claims of the Susquehannah Company was consistent with its earlier action of October, 1784, when that house apparently made a distinction between actual settlers in Wyoming and mere proprietors of the Company; see Vol. VIII, Introduction, note 66. The action of the upper house, of course, ended consideration of Franklin's petition. According to Stephen Mix Mitchell, "Mr Franklin & his freinds exerted every Nerve with their petition ...."; Mitchell to William Samuel Johnson, July 26, 1787; C. H. S., William Samuel Johnson Papers, II, 124.
[81] ^{1} M. H. S., Pickering Papers, LVII, 229, in Wadsworth's hand.
^{2} Not found.

terupted by our legislature.[3] Your correspondence with me on the Subject must be kept to your selfe but you may Always Assert any of the facts. I write you and pledge your selfe for their proof, which I will furnish in case of need. I am d' Sir Your very h[b] S[t]

Jere Wadsworth

[82] Samuel Hodgdon to Timothy Pickering.[1]

Philadelphia 10th June 1787

Dear Sir

Though we every Moment expect your arrival, yet as an Opportunity presents we cannot satisfy ourselves without making a communication supposing it possible that you may be detained. In the first place then know that the family are all in perfect health, and as happy as they can be in your absence. And with respect to business, nothing either Public or Private, has turned up very particular since you left us. On the affairs of Wioming I shall be silent, what is doing you will best learn from the enclosed Paper,[2] and these doings you will readily believe take their rise in this City. every art is trying to embroil affresh this happily terminated dispute, reports are circulating with malicious intent, but as far as I can learn no One is injured by them. it has been my business to detect and expose some of them. Nothing transpires from the general Convention but much is expected from their deliberations—much I am sure is Necessary. All friends desire a kind rememberance. With Affectionate regards I am sir, Your Most Obedient servant

Sam Hodgdon

[83] Extract from the Minutes of the Pennsylvania Council.[1]

Philadelphia, Wednesday, June 13th, 1787.
Council took into consideration a paper signed Andrew Led-

---

[3] Wadsworth means that the legislature will not support the extravagant claims of the Susquehannah Company. These claims interfered with Pickering's aim to carry out the Confirming Act, which, of course, applied only to those who had settled before the Trenton decree.

[82] [1] M. H. S., Pickering Papers, LVII, 231.

[2] Hodgdon is probably referring to no. 77, *ante,* which appeared in the *Pennsylvania Packet* on June 9, 1787.

[83] [1] *Pa. C. R.,* XV, 224-25.

lie, Chairman, containing divers resolutions of the inhabitants of Easton, in Northampton county, at a town meeting lately held in that place,[2] respecting the late act of General Assembly, passed on the twenty-eighth day of March last, for confirming to the people called Connecticut claimants the lands by them claimed in the county of Luzerne; and thereupon,

Ordered, That the Honorable the Judges of the Supreme Court and the Attorney General be requested to hold a conference with Council, upon the subject of the said resolutions, at five o'clock this afternoon, at the President's House. * * *

The Honorable the Judges of the Supreme Court and the Attorney General attended, agreeable to notice given them this morning, and a conference was had upon the subject of the late resolutions of some inhabitants of Easton, signed Andrew Ledlie, Chairman.

Council resumed the consideration of the remonstrance of certain persons stiling themselves inhabitants of the town and township of Easton, in the county of Northampton, and certain resolutions signed Andrew Ledlie, Chairman, transmitted with the said remonstrance; and being of opinion that the said resolutions have a tendency to incite the good people of this State to desist the government thereof, and are of criminal and seditious nature,

Resolved, That the said remonstrance and resolutions be transmitted to the Attorney General, and that he be directed to commence a prosecution against such persons as shall be found to be principally active in framing and circulating the said seditious resolutions, and to take proper measures for bringing the said persons to trial.

[84] Letter from Northampton County.[1]

Extract of a letter from Northampton County, June 18.

"I received your favour of the 13th instant, and observe by the papers, that the petition and resolves of this and some other townships in this county have been published.[2] We did expect that the advocates for the Luzerne law [3] will be very industrious

[2] No. 77, *ante.*
[84] [1] *Pennsylvania Packet,* June 29, 1787.
[2] No. 77, *ante.*
[3] No. 38, *ante.*

to torture some expressions in the resolutions to the disadvantage of the subscribers; for it is an old and true remark, that he who is so wicked as to injure his neighbour or friend without cause, cannot after be at peace with him, even though the injured should require no concession: But our assurance rests in the justice of our cause. We have not a doubt but that there does yet remain public virtue in the councils of this state, and spirit and honesty in our fellow citizens, to set all things to right. When the people at large are informed of any sufferings for the laws of Pennsylvania, the eyes of all the brave, the just and good, will point to essential and speedy redress. It cannot be that a number of honest peaceable citizens, attached to the laws and customs of the state, will be expelled from their fair fields, purchased and held under the faith of government, to make room for a banditti, composed of the dregs of all nations, and for many years disowned by all. Such a band of unprincipled ingrates cannot be suffered to possess the well-earned property of those who lost their all in support of the government of Pennsylvania. Is the murder of Capt. Ogden already forgot?[4] Was the Luzerne law designed as a repository for the remains of Jesse Lukens?[5] Was it necessary to stop the courts of justice, and by a summary law, or a smuggled act, at once put an end to all open enquiry, or trial by jury? We see the design of this act, and the fatal consequences that may arise from its operation. Should it be carried into effect, whose property is safe, whose title secure? Can any reliance be had on the standing laws of the land, or the constitution we live under? I learn that General Muhlenberg and Mr. Montgomery have resigned[6] the invidious talk of granting away, without judge or jury, our property at Wyoming, to the motley groupe; these they have by this refusal given farther proof of their integrity, hitherto so well known. In a few words, think as you will at Philadelphia, it appears to me, that the Luzerne act, and all the evils it contains, will fail together, as soon as the legislature meet. It is too base and partial to remain on the records of Pennsylvania."

[4] Ogden was killed in January, 1771; see Vol. IV, Introduction, pp. xiv-xv.

[5] Lukens was killed in Plunket's Expedition in December, 1755; Vol. VI, 426.

[6] Peter Muhlenberg and Joseph Montgomery; see no. 38, *ante*, note 2.

[85] Timothy Pickering to Benjamin Franklin.[1]

Philad. June 25th, 1787.
Sir,

The Justices of the Peace for the County of Luzerne are destitute of the laws of the State. It seems that heretofore Justices of the Peace have been furnished with the laws at the expence of the State, the Justices of Luzerne have expressed their hopes that they may be supplied in the same way, and requested me to make the application in their behalf. I beg leave to express my hopes also, that they may be so furnished; otherwise I fear they will, for the most part, remain unprovided, & the laws unexecuted. At the same time it is proper that I should add, that there was manifested a general disposition to conform to the laws, with great punctuality and many were solicitously enquiring what were the laws in particular cases, that they might not transgress them. I have the honor to be, Sir, your Excellency's most obedt. servant,

T. Pickering.

[86] John Franklin to Caleb Benton.[1]

These may Certify that William Patterson has Liberty to Repair to the town of Hamelton[2] and tack up one hundred accers of Land in S⁴ Town agreebly to the Regalations of the Setlers therof and to have the Saime Confirmed to him on the Saime Conditions as others Setlers of S⁴ Town Or otherwise if he Shall not be Satisfied to tack his Right in S⁴ Town of Hamⁿ he has Liberty to Loacate and Survey tow hundred acres on aney of the unlocated Lands in the Susquehanⁿ Purchass agreeably to a Resolve of the Susquehanah Companey of the 26ᵗʰ of December Last[3] to be Granted to him as a Setler Provided he Shall Setle and Conform himself as the Resolves of the Companey in that Case Dericts. Given under my hand at Athens

[85] [1] *P. A.,* XI, 159.
[86] [1] M. H. S., Pickering Papers, LVII, 232, a copy furnished by M. Hollenback, according to an endorsement in Pickering's hand.
  [2] For Hamilton, see no. 119, *post.*
  [3] *Susquehannah Company Papers,* VIII, no. 268.

John Franklin Commissioner
June 26ᵗʰ 1787 To Dotʳ Benton [4] or To Whome it may Concern

[87] Extract from the Minutes of the Pennsylvania Council.[1]

Philadelphia, Friday, June 29th, 1787.
The memorial [2] of sundry Pennsylvania claimants of land in Luzerne county, praying Council to direct the officers of the Land Office to receive no more locations of land in the counties of Northampton and Luzerne, untill the General Assembly shall meet and make order respecting them, was read, and an order taken that the same be laid before the General Assembly at their next meeting.[3]

[88] Wyoming Commissioners to Benjamin Franklin.[1]

Philadelphia June 29, 1787.
Sir,
As the examination of the Connecticut Claims to lands in the county of Luzerne will be of several months continuance, and we may not return hither until the business shall be accomplished, we are desirous of receiving some part of our pay in advance; and if this shall be thought proper by Council, we request such grants may be made to us and Mʳ Evans (whom we have appointed our Clerk) as Council shall judge expedient.
The law for confirming the lands of the Connecticut Claimants required that it should be published in the News-papers of Connecticut: But there are divers claimants under Connecticut, who live in the State of New-York; and other claimants under Pennsylvania who live in New-Jersey: We submit to the consideration of Council, whether it is not expedient to cause the

---

[4] See no. 119, *post.*
[87] [1] *Pa. C. R.,* XV, 235.
[2] Not found.
[3] In the fall the General Assembly received a number of petitions for and against the Confirming Act, as well as petitions for better compensating Pennsylvania claimants.
[88] [1] L. C., Pennsylvania Miscellaneous Papers, XI, in Pickering's hand but signed by each of the three men.

law to be published in one of the news-papers of each of those States. It may supersede applications which may hereafter be made for allowing further time to make their claims, under pretence that they were not informed of the law. We are respectfully, Sir, y^r most h^{ble} Servants

T. Pickering
Dan Hiester [2]   }   Commissioners
Stephen Balliet [3]

Endorsed: Read in Council July 3^d 1787 and an order drawn for £150.0.0 in part of their pay & for purchasing Stationary &c.

[89] Obadiah Gore and Mathias Hollenback to Timothy Pickering.[1]

Tioga Point July 3^d 1787

Dear S^r

These are to Inform of a Certain Character now with us and to Get your advice and assistance in the affair. one Jn° J Acmoder as he calls himself has been Exceedingly Officious in Endeavouring to Sour the minds of the people in these parts against the Law takeing place. he has threatned those who was forward in holding the Election for Justices with being Drove from their Settlement or they Should Shortly be in hell. Others again with yokeing together & Sending out of this Settlement that if he had been here at the time of the Election he would be Damnd it had Gone on or he would have Died in the Cause of opposition. these and many Other matters we Can make appear and that Mr Thos Wigton will Testify that he heard AcModer Say both at his house and at the Point, he had Great Influence over the Indians and that he would fetch the Indians Down and Kill Every Dam^d villian that Accepted of the Law. as to this Last you will Enquire of Sheriff Butler. on the whole he is promoting a settlement up on the Tioga [2] about 40 or 50 miles from this in the County of Northum^{bd} and has about 20 persons there in Defiance

---

[2] Hiester had been appointed a commissioner on May 22, 1787, in place of Peter Muhlenberg; *Pa. C. R.*, XV, 217.

[3] Balliet had been appointed in place of Joseph Montgomery on June 1; *ibid.*, 221.

[89] [1] M. H. S., Pickering Papers, LVII, 233, in Gore's hand but signed also by Hollenback.

[2] In modern Tioga County.

of the State of Pennsylvania. we Esteem him a Troublesom Dangerous & mischievious fellow and if Consistant with Good pollicy we wish you to Send a State warrant for him and Confine him in Some Goal or Avise us to the most proper measures to be taken. also the Draught of a State Warrant. from your Hum^{bl} Serv^{ts}

Obad^h Gore
M. Hollenback

[90] Samuel Hodgdon to Timothy Pickering.[1]

Philadelphia 25th July 1787
Dear Sir
I wrote you on saturday from Learns, to go by Mr Smith, this you must have received.[2] I address'd you again from Bethlehem and left my Letter with Mr Oakley who promised to forward it by the first Opportunity that presented, I hope it has come to hand.[3] this Morning I wrote again by Mr Blakeley Via Bethlehem [4] who also promised to do his utmost to get it to you. this comes by Mr Baliot, (if he comes) for in my Letter of this Morning I informed you that General Heister had resigned, and that William Montgomery was eleted in his place, since then I am informed that Baliot takes on Montgomerys [5] Commission, and intends either resigning or serving as he finds Montgomery disposed. hints are thrown out, that the business is *Managing* to prevent any *execution* until the assembly sets, which is on the 4th September Next. the appointment of Montgomery gives a colour to the suspicion for he is known to be obnoxious to those people.[6] time will set all right. conjectures may be ill founded. I have seen *Francis* and *Coxe*.[7] the divission of the Lands in your County has taken place; the *Great Bend* [8] was divided into thirds. we drew N° 1 which comprehends all the Eastermost part, and the Opposite surveys, the *Mill Seat* which you spoke of con-

[90] [1] M. H. S., Pickering Papers, LVII, 239-40.
[2] *Ibid.*, 236-37.
[3] Not found.
[4] *Ibid.*, 241.
[5] That is, Joseph Montgomery, who resigned on May 31, 1787.
[6] See the protest against William Montgomery; no. 121, *post*.
[7] Tench Francis and Tench Coxe.
[8] The Great Bend is that area where the Susquehanna River dips down into Pennsylvania from New York in northern Susquehanna County. For Pickering's statement of his land holdings, see no. 134, *post*.

sequently is ours. Francis drew N° 2 & 3, which includes the *Apple Tree* Town and the whole intermediate Lands up to us. Lukens chose for the heirs of his Son *1500 Acres* on Whapasining and the extreem Nook containing three thousand acres was set of to Francis. then the remainder was divided as the bend N° 4, 5, 6. we drew the eastermost divission, which it seems includes a part of the Tract that frightened Mᵣ Horton but on the whole all agree we have been fortunate. Wallis[9] has agreed that the Money due him shall be appropriated to the purchase of Certificates to Warrant the remaining surveys, and *Mᶜ Connell*[10] is accordingly employed to purchase the whole. I have declined any concern in the *Gore*,[11] *Francis Wallis* and *Coxe* have taken it to themselves, and the whole business will be very soon finnished, and I believe to our Mutual satisfaction, of which more hereafter. Rea has written to you by this conveyance and inclosed an Inventory of the articles that remain. No Waggons as yet have appeared, but no time shall be lost in procuring transportation for the articles most wanted. The house is not let, and from appearances it will remain long empty. everything in your Memorandum shall be attended to, and I shall be always happy in receiving your commands. inclosed you have this days papers. all friends are well, Mᵣ Doz and family are at the Farm. present my respects to the family and beleive me to be as ever, affectionately yours

Sam Hodgdon

[91] Samuel Hodgdon to Timothy Pickering.[1]

Philadelphia 30ᵗʰ July 1787

Dear Sir

This comes by Mᵣ Clark who has made a journey here, as he says to see his daughter, but finding her gone determines to see her and comes to Wyoming for that purpose. It pains me to inform you that all your goods yet remain here, not a Waggon has

---

[9] Samuel Wallis, Philadelphia merchant and land speculator. In 1774, Wallis with Timothy Matlack had acted as agents for Richard Penn to locate lands in what was then Northampton and Northumberland counties. The lands so located were finally divided by lot in 1787 among the men mentioned here. See Wilkinson, "Land Policy and Speculation in Pennsylvania," p. 96 (microfilm copy).

[10] Matthew McConnell; *ibid.*, 104.

[11] See Vol. VIII, no. 182, note 8.

[91] [1] M. H. S., Pickering Papers, LVII, 243, in Hodgdon's hand.

come from any quarter that could be procured to take them on. I have by this conveyance written out both to Pennypackers Mills, and Mʳ Oakley at Bethlehem to send in *Two* for the purpose of transporting them to Hallers; I hope they will be shortly on the way. Mʳ Balliot is yet here but talks of setting of to-morrow. he has been going every day since I returned. I have wrote you fully by him. *Heister* has resigned, and William Montgomery is appointed in his place of Commissioner but it is uncertain whether he will serve and I have heard that if he does not, *Baliot* will also give up. Shall only observe that something is wrong—delay is intended I beleive. much is expected from the next Meeting of the Assembly, or rather much is pretended to be expected. but who is to move I cannot learn. The Reverend Doctor [2] is absent, and will be so for Many Months, and he seems to be the spring that moves the whole Machine—more of this hereafter. A ship is now unlading fine salt at the Wharf and storeing it with out in the brick store. I can procure any quantity at fifteen pence per bushel or under. Shall I buy *100* bushels or more for you? this leads me to another thought, will it answer and are you disposed to engage in a store at your place, and on what conditions? I think I can from time to time supply one, at a cheaper rate, than most others. sometimes by Vendue purchases and sometimes from imm[ediate]ly on board the Vessels in which suitable goods are imported, and Credit I can obtain at any time and for any reasonable amount. let me know your sentiments on this subject. I have plaistered the Counting room, and put windows into it, with intention that Rea should reside there while closing the books. I have a Commission from Mʳ Derby for purchasing *200* Barrells superfine flour and *200* barrells porter to be ship'd to the *Indias*. A ship is arrived to day from Belfast with *250* Passengers—Carpenters, Masons, &c. can they be made profitable to you in your present pursuits? inclosed you have the Papers of the day and a subscription Paper for the publication of a certain book. Mʳ Merideth this Moment call'd on me and informs that Stewart (Charles) has come to Town, and is quite full of spirits, having heard of Massey's being dispossess'd, and some other disorders.[3] I am to meet him at Balliots quarters in half an hour to learn particulars, as well as to know whether he means to go

---

[2] The reference here remains obscure.

[3] Samuel Meredith, merchant and land speculator, and Charles Stewart of New Jersey, who had large claims of long standing in the Wyoming Valley; see Vol. VI, Index. "Massey" should be Marcy, probably Zebulon Marcy of Tunkhannock; see no. 92, *post.*

on, which Merideth very much doubts. he hinted to Merideth
that a confirmation of the claims under *the Act* was confirmation
of the whole Country, for the *Milk* would follow the *cream*—this
under the rose, that you may guard *against* a *weak Man,* should
he come on.

Just returned from seeking Balliot—did not find him—but am
informed he certainly goes of in the Morning. The house remains as yet, your own hired house like Pauls. Today I go to my
new lodgings at Mrs Millers front Near Market street. adieu,
sincerely yours

Sam Hodgdon

[92] Timothy Pickering to Samuel Hodgdon.[1]

Wilkesbury Augt 9, 1787

Dear Sir,

Your letter of July 21. (from Learns) [2] was del^d me by M^r
Smith, who had no demands for bringing back the horse. Your
other letters of the 25th & 2 of the 30th [3] were del^d me by M^r
Clark.

It was a surprize to find that Heister had resigned. if he
offered any reasons for it I wish you had intimated them: you
can yet do it; for I wish to know his motives. I am glad W^m
Montgomery is appointed in his stead, as Mr Hollenback says he
is rightly disposed. I wrote by him to Montgomery last Tuesday,
pressing his acceptance, and coming up immediately, that we
might begin the examination of Claims. 'Tis of the highest importance: for till then the laws will operate faintly. If Montgomery comes up we shall not wait an hour for Balliot. People
are growing more and more uneasy, and their jealousies are increasing—lest they should at last be deceived. Deceived indeed
they may be, by every idle tale & ridiculous lie which Franklin
& his party can invent. Yesterday I rec^d good information That
Franklin on his last return from Connecticut came down the
Susquehanna, and that about Unundilla (in York state) and
at other places along the river, told the people to be under no apprehensions about their lands—*that he had a commission from
the Governour of Connecticut to erect a seperate and independent*

---

[92] [1] M. H. S., Pickering Papers, LVII, 245-46, in Pickering's hand.
[2] *Ibid.,* 236.
[3] Nos. 90 and 91, *ante.* Other extant letters from Hodgdon were written
on July 26 and 27; Pickering Papers, LVII, 241 and XL, 218.

state, in those parts of the country. This incredible story was listened to, and one person, in particular, from about Unundilla, came down (to Tioga I think) and *seriously* inquired if it were true : This information I have from Esqr Gore, president of our Court of Common pleas. A number of Franklins adherents are making a considerable settlement at Newtown in York State (or the Tioga river) about 15 miles from Tioga point.[4] They have met and chosen a Committee to govern them with powers similar (I suppose) to the powers formerly given to the Committee of Directors here. It would seem, from all I hear, that this is to be the place of retreat of Franklin's partisans when obliged to quit Pennsylvania. Some people of the same cast are forming a settlement on the Tioga river, where it bends into Pennsylvania about 40 miles westward of Tioga Point.[5] These are [the persons referred] to in Col° Porter's letter, which I inclose.[6] Only my information from Esq^rs Gore & Hollenback [7] is, That one *Accomber* is at the head of them and that he bid, defiance to the laws of Pennsylvania. *Many* among these frontier settlers are lawless men, and in case of disturbances, w^d naturally assist one another. 'Tis perhaps of equal importance to New-York (as Pennsylvania) that regular government be introduced in all those places ; *and the cooperation of New York, might render it more easy for this state to enforce the laws in the county of Luzerne.* By M. Hollenback, who is to return from N°umberland to-morrow or next day, I shall know Whether or not Mr Montgomery will serve. Immediately after which Col° Denison will go to Philadelphia. (By him I shall write you again.) It is curious to observe That the warm *Pennamites* and *Franklin's party,* are both arriving at one point—to prevent a *peaceable* settlement of the dispute about these lands, and consequently to raise a *civil war* in the state. Col° Stewart need not triumph at Marcy's treatment.[8] Upon enquiry we found that Marcy's title was not an *old* Connecticut one ; but one acquired *since* the decree of Trenton. He has gone home, and is quietly getting in his harvest. But the half sharemen there say he shall not continue to *hold* the *land;* tho' he may live at his mill (3 miles from the disputed land) undisturbed ; having *there* a good title. It was not judged expedient, for several reasons, to attempt to take up the breakers of the Peace who assaulted Marcy.

---

[4] The vicinity of modern Elmira, New York. See no. 112, *post,* note 4.
[5] In modern Tioga County.
[6] Not found.
[7] No. 89, *ante.*
[8] See no. 91, *ante,* where Marcy is called Massey.

154

One was, that his title was that of *late possession* only. Another that there was no jail in which to confine the Offenders, if they refused (as they certainly would) to give bail. third That it might be doubtful whether the people would readily assist to inforce the laws while the law for confirming their titles was in suspence by the delay of the meeting of the Commissioners. This law, you know, was the *sine qua non* of their submission to government, and the delay of execution excites a prevailing jealousy that it is intended to leave it unexecuted until the limited time for recev^g their claims shall expire.

You mention the storing of salt in our brick store, & ask whether you shall purchase 100 bushels or more for me at 1/3 a bushel. I should be glad of a 100 bushels, at least, and to have it, in the course of the fall, put into old cider barrels, that are tight (you may get them of Lockwood) and forwarded by return waggons to Hallers, or Levers's, whence I can fetch them in sleighs in the winter. Haller told me he often got such loads brought to his house at 50/per ton; tho' in the summer that is the price to Bethlehem only.

To keep a store here would answer very well, provided *money* could be obtained for making remittances: but I know not whence it is to come. Hollenback takes furs: but experience is requisite to judge of their value. Scarcely any produce will bear transportation. They will have no surplus of beef or pork. Flax will be tolerably plenty. I have engaged a little for family use at 9^d per lb exchanged for goods. What price will it bring in Philadelphia, & in Cash, or payment of Goods? Two years of peace w^d make a plenty of flax & perhaps of hemp, and yield some beef & pork. A good road too w^d enable us to carry our grain to Easton, for the Phila^a market. Perhaps some might be carried even the ensuing winter. Did these means of remittance exist at this moment, I should not hesitate to be concerned in a store: Grain is plenty now, and daily pressing upon me for all sorts of goods. I must think farther of it & write you by Col^o Denison. An Irish bricklayer, and a carpenter, would be of great use to me in carrying forward my buildings, particularly a bricklayer, if master of his business, for I do not know of one in the settlement, tho' I have (as you saw) a good *stonemason*. It would be agreeable to me to have one carpenter & one mason, if they can be purchased cheap, & money can be found to pay for them.[9] I would choose to have them engaged to perform labour in husbandry,

---

[9] Pickering is referring to obtaining these skilled workers as indentured servants.

when not called to exercise their trades. This brings Wm George's business to mind. His tools were to be made by Hendrick's in Market Street, up an Alley near Dr Franklin's. Besides his tools & box of tin, he will want some pieces of old Copper kettles & copper rivets to patch kettles, & repair the Hollenback's stills. Mr Harbeson (near Jn° Hall's) can tell what would be suitable & perhaps can supply them. William George is tolerably steady; but is too apt to boast of more than he can perform.

I am just informed of two of Franklin's adherents, (one of whom lives at Kingston [)] the other (Baldwin) at Lackawanock who have offered their houses & lands about them (all they own) for sale—giving as a reason, that they are going up the river. Esqr Gore also told me last evening that one of the Earls at Tunkhanock (where Marcy lives) [10] was also packing up and moving northward. This certainly indicates despair of effecting their wishes *in this quarter*. They may endeavour to hold fast their half share claims at Tioga: but not below it. Thither and to Newtown they will probably resort. Since Marcy's affair, the under-sheriff served a capias on one of the Earls at Tunkhanock. He refused to come with the Sheriff; one Cady came to his assistance. However, when the under sheriff told them that he was an officer regularly appointed (& not deputized for that particular writ) they dropped their weapons, and Earl told the officer that if the Creditor (John Hollenback) w^d write him a line & fix his terms of payment, that he would settle with him. Since then also the son of another of the Earls (indebted to Hollenback) has been down to Hollenback, & told him that if he w^d take grain his father would pay him. The Justices also, in this quarter issue their processes, which have not been resisted. One trial by jury, for forceable entry & detainer has been regularly held; tho' one of Franklin's adherents (& a half share man) was a party, & the defendant in the action. Upon the whole, I feel a confidence That if the Commissioners were here & had once begun to receive claims & confirm titles, the clouds of doubt & fear & suspicion would immediately be dispersed.

I trust my goods are on their way ere this time. Some of them I am anxious to receive; particularly the articles necessary for Mrs P. The moment I get intelligence of their being at Lever's or Haller's I shall send for them. The large hair trunk with a flat top, and the pine chest that was in the back parlour

---

[10] Zebulon Marcy.

are of the first necessity. The roll of Ficklenburg that was in the office is wanted by the workmen & people for trousers while the weather is warm. We have nothing to mix with water but the few bottles (3) of gin, and ill flavoured rum save a little wine which I reserve for sickness or extraordinary cases: if I could obtain half a barrel of good Antigua rum I should be glad. We have begun to make good spruce beer: but Betsey [11] drinks no beer. The rum sh^d be of the highest proof. My wife & Betsey earnestly desire some hard biscuit may be sent up. Pray embrace the first conveyance by 28^{lbs} of water biscuit, & 28^{lbs} of pilot bread not flinty. Can you get half a piece, or a piece of strong check, that will do for workmen's shirts and checked aprons? Mrs P. says she knows not how to do without it.

I owe J. Hazlehurst & Co £16.10. & Ely & Paxon £7.16.8 which should be paid immediately. If Thompson, the blacksmith sh^d want money, pray let him have some. I forgot to make him any payment. His account is upwards of £8.0/0.

You did not mention Mr Doz: but only generally that all our friends were well; and so we include him. Betsey writes for her self. Mrs P. joins me in the kindest remembrance of them.

You kindly offer to execute my commands. I hope they will not too often occur. Affectionately adieu!

T. Pickering

P. S. You will convey Col^o Porter's Letter inclosed to his wife.

[93] Caleb Benton to John Franklin.[1]

Aug. 9, 1787.

Sir,

I have carefully perused your's dated the first of Sept., [?] [2] & think your policy good—with regard to letting the Towns on the Tioga.[3] I think it best that it should be done immediately, that any man who goes on may immediately occupy his own farm. You requested me to repair to the Tioga without loss of time but I think if you reconsider the matter you will determine to the contrary, for I am sensible that if I at present leave home for any considerable time there will be no possibility of my throw-

---

[11] Mrs. Pickering's sister.

[93] [1] *P. A.,* XI, 175; M. H. S., Pickering Papers, LVII, 279, a copy certified by James Trimble. See no. 148, *post* note 2.

[2] The certified copy also has September.

[3] See no. 119, *post,* where Benton is also identified.

ing on many settlers this Fall, for which reason I shall not go on at present, but determine to exert myself to the utmost to throw on settlers & I think I shall send on a very considerable number this fall & fix a plan to fill the Country in the spring—your policy will undoubtedly induce you to not suffer provisions to be carried from your settlement, but above all I most earnestly advise you to crush your enemies & pursue them to the pit & depend I will assist you so far as in my power & shall expect that when I hear from you again, there will not be an Acan found in your Camp & trust you will not suffer the unhallowed feet of a Penimite to tread on the Land which the Lord hath given you. I am, Sir, with Respect, yr. mo. obedient humble Servant,

Caleb Benton.

N. B. Please to present my compliments to Major Jenkins & inform him I am determined that his God shall be my God.

[94] Notification from the Susquehannah Company Commissioners to Newport.[1]

NOTIFICATION

Whereas the Susq^h Company at their meeting at Hartford on the 26th day of Decemb^r 1786 Authorized and empowered their Commissioners to ascertain the claims of former grants, and to fill up any vacancies in towns formerly granted We therefore hereby give notice to the proprietors of the town of Newport to exhibit their claims to the Commissioners by the 13th day of this instant Aug^st, that they may be enabled to Judge of the Validity of the Same and to fill up the vacant rights in s^d town Sign'd by order of the Commissioners

Asa Starkwather Secr^y

[95] Timothy Pickering to Samuel Hodgdon.[1]

Wilkesbury Augt 12, 1787.

Dear Sir,

Last evening Col° Irvin of Bucks County arrived here (on his way to Tioga, where he owns Lands in the New Purchase) [2] &

[94] [1] M. H. S., Pickering Papers, LVII, 248, in Starkwather's hand.
[95] [1] M. H. S., Pickering Papers, LVII, 249-50, in Pickering's hand.
[2] Land purchased from the Indians in 1784, the last such major purchase within the state.

del me your letters of the 3ᵈ 4th, & 5th,³ with an inventory inclosed of the loading of the waggons. Two letters also from Mʳ Rea came with them;⁴ and one from Haller informing me of the arrival of my household goods at his house. Two newspapers (Oswald's) ⁵ were also inclosed; the first and only Newspapers I have recᵈ. You either forgot to inclose Newspapers, as mentioned in your letters by Mʳ Clark, or they were intercepted.

I have read the ordinance of Congress relative to the government of the Western territory, and like it: I hope men to fill the different offices there may be found, who will be incapable of committing abuses, although remote from the arm of the federal power: *I* do not desire to ramble *any farther,* if I can live here in peace; and believe there will be no occasion for my debating the question you propose to me.⁶ That event is so improbable in itself, that I have not dropped a hint of it to my wife or Betsey—nor mean to do it—especially as my wife is not as well as I could wish. She has fatigued herself too much, and is daily complaining of pains.

Mʳ Clark left this place last Thursday, by whom I wrote you two letters; one relative to our lands with Wallis &c.⁷ in which I gave you as particular a description of the lands in the Bend and eastward of it, as was in my power, & my clear opinion that the three surveys eastward of the Bend, were of more value than the whole ten surveys in the Bend marked P. and then intimated, either that Wallis shᵈ divide, & you & Mʳ Coxe choose; or draw lots with him.

In my other letter ⁸ I made some observations about your proposal for supplying a store at this place, & reserved a final decision to Colᵒ Denison's going to Phila°. But I must farther suspend it. I desired you to engage at least one hundred bushels of the fine English salt for me, which you said was storing in the Brick store. I also desired you to engage a complete bricklayer, if to be had from the Irish vessel—and a carpenter—provided money could be found for the purpose. I mentioned William George's tinners tools that were in making by Hendricks in Market Street; & I do not now see them mentioned in the list

---

³ Extant letters from Hodgdon dated August 3 and 4 are in *ibid.,* XL, 223 and 220.

⁴ A letter from Sampson Rea dated July 25 is in *ibid.,* XIX, 105.

⁵ Eleazer Oswald, printer of the *Independent Gazetteer,* Philadelphia.

⁶ Hodgdon had stated that the choice of governor for the Northwest Territory was between Arthur St. Clair and Pickering but that St. Clair was expected to get the office; Pickering Papers, XL, 223.

⁷ See no. 90, *ante,* note 10.

⁸ No. 92, *ante.*

of articles forwarded; the tin and lead will be useless till they arrive; perhaps they are packed up with other things & so not noted. I desired you to procure of Mr Harbeson (or elsewhere) some old pieces of Copper kettles, to repair kettles & stills here, and copper rivets also. I requested to have 28^{lbs} water biscuit & 28^{lbs} pilot bread sent up; and ½ bbl of high-proofed Antigua rum. The former will be grateful to M^{rs} P & Betsey, and the latter to Betsey in particular, who has only water to drink as she will not taste of spruce beer, & my rum is so ill flavoured that neither of them can touch it. These things I desired, thinking it *possible* that the waggons might not have come away. *Now* they may be forwarded to Hallers by a return waggon, *when* one can be met with. I have repeated the various requests made in my letter by Mr Clark (as far as I could recollect them) lest he should loose it: for I perceived he was as fond of *Sir Richard,*[9] as ever; and retained the same hypocritical cant in conversation. He proposed to Mrs P. that she sh^d let Dolly go to Phila^a with him! & thence to Carlisle—that the two sisters might live together. This not being agreed to (& it did not appear that Doll wished to accompany him) he afterwards proposed to me that his Carlisle daughter should come here; adding that he could not be easy while they were asunder and that for his *own part* he could do as much work as would support him. I told him I w^d think of the matter; & that by the Fall I sh^d know whether his other daughter would be useful or not in my family. & then, at his earnest request, I am to write to him on the subject. I see the old man wishes to get again into my family: but all that know him can entertain no such idea. As his daughter is (it seems) a complete spinner, & serves at 3/ a week, my wife may be disposed to employ her, *for the sake of her spinning,* if circumstances should hereafter render it convenient.

I sh^d have been glad to have saved the extraordinary expence of the transportation of my goods, but as matters are circumstanced, I am happy & obliged that you have forwarded them as you have done: I began to be alarmed lest my *wife's* necessary articles should not arrive in time. Tomorrow (Monday) I shall have my waggon & horses got in order to set out for Hallers, either in the afternoon, or on Tuesday morning, to bring in first the few things of indispensable necessity, and get in the rest as fast as I can. We have had more or less of rain about 2 days out of 3 since you left us. Now fair weather appears

---

[9] Drink?

again to be fixed. I was fearful the Swamp was rendered nearly impassable, but Colo Irvin says it is very tolerable, there appearing not to have been so much rain there as here.

I am glad you have a prospect of selling part of our wines, & that you have concluded to take £60. if more cannot be got. As to the half pipe which we have been drinking of, I should be glad to divide it with you, and tho' the half of it might *here* last me two years, yet it will come cheaper than any I could purchase a year hence.

Since I wrote you by Mr Clarke, I have heard reports which indicate a more serious determination of disturbance from Franklin. As soon as I rec^d advice from you of Willm Montgomery's appointment as a commissioner, I made it known, as Heister's resignation had been before published. The Tuesday following (Augt 7th) I wrote a letter to Mr Montgomery,[10] pressing him, in the most urgent terms, to accept of the office. Last evening Mr Hollenback Esqr (who was going to Northumberland, & carried my letter) returned, with an answer from Mr Montgomery,[11] in very sensible terms, expressing his consent to serve: but saying that *my* letter contained the first advice of his appointment!! altho' he knew of a good conveyance by which Council might have sent him notice of it, if not his Commission. I begged him to come up before Col° Denison went to Phila^a because he must take the oath before a Councillor or Judge of the Supreme Court: He would have come accordingly, had his appointment from Council reached him. Franklin is I believe now endeavouring to raise objections against *him* as he did against Joseph Montgomery—not I suppose, that he apprehends harder measure from him, than from another; but it may answer his views—procrastination—till his scheme of independence is grown riper; for this scheme, chimerical as it is, most assuredly is yet in contemplation. I have now in my pocket an advertisement signed by Starkwather,[12] as Secretary to the Commissioners nominated last December by the Susquehanna Company, calling on the claimants of land in Newport (8 miles below this) to present their claims to those commissioners to-morrow; as all forfeited & vacant rights are to be filled up by them agreeably to the resolutions of the company: but I inclose you a copy of it. It was nailed up at the ferry house here. The rights in Newport are not all taken up; consequently the vacant lands belong either to Pennsylvania claimants, or to the state, & which these Com-

---

[10] Not found.   [11] Not found.   [12] No. 94, *ante.*

missioners now mean to grant. Franklin, indeed, does not appear to have shut up his land office at all; but his grants hitherto have been of lands up the river. Hints are thrown out that I am to be driven back thro the swamp: but I have hitherto slighted them. A multitude of idle reports are made with a view to alarm people and with a hope that they may produce of themselves the effects which are threatened. I mean to collect the best information to be obtained & be on my guard; but I think I shall not willingly go thro' the swamp again. We shall urge Col° Denison to stay till Mr Montgomery comes up and is qualified; and therefore conclude (if the Col° Will stay) that Mr Evans sh^d go to Phila^a for Montgomery's commission, or a certificate of his appointment if his commission should have been forwarded. I remain with much affection yours

T. Pickering

P. S. Present my Compliments to Rea; & excuse my not writing him, as I have not time. I was a subscriber for Mr Pike's book of arithmetic: if tis ready for delivery at Bookstores, I sh^d wish to receive mine, & have sent by Mr Evans.

[96] Timothy Pickering to Benjamin Franklin.[1]

Wilkesburg, County of Luzerne,
Aug't 13, 1787.

Sir,

A letter from a friend [2] advised me that Council had appointed William Montgomery, Esq'r, a Commissioner to examine the claims of the Connecticut Settlers in this County, in the room of Genl. Heister, resigned. I had an opportunity of writing to Mr. Montgomery to inform him of it, or rather to urge his acceptance of the office. I rec'd his answer last evening; by which I find that my letter which reached him last Thursday gave him the first notice of his appointment. He has consented, nay determined, to serve. I expressed my opinion to him, that not only the peace of this county, but perhaps of the state, depended on an immediate execution of the law for confirming the Connecticut titles. The uneasiness of the people of the delays which have happened is greater than I could have imagined; and John

---

[96] [1] *P. A.*, XI, 176. [2] No. 90 or 91, *ante.*

Franklin and his adherents are very industrious to infuse suspicions into the minds of the settlers that these delays are designed, and that the law will never be carried into execution. Until this law begins to operate, to undeceive the people, misled by Franklin's predictions and falsehoods, the execution of the laws in general will be difficult. The people, with such doubts on their minds, will be averse from aiding the sheriff and magistrates, or yield them but a faint support.

If Mr. Montgomery's commission should have been forwarded, I pray that a certificate of the appointment, duly authenticated, may be furnished to Mr. Evans who will return hither without delay;[3] and that certificate forwarded to Mr. Montgomery (if his commission should not sooner reach him,) would authorize his coming hither & being sworn; for which reason, Colo. Denison (who was going to attend in Council,) will remain here, to administer the oath to Mr. Montgomery; because the law requires that it be taken before one of the Council, or a Judge of the Supreme Court. I have the honor to be, very respectfully sir, your Excellency's obed't servant,

Timothy Pickering.

[97] Samuel Hodgdon to Timothy Pickering.[1]

Philadelphia 16ᵗʰ August 1787

Dear Sir

Yesterday Mʳ Clark arrived with your first Packet & today I am favoured with your other by Mʳ Evans. When you receive my Letters by Mʳ Balliot, you will read my suspicions relative to Heisters resignation.[2] I am glad you are satisfied with Montgomerys appointment. our freinds here were doubtful whether it would be pleasing. It has been said Franklin was as artful as designing—he hazarding such a foolish tale as the "Commission from the *Governor* [of] *Connecticut*," gives the Lie to that assertion.[3] Strange that credulity or ignorance should countenance it for a moment, it must eventually injure him—the more idle tales the better. Let the Vipers retire and settle in York state, for Pennsylvania can well spare them, that state being well

[3] A second commission was issued to Montgomery, dated August 16, and Pickering was instructed to use either this or the earlier one and destroy the one not used; M. H. S., Pickering Papers, LVII, 251 and 252.

[97] [1] M. H. S., Pickering Papers, LVII, 253-58.

[2] See no. 90, *ante.*   [3] See no. 92, *ante.*

aware of Franklins former conduct, will suspect his future designs and guard against him accordingly. As Law approaches anarchy will fly, and order rear her head. I am glad that on investigation the cause of Triumph on Marcys affair is done away. It was much talked of, and Mighty advantages were to flow from it. The reasons you give for not apprehending the offenders are to me abundantly sufficient.[4] no attempt should be made without a certainty that the people will assist to enforce the Laws. a miscarriage here would be attended with serious consequences. it is clearly my opinion that the confirmation Law will prove the ground work of all Law in your County. let nothing then be hazarded until it is compleated. The Ship I mentioned did not unlade her Salt as was expected. only *ten pence* per bushell was offered for it and the owner at length sent it to Baltimore but I can procure what you want at the rate you Mention and it shall be done. I shall expect to hear farther from you relative to opening a store at your place, more experience may be Necessary to determine its propriety, but if it will answer dont let another take place and exclude you. To inform you of the price of flax and others articles I enclose the last current price, which may be in general depended on. Wheat will be cheap, there is the greatest crops *this Year,* known for many years, and its quality is equal to its quantity. flour super fine may be had already @ *35/* per Barrel and common @ *30°/.* I will immediately enquire for a *Carpenter,* and *bricklayer,* and if to be found properly recommended, as well for their good demeanor, as for their knowledge in their respective branches I I will purchase them. *William George*'s business [5] shall be attended to in every particular, of which more hereafter. The conclusion of the *Capias* business I think favourable, for when once the people reverence the *Law,* order will be restored.[6] I hope before this reaches you the Commissioners will be with you, and their work begun. All the goods you were most anxious about are with you. the Antigua Spirits for *M"ᵖ P & Betsey* shall be sent on by the first conveyance that presents, with all the other articles named Viz* *Biscuit Pilot Bread* and *Check.* The several sums mentioned shall be paid. Colonel Porters Letter to his Wife is covered and forwarded.

Wallis's proposal I find was of a piece with all his other conduct, I shall suspect his least suspicious actions in future. I have shewn your Letter to M⁰ Coxe. we will eneavour to ob-

---

⁴ See *ibid.*   ⁵ See *ibid.*   ⁶ See *ibid.*

tain a just divission. I am sorry the Land in the *Bend* which has fallen to us are not of a better quality.[7] my Memory in this particular must have failed me. I thought the *eastermost* part the best, but fate has determined it, and I will not repine.***

you do not mention how your house goes forward, you know it was clearly my Opinion that you would not get into it 'till spring. I hope you will have plenty of vegetables for the winter. how does Hollabach manage relative to lodging and rooms. can he accomodate you 'till spring if need be? I have seen Doctor Rush, he informs me he has something to communicate and promises to write by this conveyance. The conduct of the persons appointed as Commissioners and resigned, is severely reprobated and marks pointedly the justness of the House in censuring the *executive* by Making the first appointment themselves.[8] says One their conduct in this business, is part of an infernal plan begun at the commencement of our troubles and continued to the present day, but, adds he, the discriminating day is at hand, when "*Cain* and his whole party will call on the rocks and Mountains to cover their guilty heads," Meaning the doings of the setting Convention.[9] I had written so far when I was call'd of to attend to the subdividing our Lands with Wallis. I have been and the event has been (I think) favourable. I proposed his dividing, he agreed, but from your previous information you will judge I was surprized. he had clased all the good and valuable together and all the indifferent and bad. I objected at first, he persevered and we M[r] Coxe and Myself, as it was a Lottery, consented though at the same [time] relying on your information we declared that we believed a sacrifice would be made. We drew and N° *200* the eastermost in the Bend is ours. we proceeded and the westermost of the remainder N° 250 is ours as you will perceive by the inclosed papers, when the business was thus closed for the first time. Wallis appeared chargrind for it is evident, we have got the best situation on the eastern surveys and the best Land on the western in the great Body drawn against Francis. Francis Laughs, he says the Devil is lit. when you have perused the papers give your opinion on them. I venture however to congratulate you and with the congratulation dismiss the subject for this time. I presume you have some communication from Council of a private Nature. am therefore cautious relative to a confidential story just related to

---

[7] See no. 95, *ante.*   [8] See no. 39, *ante.*
[9] That is, the Federal Convention.

me, however, right or wrong it can't be an injury to you, and may possibly be of use to you. A Councillor says, that two days [ago ?] a person from *your way* sent into their *board* an annonymous Letter giving information of an extraordinary Nature. The Letter was not publickly Noticed, and yesterday the Man appeared and requested a private audience.[10] this was readily granted, and he then backed his information in such a Manner as induces *some* to beleive, he really Means well and wishes to keep the peace of the County. all that has transpired of the information goes to discover a plan laid for renewing and keeping up hostilities against this state, under the auspices of F'ks party with you, and some Great Men in a Neighbouring state, not Connecticut, to the southward of it. thus I have ventured to skim the story, but doubt not if their is any design of the Kind, you have the particulars from Council and to them I leave the concern. business presses I must conclude tho' I have many things to say—adieu—you will be prudent, I know—be watchful also. Affectionately yours

Sam Hodgdon

My best regards to Mrs Pickering. I have prevailed with Mr Evans to take on some things which I thought she might want soon. I have written to Betsey.

[98] Eliphalet Dyer to Timothy Pickering.[1]

Fairfield Connecticut August 18th 1787

S^r

My son Co^{ll} Thos Dyer was one among the first who entered upon and took possession of the Lands on Susq^h River under the Claim of Connecticut & had soon after laid out to him a right of Land called a setling right of about three or four hundred acres which he soon entered upon & has possessed & Improved ever since principally by Tenants one after another. He

---

[10] Nothing in the rough minutes of the Council for this period gives a hint of the information or informer, but see Pickering's reply: no. 100, *post.* Charles Biddle sent a warning to Pickering on August 17; *P. A.,* XI, 177.

[98] [1] M. H. S., Pickering Papers, LVII, 259-60, in Dyer's hand. The whole tenor of the letter makes it plain that Dyer, long one of the strongest supporters of the Susquehannah Company, was willing to accept the Confirming Act, the benefits of which were limited to actual settlers long established on the land.

my son has been at ye whole expence on said right ever since. Y^e present Tenant I understand has been on improving under my son but about two years and now Am inform'd that he is so much of a Rascal as to lay in a Claim of my sons right for himself tho not been in ye Country till long since y^e Decree at Trenton. Such manifest wrong fraud & injustice I presume never will be favored or supported. It has been Impossible for my son who is a farmer to leave his farming business to wait on y^e Com^{tee} in person this summer and further conceives it Needless as ye whole Records are at $Susq^h$ and Co^{11} Denneson Who has a power from my son is as perfectly acquainted with his my sons Claim as he is of his own, as their rights & possessions Commence at y^e same time & they were togeather at their first entry & they lye in y^e same Township I think Kingston, & believe their home lots are adjoining. Have wrote to him to make application on behalf of my son to the Com^{tee}. he is knowing fully as is Co^{11} Butler & many others now at $Susq^h$ and can shew you the same evidence as they can for their own as to the expence or sum your Act requires each Claimer to pay the Com^{tee} upon his rights being Confirmd shall be paid without fail. Co^{11} Dennison or Butler or both will engage it or pay it. I wish for the sake of those Concerned & are Clearly within y^e benefit of your act and have not been Able within so short a time (and mostly in y^e summer season) to make a journey to $Susq^h$ to lay in & Exhibit their Claim, that the time for that purpose May be lengthned out by your assembly or much injustice will be done. beside it will much tend to quiet down any further disputes and Contentions in that Country. Can entertain no doubt of the Candor & Liberality of y^e Com^{tee} and that they will do every thing within ye most liberal Construction of the act of your Assembly referrd to, and not be over Critical with respect to those who are y^e Subjects of S^d Act when y^e whole design of it was to quiet down a long & unhappy Controversy most beneficial in the effects to y^e State of Pensylvania. Must Trouble you with a line to Co^{11} Dennison which hope you will be so kind as to Deliver him and am with respect & Esteem Y^r Hle $Serv^t$

Eliph^t Dyer

[99] Timothy Pickering to Samuel Hodgdon.[1]

Wilkesboro' Augt 26, 1787.

Dear Sir,

Your favour of August 16 by Mr Evans, reached me last Tuesday Morning.[2] The day before, Mr Hollenback & Mr Bowman returned from Wapalopy (20 miles below) whither they went to meet Mr Montgomery, to whom I sent a message near a week before that some gentlemen would meet him at that place, last Sunday evening. For I was fearful that the threats of F. and his partisans, who swore that Montgomery should not sit as a Commissioner, might discourage him from coming; & Balliot had not then (when I sent the message) arrived; and expecting Mr Montgomery on Monday, I was desirous of beginning the business with a full board. However, as he did not meet the gentlemen above named, as proposed, I would delay it no longer, & therefore mentioned to Col^o Balliot the expediency of our beginning the next morning; to which he agreed. We accordingly wrote several advertisements thereof, & on Tuesday Morning last met and commenced the examination of the Connecticut Claims. This was a terrible stroke to Franklin; he expressed his astonishment to the gentlemen who mentioned it to him, and said that *two* of the Commissioners made not a quorum for business. He was assured however, that we were determined to begin. This has frustrated his plans for the present—plans which he had been forming at various meetings held with his clan every two or three nights for a month past. The villain knew that the people in general were extremely solicitous to have the Commissioners meet, and he would not dare forceably to prevent them; and therefore was endeavouring to raise a clamour against William, as he had against Joseph Montgomery,[3] hoping it w^d produce the like effect; and thus he expected to defeat the intentions of government in passing the confirming law, without coming to open violences; for which he is not yet prepared. Being thus disappointed, he has been graciously pleased to permit Mr Montgomery (who joined us the same Tuesday in the afternoon) [4] to sit uninterruptedly as a commissioner. But really, for my own part, I did not think he would

---

[99] [1] M. H. S., Pickering Papers, LVII, 261, in Pickering's hand.
[2] No. 97, *ante.*   [3] No. 78, *ante.*   [4] That is, on August 21.

attempt to use any force towards the Commissioners, or any of them; and instead of swallowing greedily all the absurd and ridiculous stories related to me, of the intentions of Franklin and his party, (even when they respected myself) I reproached the informers & the people for their credulity & alarms, which served only to encourage the villains & advance their flagitious schemes. I have found since that I had incurred the displeasure of some persons, to whom I gave such a reception, as tho' I were unwilling to receive information. But in truth I felt as much contempt as indignation for Franklin & his partisans, and could not patiently listen to the wild chimeras reported to me as above. Nevertheless I at the same time declared my wish to be informed of any material *facts* relative to the designs of the party: but such as were reported were too absurd to deserve the least attention. I also kept myself prepared at night for any event, most deliberately resolved to put to death any who should molest me. At length, as I expected, all their threats have evaporated in smoke. They have not, however given up their opposition to government: but tis not the government of Pennsylvania only which they wish to disturb. Franklin with one Esqʳ Beach (formerly a dweller here, now in York state) set off last Evening for Tioga, to meet a number of *gentlemen* (*seditious villains*) there from Hudson [5] &c. to consult on a plan for forming an independent state of such part of this settlement as will join them, or they can seduce, & of the neighbouring parts of New-York. From all the information I have heard, I am satisfied that this measure is in contemplation. Franklin still continues to grant rights to be surveyed within this county agreeably to the resolves of the Susquehanna company; and lately an advertisement was posted up calling on the claimants of lands in Newport (8 miles below) to exhibit their claims, to the Commissioners appointed by those resolves; it was signed by one Starkweather (who lives with Franklin) as their secretary.[6] Franklin & Jenkins met, & Capt. Schott (without whom a quorum could not be formed) was with them; tho' he attempts to excuse his conduct for reasons which I do not recollect, but he is too unsteady to be depended on upon either side, tho' to *me* he has ever manifested a warm attachment to government. *One* person presented a claim: but he was really a friend to government; & his motive

---

[5] Hudson, New York, was the home of Joseph Hamilton, who worked closely with Franklin. Franklin's companion was Zerah Beach, a commissioner of the Susquehannah Company.

[6] No. 94, *ante.*

was to get from them some information whereby he might establish his Connecticut title, & which he could not get elsewhere. His purpose was answered; and one of Franklin's party, & a violent one too, who was in possession of the lot, was ordered to quit it to the applicant above referred to.

After all, those people (the Connecticut Claimants generally) seem as tho' they would never be satisfied of the upright intentions of government; and even with patents in their pockets, I know not but they will fear, that they will be wrested from them. Altho' we have every day diligently examined the claims presented, yet because we have not yet given certificates that their titles are good & indefeasible, they raise premises that they will not finally be confirmed. We mean therefore to give certificates to such as desire them, altho' they can not avail themselves of them, until we make our final report to Council of the claims we find duly supported. Next Week we are to hold our County Court. Divers of Franklins men have said there would be no court: but *now* they say they shall not disturb the Court or the Commissioners; but that *great things* are to be done in the fall. More hereafter. For this time sincerely adieu!

T. Pickering

[100] Timothy Pickering to Samuel Hodgdon.[1]

Wilkesboro' August 26, 1787.

Dear Sir

Since writing the inclosed (N° 1)[2] I have recurred to that part of your letter of the 16th[3] in which you mention the information given to Council by a person from this quarter.[4] I believe the information good: the informant was supposed to be (& perhaps really was) a staunch friend to the Susquehanna Company, & acted with their warmest partisans: but he now has a large interest depending on the confirming law, & professes a fixed attachment to the government of Pennsylvania. He formerly resided in this settlement; but lives now in York State, where he received the information which he communicated to Council. His credibility in this case is supported by the relation of a per-

---

[100] [1] M. H. S., Pickering Papers, LVII, 263-66, in Pickering's hand.
[2] No. 99, *ante*.   [3] No. 97, *ante*.
[4] Who the informant was is not known.

son from Niagara (a Major Scott of Connecticut whom I recollect to have seen at my quarters at Newburgh) who mentions
the very plan; but that Col° John Butler there, & others, instead
of countenancing it (as the other informant was told by one of
the conspirators) disapprove of it. Franklin however, with some
members of the Susque^h Co & a few other desperate men at
Hudson & in its vicinity, may (like the madmen of Massachusetts,) attempt measures that may disturb the peace of both
Pennsylvania & New York. Report says that a Livingston &
another from York government were in the conspiracy,[5] and
actually came to Tioga, on their way to Niagara; but that the
information received there induced them to return. I think it
will be expedient to organize the militia of this county, and make
Col° Zebulon Butler County Lieutenant.[6] He is an old officer
of experience & bravery in the field, & will in that line [be]
respected, notwithstanding the failing which you have heard me
mention. I think also that we cannot too soon be furnished with
a few chests of arms, & amunition, to be lodged in this place.

I shall notice the several matters in your letter as they occur.
In respect to a store, I am under no doubt of its answering well
enough if remittances can be obtained. They have no money, as
I told you before. But this year they have plenty of produce.
Their wheat is sold at 5/. Rye 3/6 oats 1/10½ flax 9^d per lb
flax seed perhaps at 3/9 but I am uncertain. At present they
have no other means of payment for goods; or at least the money
they w^d bring would be too inconsiderable to deserve much notice.

---

[5] The conspiracy referred to here was led by John Livingston and Caleb
Benton, associated with a group known variously as the Lessee Company,
the New York Genesee Land Company, or the York Lessees. Having
illegally obtained from Indians leases to land in western New York, they
sought separate statehood so that their leases could be converted to full
titles. The effort did not reach a peak until 1793, but in 1787 the charge
was that they sought separate statehood through aid from Great Britain,
thus the mention of the British military leader at Niagara, Col. John Butler.
See Harvey-Smith, *Wilkes-Barré*, III, 1579n and Julian P. Boyd, "Attempts to Form New States in New York and Pennsylvania, 1786-1796,"
New York Historical Association, *Quarterly Journal*, XII, 257-65 (July,
1931).

Benton also had large interests in the Susquehannah Company purchase,
particularly in settling men in the townships west of Athens. He corresponded on occasion with Franklin and not unnaturally seemed to link
Franklin with the treasonable statehood movement in New York.

[6] He was commissioned August 30, 1787; *Pa. C. R.*, XV, 264. On
September 1, Butler received orders from Vice President Charles Biddle
to hold elections for the choosing of militia officers; *P. A.*, XI, 179.

If flax seed should be sold at 3/9 (but I rather suspect it may be @ 5/.) it might bear transportation in the winter to Easton, to be carried to Phila^a in the spring: but then the Irish ships would be gone. Flax if at 12^d in Phila^a might be a tolerable good article: but the price current sets it at 10^d @ 12^d. They have not the means of manufacturing flour, and until the roads are better I think wheat & flour incapable of transportation without loss. This indeed is to be considered, That most goods sold here will at present bring from 25 @ 50 & 100 per C^t profit, which w^d enable the storekeeper to remit produce altho' the expence added to the first cost sh^d exceed the price at market. Liquors & groceries admit of the highest advance—say 100 per Cent. Dry goods (on which I suppose the longest credit can be obtained at Phila^a) may on an average allow an advance of 20 @ 25 per Cent. on the cost and charges. If a store were to be opened for dealing to any extent, a clerk to take charge of it would be necessary. M. Hollenback's (Mr Oehmig) is engaged at a very trifling expence (I forget what) but I suspect that even a New-Englandman would hardly serve at that price. Oehmig is a clever honest young man. John Scott I am persuaded is perfectly honest, and would be a good hand in the way of liquors & grocery, & to receive produce; I know not but that he could manage the coarser articles of dry goods; & he can write well enough to make entrys in a waste book. You may consider what facts I have not stated, I also will think farther on the subject & write you again by some gentlemen who will go for Phila^a as soon as the court is over next week.

You ask about my intended house: tis in truth but intended, for the sawyer (whom I took from his general character to be a punctual man) has not yet brought down the frame. Nevertheless, I could have my house habitable by the last of November at farthest, if the frame should come down in ten days or a fortnight. I still therefore desire a good carpenter & bricklayer may be sent me, if to be procured reasonably from the Irish Ship. There is not a good bricklayer (at least I have seen no proofs of one) in the county; and next year I expect there will be a good deal of building, in which such workmen could be employed, if I had done with them myself. You will conceive the fixing my house this fall to be practicable, when I remind you, that I mean only to have it rough boarded (the boards tho' to be grooved & tongued) and all the partitions of rough boards. The floors too will be but rough planed, because, single & next summer I w^d lay a 2^d floor of well seasoned boards. So that the doors, windows & stair case would be all the parts which would be in any sort finished. Being still in expectation of living in my own house I have not asked Mᵣ Hollenback whether I can continue in his. It will be more easy to get his consent when the measure proves inevitable. You tell me Wᵐ Georges Tools &c. shall be remembered. I am happy to learn that Mʳ Doz & family are in health. Capt. Donnel's I hope is in like condition. To all of them Mʳˢ P. Joins me in kind remembrance. I am afraid Lazel will think 30/. too low for his scythes that remained unsold: but you will hear from him. I see no copy of a letter to him, to which you seem to refer. They will answer in this settlement, & I shall be pleased to receive them in the course of the winter. I wrote you in my last about the wine, & leave the sales to your discretion. I am happy in your brother's good fortune, & thank him for his remembrance of my family. I am greatly obliged by your attention to my requests, & very glad of the remittance to Nazareth. I hope to obtain some or all of those articles shortly, as I intend to send my waggon for a second load to Hallers next Tuesday; & shall write by Colᵒ Denison to Mʳ Henry to endeavour to forward the goods to Hallers: however tis only 7 miles from Hallers to Nazareth. I shall have great plenty of vegetables for winter but shall much want my own cellar to keep them in. Hollenback lodges abroad & my family has the 3 front chambers & garret. Dʳ Rush did not write me. The draught with Wallis in the Bend & eastward of it is fortunate, beyond all comparison the most valuable flats in that quarter are ours: He has the mill seat on the Starucca, but (as I wrote before) I am persuaded a more eligible one is in lot N° 1. near the river and by tracing up the creek about as far as the Mill seat on the Starucca is from the Susquehanna, we shall find one still better (as a major Buck informed us) on the Canawacta, than that on the Starucca. Wallis has that abominable tract of mountain covered with rocks & laurel (but without trees) which discouraged Horton, & reduced him indeed almost to despair. I return your congratulations for our success in the draughts.

Capt. Schott has made me an offer of some lands on terms which perhaps may be highly advantageous. But I cannot determine until I know the exact amount of his debt to Mʳˢ Kepple the corner of Arch & 4th street. Tis by bond for I think £60. Pray be so good as to enquire, & how many years interest are due, & what costs upon any action, if any has been brought. In a word, the entire sum he will have to pay, to settle her demand against him, & if I should undertake to settle the whole, within what time at farthest the money must be paid. I expect Mʳ Wᵐ

Nichols may be here at our Court: if there be opportunity, please to send an ounce of lapis Calaminaris & half a pint of the purest red rose water by him. Almost all our eyes are sore.

There is no Bohea tea in this place, except a pound perhaps that remains of mine. If it were possible to procure & send me speedily 28 or 56 lbs it would very materially serve my interest. 6^{lbs} of black pepper & 2^{lbs} of indigo would also be desireable. If Mr Williams's leather is not sold, I would gladly receive 10 or 20 sides more of it. I readily barter it for produce and labour at 2/3, & the demand will increase in the fall and winter. In one of my letters to you or Mr Rea I desired the set of brass weights which I bought of Capt. Moulder, might be sent for and forwarded: we have been and are much troubled for want of them. Carpenters tools I find are very scarce; I could get hands to advantage if I had tools for some of them. One has offered to work at 6^d less per day, & is earnest for the work, but has not tools. One Carpenter's Adz, 2 broad Carpenter's Chizzels, 2 narrow ditto (or heading ones I believe they are called,) 1 steel plate hand saw, 1 fore plane, 1 smoothing plane 1 jack plane, & half a dozen plane irons would suffice. If you should have procured me an Irish carpenter without tools, he also will require such as are of indispensable necessity. The Brick layer the same in his trade. Present the affectionate regards of Mrs P. & myself to Mr Doz & family, & Capt. Donnel & family & accept the same for yourself. Remember me to Mr Rea. Adieu.

T. Pickering

P. S. My wife just informs me that George & William George will each want a coarse woolen outer jacket, with sleeves. Double or triple that quantity will come in play. twist, buttons, & something for facing will be also wanted. She adds something suitable for breeches for them will also be wanting very soon. The same cloth may serve for both garments. Our wants multiply as I write so I stop.

[101] Warrant for the Arrest of John Franklin.[1]

Pennsylvania ss.   The Commonwealth of Pennsylvania to Zebulon Butler Esquire Lieutenant of the county of Luzerne, Lord Butler Esquire Sheriff of the same county, and to all and

---

[101] [1] M. H. S., Pickering Papers, LVII, 271, the original warrant, which was enclosed in a letter from Vice President Charles Biddle to the commissioners; no. 103, *post.*

singular the Bailiffs, Constables and other our Ministers within our said county, and particularly to William Nichols [2] of the city of Philadelphia Esquire, greeting. Forasmuch as the Chief Justice of our Supreme court has been credibly informed, and hath good reason to believe, and doth believe, that John Franklin late of the aforesaid county of Luzerne Esquire, being a pernicious & seditious man, and a person of a disquiet mind, and contriving, practicing and maliciously & turbulently intending our peace & common tranquility, to molest and disturb, hath at divers times, within the last six months, in the said county of Luzerne, in the presence & hearing of divers of our liege Citizens, denied Our Jurisdiction in and over the said county, and incited and encouraged divers inhabitants of the said county to disobey Our laws and to resist Our Government, to the evil example of all others in the like case offending and against Our peace. These are therefore to require you, or some, or one of you, immediately upon receipt hereof to bring the said John Franklin before Our said Chief Justice, or one of the Judges of our Supreme court, to answer the premises, and to be further dealt withal according to law. Witness the Honorable Thomas M⁢ᶜKean Esquire, Doctor of Laws, Chief Justice of Our Supreme courts at Philadelphia the thirty first day of August in the twelfth year of our Government, and in the year of our Lord one thousand seven hundred and eighty seven.[3]

Tho M:Kean

[102] Samuel Hodgdon to Timothy Pickering.[1]

Philadelphia 31ˢᵗ August 1787

Dear Sir

On my return from *Dover* which was last evening, I found your esteemed favour of the 26ᵗʰ instant.[2] today I hear of an Opportunity for answering but being fatigued and very Much

---

[2] William Nichols had been appointed by the Council a notary and tabellion public on June 29, 1786; *Pa. C. R.,* XV, 45. In May, 1787 he was admitted as one of four attorneys to practice before the Luzerne Court of Common Pleas; Pickering Papers, LVII, 223. Later he became a United States marshal.

[3] On the following day McKean and one of the other judges, George Bryan, conferred with the Council on "fresh disturbances in the county of Luzerne"; *Pa. C. R.,* XV, 265.

[102] [1] M. H. S., Pickering Papers, XL, 225-26, in Hodgdon's hand.

[2] Nos. 99 and 100, *ante.*

engaged I cannot riply fully. I am happy to hear the Commissioners are present, and proceeding on the business assigned them. the greatest firmness is become Necessary to stop the current that has and will prevail from delay. some of the Gentlemen have much to answer for on this score, if they think so they will now exert themselves. Colonel Zebulon Butler is this day appointed County Lieutenant, and the Militia is to be immediately arranged, the spirit of the people is up, and Government at all hazards will *now* be supported. The Assembly comes togather Next week. *Stuart* [3] says they *will repeal* the *confirming Law.* he is laughed at by all Men of sense, but persists, the event will be speedily known. Livingston scheme is well understood here.[4] he is not alone in it. Many considerable Characters in York state, and in his Brittish Majesty's Province of Canada are in the secret, and joined in the business, but here it is thought to be harmless from the colouring given. you can best judge of their designs by the Movements they make. that Country at all events will be settled, and the present commotions may facelitate what all wish. I am satisfied from your representations, that the store business should immediately commence. of this I will write you fully by the Next conveyance. the risque of a trial cannot be greatly injurious, for the expences may and ought to be circumscribed. Another arrival this day from Ireland, gives a greater probability of obtaining the Men you want, and they shall be sought affter without loss of time. The compleat draught of our Lands in the bend and elsewhere on the North East branch shall be forwarded within a few days, that you may avail yourself of any favourable offers that may be made. Francis says he will submit all his to your disposal in *any way* without instruction. I am well pleased with our Lot in that business. we have paid *Wallis* of in *full,* and have settled also with the *Land Office,* so that we have *nothing* further to do but obtain the *Patent.* this if we chuse may urge an advantageous sale. Capt Schotts business shall be attended to, and you shall have information previous to the purchase.[5] the Lapis Calaminaris and rose water shall come by Mʳ Nichols if he can take them. Bohea Tea Pepper and Indigo shall be forwarded as Opportunities present. Observe what you say relative to tools. they will come on as will the articles Mentioned by Mʳˢ Pickering. We have sustained a loss of 21 Cases of gin during my absence, by Mʳ Rea's leaving open One of the store windows. I am taking Measures for their recovery, but am not sanguine that I shall succeed. I

---

[3] Probably Charles Stewart; see no. 91, *ante.*
[4] No. 100, *ante,* note 5.   [5] See no. 100, *ante.*

find it Necessary to be present every Moment, for disipation destroys confidence. Of this more hereafter. all Matters not particularly attended to now, will be in my next. present my compliments to M⁺˙ Pickering and the family. My Brothers best regards and wishes attend you and yours. M⁺ Doz's family are well as are Cap⁺ Donnells and both desire to be very kindly remembered to you. Adieu With affection and the most cordial esteem I am yours

Samuel Hodgdon

[103] Charles Biddle to the Wyoming Commissioners.[1]

In Council Philadelphia September 1ˢᵗ 1787

Gentlemen

Notwithstanding Government are taking every measure in their power to satisfy the People of Luzerne, we are informed some wicked persons are endeavouring to deceive the People and prevent the execution of the Law. Understanding that John Franklin is at the head of this opposition, we have thought it necessary to send a warrant to apprehend him. If you are of opinion it will tend to preserve the peace of the County you can have it executed during the sitting of the Court, however we leave you to Judge of the time it should be executed, or if you think it advisable you may have it surpress'd.

You may assure the people of the County that every encouragement will be given to the peaceable Citizens, and that those who may occasion any disturbance in the Settlement shall be prosecuted with the utmost rigour of the Law. I am Gentlemen your obedient and humble Servant

Chaˢ Biddle V. P.

[104] Timothy Pickering's Charge to the Grand Jury of Luzerne County.[1]

Gentlemen of the Grand Jury!

It has been the practice of courts having cognizance of criminal causes to address the grand juries attending them in what is

---

[103] [1] M. H. S., Pickering Papers, LVII, 269, signed.
[104] [1] M. H. S., Pickering Papers, LVII, 272-73, a draft in Pickering's hand. Pickering spoke in his capacity as clerk of the quarter sessions of the peace, a court having criminal jurisdiction.

called a *charge,* therein suggesting the several matters concerning which it is their duty to enquire. These are generally the same in the courts of inferiour jurisdiction in Pennsylvania, as in those of New England; What difference there may [be] is grounded on particular statutes adapted to the local circumstances of the different states. The Offences against such statutes may be particularly pointed out at the next session of this court there having been no opportunity of inquiring into them before the present term. I will therefore only observe, in a few words, That the first breaches of the peace are the most common subjects of enquiry at the courts of general quarter sessions of the peace. The crime of fornication you are also to present, as well that the guilty may be punished, as that provision may be made for the maintenance of bastard children. In these and any other matters which may be known to you, or which may be laid before you by the Commonwealth's attorney, you will enquire with diligence impartiality and firmness, fearing no consequence for the honest and faithful discharge of your duty. I trust in God there is virtue, good sense & spirit enough in the freemen of this county to yield you effectual support. It has been the artful practice of a certain class of people here to be continually throwing out threats of doing personal injury to certain characters, & to any others who should aid them in the execution of the laws, thereby expecting to intimidate the peaceable inhabitants, who are the most valuable part of every community ; and I am sorry to say that such threats appear in any degree to have answered the wishes of the few turbulent men who have used them. I trust however that their influence is at an end ; and and that the minds of the good people of this county will no longer be disturbed, nor the introduction of peace order & law continued to be obstructed by a small knot of desperate men ; most of whom indeed, are deluded and deceived by their leaders, who seem willing to sacrifice the peace, happiness & interest of the body of the people to gratify their resentments & promote their own ambitious schemes. I need not name individuals ; you all know to whom I refer ; Beware therefore, I intreat you, of the pernicious designs of such men. They will deceive under the mask of friendship ; and pretending to be our friends, are the worst enemies we have. These indeed, and a small portion of the men whom we formerly knew under the name of Pennamites, are the only enemies of this settlement now existing, and these two parties, tho' with very different views, seem willing to league together for our destruction. Both are zealously endeavouring to prevent the happy establishment of peace and property which the late law of this state was calculated to effect. But it is our duty and our interest equally to oppose the attempts of both, and we manifest a small degree of resolution & firmness, we shall have nothing to fear from either. The government of our parent state, Connecticut, and the best and most discerning men in it, have manifested their satisfaction with the confirming law above referred to, and those good men there who are our truest friends earnestly recommend our perfect acquiescence under the government & laws of Pennsylvania; and the best wish I can form, is, that we may all have wisdom enough to follow their advice.

[105] Deposition of Tunes Dolsan.[1]

Tunes Dolsan of Tioga testifies That John Franklin John Jenkins, William Jenkins, Col° M‘Inster,[2] with others were last week assembled at Tioga (one of whom had on a light coat, a black waistcoat & black breeches, & who, I am informed, is Zerah Beech). That Uriah Stevens of the flat called Queen Esther's, near Tioga, declared to me, in company with Elijah Buck, that last Friday (being the 31st of August) he had a conversation with one Green from Fishing Creek, & an adherent to the said John Franklin; in the course of which the said Green (taking said Stevens to be of the same party) informed said Stevens that their design (meaning the design of said Franklin's party) was to erect an independent state, and that he (said Green) could bring from Fishing Creek forty men to assist them. I farther declare that said Green informed said Stevens (as Stevens declared in presence of said Buck & myself) that they (meaning said Franklin's party) had had a meeting at Thomas McClure's at Tioga Point, last Thursday the 30th of August, & that he said Green was with them. I farther declare, that last Friday evening I saw and read an advertisement put up at the Store of Matthias Hollenback Esq. at Tioga calling upon the people or inhabitants there to present the claims for their lands there to the Committee, on the Tuesday following, which is this day.
Sworn September 4, 1787.
Before Obad[h] Gore Justice of the peace

[105] [1] M. H. S., Pickering Papers, LVII, 274, in Pickering's hand but signed by Gore. The hearsay character of this testimony hardly needs comment. See no. 124, *post,* note 2.

[2] Col. John McKinstry, associated with Joseph Hamilton in land speculation schemes in New York. See nos. 109, and 128, *post.*

[106] Timothy Pickering to Benjamin Franklin.[1]

Wilkesborough, Sept. 5, 1787.

Sir,

I was honored with a letter from Council, inclosing a commission for Col. Butler, whom they have been pleased to appoint lieutenant of this county.[2] It arrived opportunely. The Col. accepted the Commission, which, by permission, I read in the County Court, in the hearing of the grand & traverse juries, & the spectators; and in open court I also administered to him the oaths of allegiance & of office, and read the Council's letter to him, repeating, with an emphasis, that part in which the aid of government is promised in support of the peaceable inhabitants of the county.

Franklin & Jenkins were at Tioga last Monday; and on Tuesday were to sit, with Beach & others, to receive & examine the claims of the inhabitants in that quarter by the lands in their possession; agreeably to an advertisement posted up at Tioga by their order. A Col., McInster, from Hudson, (Claverac) and one Allen, from Rhode Island, are said to have met them there.[3] I have a deposition declaring that one of their company confessed that their plan was to erect an independent state.[4] This deponent's information came from the person to whom the confession was made. Another person arrived this evening from Tioga, but I am not informed what intelligence he brings.[5] Two of the Justices here intend shortly to be in Philadelphia, by whom I will communicate particularly, whatever shall appear worthy of the notice of the Council. I have the honor to be, Sir, Your most obedient servant,

T. Pickering.

P. S. Council's letter to the Commissioners[6] was also received by Mr. Nichols.[7]

---

[106] [1] *P. A.*, XI, 180-81.

[2] Council's letter to Pickering has not been found, but the Council wrote to Zebulon Butler on September 1, notifying him of his commission as county lieutenant and ordering him to hold elections for militia officers as soon as possible; *ibid.*, 179.

[3] John McKinstry and Capt. Benjamin Allen.   [4] No. 105, *ante.*

[5] Possibly Thomas Wigton; see no. 109, *post.*

[6] No. 103, *ante.*   [7] See no. 101, *ante*, note 2.

[107] Timothy Pickering to Samuel Hodgdon.[1]

Wilkesburgh Sept. 6. 87.

Dear Sir

Your favours by M[r] Nichols I received:[2] His sudden departure prevents my touching on business. This is principally to acknowledge your favours & to inform that my family are well. Yesterday a second load of my goods arrived from Haller's in my own waggon, after 2 axletrees had been broken, & a third put in by the Carpenter I sent from hence 15 miles to the waggon. It was the fore axletree, & is the 4th new one since I left Phila[a] that put in at Bethlehem, having sprung to such a degree that I was obliged to throw it away. I find it will not do to bring goods by the way of the swamp till the roads are essentially altered for the better. It will be cheaper to transport every thing by the way of Middletown.[3] M[r] Hollenback will go to Philadelphia shortly, & by him I will write more fully on this & other matters. We have held a peaceable court. Franklin is still at Tioga. The Grand Jury have found two bills against him for breaches of the peace & feloniously stealing & carrying away another man's grain & hay: but I suspect in the latter case the point of law has been mistaken, & that it had been better not to have meddled with it. M[r] Nichols is waiting, & I must bid you for the present heartily adieu!

T. Pickering

[108] Jacob Weiss, Jr., to Timothy Pickering.[1]

Fort Allen September 7th 1787

Sir

The Road thro' the pine swamp from Shoops if opened this Fall would be of infinite service & am of opinion that if the £300 granted for the Road laid out by Col Balliet[2] was allowed, a

---

[107] [1] M. H. S., Pickering Papers, LVII, 275-76, in Pickering's hand.

[2] Probably no. 102, *ante.*

[3] That is, by road to Middletown and then up the Susquehanna River to Wilkes-Barre.

[108] [1] M. H. S., Pickering Papers, XIX, 111.

[2] See no. 44, *ante,* note 3.

Road thro' the swamp, and one from Nanticoke might be made.
I am told from Nanticoke to Balliets in the Nescopeck Valley
is about 10 Miles, *wanting to be open'd,* and as the Road laid
out by M[r] Owens[3] passes Balliets Farm in the Valley, it would
be a grand matter to get both opened as early as possible this
Fall, supposing £150 was allowed by Council for the pine swamp
Road, and as much for the Road from Nanticoke. this with what
Subscriptions I have already got, for both; would enable us to
open two Suitable Waggon Roads, and the whole now rests with
your getting this support from Government, and wish to hear
of such encouragement, I am with much esteem Sir Your most
obed[t] humb[l] Serv[t]

Jacob Weiss Jun[r]

[109] Deposition of Thomas Wigton.[1]

Sep[t] 8th 1787

I Thomas Wigton of the County of Luzerne declare that I
was at Tioga point the first, sencond, and third days of this Instant
that I Saw and was in Company with John Franklin Zerah Beech
and Col[o] Jn. M[c]Kinstry of Hudson who with a number of Others
were forming a plan to Oppose the laws of Pennsylvania being
Carried into Execution in the County of Luzerne. that Col[o]
Jn[o] M[c]Kinstry Said that they were fully Determined to Defend
the Cause of the Half Sharemen[2] Even to force of Arms [Jn[o]
Sheppard who runs M[r] Hollenback's store told me that the S[d]
m[c]Kinstry & Benj[a] Allen][3] brought Two Casks of powder with
them which were Deposited at the Store of Mathias Hollenback
Esq[r] at the point at Tioga which Casks I[4] Saw. Franklin and
Beech also manifested[5] their Intention of Opposing the laws of
Pennsylvania.[6] Franklin in particular said that he would Spill
his blood in the Defence of the half Share men. I[7] was further
Informed by Col[o] M[c]Instry[8] that General Ethan Allen would be
there in a fortnight with a number of men for their assistance

---

[3] Evan Owen, who laid out a road from the mouth of Nescopeck Creek
to the Lehigh River ; see no. 44, *ante.*
[109] [1] M. H. S., Pickering Papers, LVII, 277, a draft in Obadiah Gore's
hand. See no. 124, *post,* note 2.
[2] See *Susquehannah Company Papers,* VII, no. 141, note 4.
[3] The words in supplied brackets are interlined and substituted for "and
that they had." [4] "I" is substituted for "the deponent."
[5] "Manifested" is substituted for "Intimated."
[6] "Of Pennsylvania" is interlined.
[7] "I" is substituted for "the deponent."
[8] "Col[o] M[c]Instry" is substituted for "them."

and that there was no Danger but they would have men Enough and that the Pennsylvanians would never fight like those who are particularly concerned.

further that they had posted up a notification to Convert those who Call themselves the proprietors of the Town of Athens for the purposes Specifyed in S^d notification a Coppy of which is Sent by Mr Shepard to Esqr Holenback & I [9] Declare it to be a true Coppy to the best of my recollection: [10] [I am certain that it was signed by John Franklin, whose hand writing I well know] [11] also that they had Sent Asa Starkweather out into the Country (to Hudson or Vermont, as was supposed) [12] as an Express for some purposes [with orders not to rest day or night on the way], [13] which information I [14] had from Tho$^•$ McCluer at [15] whose house they the S^d Franklin, Beech, McKinstry, Starkweather & others had Conveened.

I farther declare that [16] propositions were made me [17] by McKinstry & Beech of haveing my property (which was Infringed upon by their Adherents) together with my person fully and amply Secured and all my Damages which I had Sustained by them made Good on Condition of my Association and Joining them in their Scheems or Even Lying Neuter in the Cause

[110] Samuel Hodgdon to Timothy Pickering.[1]

Philadelphia 8th September 1787

Dear Sir

* * * The assembly are setting. I have had some talk with Finley [2] and other leading Members, on your affairs in the *New County,* as it is termed, and I have the pleasure of assuring you,

---

[9] "I" is substituted for "the deponent." The notification has not been found; for its contents see John Shepard's deposition; no. 320, *post.*

[10] "My recollection" is interlined and substituted for "his knowledge."

[11] The words in supplied brackets are interlined, "I am" being substituted for "he is."

[12] The phrase in parentheses is interlined.

[13] The phrase in supplied brackets is interlined.

[14] "I" is substituted for "the deponent."

[15] "At" is substituted for "the owner of."

[16] "I farther declare that" is substituted for "and that the deponent said."

[17] The first person singular pronoun is substituted here and everywhere in the wording that follows for the third person singular.

[110] [1] M. H. S., Pickering Papers, LVII, 280-84, in Hodgdon's hand.

[2] William Findley of Westmoreland County, a leader of the Constitutionalist faction.

they are highly pleased with your conduct in the business. Finley observed, that if with Organizing the Militia within the County, the Law could be supported, he thought all would be *well,* and that Goverment ought not further at present to interfere. Farewell! sincerely yours

Sam Hodgdon

[111] Joseph Hamilton to John Franklin.[1]

Hillsdale, Sept. 8, 1787.

Sir,

I flatter myself Starkweather[2] will be able to give you that information of our Ideas of policy which will be entirely satisfactory to you all and that you will be of our mind, think as we do on the subject. Notwithstanding what I wrote about the Town of Strong[3] &c., to reserve it yet upon further consulting we give it up, into the hands of the Commissioners to settle as they think best, the other Towns we wish to have surveyed and lotted and fifty lotts in each survey in the best lands any where in your town and send us the Platt of each & we will instantly fill them with settlers as many as you please, only give no one man more or less than one hundred acres for settling, I mean of good land or an equivalent thereto, you write as though you thought us discouraged, I don't know that we have given you any just reason for such an opinion. I am not in the least discouraged in case you do as you write, nay, I can say more I am willing to risque any thing I possess upon it, I do not conceive I have given you any just reason to make the conclusions you do make, however I heartily excuse you, it is time to be jealous, your jealousy begins with your friends, it will be well if it continues & ends with your enemies.

N. B. Nothing in our power to retain our lands has been hitherto omitted & you shall never have any reason to judge that we will for the future relax in the least, from your constant friend & servant,

Jos. Hamilton.

---

[111] [1] *P. A.,* XI, 182-83; M. H. S., Pickering Papers, LVII, 278, a copy certified by James Trimble. See no. 148, *post,* note 2.

[2] Starkwather had been sent to Hudson, New York, where Hamilton lived; no. 109, *ante.*

[3] Probably the town claimed by Solomon Strong; see Vol. VIII, no. 255, note 23.

P. S. I can write no more letters at present for want of time, tell Mr. Kinsley his family is well, my best compliments to him & Capt. Allen [4] & I thank them for their letters, will embrace the first opportunity to write.

[112] Joseph Hamilton to John Franklin.[1]

City Hudson, September 10, 1787.

Sir,

I now sit down to observe on a clause of your letter which in my former was unnoticed.[2] You say you cannot concieve from whence my fears arose. I will tell you sir, how it is—principal & leading characters here will believe that you never will be able to klink up a Bubbery [3] there & act on a different scale of policy untill you have really done it & untill that is done the truth is they will not venture any further part of their property or character so that you readly see your schemes at an end, for what can I do to all out of my private pocket. moreover Sir, if I should tell them that there was something about to be done which by the way would be dangerous, our enemies may take the hint too soon, nay if I could in order to prove it show some clause in your letter which I have often done to keep up their spirits, they would immediately say this has been an old story for a long time, we do not believe it, Colonel Franklin is mistaken in his policy from what we hear almost every day, it is very probable to us that he will be in person soon if he is not already in the practice of Physic where life is in question, it is an observation of Dr. Huxham that the low & timid method of practice is as reprehensible as the bold & quirical, for while the one neglects an opportunity never to be regained, the other wafts you off the stage in a moment.

However, if you suddenly & in a proper time sever the wheat from the chaff among you, & suffer not a dissenting whisper among you, I can assure you this part of the world will be better in removing them as soon as they know of such a matter. From your friend & servt.

Joseph Hamilton.

P. S. I think you have & harbour in your Country a curious monster of two heads in one body, for what else are your two

---

[4] Benjamin Allen from Rhode Island; nos. 109 and 106, *ante.*
[112] [1] *P. A.,* XI, 185; M. H. S., Pickering Papers, LVII, 285-85A, a copy certified by James Trimble. See no. 148, *post,* note 2.
[2] No. 111, *ante.*   [3] Stir up a dispute or quarrel.

setts of Commissioners which you allow among you, granting the same lands, Gore said in his letter to me that as soon as they meddled with the title of lands he would find Indians enough to protect them. Where are Gore's Indians, are they scattered away by his new settlers at Newtown.[4]

One obervation more I think important which is that no one non-resident proprietor whatever ought to hold any piece of land out of the hands of the Commissioners to dispose of to settlers who will immediately take possession but the Commissioners ought to dispose of the Lands and keep fair Records of their Transactions and in future make ample compensation.

[113] Joseph Hamilton to [John Franklin and Others?][1]

Septem. 10, 1787.

Sir,

I am just now informed by Captain Coon of this place that yesterday afternoon Captain Strong[2] crossed this River on his way to Wyoming, that he said he had matters with him necessary to lay before the Pennsylvania Commissioners for a confirmation of his lands, that he was determined to pursue it, that he had determined heretofore to hold it under Connecticut claim, but that was over, the Laws were in exercise & it was too late. You will let your enemies secure their lands under that title, pass & repass in that Country, wait on their commissioners &c., without obstruction, but will scold at your friends, nay your best friends

---

[4] See John Franklin's opinion of Obadiah Gore in no. 65, *ante*. Apparently Gore was keeping a foot in both camps, supporting Pickering and the Confirming Act as it affected the old towns along the Susquehanna River, but promising to take some part in laying out new towns under the Company's auspices well to the west along tributaries of the modern Tioga River. The map in Vol. I shows a town of "Gorsburgh" there. But Gore also accepted Pickering's patronage. The latter wrote Francis Johnston asking that he use his influence with the surveyor-general to get Gore a surveying post; see Johnston's reply, October 1, 1787, Pickering Papers, LVII, 304.

For Newtown see no. 92, *ante,* note 4. Gore and some associates had petitioned the New York legislature for lands in 1783 and 1784. Ultimately they got grants along the Chemung River (then called the Tioga); see Vol. VII, nos. 142 and 205.

[113] [1] *P. A.,* XI, 183-84; M. H. S., Pickering Papers, LVII, 284-84A, a copy certified by James Trimble. See no. 148, *post,* note 2.

[2] Solomon Strong probably. For Coon see no. 119, *post.*

who would risque every thing dear to them for your safety and welfare, nay you will reprobate them for the most distant proposal, in short such policy appears, to me to be a very visible matter. I have known many a patient in a highly inflammatory fever, being attended by a timid physician who dare not let blood, suffer the disolution of his whole body barely for want of drawing a little Blood from the arm.

Nay Gentlemen suffer me to advise you that if you suffer Pennsylvania Politicks any longer to intermingle with yours then to take Strongs method, get a confirmation of the land from them and then find some fool to purchase of you, and so save something, for it is a pity that men who have first fairly purchased the Land paid for it at a dear rate and suffered every thing that can be named but death itself nay have lost hundreds of lives in defence of it through a long & bloody war & in that defence have defended the lives & property of those very state dignified & dirty rascals who now mean to possess it, I say now without the flash of a single Gun rifle or any of the least resistance to be manuevered trucked and jockeyed out of the whole is too much for people who have had the name of brave people, but if you should in proper time afford a manly resistance to a power exercised in the eyes of all the world, for the most villainous purposes my desire is that you should reserve an handsome seat on the Tioga point for we think it policy in such case, that either Doctor Benton or myself should remove to that place in the Spring to continue there. this matter we have talked of between us & agreed on, but we can do nothing without your exertions & that resolute ones to, we have got the money chest in possession, we are very sensible of, but then you have the key, no righteous wheel will move until you move and that in such manner as to make the world know you are in earnest, they all think you are jesting, madness in you would not surprize the world half so much as has your past conduct, for surely oppression maketh the wise man mad, we naturally reason thus either that you are not wise men or that the scripture is not true. Be assured the greatest outrages attended with a thousand inadvertencies & even large imprudence would afford much less astonishment in the eyes of the world at large, then the calm, soft, easy Lethargy & pusillanimous scenes that are now passing in that county. Another observation, True policy knows no passion, you all will therefore calmly consider the whole matter as to the precise time to begin, but sure I am, that if it is not done this fall you cannot have much succour from this quarter.

N. B. upon hearing from me, I anticipate your observations, you say Dr. Hamilton is a coward, he fights well at a distance but he will not venture his own skin, he can talk and write but that is all, &c., &c.

I own I was never bred a Warrior, I am no fighter, am of a timid make &c., but I call G-d to witness that my feelings are that in equal combat in the present cause, I would not think myself in to much danger to encounter the men you have on the ground, and if you will contrive any way that I may do Justice to my large & Tender Family who have already suffered every thing but death in that country, I will be with you in a fortnight, but then you shall make a noise or I will not tarry to die such a tapering death.

Jos. Hamilton.

[114] Extract from the *Connecticut Courant*.[1]

PHILADELPHIA, August 29 [1787]
We learn from Wyoming, that a dangerous combination of villains, composed of runaway debtors, criminals, adherents of Shays, &c is now actually forming on the river Susquehanna. *Tioga-Point* seems to be their general rendezvous. They extend some distance down, as well as up the river, including also *Tioga Branch.* They have had a gathering to council of their principal partizans, who oppose the introduction of law in that settlement. They carry every thing with a high hand, in open defiance of all government, except their own; Last week they were to try a man for his life, who refused to comply with their injunctions; but the issue is not yet known. Their avowed design is to institute a *new state;* and, if they are not timely checked and restrained, will soon become very troublesome and dangerous. They encrease very fast, and their present numbers are by no means inconsiderable. Immediate and decisive measures ought to be taken against them; but it is to be lamented that our governments admit of no decision. It is for the want of energy in this respect, that we see *banditties* rising up against law and good order in all quarters of our country.

[114] [1] September 10, 1787.

[115] Nathan Denison to Timothy Pickering.[1]

Philadelphia the 12th of Septembr 1787

Dear Sir

Esq[r] Meed[2] has been in this town Considerable time Past interceeding With the bord of property to git his Equivelent Confirmed to him in lands at the Weston Part of this State, for the Lands that he Claims in Luzerne County. it appears to me that the bord go into the measure With allmost as grate reluctance as the Comisoners Went into the buisenes of inquireing into the Claims or title of the Connecticut Claiments at Wyoming. mr Meed mets With Some Discourigments in his persutes tho Seems fully Detirmined to Comply With the late law of the State. if the Commisenors at Wyoming Can put the matter on Such a futing that mr Meed Can have Justice Don him it may indue others of the pennsylvani Claments to follow the Same Exmple. Colonal Stewart has been in town for Som Considerable time past. What Plan he is per Suing is not Knoon to me. it is Expected that the plan Come into by the Convention Will be made Public this present Week. am S[r] With Esteem and respect your most obediant and very humb[l] Serv[t]

Nathan Denison

[116] Ebenezer Gray to Zebulon Butler.[1]

Windham Sept[r] 12th, 1787

Sir

I have Just heard the Pensylvania Comissioners for quieting the Claims of the settlers are now at Wyoming on that Bussiness and that the Priniples adopted by them will include me as a settler. I intend to be at Wyoming with the Evidence of my Title to lay before them in the beginning of October. I would request you to mention to Col° Pickering that I have a claim to Wapwallapin and desire that there may not be any Determination on that spot until I can come & lay in in my Claim. Times

---

[115] [1] M. H. S., Pickering Papers, LVII, 286, in Denison's hand.
    [2] David Mead, against whom Franklin forces had taken action in 1785; see *Susquehannah Company Papers*, VIII, Index.
[116] [1] Wilkes College Library, Wilkes-Barre, Pa., McClintock Papers, in Gray's hand.

are dull no money, weak Government who have no Idea of a certain Thing called Justice or in other words no Intention of paying their Just Debts. Presenting Compliments to Mrs Butler, and am with great Esteem Yours &c

Eben^r Gray [2]

[117] Roger Sherman to Zebulon Butler.[1]

PHILADELPHIA, Sept. 13th, 1787.

SIR,—I am informed by Col. Denison that the commissioners appointed by the State of Pennsylvania are proceeding in examining the claims of the people settled under the claim of Connecticut and that they appear disposed to do justice to the claimants so far as they are enabled by the law. I hope it will be a happy means of quieting the inhabitants in their possessions—I hear that some of the claimants are opposed to the measure but it appears to me it will be for the interest of all of them to get a confirmation of their title to as much land as they can under that law, though they may not get so much as they may think themselves entitled to; whatever they get confirmed they may enjoy peaceably or dispose of as they please—the many and great calamities that the people of the settlement have undergone have given me great concern—their future peace and prosperity would give me much pleasure.

[118] Timothy Pickering to Benjamin Rush.[1]

Wilkesburg, Sept. 13. 1787

Dear Sir,

I received your favour of the 30th ult° by Mr Nichols,[2] for which I am much obliged. The advice you give me "to put a

---

[2] Ebenezer Gray was the son of Samuel Gray, long-time secretary to the Susquehannah Company. That he was willing to resort to the commissioners for confirmation of his lands suggests that not all the old proprietors were adverse to cooperation, as was John Franklin. *Cf.* also Eliphalet Dyer to Timothy Pickering; no. 98, *ante*.

On November 9, 1787, Gray gave Butler a power of attorney to act in his behalf; Wyoming Historical and Geological Society, Butler Papers.

[117] [1] Lewis H. Boutell, *The Life of Roger Sherman* (Chicago, 1896), p. 340. Sherman had long taken an interest in the Connecticut claimants. See correspondence between him and John Franklin in Vol. VII.

[118] [1] Haverford College Library, Haverford, Pa., Charles Roberts Collection, in Pickering's hand.

[2] William Nichols; see no. 101, *ante*, note 2.

bold face on things" I have been urging on the people here these six months past, and reproached them for their fears of the arch villain Franklin: but they have been so long accustomed to his yoke, that tho' it now sensibly galls them, many know not how to throw it off. On every occasion *I* express for him as much contempt as indignation. I have been repeatedly told that I, among a few others, am to be a victim of his party's revenge, if Franklin should be apprehended: but I take no farther notice of such threats than to remember then, that if there should be occasion for it, I may be on my guard. I have reflected *seriously* on such an attack, and am determined to put to death any of the villains who shall attempt to seize or injure me. This seditious crew are hatching mischief, & proceed to repeat their former violences and deceptions with surprizing impudence. They lately held a meeting at Tioga, when they ordered off all persons who did not hold lands there under Franklin's grants. I had given a lease to one man there (Epinetus Owen) in behalf of the company with whom I am concerned in the New Purchase.[3] Him they ordered off, instantly, and have advertised his corn for sale. Franklin continues to sell and dispose of half share rights in the Susquehanna Company's claims, and John Jenkins surveys them, the latter often selling the land surveyed for a trifle, to pay his surveying fees. They are thus daily cheating a number of deluded people, to whom they pretend a just right to sell these lands; and the cheapness of the bargain tempts them to buy. What crime shall this be called? What would it be called in any other county of the state, if any set of men, not authorized by the Government, should open a land office, and sell and survey the lands of the Commonwealth? I ask this question, not from curiosity; but that it may be made a subject of enquiry. It appears to me so great a crime, that fine and imprisonment are the lightest punishments which can be inflicted on the actors. As it affects individuals, 'tis such palpable *cheating,* that I presume Franklin & Jenkins might be indicted for common cheats. Pray consult Mr. Wilson on this business, and put the government in motion to apply immediate remedies to these great evils. The county will not have peace while those two men are at large. They are conscious of having offended past forgiveness, & the possibility of retrieving their characters; and are therefore ready to hazard any measure of desperation. If the present laws reach not their offences, pray let some be made to point directly at

---

[3] See no. 134, *post,* for a description of Pickering's land holdings.

them. By direction of the Justices at the late quarter sessions I have written to the speaker of the assembly, praying that we may hold the ensuing general election without the usual formalities, or, as we held the one in Febʸ last, and that we may convey prisoners to the jails of Northampton & Northumberland until our jail shall be built.[4] Without the first we can hold no election, & without the last the laws (especially the criminal laws) must remain unexecuted. At the late court of quarter sessions the Grand jury had courage enough to indict Franklin for a breach of the peace and an assault and battery, and in another bill to indict him and three or four others for stealing a man's grain and hay. The justices have ordered warrants to be issued for apprehending them; but I postpone issuing them until the law shall authorize their confinement in the jails of the two neighbouring counties: for they will be cunning enough to refuse to give bail, if apprehended, knowing that at present they cannot be put out of the county, & consequently that they must be discharged. I am dear sir with great respect & esteem yᵣ very h'ble servant

T. Pickering.

P. S. I notice what you say relative to our new federal government, & hope you are not too sanguine.
P. S. Matthias Hollenback & Obadiah Gore Esqᵣ of this county are now going to your city. I shᵈ wish you to see them to get many particulars of the practises and designs of Franklin & his party. Ask for them at Col° Farmers, King of Prussia, Market Street.

[119] Zerah Beach to [John Franklin?].[1]

Tioga 14ᵗʰ Septᵣ 1787.

Dᵣ Sir

I have only to inform you Doctᵣ Benton is sending on men, 8 arrived on Monday, have proceeded on to the town of Hamilton, Capt. Coon & family I expect every day. Owens is about going

---

[4] Pickering's letter was read in the General Assembly on September 20. The committee to whom it was referred recommended that a bill be brought in to permit use of Northumberland and Northampton jails and to permit departures from election requirements temporarily; *Minutes of the Third Session of the Eleventh General Assembly,* 229, 233 (microfilm copy).
[119] [1] M. H. S., Pickering Papers, LVII, 287, a copy in an unknown hand. The note is in Pickering's hand.

he says he is determined to have his crops or die in the attempt.[2] I am apprehensive Depue intends to finish his house. I send by Doct[r] Holbrook a letter from Doctor Benton to Gore, I believe Benton is playing out a card of policy with him. Let me hear from you as soon as possible and know if you trade with Alden. I am D[r] S[r] yours &c.

Zerah Beach

(Copy)
Taken Sept. 20, 1787.

N. B. D[r] Benton lives at Hillsdale in York state, adjoining Egremont in Massachusetts. Capt. Coon from New York State. Owens is the man Franklin & party, when lately met at Tioga, ordered to quit the lands he lived on at that place, and whose corn they advertised for sale. Depue is a friend to Government. Franklin was to treat with Alden for the purchase of his right in Athens for Beach's use. The town of *Hamilton* is on the Chemung,[3] in Pennsylvania, about 50 miles westward of Tioga. Three towns are pitched there—Goresburg[4]—Benton'sborough & Hamilton.

[120] Timothy Pickering to Samuel Hodgdon.[1]

Wilkesburgh Sept[r] 15, 1787.

Dear Sir

I expected to have written you several days ago; but M[r] Hollenbach delayed his journey. I inclose a plan and description of a large tract of land discovered by Ebenezer Marcy and his associates. M[r] Marcy is a man of sense, a judge of lands, and of a perfectly fair reputation; and as he has been over the lands, his description may be relied on. What appears in my hand writing is taken from his mouth. I have more than once mentioned the land to M[r] Meredith, & he & M[r] Cunningham appeared disposed to take it up. I request you therefore without a day's delay to make a tender of them to M[r] Meredith, in the first place, & to M[r] Cunningham. If they decline the concern, endeavour to find

---

[2] See no. 118, *ante.*

[3] Now called the Cowanesque, originally considered part of the Tioga. The fact that the word *Chemung* is used suggests that this note was written well after 1787. See map in envelope in Vol. I.

[4] See no. 112, *ante,* note 4.

[120] [1] M. H. S., Pickering Papers, XXXV, 19, in Pickering's hand.

some gentlemen who will engage in it. Mr Marcy expects one third for the discovery. If I had the means I should like it myself: but under my present burdens must avoid the concern. Every gentleman to whom You may show the discovery, will have honour enough to keep it to himself, if he declines meddling in the purchase. You will be pleased to preserve the plan, to return to me, if nobody will purchase.

Inclose an order of Noah Webster Esq. on Messrs Spotswood & Leddon for parts of his institute [2] to the am^o of £5.17.10. Since the date of the order, he has informed me that some other printers (I think Young & McCullock) had taken his work to print: Be pleased to apply to Young & McCullock, and if they have rec^d no orders for the purpose, speak to Mr Webster & get a new order. I should wish to have five spelling books to one grammar; and but one copy of the 3^d part of the institute if printed.

You repeat the subject of a store at this place, and desire an estimate of the cost of a proper building for the purpose. As to such a building, I should not think it expedient to erect one at present, even if there were time. I shall doubtless get my house in such forwardness, that I can safely lodge liquors & my other goods in the cellar, which will be, I expect a very dry one. All the difficulty I have to apprehend respects the means of remittance. I think we could not expect 5 per Cent. in money. Flax seed I suppose may be got for 5 per bushel, but this bears a high price in Phila^a *only in the fall,* when the transportation is impracticable. Indian Corn will probably be at 2/ or 2/6, rye is at 3/6 & wheat @ 5/, oats at 1/10/2, good swingled flax @ 9^d. In the spring wheat, corn & rye have always fetched good prices; last spring wheat was @ 7/6 corn @ 5/, rye @ 5/6 @ 6/, but the flood of last fall occasioned a scarcity. Next Spring however, if peace be firmly established here will bring on many new settlers, who must be supplied with bread, & this will make grain in demand. We may reckon the different sorts to rise from 25 to 50 per Cent. in their prices, especially corn and wheat.

Agreeably to your request I shall inclose an invoice of the articles which I think will be in the greatest demand, in my next, which will go by John Scott who will set out on Tuesday, the 18th inst.

---

[2] *A Grammatical Institute of the English Language,* a speller, a grammar, and a reader; Harry A. Warfel, *Noah Webster, Schoolmaster to America* (New York, 1936), 54, 130, 163. Pickering had been an admirer of Webster for several years; see Webster to Pickering, October 28, 1775 in Warfel (ed.), *Letters of Noah Webster* (New York, 1953), 38-39.

I have given M[r] Hollenback an open letter to you in which I request the payment of £53.2.6, due to him on securities I gave last winter for the lands I purchased here. He is going to Philadelphia for his Winter stock of Goods, and his end will be answered, if the merchants with whom he deals accept your notes, at such payments as can be agreed on. I remain with much affection yours

T. Pickering

[121] Remonstrance of Luzerne Inhabitants against William Montgomery.[1]

To the Commissioners appointed to enquire into and ascertain the Claims of the Connecticut settlers in the County of Luzerne.

Whereas William Montgomery Esq[r] is appointed one of the Commissioners for the Purpose of enquiring into, and ascertaining the Claims of the Connecticut settlers in the County of Luzerne, agreeably to a Law of this State pass'd the 28th Day of March last and has undertaken to Proceed in that Capacity. And Whereas a matter of Such Importance demands that it be Determined by not only wise but the most unexceptionable Characters. Therefore we whose names are hereto subscribed, settlers Proprietors and owners of Lands in the County of Luzern, under the Connecticut Claim, Do Protest against the said William Montgomery acting in the capacity aforesaid for the following reasons:

1st The Partial proceedings of the board of Commissioners sent to Wyoming to endeavour a compromise between the Connecticut settlers and Persons Claiming in opposition, in 1783, of which board, the S[d] Montgomery was one. That notwithstanding the Said Commissioners were Instructed to pursue every measure to bring about a Reasonable Compromise between the said settlers and Pennsylvania Claimants, and most solemnly Pledged their own honour, and the faith of the State, that the said settlers should have all the advantages of Civil Government secured to them with Liberty to elect Justices of the Peace agreeably to the Laws and Constitution of the State, yet in Direct violation of the solemn Promise they had made to the setlers no reasonable Compromise was ever proposed, but Pledges were De-

[121] [1] M. H. S., Pickering Papers, LVII, 294-96, in John Franklin's hand and signed by 143 men.

manded for our good behaviour, and a total Relinquishment of all Claim to our Lands that we might thereby be Intiteled to the Priviledge of taking leases of the one half of our own Improved Lands for the term of Eleven months. And an Election of Justices was holden by order of the Commissioners in Violation of the Constitution. And that the said Montgomery being afterwards appointed one of a Committee to consider the report of the aforesaid Commissioners Did Report that he was fully satisfied with the laudable zeal and Industry used by the Commissioners sent to Wyoming, and that their offers made to the Connecticut settlers were generous, and that the Said settlers ought to be Ejected from their Lands, and dealt with as Tresspassers for Refusing to comply with the offers.[2]

2dly That in December 1784 the S^d Montgomery urged the Connecticut settlers to Purchace a Tract of their own Lands of the Pennsylvanian Claimants, that the same should be Divided between the said setlers and holden by Deeds under the Pennsylvania Claim which would entitle them to the Rights of free Citizens and benefits of freeholders; at the same time Declaring that without such a title the Said settlers could neither Elect Justices or be Elected. This Proposal[3] we conceive to be made for the avowed Purpose of leading the People into a snare, that by our Purchasing a new they might Plead the Invalidity of our former title.

3dly That by a Letter from the aforesaid William Montgomery Dated June the 22^d 1786 to his friend at Wyoming,[4] he Positively asserts that Congress have granted to the Susq^h Company, a Tract of Land West of the State of New York, in Lieu of a Relinquishment of all Claim to Wyoming Lands, and that the Susq^h Company and all Parties were satisfied with the same; and that he was authorized by a Letter from the President in Council to Inform the settlers of the Resolutions of Congress, all of which Assertions appear to be without the lest colour of truth, and done with a Design to Create Divisions and Disturbances amongst the settlers to give advantage to the Pennsylvania Land Monopolizers that they might unjustly avail themselves of our Justly acquired Lands and Property.

---

[2] *Cf.* the language of this paragraph with that in no. 78, *ante.*

[3] Montgomery's proposal has not been found.

[4] To Lawrence Myers; *Susquehannah Company Papers,* VIII, no. 227.

4th We cannot but Protest against the Said Montgomery, that
the general tenor of his conduct towards the Connecticut settlers
has ever been Conformable to the before recited instances of his
Prejudices and Partiality, we humbly Conceive that the whole
Collectively considered ought to Debar him from acting in his
official Capacity as Commissioner. Therefore we wish it to be
known to the Commissioners, as well as to the State of Pennsylvania, and the World that we have borne our Testimony against
the S^d William Montgomery acting in the Capacity aforesaid
County of Luzerne
Septr 18th 1787

James Fanning	Walter Watrus
Isaac Baldwin	Stephen Gardiner
Isaac Baldwin, Junr	Samuel tubs
Frederick Budd	Joseph Spalding
Oliver Bigelow	David Holbrook
Elisha Satterlee	Abnar Kelleey
Wm Slocum	Walter Watrus Junr
Ira Stephins	William Jenkins
Eldad Kellogg	Jno J. A^{c}Moder
Stephen Hellar	Elijah Griswold
Timothy Winchel	David McCormick
Benjn Bidlack	Phinihas Stevens
Thomas Ma^{c}Cluer	Stephen Parish
Elazer Newcomb	John Finch
John St john	Thomas Gilbert
Thomas Harding	Asa Pease
Ishmael Bennet	Joseph thomas
Nathan Abbott	Thomas Heath
Peleg Burrite	Tho^m Baldwin
Stephen Burrity	Josiah Marshel
Jonathan millet	Jo$^•$ Kinney
Andrew Millet	John Fuller
John Hurlbut	Jeremiah Shaw
Mason F. Alden	Jehiel Franklin
Alex^r Jameson	Isaac Foster
Jonathan Corey	Hezekiah Townsend
Joseph Corey	Wm Jackways
Jonathan Newman	John Horton
David Morehouse	Daniel Shaw
Jno Jenkins	Ephraim Tyler
Wm Williams	David [Wodard?]

197

Stephen Jenkins
Waterman Baldwin
Abraham Vanfleet
Rogers Searles
John Dickson
Enoch Miller
Ishmael Bennet [Jr?]
Fraderick fry
Narlshell Dickson
David Dickson
Isaac Dow Tripp
Joel thomas
David Ingersoll
Elisha Harding
Corneluis Hopper
Samuel Millr
William Miller
Daniel Campbell
Samuel Miller
John Davison
Elijah haris
Wm Hurlbut
[John Camstok?]
Benjamin Crawford
Titus Ives
Elisha Matherson
Stephen Stickland
Wm Hyde
Richard Inman
Elijah Inman
Ezra Bennet
Elijah Bennet
Charles Harris
Joseph Avery Rathbun
Abraham Pyke
Ira Manvill
David Huydon
Benjamin Corey
Jedediah Stephen s^r
Robert Cooley
Reuben Wells

Zaccheus [Wyrunger?]
Gideon dudley
Joseph Dudley
Daniell Earll
Daniel Earll Jr
Zebulon Cady
Jephthah Earll
Solomon Earll
Benjamin Earll
john mangin [Jr?]
Martin Dudley
joseph Earl
Jonathan W Rolph
Wm Jones
Gideon Church
Ambrose Gaylord
John ONeil
Stephen Arnold
Jonth Bunell
Timothy Ives
Richard Vaughn
John Ventner
Joshua Vanfleet
Moses Roberts
Bennajah Ives
Stephen Mills
Jeames Makem
Isaac Sears
John Ryon
John Hyde Junr
Ichabod Shaw
Jno Swift
Corn^s Atherton
Thos Duane
Jeremiah Baker
Samuel [Ayres?]
David Allen
Alman Church
Joel Atherton
Ephraim McKay

[122] Reply of the Wyoming Commissioners to the Remonstrance.[1]

To _____ and others, subscribers to a remonstrance,[2] presented yesterday against Wm Montgomery one of the Commissioners for examining the claims of the Connecticut Settlers in the county of Luzerne, pursuant to a late law of Pennsylvania entitled "An Act for ascertaining & confirming to certain persons called Connecticut Claimants the lands by them claimed within the county of Luzerne, & for other purposes therein mentioned."

The regard we bear to the well-disposed[3] inhabitants of this county, and our desire to give that information which may tend to preserve the peace thereof, induce us to notice the said remonstrance.[4]

In the first place we must remark, That it appears very improper to have been addressed to the Commissioners, who have no authority to set aside the appointments made by the government of the state, nor to suspend any one commissioner acting under that authority. This, Mr Franklin (in whose handwriting the remonstrance appears) very well knows; and that, if there are any just exceptions against Mr Montgomery, the application for his removal or suspension should be presented to the Supreme Executive Council, by whom he was appointed.

Without attempting to determine whether the charges against Mr Montgomery are or are not well founded, we observe, that they only respect his conduct three or four years ago, when the opinions of the inhabitants of Pennsylvania relative to the Connecticut Settlers here, were very different from what they are now, and when the laws of the state would not warrant their claims. At that time any man, the best friend to the settlers here, might have given his opinion that they had no *legal* title to their lands. Of this opinion indeed were the settlers themselves;

---

[122] [1] M. H. S., Pickering Papers, LVII, 297, a draft in Pickering's hand. Although an endorsement of uncertain origin gives the date as September 18, 1787, the document, since it refers to the "remonstrance presented yesterday," must have been written on September 19.

[2] No. 121, *ante*.

[3] "Peaceable" is lined out before "well-disposed."

[4] The following words are lined out here: "altho it appears very improperly presented to the Com addressed to the Commissioners."

why else have they repeatedly petitioned the Assembly of Pennsylvania to confirm their titles? If they had been good in law, they would have needed no confirmation. We desire not to be misunderstood: The settlers here doubtless supposed they had *equitable* titles to their lands, otherwise as honest men they ought not to have contended for the possession of them: but *equitable* titles, & titles that can be supported in *trials at law,* are often very different things. But tis quite immaterial what were the opinions of any persons about your titles four years ago: a law is now passed for making them *legal* titles, which, when established agreeably to the provisions of that law, nobody can controvert. To carry that Law into execution we and Mʳ Montgomery have been appointed. We have entered upon it, and made considerable progress therein, &, we trust, to the general satisfaction of the claimants. And if the other claimants in the county lose no time in presenting & supporting their claims, we hope to be able to get through the examination of them before the time allowed for that purpose shall expire. If in performing this service, Mʳ Montgomery or either of us depart from the law, or manifest any partiality to the injury of any claimants whatever, such claimants will then have good ground of complaint, and may apply to the Assembly or Council for our removal; and their complaints will assuredly be heard & their grievances to be redressed [5]

[123] Thomas Fitzsimons to Timothy Pickering.[1]

Philadᵃ 20 septʳ 1787.

Dear sir

The business you are Ingaged [in] has been So much the Object of publick attention for some time past, And feeling myself Very much Interested in it from the Share I took in Getting the Law under Which you Act passed, I have wished to Know how farr it is likely to answer the Good intention of its promoters. And to What extent the Claims of the Connecticut people will Go, in sum & in Value. Nothing Can Exceed the Virulence & Indecency of Some of the Pensylvᵃ Land owners, but to men so

---

[5] The last two or three lines have several phrases lined out but the alterations make no changes in meaning.

[123] [1] M. H. S., Pickering Papers, LVII, 298-99, in Fitzsimons' hand. Fitzsimons was a member of the General Assembly and of the Republican faction.

disposed Little Regard will be paid.[2] There is however Serious apprehension in the Minds of a different Class of people lest some Expressions in the Law shall be Construed so as to Let in Claims To a much Greater Extent than some of us at heart had in Expectation. Original settlers, & their Legal Representatives were all that were intended to be provided for. You can Inform me Whether the Law is Construed to go further. And as we shall be Incessantly plagued with these people I should wish if I am in the Assembly Next year to be able to Speak with Certainty upon these Subjects.

You will hear of the Application to the present house for Leave to Appoint a person Who with and to be Appointed for the State shall View the Lands & Return their Valuation to the board of property.[3] They desire to have Compensation in Certificates to be Issued for that purpose & a fund Established for their Redemption in some short period.

I think both Requests Reasonable & have so Represented to the house, but I allmost fear the practicability of the Last, as the funds of the state are allready Mortgaged beyond their ful due. At any rate the present house Cannot do more than Recommend it to their Sucessors. I hope however we shall pass the bill Enabling you to hold an Election, for Secureing your prisoners, & to ascertain the NW Line.[4] it had a second Reading yesterday, & required Some pains & Management to get thro.

---

[2] Fitzsimons is referring to those living in counties bordering on Luzerne who had been driven from their farms in years past. Large speculative landholders had come around to accepting the Connecticut settlers in the seventeen towns, for stable settlements there would increase the value of their holdings in the rest of the Susquehannah Company purchase and elsewhere; see no. 185, *post,* especially note 4.

[3] *Minutes of the Third Session of the Eleventh General Assembly,* 204, 207, 239 (microfilm copy).

[4] See no. 118, *ante,* note 4. The bill was enacted into law on September 29; *Minutes of the Third Session,* 248.

The provision of the bill concerning elections caused a split vote of 41 to 20. Since the commissioners had not yet made assessments, returns of taxable inhabitants could not be made, raising a question whether elections could be lawfully held under such circumstances. The bill validated the up-coming general elections in Luzerne, but no exceptions were to be made thereafter; *ibid.,* 241.

The debate on whether to make an exception to the election laws took up a good part of the Assembly proceedings on September 27 and 28. Robert Whitehill, a Constitutionalist, led the opposition, shifting his ground as he saw fit. Men like Thomas Fitzsimons and George Clymer, who favored specific Assembly action to allow elections in Luzerne County, called attention to Whitehill's inconsistencies, implying that his real aim was to provoke confusion in order to discredit the majority party, the

I hope by perseverance We shall Overcome all difficultys, &
a friendly Communication of Sentiments & Occurrences will I
think a Good deal Contribute towards that End. I shall be
happy to Contribute to that Communication, & shall recive with
pleasure any you may make me being with Regards Sir Y^r M^o
hble Servt

Thos FitzSimons

[124] Extract from the Minutes of the Pennsylvania Council.[1]

Several papers[2] containing intelligence of an armed banditti
having assembled at Tioga, within this State, in a riotous manner,
with an intention to resist the Government, were laid before
Council; and

On consideration,

The President was desired to write a letter to the Governor
of the State of New York,[3] inclosing the said papers and requesting the concurrance of the government of that State in
concerting measures for effectually suppressing the said rioters;
and also that our Delegates in Congress may be permitted to hold
a conference with him for that purpose.

A letter was written to the Delegates of this State in Congress
upon the same subject.[4]

[125] Benjamin Franklin to George Clinton.[1]

In Council, Sept. 22, 1787.

Sir,

Your Excellency will see by the Papers & Letters of Intelligence, which I have the honour of communicating to you,[2]

Republicans. See *Proceedings and Debates of the General Assembly of
Pennsylvania*. Taken in shorthand by Thomas Lloyd (Philadelphia, 1787),
I, 103-15.

The provision of the bill concerning the boundary between Luzerne
and Northumberland running northwest from Nescopeck Creek permitted
the commissioners to run a more definite line. The commissioners had
written about the boundary problem to the Council, which had referred
the matter to the General Assembly; *Pa. C. R.*, XV, 276. See also no.
189, *post,* notes 15 and 16.

[124] [1] *Pa. C. R.*, XV, 278, dated September 22, 1787.
   [2] Probably nos. 105 and 109, *ante.*   [3] No. 125, *post.*
   [4] No. 126, *post.*

[125] [1] *P. A.*, XI, 187-88.   [2] See no. 124, *ante,* note 2.

that there are a Number of disorderly People collecting near the Line that divides our two States, who are impatient of regular Government, and seize upon and presume to dispose of lands contrary to and in Defiance of the Laws. It has appeared to us by other evidence that their Numbers are daily increasing by vagabonds from all quarters, and that they expect Reinforcements from Shay's late Partizans, and purpose defending their proceedings by Force of Arms. Your Excellency will be sensible with us of the Mischief, such a Body of Banditti may be capable of occasioning to both our States, if suffered to increase and establish themselves in that country; The Vicinity of the Boundary Line affording them at present an imaginary security, since if pursued by the Authority of one of the States, they can easily step over into the others. Your Excellency's Readiness manifested on former occasions, to aid the operations of general justice, even in neighbouring Governments,[3] leaves no room to doubt of your concurring with us in the Measures that may be necessary to defeat the projects of those people, some of whose Leaders are said to be Inhabitants of your State; for the concerting such Measures the Council of this government unanimously and earnestly request your Excellency would be pleased to permit our Delegates in Congress to have a conference with you. I have the honour to be, Your Excellency's most obedient and most humble Servant.

B. Franklin, President.

[126] Benjamin Franklin to the Pennsylvania Delegates in the Continental Congress.[1]

In Council, Philadelphia, Sept. 22, 1787.

Gentlemen,

Enclosed is a Letter to Gov. Clinton,[2] which we send unsealed for your perusal, with the several Papers of Intelligence that accompany it.[3] The Council have thought of sending a few resolute Men authorized to apprehend and bring off Franklin and Jenkins; but if they should be on the York side of the Line it might be impracticable without the Concurrence of that Goverment. You will see that we have requested the Governor to have a conference with you on the subject; in which, if it take place; we desire you would not only discuss what may be proper for the securing the Ringleaders of the sedition, but concert

---

[3] See *Susquehannah Company Papers,* VIII, no. 265.
[126] [1] *P. A.,* XI, 188.   [2] No. 125, *ante.*   [3] See no. 124, *ante,* note 2.

some general Measures for the two States to take, that it may be effectually and totally suppressed: and that you would report to us the Result of your conference as soon as may be. With great esteem, I am, Gentlemen, your most obedient, humble Servant,

B. Franklin, Pres.

P. S. You will see the Propriety and Necessity of keeping the Proceedings secret, as well as the names of the Informers, and you will return the enclosed Papers.

[127] Samuel Hodgdon to Timothy Pickering.[1]

Philadelphia, 24 Sept[r] 1787

* * * Since writing the foregoing, I am informed a Petition is handed into the House signed by upwards of four hundred inhabitants of Northampton County, praying for the repeal or suspension of the Law in favour of the Connecticut Claimants.[2] For this I have looked some time hearing that such a Paper was in being. To day is assigned for its consideration, but from appearance it will be treated as the last efforts of an expiring faction. M[r] Fitzsimons promises to write by this or the Next conveyance fully on the subject. Yours

Samuel Hodgdon

[128] Proclamation for the Arrest of John Franklin and Others.[1]

Philadelphia, Tuesday, September 25th, 1787.

The following draft of a Proclamation was read and approved:

---

[127] [1] M. H. S., Pickering Papers, LVII, 293, in Hodgdon's hand.

[2] On September 24 petitions from 420 inhabitants of Northampton County asking for repeal of the Confirming Act were read a first and second time; *Minutes of the Third Session of the Eleventh General Assembly*, 234-35 (microfilm copy). These were not the first petitions on the subject. Similar petitions had been read on September 10, 17, and 20; *ibid.*, 204, 214, 229. Their tenor was that those from Northampton and Northumberland counties who claimed land under Pennsylvania titles in Luzerne would be hurt by a law that granted away their property to Connecticut claimants. See also no. 83, *ante*.

[128] [1] *Pa. C. R.*, XV, 279-80.

WHEREAS, It appears from the deposition of John Wigton,[2] and other testimony, that John Franklin, Leriah [Zerah] Beach, John McKinstry, and John Jenkins, have violently opposed the execution of the law in the county of Luzerne, and drove many of the claimants under Pennsylvania from their habitations and the county:

And whereas, it is of the utmost importance to the good people of this State, that the perpetrators of such atrocious offences should be brought to condign punishment; we have thought proper to issue this Proclamation, hereby engaging that the public reward of four hundred dollars shall be paid to any person or persons, who shall apprehend and secure John Franklin; and the public reward of two hundred dollars shall be paid to any person or persons who shall apprehend and secure John Jenkins; and the public reward of two hundred dollars shall be paid for apprehending and securing Leriah Beach, and John McKenstry, or one hundred for either of the said Leriah Beach or John McKenstry. The above rewards to be paid on the offenders or offender being secured in the jail of the city and county of Philadelphia; and we do hereby charge and require all Judges, Justices, Sheriffs, and Constables, to make diligent search, enquiry after, and to use their utmost endeavours to apprehend and secure the said John Franklin, Leriah Beach, John McKenstry, and John Jenkins, so that they may be dealt with according to law.[3]

GIVEN in Council, under the hand of the Honorable Charles Biddle, Esquire, Vice President, and the Seal of the State, at Philadelphia, this twenty-fifth day of September, in the year of our Lord, one thousand seven hundred and eighty-seven.

Charles Biddle

Attest:—James Trimble,
For John Armstrong, Jun'r, Secretary
GOD SAVE THE COMMONWEALTH!

---

[2] No. 109, *ante.* The name should be Thomas.

[3] On September 26, the Council instructed Col. John Craig to proceed "with the greatest dispatch to Wilkesbarre," taking whatever militiamen he needed, in order to seize the men named in the proclamation. If Craig succeeded in seizing only Franklin, he was to take no more risks but return his prisoner to Philadelphia; *P. A.,* XI, 189. See also no. 150, *post.*

[129] Samuel Richards, Jr., to Eliphalet Richards.[1]

Sir

I am informed several ways that you have accepted of the office of Constable under the Legislature of Pensylvania. As I cannot with certainty judge so I shall not undertake to determine of the utility of such a measure but I concieve myself called on to suggest to you some few sentiments on the subject as they arise cursorily in my mind. It appears to me you cannot derive either honor or profit from the employment. I am very sensible in the middle states it is considered a very dependant and diminutive post: and unless you have really recieved a decent sum in advance from Mr Pickering it appears to me you will not make it profitable, for the fees ari[sing] [2] from the office in that new distracted district must be trifl[ing] for a long time, and considering Mr Pickering as he really is—a tool hired to shackle those poor exhausted settlers. In his present conduct, he will not probably be very scrupelous in performing what he shall now engage, & indeed I presume he promises officially and not personally, and if officially when you demand your fullfillment from him he will refer you to the state he serves, and you are not insensible of the value of State promises at present in general, and particularly of the feelings of Pensylvania towards you as a holder of lands in that district: [3] this is going on the idea of their really establishing & holding jurisdiction there, but should they fail of it, what will be your situation. you have declared war against the opposing party, and desperation may dictate what cool reason would shudder at. If you have not proceeded too far to retract it might be well to weigh those observations in your mind and act consequencially. I have got sight of the paper D Allen asserts to be a discharge from you. it is spelt Eliphlet and is not much like your hand, which Mr Ellsworth acknowledged on the comparison. I hope you will not fail of attending to

---

[129] [1] M. H. S., Pickering Papers, LVII, 301-02, in Richards' hand.

[2] Where the ms. is damaged, parts of words are supplied in brackets.

[3] The name of Eliphalet Richards does not appear on any of the extant lists, such as those taking the oath of allegiance, those desiring an election of justices of the peace, those signing remonstrances, etc. The letter is addressed to Richards at "Wilksbury."

Cap' Goodwin at this crisis by forwarding depositions. I am Yours affectionately

Sam¹ Richards Jun' [4]

Farmington Sep' 25, 1787.

This is really a crisis in the affairs of your settlement & I hope you to take into your acc' the agitations which will succeed the federal convention in every State: Vermont rose in such a storm too strong to fear an attack, whether Westmoreland [5] will, time is to determine. This is certain those you attempt to expell will make efforts to hold or regain what they esteem their rights: and will not the general commotion we are entering increase their strenght faster than it will yours?

[130] Instructions to John Craig. [1]

In Council, Sept. 26, 1787.

Sir,

You are to take what number of Militia you think necessary and proceed with the greatest dispatch to Wilksbarre, in the County of Luzerne. When there, if you think it necessary consult Col. Pickering on the best method you can take to apprehend John Franklin, John Jenkins, Zerah Beach and John McKinstry. Should you take all or any of those men Prisoners you are to bring them to Philada. If you take Franklin at Wilksbarre do not proceed any farther, or run no risque of losing him by endeavouring to apprehend the others.

Council have the utmost reliance on your secrecy and your prudence in conducting the affair. If opposed by force, you are to use force and execute the warrant [2] at all events.

---

[4] A Samuel Richards is listed among those in possession of land in 1762; *Susquehannah Company Papers,* II, 190.

[5] The old name for the Connecticut town and county comprising the settlements in the Wyoming Valley.

[130] [1] *P. A.,* XI, 189.

[2] The warrant for their arrest has not been found. See no. 163, *post,* note 3.

[131] Arthur St. Clair to Benjamin Franklin.[1]

New York, Sept. 28, 1787.

Sir,

In pursuance of your Excellency's Letter in Council of the 22d, instant,[2] The Delegates of the State had yesterday a conference with Governor Clinton upon the subject of the Intelligence contained in the Papers inclosed to him.

Governor Clinton seems perfectly well disposed to concur in any general Measure that may tend to preserve the Peace of the two States; but he apprehends no danger from most of the Persons mentioned in those Papers; on the contrary he seems to think they are disposed to become peaceable and orderly Citizens of the State of New York, Particularly, Ar. Moodrey,[3] in whom he appeared to have a confidence. As General Irwin and Mr. Bingham, are both going to Philada., I beg leave to refer your Excellency to them for more particular information.

As to Franklin and Jenkins, The Delegates are of opinion that no more proper method can be pursued than that suggested in your Excellency's Letter, of sending a few resolute men to take them off; and should they be on the York side of the Line, or take refuge within that State, the apprehending them will give no offence to the Government. On the contrary the Governor is ready to concur with the Measure, and to that end has proposed that the warrant that may be thought proper to issue against those Men, be sent here, when he will get it backed by the Chief Justice, and accompany it, so backed, with his own warrant under the privy seal commanding all the Inhabitants, (for they have no Magistrates) of that District to be aiding and assisting in apprehending them. Should Council then adopt the Measure, if you will please to enclose the warrant to me no time shall be lost in presenting it to Governor Clinton, and returning it to your Excellency. I have the Honor to be, with the greatest Respect, Sir, Your Excellenc'y most obedient Servant,

Ar. St. Clair.

---

[131] [1] *P. A.,* XI, 189-90.   [2] No. 126, *ante.*

[3] John J. AcModer; see no. 89, *ante.* It would seem that Governor Clinton's confidence was not shared by those supporting Pickering. AcModer was one of those who signed the remonstrance against William Montgomery.

[132] Nathan Kingsley to Zebulon Butler.[1]

Wyalusink Sept 29 1787

Sir
  I am this instant inform⁴ By Cpᵗ Landon that you intend to
Git one Battalion of the Melitia to Gather as quick as the Law
will admit whitch Gives me Grate Satisfaction—Inform you that
Esqʳ franklin Has Sent Letters up the River to tuncanneck
Wialusink Tioga and Nutown By young Isac Baldwin who Stade
at my House Last Wensday night. He Left one of the Letters
With Joseph Eliot Derectted to him or Amasa Wells to warn all
the halfe Shear men in theas Parts to apear at the House of
Abel Yerinton on the Ninth Day of Octoʳ Next Compleat in
arms With out fail.[2] my Son Has Red the Letter I find thar is
Som in these Parts are varey Sperrited and are Detamend to
Prosed as they are military men. I hope you Wil Be able to
Receue [Rescue?] them in that Line &c I hope to Be Down and
Se you at the aletion So I Remain yours to Serv
                                                  Nathan Kingsley

[133] John Franklin to Jehiel Franklin.[1]

Mʳ Franklin,[2]
  Sir you are Requested to notify all the half share men &
others at Wysock and Towandee who Expect to support their
Rights under the Susqʰ Company that they meet at the house of
James Lasly in Hanover on Monday the 8ᵗʰ of Oct at 9 in the
Morning Completely Armed & equiped[3] as that is the Day the

---

[132] [1] Originally in Wyoming Historical and Geological Society, Butler
Papers, but now no longer extant.
  [2] See no. 133, *post*, note 3.
[133] [1] P. H. M. C., Div. of Arch. and MSS., Record Group 27, Series:
Exec. Corr., 1777-90, in Franklin's hand; M. H. S., Pickering Papers,
LVII, 303, a copy in Pickering's hand.
  [2] Jehiel Franklin, no relation to John apparently.
  [3] This order replaced one issued on September 25, which had called for
a meeting on October 9 at Abel Yarrington's in Wilkes-Barre; Pickering
Papers, LVII, 303. The originals were sent to Philadelphia; no. 285, *post*,
note 22. This order was the basis of the Commonwealth's later presentment
of Franklin and others for treason for their effort to erect "a new & independent Government" within the state's boundaries; no. 319, *post*.

Pennsylvania Loyalists intend to regulate their Militia to Subjugate us, which we are Determined to Prevent.

John Franklin
Col° Comdᵗ

Wilkesbarre Sept 29, 1787
Endorsed: Mʳ Jehiel Franklin
Claverack
hand by Mʳ Baldwin

[134] Timothy Pickering's Proposed Address to the Inhabitants of Luzerne.¹

To the Inhabitants of the County of Luzerne.

Countrymen & Fellow Citizens:

I address you by the first title as being by birth & affection a New England man, by the latter, as being by residence, like each of you, a citizen of Pennsylvania and under both as your sincere friend, who from my earliest knowledge of you, have been your advocate, when your enemies out of the settlement sought your destruction. Such enemies you still have: I mean a small band of Pennamites who rejoice at every disturbance among you, at every instance of resistance to the laws of Pennsylvania, hoping that the state by repeated provocations will at length arm itself against you; and drive out all of you, as well the innocent as the opposers of government, that they may get possession of your lands. But, believe me my fellow citizens, these enemies can do you no harm, unless you furnish them with the means, by resisting the authority of the state. But you have dangerous enemies among yourselves, who are endeavouring to stir up the people to rebel against the government & who openly avow their design of opposing the laws, strangely thinking that they can defend themselves against the power of the State. So mad a project never before entered into the hands of any men. Pray consider for a moment & compare the strength of this party with the power of Pennsylvania. It appears by the returns just made to Col° Butler, the County Lieutenant,² that all men in the county,

---

[134] ¹ M. H. S., Pickering Papers, LVIII, 1-4, a much-corrected draft in Pickering's hand. Its probable date is September 1787.

² Butler was commissioned county lieutenant on August 30, 1787; *Pa. C. R.*, XV, 264.

210

between the ages of 18 & 53 fall short of 700, and only one small town has not been returned, which added to the returns received may make the whole number a little overrun seven hundred. On the other hand view the great population & power of Pennsylvania, which during the late war furnished one eighth part of the men & means by which the United States successfully opposed the mighty force of the British empire! and which numbers on her militia rolls fifty or sixty thousand men! But with this great force compare the small part of this county militia who may be unwise and desperate enough to oppose it! And then you must conclude that no men in their right minds would attempt it. I well remember it was said last winter, in some of your town meetings, that the people of Pennsylvania were your *friends,* & would not turn out against you: and many of you will also remember, that I owned you had many friends in the state—that your *suffering* had made you *many friends*—and you find I told you the *truth.* You had so many friends among the people, and in government, that the Assembly have passed a law by which your old possessions and your other lands particularly assigned to you before the decree of Trenton, & whether improved or not, are confirmed to you, according to your petition.[3] The Assembly have thus done what I assured you they were disposed to do—what your friends in the state wished them to do—what your *real* friends in Connecticut & the *government* of that state are satisfied with. And what more was to be expected? Or if more be desired, and there are just reasons for granting more, why not ask it? Why appeal to arms? When all that your petition prayed for has been granted, what pretence can there be for resisting the authority of the state? Do you not see that such conduct will make enemies of friends? Yes, rest assured, that any farther resistance to the laws will turn every man against you. While you were oppressed and denied your possessions, you had many to take your part: but now that oppression has ceased, & your lands have been granted to you, if you persist in your opposition, you will have no friends, either in the government, or among the people; on the contrary, both will be exasperated & enraged against you; and in that case will not fail to send a sufficient military force to reduce those who will not submit to the gentle government of the laws. Having thus shown you the folly & madness of the project of resisting the power of

---

[3] That is, the petition which had resulted in the Confirming Act; no. 16, *ante.*

Pennsylvania, suffer me to point out the desperate wickedness of the attempt.

While Connecticut claimed & exercised the powers of government in this settlement, it was your duty to submit to it. But Pennsylvania laying claim to this country, the dispute was submitted to Judges chosen by the two states, agreeably to the articles of confederation of the United States; and these Judges unanimously determined that the Jurisdiction & right of soil belonged to Pennsylvania. Accordingly Connecticut withdrew her jurisdiction & you became subject to the Government of Pennsylvania; and her right to govern here has been acknowledged; & most of you have taken an oath of allegiance to be true and faithful to the state of Pennsylvania: & how can such persons now attempt to disturb its peace? Are they so abandoned to wickedness that they pay no regard to the oaths they have taken?[4] Are they willing to add to a breach of duty, the heinous crime of perjury? It would seem that some few are so disposed: & to these few let me address myself. What can you promise yourselves by ingaging in so desperate an undertaking? It is said you want certain lands to be secured to you: and do you expect to get them by rebelling against the state? If the whole force of this county were united, it would be insignificant compared with the force of the state: how much more insignificant must be the small part of the county which has been persuaded, by misrepresentations and deceitful stories, to engage in this wild attempt? an attempt that will certainly bring you to destruction, or oblige you to flee from the state, and which may also bring ruin upon the whole county. Has not this settlement already endured miseries enough that you would again involve it in war and bloodshed? and without even the possibility of succeeding? but with a certainty of losing your lives as criminals, or of being under the necessity of fleeing from the state, and leaving all the property which by the law is confirmed to you? I again address all the people of the county. It is said you ought not to be *saddled* with the laws of Pennsylvania until your lands are finally confirmed to you: and can you believe that the lands will not finally be confirmed? Is it possible that you can give credit to the persons who tell you so? when for eight or nine months past you have found them false prophets in every thing they have said against Pennsylvania? Last winter, when I met you in town meetings, & assured you of the kind disposition of

---

[4] The names of Franklin, Jenkins, and many of their die-hard supporters are not included on the list of 141 men who took the oath in 1787; nos. 11, 62, and 70, *ante*.

212

the state towards you, I was answered, That the state had formerly deceived you and you was affraid she meant to deceive you again, and one of your present mis-leaders, in particular, not only said that the state would deceive, but that *I* came on purpose to deceive you![5] Both of these assertions you see have proved false. He also said, if the Assembly means not to deceive us, why does it not pass a law to confirm our lands? Well—the Assembly has passed a law to confirm all the lands you petitioned for; & why is not that man content? If the petition was not large enough, why did not he and his leading companions ask for more? and why did not your representative attend his duty in the Assembly [6] to show the propriety & justice of larger grants? If he could have shown this, such grants would have been made as readily as those now included in the law. He was even pressed to write another petition, agreeable to his own mind: but he would not do it, and chose rather to let the petition which was then signed by a large proportion of the inhabitants go forward, determined still to persist in his opposition whether the Assembly granted or rejected the petition. For, says he to Col° Denison, who was then going down with the petition, "If the Assembly grant the petition, then we will remonstrate against it, as not speaking the minds of the people: but if the Assembly reject the petition, then we will say it spoke the voice of the county."

Commissioners being appointed by the law for examining the Connecticut Claims, a remonstrance was drawn up against one of them [7] & sent to Council that Commissioner resigned. Another also resigned, & a third newly appointed also resigned.[8] These resignations with other accidents occasioned considerable delays in beginning the examination of the claims; and then it was publicly reported that the Commissioners would never come, that they were appointed only to annoy & finally deceive you. And tho' I had said when I last went to Philadelphia that I was going to bring on my family it was reported that I had no intention to bring my family here, and this was said by Esquire Franklin until the very day on which I arrived with them; In all these things you see the makers of these reports were false prophets. I am only surprized that such stories should gain any one's belief. Could any reasonable person think that I would

---

[5] Pickering is referring to the language of William Judd's address to the settlers; no. 49, *ante.*

[6] A reference to John Franklin's failure to take his seat in the legislature.

[7] Joseph Montgomery, who resigned on May 31; *Pa. C. R.,* XV, 221 and no. 78, *ante.*

[8] See no. 38, *ante,* note 2.

go to the expense of building an office and a large house unless I meant to use my office & bring my family here. Without a family here, what should I want of a house? & without an intention of living here myself, what should I want of an office?

But a story has been lately raised & industriously spread in the settlement, that I also have been guilty of falsehood, and am a second Armstrong: But, fellow citizens, I defy all my enemies, & the whole world to prove a single falsehood upon me during my whole life. The pretended falsehood as I am informed is this— "That I had said I owned no lands in the county under a Pennsylvania title whereas it now appeared that I did own such land & had given a lease of a tract to a man at Tioga; and it seems that the persons Who got possession of this lease or letter, plume themselves upon the acquisition! Why if those persons had asked me for a copy of the lease I would have given it without the least hesitation; because there was nothing in the transaction that I desired to conceal from them or the world. In the first place, I declare the charge itself to be a gross falsehood. I never said I had no lands in the county under Pennsylvania; on the contrary, at one or more of the town meetings last winter I said that I did own such lands, & told precisely what they were. That I was interested with a company who owned a large tract between the Susquehanna & the Delaware, about the great Bend, in which my share would amount to ten thousand acres, but that I believed no part of this tract came within [   ] miles of the Susquehanna at Tioga, and consequently was not within the Susquehanna purchase. I also said that I was concerned with another company who had four surveys amounting to about two thousand five hundred acres within the county, & the New Purchase made by the state of the Indians—that when I entered into this company, I did not know that the Connecticut claims took in any part of the New Purchase—that, however, my share of the twenty five hundred acres was only an eighth & a half, amounting to about 450 acres; an interest too trifling to influence my conduct for or against the people. This was the substance of what I declared, & I appeal to the persons present at those meetings for the truth of what I say. You thus see that this report to my discredit, is utterly without foundation. But I must tell you further when I proposed to buy lands enough at Wilkesborough under the Connecticut Title to make me a farm & it was objected, that I might get it secured under Pennsylvania, I then declared & solemnly assured the people that I would hold those Connecticut rights under no other title, until they held by another title: and I have kept my faith: And as the late law has provided for

214

the confirmation of your titles so it of course has provided for mine; & I now stand exactly on the same ground with you. Perhaps this fact has been blended with the former & thus by mistake the gentlemen who raised the report may have charged me with falsehood; & When I have not particular evidence of any man's disposition to say untruths, I am willing when any circumstances will admit of it, to apologize for their reports, by supposing that by mistake & without design they have reported what is not true.

And now, my fellow citizens, as I have uniformly told you the truth in times past, be assured I will not deceive you in time to come; that as I have embraced every occasion heretofore to establish the peace & promote the real good of the county, so the same shall be my constant study & endeavour in future; And if I suffer in my person or property, it will be the suffering of an innocent man, against whom no crime can be alledged; I am aware that innocence is not a certain guard against murderers, & robbers: but I should hope we have no such characters among us, or trust at least that no such characters can have any influence among this people. At one time I hear that I with my wife & family of small children am to be driven out thro' the swamp, at another that I am to be sacrificed: but tho' either of these might prove destructive to me, I am certain it could do no good to the opposing party; on the contrary, it would only be as a watchword to the State to send an armed force against them to destroy them, or drive them from the county. When any such outrage happens, the vengeance of the State will no longer sleep. Of this I solemnly warn the people; and call God to witness the purity of my intentions and conduct towards you—that from the beginning I have faithfully sought and endeavoured to secure & promote your interests—and that if I suffer or die, I shall suffer or die for your sakes.

Endorsed: Rough draught of an address intended to be made to the Inhabitants of the County of Luzerne.

[135] Agreement of Susquehannah Company Members.[1]

Whereas we the Subscribers being Proprietors, Purchasers & Settlers of a Tract of Land known by the Name of Susquehanna

[135] [1] M. H. S., Pickering Papers, LVII, 25, a contemporary attested copy; P. H. M. C., Div. of Arch and MSS., Record Group 27, Series:

purchase and are in Consequence of a Royal Chartered Right, together with that of an absolute purchase from the Aboriginal Proprietors (with our Associates to wit the Susquehanna Company) in possession of the whole of the Aforesaid purchase, and Whereas the Setlers and their Associates, are and were joint Tenants of the Whole Territory of Country aforesaid, and the possession of the Settlers is, and ever hath been the possession of themselves and their Associates; agreeably to an observation of a Celebrated Law writer who saith that a possession of part in the name of the whole is a possession completely for every part; and Whereas the aforesaid Company of which we are a part, were the first in possession and Occupancy after the Aboriginals and neither have been or can be legally dispossessed by a Tribunal short of a Federal Court instituted agreeably to the Articles of Confederation, it therefore follows that no one State in the Union has a right to determine the Title or Right of possession to any of the Lands in the aforesaid purchase until the Institution and exercise of a Federal Court as above mentioned. Therefore we hereby jointly and Severally pledge our Honors & all our properties Real and Personal that we will use our utmost exertions for the protection and defence of each other in the possession of the Lands aforesaid, against all invaders, and also for the defence of all such as will join with us in this Combination, and that we will unequivocally adhere to every thing comprized in the foregoing declaration. We also hereby declare to the Public that we will lay no claim to the Lands under any other Title but that of the Susquehanna Company in the beforementioned purchase. In testimony whereof we have hereunto voluntarily Subscribed our Names.[2]

John McKinstry	Cornelius McDaniel	John Cole
Serach Beach [3]	Nicholas Depue ju^r	Simon Spalding
Benjamin Allen	Peregrine Gardner	Abel Maringer
Thomas McClair [4]	John McCluer	Thomas Spalding
Samuel Gore	John Fuller	Jonathan Harris
Peter Downin	Walterman Baldwin	Eldad Kellogg
Jacob Snelf	John Spalding	Chester Bingham
Christian Kress	Joseph Marchell	Stephen Fuller
Nathan Herrington	Avery Grove	Lebeus Hammond

Letter Books, Nov. 4, 1782–Oct. 6, 1787, pp. 424-25; *Hudson Weekly Gazette*, November 8, 1787; *P. A.*, XI, 194-95. The agreement was drawn up "at Tioga sometime in the month of September"; no. 173, *post*. This agreement was referred to as the "Combination."

[2] The copy in the *Gazette* does not include names.   [3] Zerah Beach.
[4] Thomas McClure.

Abraham Brohaw	Simon Sheppard	Stephen Dolson
Samuel Southward	James Therinlon	John Dolson [8]
Othniel Campbell	Solomon Bennet	John Moorcraft
Reuben Compton	Joel Thomas	John Kortright
Abraham Spalding	Benjamin Clark	Jacob Collins
John Gary	Jeremiah Skeer	James Witney
Thomas Brown	Joseph Spalding	Jacob Kress
Samuel Bewelman	Joseph Hinney [6]	Nathan Herrington ju
Jonathan Harris jun[r]	Joseph F. Thompson	Moses Depue
Martin Young	Joseph Thomas	Jacob Herrington
Walter Watrue [5]	James Faming [7]	Prince Bryant
Abraham Minier	John Oneil	John Simpson
Joseph Tyler	James Dolson	John Simpson jun[r]
Alex[r] Sempson jun[r]		

[136] Timothy Pickering to John Swift.[1]

Savages [2] Thursday October 4th 1787

Sir

I am informed that you commanded the party which surrounded M[r] Hollenback's house last Tuesday night, and that my Wife is kept there a prisoner. I am farther informed that it has been proposed to send her [to] Tioga.[3] But so cruel a measure I cannot think you will suffer to be carried into execution. I profess myself to be innocent; unless it is a crime to have laboured for near a year past to promote the welfare & interest of the Connecticut Settlers in the county of Luzerne. But what ever misrepresentations and lies may have caused any to believe concerning *me,* certainly my *wife* is *innocent,* and ought not to suffer; and I rely upon you to prevent any insult or abuse being offered to her; and a greater injury perhaps could not be done to her, than to send her to Tioga. She is of a tender frame, and has an infant at her breast but about three weeks old, besides

---

[5] Walter Watrus.   [6] Joseph Kinney.   [7] James Fanning.

[8] This name is missing in *P. A.*

[136] [1] M. H. S., Pickering Papers, LVII, 306-07, a copy in Pickering's hand; Harvey-Smith, *Wilkes-Barré,* III, 1588-89. John Swift had long been an activist on the Connecticut side; see *Susquehannah Company Papers,* VIII, Index, and Harvey-Smith, *Wilkes-Barré,* III, 1406 n.

[2] Savage's or Savitz's Tavern on Sullivan's Road; Harvey-Smith, *Wilkes-Barré,* III, 1588 n. Pickering had left Wyoming when warned that his own capture was imminent. He proceeded to Philadelphia to seek official help; see Pickering to his son, Dec. 31, 1818, Pickering Papers, XXXVIII, 246.

[3] Tioga was the strong point of those opposing the state under Franklin's leadership.

four other young children, to look after. To compel her to make such a journey, either by land or water, and in such circumstances, & a prisoner may be fatal to her And any injury done to her I shall not consider as I should injuries done to myself: for these I can easily forgive but any injuries to her I shall not forgive. I was glad when I heard you had the command, because I think you naturally possess both honor and humanity; tho' you are sadly misled to engage in your present undertaking.

I long ago heard, that in case Franklin should be taken, the Vengeance of his party was to fall on me: But why, if any regard was had to Justice, it was not easy to determine. If I have been guilty of any crimes, I am ready & willing to answer for them; and no more will be required of Esq' Franklin. He will not be condemned unheard: He will have a fair trial by a Jury; and the Constitution of Pennsylvania requires that persons accused of crimes to be tried in their own county. This is the sense put on that part of the Constitution, by a law of the state, agreeably to the opinion of the Council of Censors. Why then should men rise in arms to seize me, unaccused, & without any lawful authority for it, because Esq. Franklin, accused of conspiring with others to levy war against the state, had been apprehended? The warrant [4] required the persons taking him to carry him before one of the Justices of the Supreme Court, and consequently to Philadelphia, where, in case the charges alledged against him should be supported by evidence, he might be confined for trial. If found innocent by a jury of his peers, he will be acquitted: if guilty, he must doubtless suffer the penalty which the law prescribes for the crime of which he shall be found guilty. And will not this be right? What freeman of any state can require more?

On this occasion I wish to say something more to you. Let me ask What can you & those who joined you, propose to yourselves in taking up arms? Is it possible you should think Franklin's party able to withstand the power of Pennsylvania? Do you not see how much the present situation of the settlers differs from their situation before the law passed for confirming their lands? Then not only the settlers, but the people of Connecticut, and the majority of the people of Pennsylvania might excuse your opposition to government, because they thought the settlers ought to be quieted in their old possessions. But now

---

[4] The warrant charging Franklin with misprision of treason has not been found.

218

that a confirmation has been made of those possessions, and a great deal more, your opposition will be condemned by the whole world; you will be left without excuse; and can obtain no assistance, unless from a few turbulent men who have wickedly disturbed the peace of their own states, and are unfit members of any government whatever. If you think Pennsylvania will lay still as formerly, when her government is trampled on, you will find yourselves mistaken. Now that she has done what justice and your own petition required, she will feel herself justified before God & the World, in sending a sufficient military force to crush at once all opposition and rest assured that she will do it. I do not speak thus to frighten you, but as of a fact that will certainly be done, if the opposition be continued. What miseries this may bring on the opposers and their families and friends, it is not hard to forsee, nor is it necessary to relate. At the same time it is inconceivable what reasons Franklin could give his followers to make them believe his project would be successful. For I believe a wilder one never before entered into the head of any man in his senses. Who but a madman with his handful of associates could imagine that he could successfully oppose a state that is equal in power to one eighth part of all the United States? Or that because you baffled the handful of troops she sent against you formerly, therefore that you can maintain your ground against the whole force of the state, which, for the reason before mentioned, will be ready to arm against you? All who before were your friends & well wishers, now that your lands are confirmed, & you still refuse submission to the laws, will be your enemies. The Government & people of Connecticut are satisfied with the confirming law, except, I suppose, some members of the Susquehanna Company. Doctor Johnston & Mr Sherman two of the Connecticut Delegates in the late Continental Convention, in particular, were satisfied with it.[5] And Doctor Johnson, I understood, sent a message by William Ross, to Franklin, to this effect, "That if he did not abandon his measures of opposition, he would bring himself to ruin." But he would obstinately persist in them, and you now see the Consequence. This reminds me of what I said to Franklin last April, the Friday evening after the election at Forty Fort was violently broken up. He called to see me at John Hollenbacks, where we consed [con-

---

[5] Roger Sherman did not serve in Congress at the time of the passage of the Confirming Act; Johnson's colleague was Stephen Mix Mitchell. See no. 38, *ante,* note 1.

versed] together two or three hours on the subjects then in dispute, at the close of the Conversation, when he rose up to go home, I addressed him in words to this effect. "Mr Franklin, you have heretofore had great respect paid you in this settlement, & taken the lead in its affairs: & notwithstanding all that is past, notwithstanding all your opposition to government, it is not too late to retreat: if you now change your course of conduct, if you submit, as every good citizen ought, to the Government of the State, your past conduct will be overlooked, you may still be respected still take the lead in the Settlement." This sentiment I expressed to him in language as serious and affecting as I could frame, hoping it might have the disired effect, and induce him quietly to submit to the laws, & take his seat as your representative in the General Assembly, where, as I often told him, if any demand could be made on just grounds, for persons not provided for by the present law, it was his duty to make & support it with what arguments he could urge in its favour. But all my words and arguments were thrown away upon him; for if he had regarded them, he must have given up the dareing tho' ridiculous idea of forming a new & independent state. That this was his plan, is now pretty clearly seen & generally known, and it was to be accomplished by the slaughter or banishment of all the good & faithful citizens of Pennsylvania in the county. Government have from various quarters been apprized of his proceedings and wicked designs; and for some time past proposed to apprehend him. The three Commissioners received a state warrant a month ago for that purpose:[6] but we did not think it expedient to put it in execution. He was taken last Tuesday by another warrant, directed to sundry officers, particularly to one of the Gentlemen who took him;[7] but of this we knew nothing till they arrived.

I have written thus much hoping it may induce you and others engaged in an undertaking so desperate, & which must necessarily fail, to give it up, and be at peace. I am not revengeful. I wish that lives may not be taken away, Government will be ready to pardon on on submission, perhaps all Franklin's adherents: I will &c; but if they persist in their opposition, the vengeance of the State will overtake them. They will be pursued not only in this state but into any other into which they may flee. I myself, tho' injured & slandered by them, will nevertheless be their advocate.

---

[6] Nos. 101 and 103, *ante.*   [7] John Craig; see no. 128, *ante,* note 3.

[137] Samuel Hodgdon to Timothy Pickering.[1]

Philadelphia 4ᵗʰ Octo 1787

Dear Sir

Another Opportunity presents and I again address you. but a few things of your last indent are yet purchased, those will come on with Mʳ Hollenback and the remainder shall be forwarded with all possible expedition. inclosed you have the papers and the Minutes of the house to the close of the session, and the curious defence made by the *abandoned Nineteen* for their secession from the Assembly on friday and saturday last.[2] *State warrants* were talked of to apprehend certain obnoxious characters For aiding the sergeant of Arms in bringing them to their duty but the Cheif Justice being consulted put an end to the Measure; he declared that the Mass of the people were so incensed at their conduct, that tumult and Further outrage would be the inevitable consequence, so the Matter rests for the present. you will see *Whitehill*[3] the Jesuit conspicuous in the debates on the last Wyoming bill.[4] distraction and confusion are essential to the existance of such consummate villians. the terms are harsh, but I confess I am exceeing angry with them. I will leave them and politicks at this time. Inclosed you have Mʳ Marcys Plan of the Land newly discovered,[5] Mr Meredith does not understand enough to engage. he supposes he might be willing for a stroke at one third, or one half the quantity provided. he was sure it was unlocated, and that the part he might engage for should be the cream of the whole tract. he seems to have no idea that so great a quantity of *good* Land togather remains unnoticed in the Old purchase. I am of his opinion, but both may be mistaken. * * *

[137] [1] M. H. S., Pickering Papers, XL, 233-34, in Hodgdon's hand.

[2] His reference is to the Antifederalists who sought by preventing a quorum to postpone calling a convention for ratification of the Constitution of the United States.

[3] Robert Whitehill.   [4] See no. 123, *ante,* note 3.

[5] See no. 120, *ante.*

[138] Lord Butler to Timothy Pickering.[1]

County of Luzerne Octr 5th, 1787

Dear sir

I am verry ancious to hear from you I cant express my feelings on the Cruel and ungenerous treatment of the people of this County towards you, who out of the motives of frindship to them and a frind to good Government have Spoused their cause and become a Citizen with them. I Beleive there is some of my Neighbours that is as ancious as I am but dare not say any thing for Franklins party is so strong that those in favor of Government do nothing. the Authority is stop^d acting. you knowing my Attachment to Goven^t may expect when I found that the authority could not Stop the riot, that I was Distress^d to see the Destruction coming upon us. your family is well and you may rest asured that they will not be hurt. excuse the irregularity of my writing for I am crazy to think Distruction is going to come upon the unhappy County &c. I am Dr Sir your friend sincerely

Lord Butler

I was coming to philadelphia myself But it is thought best to try to carry on the Ellection[2] which I am Determind to do if their is but ten Votes and make the Return to you by which time I hope to see you. I am &^{c} LB

since I wrote Swift, and some others seem to wish A Compromise if they can be forgiven

[139] Samuel Hodgdon to Timothy Pickering.[1]

Philadelphia 5th Octo 1787 2 oClock P M [2]

Dear Sir

At One oClock this day Franklin was brought to Town and lodged in Jail.[3] It seems six Men were deputed to take him, un-

---

[138] [1] M. H. S., Pickering Papers, LVII, 308-09, in Butler's hand. He sent his letter to Philadelphia, where Pickering had fled when he and the other commissioners were expelled from Wyoming.
[2] The annual elections scheduled for October 8.
[139] [1] M. H. S., Pickering Papers, LVII, 310-11, in Hodgdon's hand.

der a charge of Misprison of *Treason*. They say he fought the whole of them for several Minutes, before he would surrender. Five of them have receipts to prove the assertion—One black eye each, Franklin has a black eye, and is otherways bruised. How this will affect you time must discover, but I hope his party is too contemptible to affect *you*, or alarm any one. It affords a great triumph here, and I sincerely hope that peace may follow violence. I have not yet quite filled the box prepared for your things, yet shall forward the invoice of what is already in should Hollenback set off as he talks before the other articles are purchased. I have paid the specie Cash in hand for every article forwarded and I am sure they are laid in very low. Dennison has this Moment called on me. he has seen Franklin. He informs me he seems disposed to be composed, though it is manifest he is in the horrors. his Plan for Independency seems to lay heaviest against him. he will not at any rate trouble you again soon. I hope you are going forward rapidly under the examination Law. once settle and adjust the claims, and Peace will be restored, which I know is your *only* wish. Everything agreeable to invoice is in the Box and it is nailed up and ready for transporting to you. adieu. Affectionately

Sam Hodgdon

[140] Obadiah Gore to Timothy Pickering.[1]

Wilksbarre Octr 6th 1787

Dear S^r

I this morning arived here and was very agreeably Disappointed in finding your family Safe and I am Induced to believe the Idea of removeing them is at an End, and I have an assurance from Capt Swift & Capt Baldwin [2] that no Opposition will be made to Either of the Elections of Civil and military Officers.

This letter may not have been sent, for no address was given or person named to carry it. Pickering was on his way to Philadelphia or had arrived.

    [2] Harvey-Smith, *Wilkes-Barré*, III, 1586, says the arrest gave great satisfaction, and that Hodgdon wrote Pickering *"at 2 A. M."* (italics theirs) ; yet the letter clearly gives "P. M."

    [3] Franklin was arrested on October 2; see no. 136, *ante*. According to his own account, Pickering assisted in the capture of Franklin; see Pickering's statement of March 2, 1790, in *Susquehannah Company Papers*, X.

[140] [1] M. H. S., Pickering Papers, LVII, 312, in Gore's hand.

    [2] John Swift and Waterman Baldwin.

Should that be the Case you may Depend on hearing further from us Soon. I am Sʳ your humbˡ servᵗ

Obadʰ Gore

my Present Sentiments are that no further opposition will be made and that the Commisioners may (as soon as convenience will permitt) return to Execute their Trust.

[141] John Swift to Timothy Pickering.¹

Wilkesborough October 6ᵗʰ AD 1787

Sir

I recieved you letter dated the 4ᵗʰ insᵗ in which you express much concern for your family; I expected it.² Scott (one of your Domestics) unluckily set our [out?] for Philadelphia a few minutes too soon. Some one of the party had told Mʳˢ Pickering to prepare to go up the River to be kept as an Hostage till Col° Franklin shou'd be restored; but As soon as I heard such orders had been given, I repaired immediately to your family, to relieve Mʳˢ Pickerings Anxiety. Your family has not been removed nor any way injured to my knowledge. Mʳ Bowman can inform you the particulars. I write this, to inform you that your Family & effects shall be safe & till you return, that they are not under any kind of Confinement that Col° Franklin's friends are disposed to submit to Govᵗ & Law in all things, that you will think differently of them from what you have done, & that we wish your return with the rest of the Commissioners. Upon my honour the Notion of Independancy was not in our heads, Neither was it (to my knowledge) Franklins object, at the time he was taken. You may expect me & my influence in favour of Law. One thing for myself and for his friends in this County, I ask of you; that is, I wish you to use your influence that Col° Franklin (whom you know I love) shou'd be dealt with fairly, & that as much lenity as possible be shown him. This you can do, this will lay us under an obligation [to] you, & will tend greatly to the peace of this County. Majʳ Jenkins, Capᵗ Baldwin & Satterly, Lᵗ Slocum & Mattison concur with me.³ We have spent two days in Wilkesbarre to convince the Authority of our peacable disposi-

---

[141] ¹ M. H. S., Pickering Papers, LVII, 313-14, in an unknown hand but signed by Swift.

² No. 136, *ante*.

³ John Jenkins, Waterman Baldwin, Elisha Satterlee, William Slocum, and Elisha Mathewson; see no. 143, *post*.

tion. I hear there is a State warrant out to take off, as Franklin was taken, Myself and others for our past conduct. we must not be taken off in that manner, 'twas too cruel. I am Sir Your humble Servt

John Swift

[142] John Craig's Reward for Capturing John Franklin.[1]

IN COUNCIL, Philadelphia October 6th 1787

Sir

Pay to Colonel John Craig or order the sum of three hundred Pounds as a reward for apprehending and securing John Franklin under orders from Council.[2]

Chas Biddle

To David Rittenhouse Esqr, Treasurer

Endorse: Ent^d Jno Nicholson

On presenting this Order to Mr Rittinghouse Treasurer, He informed Me that at present he could not pay it: But on meeting Jno Lukens Esqr Survey^r General, he said That he would advance the amount, to enable Me, to make a dividend forthwith to the Gentlemen who had Rendred such essential Service to the State, and paid me three hundred pounds accordingly.

Philad: 6^h Oct^r, 1787

John Craig

Endorsed: Rec^d Oct 8th 1787 of John Lukens Esq in part of his payment

[143] John Swift and Others to Nathan Denison.[1]

Wilksbarre October 6th 1787

Sir

By this [time], we imagine that you have heard that we in company with Others assembled on the Night suceding the day

[142] [1] Tioga Point Museum, Athens, Pennsylvania. The order for payment is signed by Biddle; Craig's communication is in his hand.

[2] See no. 128, ante, note 3.

[143] [1] P. H. M. C., Div. of Arch. and MSS., John Franklin Papers, signed by each of the five men.

in which Col° Franklin was taken. We were in the heat of passion and wish that the whole transaction may be viewed in that light. The manner in which the Col° was taken roused us. We supposd that he was taken without a warrant and by Men too especially one of whome who had in the Year 1784 treated us with the utmost cruelty. had they declard their Authority we should have turnd our behaviour very differently. You are sensible of what advantage Col° F. hertofore has been to the settlement and we now wish that you would plead for the unfortunate Man. Do your utmost that his confinment may be easy as possible. Let him want nothing. Strive for what you think will ease our minds, for they are anxtious for the want of the Poor Man. We are determind to be quiet and submissive to the laws of Pensylvania. believe us Sir for we are sincere. A total end, we are determind there shall be of disturbance. No longer shall there be two parties in this Settlement. We will now unite like one great family and make peace bless our land. Now Sʳ we have spoken to you the language of our hearts and we expect your natural generosity will lead you to do everything for Col° Franklin that you can [to] Get him to bail if you can for it will give us great satisfaction and I dare say every other person in the settlement. In compliance with the above request you will oblige your friends and humble servants

> John Swift
> Waterman Baldwin
> Wm Slocum
> Elisha Satterlee
> Elisha Mathewson

N B Send us an answer if you please. Yours as above

Endorsed: Appointed by all who have been under arms to do what to us seemed most proper.

[144] Zebulon Butler, Obadiah Gore, and William Hooker Smith to Benjamin Franklin.[1]

His Excellency, Benj'n Franklin, Esq. Pres. of State.

Wilkesbarre, Luzerne Co., Oct. 6, 1787.

Sir,

Doubtless your Excellency & the Hon. Council have heard of the disturbance in this place on the night of the second inst.,

[144] [1] *P. A.*, XI, 192-93.

caused by the taking of John Franklin (as now supposed) with a state warrant; with pain we should give a statement of all the circumstances, did we suppose your honors not informed thereof. Yet we conceive it now our duty to acquaint you with the state of this County. We have reason to suppose that various & shocking accounts of the late disorders in this county have arrived at Philadelphia, and while we lament the abuse offered to Colonel Montgomery by an individual, we can inform you that no other person has been hurt on the occasion, & that those persons who fell into the hands of the disturbers are liberated. The disaffected party dispersed the next day, regreting exceedingly their disorderly conduct. We believe they feel a degree [of] Compunction equal to the magnitude of their Crimes. This day we met the principal of that party who made the disturbance, upon their request by them, we were informed that they supposed the manner of taking Franklin was illegal, that those persons who seized him had formerly exercised cruelty in this settlement, & by the Report of a number of pistols, their intention was to take his life; We can assure your Excell'y and the Honorable Council that we are convinced of their penetence, & have reason to believe that in future the administration of law will not be interrupted in this County, that Elections will not be opposed & that they will demean themselves as peaceable citizens of this State. They have expressed to us their wishes that the Commissioners for ascertaining claims in this County would return for the Completion of their business again; we would inform your honors that we believe them sincere, & with them join in requesting that the said Commissioners would return and proceed in their business. Had we reason to doubt of the future submission to law & Civil government in this County, we should deviate far from our duty when we represent that the situation of this County at present is not such (in our opinion) as calls for the immediate exertions of a military force. Messrs. Wells & Bowman (the bearers of this letter) will be able to give an account of the particulars of our situation, Col. Pickering's family, &c.

Those persons who assembled under arms upon Franklin's being taken (and now disposed for peace, good order, and submission to Government) have in the most humble manner solicited us to represent their submission & orderly disposition to your Excellency & the Hon'ble Council, begging that Franklin's person may be treated with as much tenderness as the nature of his charge will possibly admit, & if consistent with the laws & dignity of this State, that he be admitted to bail. We also join with them in this last request, observing that many people in this country, entirely submissive for Law & Gov't, wish Franklin to be treated with as much lenity as will be consistent with his [position.] We have the honor of Being, Your Excellency's humble servants,

Zebulon Butler,	⎫	Lieutenants
Obediah Gore,	⎬	of
Wm.Hooker Smith.	⎭	County.

P. S. The principals of the party above mentioned have in their Letter to Col. Dennison [2] said something in Corroboration of our Opinions to which Letter we would refer your Excellency.

[145] Francis Smith to John Armstrong, Jr.[1]

Lower Smithfield, 6th October, 1787.

Dear Sir,

Yesterday morning, being on the Wyoming Road, at a small distance from Larner's house, I met Timothy Pekrin, Esqr., and Mr. Evans, secret[y] entering our settlements in a distressed situation. Informed of the coup de main executed on Franklin, and apprehensive of the natural consequences attending such Conduct, I asked for information, when to my great surprise I understood by Mr. Pekrin that although he narrowly escaped the vengeance of the Connecticut Banditti, and had Left behind him his Lady and children, Likely to be taken as hostages for Franklin, he was going to Philadelphia to compromise matters with John Franklin; his expressions, I believe, started from a repenting and disappointed heart, in the expansion of which I understood that he had wrote a Letter to John Swift,[2] the present Leader of the faction, promising an act of administy for him, Franklin & Party, provided they would submit to his fugitive plan of Submission to our Laws; he further added that his first exertion in the city would be to pay a visit to the Prisoner, John Franklin, and should propose him once more to make him and Swift men of great importance on the above Conditions, it hurted my feelings to conceive that one individual as Mr. Pekrin, in a free and Constitutional Government, should cousin or pretend to dispose of the three Branches of our Political existence in the same time that he confesses the necessity of coercive measures, and sees the dignity of Government exposed.

[2] No. 143, ante.
[145] [1] P. A., XI, 195-96. Major Smith had briefly been in command of state troops at Wyoming in November, 1784.
[2] No. 136, ante.

The tumult continues in Wyoming, the apprehending of Franklin, I believe, has only hastened the Period of their clandestine opposition to Government, I hope it will convince our Legislators of the impropriety of purchasing Peace at the expence and ruin of individuals from a set of men devoted to disturb publick tranquility. I remain with sincere esteem and respect, Dear Sir, your most humble and obed't servant,

Francis Smith.

[146] Benjamin Franklin to George Clinton.[1]

In Council, Philad'a, Oct. 7, 1787.[2]

Sir,

The Bearer Mr. Redick is a Member of this Board, and goes to New York on a Business of Importance to both our States. The Council earnestly request of your Excellency to take the Information he may communicate into immediate Consideration, and afford this State the Aid that you will perceive to be necessary for securing the Person and Papers in question, in order to compleat the Evidence against the Conspirators,[3] so that they may be brought to condign Punishment, & their Schemes of Mischief defeated. With great & sincere Respect, I have the honor to be Sir, your Excellency's most obedient & most humble Servant,

B. Franklin.

[147] Extract from the Minutes of the Pennsylvania Council.[1]

Philadelphia, October 8th, 1787, Monday

Council taking into consideration the intelligence received from the county of Luzerne since the capture of John Franklin, the principal of the banditte lately assembled at Tioga, and the

[146] [1] *P. A.*, XI, 196.
   [2] Since the Council did not authorize Redick's mission until October 8 (no. 147, *post*) Franklin's date must be a slip. He probably wrote on October 8. Leonard W. Labaree, Editor of *The Papers of Benjamin Franklin,* who has a photocopy of the original letter, kindly informed me that the *P. A.* version follows the original in dating and wording.
   [3] See no. 100, *ante,* note 5.   [147] [1] *Pa. C. R.,* XV, 291.

public safety at this time requiring that the said John Franklin should be closely confined, therefore,

Resolved, That the Sheriff of the city and county of Philadelphia be directed to confine the said John Franklin, in one of the upper rooms of the jail, in irons, to suffer no person or persons what-ever to speak to him without leave from Council, or one of the Judges of the Supreme Court, and to debar him the use of pen, ink, and paper.[2] * * *

Resolved, That Mr. Redick, member of this Board, be requested to go immediately to New York [3] to communicate to his Excellency the Governor of that State some important intelligence, this day received,[4] respecting the late riots in the county of Luzerne, and to request that he will afford this State the aid that he will perceive to be necessary for securing sundry persons now in the State of New York, together with their papers, in order to compleat the evidence against the conspirators, so that they may be brought to condign punishment, and their schemes of mischief defeated.

[148] Charles Biddle to David Redick.[1]

In Council, Philadelphia, October 8th, 1787.

Sir,

We send you several letters received this day from Luzerne —by those letters you will perceive that Hamilton and Benton have been doing every thing in their power to disturb the peace of this Government.[2] The Insurgents appear to repent of their rash proceedings—however, to keep peace in that County, we think it will be necessary to send a few militia, to be stationed at Tioga and Wilksbarre.[3] If the Government of New York

---

[2] A copy of this extract from the minutes directed to Sheriff Joseph Cowperthwaite is in H. S. P., Conn. Claims in Pennsylvania, I, 27.

[3] See no. 146, *ante.*   [4] See no. 148, *post,* note 2.

[148] [1] P. A., XI, 459.

[2] Biddle is probably referring to copies of letters written by Joseph Hamilton and Caleb Benton; see nos. 93, 111, 112, and 113, *ante.* These Hamilton letters were seized from Asa Starkwather on October 2; no. 238, *post.* The letter from Benton was probably taken from Franklin after his arrest. Copies of all four letters are in P. H. M. C., Div. of Arch. and MSS., Record Group 27, Series: Letter Books, Nov. 4, 1782–Oct. 6, 1787, pp. 422-24.

[3] On October 9, the lieutenant of Berks County was ordered to detach a force of "seventy privates, properly officered and equipped," presumably to

would send a few men to Newtown, to act with those we send to Tioga, it would preserve the peace of both States. After you have perused the letters we send you, and shewn them to the Gov. of N. Y., you will please to send them back. I am, Sir, your obedient and very humble servant,

Charles Biddle, V. P.

[149] Timothy Pickering to John Swift.[1]

Philadelphia Oct. 9, 1787.

Sir,

M[r] Bowman arrived yesterday with your letter[2] of the 6th. It is very well that my family and property have received no injury; and for your attention to preserve both I thank you. I have, from my first knowledge of you, been made to believe, that your natural disposition was such as would become a good citizen; and I am yet fully persuaded, that if you had not been deceived & misled by Franklin, you would faithfully have stood to the allegiance you owed to this state. For a man naturally so well disposed I feel a regard; and if you renounce Franklin's cause, which is that of treason against the State, and manifest in future a steady attachment to Government, I shall take a pleasure in showing myself your friend. You say I shall think differently of Franklin's friends from what I have done; I wish there may be reason for it. By their future conduct they must show that they deserve any degree of confidence: for what trust can I place in the promises of men who pay no regard to their solemn oaths? You know that most of his friends have taken the oath of allegiance to the State; and yet they have since damned its laws & government, and at last have taken up arms against it! What confidence can the government place in the promises of such men? Government, however, is disposed to receive favourably every sign of repentance & return to duty.

As to Franklin's treatment, you may expect it will be such as will be proper for one charged with crimes of so deep a die; and in whatever respect it may be severe, it will be so, no farther

---

be sent to Luzerne; *Pa. C. R.*, XV, 292. There were, however, long delays before the militia got to Wyoming. President Benjamin Franklin was still drafting instructions for them in mid-November; no. 179, *post*.

[149] [1] M. H. S., Pickering Papers, LVII, 314-16, a copy in Pickering's hand.   [2] No. 141, *ante*.

than Government shall think absolutely necessary effectually to secure so dangerous an enemy to the State; and these severities I dare say will be abated as soon as order & tranquility shall be perfectly restored in the county of Luzerne. You say you love Franklin, and desire me to use my influence that he may be dealt with fairly, and that as much lenity as possible may be shown him. As to the latter, I have answered already; and to procure him a fair trial, no influence of mine or of any other person is necessary in *Pennsylvania*. The constitution and laws of this state are free and favourable to its subjects, and will give a fair chance to the greatest offender—even to Franklin—whatever lies he may have told you and his adherents of the injustice of its laws & the cruelty of its government. He knew better; but has used falsehoods & misrepresentations to poison the minds of the inhabitants, and gain them over to his interest. I am sorry that so many have been deluded by his deceitful stories. If you are his warm friend, you will start perhaps, at my applying so freely, lies and falsehoods to Franklin, but you will recollect I said as much to his face, at Forty Fort, last April: and I can support my charges with sufficient evidence. And again I assure you that he has most abominably deceived you and his other friends; and instead of still espousing his cause, you ought to feel much resentment against him for the deceits he has practised upon you. I have always spoken freely; and I have always told you and the people the truth; and you and they must now see it. Even Franklin told the Gentlemen who took him, that I was a man of my word. Yet Satterly and Slocum, I was informed, raised and propagated a lie against me as they came from Tioga; pretending that I said I owned no lands in the county under Pennsylvania: but I never said so: on the contrary, I told the people, last winter, that (besides my lands about the Great-Bend) I did own such lands within the New-Purchase of the State, partly about Tioga; but that my share amounted only to about 450 acres. This many must and do remember. Ask Lawrence Myers, William Ross, & others. Satterly & Slocum needed not to take such pains to get my lease to Owen: If they had asked me, I would have given them a copy of it. And I defy them and all the men on earth to prove a single lie against me during my whole life. I hope this lie [was] not raised by them designedly, but thro' mistake. But what has Franklin told you? Recollect well; and then compare what he has said with what you since find to be the truth; and you will see how widely the truth and his words differ. Has he not also, been perpetually prophesying falsely? Has he not often told the people that Pennsylvania was cruel and unjust, and would never confirm the Connecticut titles? After the confirming law passed, did he not say that it was all a sham, and the Commissioners would never sit? Though I was building an office and a house, & had said I was going to bring up my family, did he not say I would never move my family to Wyoming? Did not he say this on the very day on which I arrived with them? And after he found I was arrived with them, & was twitted with his false prediction, how did he turn it off? Why by asking "What I should think of being driven back again thro' the Swamp?" And this I have no doubt he resolved on. From various quarters I heard that I was to be driven out; and 'tis not above a fortnight since Waterman Baldwin said (as I was well informed) that I was to be moved off in ten or twelve days.

You say (speaking for yourself, Baldwin & others) upon your honour, that the notion of independency was not in your heads: But was it not in Baldwin's head when he asked Col° Denison what he thought of independence, & what advantages would attend it, if they could carry it? What has been the business of so many meetings between Franklin and his partisans? What was meant by Franklin at your meeting last Thursday week, at Shawnee, when he (as I was credibly informed) swore by God his maker, that the laws of Pennsylvania should never circulate in the settlement? Did he not also openly declare that there should be no election of militia officers? For what did he send orders up the river, for all his men to appear at Wilkesbarre yesterday with arms and ammunition? For what were several kegs of powder brought to Tioga, & thence down to Exeter or Kingston? For what was there such a collection of flints at his house? What did he say last Sunday or Monday (Septr 30th or Octr 1st.) to the people at Wapolopen, when you, Satterly, & Abraham Nisbett were present? What was the object of the Convention, as it was called, of Franklin, Beach, McKinstry, & other leaders, at Tioga? Have you never been informed? Recollect all that you have seen and heard, and then say if you think Franklin did not intend entirely to cast off the government of Pennsylvania, and out of the Wyoming settlement, and perhaps the parts of New-York round about Tioga, to erect a New State? Let me assure you (and as you are all witnesses that I have ever told you the truth, what I say deserves some attention)—let me assure you that this is at the bottom of all the machinations of Franklin, Beach, Hamilton, Judd, and the rest of the leaders.

233

If this was not the design, there proceedings were madness and folly in the extreme. But there is abundant proof that this was their design. All the writings of Hamilton, Judd & others clearly prove it, to those who have not been blinded by the lies & artifices of the leading conspirators. And the intercepted letters taken with Starkweather, from Hamilton & Benton, call for blood & slaughter. Hamilton in particular, upbraids Franklin for delaying it.[3] With so many proofs of this wicked plan of destruction and rebellion, which Franklin was to carry into execution, can you wonder that Government should order him to be apprehended? And do you not know that it was my duty, & the duty of every faithful citizen, to give all necessary aid in the execution of every legal warrant? Perhaps you have been told that Franklin's capture was illegal: but this is the declaration of ignorance or something worse. The warrant for taking him was issued by the Chief Justice of the State; and I presume his law-knowledge is rather superiour to that of any lawyer in the county of Luzerne. I presume also that both the Chief Justice[4] (who is an old & able lawyer) and the Supreme Council of the state, know what is Constitutional as well as any sagacious gentleman in Wyoming.

You are apprehensive that a State-Warrant is out to take you & others, as Franklin was taken; and you say *you must not be taken in that manner*—that *it was too cruel*. This, let me tell you, is very improper language in the same letter in which you say "Franklin's friends are disposed to submit to law & government in all things:" For it contains a threat that you & they would resist the government in such case; & indecently reproaches the government with cruelty. But no cruelty was exercised on Franklin. It is true he had been struck, and was bloody; but this was wholly owing to his obstinate resistance. His hands were never at liberty but he struck with all his might one or another of the gentlemen who took him. He says himself that he was well used by them after he surrendered. To relieve your apprehensions, I now inform you, that I know not of any warrant against you or any of the men who assembled in arms the night after Franklin was taken: and if you and they keep the promises of submission to the laws expressed in the letters to Col° Denison and me, I suppose the Government will pass over your & their offences; imputing your misconduct to Franklin as the cause of it.

---

[3] See nos. 112 and 113, *ante*.   [4] Thomas McKean.

234

I request you to speak to Slocum, who commanded the party at Kelly's, & who I suppose detached the six men who lay in wait to take me, between ten-mile-run & Bear Creek, & desire him to call upon them for the 17 hard dollars of which they robbed John Scott.

I have written thus largely to excite you and your associates to consideration. I have written, I see, not in the softest terms; and you must suppose I cannot but feel some resentment at the ungrateful treatment I have received—to be hunted and pursued like a wild beast, or criminal—I who far from injuring, have made it my study to promote the peace & welfare of the settlement—who on every occasion have shown myself its friend—and never more, than in assisting to secure its *greatest enemy*—I mean *John Franklin*. I am &c.

T. P.

P. S. Since writing the above, I have seen two of the gentlemen who took Franklin, and of their own accord they told me of the conversation between them & Franklin on his way to this city, in the course of which he told them that it was his determination to prevent the election of any militia officers last Monday, and to break up the annual election to be held yesterday; and that he intended to set up a new state, which was to extend to the West Branch of the Susquehanna. This they are ready to depose on oath, & will do it before they leave this city.

[150] Benjamin Franklin to John Craig.[1]

In Council, Philadelphia, October 9th, 1787.

Sir,

The Council on Consideration have thought proper, to suspend for the present the execution of those warrants which are in your hands for the apprehending of Jenkins Beach and McKinstrey. You are therefore to retain those Warrants in your hands until you receive further orders from Council. I am Sir, your obedient and very humble servant,

Benjamin Franklin.

---

[150] [1] *P. A.*, XI, 196. Craig was lieutenant of Northampton County and had led the men who captured John Franklin.

[151] David Redick to Benjamin Franklin.[1]

New York, 9th October, 1787.

Sir,

I arrived in this city at 12 to day, and waited on Genls. St. Clair and Irvine before I sat down they went with me to Governor Clinton so that I had an interview with him before dinner. The governor discovered the greatest cheerfulness to pursue any measure, in concert with Pennsylvania or otherwise, to secure the peace and quiet of his own Government and at the same time to promote that of Pennsylvania, we entered very seriously into the business, he appears now fully convinced that Hamilton, Baynton, Aughmuterry and McKinstry[2] are wicked men, he rejoices much at Franklin's being secured, as he thinks it equally favourable to the happiness of both our States. We waited this afternoon on the Chief Justice;[3] who with equal readiness, and earnest intent on his part, went into the necessary measures for apprehending the persons and securing the papers of Hamilton and Baynton. I mentioned to the Governor & Judge that my anxiety for the certain and effectual execution of the business was so very great, that if they thought, that my personal attention to it would contribute to its success, I would freely go to Hudson;[4] this proposition had the desired effect, that was to lead to a conversation respecting the person (as well as the manner of doing it,) to whom it would be intrusted. After several proposals or rather plans, still observing symptoms of doubt on my brow, for I did not think it prudent to impress them by words, he assured me he would endeavour to get Col. Willet, High Sh'ff of the city to go in person; and that he would answer for the completion of it; he accordingly waited on Col. Willet who will undertake to do it; but some matters of much importance obliges him to attend to them tomorrow; next day early he intends setting out. I have been with Col. Willet since night and mentioned to him my Ideas respecting the propriety of Securing or rather apprehending both the persons at one and the same time lest an alarm might put the other on his guard; he has satisfied me.

---

[151] [1] *P. A.*, XI, 197.

[2] Joseph Hamilton, Caleb Benton, John AcModer, and John McKinstry.

[3] Richard Morris; *P. A.*, XI, 340.

[4] Hudson was the home of Hamilton.

The Governor assures me, that authenticated transcripts of every material paper shall be immediately transmitted to your Excellency & the Council upon their arrival in New York, and he further declares that the moment in which it may be found necessary to send force he will in conjunction with Pennsylvania crush them at once.

After all, I do not find myself at liberty to return to Philadelphia until I see Col. Willet fairly set off. Sir, I have the honor to be your most obedient & very humble S't,

David Redick.

[152] Extract from the Minutes of the Pennsylvania Council.[1]

PHILADELPHIA, Wednesday, October 10th, 1787.

On consideration,

Resolved, That Colonel Dennisen be requested to go immediately into his county of Luzerne, in order to inform himself minutely, and to furnish exact information to Council of the state of affairs there; and that, if he shall judge it proper, he proceed as far as Tioga himself, or send thither some other suitable person, to view the situation of the mal-contents there, and obtain what knowledge he can of their designs, numbers, force and probable means of support, if they mean to establish themselves within the boundaries of this State: of all which he is to make report as soon as possible to the Council.

The President offering to advance what specie may be necessary in part of his expence for this service, it was agreed to, and he was accordingly furnished twelve dollars to Colonel Dennison.

Colonel Dennisen's instructions are as follows, vizt:

In Council, October 10th, 1787.

Instructions to the Honorable Nathan Dennisen, Esquire.

On consideration of the letter communicated by you,[2] which you received from sundry of the persons principally concerned in the late riot in the county of Luzerne, upon the apprehending of John Franklin, representing that the same was committed in the heat of passion, occasioned by the supposition that he was carried off illegally, without the authority of any regular writ or warrant; and that being now better informed, they were sorry

---

[152] [1] *Pa. C. R.,* XV, 292-93.   [2] No. 143, *ante.*

for their misconduct in that affair, and determined to submit quietly to the operation of the laws, hoping this their offence might be passed over:—The Council, ever desirous to promote and establish peace and good order in that county, and giving credit to the aforesaid declaration of the offenders, do hereby authorize you to assure them that if they hereafter behave orderly, as good citizens of the State of Pennsylvania, no prosecution shall be commenced against them on account of their said irregular and criminal conduct, but you are at the same time to acquaint them that the Government, having already taken every measure for securing to the settlers the future quiet possession of their lands, are now determined to carry into execution the laws of the State, to the full extent of its boundaries, and purpose to send immediately into that county a force sufficient to support the public officers in the discharge of their respective functions against all opposers, who, if they persist in their evil practices, are to expect no further favor.

B. Franklin, President.

[153] Zebulon Butler to John M. Breed.[1]

Wyoming 11 Oct' 1787

Sir,

I am informed by M' Storey that you had A Letter wrote to Send to me. I conclude it was on the Subject of the Land that I wrote to M' Cleveland to Communicate to you.[2]   Now Sir I can only Say as I did before that is I would wish to have the Land on Good terms. I have communiated to M'' Deany and the Family all that has passed on the Subject. I have Examined the Inventory of the Estate of M' Deany. I Find that the Lot Deaded to Cap' Breed is not Included in in the Inventory of that Estate. So that if some one does not put in a Claim for it, it will of cores Revert back to Pennsylvania Claments and you will Lose your Money.[3]   Now Sir if you can forward A

[153] [1] MS in the possession of George O. Pratt, Southport, Conn.

[2] In May, 1787, Butler had written a letter to Aaron Cleveland expressing a wish to buy land which apparently had been deeded by Breed to Deany, but for which Breed had never received payment. Cleveland wrote Butler on May 29 that Breed had said that the Deany family should have first refusal if they would pay what was due plus interest; Wyoming Historical and Geological Society, Butler Papers.

[3] According to the Confirming Act, Connecticut claimants could establish title only to lands settled and assigned before the Trenton decree.

Power of Attorney to me or any man that you chuse to put in your claim to the Land it will be Entered and the Land Saved to you but it must be done in the Corse of one Month. I am Sir tho Not acquainted your Friend and Hbel Servt

Zeb^n Butler

[154] Aaron Cleveland to Timothy Pickering.[1]

Norwich Octr 13 1787

Sir

I have lands lay'd out in the county of Luzerne, but Subsequent to the decree of Trenton. as I have it in contemplation to Settle there, should wish you to befriend me in the security of those lands as far as you can consistent with the Spirit and intention of your Comm^sn. Mr Benjamin Bailey is furnish'd with A power of an attorny to act for me. I don't know what chance I can have unless your commission be Some what enlarged. am in hopes all things considr'd that will be the case in order to give general quiet. * * *

[155] Lord Butler to Timothy Pickering.[1]

Luzerne Octr 15th, 1787

Dear Sir

Since I wrote you we have held the Ellection in peace. our Opposers Join^d verry freely & Run with us in the same Tickett. what their Views is I Cannot say. Col° Denison is now with us. they profess their Submission to the Laws and say they will support them. I cant say but I a Little Doubt them. However I wish for peace, & Wish you to Return with safety. I proposed to be with you soon After the Ellection but am not Able to come. I wish that the Officers that is to be Commission^d might be Commission^d by yourself as they were before in order to keep the wheels of Government moving. Col° Denison has wrote to Councill that he Believes they will be sbmissive & is now gone to Tioga himself. we expect we shall see you before Col° Denis-

[154] [1] M. H. S., Pickering Papers, LVII, 317, in an unknown hand but signed by Cleveland.
[155] [1] M. H. S., Pickering Papers, LVII, 318, in Butler's hand.

son Returns &c. Excuse hast. I am Dʳ Sir your freind & well wisher

Lord Butler

[156] Samuel Gordon to Obadiah Gore.¹

Wylusing 15ᵗʰ Oct, 1787

Dear Sʳ,

It gives me some concern to hear of Capᵗ Shotts & others ingaging themselves to the halfshare-men that they will get a grant or a something from the Legislature of Pennsylvania, to confirm their Lands to them, on their petitioning. It would be no grief to me were they to have their lands laid out where it would not interfere with Surveys formerly made to old propriators, who were Settlers & Sufferers: But, they have laid their rights on old Surveys made in the year 1776,1777 for men, many of whome are dead being killed by the Savages or died in the Service of their Country their widⁿˢ & Children have not had it [in] their power to Settle their Lands before it was granted to halfshare men ² (many of whom have fled hither to escape Justice) who are now in possession of the land & keep the original propriators off by force. None can be more injured by establishing the ½ share men in the right of the Land they possess than your Sisters, as each had a right in Braintrum Township which is now chiefly possessed by Franklins desciples. If there is a petition in their favour, or in the favour of Old Rights unlaid out, pray, let them pray for Lands unlocated, & not have it in their power to take our improved lands, and also lands laid out to Old setlers & Sufferers, By consenting to this Capᵗ Shotts & those concerned would open a door for further dispute & confusion; which would be music to those who wish to supress government, that they may roam at learge & impress on the minds of the discontented with the many advantages they must unavoidable reap to themselves & posterity by Returning under the protection of the British. There are many now engaged in this business; and as no argument is more forcible than gain, to

---

[156] ¹ M. H. S., Pickering Papers, LVII, 320-21, in Gordon's hand. Gordon was a surveyor engaged by Pennsylvania in the boundary dispute with New York; Harvey-Smith, *Wilkes-Barré*, III, 1619.

² If what Gordon says was true, it was in violation of the rules of the Company, for its latest resolves specifically protected the claims of widows and orphans; see *Susquehannah Company Papers*, VIII, no. 268.

Lord Butler (1761-1824), reproduced from Oscar J. Harvey, *A History of Wilkes-Barré*, II, facing p. 1176.

unprincipal'd wretches, there are now a Number Leasing land
from the Indians for a long term of years & offering the same
gratus to those who will Settle it. the brittish are very active in
this business and have influenced the setlers to Refuse asking
the protection of any state; these Brittish emissaries are now at
Buffelow Creek (Genosee) with Col Harfner & Livingston from
York state [3] and others from other states treating with the Indians for all the Genosee country; as soon as the treaty is over,
they will givery every encouragement to Setlers & introduce
british Government. If the Legislature of New York are unacquainted with this matter it is Capt Shotts' duty to inform
them of it, and crop their proceedings in the bud. Please to inform Capt Shotts how uneasy his offer has made a considerable
number of respectable people, that if he means to have the Lands
confirmed to the halfsharers where they possess a Remonstrance
will be sent into the Assembly against it. It is the opinion of
the most of people that if those known to be old Settlers & Sufferers were allowed to locate a tract of Land & have it survey'd
where it would not interfere with former Surveys that all parties
would be perfectly pleased, and content sit smiling on the brow
of every man or woman interested: moreover those old propriators, setlers & suffers should be intitled, on producing a certificate from Col^r Denison, Butler or Esqr Gore that they were old
priators & Sufferers & that they have not had any land laid out
on their Rights. In order to satisfy the minds of the people
please to let me know by the Bearer what the Substance of their
petition is & with many others you'll oblige your Most obed^t
Servt

Saml Gordon

[157] Instructions to Wyoming Commissioners.[1]

In Council, Oct. 16, 1787.
Instructions to the State Commissioners now in the County
of Luzerne for settling the Claims of Landed Property there, and
to the Civil Officers of the said County.

---

[3] See no. 100, *ante*, note 5.
[157] [1] *P. A.*, XI, 205. Similar orders were given to the military; *ibid.*,
204.

Gentlemen,

The Council on Consideration of the late Disturbances in the County of Luzerne, and the opposition there given by some Disorderly People to the operations of Legal Government, have ordered a Company of Militia thither from the County of Berks, to be employed under your Direction in supporting the Civil Authority and protecting its officers in the Exercise of their Duties and the Execution of the Laws of the State; but not to be used in acting offensively, (unless impell'd by Necessity) against any Place, Person or Persons whatever; you are therefore to take the Direction of the said military Force, and to call on the Lieutenant of the County for such Addition thereto by drafts out of his Militia as you may judge necessary and convenient; and the whole being under your orders, you are to take especial Care that the strictest Discipline be observed, and that no Insult or Injury be offered or done to any of the Inhabitants, they behaving quietly and inoffensively as becomes good Citizens of the Commonwealth. And if any Circumstances should arise which may make it appear to you that a greater force is necessary to secure Peace and establish good order in the said County, you are to inform Council thereof by the speediest Means, that Bodies of Militia from other Counties may be sent to reinforce you accordingly.

[158] Ebenezer Bowman to Timothy Pickering.[1]

Sir

We arrived here Saterday evening and found the settlement nearly in the same situation as when I left it. Beach and McKinster with a party of the half sharemen were here; some of them on the night I left this place for Philadelphia abused Esqʳ Gore in a shameful manner, the particulars you will learn from Capt Schotts; on monday the fifteenth we had a meeting at which time Coll Dennison communicated the determination of Council[2] concerning the disturbances on the night of the [2nd] Instant; the offenders seemed much pleased, with the lenity of Council towards them; and manifested their readiness to submit to Government. Beach & McKinster were present, but made no

---

[158] [1] M. H. S., Pickering Papers, LVII, 322-23, in Bowman's hand. Bowman, a lawyer, lived with the Pickering family in Wyoming and managed Pickering's legal business in his absence; see no. 181, post.

[2] See no. 152, ante.

remarks upon the letter from Council nor did they give any advice (publickly) to the people. I am told however that Beach is still very busy endeavouring to persuade the people to sign the Combination (as they call it) [3] it is similar to that which is before Council; and some thro fear and others from a mistaken Notion of promoting their own Interest have been induced to sign it in and about this place lately; Beach is certainly a disturber of the peace, and as such ought to be punished. I delivered your Letter to Swift; [4] Slocum was present, and they both declared they had kept their promises in behaving themselves in a peacible manner; and further promissed to exert themselves to support the Laws and Assist the Officers of Government in the discharge of their respective duties; the Idea of of Troops being sent (I find) is disagreeable to many and particularly to those who have no Just claims to any property in this settlement. The election for Military Officers was adjourned to the twentieth Instant; had it gone on Franklin undoubtedly would have been Colonel; I am informed that Jonah Rogers was very busy giving out Votes for Franklin and I believe it is the determination of that party still to make him their leader if possible, but they will meet with greater opposition than they expect. The election for Civil Officers was held peacibly. W Ross & M F Alden were in the ticket with Lord Butlar for Sheriff and had an equal number of Votes (Ross & Alden). [5] the Sheriff was at a loss whether to return them both. Aldens conduct merits no favour from Government. publick as well as private business call for your immediate return. I am with every sentiment of esteem your friend and hum^b Servt.

Eben^r Bowman

Wilkesborough Octr 17th 1787

[159] Timothy Pickering to Samuel Hodgdon. [1]

Easton, Friday Morn^g Oct. 19, 1787.

Dear Sir,

Yesterday afternoon I set off from Bethlehem with my horses, provided with side-saddles, for my Wife & Betsey to ride out

---

[3] No. 135, *ante.*   [4] No. 149, *ante.*

[5] On October 22 the Council ruled that Butler and Alden were elected sheriffs; *Pa. C. R.,* XV, 300.

[159] [1] M. H. S., Pickering Papers, LVII, 324-25, in Pickering's hand.

thro' the Swamp; intending to send Jnᵒ Scott & George for them, and to wait myself their arrival at such place as I thought safe: But when half way to Nazareth, I met Mʳ Horton returning, who told me that he came from Wyoming with Capt. Schott, who had letters for me, but had turned off from Hallers, & gone to Easton, which place he was to leave this morning. After such enquiries as occurred, I parted with him, & at the first opening turned off for Easton; Jnᵒ Scott & George having gone forward to Nazareth. At Easton I found Capt. Schott (who is elected member of Assembly for Luzerne & is now on his way to Philaᵃ) who delivered me a letter from my wife, & one from Mʳ Bowman.[2] By the first I found that my wife was quite at ease, & entertaining no idea of leaving Wyoming: at the same time she expresses some apprehensions for my safety if I return. Mʳ Bowman's account of Swift & Slocum is favourable. He says They have not only been quiet themselves, since the first rupture, but repeat the most solemn promises, not only of remaining so, but of assisting the officers of government in the execution of their duty; and concludes with these words "Public as well as private business call for your immediate return." Capt. Schott tells me he left the insurgents with their friends preparing an address or petition to Government, giving assurances of their future good behaviour: That Slocum expresses much sorrow for his conduct towards Mʳ Montgomery; and with others was going to send a letter requesting his immediate return: That not having time before he (Schott) parted with Horton, to write to Colᵉ Balliet, he had desired Horton to do it in his name, to urge his return to Wyoming without delay: Capt. Schott urges me to do the same. All things considered, I have concluded to return; and shall send Jnᵒ Scott & George back to Bethlehem for my waggon which I left there because it needed some essential repairs. I expect it will be done so that they may get to Nazareth again to-night: To-morrow we shall put into it some necessaries at Hallers, & by Monday night we may arrive at Wyoming. I shall myself go in in the evening; and if I find I may do it with safety, shall remain there; tho' with watchfullness of any attempt against me.

The last words I said to you, expressed my opinion that the sending out my children was too precipitate; & my Wife says she did it "contrary to everybody's opinion that she talked with": however, I do not blame her, because she was actuated by the

---

[2] No. 158, *ante.*

deep anxiety of a mother, who cared for her children's safety more than for her own. On the same principle I set out on this journey, to relieve her distresses, & intending to consult her *feelings* only, not her reason, in respect to hers & Betseys removal. I wished to know Betseys sentiments; and was tempted to open her letter to you, in which I supposed she had spoken her mind freely: but on the whole being tolerably satisfied by some passages in my wife's letter & Mr Bowmans, & with capt. Schotts detail & opinion, that it was best for me to go in, I left Betsey's letter untouched.

Capt Schott, has this moment called, & delivered me two more letters, one from the Sheriff,[3] the other from Esqr Gore.[4] The former expresses himself cautiously, tho' at the close says he expects to see me there before Col° Denison returns from Tioga. Esqr Gore gives me a detail of the abuses he rec^d from some of the Tioga & Newtown ruffians who came down with Beach & McInstry the Saturday evening after Gore's arrival "but the next day (says he) the party who came down the river finding that those who committed the disorders the evening after that Franklin was taken, *had retracted, & would not join them,* it calmed them down, that a number returned on Monday evening (the 15th) or Tuesday morning; the remainder appeared disposed to countenance the elections, & to have the exercise of law take place uninterrupted."—"I attended the election of county officers, administered the necessary qualifications, and the election went on very orderly, and those who came down the river have generally returned I believe much chagrined."

Capt. Schott also informs me that Col° Denison has written by him to Council, expressing his opinion that all would remain quiet. I am satisfied they will, until the Sheriff, on the proper process, shall go to turn the half-sharemen out of possession of their ill-gotten lands; and then the opposition will begin again. Nothing is clearer to me, than this, That if Pennsylvania & New York wish to extend their authority to Tioga and Newtown, they must send each one company of 50 good soldiers to take post at Tioga, and remain there *at least one year* and that the sooner this is done the better; for the numbers of lawless men will be encreasing in those parts, and the longer they remain uncurb'd, the more difficult it will be to reclaim & reduce them. Such a permanent post at Tioga would soon, if not immediately, supersede the necessity of troops at Wilkesburgh. I therefore ear-

---

[3] No. 155, *ante.*   [4] Not found.

nestly wish that the raising such a permanent body of soldiers might be strongly urged by you with such gentlemen as you think proper to speak to, & who have influence in the government. If New-York will not join (which is not to be believed) Pennsylvania ought to do the whole herself if she consults her peace & interest. I remain dear Sir with great affection & esteem yʳ friend

T. Pickering

Endorsed: Mʳ Pickering Oct 19 1787 Recᵈ 21ᵗᵗ.

[160] Timothy Pickering to Samuel Hodgdon.[1]

Nazareth, Oct. 19, 1787.

Dear Sir,

I wrote you to day by Capt. Schott from Easton,[2] I think the intercepted letters of Hamilton & Benton[3] which are with Council, would be useful to me at Wyoming. I wish you therefore to get copies of them, & forward them by Mr. Evans, who indeed can easily obtain the copies, or may have leisure to make them himself, I shall be sorry to miss of them, & the sooner I have them the better.

On my arrival here this morning, I found that Jno. Scott & George had gone forward to Hallers, expecting I should go thither directly from Easton, This has obliged me to pursue them, & I am just returned. I have sent Jno. Scott forward on foot directly from Hallers, & I expect he will be in Wilkesborough, on Sunday. If there should be any ground to apprehend danger to my person, he is to come out to meet me. I shall accompany George with the waggon in which I shall put on a few of the goods remaining at Hallers.

4 o'clock P. M. George is just ready to start for Bethlehem for the waggon. affectionately adieu,

T. Pickering.

---

[160] [1] *P. A.*, XI, 205-06.

[2] No. 159, *ante*. Actually Pickering wrote twice from Easton. His other letter, which concerned only business affairs, is in M. H. S., Pickering Papers, XXXV, 25.

[3] Nos. 93, 111, 112, and 113, *ante*.

[161] Benjamin Franklin to the Pennsylvania Delegates in the Continental Congress.[1]

In Council, Philadelphia October 20th, 1787.

Gentlemen,

Your letter of the 18th is received,[2] containing the pleasing intelligence of the apprehending of Hamilton with his papers. The Council are extremely sensible of Governor Clinton's very neighborly and friendly conduct on this occasion, and desire you would express their thanks to his Excellency in the strongest terms, and they leave entirely to his judgment the expedience of admitting the prisoner to Bail, only wishing that if he is permitted to go back to Hudson, some measures may be taken there to watch and intercept his future correspondence, and that we may as soon as convenient be favoured with copies of such parts of the past as you may think of importance. I am with sincere, and great Esteem, Gentlemen, your most obedient, and most humble servant,

Benjamin Franklin.

Hon. Arthur St. Clair, William Irwine, & John Armstrong.

[162] Ebenezer Bowman to Timothy Pickering.[1]

Sir

Scott arrived last evening.[2] By him we learn you are on the way for this place. I supposed you had determined (before I left the City) not to return untill you had troops to protect you; In my letter by Capt[n] Schotts I mentioned the determination of a number to choose Franklin Col[l] of the Militia and thought that would be sufficient to convince you that no great dependence could be put in those people, and I can assure you Sir nothing has since taken place to convince me that they have entirely re-

---

[161] [1] *P. A.*, XI, 460.   [2] Not found.
[162] [1] M. H. S., Pickering Papers, LVII, 326-27, in Bowman's hand.
[2] See no. 159, *ante*.

linquished their former plan; last evening a person who has always appeared to be friendly towards you told me he had within two or three days been in Shawanee and that the people there were yet determined to take you if possible in order to secure the return of Franklin, and their conduct yesterday at the election of Militia Officers shews that they are not so peacibly disposed as they have pretended. They did not vote for Franklin, but gave this reason that they feared it would opperate to his disadvantage; they however came determined to put Swift in Col¹ and Matthewson Major; but they failed in both. M. Hollenback was chosen Col° and L Myers Major; Scott says that you do not expect any troops will be sent; as I suppose he is Kept in Ignorance about their comming I feel easy; but if I thought they would not be sent I think I should soon determine to leave the settlement for I believe we should be in a worse situation than ever in a little time; Beach and McKinster endeavoured (while here) to persuade the people that they were friends to the settlement, and would assist in establishing the Laws, and Beach said he was sure the people would all join to protect the Commissioners, and the Civil Officers of the County and that he thought it unnecessary to send troops as it would put the Government to expence; and greatly destress the inhabitants and at the same time he was appointing and ordering persons to survey all the good lands lying on Wysockings Creek and gave them particular orders to admit all the able bodied men (as settlers) that should Report, and also to allow them an hundred acres each, and said also that he should be able by Spring to bring on near two thousands; by this you will be convinced of his reason for wishing to prevent military force coming here; When I saw you in the city I said much in favour of Schotts and I wish his conduct since would justify what I said but at present it is beyond a doubt in my mind that he got his election by making interest with Beach and McKinster and promising to do great things for the half sharemen.³ This you will be convinced of when you hear the Circumstances; one thing I believe he promised was to prevent troops coming. Of this however I am not certain, you will learn something perhaps by Doc⁂ Smith who sets out for the City on Tuesday; my reason for writing, is it possible to prevent your coming here before the troops for I do not think you would be

---

³ Schott was elected to the General Assembly. This view of Schott should be compared with that expressed in no. 156, *ante*.

safe. However you will see the Doct^r and take his advice. from your humb^l Servt

Wilkesborough Octr 21st 1787   Eben^r Bowman

[163] Extract from the *Connecticut Courant*.[1]

On Saturday last John Franklin was brought before the supreme court, to show cause why he should not be committed upon a charge of high treason. The chief Justice stated, that many depositions and proofs of his treasonable practices, were in possession of the executive council, besides the affidavit upon which issued the warrant for apprehending the prisoner and several other persons whose names, it would be improper at this time to divulge.[2] In this affidavit it was sworn, that Franklin and a number of the Luzerne malcontents, had assembled, for the purpose of opposing the authority and laws of the common-wealth, and that a paper subscribed with his name, and in his hand writing, was posted up in different places by which the people were invited to throw off their allegiance to the state of Pennsylvania, and to erect themselves into an independant state.[3] It appeared likewise, that the insurgents had appointed a court, consisting of three judges, which was vested with jurisdiction in all cases criminal and civil, whether capital or otherwise. These facts, being read, the chief justice observed that if proved, they would clearly constitute the crime of high treason, but that the laws of the government had prevailed upon them to institute a prosecution, for misprision of treason only: and the prisoner being accordingly asked, if he could assign any reason why he should not be committed to take his trial for that offence, he answered, respectfully, that he was not guilty of the practices with which he was charged, and referred his defence to Mr.

---

[163] [1] October 22, 1787.

[2] The warrant for the arrest of Franklin has not been found. The other men were John Jenkins, Zerah Beach, and John McKinstry, warrants for whose arrest were suspended; no. 150, *ante*.

[3] The affidavit referred to was probably that given by Thomas Wigton (no. 109, *ante*), which was also the basis for the proclamation issued on September 25 (no. 128, *ante*). This affidavit, however, which mentions a notice signed by Franklin, does not specifically state that the notice invited people to form a separate state. For its contents, see John Shepard's deposition; no. 320, *post*.

249

Daniel Clymer and Mr. James Biddle, his council, in which the prisoner should give bail; but the chief justice observed, that however, inclined he might have been to consider that subject yesterday, the information which had been since received from Luzerne was a conclusive bar to the application; for it appeared that the insurgents, of whom Franklin was the leader, had proceeded to acts of open rebellion, in consequence of his imprisonment, that they had surrounded the house of Col. Pickering, and seized his family as hostages, and that Mr. Montgomery, one of the commissioners, had escaped with difficulty after suffering the greatest personal violence. Upon this the attorney general stated, that as the circumstances were now essentially altered, it became his duty to pray, upon the commonwealth, that the prisoner might be committed for the crime of high treason, which was incontrovertibly charged in the deposition that had just been read. The judges, unanimously agreed to make out the warrant accordingly; and as the commitment is by the whole court, a single judge will not, of course, admit the prisoner to bail during the vacation.

[164] Samuel Hodgdon to Timothy Pickering.[1]

Philadelphia 24ᵗʰ Octo 1787

Dear Sir

I received your Letters by Mʳ Schott, & from the information they contained I shall be doubly anxious to hear again. Most people here blame you for going to Wyoming until properly supported, but all hope the Measure may end well. The Assembly have not yet made a house, as soon as they do, which will probably be to day or to Morrow, your Counties concern will command their attention. General Armstrong has resigned his secretary ship and strange to tell, the late *Vice President* Biddle is elected to supply his place, and the complexion of the House being in degree changed, James M'Clean is to fill the Speakers Chair, but this with the choice of Clerk as usual is to try the strength of the different parties. Inclosed you have the Missing pages of the Minutes. I believe you now have them for the late sitting compleat.* * * You must have heard that *Hamilton* is

---

[164] [1] M. H. S., Pickering Papers, LVII, 328-30, in Hodgdon's hand.

taken and safely lodged in Jail at York.[2]   Important discoveries are said to be made—of which more hereafter.* * *

[165] Extract from the Minutes of the Pennsylvania Council.[1]

Philadelphia, Friday, 26th, 1787, October.
The following draft of a message to the General Assembly, was read and adopted:

A message from the President and the Supreme Executive Council to the General Assembly.

Gentlemen: Since the last session there has been a renewal of the disturbances at Wyoming, some restless spirits there having imagined a project of withdrawing the inhabitants of that part of this State, and some part of the State of New York, from their allegiance, and forming them into a new State, to be carried into effect by an armed force, in defiance of the laws of the two States. Having intelligence of this, we caused one of the principal conspirators to be apprehended and secured in the gaol of this city; and another, who resided in the State of New York, at our request has been taken up by the authority of that Government.[2] The papers found on this occasion, fully discover the designs of these turbulent people, and some of their letters are herewith laid before you.[3]   The Government of New York, has in this affair, manifested the most friendly and neighbourly disposition towards this State, and has promised to concur with us in such future measures as may be necessary to secure the due operation of the laws, and restore quiet in those parts of both States, where these irregular and ill-disposed settlers have their habitations. To protect the civil officers of our new county of Luzerne in the exercise of their respective functions, we have ordered a body of militia to hold themselves in readiness to march thither,[4] which will be done, unless some future circumstances and informations from those parts may, make it appear unnecessary.[5] * * *

___

[2] New York State is meant.

[165] [1] *Pa. C. R.,* XV, 304.   The message went out over President Benjamin Franklin's name and was dated October 27.

[2] The reference, of course, is to John Franklin and Joseph Hamilton.

[3] See no. 148, *ante,* note 2.

[4] See no. 148, *ante,* note 3.

[5] This part of the president's message referring to disturbances at Wyoming was referred in the Assembly to a committee composed of George

251

[166] Obadiah Gore's Memoranda.[1]

Almarina Marshal said in the hearing of Wm Gallup & several others, that if Col° Pickering should ever come into this settlement, he would be the death of him, and that Col° Butler was a damned rascal And further, that he did not regard the authority of this county. Thomas Bennet says That lately he heard Gideon Church say he would be damned if ever Penn^a Law came through the Great Swamp. Samuel Allen overheard Beach and several others talk that if they could keep troops out of the Settlement, and get those of Franklin's party to the command of the battalions, they did not care for the Authority, and that they should have matters to their liking in the Spring. Lawrance Myers says that not long since John Swift told him that about the time of the election there would be a great disturbance, and (says he you must think I know) the disturbance will be such as the Government party do not expect.

Endorsed: Copy of Esqr Gore's Memorandums, rec^d Octr 26. 1787, by the hand of Col. Denison.

[167] Extract from the Minutes of the Pennsylvania Council.[1]

Mr. McLene, Mr. Hiester, Mr. Wynkoop, Mr. Clymer, Mr. Lowry, Mr. Piper, a committee of Assembly, attended in Council, agreeably to the request of yesterday.[2] The intelligence received and communicated by Colonel Pickering, containing information that the rioters lately assembled at Tioga still persist in their intentions to oppose the Government and laws of this State, was taken into consideration, and some time being spent in

---

Clymer, Gerardus Wynkoop, Samuel Evans, Alexander Lowrey, James McLene, Gabriel Heister, and Thomas Kennedy, which reported first on November 3 and subsequently on November 12 and 14; *Minutes of the First Session of the Twelfth General Assembly*, 12, 18, 42, 56-57 (microfilm copy). See no. 170, *post*, note 22.

[166] [1] M. H. S., Pickering Papers, LVII, 330, in Pickering's hand.

[167] [1] *Pa. C. R.*, XV, 307, dated October 30, 1787.

[2] *Ibid.*, 306.

conference thereon it was deemed proper and necessary to make application to Congress for their consent to raise and employ a body of troops, not exceeding five hundred, to be stationed in the county of Luzerne, for protecting the officers of government and well affected inhabitants of said county.[3]

[168] Peter Muhlenberg to Timothy Pickering.[1]

In Council, Philadelp. October 31st, 1787

Sir,

Col° Dennison, on his arrival, laid before Council, several papers relative to the present situation of Luzerne County, together with a representation from the Magistrates.[2] Council wish to take some time to deliberate on the necessary measures, but wish you, in the mean time, to inform the Magistrates & County Lieut., That a sufficient number of Troops will be sent in good time, if necessary, to take part at Tioga. Council have also commissioned Capt[n] Ross, whose name was formerly omitted by mistake. Those other Gentlemen who were return'd, and not Commission'd,[3] may still be brought forward, if it can be made appear to Council that They have not disqualified themselves by Opposition to Government. If you, therefore, in Conjunction with the County L[t] & others, will make inquiry into the matter & report, Council will take order thereon.

The increase of Magistrates for Luzerne will be taken up by

---

[3] On October 31 the General Assembly authorized the request of the Council for an appeal to the Continental Congress; *P. A.,* XI, 206-07 and *Minutes of the First Session of the Twelfth General Assembly,* 14 (microfilm copy). The Pennsylvania delegates were unable to present the request because Congress lacked a quorum; no. 173, *post.*

[168] [1] *P. A.,* XI, 208.

[2] What papers Denison brought is not certain. He may have brought nos. 135 and 144, *ante,* copies of which are in P. H. M. C., Div. of Arch. and MSS., Record Group 27, Series: Letter Books, Nov. 4, 1782–Oct. 6, 1787, pp. 424-27. He may also have brought nos. 143 and 166, *ante.*

[3] No return of the election of militia officers for Luzerne for the year has been found, but see no. 237, *post.* Capt. William Ross commanded the Third Company of the Lower District of Wilkes-Barre; Harvey-Smith, *Wilkes-Barré,* III, 1580. According to William Hooker Smith, Ross's commission was held up because of opposition to it by one of the Luzerne magistrates; no. 190, *post.*

Council as soon as possible. Council wish further to inform you, that They have rec^d a Letter from Col° Buttler Apologizing for part of his Conduct during the late riot, & stating the reason for such Conduct;[4] That Council are happy to find the charges ag^t Col° Buttler are on slight grounds, and flatter themselves He will, by his future Conduct, justify the Choice of Council in his Appointment. Council having likewise rec^d information That proper & legal notice was not given for the choice of the upper B.[5] Militia Officers; They have therefore set aside the election & directed the Lieut. to order another. I am, sir, your obedient and very humble servant,

Peter Muhlenberg, V. P.

[169] William Hooker Smith to Timothy Pickering.[1]

Sir

I feal Sencably affected for Coron^l Butler. Whilst in Bead at Harts This morning being Sabath Day I have Run over his Conduct by way of questⁿ To which I have fixt ansr^s. 1st who went To varmount after Ethⁿ Allin To bring him Into wioming. ansr. Soloman Strong.[2] qs^t where Did allin Log [lodge] whilst at wioming. ansr. at Butlers. qs^t What did allin Do whilst at wioming. ansr. Urge The People To Rebellion. qs^t. was Butler Ever Urgd To Declare on The Side of Goverment in oposition To The Notion of a New State. ans^r. yes. qs^t. what was Butlers Reply. ansr. he Chose To be Nutral whilst allin was at wioming. Dr Smith Brot Sum advertisements Urging The people To Thare Duty in Conformety To Goverment which allin and Strong Puld Down with Rage & Thretning of Doctr Smiths Life Strong being in The upper Part of wioming & finding on [one] of Dr. Smiths Papers Thare Tore it Down in Grat Rage & wrot a Letter To Butler & Captn Shoot[3] To Call Smith to an accont & if he wold Not Stop his hand & alter his Conduct The wild yankeys Swore Thay wold Distroy him. a Copy of This Letter you have Read as To Butlers Late Conduct you are Informd. qs^t. by whose Influence & on whose bisness Did wells

---

[4] Not found, but see no. 193, *post*.   [5] Upper Battalion.
[169] [1] M. H. S., Pickering Papers, LVII, 331, in Smith's hand.
[2] See *Susquehannah Company Papers*, VIII, no. 186.
[3] *Ibid.*, no. 204.

& Catlin Come To wioming.[4] ans[r]. by Recomendation & appointment of The Susquahannah Company & Propriators. qus[t]. To whome was They Directed & with whome Did They quorter. ansr. Butlers. I am well Informd That when makinster & Beatch Came Down The River Thay Told People on The way That Butler had Joynd Them. These are facts. I am hartely Sorrey for Butler Dear Sir. Honesty is Best Policy.

W[m] Hooker Smith

P. S. Shoots [5] was Put in by The Insurgants.

Endorsed: rec[d] Oct[r] 1787

[170] Timothy Pickering to George Clymer.[1]

Philadelphia Nov. 1. 1787.

Sir

The facts within the knowledge of government clearly show [2] that John Franklin & his associates had formed a dangerous conspiracy against this state, the object of which was to prevent its disposing of or exercising any jurisdiction over that large tract of country which has been claimed by the Susquehanna Company; [3] and that Franklin was principally relied on to carry this plot into execution.[4] It also appears that this design is not relinquished. It seems also that this plot was only part of a more extensive scheme for acquiring the property and dominion of a large tract of country belonging to [5] Massachusetts & New York, lying in the Northward of this state, & which with the Susque-

---

[4] Rosewell Wells and Putnam Catlin had been admitted as attorneys to practice before the Luzerne Court of Common Pleas; Pickering Papers, LVII, 223. As a newcomer, Wells was recommendel to Zebulon Butler by William Judd; no. 27, ante.

[5] John Paul Schott.

[170] [1] M. H. S., Pickering Papers, LVII, 332-33, a draft in Pickering's hand. Merely stylistic changes are not indicated. Clymer, one of Philadelphia's representatives in the Assembly, was a member of the committee appointed on October 29 to consider the Wyoming disturbances and recommend action.

[2] The original beginning of the letter is lined out: "From the information contained in the various papers now produced, and others."

[3] The following words are lined out here: "and this by force of arms."

[4] The following words are lined out here: "And by the papers now produced." Crossed out above "now" is "since."

[5] "Belonging to" is substituted for "within the states of."

hanna Purchase were probably intended to form a New State.[6] It further appears, that altho' the body of Franklin's adherents may be convinced of the folly and madness of the project, & be [7] disposed to submit to Government; yet there are some abandoned villains of his party who entertain no such ideas of submission, and stand ready to seize the officers of government, or commit any other outrage which may [8] advance their cause, or gratify their revenge. The natural instability of the common people, but especially of that settlement, where during so many years they have lived in anarchy—where they have been taught to abhor the government of Pennsylvania—& where the present generation of young men have grown up without any experience of the blessings of regular government—warrants the suspicion that a large number of those [9] who have enlisted under Franklin's banners, would again easily be wrought up to a pitch of violence like that which they lately exhibited on his capture. Under these circumstances, the expediency of establishing one or two military posts in that country seems very evident. And if this be done immediately, while the disappointment & dismay occasioned by the capture of Franklin remain forceably impressed on the minds of his followers, the authority of government may be established at comparatively a small expence, and probably without bloodshed. But if the measure be delayed, that party will gather strength, and a considerable expenditure of blood and money may then be necessary to reduce them to obedience or expel them from the state. This evil will be the greater because [10] of the connexion between those seditious citizens and their neighbours in the state of New York; whose numbers also will be increased by a multitude of discontented people elsewhere in that state & in New England who stand ready to remove at the word of the leading conspirators, when the extensive scheme before mentioned shall be ripe for execution.

The discontents in the county of Luzerne are not the result merely of disaffection to the government of Pennsylvania. The peculiar circumstances of the United States have encouraged bad men in several of them to throw off their allegiance to excite the

---

[6] The following phrase is lined out: "or become [?] a member of the British government."

[7] "Be" is substituted for "therefore are."

[8] "May" is substituted for "they may think" and for "will."

[9] Three words lined out after "those" are illegible.

[10] The following words are lined out here: "the opposition to the Government of Pennsylvania is but part of an extensive plan of."

common people to rebellion & to attempt the erecting of New States. The strongest ground of hope for success, entertained by Franklin, Beach, Judd, & others of the Susquehanna Company, was the speedy dissolution of the federal union. Major Judd, (a lawyer in Connecticut) has written several inflammatory letters to disuade the inhabitants of Luzerne County from submitting to the government of Penn³. In one he tells them they are more than a match for that gasconading power which has so often cruelly oppressed them, reminds them of their former brave resistance, & for their encouragement to hope for final success, tells them "That the federal government is upon its last legs," and that if they are not wanting to themselves they will stand as good a chance as the rest of mankind; [11] that is, to erect themselves into an independent state: Expecting that on the dissolution of the federal union, general confusion would ensue, and during its contrivance by a manly exertion, they might with little hazard throw off the government of Penn³ & set up for themselves.[12]

One thing which has contributed to keep some of the inhabitants of Luzerne County wavering & unsteady has been a jealousy that the law for confirming their Connecticut titles would ultimately be repealed; that it was originally designed as an opiate to lull them into security, until the Government should have firmly fixed its yoke upon them; after which they would be stripped of their lands. This is the doctrine which Franklin and his principal associates have been preaching among the people ever since the law was enacted, and before that time, they were continually declaiming against the government of Pennsylvania not only as cruel, but as faithless: That it had often deceived them; & that there was no safety in trusting to its acts and assurances. This opinion was last Winter almost universally prevalent [in] the county and it was the more easy to mislead the body of the people into such a belief because they had themselves been witnesses to some deceptions practiced upon them by agents of the state because the mass of the people was credulous; and because Franklin & other artful villains stuck at nothing to promote their views; Truth or falsehood was used by them indifferently, as one or the other would serve to Confirm the people in that belief, & strengthen their prejudices & hatred against

---

[11] No. 4, *ante.*

[12] The conclusion Pickering draws here is not the only possible one. Judd may have meant only that upon the dissolution of the federal government the Trenton trial decision would not stand.

257

Pennsylvania. One declaration often repeated last Winter by John Jenkins at the town meetings was this: That an honourable member of the Council last year, when he & Franklin were waiting on the Assembly speaking of the lands claimed by the Conn^t people told him that the land was theirs by the laws of God & Nature; but that the laws of Penn^a would take it from them. I did not believe him: and I presume that honourable gentleman (who I take it is now in the Assembly) would pronounce Jenkins a liar.[13] But by such lies & artifices those people have been misled; and my most difficult task last winter was to allay their prejudices so far, & to inspire them with such a degree of confidence in the government as would induce them to come into the election, if it were only by way of experiment, & to put their enemies in the wrong.

I readily acknowledge that besides the half share men, who have no claims to land but under Franklin's grants, there are some who have acted an ungrateful part towards this state, and do not deserve any favour: but there are others, & I believe a great majority of the old settlers, who really wish for the full establishment of the authority of this state: but these are the most quiet part of the people: and such, in every community altho' far the most numerous party, yet are often controuled & directed or kept in awe, by the turbulent, active minority.[14] Hence many in that settlement have been induced to temporize, partly from urgent necessity, to preserve their present crops & improvements, and perhaps partly from a fear that the state would still delay effectually to enforce its authority. And these causes have greatly swelled their lists of associators; the greater part of whom I believe would drop off on the appearance of a small military force, & the rest be either awed into submission, or voluntary banishment, without shedding of blood.

But if the law for confirming the lands of the old settlers should be repealed [15] or suspended the case would be widely different: the whole body of the people finding themselves out of the protection, would no longer think of submitting to the laws

---

[13] Neither Jenkins' diary for this period nor Franklin's letter to Joseph Hamilton recounting the mission to the Assembly mentions this episode; *Susquehannah Company Papers*, VIII, nos. 250 and 255. But see no. 18, *ante*, note 26.

[14] The following words are lined out here: "Franklin and his adherents having an object in view."

[15] The following words are lined out here: "for a suppression of it is unnecessary."

of the state. They w^d join the present malecontents in resisting the government. The neighbouring inhabitants of York State would be their immediate auxillaries. Discontented Spirits from New England would come to their aid. A great many persons of talents, but of desperate fortunes, in those states, New York, Vermont, & other places would put themselves at their head; and at the outcry of the injustice perfidy and cruelty of Pennsylvania, the inhabitants of Connecticut in particular would take fire, and altho the Government might not openly afford assistance, yet it would not discountenance its citizens in doing it,[16] and, from the interests of many & the general resentments of the body of that people, the inhabitants of Luzerne w^d derive no small support. In short, no one can say what would be the final issue of the contest, in the present weak state of the federal union, & general discontent & spirit of revolt so prevalent among the people of these states. I will add but one more remark[17] which is this. That there are two events which of all others would give Franklin, Beach, McKinstry, & the rest of the conspirators, the highest pleasure: One, the repeal[18] of the confirming law. The other, a rejection of the proposed federal constitution, & consequent dissolution of the United States.[19]

I hope, sir, you will excuse the length of this letter. The subject is important. I feel myself deeply concerned to prevent, if possible, so fatal a step as the repeal or suspension of the law for confirming the Connecticut titles.[20] The next must be to raise a body of troops equal to the expulsion of seven hundred fighting men with all the auxillaries who from various quarters w^d join them, from lands to which they feel a most powerful attachment —an attachment indeed which has been rendered invincible by their unexampled[21] sufferings in defending them, & the alternative of utter ruin to themselves & families if they cannot maintain them. The misery or comfortable subsistence of three thousand souls is suspended on the breath of the Assembly. This Govern-

---

[16] Words lined out here are illegible.

[17] Words lined out here are illegible.

[18] Two words are lined out here which are not really legible but could be "or suspension."

[19] The following words are lined out here: "But what would then gratify the wishes of these unprincipled men can never be adopted by the enlightened patriots of Pennsylvania."

[20] The following words are lined out here: "It would be destructive to that settlement."

[21] "Rendered invincible" is substituted for "strengthend" and "unexampled" for "repeated."

ment will be pronounced stable & faithful, or inconstant and perfidious, as the measure proposed [22] shall now be adopted—or rejected. With great respect, I am &c.

T. P.

[171] Extract from the *Hudson Weekly Gazette*.[1]

For the Hudson Weekly Gazette.

Mr. Printer,

Please to publish the following, and you will oblige your humble servant, the Subscriber.

WHEREAS a torrent of odium is drawn on the people of Tioga, Wyoming, and the intervening setlements on the river Susquehannah, occasioned by the malicious insinuations, and false representations of enemies lurking among the inhabitants of that country, who have industriously laboured to brand them (and their associates, to wit, the Susquehannah Company) with the approbious epithets of Disobedient, Refractory and Rebellious, insinuating at the same time that they were entering into an alliance with the British government within the limits of the United States; [2] or that a New State was to be instituted, by which means the characters and properties of the settlers and their associates have sustained repeated injuries, and still are suffering unjustly: And whereas the above representations are entirely contrary to the ideas and intentions of the people on that ground, who have uniformly declared that they wanted nothing

---

[22] Apparently George Clymer had told Pickering about the committee's report, which was not read in the General Assembly until November 3. The committee made further reports on November 12 and 14. It favored continued operation of the Confirming Act in modified form, and out of its reports grew several Assembly resolutions collectively considered as a supplement to the Confirming Act. These resolutions would have required from Connecticut claimants fresh oaths of allegiance to the state, would have extended the time limits of the act, and would have given Pennsylvania claimants a choice between taking fresh lands elsewhere or accepting interest-bearing certificates as compensation. See *Minutes of the First Session of the Twelfth General Assembly*, 18, 42, 43, 56-57 (microfilm copy).

[171] [1] November 8, 1787. A clipping of the article is in M. H. S., Pickering Papers, LVII, 334.

[2] Apparently Pickering had had second thoughts about this charge; no. 170, *ante*, note 6. Beach, of course, would have no way of knowing about Pickering's latest opinion on the matter.

more than the peaceable possession of their properties; but was (as there is great reason to believe) done by the internal enemies of that country, who have been bought by the land-jobbers in Pennsylvania; the latter of whom would willingly use every exertion in their power to root out the Connecticut settlers at Wyoming, and who, for the same reason, are ready to catch at, and exaggerate every aspersion, which has been, or may hereafter be levied against the characters of those individuals, who have taken the lead in the affairs of that settlement.

And whereas it further appears that the influence of those land jobbers has furnished the state of Pennsylvania, with a pretext to exclaim Treason, Rebellion, &c to quell which the settlement is now threatened with an armed force, the bottom of which machination looks like a design to add to the distresses of the people at Wyoming.

Therefore, to prevent these evils in future, and that the public may be undeceived, and the real intentions and ideas of the settlers and their associates made known, I think it my duty to republish the following combination, viz.[3] * * *

The foregoing combination was drawn at Tioga sometime in the month of September last, and was readily signed by nearly all the people at and near that place, and from repeated conversation with Col. Franklin on the subject, I was confident that it would meet his approbation, therefore, by the advice of Col. M[c]Kinstry, Capt. Allen and others, I sent it on to him at Wyoming by Mr. Starkweather, but before it reached that place Col. Franklin was made a prisoner and gone to Philadelphia. I have since been at Wyoming, and upon exhibiting the combination was happy to find that it was generally approved of by the people in that settlement, And I have frequently conversed with able lawyers on the subject, who have uniformly acknowledged it to be founded on principles of law. Now if the above recited combination contains any thing of Treason, or Rebellion, I confess I am guilty; and have reason to believe that nearly all the inhabitants of Wyoming and parts contiguous are equally so; if not, I am innocent; for I hereby pledge my loyalty as a citizen, and my veracity as a man, that I have nothing further in idea than what is comprised in the foregoing declaration; nor do I know of any person that has. Nor is this all, but I believe as do others, that we are supporting the federal government, by acting in conformity to this our declaration; and that the state of

---

[3] See no. 135, *ante.*

Pennsylvania has no right, by her acts, laws, or courts of commissioners to personate a federal court to determine a cause in which she is deeply interested; to take away, by a legislative act, the property of one citizen and give it to another; or to disturb the Susquehannah Company in the peaceable possession and occupancy of the whole of their purchase, which, if she has done, or should hereafter do, is she not guilty of violating the federal government? and will not all opposition to any such acts, laws, or court of commissioners, be considered as a warrantable resistance of cruel and arbitrary measures? For, if any kingdom, state, or people, have any claim, challenge, or demand, within the limits of the Susquehannah purchase, is it not their duty to bring forward their claim? agreeably to a clause in the ninth article of confederation, which is as follows, viz.[4] * * *

Now as the method for determining the dispute, is clearly pointed out by the above recited clause; and as the settlers and their associates, are actually in possession of the disputed territory, would it not be ridiculous for them to apply for a trial, inasmuch as, by consequence of their possession, they are necessarily the defendants?[5] If this is not the true intent and meaning of the above mentioned clause, and the Susquehannah Company have not a right to remain in peaceable possession upon the principles therein contained, I confess myself ignorant, and shall consider myself indebted to any of the more knowing, who, from a principle of benevolence, shall correct my mistake, and lead me to a right understanding of the matter. For, in this exigence of affairs, humanity demands that the authority of the United States, and every individual, whose means of knowledge have rendered him capable of becoming serviceable to a distressed people, now to interpose in their behalf. True it is, that a few individuals have received a confirmation of the title to their lands, by a late law of the state of Pennsylvania;[6] but no more than one third of the inhabitants, it is presumed, have obtained

---

[4] Beach quotes from the Articles of Confederation the paragraph that provided for settlement through judicial process initiated by the petition of one of the disputing parties of the private right of soil where grants had been made by two different states before territorial jurisdiction had been established. It was Pennsylvania's contention, of course, that the lands of the Susquehannah Company had not been granted by Connecticut.

[5] Beach ignores the fact that the Susquehannah Company had indeed sought through its agent, William Samuel Johnson, a trial under the auspices of the Continental Congress to determine the private right of soil; see Vol. VIII, *passim.*

[6] No. 38, *ante.*

a sufficient farm to support a family; while the principal part of those sufferers, who have fought and bled in the defence of the country, are entirely neglected! Now for those people, who have obtained nothing by the confirming law of Pennsylvania (which, by the way, are about two thirds of the inhabitants in that country) to be obliged to leave their farms, and flee out of the country with their families, with no other prospect of any support, than what the world shall see cause to afford them, and that even without the formality of a trial by law, merely because superior strength are invading them, is insupportable cruelty, and cannot fail to throw them into a state of inexpressible wretchedness!

Therefore we hope and believe that all friends to the distressed settlers in that disputed country, will be excited to point out and publish whatever errors they may discover in the forgoing composition, and offer the reasons, if any there be, why the Susquehannah Company ought not to remain in the peaceable possession of the whole of their purchase: And if nothing shall appear against the sentiments herein contained, I shall consider the silence of the public as an acknowledgement of the righteousness of our cause, and shall expect, the ensuing year, that, while we demean ourselves as good citizens of the state claiming jurisdiction over us, we shall receive no molestation, in the prosecution of our lawful business, in that country.

Therefore, that our wishes and intentions may be universally made known, the Printers are hereby earnestly requested to publish the foregoing in the several News papers, throughout the United States. I am the Public's most humble Servant,

Zerah Beach.

Amenia Precinct, State of New-York, November 5, 1787.

[172] Advertisement from the *Hudson Weekly Gazette*.[1]

Whereas, on the 3d day of October last, I was taken a prisoner by a party of men under the command of William Hooker Smith, on my way from Tioga to Wyoming, and confined in the house of Matthias Hollenback, in Wilksbury, until late in the night, and in the mean time robbed of certain writings with which

---

[172] [1] November 8, 1787. A clipping of this advertisement is in M. H. S., Pickering Papers, LVII, 334.

I was entrusted;[2] and my own things, viz. my hat, my handkerchief of clothes, and the great coat which I had on when captured
(which last is the property of Col. John Franklin) deposited in
different parts of the room, where they remained until I was relieved by a party of men who surrounded the house for that purpose, in the midst of which confusion, there being no lights in
the room, I took a great coat which I afterwards found was not
the one which I wore there. Therefore, the owner may have it,
by proving property and applying to James Bryan, Esq. in
Nobletown.[3]

Asa Starkwather.

Nobletown, November 5, 1787.

N. B. The last mentioned coat is supposed to be Devonshire ker-
sey, of a light brown colour and trim'd with basket buttons of
the same colour.

[173] Extract from the Minutes of the Pennsylvania Council.[1]

Philadelphia, Wednesday, November 8th, 1787.
The following draft of a message to the General Assembly
was read and approved, vizt:

*A Message from the President and the Supreme Executive Coun-
cil in the General Assembly.*

Since your resolution, of the thirty-first ult., was forwarded
to Congress, Council having received information that the members remaining at New York, were not sufficient to form a
representation of the United States.[2]

As the danger to the State appears to be pressing, and the
permission solicited from Congress cannot now be obtained,
Council, therefore, recommend it to the General Assembly to
adopt effectual measures, for inforcing the laws of the State in

---

[2] Among other papers, Starkwather was carrying the "Combination"
(no. 135, *ante*), according to Zerah Beach; no. 171, *ante*. He also carried
letters from Joseph Hamilton to John Franklin, which were seized and
copied; no. 238, *post*.

[3] How much Starkwather wrote tongue-in-cheek may be guessed from
Pickering's indignant account of the episode; no. 238, *post*.

[173] [1] *Pa. C. R.,* XV, 314.   [2] No. 167, *ante,* note 3.

the county of Luzerne, which they are of opinion cannot be done without a permanent force.[3]

The expulsion of the Commissioners from Wyoming will occasion a delay in the execution of their duty under the late law.[4] Council, therefore, recommend that a further time be given for compleating the services expected from them under their present appointment. * * *

[174] Zebulon Butler to Nathan Denison.[1]

Wilks Barre 12th Nov[r] 1787

Dear Sir

By this you[ll] be inform[d] I Recivd yours of the 27 of Oct[r] Last Mentioning the Commissions &c which I have Recieved and Delivered to the Gentelmen.[2] You mention the Number & Rank of the Regiments which Law has Pointed out by the Drawing Lotts of Battallions & Companys and of Course Must Suppose the Counsel have no Occation to give themselves any troubel of Ranking them. You Mention that the affair of the Conduct of the peopel at this Place on the Evening after Frankling was Taken was Laid before the Counsel, &c. and Refer me to Doct[r] Smith for Particulars. I applyed to him and all that I have got from him yet is he Believes I am under Censheur. Ill thank you to Let me know what is true on that Subject for I can not Serve in any Office Under Censheur.[3]

I have Compleated the Officering one Battalion and now Send the Return of them for their Commissions when they Recieve them I Shall think I have Some Strengh as I then Shall have Some under command.

[3] This desire for a permanent force was presented in the General Assembly on November 8; *Minutes of the First Session of the Twelfth General Assembly*, 20 (microfilm copy).

[4] That is, the Confirming Act, which was effective for only eight months from the date of its passage on March 28, 1787; no. 38, *ante*. A resolution to extend the operation of the law to give the commissioners more time was introduced in the Assembly, receiving its third reading on November 22, but final action was postponed when the whole question of amending the Confirming Act remained unresolved at the end of the first session; *Minutes*, 42, 60, and 83.

[174] [1] Wilkes College Library, Wilkes-Barre, McClintock Papers, in Butler's hand.

[2] Denison's letter of October 27 has not been found. The commissions mentioned are those for militia officers recently elected.

[3] See no. 193, *post*.

I have Sent Notifycations up the River for the other Battallion to Meet on the 22^d Ins^t for the Purpose of Chuseing the Field and Comp^y Officers which I expect to be Compleated before I Return and as soon as Possabel after that I Shall Make my Returns to Counsell. I am Sir your Humbel Servt

Zeb^n Butler

[175] Obadiah Gore to Timothy Pickering.[1]

Wilkesbarre Novr 12 1787

Dear S^r

You will Doubless by Mr Butler receive an appointment from this County to attend the Convention. how far you will approve of our policy in the appointment I Cannot tell. when you are So much wanted to attend the office of a Commissioner but as Mr Wm Stewart & Some Others were makeing an Interest among the Opposers to Government put us on the plan of runing one person only in our ticket and by that means you had it by a Great majority, but I wish that the Other Commissioners might Attend as Soon as possible to the Examination of our Claims after the arival of Troops.

there is a number of people that have been and are now waiting to See the Commissioners. Colonels Thos Dyer & Eben^r Gray have been here Some time. Dyer told me that the plan of Independance here Originated in the Circle of a few Such as Judd & [Ham]bleton &c and that the plan was not known by the Committee in windham untill Since Franklin was Taken.

Col^o Gray Inform^s me that Judd about Two months ago Wrote to him Desiring that Coppys of the Comp[anys] reecords might not be Sent to Wyoming as a bad use wou^d be made of them and that their Quandram friend such as Butler, Gore & others Could not be Trusted &c which was Enjoined on him to keep secret from Col^o Dyer and when they (Dyer & Gray) were on their Journey for this place they Called on Judd who told them that the Devil and all was to pay at Wyoming, that they had not only taken Franklin and Hamilton but that he had but little before Sent on a Constitution [2] for the Government of that

[175] [1] M. H. S., Pickering Papers, LVII, 335-36, in Gore's hand.

[2] No such constitution has ever been found. It may be that the "Combination" (no. 135, *ante*) was meant. Harvey-Smith, *Wilkes-Barré*, III, 1619-20, discusses this possible confusion of terms. See also no. 172, *ante*, note 2.

people together with a number of letters attending which he Concluded had fell into the hands of Government and he feared would prove fatal to Franklin as he had no[t] veew^d them. on Dyer & Gray Informing him that their business to Wyoming was to Exhibit their Claims to the Commissioners, Judds reply was that his Stomach was too big Ever to hold lands under Pennsylvania. they told him that what suited one^s Stomach would not another but for their part they should be happy to secure their lands under the Confirming act. after much was Said Judds Stomach Came down and he has Sent on his Deeds & Writings to Mr Wells Desiring him to Exhibit his Claims.

I am frequently Informed that the halfshare men Up the river are breathing out Threatnings particularly Wm Morgan Solo^n & Danl Earle Junr make use of the most Blasphemous Expressions that I ever heard being Uttered from any person.

we have been Trying Some time to have them once more apprehended but do not yet succeed.

I have not thought prudent to return to my family yet. Col^o Butler has appointed the 22^d Instant for the Upper Battalion to meet at Wylusing to Chuse the field Officers I propose to Go up with him, and return soon to attend the Court at Which time I Shall Expect to See you.

I have Wrote Some matters to Col^o Denison ^{3} which are not mentioned here. wou^d therefore refer you to him. I am S^r your Hum^{ble} Servt

Obad^h Gore

[176] Samuel Gordon to Nathan Denison.^{1}

Wilksborrough Novr 12th 1787

Dear Sir

It is impossible to paint to you either the Anxiety of the friends to government, occasioned by the Oposite party, who exultingly say the Commissioners will never come here again or, that they darnot or that the Legislature of Pennsylvania will not take any further notice of us, having us now fast under the Jurisdiction of the State from w^e we cannot revolt if we were so disposed, knowing that they (the opposers of Government)

---

^{3} Not found.

[176] ^{1} M. H. S., Pickering Papers, LVII, 337, in Gordon's hand. For Gordon, see no. 156, *ante,* note 1.

would not view us in any better light, than that of Traitors.
They are lifted up with the notion that they will have the whole
Country confirmed to themselves, by a Fedral Court, and think
they can keep possession untill they can procure a trial before
such a Court. As to Troops, they say, the do not blieve any
will be sent here. if there are, they will pick them off as they
have Oportunity, that for that purpose they mean to turn Indian
&c. Thus I have given You a few hints of hopes & fears. We
have prefer'd a petition² to the Honourable Legislature the
prayer of which is to have the time lengthened for the Commissioners to Receive our Claims; I think there might be an addition made there to, intimating that if the Confirming Law is not
continued the prayer should be, that the Honourable Legislature
might Adopt some other eligable mode of confirmation agreeable
to the design of S⁴ Law.

There are but a fiew who appear opposers of Government,
there are a greater number who wish to continue nuter untill
the are able to form a Judgement from Occular demonsteration.
And there are a few who would not Sign the petition least they
should give offence, as it bore hard on the conduct of those who
were Active in the late insurrection; with a view, to exculpate
the Signers from every imputation of that nature.

You will please to write me a line ⅌ Mˬ Butler, I am to tarry
here untill Court then mean to go home & prepare for moving
into this Settlement, I am about building a Grist-Mill in Han-
nover my Timber &c will be procured this winter. I begin to
Lott the Town of Exeter this day. I am dear Sˢ your Obliged
Humble Servᵗ

Samˡ Gordon

[177] Ebenezer Bowman to Timothy Pickering.¹

Dear Sir

I am happy to inform you the people here have made choice
of you (by a great majority) to represent them in Convention,²
I was particularly busy at the election of military Officers, but

---

² Not found. It was presented in the General Assembly on November
17; *Minutes of the First Session of the Twelfth General Assembly,* 61
(microfilm copy).
[177] ¹ M. H. S., Pickering Papers, LVII, 339-40, in Bowman's hand.
² *Cf.* no. 175, *ante.*

was determined not to be active again in that way, and should have kept my resolution had I not been informed the evening before the election that a plan was on foot to send a constitutionalist.[3] I then thought it my duty not merely as an inhabitant of this County of Luzerne, but as a Citizen of the United States and a well wisher to the federal union, to exert myself to prevent if possible a person being chosen who would object to the proposed Constitution, Christopher Hurlbut was the person proposed, and being in favour as well with the opposers as the supporters of Government it appeared highly probable he would be chosen. As you had informed Hollenback and Doc[r] Smith that it would not be convenient for you to attend (if chosen) no proposal of the kind had been made but at that late period it was necessary that some person should be run in whom the people would be most likely to unite or the other party would succeed; you was proposed and it took generally with the people, the only objection was that your attendance would interfere with the business of the County, and this was removed by assuring them you was not expected under three weeks. It is my sincere wish that you would attend, and I am sure you will, provided it appears by the returns that any considerable number of Constitutionalists, are chosen. The other Commissioners may come in with safety and the business of the County go on. I recieved by Doc[r] Smith (from you) a number of addresses to the Citizens of Pennsylvania[4] and distributed them among the people but had it not been your particular desire I should not have done it, for I had carefully avoided letting them know that any objections were made to the Constitution as I knew they were so prone to opposition that they would readily join in any to prevent that excellent plan from taking place; and altho, the addresses contain sufficient to convince any rational mind of the excellenc of the proposed Constitution, yet as they discover that some persons oppose it I thought they would do more hurt than good in this place. The Comptroller General sent four Pamphlets into this settlement each containing the new Constitution with a number of futile remarks upon it. Had he known the Character of those to whom he sent them I am sure he would not

---

[3] That is, a member of the political faction which had long supported the Pennsylvania constitution.

[4] *Addresses to the Citizens of Pennsylvania. Calculated to Shew the Safety—Advantages—and Necessity of Adopting the Proposed Constitution of the United States. In Which Are Included Answers to the Objections that Have Been Made to It* (Philadelphia: Hall and Sellers, 1787).

have taken so much trouble, (Coll Butler Doc^r Smith Esq Gore
& Esq. Hollenback). Gore who is a person of some enquiry
undoubtedly read his but the other three I am convinced never
have. I had the Curiosity to enquire of Butler just before the
poll was opened, concerning the pamphlet he had recieved from
Nicolson. it turned out as I expected, he was not able to determin whether it was the Constitution or an almanac; upon the
whole Mr Nicolson has really lost his Pamphlets, and as he has
shown his good will in this last struggle, I think it but reasonable that his Bretherin (of the Constitutional party) should make
him some amends.

I was informed by Doc^r Smith that an enquiry would be made
concerning the Conduct of some particular persons in this Place,
and that Lord Butler (in consequence of his having met with
the Commissioners appointed by the Susquehannah Company,
and also for neglecting his duty at the time of the riot here)
would not be Commisionated, the first of these charges I believe
to be groundless as I cannot learn that he has ever acted as Secretary to that Board since his appointment as Sheriff;[5] and I
think it my duty to say that from my first acquaintance he has
ever appeared friendly to Government; with respect to his conduct at the time of the Riot, as an executive (officer and one
whose particular business it is at all times to supress mobs and
riots) he certainly has laid himself open to Censure; but I believe his conduct ought to be imputed more to the want of
Resolution than attachment to Government. I am sensible that
no motives of fear (in general) are sufficient to excuse an Officer from attempting to discharge his duty; yet considering the
critical situation of the County at that time, and the violence of
those who were opposed to Government I do not think him to
blame for not attempting to disperse the people. I am sure he
would have met with great personal abuse.

I recollect to have been present at Concord (Massachusetts)
where a number of people collected for the purpose of preventing the Court setting, the Sheriff was nigh but did not attempt
to disperse them (altho, he might have done it with safty, for
they were under such Regulations as that no abuse would have
been offered to any officer in the execution of his office). Yet
the Sheriff was not censured for his conduct, because it was well
known that had he attempted to disperse them he would not have

<hr>

[5] According to extant records, Lord Butler last signed the minutes of
the commissioners of the Susquehannah Company on April 1, 1787; no. 68,
ante. He was commissioned sheriff on April 7; no. 43, *ante*, note 3.

succeeded; if this behavior in an experienced Officer (as the Sheriff was) and in a place where Government had been establised for more than an hundred Years was thought proper, truly the same behavior in a young unexperienced Officer and in a place where Government has never (properly) been established will be overlooked.

Doc^r Smith I suspect said more against L Butler than he ought to. I believe the Doc^r to be a true friend to Government but he undoubtedly is wanting in that excellence of which he is so often boasting (Viz Courage) and like others of that Character is very ready to censure any who thro', fear (altho', the Cause is ever so great) neglect their duty; But should his Commission be witheld to whom would it be given? I know of no person who was not as guilty of neglecting his duty at that time as the Sheriff; But as he will be present in the City he undoubtedly will be able to answer for himself.

Esq Gore is here and does not think it safe for him to return, he some expects an appointment as Deputy Surveyor of the County in which Case he is determined to move his Family into this Town immediately. He wishes you to assist him in procuring the appointment; it will be an advantage to the County (as well as to the individual) to have a person who is an inhabitant appointed to that office.

Mr John Pierce informs me he left with the Commissioners three powers of Attorney (to be recorded) the day before you left this settlement; he is in want of them but they are not to be found, if you can give directions where to find them you will greatly oblige him, I have sent some blank letters of administration to be figured, as some persons wish to take administration immediately in order to secure the minor debts due to the estates of Intestates; Mr Butler expects to recieve some money in the City, if he should I would request the favour of you to purchase some books which will greatly assist us at the court, Viz Crompton in two Volumes upon the practice of the Common Pleas and Kings Bench, and Burnes Justice;[6] they will cost about twelve dollars, which Mr Butler (if he recieves) will let you have as they are not large Volumes he can bring them up.

If you can procure the following Forms and send them by

---

[6] George Crompton, *Practice Common-Placed; or, The Rules and Cases of Practice in the Courts of King's Bench and Common Pleas, Methodically Arranged* (London, 1780, 1783, 1786). Richard Burn, *The Justice of the Peace and Parish Officer* (London, 1755 and many subsequent editions).

271

the Sheriff they will be of service to me (Viz) Scire Facias on a Mortgage a Writ of Estrepment a Writ in trover. from your hum^b Servt

Eben^r Bowman

Wilkesborough Novr 12th 1787

[178] Mathias Hollenback to John Nicholson.[1]

Wilkesborough Nov^m 13th. 1787.

Dear Sir

I rec^d your pamflet by Esqr. Smith[2] & when our Election cam on finding the pople so Divided I thought better to have a Good man in Convention than one that we Did not know whether he was a friend to Goverment or not so by that mains run Coll. T. Pickering and he goot the apointment. when I Left the City I Expec^d to have had the Troops here before this time but as the are not here wood be Glad to know when the are to be here or wheather we shall Expect them or not as the time will be Short for me to percure a Supley for them through the winter &c. I have nothing new the pople in this Settlement Do apair more Lick Pacable Inhabitants then what the have Done here to fore though there is a Number of men at Tunkhannah that Capes under armes and Defies the Laws also threatons to send all the othority a Beaver hunting &c &c though there is but Very Little of the Lick in this Settlement though Som thinck if Troops Dow not Come they may again keep under arms or in opesision to Government. Coll. John McKinstry and Zerah Beach has Left Tyoga and Gone to their homes as it is Said. We find by an Entersepeted Letter that the Constitution of this Intended State was formed by a Cartin Wm Judd and the nam was to be Westmoreland.[3] I am in hast Dr. Sir Yours &c

M. Hollenback

Plase to Give my Compliments to Mr Saml Jackson & Mrs Jackson and inform him I have his Toles readey for him to Go to work in the Spring &c.

M. H

---

[178] [1] Originally in Wyoming Historical and Geological Society, but no longer extant.

[2] See no. 177, *ante,* note 4.

[3] *Cf.* no. 175, *ante.* What intercepted letter Hollenback refers to is not clear. When Asa Starkwather was seized, several letters were taken from him and copied, but none mentions a state of Westmoreland. See no. 148, *ante,* note 2.

[179] Benjamin Franklin to the Commander of Militia Intended for Luzerne County.[1]

In Council Philadelphia November 14th 1787
Instructions to the officer commanding the Militia to be sent or raised in the County of Luzerne [2]

Sir the Intention of Gov[t] respecting the forces under your command not being to act offensively against any place, person or persons in that County but merely to protect the Civil officers in the exercise of their functions & to secure the peace of the County & the due operation of Laws of the State against the attempts of the disorderly part of the people who have lately opposed the same. You are to take Special care that your men observe the strictest discipline in neither injuring nor molesting any of the Inhabitants in person or property.

And you are to take your orders from the State Comiss[rs] & the civil authority of the County.

And if circumstances shou'd appear to you on any occasion to require additional force, you are to apply to the Lieu[t] of this County for his assistance & also to consult & advise with him in all cases of importance. I am Sir your obed[t] & very Hb[l] Servant

Benjn Franklin
President

[180] Debate on a Supplement to the Confirming Act.[1]

Mr. [John Paul] *Schott* called for the third reading of the bill, entitled "a supplement to an act, entitled an act for ascer-

---

[179] [1] Harvey-Smith, *Wilkes-Barré*, III, facing p. 1582, reproduced from a photograph of the original once in the possession of Smith.

[2] These instructions were delivered by Nathan Denison to the militia commander, then at Fort Allen. Denison was also enjoined to prepare the minds of the people of Wyoming for reception of the militia; Franklin to Denison, November 15, 1787, in *P. A.*, XI, 212. The number of militia Council intended to send amounted to 70; *Proceedings and Debates of the General Assembly,* II, 159. On November 16 the Assembly was still debating whether to empower the Council to raise a permanent force; no. 180, *post.*

[180] [1] *Proceedings and Debates of the General Assembly,* II, 111-19, 122, 124-26, November 16, 1787.

taining and confirming to certain persons called Conecticut claimants, the lands by them claimed within the County of Luzerne,
and for other puposes therein mentioned."[¹]

After reading over the same it was agreed to be considered
by paragraphs.

The first enacting clause being read by which the supreme
Executive Council are empowered and directed to raise and keep
up such military force in that County, as they may judge necessary to preserve the peace and enforce the execution of the laws,
and to draw on the treasurer for the monies requisite for that
purpose, provided that this force do not exceed five hundred men,
nor be kept in pay for a longer time than one year from the
passing of this act.

M. [James] *M'Lene* confessed he had his doubts on the propriety of this clause, for agreeably to the articles of confederation, this state cannot raise an army without the consent of Congress; it is there provided, that *no state keep up a body of troops
in time of peace, except such number only as in the judgment of
Congress shall be requisite to garrison the forts,* but every state
shall keep up a well disciplined militia. Now it appears from
the article, and the resolution which was agreed to by the House
the other day that it was understood by us to be improper, until
the consent of Congress was obtained; Council was instructed to
apply to Congress for leave to raise these troops, but by some
means that has not been got:[²] I wish gentlemen would therefore
think whether we are at liberty to raise forces for the occasion
proposed in the bill, without the assent of Congress, and in violation of the articles of confederation—for my own part, I confess
I have doubts; but if any gentleman can remove them I shall
be in favor of the clause, if not I must move to postpone the bill,
until I can be satisfied. Another great difficulty with me is to
raise the money necessary to make provision for these five hundred troops. What funds can we provide sir, out of which they
may be paid, when we know we are already distressed? For my
part I dont see how the law is to be carried into effect if it is
agreed to—but I shall wait and hear what other gentlemen have
to say, and what their sentiments are on this subject, before I
move the postponement.

Mr. [George] *Clymer.* I am very sorry sir the observation
has been made, that we were unsuccessful in the application we
directed Council to make to Congress, because I consider it of
no service to our cause or to the state.

---

² See nos. 167, note 2 and 173, *ante.*

274

I wish also that Council had not mentioned it in their message, because it was not necessary to be known. Council had gone far enough, when they paid the compliment to Congress, who no doubt would have complied with the request had they been sitting. The business might have rested here, and the world could not have supposed but we had obtained the consent of Congress.

Tho' we have been disappointed by a circumstance which was not adverted to at the time, yet sir, self-preservation is the paramount law of nature. We are not to neglect our own safety or remain inactive, when force is required for the protection and support of our authority, against a lawless banditti of perverted citizens, or to keep the turbulent in subjection. We ought not to lose the substance in striving to obtain the shadow, or attend to forms when such attention eminently risques the peace and welfare of the state. As to the other objections which he has taken, that our funds are so low as not to furnish the means of raising troops, there may be some weight in it—but as Council are left to the management of this business, they are sure to go no further than the means will permit. If money enough cannot be found to comply with the full extent of the demand, enough may be had to raise a force which may still be adequate. The act being of absolute necessity, it was perfectly warrantable; for if it either was neglected or delayed, the most serious consequences were to be apprehended.

The *Speaker* recommended to the member who had stated the objections, to read the part of the articles of confederation which followed, where he had chosen to stop.

Mr. *M'Lene* looked over it, and being about to read aloud, a member requested that the Clerk might read it—the clause was to the following effect: That no state shall engage in any war without the consent of Congress, *unless such state shall be actually invaded by enemies, or shall receive advice of an attack from the Indians, and the danger is so imminent as not to admit of a delay, until Congress can be consulted.*

Mr. [William] *Findley.* It is with great diffidence that I rise to say any thing on this occasion, because I have not had an opportunity of digesting and examining the principles of the law now before us. It is allowed on all hands to be a matter of much importance, and it is more so as it is without precedent, which if now adopted wrongly, may be in great danger of fixing a continuance in the same improper road. We have all along in this business sir, gone on in the dark, and been deceived both as to the object and magnitude; in saying we have been deceived,

I dont mean that we were any otherwise deceived than as we deceived ourselves; it is therefore that I go with great timidity into this business. We are to pass a law again without knowing its consequences, and may continue to give that uneasiness which the former one has done, beside laying the foundation of an enormous debt, tho' the last law [3] may be said to be the foundation on which the whole is created. The reason, If I recollect aright, for passing, that, was to prevent a war. We allowed then that it was right to give up the property of a number of our fellow citizens, in order to avoid coercive measures. I believe we gave up much more than we thought we were doing; still we were justifiable, because it was done to prevent a war, and consequently a greater expence. But now we find a war is not prevented; for the truth of this I appeal to the clause before the House—here you find it necessary to raise an army, and therefore you encrease the debt, and encrease it again in the dark, for you do not know how much further you are to go.

Suppose we raise 500 troops, and send them to hold possession of that country by the sword, if they are found insufficient, shall we stop here? certainly we shall not. We shall have still to furnish more. When once we pass the Rubicon, when once we commence the war, it will be impossible to stop short of the perfect attainment of our object, therefore I would wish gentlemen to consider well, to deliberate on the consequences before they decide the present question; for my own part, I am not clear to vote for raising troops at all; and to raise and pay those troops out of funds which are already appropriated, and we know all our funds are appropriated; for no more funds should be required than are necessary to pay that for which they are appropriated. When an occasion demand an increase of the funds, the funds should be sought for; and it is for this reason that I am not clear for raising troops; but were I in favour of going to war, I should not do it without I knew where to lay my hand on a fund that should defray the expence. Are we to consent to embarrass our funds created for the relief of the public creditors? or are we to call upon Council to go into the measure of raising troops, without providing any means for them to defray the expence? I don't know on this occasion but we ought to be certain, and see the fund before we agree to the clause, and know the amount of the expence we are to incur. Yet that my opinion may not have an improper weight, I shall not further oppose the

---

[3] A reference to the Confirming Act; no. 38, *ante.*

bill at this reading; but I have learned caution too late in the affairs which relate to the unfortunate district of Wyoming, and I do not wish to proceed without some degree of certainty.

Mr. [Thomas] *Fitzsimons*. That the business we are now deliberating on is of great importance, I agree with the gentleman who was last up, and that its consequences ought well to be considered—this I apprehend will be done by the House; but he has thrown out a hint that the business has already been gone on too fast, and that it will be proper now to draw back. We are says he, about to engage in a war, and should therefor consider well the consequences. Many of the gentlemen on this floor must remember the rise and progress of this business in the late House, whose object in passing the law to which this is a supplement, was to prevent a war; this the gentleman allows, but tells you the war is not prevented; but sir I believe the intention of the present House is the same as the last, and all that is meant by the bill before you is to *prevent a war,* and not *declare one.* I believe it is general opinion of the members of this House, that by raising immediately a few men, and establishing a post in that country you prevent a war; but without this a war is inevitable, therefore his arguments for deliberation, before we decide in favor of the war, do not apply.

If the information which was received from that country in the last year was well founded, I think sir nothing but the measures we then adopted could have saved us from being shortly after engaged in a long, formidable and expensive war; by the measures we then took, we divided the opposition to our government; in its consequence it not only weakened the number of incendiaries, equal to the separation that took place, but strengthened the hands of government by the accession; and further it prevented a much greater number from coming and joining with them than has done: Again sir, it has taken off the assistance which the state of Connecticut would have given her own citizens, complaining of the injustice of Pennsylvania. All these objects have been accomplished by that very measure which the gentleman insinuates he was deceived into; certainly the interest of the state has been attended to, otherwise it could not have had these good effects. From further information which has been received it appears, that there are a number of inhabitants in that part of the country who are dissatisfied and opposed to the government of Pennsylvania; they have declared by the measures they have taken, that nothing short of an absolute secession from this state, and an independent government of their own, will give peace or

277

quiet their discontents.[4] The intention of the present bill I apprehend is to prevent them from embroiling that part of the country in feuds, dissentions, and to preserve it from bloodshed. I believe the information which has at various times been laid before the House, the dispatches from the governor of New-York, and the evidence of gentlemen from that country, all prove the necessity of sending up such a force, and that soon too, lest it be employed to cure what it may be too late to prevent; nor do we know where it may stop—for if the frontiers are suffered to insult your government, the contagion spreads more and more wide, by the accession of all the disselute and idle, until it may reach the centre, and all be anarchy, confusion and total ruin.[5] * * *

The gentleman enquires how far we are to go, after having once more engaged in this business? I must own I do not know how far—but I will observe, that at the time when the first law passed in the last year, the situation of America was much worse than at preset; it is well known that the rebels in the state of Massachusetts were but just defeated, and would instantly have sought an assylum on the frontiers of Pennsylvania, could they have found encouragement; that they would have been there, if the Legislature had not divided the claimants, is I believe clear from the various letters which have been laid before you, so that not a member of this House entertains a doubt on that head.

If as the gentleman asserts, it is necessary to find funds for these so necessary expences, I trust they will be found: But we know that the House in many cases orders Council to apply monies to such uses as they see occasion for, because it is supposed that the funds of the state make a general fund, and amount to more than what is appropriated; I hope therefore the House will agree to the bill, and if it shall be found necessary to obtain additional funds to provide for the troops, that the House will engage to make the supply by the best means in their power.[6] * * *

Mr. [Richard] *Peters.* Whether all the observation that have fell from the gentleman are strictly in order, and apply to the clause before the House, I shall leave to the Speaker to determine. I mean to consider only whether it is necessary to conduct a permanent force into that country, for the support of good

---

[4] See Introduction, section III.

[5] In the omitted portion of his speech Fitzsimons discusses state finances.

[6] Omitted is a reply made to Fitzsimons by Findley concerning the indebtedness of the state.

government, which can never be done by want of firmness; for when the civil authority is too week the aid of military is requisite. The gentleman who first objected to the clause before you, objected sir upon the ground of the confederation. The more Mr. Speaker we examine that confederation, the more unfortunate and inadequate does it appear, for the protection of this country. But sir if we turn to it on the present occasion, we shall find it justify this state in the measure we are now about to adopt. I shall say very little about what kind of funds ought to be provided, because I consider the question at present to be whether it is necessary to send troops into that country. I am not alarm'd sir at this time of day, by a breach of the confederation; I have known them happen frequently in cases somewhat like the one before us, when Congress could not be consulted, or were in such a situation that they could not assemble: yet individual states have not suffered themselves to be ruined through a strict attention to formalities directed in those articles; and shall we, so critically circumstanced, attempt to secure the shadow but lose the substance? it is written that the spirit healeth, but the letter killeth. I am not alarmed sir because we have done every thing to pay a proper compliment to Congress; we have sent to them for advice and approbation, but they are not together, nor cannot apply the remedy to the disease. Shall the state of Pennsylvania be overrun by a lawless banditti; because Congress are not assembled? can any gentleman rely upon such argument, to defeat the present object? as for the observation of the gentleman from Westmoreland,[7] that the former measures have proved ineffectual I would just remark, that they have not yet been fairly executed; when I first heard of a law vesting the Connecticut claiments in their claims, I thought it an improper measure; since that I have heard the subject more fully discussed, and greater lights thrown upon it; I must own I do not see what the Legislature could have done more prudently, and I do insist that the pacific disposition shewn by the state of Pennsylvania, in offering those misguided people what they contended was their property, is an instance of lenity that will justify her conduct to the world, if it is now found necessary to coerce these people into an obedience to her laws. The gentleman is apprehensive that we are about to begin a war, but I say sir it is defending against a war being begun. Will these people commence hostilities the sooner because Pennsylvania is prepared—or are they to be suffered to

---

[7] William Findley.

collect their force together? The lawless and abandoned from every part, and consolidate them so as to bid defiance to your government before you are prepared. *Venienti occurrite morbo,* let us prevent the disorder in the beginning, and no longer suffer them to contemn your lenity, dispise your pusillanimity, and defy your government, then your expences will be increased in a ten fold proportion, if we act with decision now it will save money to the state, which is perhaps as necessary as to support her violated dignity. We ought to know the consequences of permitting these men to have an accession of force, for then their decisions will not depend upon justice, but the strength of arms; and the more they increase in number, the more they extend their influence. We must not make an exertion to prevent the ill consequences that arises to the state, because we are not to embroil ourselves in the suppression of the insurgents; and because it will be expensive, now I conceive the only way to save expence, on such occasion, is to keep up a proper force in every county where disturbances may arise.[8] * * *

Mr. [William] *Robinson* [Jr.]. A question seemed to be made by the member who spoke first, whether it was in the power of the House to raise troops, without a breach of the confederation. let me sir endeavour to determine this point. By the sixth article of the confederation, no state can keep up a body of forces without the consent of Congress; in the clause following, an exception is made, in case of such state being actually invaded by enemies; if this article is taken in its strict, literal sense, it can only apply to forces raised against external enemies, and not to those within, as in case of rebellion; but if even it did apply in our case, the exception that follows determine for us beyond the possibility of a doubt: the words are, *unless the danger is so imminent as not to admit of a delay till the United States in Congress assembled can be consulted;* but enemies arising within the bounds of a state are to be suppressed by the exertions of government, as in case of riots; and I presume it was not intended by the confederation to lay such state under the necessity of applying to Congress, to be enabled to ward off these dangers to itself which would be breaking down the natural barrier of its own security; therefore I should conclude, that the application to Congress in the present case is unnecessary; *but if necessary,* we are warranted to raise the troops, *because the danger is so pressing*

---

[8] In the omitted portion of his speech, Peters briefly insists that discussion of state funds is not germane to the issue.

as not to admit of a delay. To establish this point it will be necessary to enquire whether such is our situation? We must now turn to the communications that have been made to this House by Council; from which we shall be able to prove the precarious tenure by which we hold that country. You find its inhabitants are associating for the purpose of defiance; you find that combination sir breaking out in acts of extreme violence, the expulsion of your Commissioners, and rejection of those benefits which have been offered them; so that it appears clear not only from the spirit but the letter of the confederation, that we are perfectly justifiable in passing the clause before you; with respect to the question on funds, it is necessary to say but little upon it: but if it was so that we could not lay our hands upon any, and the question was to determine whether the state should be exposed to all the miseries and difficulties of a rebellion, and the officers of government remain for a time unpaid, I should not hesitate *salus populi suprema lex est*—the public good should be the first consideration. But a breach of any appropriation is not necessary in the present case; for even were the funds insufficient, the good people of this state would contribute cheerfully, rather than endanger the safety of their government and laws. With a view to execute this it is necessary to pass the law; Council will judge how far it is requisite to embody the troops, and it will then become our duty to supply such funds as are necessary.[9] * * *

Mr. [William] *Lewis.*[10] * * * The second point to be considered is, that a case of this momentous concern ought well to be deliberated and adjusted, lest we err beyond correction. I join perfectly in sentiment with the honorable gentleman from Westmoreland (Mr. Findley) that it is a good rule to deliberate seriously in the first place, and to act afterwards with firmness and decision; but what would be the situation of Pennsylvania, if those incendiaries are permitted to continue their violence and disorder much longer? it is known to a demonstration, that a rebellion exists in that country, and that measures of a milder aspect have hitherto proved ineffectual to allay that rage for opposition. Has not the state of Pennsylvania hitherto pursued measures of uniform lenity towards them, even until we are become contemptible in the eyes of the surrounding states? Has not the ground of difference been decided conformably to the

---

[9] Omitted is Fitzsimons' discussion of available state funds.

[10] The first part of Lewis's speech is a long discussion of the war-making power under the Articles of Confederation.

articles of confederation by the decree at Trenton? Has not the Legislature of Pennsylvania passed an act, confirming to the Connecticut claimants certain lands which they held under that state? Have they not abolished the rights of their own citizens as a peace-offering? Have they not been allowed a sufficient time to return to their duty, instead of which they have applied it solely to increase their force and usurp the jurisdiction over that part of the state? Let me ask Mr. Speaker, if after all this lenity—lenity so ineffectual, we shall one moment longer deliberate on the propriety of adopting measures of a different cast, and on which we have to reply. I admit sir it is a good rule to deliberate, but not to deliberate until all oportunity of acting is passed away. When we find these people here so long been dealt mildly with, and that the consequence is adding strength to their opposition, we ought not longer to hesitate on drawing the word of self-preservation.[11] * * *

Mr. *Clymer*. When I was first up, I replied to the member from Franklin [12] upon the broad bottom of the rights of sovereignty. But confining the argument to what relates to our articles of confederation, I think the several gentlemen who answered from this side of the House have fully obviated his objections, as to the spirit of the articles; but I consider our case sir as coming within the letter. I have heard of armed men coming from the borders of other states, to oppose the execution of our laws; some from New-Town and various parts in its neighbourhood, have associated with the refractory of our own citizens, that we have to combat enemies from without as well as incendiaries within—and if it is once viewed as an invasion, which it may with propriety be considered to be, no member I apprehend will hesitate to declare, that it comes within the letter of the confederation, as contained in the clause where an exception is made to favor such states who are absolutely invaded, and whose time cannot permit them either to send or wait for the consent and approbation of Congress, to take necessary measures for their own defence and preservation.

Mr. *Schott*. I rise, Mr. Speaker, to offer some remarks upon what has been said by the gentleman who spoke last but one (Mr. Lewis) when he alleged that uniform lenity had been shewn by the government of Pennsylvania to the settlers at Wyoming: That gentleman must be mistaken in his information, or

---

[11] Lewis concludes by suggesting the dangers in delaying the sending of a permanent force just for lack of funds. Also omitted are a rejoinder by Findley and further remarks by Lewis.

[12] James McLene.

I do not believe he would assert what he has just done; because if that lenity which he mentions had been observed after the decree of Trenton, this House would not now be pursuing such harsh measures as are offered in the present bill. If at that time instead of marching an armed force into that country, a proclamation holding out the language of reconciliation, and confirming those claims which have since been given was issued, I am confident in asserting sir that Pennsylvania would not at this moment contain more loyal or better disposed citizens than the Wyoming settlers. That opportunity was unfortunately lost, but I still think the object of restoring peace and harmony within our reach, and that without the exercise of military force; for the persons who are deemed so lawless are not I hope so numerous as to make it necessary. The majority of the House will decide as they judge proper on the subject before them; but sir I cannot admit that Pennsylvania has shewn every lenity which she might and ought to have done.

The question on the first clause of the bill was now taken, and agreed to almost unanimously.

The following clause was considered:

And be it further enacted by the authority aforesaid, That within sixty days next after the   day of   every free male inhabitant of the said county of Luzerne, of the age of eighteen years or upwards, shall take and subscribe the oath or affirmation of allegiance, and make and subscribe the following declaration before some one of the justices of the peace of the said *county,* to wit: "I A. B. do acknowledge and declare that the state of Pennsylvania have lawful right to extend her jurisdiction to the whole county of Luzerne, to exercise her government and enforce the full execution of her laws therein; that I do and will rest satisfied with the provisions of the late law of the said state, entitled 'an act for ascertaining to certain persons called Connecticut claimants the lands by them claimed within the county of Luzerne, and for other purposes therein mentioned,' and of the law which is a supplement thereto, and I renounce and forever give up all claim to land within the state of Pennsylvania under any title derived or pretended to be derived from the colony or state of Connecticut, or the Susquehannah company, or its consequence of any purchase said to have been made of the Indians, or from any of the commissioners, or from any person or persons whomsoever, acting or pretending to act under the authority or orders of the company, excepting only such lands as it is declared by the act aforesaid, shall be confirmed to the Connecticut claimants. And I do solemnly engage to appear at the call of the civil and militia officers of the said county, or any of them, and to the utmost of my power support them in the full execution of the laws of the Commonwealth of Pennsylvania."

Mr. [Thomas] *Kennedy* wished to amend this clause by inserting after the word "county" (printed in Italic) "unless he has already taken the oath prescribed by law." He wished this to be inserted, because he considered that if the persons disregarded their former oath, they would disregard this also.

Mr. *Clymer*. The reason that influenced your Committee to subject all the inhabitants to this oath, was, because it is alleged, that the mode in which the former was administered, did not correspond with the one, which the custom of their country imposed; the New-England people having generally been used to swear with uplifted hand, and this had been taken by another mode.

The question was put on the amendment, and determined in the negative.

Mr. *Findley*. I am not going to vote against the clause, but I do not like it altogether, as it is without a precedent to extort an oath from one part of the citizens, while others are left at liberty; it is creating not only an extraordinary oath, but new crimes and punishments in its consequence—such precedents as we are about to establish, is extremely dangerous, and may hereafter be extended to an engine of oppression; it is certainly important, and ought to be well considered before it is gone into.

Mr. *Peters* thought there was a good deal of propriety in the observation made by the member, but on this occasion he thought it necessary to have some criterion, to determine the fidelity of those who accepted the lenity of government, in substantiating their claims to the lands in Luzerne; he was as much opposed to multiply oaths on any occasion, as any person, but could think of no other means to substitute; he thought it proper to forget and forgive those who should now come forward, and pay obedience in future to the laws.

Some further conversation took place, when the clause was agreed to.[13] * * *

---

[13] The other clauses of the supplementary bill were debated at less length, and the members moved on to discuss the cost of compensating Pennamites for their losses. On November 22, the question of a permanent force was debated further, Thomas Kennedy moving that the number of troops be reduced to 150. The Assembly finally decided to stipulate no definite number; *Proceedings and Debates*, II, 153-59.

[181] Timothy Pickering to John Pickering.[1]

Philadelphia Novᵣ 17, 1787.

Dear Brother,

You will have heard of the disturbances at Wyoming, whither I had moved my family. I have forborne to write particularly, because I could write nothing favourably. However, the prospect is now changed; and I expect peace will be shortly fully established in that country. The Government of Pennsylvania appears disposed to do every thing requisite for that end. The troubles originated with a few villains of some ability, but chiefly of desperate fortune, who had formed a plan to erect a new state in that and the adjacent country of New-York; and taking advantage of the disaffection of a number of the Connecticut Settlers at Wyoming, whose prejudices & resentments against Pennᵃ had been coeval with their settlement in this state, had really drawn into the plot a considerable number of men. But the capture of John Franklin who was their leader to execute the plot has disconcerted all their measures. The State have ordered in some militia for the present; & a bill has had two readings to authorize the Council to raise and post there a permanent military force. This will effectually overawe the insurgents (who are all dispersed) & effectually establish the authority of the state & peace of the county, I trust without bloodshed. The principal conspirators lived in the states of Connecticut & New-York. Their plot was so far advanced, that Major Judd, a Connecticut lawyer, had actually drawn up a constitution [2] for their intended new state, which was to be called *Westmoreland,* the name of the Wyoming district when a county under the Connecticut Jurisdicdiction. The pretence of the conspirators, who were members of the Susquehanna Company, by which they deluded the people, was, that this company having made a fair purchase of the Indians of the *soil,* they had still a right to hold it; and that no act of Pennsylvania & Connecticut could divest them of it. The fact is that the whole country in dispute lies within the bounds of the Pennᵃ charter. Connecticut claimed a right to it as falling within her charter, extending it, according to the word of it, to the South Sea. This dispute was referred by the two states (agree-

---

[181] [1] M. H. S., Pickering Papers, XXXV, 26-28, in Pickering's hand.
[2] See no. 175, *ante,* note 2.

ably to the articles of confederation) to a Continental court, the members of which were mutually agreed on by the two states. This court sat at Trenton in Dec.ʳ 1782 and after a hearing of counsel on both sides during many days, they decreed, *unanimously,* that both the soil and jurisdiction did of right belong to Pennsylvania.³ This gave a terrible shock to the Susquehanna Company and their settlers at Wyoming; and if Penn.ᵃ had then manifested any degree of generosity & magnamimity—if she had indeed consulted merely her own interest—she would have quited the *settlers* in their old possessions, which they had had derived by titles, which they supposed to be good, from the Susquehanna company. But instead of this, the Conduct of the state has consisted of a series of impolitic measures, sometimes lenient, sometimes severe, and, thro' the abuse of power by the persons appointed to execute the orders of the state, sometimes cruel & oppressive. These circumstances, together with the discontents generally prevailing through out the United States, the rebellion in Massachusetts, and the prospect of an entire dissolution of the federal union, have encouraged the villains before referred to, to form & prepare to execute their wicked plot before mentioned.

I have just heard from my wife at Wyoming: She is very well. She expresses much solicitude to hear from her son John. Tim, Henry, Charles & William are with our friends in this city. The infant, Edward (born the 12th of September) is with my wife at Wyoming; her sister also is with her. A M.ʳ Bowman a lawyer, & a very clever man, is in my family, & has remained at Wyoming during all the disturbances. He was educated at Cambridge, and is known, I believe, to Samuel & Timothy Williams. He attends the business of my office during my absence.

The Sheriff of Luzerne has brought down the return of the election of a member to sit in the convention of this state for considering of the federal constitution. I am chosen. The Convention is to meet the 20th instant. This will keep me here a few weeks. I wish to hear from you and my friends before I go up to Wyoming; or if you address a letter to M.ʳ Hodgdon's care, he will forward it if I should be gone. Should it be perfectly convenient to you, I shall be obliged by a remittance of any sum of money more or less; as you can spare it. This also may be directed to M.ʳ Hodgdon's care. After I return to Wyoming, I shall embrace an early opportunity to make & forward you a

---

³ See no. 8, *ante,* and note 2. Pickering does not make clear that private right of soil was not decided at Trenton.

deed of the land you proposed to take of me. Your letters on the subject are there, the particulars of which I do not fully recollect.

Give my love to my son, & persuade him to write a short letter to his mamma or me. I will write Mr Williams, if I have time. This I expect to send by John Blanchard, brother to our Cousin; & I must go to him immediately lest he should be gone. I bid you, dear brother, a most affectionate adieu! & pray you to present my kind love to all my sisters & their children, whom I remember with tenderness; & Mr Williams Mr Gardner & Mr Dodge are not forgotten.

T. Pickering

[182] Extract from the Minutes of the Pennsylvania General Assembly.[1]

It was moved by Mr. [William] *Findley,* seconded by Mr. [John] *McDowell,*

To insert the following clause, immediately after the seventh section, *viz.*

"And whereas doubts have arisen with respect to the true intent and meaning of the term *'acquired,'* in the act to which this is a supplement: Be it therefore enacted and declared by the authority aforesaid, That none but such person or persons as have made a real settlement at or before the decree of *Trenton,* or the legal representatives of such person or persons, shall be esteemed or judged to have acquired any title under the aforesaid act; and that an actual settlement or occupancy, made previous to the decree at *Trenton,* shall enable such person or persons so claiming to enjoy a tract of land, not exceeding three hundred acres, and the allowance of *six per centum* for roads.["] [2]

---

[182] [1] *Minutes of the First Session of the Twelfth General Assembly,* 84-85 (microfilm copy), dated November 22, 1787.

[2] Findley offered this clause as part of the supplement to the Confirming Act, which the Assembly was working out; see no. 170, *ante,* note 22. His proposal passed by a vote of 46 to 15. Among those voting *nay* were Thomas Fitzsimons, George Clymer (see no. 170, *ante*) and John Paul Schott, the representative from Luzerne. On November 24, Fitzsimons tried unsuccessfully to get a reconsideration of this amendment; *Minutes,* 87. A second unsuccessful attempt at reconsideration came on November 27; *ibid.,* 90. This amendment, however, did not become part of the law, for the supplement never received final action in the Assembly.

[183] Debates on the Findley Amendment to the Confirming Act.[1]

Mr. [Richard] *Peters* was of opinion, that the great truth contained in divine writ, ought to influence the conduct of individuals, and perhaps might not be improper to be adopted by the Legislature—that is *charity begins at home.*

I am as much in favour of our own citizens as any person can pretend to be, and I confess if any people are to suffer, it ought to be those who are seizing the property to which they have no legal claim, unless from the bounty of the state; but we are also to consider that the object of the Legislature is to reconcile the Wyoming settlers, in order to preserve peace and extend the jurisdiction of the Commonwealth to that territory. Such I apprehend was the object of the bill passed last March,[2] and whether that law was or was not politic, forms no part of our present consideration; but be it as it may, we are now obliged to carry it through, and must adhere to the principle of justice which is there laid down. This clause [3] I suppose sir is intended to serve my old fellow-citizens, to whom I am greatly attached, by preventing our *adopted brethern,* whom I confess I do not like to well, from obtaining an accumulated number of estates in that country. Had this been the principle of the first law, it might have been proper, but now sir that these people have come forward and laid in their claims under that law, and conducted themselves according to its direction, I cannot think the state at liberty to recede from their part of the contract. This amendment sir bears down the principle of the old law, and appears to me very unjustifiable; but as I have not perfectly made up my mind, I shall wait until I hear the sentiments of others on the subject: but I have prepared something like what the gentleman has proposed—but it is not contrary in its principle, as I take his to be to the old law, and which if I am seconded, I will read and present to the table.

This being done, it was put as an amendment, and after stating the doubt of the meaning of the term *acquired,* it went to explain by reciting, that those should be deemed to have ac-

---

[183] [1] *Proceedings and Debates of the General Assembly,* II, 160-66, 172, November 22, 1787.
[2] No. 38, *ante.*   [3] No. 182, *ante.*

quired titles who had made a real settlement, whether by themselves or by others, agreeably to the rules and regulations of the Susquehannah Company or state of Connecticut, before the decree of Trenton; and that those who were the heirs or assigns of such original settler or occupant, whether by purchase or otherwise, should be entitled to such tracts not exceeding 300 acres each, as they should establish by sufficient proof, according to the prayer of the petition upon which the original law was founded, and which prayer was constituted a part of the amendment.

Mr. [James] *M'Lene* requested that the petition and report of the Committee which had been the foundation of the former law might be heard. The petition was read, but the report of the Committee was mislaid.

Mr. [William] *Findley* had expected, and he believed a majority of the House expected something of this kind to be offered, to make the present bill go down: his amendment has been hastily drawn up at the table, and might not be so accurate as the one presented by the gentleman from the county (Mr. Peters) and as he was not so good a judge as he could wish to be of the superiority of the one over the other, he was very willing to let them both lie over. This observation he made to induce the House to allow further time to acquire information.

Mr. *Peters* had no objection to postponing both.

Mr. [George] *Clymer* would willingly agree to postpone them, provided they were never to be brought forward again; if one of these were, he would oppose the bill itself. Sir, if the House was to agree to the amendment proposed by the member from Westmoreland (Mr. Findley) I apprehend a very serious consequence would result; it will be entering upon ground which no Legislature has yet hazarded itself upon. To say what was or was not meant by an expression in our former law, belongs not to us; it is no part of our duty to put constructions on the meaning of the word *acquired:* having granted the occupants, their heirs and assigns, all their lots and rights they had *acquired,* upon condition that they conform with certain terms held out to them, is it for the Legislature to step in and restrict that term to what they think proper? if it is, what are the consequences sir? the Legislature after granting lands upon conditions, may notwithstanding a compliance on the part of the individual, resume that grant or so much of it as their will and pleasure may direct. I think sir it would be better to abide by the loss of a few acres more than what even the restriction allows, than thus commit the faith of the state, and moreover hazard the consequences of detaching a great number of the well affected people at Wyoming, who have complied and hitherto shewn a disposition to comply with the laws of the state.

Mr. [Thomas] *Fitzsimons.* If the gentleman's object in moving a postponement is no other than to get information of the analogy between the two amendments, I think there is little call for the House to be detained here long on that account. This bill has been postponed from day to day, and week to week, for a long time past, in order, as gentlemen tell you, to get more and more information, yet not satisfied with the frequent postponements already made; you are solicited once more to postpone for the purpose of comparing two motions, whose objects are different; if this is a sufficient reason to postpone, the House will decide so: But I beg before that is done, to call the attention of the members once more to the object of the bill generally. I do not consider this measure as proper sir, for any other reason than necessity; and I contend sir that necessity justified the first bill, and I contend further sir, that we are bound in every particular by what the first bill enacted; and if it was necessary at first, I consider the necessity of completing the measure to be now in existence. What was the object of the bill passed last March? was it not to prevent contention and bloodshed? was it not to quiet the settlers at Wyoming under the Connecticut claims, supposed to be enemies to your government, in order to preserve the peace of the state, which appeared in extreme jeopardy? and shall we now for the paltry consideration of a few acres of land, risque the welfare and happiness of Pennsylvania, the lives of her citizens, and that too by a breach of our plighted faith? the acres you will thus save must be few, for I have too high an opinion of the Commissioners and board of property who are to decide their claims, to believe a single acre will be given that is not right; by proceeding in this manner, sir, the whole business of conciliation will be defeated.

Mr. *Findley.* I find the worthy gentleman last up differs with me in the design of postponement, because I wish only for the time to examine more particularly what the other contains; but we agree sir in one observation, that it is difficult and dangerous for the Legislature to explain laws; this is true sir, but it is well known that doubts have arisen on the import of the word acquired; doubts have arisen with a number of members of this House, and it is well known *that the judges have differed in opinion on this and other subjects; Colonel Pickering has had an opinion of the term acquired, which the other judges had not.*[4] We generally enact laws, and leave the explanation to the judicial department, but if doubts arise in carrying the law into execution, we have a right to explain, though it may be a right that ought not to be generally exercised. This law sir that wants our explanation was the child of necessity, for can any thing but necessity justify the Legislature in taking away the property of individuals without their consent, or without a trial by jury? I think if we give up the plea of necessity, we must give up the law—now I don't wish to destroy the law; and if it was necessary, it ought to be restricted, so as not to be greater than the necessity: I do not wish to allow so large a field for speculation. The amendment which was proposed I conceive to be necessary, and I believe the bill is also necessary, but unless this or something like it is adopted, the bill may not be enacted this session. I wished therefore sir that the amendment might be postponed, to give us time to accommodate it to the necessity.

Mr. *Peters* did not like half-hasty business, and was at first willing to let the amendments lie over, that the member might examine and correct any loose expressions they contained.

But I am perfectly decided sir, that unless we support the faith, honor and dignity of the state, we risque its peace and happiness in future: if I thought sir that any amendment of mine would either tend to alter, defeat or delay the business, I would withdraw it instantly.

I know sir that there are some part of the members in this House who differ very widely from their colleagues, and it was with a view to conciliate those who are so averse to the insurgents at Tyoga, and others that are apprehensive the Pennsylvania claims will be insupportable, that I introduced my amendment; but sir it will be remembered, that when I presented it I did not even pledge myself to vote for it, nor do I know that I should— yet rather than retard the great object or embarrass the House, I would withdraw; but I should expect the gentleman to withdraw his also: For if the business is not now finished, I think we had better never begun, for my own part I am willing to let the terms of the old law stand, and it was not from any doubts I had myself that I introduced the clause—I say sir let the old law be what it may, it ought to stand, for tho' I find many laws

---

[4] Pickering, in keeping with the views of the Connecticut settlers, included in the term *acquired* rights assigned prior to the Trenton decree but not actually occupied because the lands were exposed to Indian attack; see no. 184, *post.*

that are not as I could wish them, I submit to them without murmuring, whatever my feelings may be, because I consider that they ought to be obeyed for the general good. I think in the most decided manner, that the Connecticut claimants ought to have titles to the full extent of the first law, be that what it may, but I am well convinced that if the word acquired is explained in the most extensive sense, but a few persons will receive more than 300 acres. I know a different opinion obtains in the House, but without any other foundation I apprehend than mere surmise; to be sure sir I will grant that neither the commissioners, nor any other person, know precisely the number of these claims, yet I conjecture it will be allowed, that they are better able to make the estimation after being upon the spot, and receiving the number they have already done, than any of us, who know so little of both the country and the people. By the short extension of the time already agreed to by the House, in which claims are allowed to be exhibited, I apprehend there is small ground to expect these applications will be numerous, even if the commissioners are properly supported in the exercise of their duties, so that there is less occasion for this restriction, than there would be if the claims were allowed to come forward for a longer time hereafter. I think very little alteration if any, in the quantity of land, could take place; at all events I am for supporting the old law, and not for joining in what must involve a breach of public faith with even a single individual.

Mr. *Findley*.[5] * * * The gentleman from the city [6] alleges, that the term acquired ought not be restricted, yet the intention of the first law ought to be complied with; this is the object of my amendment, for as doubts have arisen even among the judges, of the meaning of the word, they may be supposed to have been misunderstood by the House; and I would appeal to the gentlemen present, who were members of the last House, for their opinion of what was the intention of the Legislature, whether their lots were not supposed to be but 300 Acres: I am very certain sir that such was the intention.

This law I have already observed was the child of necessity; being such it cannot be supposed so perfect as it ought to be— many people are of opinion sir that the whole plan is indigested, and I am one who am of this opinion; and I think there is room

---

[5] In the omitted part of his speech Findley explains his unwillingness to withdraw his amendment. He asserts that various members in both parties have expressed a wish for such a change.

[6] George Clymer.

to believe that the term *acquired* was *insiduously* inserted in the law :[7] I did think that our plain and only meaning was, to allow no more than one right to each settler ; no man occupying land under Pennsylvania, could be entitled to a greater quantity, then what right is there to allow more to these people? yet sir the judges themselves acknowledge, that they have admitted, some to have 6 or 8 shares or lots, and I don't know how many more. Why sir, on this principle of allowing them all they have acquired, I don't see where it is possible they are to stop ; if the lines of the county itself are found to circumscribe their demands, it will be happy for us.

These considerations give ground of suspicion and jealousy, when we must not explain a law that cannot explain itself.

That this law sir was designed upon the principle of conciliation, I admit ; and that it is a valuable consideration to reconcile the people to the government ; but why don't we extend the principle sir, and take in the half-share men? yet the term acquired may be construed in some manner to apply even to them ; why sir don't we accommodate the whole? I admit we cannot ; and I admit it would be improper [8]—but yet such is the effect if [of?] the term acquired rights, as defined and explained by the conduct of the judges in allowing so many claims to one person. My judgment tells me this is going beyond what was the intention of the Legislature, and if the members are also clear to decide I am willing, and will therefore withdraw my motion for postponement.

Mr. *Fitzsimons.* As I was by no means in favour of postponement, I am glad the motion is withdrawn. I would just beg leave therefore to observe sir, that the gentleman gives as a reason why the House should adopt his clause, that in several instances the commissioners have admitted 8 or 10 claims made by one person ; if the commissioners have admitted such claims, I venture to pronounce it was in obedience to your law ; and those claims were made as heirs or assignees of original settlers, before the decree of Trenton—this sir I take to be the clear and plain import of the word *acquired,* and I am surprised how the gentleman can torture it to make it appear otherwise.

I hope the House do not mean to make a distinction between alienated and unalienated rights ; for certainly the purchase of *an estate* has as good title to it as the original occupant or holder ;

---

[7] This was a charge which Pickering was at pains to deny ; no. 184, *post.*

[8] Yet later Findley did unsuccessfully move that half-share men be included within the law ; no. 186, *post.*

but moreover your faith is plighted to these people by the express words of your former act, where it is declared, that you will confirm all these lots to the heirs and assigns of the first settlers or occupants.

It is true that I considered these people as intruders, but then they did not consider themselves such; they had the claim of occupancy or first settlement; a pre-emption is a right in many instances; many other persons settled within the state of Pennsylvania, have no other claim. These had settled themselves under the state to which they belonged, had conformed to the rules and regulations laid down for that purpose, and absolutely paid a valuable consideration to the state of Connecticut for what they thought were good titles; many of them have been several years living there: the mere settlement was supposed in Pennsylvania to give a right, but these people have been confirmed in their right by an express law: the half-share men were invited by the Susquehannah Company, for the particular purpose of keeping possession of the county, not only in defiance of the laws and authority of the state, but in direct opposition to all good government, and I believe no gentleman in this House had ever an intention to reward these people—the other class were tenacious of their property, because they have purchased or procured it by that mode which our sister state had directed. But I would ask the gentleman what will be the consequence if his motion is enacted in the law? The people in that country whom you intend to conciliate, and many of whom in fact are now your friends, will disengage themselves from you, declaring they can have no confidence in a government that refuses to confirm their own contracts: great pains are taken to seduce them from their allegiance, and it wants but such a mistaken, nay, unjust stroke of policy as this, to throw the whole country again into confusion and disorder. They are already told that there is a strong party against them throughout Pennsylvania; jealousies are already sown amongst them, and this will be a weighty proof.

The gentleman tells you that the former act was ill digested, and the plea was bad; if sir the last was an impolitic law, let us make no more such; but if it was policy, true and necessary policy at that time, when the danger of an encrease of force on their side was so very much to be apprehended, and if that necessity exists, by the peculiar temper and situation of the settlers at Wyoming, let the principle of conciliation be continued; and this when aided by a small force, will restore harmony and contentment to that district—for disorder is to be principally apprehended from them, who having little to lose, but much to gain, by an effectual opposition to your government, will be the most mature for acts of violence and outrage. I hope when gentlemen reflect on the dreadful consequence of setting this business afloat, and the injustice that is about to be done, they will agree to reject the motion.[9] * * *

Mr. *Clymer* being in some degree instrumental in procuring the former law, wished to be heard in a few words on the subject. One gentleman (Mr. Peters) said he did not like the law, but he would submit to it as he found himself strapped about the neck with it; another gentleman (Mr. Findley) goes farther, and declares the law to be a violation of the constitution; I know nothing in the constitution adequate to repel the dangers that may arise from insurrection, but I am certain that the power held by all nations extends to every measure necessary for the preservation and safety of the government, and therefore authorise a law founded in state necessity. It has been conceived by that gentleman, that this law was necessary from the danger to which we were then exposed, and without a law of this kind I apprehend that country would at this time be totally seperated from our dominion. I say there was a necessity for this law, and those persons ought to be most silent who were instrumental in producing that necessity; those who have exerted themselves from time to time to defeat every measure that has been for some years past proposed, unfortunately for the state their opposition has been adequate to this end. When it was in contemplation to use other means, a party in this state opposed it, and defeated the intention.[10] For it is a well known fact, that the friends of good order were obliged to give up their attempts to restore the defeated Pennsylvania claimants to their property. When this had been effected, it only procured an addition of force to the settlers at Wyoming, and we were, by such policy, reduced to the necessity of giving up to those people a part of their claims, in order to put an end to the numerous evils with which that settlement was surrounded.

It was state necessity alone that compelled the measure, a ne-

---

[9] Omitted here are a brief rebuttal by Findley and long speeches by William Lewis reiterating the contractual obligation incurred by the state with the passage of the Confirming Act. He was supported by Richard Peters, but Findley denied that the settlers' petition put a binding interpretation on the law.

[10] Clymer's reference is to the Constitutionalists, who earlier had criticized the use of force against the Connecticut settlers; see Vol. VIII, no. 47, pp. 59-60, 65-67.

cessity that arose from the opposition given by certain persons to coertion. And I would beg to observe farther, that those persons who forced this act upon the state, are now most desirous to prevent its operation, knowing if they can defeat this, the country will be involved once more in contention; if their object sir is not to embroil the state, it is impossible to ascertain what it is—but their conduct appears to me similar to what it was when they opposed the former measure, and I have no doubt but their object is the same, though they pursue another mode of accomplishing it.[11] * * *

[184] Timothy Pickering to the Speaker of the Pennsylvania General Assembly.[1]

Thursday Evening Nov' 22, 1787

Sir,

Deeply Impressed with a sense[2] of the mischievous consequences of the material alteration of the law relating to the Wyoming lands, which will be effected by the Clause just adopted by your Honourable House,[3] I beg leave to state some facts, which appear to me important, and which, perhaps, may induce a reconsideration of it. The part I have taken in this business, the safety of myself and family which depend on the issue of it, and weighty public considerations, compel me to enter on the subject; & I pray for the indulgent attention of the House.

After the law had been enacted for erecting the northern part of Northumberland into a separate county,[4] by the name of Luzerne (a measure of which till then I was wholly ignorant) it was proposed to me to apply for the office of prothonotary for the new county. I objected: but it was urged upon me, chiefly on this ground, that the views of government being conciliatory, my particular situation would enable me more than any other

---

[11] After Clymer, Richard Peters, Robert Lollar, and William Lewis each spoke. Lollar, favoring the amendment, saw no breach of faith. Lewis spoke against the amendment because the state had been committed by the terms of the Confirming Act.

[184] [1] M. H. S., Pickering Papers, V, 409-11, a draft in Pickering's hand.

[2] "Painful" is lined out before "sense."

[3] See no. 182, ante. Findley's amendment would have limited the Connecticut settlers to 300 acres each and would have recognized the claims only of those who actually settled on their rights before or at the time of the Trenton decree. Pickering explains below the full meaning of this change.

[4] September 25, 1786.

probable candidate for the office [5] to promote them. I yielded to these solicitations; and applied for that office, & the others usually joined with it in new and thinly peopled counties.

Afterwards, the Assembly having passed a law to enable the electors of Luzerne to choose a counsellor, representative, Sheriff & other county officers,[6] and therein authorized me singly, or in conjunction with the other persons therein named to conduct those elections, I went thither with the law; and during the space of three weeks was unremitting in my endeavours to persuade the people to make their elections, & peaceably submit to the government of this State. With extreme difficulty I prevailed. The Councillor took his seat: but the Representative, John Franklin, having other views, remained at home; and by his artifices and misrepresentations seduced a considerable number of the people from their duty; so that on my return to that county in April, I had to repeat my labour; but again I succeeded; and the elections of the Justices were ultimately held with the very general approbation of the inhabitants.[7]

Immediately After the first election, in February, I consulted some of the principal persons who had attended the election & who had been old settlers, &, as I supposed, were best acquainted with the claims & expectations of the people. Those claims & expectations the petition which has been read this evening [8] was intended to describe; the law for confirming the lands so claimed, was grounded on this petition: and such words or passages as were inserted into the law, to extend the confirming clause beyond the limits of the Committee's report, I trust I may be permitted to say were not "insidiously" introduced. I did not wish [to] con[ceal?] a single fact or motive from the committee.[9] The principle of public policy which led to the adoption of the bill, was that of securing the submission & future attachment of that great majority of the Connecticut settlers within the county of Luzerne who had equitable pretensions to lands granted them

---

[5] The words after "enable" are interlined; the words lined out are illegible.

[6] A number of words that follow are lined out and are illegible.

[7] The following words are lined out here: "In May the first county court was held without opposition."

[8] The petition of February 5, 1787, which Pickering had drawn up with the settlers; no. 16, *ante*.

[9] Originally this sentence apparently read: "I believe every fact or motive within my knowledge was laid before the committee." The charge that the term *acquired* was "insidiously" introduced was made by William Findley; no. 183, *ante*.

prior to the Trenton decree; and to effect that it appeared expedient to extend the confirmation beyond the occupied rights: but so far was I from wishing or attempting to conceal that extension, I well remember to have told one honourable member who supported the bill, & who is also in the present house, that it might perhaps comprehend, one hundred [10] such unoccupied rights. The case of the claimants of such rights, as originally stated to me, struck me very forceably. In all my communications with that people before the first election, I held up no ideas of confirmation beyond the rights they had occupied before the Trenton decree: but the gentlemen there whom I afterwards consulted, represented That besides such occupants, there was a considerable number of persons who, or those whom they represented, were actual settlers there prior to the said decree but who had not taken actual possession of their rights before the passing of the said decree. These persons, they said, were obliged during the late war to live with their friends in the compact part of the settlement, for their mutual safety and protection against the Indians: That they had suffered and bled in common with the other settlers in the defence of that frontier; and that it would be singularly distressing to reduce them or their orphan children to beggary, merely because their lots had fallen to them in places remote from the heart of the settlement. I need not be ashamed to own that humanity as well as considerations of equity & public policy, prompted me to wish such sufferers might be provided for; and to such the petition specially referred. These sufferers sir, I yet hope may experience the commiseration & favourable regard of your Honourable House.

There are, sir other circumstances respecting the Connecticut claimants which seem necessary to be made known [11] before the bill now pending is passed into a law.

The first township granted by the Susquehanna company & called Kingston was to be divided into forty three parts,[12] each of which, as the township was five miles square, would contain about three hundred & seventy two acres without any allowance for roads.

Another township, called Hanover, was to be divided, agreeably to the latest resolution of the Susquehanna Company that

---

[10] Several illegible words are lined out before "one hundred."

[11] The following words are lined out here: "to prevent the confirming Act."

[12] Apparently Pickering originally wrote that Kingston was granted to forty settlers.

I have seen, into thirty six parts. And I think there is one other township which was also granted to about six & thirty settlers. The other townships as well as I recollect, were to be divided into fifty three parts; which gives about 300 acres to each right.[13] In each of them three rights were to be reserved; one for the first settled minister in fee; one for a parsonage; and one for the support of a town-school. The manner of dividing the townships has been various. In some they made as many four several divisions. In Wilkesborough, for instance, each settler had a meadow lot (being part of the flats) of about thirty acres—a town-lot of three acres and a half, or three acres & three quarters, a back lot of about two hundred & fifty acres, and a fourth lot containing five acres; and the land reserved for the three public uses aforementioned was left in one entire body. In some townships those three public rights were drawn in several lots. And in other townships some parcels of land have been reserved to accommodate a mill, or for other uses, of common benefit to the inhabitants. Now, whatever lands shall be confirmed, it seems necessary to advert to these circumstances, to prevent the confusion & mischief which a departure from the usages of the people might produce.[14] The surveys of townships which have been made by order of the commissioners, have been conformed to those usages.

I would here beg leave to mention the alteration lately made in the lower line of the county of Luzerne. In the first law it was declared that it should run west from the mouth of Nescopeck Creek. In the supplement to that law it was declared that it should run northwestwardly [15] "from the mouth of Nescopeck" —and in the law passed on the [   ] day of September last this word "northwestwardly" was interpreted to mean "North one degree west." Sir, I am well informed that this last line will [16] never strike the ridge dividing the waters of the east & west branches of the Susquehanna: I am also informed that it will cut off one half, and perhaps the whole of the township of Huntington, which is one of the seventeen townships mentioned in the petition, and in which there are sundry Connecticut set-

---

[13] Three and a half lines are lined out here, the ideas being repeated below. In addition the following sentence is crossed out: "The rights in these Townships will consequently be larger or smaller according to the number of parts into which they are divided."

[14] Lined out here are the following words: "I would also request the attention of the house."

[15] The word "until" is interlined over "northwestwardly."

[16] Lined out before "will" is "will continued."

tlers who occupied & improved their lots long before the Trenton decree. A number of them have already presented & regularly supported their claims.

I would here cease, sir, to trouble the House with any farther observations, had I not reason to believe that pains have been taken to lessen the weight of any oppositions [17] I should make in this business, by false suggestions of their proceeding solely from interested motives. Permit me sir, to declare that I claim no lands under a Connecticut title except those mentioned in the inclosed paper: [18] that I cannot acquire a single acre by extending the confirmation beyond the rights actually occupied prior to the decree of Trenton; all the lands I purchased being parts of very old settled rights: and that I can lose nothing from the lessening of the original grant by the clause just adopted: unless by that restriction numbers of the inhabitants, who will lose their expected rights should murmur, and a general discontent & jealousy be excited [19] by an apprehension that this step is only a prelude to total repeal of the law, which indeed to stir up the people to rebellion, Franklin has been continually predicting. Such general discontent should it arise would oblige me to remove my family and abandon the country forever.[20] I am sir, very respectfully, your most obedient servant,

Timothy Pickering

Lands purchased by Timothy Pickering within the county of Luzerne under Connecticut titles the whole lying within the town of Wilkesborough.

2	town-lots of Colonel Butler fenced containing	}	7½ ....£37.10.—
1	town-lot of M. Hollenback Esq' agent of Benj* Clarke } not fenced }	3¾ .... 15.—.—
		11¼	
1	meadow lot of 30 acres, & 8 acres adjoining, of Asa Bennet }	.... 38 .... 90.—.—
½	of a meadow lot 15	
½	of a back lot, about .... 135 } .... 65.—.—
1	five acre lot 5	
1	back lot of Jabez Fish & John Corkin .... 250 .... 78.15.—
1	back lot of Captain Schott .... 250 .... 80.—.—
	total 704¼ acres £366.5.—

---

[17] "Oppositions" is substituted for "propositions."

[18] In the draft the list of his holdings is simply added to the letter, as below.

[19] The words in the sentence after "excited" are interlined and added on.

[20] The phrase "the country forever" was substituted for "my property & improvements there."

Of Flats 64¼ acres—other lands 640 acres, of which the total cost, payable in short instalments, amounts to £336.5.— [21]

T. P.

[185] Pennsylvania Landholders' Memorial to the Pennsylvania General Assembly.[1]

To the hon. the general Assembly of the commonwealth of Pennsylvania, the representation and petition of sundry Landholders in the County of Luzerne:

Your petitioners beg leave to represent that they have the most serious apprehensions for their property and for the peace of the State in consequence of a clause introduced into the bill [2] relating to that county now depending before your hon. house;

That they conceive the laws last past on that subject are of the Nature of a solemn compact between this independent State and a body of citizens of another independent State connected with and acknowledged by this commonwealth;

That in the present state of the finances of Pennsylvania they fear the expense of a large and permanent force will be necessary to crush an opposition rendered more firm and determined by breach of public faith, destructive of all confidence in this government;

That the law of 1787,[3] by dividing the opposition, has rendered the business of reducing the *late* intruders easy, certain and much less expensive to Pennsylvania than any other mode that can be adopted;

They, therefore, most earnestly pray your hon. house not to alter in any particular the footing on which the actual residents in any County, before the decree of Trenton, were placed, as they are perfectly convinced and satisfied that it will render nugatory any compensation the State may offer to the Pennsyl-

---

[21] For some puzzling reason Pickering blotted the correct total for the value of his holdings after he had added it up and wrote this new total here.
[185] [1] *P. A.*, 2nd ser., XVIII, 671-72. This petition was presented to the General Assembly by Thomas Fitzsimons on November 23, 1787, and led Fitzsimons to move that the Wyoming commissioners be called to the bar of the House to testify on proposed changes in the Confirming Act; *Minutes of the First Session of the Twelfth General Assembly*, 85 (microfilm copy) and *Proceedings and Debates of the General Assembly*, II, 178.
[2] The clause was that successfully introduced by William Findley on November 22; no. 182, *ante*.
[3] That is, the Confirming Act of March 28, 1787; no. 38, *ante*.

vanians, and finally prove the most injurious and expensive mode that can be pursued.

They beg leave further to pray that an attention to compensating their just demands on the State may not so far influence the honorable house as to induce to take any measures at this time to their favor, if it is to lead the legislatures into a breach of the sacred obligations of public faith.[4]

> Sam'l Meredith,
> Tench Coxe,
> Reuben Haines,
> Tench Francis,
> Levi Hollingsworth,
> John Sitgreave,
> Tho's Affleck.

[186] Extract from the Minutes of the Pennsylvania General Assembly.[1]

It was then moved by Mr. [William] *Findley,* seconded by Mr. [John] *McDowell,* to postpone the said ninth section, in order to introduce an additional clause, to precede the same in the said bill. Which was carried in the affirmative.

And the additional clause being read in the words following, *viz.*

"And whereas it hath become expedient to quiet in their possessions, not only those who were actual settlers upon lands in the county of *Luzerne* aforesaid before the time of the decree of the court of *Trenton,* but that such also as have at any time since seated themselves upon lands and improved the same, and are

---

[4] Whether these men spoke only for themselves or for others as well cannot be determined. The spirit in which they wrote was far different from that animating Pennamites like Alexander Patterson and his supporters in 1783 and 1784. While these signers were holders of lands with Pennsylvania titles, some of them within the Susquehannah Company's purchase, they were not likely to become actual settlers in the seventeen towns. A peaceful settlement would enable them to get on with their land sales. Some of them, however, had not always felt this way, for in 1775, they had taken the lead in trying to get the Connecticut settlers wholly expelled. See Vol. VI, nos. 187, 193, 194 and 200.

[186] [1] *Minutes of the First Session of the Twelfth General Assembly,* 88-89 (microfilm copy), dated November 24, 1787. The Assembly was putting together a supplement to the Confirming Act.

now resident thereupon, should, upon their taking the oath of allegiance and renunciation therein before prescribed, and demeaning themselves as good citizens, have the lands upon which they have so improved and become resident, secured to them in like manner: Therefore be it further enacted by the authority aforesaid, That all and every person actually resident within the said county of *Luzerne* at the time of passing this act, who is seated upon lands improved and held by him, and upon which he hath erected a dwelling-house, shall have, and he is hereby declared to have, the same confirmed to him, his heirs and assigns forever, subject to the like limitation for making their respective claims as is herein after provided. And the commissioners who are or may be appointed to receive claims shall in like manner proceed to receive, enquire into, examine witnesses on oath, and determine upon every such claim, cause the same to be surveyed, at the expence of the party, within some one of the eighteen towns, and in such manner as the said half shares have been already surveyed and allotted; provided that it do not exceed [   ] acres to each lot or half share.[2] And the return of the same shall be made to the Supreme Executive Council, who shall grant patents therefore, in like manner as is directed by the act to which this is a supplement: Provided always, That no person so occupying and claiming shall receive any benefit from this act, unless he take and subscribe the oaths herein before directed within the time prescribed."

It was, on motion of Mr. *Findley* and Mr. *Rittenhouse,*

Ordered, That the same be referred to Mr. [George] *Clymer,* Mr. [Richard] *Peters,* Mr. [Gerardus] *Wynkoop,* Mr. [Samuel] *Evans,* Mr. [Alexander] *Lowrey,* Mr. G.[abriel] *Heister,* Mr. *Findley,* Mr. [James] *McLene* and Mr. [John Paul] *Schott,* to report thereon.[3]

The ninth section being then again under debate,

A motion was made by Mr. *Peters,* seconded by Mr. *Findley,*

To strike out the remainder of the said section, after the

---

[2] Findley's language here not only recognized the rights of half-share men, who had begun coming onto the Company's land in 1785, but the right of the settlers to Athens, the eighteenth town, where many of the half-share men went, threatening the speculative ventures of Pickering and his associates. In spirit, it was quite the opposite of the amendment he had successfully proposed two days earlier; no. 182, *ante.* Findley proposed to give the half-share men 200 acres each as a way of eliminating the need to send troops; *Proceedings and Debates of the General Assembly,* II, 180.

[3] The committee reported on November 28. After debate, the Assembly voted down Findley's proposed addition to the law by 42 to 18; *ibid.,* 93.

words, *"quality and value,"* and in lieu thereof to insert the words,

"And it is hereby declared and enacted, That this House shall and do pledge the faith of the state to provide funds, so soon as the said valuation and appraisement shall be made and communicated to this House, for the payment or satisfaction of the said claimants, in such mode as shall be consistent with the justice due to the citizens of the state, whose property is, may or shall be affected by, this act, or by the act to which this is a supplement." And after some debate thereon,

On motion of Mr. [Thomas] *Fitzsimons,* seconded by Mr. *McLene,*

Ordered, That the said clause and amendment be referred to the last named committee, to report thereon.[4]

Ordered, That the further consideration of the said bill be postponed.

Adjourned until half past nine o'clock on *Monday* next, A. M.

[187] Samuel Gordon to Nathan Denison.[1]

Wilkesbarry, 24th Nov'r, 1787.

Sir,

In my epistle to you whilst you were in Philadelphia I forgot to inform you of a certain Smith, a scotchman, long visaged, much broke with the small-pox; who I take to be one of Mc-Kinstry Beach Levingston's & Co's., emissaries,[2] who taking me to be of a like turn of mind with himself informed me their in-

---

[4] The Peters motion, although reported out by the committee on November 28, was not considered on that date. On March 5, 1788, a substitute motion was offered; no. 206, *post.*

Dissatisfied Pennsylvania land claimants had for weeks been complaining about the inadequacy of compensation payable to those who lost out to Connecticut claimants. Petitions in opposition to the compensation provisions of the Confirming Act had been read in the Assembly on September 10 and November 12; *Minutes of the Third Session of the Eleventh General Assembly,* 204, and *Minutes of the First Session of the Twelfth General Assembly,* 42. On November 14 a committee had recommended resolutions calling for compensation in either land or interest-bearing certificates; *ibid.,* 56-57. See also no. 188, *post.*

A petition opposing a change in compensation was presented on November 22 by "several members of a committee of public creditors"; *Minutes of the First Session,* 68.

[187] [1] *P. A.,* XI, 213.

[2] *Cf.* with no. 156, *ante.* See also nos. 100 and 102, *ante.*

tention was not to ask the protection of any state, that they ment to govern themselves, and if molested protect themselves against any, or all the states. If they found themselves unable to stand against the States, call for the assistance of the British, being an independent people, should have a right to request & receive the Protection of any state or Power.

In order to incourage Settlers to come into their country & settle, I see a writing in the hands of the above Smith signed by McKinstry & Allen signifying that Each settler should have a certain Quantity of Land gratis, &c., &c., Subtill arguments are made use of to persuade the people to repair to a new Country to avoid the heavy Taxes their new masters lay on them, that they would be much easier under the former yoke.

I shall not trouble you with the arguments I have made use of to deswade some, who I think have seen their error. I am S' your most obed't Serv't.

Saml. Gordon.

[188] Extract from the Minutes of the Pennsylvania General Assembly.[1]

The House met pursuant to adjournment.

A motion was made by Mr. [James] *McLene,* seconded by Mr. [Richard] *Peters,* in the words following, *viz.*

"*Resolved,* That the Supreme Executive Council be, and they are hereby authorised and requested to issue a grant or grants in favour of such *Pennsylvania Claimants,* who have or may be divested of their lands in the county of *Luzerne,* by the operation of an act, entituled * * * [The Confirming Act], which grant or grants shall give such claimant or claimants a right to take up and settle upon a quantity of land, in any part of the residue of the donation lands not already appropriated,[2] provided the quantity of lands so granted do not exceed the quantity of land of which such person or persons have been or may be

---

[188] [1] *Minutes of the First Session of the Twelfth General Assembly,* 94-95 (microfilm copy), dated November 29, 1787.

[2] The effect of this resolution would have been to set aside procedures in the existing law, which required the Board of Property to grant compensation after consulting the records of the Wyoming commissioners and ascertaining the validity and extent of claims. In debate a number of members declared that granting land by resolution was illegal; *Proceedings and Debates of the General Assembly,* II, 186.

divested as aforesaid; which land, so granted and accepted of, shall be considered as a compensation to such person or persons, either in whole or in part, as shall hereafter be determined."

And on the question,—"*Will the House adopt the same?*"— the Yeas and Nays were called by Mr. *McLene,* and Mr. *Peters,* and were as follow, *viz.*[3] * * *

So it was carried in the negative.

A motion was then made by Mr. *McLene,* seconded by Mr. [James] *McCalmont,* in the words following, *viz.*

"*Resolved,* That it is the opinion of this House, that all proceedings of the commissioners appointed to carry into effect the act, entituled * * * [The Confirming Act], shall cease and determine, until this House shall take further order therein."[4]

The previous question was then called by Mr. [Thomas] *Fitzsimons,* Mr. [William] *Robinson,* [Jr.], Mr. [Richard] *Thomas* and Mr. [Samuel] *Evans, viz.*

"*Shall the main question be now put?*"

And carried in the negative.

[189] Proposed Amendment to the Confirming Act of 1787.[1]

And whereas doubts have arisen about the extent of the confirmation intended by the act aforesaid[2] of the lands claimed by the said Connecticut claimants, and it is necessary to define the same: And whereas in the petition[3] of the inhabitants of the county of Luzerne presented to the last Assembly on the sixth day March last, on which the act aforesaid was grounded, it was set forth, that the lands claimed by the said Connecticut claimants were generally assigned to them in lots of three hundred[4] acres each; and that besides the lots by them occupied within the seventeen townships & in some detached places, capable of

---

[3] The vote was 38 to 20 against the motion. On November 14 the Assembly had called for a bill providing compensation in either lands or interest-bearing certificates: *ibid.,* 56-57.

[4] On November 17, a petition calling for suspension of the Confirming Act had been presented to the Assembly. It was signed by Garret Broadhead and Cornelius Vanhorne in behalf of themselves and others; *ibid.,* 60. For petitions demanding outright repeal of the act, see no. 127, *ante,* note 2.

[189] [1] M. H. S., Pickering Papers, LVIII, 5-6, a draft in Pickering's hand. The probable date for this proposed amendment is November, 1787, when amendments were being considered by the Assembly; see no. 182, *ante.*

[2] The Confirming Act; no. 38, *ante.*   [3] No. 16, *ante.*

[4] "Three hundred" is interlined above "about 300," which is lined out.

306

cultivation between the townships [5] mentioned and referred to in said petition, certain similar lots falling within those townships and detached places [6] had been particularly assigned, prior to the decree of the federal court at Trenton, to divers persons who before that time had been actual settlers within the limits of the county of Luzerne, but of which lots so assigned them, they had not been able to take possession during the late war, thro' fear of destruction from the Indians; and the lots occupied & particularly assigned as aforesaid were those alone of which the said petitioners prayed a confirmation: And it being well known to have been the intention of the said Assembly to confirm the lands of the said Connecticut claimants agreeably to the spirit of the said petition, so that [7] none of those claimants actual settlers, within the limits of the county of Luzerne before the decree aforesaid who had such lots by occupancy or particular assignment as aforesaid prior to the said decree, should be left destitute of a reasonable provision for the support of themselves and families:

Be it therefore enacted by the authority aforesaid [8] that the confirmation aforesaid [9] shall comprehend all the lots within the seventeen townships & detached places [10] aforesaid, of which the said Connecticut claimants respectively had the possession [11] & occupancy prior to the decree aforesaid, and also one lot not exceeding three hundred acres, within the same townships & detached places [12] for each of the said claimants who was an actual settler within the limits of the said county prior to the said decree and to whom, before that time, such unoccupied lot has been particularly assigned, as aforesaid,[13] And no claim shall be admitted to any other lots than those comprehended within the plain meaning of this paragraph.[14]

---

[5] The phrase "capable of cultivation between the townships" is interlined above "called pitches."

[6] "Detached places" is substituted for "pitches."

[7] There follow three and a half illegible lines that have been crossed out.

[8] A following line and half has been crossed out.

[9] Several following words have been crossed out.

[10] The phrase "or pitches" is crossed out here.

[11] An illegible word is crossed out before "possession."

[12] "Detached places" is interlined for "pitches."

[13] About four illegible lines are crossed out here.

[14] This amendment was designed to correct the injustice which Pickering felt was threatened by the amendment proposed by Findley; see nos. 182 and 184, *ante*. Along the margin is written "Mess[rs] Peters & Schott." Richard Peters was particularly active in the Assembly in trying to bring about modifications of the Confirming Act. John Paul Schott, of course, was Luzerne's representative.

[And whereas by an Act passed on the 29th day of September last [15] it was declared that the line of the said county from the mouth of Nescop[eck] sh[d] run North one degree west until it should intersect the line which divides the waters of the east branch from those of the west branch of the river Susquehanna: And this Assembly is now informed that a line running North one degree west will not intersect the other line aforesaid: Be it therefore enacted by the authority aforesaid That the the line of the said county of Luzerne from the mouth of Nescopeck shall run in such direction northwestwardly as to comprehend the township of Huntington on Fishing Creek within the county of Luzerne; & from said township the said line shall be continued in such a direction as shall in the shortest distance intersect the line aforesaid dividing the waters of the east & west branch of the Susquehanna.] [16]

[190] William Hooker Smith to Timothy Pickering.[1]

Sir

I Think Thare is but a Dul Prospect of Peace at Wioming. The Upper Batallion have bin Lead To a Choice of Field offisers by The Leftennant of The County.[2] Thare was Not To Exceed Thirty Voters assembled Not more Than Six but what ware half Share men however The Election was Excepted by The Leftennant. John Jinkins was Chosen Coronal & Thomas Baldwin Mager. The Companies In The Upper Batallion have made Choice of Thare officers. Dudly who Lives at Wigtons Sawmill Is Chosen Captin of one of The Companies & almost The whole of The offisers are Enemies To Goverment. I am Glad That all That ware Chosen in The Lower Battalion are Not Commissioned as To William Ross how has it hapned That he has Not

---

[15] Mitchell and Flanders, *Statutes at Large*, XII, 587-89, Chapter MCCCXXIII. The description of the boundaries of Luzerne County that was part of this law was the third attempt to describe them properly. The earlier ones appear in the original act of September 25, 1786, establishing the county and in the supplement to that act passed December 27, 1786; *ibid.*, 300-03 and 339-43.

[16] The passage in brackets is marked out with a large X. There is no record in this period of any consideration by the Assembly of this proposed change in the description of the boundaries of Luzerne County.

[190] [1] M. H. S., Pickering Papers, LVII, 344, in Smith's hand.

[2] Zebulon Butler had set November 22 for the election of officers in the Upper Battalion; no. 174, *ante*.

bin Commissioned.³ Captⁿ Shoots Reports That one of The magistrates Rote against him. I Cannot Conceive wich it Should be Unless Kingsley. He Keept Company with MᶜKinster & Beach. The most of The Time Thay ware Down & with Utmost Complesance accompanied Them To Tioga It must be him or Nesbet. Pray Inquire who It was. Ross is a friend To Goverment has Exarted himself Ever Sence he as acted as Under Sherief. I hope you will Inquire Into The matter & Indavor That Ross may have a Commision. I am Sensable of his atatchment To Goverment. Boldwin Come with Uttermst vennom Down The River with MᶜKinster. Captⁿ Shoots accounts are That The half Share men have many friends in The house of assembley. I Expect That Shoots has Exearted him Selfe for The halfe Share men agreable To his Ingagments To Them it was Thay That Sent him. If The offissers Chosen in The Upper Battallion Shoold be Commissioned by Next Spring Thay may Git assistance from Thare friends abroad & will be able to Command The Lower Battallion Unless Goverment Interpose. I am of opinnion That Nothing Short of a miletary Post at Tioga will Istablish Peace in This County. The halfe Share men are amaisingly Incoraged by The Reports of Shoots which was That Sum in The house have Proposed an appeal of The act others amendments To wit That No man Should hold more Land Than Three Hundred acres & That No man Should hold any Except he Shall have Bult and Improved on The Very Lot which he Drew or Pitchd.⁴ If This Should be The Case Thare will be a General Revolt & you & I must flye or fall into The Hands of The Insurgants. Sir I am your most obdᵗ Humble Servᵗ

W ͫ Hooker Smith

Wioming 7ᵗʰ 1787

Endorsed: Decʳ 7, 1787.

[191] Petition of Isaiah Hallsted and Others to the Pennsylvania Council.¹

To the Supreme Executive Council, holden at Philadelphia in and for the State of Pensylvenia, Honorable Gentlemen We being sensable of the Ties and obligations we are under to return

---

³ See no. 168, *ante*, note 2.

⁴ *Cf.* Pickering's memorial to the Speaker; no. 184, *ante*.

[191] ¹ P. H. M. C., Div. of Arch. and MSS., Record Group 27, Series: Exec. Corr., 1777-90, signed by each individually.

our grateful Thank offerings for those inestimable favours that We have already Receved from the hands of this Honorable body in Giving us Protection under the hands of Civil government and in Erecting us into a seperate County and organizeing the same with Civil, as Well, as military officers, the manefest Cander of this Honorable body induceth us Come as Children to a Parent, to make known further Necessity with assurance of an indulgent ear ———

And Now gentlemen being Convinced that it is the Study of this Politick body to Communicate good to this infant settlement shall beg leave to inform your Honours ———

First Notwithstanding the Gratious indevers of this Executive athority in indevring to organize this County With Civil officers Yet we think that there is many more yet wanting to answer the Necessity of the Circumstance of the Settlement in this County as these settlements Do Extend more than a hundred and thirty miles in Lenghth and on booth sides of the River and only six Justices of the peace and less Constables in Number ———

But as to us your Honours Humble Potitioners Cituate in the Township of Putnam on the mouth of the Crick Tuncennick and the a Joining settlers have it to Regret that we are Twenty seven miles from Either Justices of the Peace or Constables and the settlement is Twelve or fifteen miles further up the Crick Who must first Come hither in order to go Either up or Down the River so that some of the inhabitance must Travil as much or more than forty miles in order to Come to a Justice of the Peace or Constable ———

Please Gentlemen to Consider the the Vast Expence that We must be at in order to be in any Way benifetted by the Civil administration of law

But this is Not all but When Visious men, Do Take Part of our little property and before we Can pass this Distance and Rough Road to Procure legal athority to aprehend them they are gone out of our Reach, and our substance lost, but should we be so fortunate as to Take the Visious and bring them to Justice and regain our Property it must be With Vast Expence and geat Trouble as the Roads as Well as the People Uncultivated therefore We think that so long a Space uncloathed of aThority must be a greate incouragement to Vice and immorallity as Well, as wearisum to Virtue ———

Lastly We your Honours Humble Potitioners Humbly Pray that your Honours Would Take the matters aforesaid into your Wise and Serious Considration and Provide measures Whereby some fit Parsons may be soon Cloathed with the athority of a Justice

310

of the Peace and Constable in the aforesaid Township and your Honours Humble Potitioners as in Deuty bound shall Ever Pray

Luzerne County
December 10ᵗʰ A D 1787

Eben Bartlett	Eliphalet Stephens, Sener
Jonathan Rolph	Caleb Newman
Josiah Arden	Jephthah earll
Ebenezer Stephens	Jeremiah Osterhout
Samuel holsted	Zebulon Marcy
Isaiah Hallsted	Gideon Osterhout
Ephraim Sanford	Elisha Drake
Benjamin Jones Jun.	Darius Parks
Elijah Oakley	Daniel Earl [2]
Joseph Arthur	John Harding
Asahel atherton	Isaac adams

Endorsed: recᵈ Janʳ 1788
Read Febʳ 21ˢᵗ 88

[192] Obadiah Gore and Mathias Hollenback to Benjamin Franklin.[1]

We have made it a matter of Enquiry of the necessity of the State keeping up Troops to secure the Allegiance of the Insurgents of this Country, and have Consulted a number of those We Esteem friends to Government, am Informed from Good authority that it is the Determination of the leaders of the Insurgents to get on as many half Sharemen (so called) as possibly they can in the spring, & possess themselves of all the lands Capable of Cultivation that is not now Occupy'd, and set up their Claim and support it in their way.

Now whether it wouᵈ not be policy to send a Company Immediately to Tioga, Inlisted for one year, unless sooner Discharged, and let the reasons be published why they are sent, which will prevent in a Great measure people being prevailed on to commence half sharemen by mischievous Designing persons

---

[2] That this petition for more justices should have been signed by Darius Parks and Daniel Earll, both strong partisans of John Franklin, who himself wanted nothing to do with authority under Pennsylvania's laws, perhaps suggests a temporary weakening in the Franklin forces. Both men a few months later were involved in the abduction of Pickering as a way of getting Franklin out of jail.

[192] [1] *P. A.*, XI, 216-17. The endorsement gives the date as December 22, 1787.

to Engage in that undertaking, and turn the Drift of them another way. Should the Troops (under smart, active Officers,) continue there until about the first of June next, while people Generally Get settled for a season's work, it is highly probable they may be Discharged.

It is but of little consequence to continue the troops here, as it does not secure the allegiance of the Insurgents at Tioga, (where they chiefly are and Going) but the Troops being there secures the whole. We should have advised to the measure of removing the Troops which are now here to Tioga, but the time of their Inlistment was so short we apprehended it wou^d have been attended with a bad consequence unless we were sure of a relief arriving Immediately upon the Expiration of their Inlistment.

This County from the Nescopeck to the north line of the State is about 120 miles, and only six magistrates within it, we should suppose an additional number wou^d be Necessary, and could Messrs. Buck & Hurlbutt be Commissioned on their former appointment it might answer a Good purpose,[2] as there is some complaints among the militia officers who have not received their Commissions, that the Councill have received some unfavourable Information against them.[3] Wou^d it not be adviseable to Order a board of Enquiry, that the aggreaved party may Exonerate themselves by Testimony, and by that means the Councill may be Informed of facts, and capable of Doing Justice to the parties. We are, Sir, your most Obedient, Humbl. Servts',

Oba^d Gore,

M. Hollenbach.

[193] Zebulon Butler to Nathan Denison.[1]

Wilksbarre Decemb^r 22 1787

S^r

In conformity to my request, you have sent me the allegations, on which Council have founded their censure.[2] I thank

[2] Council gave consideration to increasing the number of justices of the peace on January 7, 1788; *Pa. C. R.,* XV, 366.

[3] *Cf.* no. 168, *ante.*

[193] [1] P. H. M. C., Div. of Arch. and MSS., Record Group 27, Series: Exec. Corr., 1777-90, in an unknown hand but signed by Butler.

[2] Butler had written on November 12 to ask whether he was under censure for his conduct on the evening when John Franklin was arrested; no. 174, *ante.* Denison's reply to Butler has not been found.

you for the information, and cannot, but at the same time remark to you, my astonishment at the misrepresentations which have been made to Council. To whom, I am indebted for this ungratful and malicious attack upon my reputation, I know not; but were I to hazzard a conjecture I should say it is some insideous Wretch living not far from the place of my abode. Carried away by an ill temper'd Zeal, and ever wishing to raise his own character by injuring those of others; without provocation or cause—but merely to gratify the wickedness of his heart and to accomplish his sordid purposes has for this once, made my character the ground of such an ungenerous experiment. But unnecessary is it to comment longer in this manner. It only remains then, for me to relate naked facts, and show the reasons on which, my late conduct was founded, and leave the construction to yours and the rest of the honourable Counsellors deliberate judgement.

The first allegation against me, it seems is, being often disguised with liquor and particularly on the evening after John Franklin was taken. This charge I solemnly and expressly deny and for the support of my observation I appeal to my Neighbours.

The next is, on the same evening, I was applied to, by a party in favour of goverment for powder, whome I denied but gave on the same evening to those against goverment.

The former part of this allegation is true, but the latter, is a most palpable falshood. A fact is it, that one Wᵐ Smith, a son of Wᵐ H. Smith applied to me for powder but I knowing him to have been an Intimate of Swifts party formerly, and he also showing me no written instructions from the Officer of the guard authorising such an application, I thought it not prudent to deliver him powder or even to let him know that I had any in my cottage. About eight pounds I had which was sent me by the Susquehannah Company three or four years since, but I supposed no Man (myself excepted) on the ground knew any thing of it. However, after my deniel to Smith, I immediately returned home with a determination to send, in a private manner, the powder to Capt Gore who commanded the Party in favour of goverment but before I could accomplish this, the Insurgents appeared and put it entirely out of my power.

As to my delivering powder to the Insurgents, that evening I solemnly avow I did not. They made no applications to me and the whole evening I spent in soothing their turbulent and rebellious passions. To accomplish this and effect the security

313

of Col° Pickerings family engrossed my whole attention that night. The next day the Insurgents, being still tumultuous & informed that I had powder belonging to the Company came under Arms, accompanied by one Starkweather,[3] from whom if from any body, they must have learned their information, and demanded the powder. I gave them no direct answer. Upon this Starkweather who had been a Boarder in my house and lodged near where the powder lay unbeknown to me had discovered it, led the armed Men to the Chamber, took the powder and soon after which, despersed and went to their several homes.

Thus Sir were matters circumstanced and if the truth of them be admitted, as I flatter myself it will be, Council upon a candid examination will not, I presume think me so culpable as has been represented. It is a matter of no small dissatisfaction to a Man of feelings, to be counted unworthy to wear by those who gave it, his commission. At different Periods of my life I have been honoured with offices of no small distinction and in no one instance has my conduct been stigmatized with unworthiness and infidelity like the late which moves my guil in vindication. If I have erred, the inability of acting with true policy on such an occasion must plead my pardon. My whole conduct proceeded from as pure moti[ves] of attachment to goverment as ever found place in the heart of Man. From the moment I laid myself under the solemnity of an Oath to be a faithful and loyal subject of Pennsylvania; to this day, I defy the Man to give to the impartial World the least proof of my disaffection to goverment. From observation and experience, finding it to be one of the impossibilities in Nature to live in security without law and regularity, I chearfully embrace the protection of this Commonwealth, with the fullest assurance of sharing every advantage, warranted by her Customs, Laws and Constitution. As far as was in my power I have endeavoured to establish order and tranquility in this County, and if now my greatest exertions and surest intentions must terminate in the destruction of my reputation through the instrumentality of malignant Callumniation I must only say that I am a very unfortunate Man. At the close of the War, I returned to the humble walks of private life, with a resolution to devote the remainder of my days in retreiving an Interest much expended and wasted by seven years absence. In the commencement of this I resolved never more to accept an office either military or civil: but to serve my Country by an aggricultural pursuit was my only intention and wish. How-

---

[3] Asa Starkwather, who had served as secretary to the local committee of the Susquehannah Company; no. 68, *ante.*

ever, when I saw that the State were about to do justice to the People on this ground I was willing to sacrifice a former resolution and accept an office that by the exercise of which, I might in all probability contribute something to the establishment of peace and Law in this County. But it seems by the information which Council has receiv'd, that I have fell far short of doing this in their opinion. If the statement then of my conduct in this letter relative to that nights transactions should be found insufficient to exculpate me, my only wish is that I may be brought to the bar of trial and have an hour to prove to the satisfaction of Council, the truth of what I have now asserted. I have the Honour to be your most Obedient & humble Servt

Zeb^n Butler

[194] Extract from the Minutes of the Pennsylvania Council.[1]

Information being given to Council that proper and legal notice was not given in the late choice of officers for the upper battalion of militia, in the county of Luzerne;[2] therefore,

Ordered, That the late election for officers in the said battalion be and hereby is set aside and made void, and the Lieutenant of the said county is hereby directed to hold another election, according to law.

A letter was written to Colonel Pickering,[3] in answer to the several letters of intelligence received from Luzerne county, in which was enclosed the foregoing order of Council.

[195] Reuben Herinton and Others to Timothy Pickering.[1]

Tioga Luzerne December 1787

Sir

How to exculpate ourselves from the scandalous imputation of being considered as enemies to the Commonwealth of Pennsylvania is a task we dare hardly attempt. We confess our conduct of late evinces us to be such, but, when the Honourable Legislature and the World are assured that we were compelled

---

[194] [1] *Pa. C. R.,* XV, 362, dated December 31, 1787.
[2] *Cf.* no. 190, *ante.*   [3] Not found, but see no. 237, *post.*
[195] [1] M. H. S., Pickering Papers, LVII, 343, signed by the six men.

or deluded, we presume to think, they will not blame us; and, as we have reason to think the Legislature is exasperated against us, We take the liberty to convey to you the motives which led us to subscribe our names to a Combination we either did not understand, read it, nor heard it read, and some of us were assured it was an Instrument to be sent to the Assembly praying a confirmation of our lands.[2] Sir, your Humanity and friendship for mankind in general & for the Citizens of this County in particular, in which we hope you mean to reside, induces us to take the liberty of conveying to that Honourable body thro' you, our dislike to everything that may bear the appearance of opposition to the free Operation of Law and good order. We shall not trouble you with the Artfull arguments made use of to alieniate our minds from the Government of Pennsylvania and to induce us to Sign the aforesaid Combination. When Arguments failed and a reluctance shewn [i]n arguments made use of against it we were ordered out of the Settlement, immediately: and having nothing to support our Families on, but the Crops we had then on the ground, were, for our own safety, & principals of self preservation compelled to sign it.

We do assure you S[r] we mean to do everything in our power to support the civil Authority under Pennsylvania & use the utmost of our power to root out from amongst us all disorderly persons, & those who flee from other countries to this place to escape Justice. We are sir your most Obedient Servants

> Reuben Herinton [3]
> Jacob Herinton
> Solomon Benit
> Nicholas Depue
> Christian Kress
> Jacob Kress

[196] *A Few Facts That Cannot Be Controverted.*[1]

1st. That when the citizens of Pennsylvania settled at Wyoming, they had the orders of government for so doing; they built their

[2] No. 135, *ante.*

[3] Reuben Herinton's name does not appear on Pickering's attested copy of the Combination.

[196] [1] *The Pennsylvania Packet,* February 9, 1788. Apparently this piece circulated as a handbill; see no. 198, *post.* It probably appeared in early January, 1788.

houses, enclosed their fields, and had not even an idea that intruders would come to disturb them.

2d. That when the first party (composed of stragglers from many states) arrived at Wyoming, they found the people of Pennsylvania in full and quiet possession of the lands there, and attempted nothing hostile, but solemnly promised to return to their own country in peace.[2]

3d. That their next attempt was to possess themselves of a tract of land at Lahawanack, ten miles above Wyoming, for which they were apprehended, and conducted to Easton goal.[3] (See the records of Northampton county.[ )]

4th. That their third attempt to possess themselves at Wyoming was equally abortive; for, although their numbers exceeded four hundred, they were apprehended by the sheriff of Northampton county, at the head of his posse, and their leaders lodged in Philadelphia and Easton goals, where they continued until the lenity of Governor Penn released them from prison, on their most solemn engagements, not further to disturb the peace of the state.[4]

5th. That their fourth attempt was equally futile, for although they again took possession at Wyoming and drove off great numbers of the Pennsylvania settlers, the appearance of the sheriff and his posse obliged them to submit to the laws, and the prisons of Philadelphia and Easton were once more filled with their leaders [5] (the agreement then entered into between their committee and the agents acting under Governor Penn, is lodged in the secretary's office.)

6th. Their next attempt was of a different kind. Stratagem became needful; and to avoid the charge of a breach of oaths &c.

---

[2] The first men to go to Wyoming in behalf of the Susquehannah Company were armed men from Connecticut, who arrived in the summer of 1762. The first attempted settlements came in the summer of 1763 and were destroyed by the Indian uprising of that year; Vol. II, Introduction, *passim.*

[3] These events occurred in the spring of 1769, but despite the arrests, settlements were made in the summer of 1769; Vol. III, Introduction, pp. xxvi-xxviii.

[4] Sheriff Jennings made his arrests in November, 1769; *ibid.,* p. xxix.

[5] The arrest of the Connecticut settlers occurred in September, 1770; Vol. IV, Introduction, p. xiv.

on those persons so lately discharged from goal, the unfortunate though enterprizing Lazarus Stewart was induced by promise of a township, to surprize and dispossess the settlers at Wyoming, which he effected, but soon after he and his adherents were obliged to fly from Wyoming to Connecticut for the murder of Capt. Ogden, plundering the inhabitants of their property, and other attrocious crimes.[6]

The decree of Trenton having established the title of Pennsylvania, the settlers under this state expected to be restored to their possessions, but the very reverse happened, and their lands, by the law of the 28th of March last,[7] are granted to those persons who by force and violence dispossessed them. They are told that they may have an equivalent in lands or in certificates, but does either the one or the other deserve the name of an adequate compensation? Surely they do not. They have submitted to give up their property and claims to the state on the most reasonable terms for money, agreeable to the valuation of impartial and disinterested men; but this has not been granted. They now look up to the dignity and justice of the legislature, either to grant them the above compensation, or to repeal the law of the 28th of March last, and likewise the law erecting the county of Luzerne;[8] thereby restoring to Northampton county its former extent and jurisdiction, that law and justice may again reach that part of the state now called Luzerne, and relief be afforded to the distressed citizens of Pennsylvania now suffering under the operations of the aforesaid acts. By this act of general justice the state will be exonerated from the charge of wantonly sacrificing the interest of good citizens to gratify a band of plunderers and murderers.

If any speculator in new lands does not fully understand this address, he may have it explained by

A REAL SUFFERER.

----

[6] The attack was led by Lazarus Stewart in December, 1770. Ogden was murdered in January, 1771; *ibid.* The Connecticut claimants, gaining renewed possession of Wyoming in 1771, retained control all during the Revolution.

[7] No. 38, *ante.*

[8] During 1787-88, while numerous petitions went to the General Assembly asking for repeal or suspension of the Confirming Act or asking for a change in the system of compensating Pennsylvania claimants, only one petition in this period called for the repeal of the law establishing Luzerne County—that read on March 8, 1788, from John Van Campen and others. Their plea may offer a clue to the authorship of this handbill.

[197] Richard Peters to Timothy Pickering.[1]

Belmont Jany 27. 1788

My dear Sir

I recieved your Letter [2] & was very happy to hear you were well & unmolested. I have not the same Opinion of your Security you seem to have & beseech you not to trust too far to it. You are I confess a better Judge of Circumstances than I am but consider you have been decieved. It is natural for you to wish your Children about you; [3] but I am sure Tim is better here under my Ideas of Matters than he would be at Wioming. I dont know however whether I should have taken the Liberty of acting against your Desires had the Weather been more favourable & Tim been perfectly well. But he is now mending fast having had a bad Cold which would be increased by such a Journey. I have thought it best to detain him here where he is very happy & really wishes to stay. He goes constantly to School & I think improves. I have done under all Circumstances what in the same Situation I should have wished to be done by me & this is a Rule I hope you will not blame me for tho' it may not meet entirely your Wishes.

M*rs*. Peters begs her affectionate & sincere good wishes to be presented M*rs* Pickering & yourself. I hope to see you at the Meeting of the Assembly & that you will have a better Opinion of our Majority than their late Proceedings have entitled them to.[4] Many of them I am sure mean well but are either bewildered or misled. I hope some Plan of Compromise will be fallen upon & it will accelerate it much to bring with you the Means of clearing up many Prejudices which seem strangely to operate with them. There is no Man less interested than I am & I believe I think dispassionately about it. I have turned the Subject over since I have had Leisure & really am more confirmed in the Opinions I had on the sudden adopted when the Matter was

---

[197] [1] M. H. S., Pickering Papers, XIX, 119-20, in Peters' hand.

[2] Not found.

[3] Pickering had written Samuel Hodgdon twice about his desire to have his children return to Wyoming; Pickering Papers, XXV, 33 and 35-38.

[4] A reference to the many votes taken on the Confirming Act in the recent session of the General Assembly; see nos. 182, 186, and 188, *ante*.

agitated in the House.[5] I wish you every Happiness I am very affectionately yours

Richard Peters

[198] Article by *A Citizen of Northampton County*.[1]

To the Printers of the Pennsylvania Packet,
Messrs. Printers,

A few days ago I met with a handbill published in Philadelphia, entitled, "A few Facts that cannot be Controverted," [2] signed by "A Real Sufferer," on the subject of the Wyoming business, which has attracted so much of the public attention. I am also a sufferer by the late unconstitutional acts of our legislators; [3] and can, from my own personal knowledge, vouch for the truth of every one of the facts represented in the said publication. I beg leave, thro' the medium of your paper, to communicate to the public and to people in power, one other fact equally incontrovertible, & which will evince to demonstration the very great influence of a law which confers the property of the citizens of Pennsylvania to strangers.

My deceased father was born in this state, (then a province) and in his life time borrowed a considerable sum of money, which he laid out in the purchase of a valuable tract of land at Wyoming, fondly hoping that it would prove a competent provision for his children. For the payment of this sum he mortgaged the plantation I now live on, which has descended to me saddled with this encumbrance. Not in the least dubious of my father's title to the purchase at Wyoming, or of the right of the late proprietaries, from whom he purchased, I have in conjunction with others in the same predicament, at the expence of much time & money, endeavoured to maintain a property acquired under the faith of government, and in the spirit of the intention and express orders of the then legislators, have spared no pains, either as a magistrate or a private individual, to oppose the Connecticut intrusion. I have been mortified to find that all this expence of time and money, this perseverance in duty has been in vain, but

---

[5] See the motion made by Peters on November 24; no. 186, *ante.* He also seconded a motion on November 29; no. 188, *ante.*
[198] [1] *The Pennsylvania Packet,* February 9, 1788.
[2] No. 196, *ante.*   [3] A reference to the Confirming Act; no. 38, *ante.*

320

I have been more accutely injured by having my inheritance wrested from me without the constitutional judgment of my peers, and even without a hearing. To make the measure of my misfortunes complete, the money which my father borrowed is not yet paid, and will the lender accept the paltry compensation which is offered me by the state for the land which is torn from me, in discharge of my father's mortgage? He assuredly will not and the only remnant of my paternal estate must be sold to produce the means of payment. Let me here ask what have been my father's crimes or my own, that I am thus treated like a step child in the land of my nativity. I have been educated myself, and have brought up my children in sentiments of veneration for the laws and inviolable attachment to their country. The blood of my family has been more than once spilled in her service; and we have taken pride in these proofs that we were not undeserving of the name of citizens. But will not injustice so great produce a revolution of sentiment? Will not veneration be converted into abhorrence, and attachment into resentment and revenge? For my own part, the expectations of my old age are blasted, and will sink with sorrow to the grave. But I shall leave behind me a numerous list of descendants, who when they find themselves robbed of their patrimony, and reduced to poverty when they looked for competence, will curse the head that devised and the heart that consented to their ruin.

But one word more—it may be depended upon that this picture is not the offspring of fancy; but the simple and true narration of the humiliating situation of

A Citizen of Northampton County

Jan. 27, 1788.

[199] Petition of John Franklin to the Pennsylvania Council.[1]

His Excellency the President, The Honble Supreme Executive Council of the Common Wealth of Pennsylvania

The Address, and Petition of John Franklin of the County of Luzerne, and State of Pennsylvania, now a State Prisoner in the Goal at Philadelphia most respectfully sheweth

That on the 2d Day of October 1787 he was taken Prisoner at Luzerne afores.^d by Capt Craig and others, by Virtue of a

[199] [1] Lackawanna Hist. Soc., Wilcox MSS., in Franklin's hand.

Prosecution Instituted for Misprison of Treason by the Honble chief Justice of this State. That on the 6th day of Oct afors^d he was brought before the Honble Justices of the Supreme Court, then sitting in this City, to assign Reasons why he should not be committed to take his tryal for that offence at which time new complaints were exhibited against him, founded on certain Depositions stating that since, and in consequence of his Imprisonment, a Party at Luzerne Afos^d (of whom he was said to be the leader) had proceeded to Acts of Rebellion, seized a family as hostages, and other Misdemeanours done, whereupon a Warrant was made out against him for high Treason, and he accordingly committed to take his tryal for the offence. That since which time he has been loaded with heavy Irons (a few days excepted) and closely confined to a single Room in one of the Wings of the Goal where he has been near four months, and is still languishing under his lonesome Confinement, in an Inclement season, being Destitute of Money, and Remote from his friends, he is entirely Dependent on the Liberal Donations of Government, and Charitable Disposition of a single acquaintance in this City for his daily support, that the longer he is confined the more unable he shall be to make Restitution therefor.

Your Petitioner begs leave to observe that the hostile Acts since and in Consequence of his Imprisonment, the Capture of a family as hostages &c. were not only Committed without his Consent or knowledge, But (by Information) were not so aggravating as Represented at the time of his Commitment. However he submits that to your Hon^{rs} who have the knowledge of the facts.

He farther begs leave to State to your Honble Body that however he may have been mistaken in any of those matters laid to his charge, and hereafter to be determined, yet he trusts to Prove himself Innocent, though open to Conviction if found guilty on a tryal by the Laws of this State, and the Judgment of his Peers; to which he submits, yet he feels himself happy (that he is able to maintain) that during the late War, he cheerfully, and voluntarily took an active part in his Country's cause, expended both Blood and Treasure in defence of the United States in general and the frontier Settlements in Particular, that as an officer, Soldier and Citizen, he endeavoured to render himself faithful and serviceable, according to his abilities, and to the trust repos'd in him, and Freely Cast in his Mite towards Purchasing that *Freedom, Liberty,* and *Independance* which the United States now Enjoy.

That a Close Confinement in Chains (as before represented) renders his Life unhappy, Destroys his health, Deprives him of that Liberty that every man that is free born wishes to enjoy, Renders him unable to make that Preparation that is Necessary for him to make his defence, and Disables him, not only from making any provision for his own support, but from Contributing any thing towards the support of his family (Consisting of three Children) who During his Confinement must Consequently Depend on the Clemency of his Aged and Hon^d Father for their subsistance.

Your Petitioner Therefore Relying on the Lenity of Government, Prays your Excellency and Honble body to take his Case afores^d under your Wise Consideration, and grant (if the Nature of his Cause will Permit) that he may be admitted to Bail, under such Assurances as you shall Judge Right and Requisite or in such other way grant him Relief as you shall Judge Just and Equitable. And he as in Duty bound will ever pray

Philadelphia Goal   John Franklin
Jany 31st 1788.

Endorsed: Postponed to Tuesday next.[2]

[200] Extract from the Minutes of the Pennsylvania Council.[1]

The memorial of John Franklin being read,[2]

Resolved, That the Honorable Frederick Watt and Nathan Dennison, Esquires, be a committee to inquire into the truth of the facts stated in the memorial aforesaid, and report to Council.

The committee report to Council that they have visited John Franklin, in the jail of this city, and find that his health is greatly impaired, and that unless his irons are taken off he may greatly suffer; Council having attended to the above report, and regarding as far as lies in their power the favorable interposition of his Excellency Governor Huntington,[3] are well disposed to mitigate the severity of the said Franklin's confinement.

Resolved, That the Sheriff be directed to have the irons taken off the said Franklin, and otherwise mitigate the severity of his

---

[2] For the action of the Council on this petition, see no. 200, *post.*
[200] [1] *Pa. C. R.,* XV, 385, February 8, 1788.   [2] No. 199, *ante.*
[3] Huntington had written to get the severity of Franklin's treatment mitigated; *P. A.,* XI, 238-39.

confinement as much as the Sheriff shall think consistant with the safe keeping of the prisoner.

[201] Peter Muhlenberg to Samuel Huntington.[1]

In Council, Philada., February 11th, 1788.
Sir,

His Excellency, Doctor Franklin, president of this State, being indisposed, Council have directed me to acknowledge the receipt of your Excellency's favor relative to John Franklin, a State prisoner now confined in the Jail of this City.[2] Your Excellency will perceive by the enclosed Resolution[3] That the Supreme Executive Council of this State, in compliance with your Excellency's friendly interposition, have mitigated the severity of Franklin's confinement as much as lay in their power, but as his admittance to Bail depends on an act of the Legislature, and the General Assembly are not conven'd at present, Council will probably recommend his case to the next House;[4] provided the Inhabitants of Wyoming continue their present peaceable disposition. I have the Honor to be, With great Respect, Your Excellency's most obedient servant,

P. Muhlenberg, V. P.

[202] Petition of Cornelius and Jacob Van Horne.[1]

To the Honourable the Representatives of the freemen of the Common Wealth of the State of Pensylvania Assembled

---

[201] [1] *P. A.*, XI, 238-39. [2] Huntington's letter has not been found.

[3] Huntington was sent a copy of the Council's resolution of February 8; no. 200, *ante*.

[4] The Council included the treatment of Franklin among a number of matters communicated to the Assembly on February 21; *Pa. C. R.*, XV, 393-94. On February 23, Franklin petitioned the Assembly to be released on bail. Although a committee recommended favorable action on his petition, the recommendation was rejected; *Minutes of the Second Session of the Twelfth General Assembly*, 104 and 110 (microfilm copy).

[202] [1] P. H. M. C., Div. of Arch. and MSS., John Franklin Papers, a copy in an unknown hand.

324

Wee Your Petitioners beg leave as we think it our Duty to inform Your Honours, that wee are possess'd of a right, to two Lotts of Land granted to us which is all the Legacy and Dependance left us in Land by the Last Will of our Deceased Parent, who shortly after Penns Purchaseing the Northren Lands of this State of the Indian Nations he Contracted with the Honourable proprietor Governor Penns Agents to whome he paid his money & had two Pattons granted to him for the Two sd Lotts of Land, he Imediately sent planters thither & furnished them with Provision, Team, & Utentials for Farming. They Built a House & Dwelt in it untill they Planted Corn & rais'd a Crop of Wheat the Latter they Harvisted, they then being over power'd by numbers of the Connecticut party, who slew and made Beefe of our Oxen, drove the s^{d} setlers out of their Habitation & sent them away empty. Our Parent still being confident his title for the Land was best & that in a short time right would take place when he or his posterity might injoy the same in peace, in trust & confidence of which, he thirteen Years past last May dispos'd of Land in Jersey state to the Value of Seven Hundred pounds in Gold or Silver Coin; our Parent three Months after departed this Life the payments of the s^{d} money being detained untill made in Continantle Currency at a Very low rate, and at length sunck to no Value; we then haveing no other hope from our Parent for a livelyhood then the two Lotts of Land and after the Decree past at Trenton as Ordered by Congress between Connecticut & Pensylvania wee moved thither & setled on our two Lotts of Land as we thought in peace made some improvement thereon as Building & raising grain. The Connecticut people being disturbed and giting Angry with us, for Claiming the Land which they pretended they had a right unto, they took of our property as suited them and by the Friendly Countenance shewn them by the Indulgent Legislature of Pensylvania, we where by real necessity Obliged to Quit our Houses & Land, much to our Damage of both time & property these Damages with much more too tedious here to mention is what we have suffered, in trusting & Depending on our title to this Land at Wyoming being sure. These Assertions are the real truith and if scrupled there are numbers of liveing Witnesses by which we can prove the same to satisfaction.

To these things we beg your Honours will plese to here, & when you have concidered, we trust with all Assurance, (that you who are the trustees and guardians of the state in geniral will

325

not sacrifice the property of any Individual of the state to the Peace & good of the same without granting an Inediate & full Compensation to the party or Parties Ingured.

And as your Honours are now mett agreeable to your proposition the last Session,[2] Wee do therefore hertily Pray you to make a final Desition, in regard of granting the Wyoming Lands to the Connecticut Claimants, or repeal all Acts made in relation thereto, that the former Laws of the State may descide between man & man.

And if it be your Honours pleasure to make a Sacrifice of our Land for the profit & peace of the State, wee do heartily agree thereto, with your making us a just Compensation, strict justice is all wee ask. In granting the same we prey Your Honours will appoint one Man on the part of the State, and wee the Pensylvania Land Claimants may have choice of a second, the two Men to appoint a third, the s^d three Men so appointed shall after vewing our Lotts of Land judge the real Value thereof and give a Certificate of the same from under there hands, which laid before the Board of Property, who may judge of our Title to the same, and grant us such Compensation as your Honours may appoint.[3] And as to the Value of our Land, & the payment sure, we wish it to Valued Equal to Gold & Silver and the Faith of the State Pledg'd in payment thereof, and bearing Annual Interest, from thet time our Land was dispos'd of untill paid. And as Your Honours propos'd the last Session, to grant the suffering Land Claiments other Vacant Lands in lew of those taken from them, wee wish to have it at our own Option to Chose either the Value paid in money, or Land, or a part of either, as we may know what will best suit our wants. As our Property is thus dispos'd of, wee are of corse reduced to want which craves an Imediate relief. for these, and what else Your Honours sees best for us, & the Honour of the State Wee Your Memorialists will every Pray

Cornelius V^{n}horn
Jacob Vanhorn

February 23rd 1788

Endorsed: Read 1 time Feby 25. 1788

---

[2] Probably a reference to the several proposed amendments to the Confirming Act which had not received final action in the first session; for example, see nos. 182 and 186, *ante*.

[3] The scheme proposed here parallels a committee recommendation made on November 14; *Minutes of the First Session of the Twelfth General Assembly*, 56-57 (microfilm copy).

[203] Minutes of a Meeting of the Pennsylvania Landholders.[1]

Wednesday, Feb'y 27th, 1788.

At a meeting of a number of Landholders, &c., James Moore appointed Chairman, The Committee appointed at last General meeting on Friday evening, the 22d Instant, made the following report, viz:

The Committee of the Landholders of Luzerne and Northampton in Pennsylvania, and of Montgomery County in Newyork, beg leave to report that they have confered with and made enquiries of several persons acquainted with the Country above mentioned, and find an uniform opinion prevailing among them, that the most useful road which can be laid out therein, must run from the place known by the name of Pocomo point along the ridge dividing the lesser waters of the Delaware from those of the Susquehanna, (or the Moosic mountain) up to Mount Ararat, & that upon a careful consideration of such facts as could be ascertained concerning the nature of that Country, they found very strong reasons for adopting the same opinion, wherefore they unanimously recommend to the Landholders to take immediate and effectual measures for laying out and opening a road as nearly in a direct line from Pocomo point to Mount Ararat as may be found practicable.

The Committee are also fully convinced that to secure all the attainable advantages of the measure now in contemplation, it will be necessary that the views of the Landholders should be extended to the opening of two forking roads from the road above mentioned, *the one* to the line of Newyork, at the carrying place between the river Delaware and the bend of Susquehanna, and *the other* towards the Mouth of Tioga Creek. The Committee found it impossible to ascertain with precision the expence of this undertaking, but they conceive the sum of Five hundred pounds will be sufficient to open a two-perch road from Pocomo point to Mount Ararat, on which may be formed a Judgment of the whole expence. For obtaining the Funds necessary to accomplish the opening of the several roads above described, your committee recommend that a subscription be immediately opened to be offered to all such persons in this State & in Newyork, as

---

[203] [1] *P. A.*, XI, 246-47.

are interested in the Lands above mentioned, as well as to all owners of water Estates, and of lots in the Northern and North-western parts of the City of Philadelphia and Liberties, whose property will be considerably advanced by the settlement of that Country. They also submit to the consideration of the Landholders, the propriety of an application to the Legislature for their aid in a matter that will so greatly promote the domestic & foreign Commerce, & the internal resources of the State.

In order to carry the above plan into execution, your Committee further recommend that persons be appointed to obtain subscriptions [2] to be paid into the hands of a treasurer, the appointment of whom they also recommend, & that a Committee of *seven* persons (of whom *five* to be a quorum,) be also appointed to make application to the Legislature and to lay out, in opening the roads above mentioned, such monies as the Legislature may be pleased to grant or which private persons may subscribe. After maturely considering the same, it was agreed to, and thereupon unanimously

Resolved, That the following Gentlemen be appointed a Committee for the purpose of applying to the Legislature for their aid,[3] and the other purposes expressed in the report, viz: John Nicholson, Henry Drinker, Tench Coxe, Mark Wilcox, Tench Francis, James Wilson and Reynold Keen.

Resolved, That Samuel Powell, be appointed Treasurer.

Resolved, That the following Gentlemen be appointed to receive subscriptions. (Not named.)

[2] See no. 204, *post.*

[3] Application to the General Assembly was made on March 7, and at the second reading of the landholders' petition on March 10, the matter was referred to a committee composed of Richard Peters, Peter Ealer, and William Findley. The committee's report, given first on March 14 and again on March 17, was accepted by the Assembly and a bill was ordered to be brought in. The committee's report read in part as follows: "That although the petitioners, who are interested in lands which will be benefited by these roads, have raised by voluntary contributions a considerable sum toward the expense of opening and clearing the intended roads, yet the cost will far exceed what ought reasonably to be expected from private exertion.

"That as the public are interested in the said proposed roads, and should from public motives encourage the population and commerce of the state, your committee are of opinion that a sum of money should be granted in aid of the private contributions of the petitioner." *Minutes of the Second Session of the Twelfth General Assembly,* 127, 132, 142, 146-47 (microfilm copy).

The roads bill was passed on March 28, the state furnishing £1000 towards the expense; Mitchell and Flanders, *Statutes at Large,* XIII, 48-50, Chapter MCCCXLII.

Resolved, That The Committee for applying to the Legislature, &c., be requested to have subscription papers printed, and distributed to the Gentlemen appointed to solicit and receive subscriptions, and perform all other matters for carrying the object of this meeting into effect, and that the Committee shall call a General Meeting of the Landholders as soon as circumstances may make it necessary. Adjourned.

Indorsed,
Report of the Landholders in the County of Luzerne. Commissioners appointed, April, 1788.

[204] Subscription List for Road for the Pennsylvania Landholders.[1]

(N. 6.)

WE, THE SUBSCRIBERS, being sensible of the great Benefits that will result to the City of Philadelphia, and the Commerce of Pennsylvania, and to the Owners of Lands in the Counties of Northampton and Luzerne, in Pennsylvania, and in the County of Montgomery, in New-York, from Roads leading from Pocomo-Point beyond the Windgap in Northampton County Northerly to Mount Ararat, and from thence to the Carrying-Place at the Line between Pennsylvania and New-York, and from the aforesaid Road to Mount Ararat, over to the River Susquehanna at or near the Mouth of Tioga River,[2] do agree to pay to the Order of John Nicholson, Henry Drinker, Tench Coxe, Mark Wilcox, Tench Francis, James Wilson and Reynold Keen, or any five of them, the Sum set against our respective Names, for the Purpose of laying out and opening the Roads above mentioned. Witness our Hands, in Philadelphia, this 28th February, 1788.

Copied from Number one

Coxe & Frazeir eleven Guineas	£19.	–5.	–
Tench Coxe eight Guineas	14.	–	–
Henry Drinker Twenty five Guineas	43.	15.	–
James Wilson Eleven Guineas	19.	5.	–

[204] [1] P. H. M. C., Div. of Arch. and MSS., Record Group 27, Series: Exec. Corr., 1777-90, the names being all in an unknown hand. The statement is printed, but the designation "N.6" is written.
[2] See the map drawn by Tench Coxe; facing p. 374.

John Nicholson Fifteen Guineas	26.	5.	–
Tench Francis Fifty Guineas	87.	10.	–
Sam¹ Meredith Fifteen Guineas	26.	5.	–
Sam¹ Powel Two Guineas	3.	10.	–
John Shields Six Guineas	10.	10.	–
Joseph Lowns One Guinea	1.	15.	–
Edward Evans Ten Guineas	17.	10.	–
Levi Hollingsworth One Guinea	1.	15.	–
Edward Milner One Guinea	1.	15.	–
Benjⁿ Rush One Guinea	1.	15.	–
James Hutchenson One Guinea	1.	15.	–
W Shippen jⁿ One Guinea	1.	15.	0
John L Coxe Two Guineas & an half	4.	7.	0
Coxe & Farman by Tench Coxe One Guinea	1.	15.	0
Mark Wilcoxe Three Guineas	5.	5.	

Copied from Number 3

Francis Johnson One Guinea	1.	15.	0
Caspar Singer Five Guineas	8.	15.	
Reuben Hains 2½ Guineas	4.	7.	6
Sam¹ Howell 2½ Guineas	4.	7.	6
John Wilson	0.	12.	0
Sam¹ Wallis 15 Guineas	26.	5.	
Wᵐ Craig 1 Guinea	1.	15.	
Isaac Wharton 2½ Guineas	4.	7.	6

[205] Observations by the Committee of the Pennsylvania Landholders.[1]

Observations by the committee of the land-holders on the utility and importance of the roads proposed to be laid open in Northampton and Luzerne.

It is of consequence to the public, as well as the land-holders, that an adequate idea should be formed of the importance of having roads laid out and opened in the counties of Northampton and Luzerne, between the rivers Delaware and Susquehanna.

If the expence to the public be an objection, we are fortunate in having thought of an adequate means of obviating it. Let us suppose seven hundred and fifty pounds to be granted in aid of

[205] [1] *P. A.*, 2nd ser., XVIII, 672-75. A broadside version of this document printed by Joseph James is among the Tench Coxe Papers in the H. S. P.

the plan. Sixty tracts of four hundred acres each, at the rate of the old purchase, being ten pounds certificate per hundred acres, and five pounds per tract for warrants and patents, will produce a greater sum, besides the benefit of sinking one thousand nine hundred and twenty pounds more in certificates. For example,

	Certificates.	Specie.
60 tracts of 400 acres, at 40 per tract is	£2400	
Certificates being about 4s. per 20s. deduct } 4-5 ths to make it specie, which will be sunk }	1920	
		£480
60 warrants at 31s. and 60 patents at 60s.		300
Whence it appears there will be sunk in specie,		£780

Now if we consider the quantity of vacant lands which lie in the intervals of Northampton and Luzerne, there can be little doubt but that sales in consequence of such capital and extensive roads going thro' the centre of so great a country, will take place, to the amount of sixty tracts, or twenty-four thousand acres. But when we recollect that it is part of the plan to extend the road over to Tioga Point, which will lead the population and purchases into the district of William M'Clay, Esquire, being No. 1 in the new purchase,[2] where the lands will probably be from thirty pounds per hundred acres, down to twenty or fifteen pounds, we cannot have the least doubt that the state will be immediately refunded all its advances, and sink a handsome part of its debt in certificates besides.

A second object of great importance at this moment is the effect this measure will have in quieting any remaining dispositions to disorder in the county of Luzerne. A new[3] easy road will be opened from the thick-settled and well-affected counties of Philadelphia, Montgomery, Bucks, &c. and from the lower parts of Northampton county to Tioga, by which a force, if necessary, may be rapidly moved to that place. Disturbances will be rendered much more improbable and less dangerous from the constant progress of settlement under Pennsylvania titles in the parts of Northampton and Luzerne, which lie on and near the courses of the proposed roads. This consideration, it is conceived, is of great consequence.

These roads will necessarily be about one hundred and fifty

---

[2] The purchase from the Indians made in 1784.
[3] The broadside has "fine" for "new."

miles in extent; and the country through which they are to be laid out is above seventy miles in length, north and south, and about sixty miles wide on a medium, and consequently contains four thousand two hundred square miles, or about two millions eight hundred thousand acres of land. How grand an object then does this appear to the manufactures, internal and foreign commerce, agriculture and general resources and powers of the state.

If we extend the idea further, as we justly may, to the numerous tracts of land belonging to New York, which lie on the Delaware, Susquehanna, and Tioga Rivers, from the first to the hundredth milestone, we shall see the importance of this plan in a yet stronger light. We shall at once perceive that a very large part of the state of New York will be rendered, as to all purposes of commerce, a part of Pennsylvania by these roads, and by the improvements of the navigation of the Delaware and Susquehanna, which the settlement of this country will enable and induce the owners to effect.

A great part of New York, New Jersey and Massachusetts, and nearly the whole of Connecticut and Rhode Island, lie due east of the Lands thro' which these roads are proposed to pass; so that all the emigrants from those parts, now known to be too full of inhabitants, will be induced by good roads to take this country in their way westward, which will give Pennsylvania a great opportunity of acquiring settlers, citizens, and taxables. It is conceived that time should not be lost, for by getting the start of a season we may turn the tide of emigration into this channel.

From the habits of our own countrymen, meat has become an indispensible article to our laborers and hired hands. The settlement of the country under consideration appears therefore of great importance to the manufacturers of Pennsylvania, for it is well known to contain a great proportion of meadow and pasture lands, and of course that it is adapted to raising cattle. It is surely a matter much to be desired that the farmers of New England may be induced to settle among us as citizens of Pennsylvania, and furnish us with this important article of domestic support and foreign commerce, which we have been used to obtain from other quarters, especially as we have several millions of acres suitable for breeding and raising cattle. At present we are tributary to foreign countries for barrelled beef, which is imported from Ireland by a voyage of three thousand miles.

A road to Tioga, whose waters nearly approach those of Lake Ontario, appears to be of great importance to our Indian trade.

332

Tho' it be very probable that the most eligible [route] [4] will be through the Sinnemahoning river, yet the chances of securing that trade will be encreased by opening this practicable route thro' the Genesee country to Lake Ontario. The channels of commerce as they offer, should be immediately secured whenever the expence is moderate.

The article of potash forms a part of the export of New York to the amount, it is said, of two hundred thousand dollars per annum. The woods of the country through which it is proposed these roads should be laid out are proper, for the manufactory of this article, and enough can be spared to make it in very great quantities.

The proceedings of the land-holders will not be deemed an improper subject of observation. For while their numerous and generous subscriptions will prove their conviction of the public and private advantages that will result from these roads, they show a liberal and equitable disposition not to withhold their money in a case wherein they acknowledge they will be benefited. It may not be improper to add that several private owners of New York lands have exerted themselves in promoting these roads, and that they are proportional contributors to the plan.

> John Nicholson,
> Tench Coxe,
> Mark Wilcox,
> Tench Francis,
> Henry Drinker [5]
> Committee.

Philadelphia, March 5, 1788.

[206] Extract from the Minutes of the Pennsylvania General Assembly.[1]

Agreeably to the order of the day, the House resumed the consideration of the bill, entituled *"A Supplement to an act, entituled* * * * [The Confirming Act]."

And in debating the ninth section of the said bill, together

---

[4] The word "route" is supplied from the broadside.

[5] The broadside lists the names of James Wilson and Reynold Keen but omits that of Henry Drinker. All were actually members of the committee; no. 203, *ante.*

[206] [1] *Minutes of the Second Session of the Twelfth General Assembly,* 125 (microfilm), dated March 5, 1788.

with the amendment moved by Mr. [Richard] *Peters* and **Mr.** [William] *Findley, November* 24th last,[2]

A motion was made by Mr. [George] *Clymer,* seconded by Mr. *Peters,*

To strike out the remainder of the said section, after the words, *"quality and value,"* and in lieu thereof to insert the following paragraph, *viz.*

"And whereas it has been the petition [3] of some of the *Pennsylvania Claimants,* that an optional equivalent be made to them in lands or money, which it is not in the present ability of the legislature to comply with, by reason of the low state of the public funds and of the great burthen of public debt, but which petition may lie over for the consideration of some future Assembly:

"Be it therefore enacted by the authority aforesaid, That any *Pennsylvania Claimant* as aforesaid, willing to accept his equivalent in lands, may signify the same to the board of property, which board thereupon are authorised and directed to allot such quantity of the public lands to the said claimant, as in their estimation shall be reasonably equivalent to the loss sustained by the said claimant, according to the valuation made; and the board of property shall order a warrant for the same to be issued by the proper officer; and the equivalent made shall be in the residuum of the donation lands, or in any other public lands either in the old or new purchase, not reserved for the use of the commonwealth." Whereupon,

Ordered, That the said section and amendment, together with the one proposed as a substitute, be referred to Mr. *Clymer,* Mr. [William] *Lewis,* Mr. *Peters,* Mr. [Gerardus] *Wynkoop,* Mr. [Samuel] *Evans,* Mr. [Alexander] *Lowrey,* Mr. G.[abriel] *Heister,* Mr. [Thomas] *Kennedy,* Mr. *Findley,* Mr. [John] *McDowell,* Mr. [James] *McLene,* Mr. [Robert] *Lollar* and Mr. [John Paul] *Schott,* to report thereon.

Ordered, That the further consideration of the said bill be postponed.

Adjourned until nine o'clock to-morrow, A. M.

---

[2] No. 186, *ante.*

[3] Petitions asking for alteration in the compensation provisions were read on November 12, 1787, and on March 5, 1788; *Minutes of the First Session,* p. 42 and *Minutes of the Second Session,* 124. See also no. 202, *ante.*

[207] Timothy Pickering to Peter Muhlenberg.[1]

Wilkesboro', March 10, 1788.

Dear Sir,

With much pleasure I inform you that last week we held the courts of quarter sessions & common pleas in perfect quiet. So much business had resulted to this from the two preceeding terms, in the pleas, that, joined with two or three criminal prosecutions in the sessions, the court was fully occupied from Tuesday till Saturday evening. Some of Franklin's quondam officers were on the grand & petit juries, & behaved unexceptionally well.[2] There is every appearance of a determination to admit the regular execution of the laws. I am, respectfully & affectionately, dear sir, your obed[t] serv[t],

T. Pickering.

[208] Samuel Hodgdon to Timothy Pickering.[1]

Philadelphia 15th March 1788

Dear Sir

This Morning M[r] Bowman handed me your Letter of the 10th instant.[2] I was happy to find you so comfortably reached home and found all well. Colonel Strowds draft has been presented and paid. I wish it was in my power to inform you that the Wioming business was agreeably settled but it yet remains much in the state you left it in. The Pennsylvania claimants have had Meetings, but cannot as yet agree upon any mode which will satisfactorily adjust their claims. Some were instructed to receive nothing but *Cash* for the Lands confirmed to the *rioters* and *vagabones* as they good naturedly call them. Other proposed Certificates bearing interest, but not Fundable, yet admissable at the Land Office; others declared nothing but the land would

---

[207] [1] *P. A.*, XI, 256.

[2] In a letter to Samuel Hodgdon of this same date, Pickering said that John Swift sat on the grand jury and Elisha Mathewson and William Slocum on the traverse jury; M. H. S., Pickering Papers, LVIII, 11.

[208] [1] M. H. S., Pickering Papers, LVIII, 13-16, in Hodgdon's hand.

[2] See no. 207, *ante*, note 2.

satisfy them. On the whole the Committee have reported that none of the Motions relative to the business appear eligable, and having offered none other in their place all remains as express'd in the inclosed Letter from Mr Clymer ³—strange policy surely. I have seen Mr Francis on the subject of your last address to him.⁴ He declines the purchase and calls for his Money, which by some means must be raised and which I am certain will embarrass me, as I have received nothing on any of our demands since you left me. Therefore at present cannot encourage you to expect the assistance you solicit so early as April or May. From present appearances I shall not be in Cash, unless procured from fortunate sale or outstanding debts, yet I will do what I can and advise you. Francis would purchase your land on the North East branch, (the whole of it) @ 2/ per acre, but the other he says is too far from home.⁵ I am however in treaty with another person for those lands, and shall be happy to inform you in my next that they are sold on the conditions tendered to the person who has the matter under consideration—but am fearful it will not succeed. The subscription for the New roads goes on rapidly.⁶ £600 is already subscribed and the Bill before the Assembly is so cordially received that we promise ourselves £1000 more from the state.⁷ This will effect all we have in view—Viz^t from the wind gap due North to Mount Arrarat, from thence forking to the Mouth of Tioga, and the North line of the state.⁸ I put you down for twelve Guineas. Wilsons Creditors gave Eighty guineas and all others in proportion. The politicks of the times you will learn from the inclosed prints. * * *

[209] George Clymer to Timothy Pickering.¹

Dear Sir

Col. Hodgson just calling me out, to let me know that would be an opportunity to write you this Morning on the Wioming business. I shall in 3 words tell you it is in the worst possible

---

³ No. 209, *post.*

⁴ Pickering's letter to Tench Francis has not been found.

⁵ That is, Francis was willing to purchase Pickering's lands in the Old Purchase in the area of the Great Bend, but not those in the New Purchase; see no. 226, *post.*

⁶ See no. 204, *ante.*   ⁷ See no. 203, *ante*, note 3.

⁸ See the map drawn by Tench Coxe, facing p. 374.

[209] ¹ M. H. S., Pickering Papers, XIX, 123, in Clymer's hand.

state. We have two parties in the house—one I detest, the other I despise. The Constitutionalists would rather stimulate than repress any thing that tended to insurgency and civil war, and so systematically refuse any measures likely to settle the peace of the Country.[2] The Republicans are bewildered about compensations, and not agreeing in the mode, fatally acquiesced in doing nothing.

I have been urging the necessity of seperating the confirming and compensating parts of the bill not necessaryly connected, as the only means of saving us from confusion but can get no second. I have no hope left. Your humb[l]

Geo Clymer.

Assembly room, March 15.

[210] Timothy Pickering to Samuel Hodgdon.[1]

Wilkesboro' March 16, 1788

Dear Sir,

* * * We had a rumour yesterday, that the Assembly had repealed the confirming law; I doubt the truth of the report, tho' I shall not be surprized at that event.[2] The people here continue to manifest a disposition to remain quiet. The day before yesterday I heard something entirely new; it came from a gentleman in the confidence of Franklin's principal adherents, to whom some of them at a meeting on the Monday after Franklin was taken, made the declaration. It was this—That they really

---

[2] Clymer is probably referring to the motions made by William Findley and James McLene, prominent Constitutionalists both. Findley's motions of November 22 and 24 angered many Connecticut claimants; nos. 182 and 186, *ante*. It was McLene who on November 29 had moved unsuccessfully that the activities of the commissioners be suspended; no. 188, *ante*. Five days after Clymer wrote, McLene's move to get the Confirming Act suspended was successful; no. 211, *post*.

In 1784 the Constitutionalists had berated the Republicans for their mishandling of the Wyoming dispute, alleging that they were unduly influenced by Pennsylvania land-jobbers. But Constitutionalists were not friendly to the Connecticut claimants' cause as such. In 1788 the Constitutionalists were a small minority in the Assembly; they probably used amendment to the Confirming Act as a weapon to embarrass the majority. See *Susquehannah Company Papers*, VIII, Introduction, and Brunhouse, *Counter-Revolution in Pennsylvania*, chap. VII.

[210] [1] M. H. S., Pickering Papers, LVIII, 16-17, in Pickering's hand.
[2] The Confirming Act was suspended on March 29; no. 220, *post*.

thought, upon the whole, that it was time to seize Franklin, to prevent the execution of his scheme, which would have brought destruction on the settlement. That they had told him of the fatal consequences to the settlement of the prosecution of his designs; but that he seemed invincibly bent on the execution of them; that his vanity & ambition were perpetually excited by the letters from Hudson;[3] and that every letter rec^d from thence, so pleased him, that he made a constant practice to ride about among his partizans to show it, of however trifling a nature. I wish government to be impressed with the importance of effectually securing that arch villain. His confinement is sufficient bail (& indeed the only certain security) for the good behaviour of *the most abandoned* of his followers. The inclosed letter to Genl Muhlenberg[4] is to suggest the necessity of vigilance to prevent Franklin making his escape. As his irons have been taken off, I see not how they can be put on again, without some fresh attempt to break jail: but the goaler may be required to inspect his apartment daily, to see whether any attempt is begun towards an escape. * * *

Endorsed: Rec^d & Ans^d 21st April.

[211] Extract from the Minutes of the Pennsylvania General Assembly.[1]

Agreeably to the order of the day, the House resumed the consideration of the bill, entituled *"Supplement to an act, entituled * * * [The Confirming Act]."*

It was then moved by Mr. [James] *McLene,* seconded by Mr. [John] *Piper,*

To postpone the further consideration of the said bill, in order to introduce another, which he read in his place.

A motion was then made by Mr. [George] *Clymer,* seconded by Mr. [Richard] *Peters,*

To postpone the said bill and motion of Mr. *McLene,* in order to introduce a bill,[2] which he requested leave to read in his place.

---

[3] That is, from Joseph Hamilton in Hudson, New York.
[4] Not found.
[211] [1] *Minutes of the Second Session of the Twelfth General Assembly,* 153-54 (microfilm copy), dated March 20, 1788.
[2] See no. 212, *post.*

And on the question, *"Will the House agree to the postponement moved by Mr.* Clymer *and Mr.* Peters?" the Yeas and Nays were called by Mr. [John Paul] *Schott* and Mr. [Thomas] *Kennedy,* and were as follow, viz. [3] * * * *

So it was determined in the negative.

The motion of Mr. *McLene* being again before the House, and he having obtained leave, presented to the chair the bill he had read in his place, entitled *"An Act to suspend an act, entituled* * * * [The Confirming Act],"* [4] which was read the first time; and on motion, and by special order, the same was read the second time, and debated by paragraphs.

Ordered, That it be transcribed, and in the mean time printed for public consideration.

Adjourned until nine o'clock on *Saturday* next, A. M.

[212] Debate on James McLene's Motion to Suspend the Confirming Act.[1]

Agreeably to the order of the day, the house resumed the consideration of the bill, entitled, a supplement to an act, entitled, an act for ascertaining and confirming to certain persons called Connecticut claimants, the lands by them claimed within the county of Luzerne, and for other purposes therein mentioned.

It was then moved by mr. [James] *M'Lene,* seconded by mr. [John] Piper, to postpone the further consideration of the said bill, in order to introduce another, which he had in his hand.

Mr. [George] *Clymer.* I am against the motion for postponement on this ground, that it is not for the legislature to interfere in the explanation of a law. I always consider it political and right to sacrifice a part to the whole, and it is justified on the principle of state-necessity: on this principle, the conduct of a late assembly was just and proper in giving up to the Connecticut claimants, the lands by them claimed, and to sacrifice the property of the Pennsylvania land-holder to the general welfare, but to whom common distributive justice requires that we make ample compensation: the Wyoming bill of 1786,[2] is a state necessity which existed, to effect a compromise, and all the in-

---

[3] The question was defeated by a vote of 42 to 24.   [4] No. 220, *post.*

[212] [1] *Proceedings and Debates of the General Assembly,* III, 175-91, March 20, 1788.

[2] This date should, of course, be 1787; no. 38, *ante.*

formation we receive from that country plainly evinces that the same necessity continues, yet the gentleman, by the bill which he has mentioned to you, endeavours by implication to repeal the law, which he would be ashamed to do by an avowed and public declaration; I do not think it honorable to get rid of the bill before us by this mode, and it can add little to the peace and happiness of that country; but if the house are determined to make the sacrafice, it will be of little avail to reiterate or call to their remembrance the solemn act by which our faith is plighted to those people; the suspension of the quieting act is the suspension of our public faith, and in my humble judgment sir, it will be attended with all the bad effects of an immediate and direct repeal. We have been much embarrassed sir, because we have attempted to combine two objects which are not necessarily combined, namely, that by which we confirm the rights of the Connecticut claimants to the lands by them claimed, together with what regards the compensation to be made to the Pennsylvania land-holder; if these two could be separated and form the basis of independent bills, there would be no necessity of taking such unwarrantable steps to rid ourselves of the one now before you. As I do not see they are indispensably mixed, I think they may and ought to be separated. Although necessity obliges us to confirm the rights of the Connecticut claimants, and compels us to make compensation, yet that necessity does not require us to do both immediately; the first part, to quiet the Connecticut claimants, is what I apprehend the house are perfectly unanimous in, the difficulties in the other are, that we cannot agree upon the mode of compensation, and when it shall be made, but because we cannot agree on the latter, it is no reason why we should not upon the former. In the *interim,* the original bill assures, that the compensation shall be made, and when or in what, we can at our leisure more deliberately determine; by this we shall preserve inviolate our faith on the one hand, and the peace and safety of the country on the other, and I think the Pennsylvania land-holder ought to be well satisfied at seeing the claims of the Connecticut people well secured to them, as their interest will eventually be served by that measure; for I see no reasonable hope that they can have either to obtain their property at all, or any kind of compensation, without the highest degree of inconvenience resulting to the state of Pennsylvania; moreover, if they have lands in that neighbourhood they will be unable to settle them unless the contest subsides, neither will their lands encrease in value without settlers. Upon the whole, I consider that the

Pennsylvanians may rest assured under the general words of the former act, that the state will make them a compensation adequate to their loss; in the mean time the lands in their neighbourhood would be improved and rise in value in consequence of the restoration of peace at Wyoming. It was under these impressions and ideas that I have drawn up a little bill as a substitute to the one before you, I will read it in my place, and leave this house to judge which is the best, as I think an act of the kind will both preserve our faith and give general satisfaction. Mr. Clymer now read the bill in his place, and it appeared to be grounded upon the principles he had mentioned: in one clause of which the commissioners were directed to make a return of the value of the estates that were claimed; upon this, mr. Findley asked whether the return of property was to be made before or after the rights were confirmed. Mr. Clymer thought they might do as they pleased, having full and complete powers under the former act, which were not intended to be altered.

Mr. [Richard] *Peters* understood mr. Clymer's motion to go to the postponement of the Wyoming bill, and the bill just offered by mr. M'Lene, in order to introduce that which he had just read in his place: If this was the true state of the question, he should second him with pleasure, nor did he believe that gentlemen could suppose he had changed his principles, which all along had been to do justice to both parties. The foundation of mr. M'Lene's motion he looked upon to be a direct and open violation of the public faith, nor was it the less so because the gentleman had given it the soft title of a suspending bill, a title that it did not merit. Its features were as harsh and as detestable as they were unwise and impolitic: I believe that gentlemen are desirous to do what is right, but their apprehensions are too much alarmed to be able to distinquish justly, and are afraid to support the old bill which seems to be given up on all hands, at least for the present session. They dread the consequences, and think if the Connecticut claims are confirmed, the expence will be so enormous that they will be unable to pay, but I cannot conceive how the house will ever ascertain their amount with any degree of accuracy, unless they suffer the commissioners to proceed in their business. Gentlemen complain that if they grant any thing at present, it will be granting in the dark; inferring from hence that they would agree to a reasonable and adequate compensation, if they knew what would be such: now if the whole operation of the law is suspended, how are they ever to acquire information? and if nothing can be done without it, another and

341

another session may pass as inactive as the present; everything being thus left in jeopardy, will give disgust to both parties, and all the good intention of the former act be defeated.

Mr. [Thomas] *Kennedy* was against postponing in order to introduce mr. Clymer's bill: he observed the gentleman laid great stress upon mr. M'Lene's bill being a breach of the public faith, which no doubt is in some degree sacred, and ought not to be varied from, where it can with justice and honor be kept. But it is essential to the nature of a promise that justice should be the foundation of it: a promise is imperfect unless both sides are justified in receiving or granting it. Now these New-England people who have come among us and disturbed the state have never done any thing that could be a foundation for granting them the land belonging to others, therefore if the state has promised them any thing, I don't think they are bound by that promise.

Something has been said with respect to the amount of what is intended to be given to the Connecticut people, but I think it very clear that the commissioners may be able to point out what that will be, without the power of confirming the claims; they can certainly make the enquiry without deciding, and the result may be sent up for this purpose.

Mr. [John Paul] *Schott.* The gentleman who was last up, I observe sir, says that we should send up commissioners into that country, in order to enquire what may be the probable expence of our keeping sacred our solemn engagements, and would have them totally destitute of power to confirm the claims of those people; now sir, it is my opinion that such a measure would answer no good purpose, but would rather tend to create a jealousy and suspicion in those persons who are now very well disposed to render essential services to the state, in establishing its laws and jurisdiction throughout the county of Luzerne: besides mr. speaker, I have known people in that country who presented their claims to the commissioners when they were up there last summer under the necessity of sending to the capital of Connecticut for the documents necessary under your law to establish their title. This being the case heretofore in many instances, we are justifiable in supposing that the like will occur in many more to come, and if the commissioners are sent up for mere parade, I am led to believe that these people will not be at the expence of sending so far for the materials necessary to support their claims, without which the design must prove abortive, for it will be found requisite to know how far every claim is well founded; for one man may claim property worth ten thousand pounds, but the question is whether he is really entitled to it, and perhaps upon investigation his claim may not be worth a single farthing. There were such instances sir, and a great many pretended claims were presented, but they could not support them agreeable to the rules of the Susquehannah company, which are made essential under the law to establish the point of right. There is also a great deal of land claimed that does not interfere with that taken up by any other person, and there are many demands made that it is not known whether they will come under the law or not, from which circumstance it will be impossible to ascertain with any degree of accuracy what will be necessary to make a full compensation; on these considerations sir, I should rather wish a new law could be passed to revive the old without alteration, for any measure that is not decisive will only bring on disputes, and prevent the country from being settled and cultivated, and as the faith of the state is pledged to grant them their well supported claims, a retraction on our part, or a neglect to reinstate them, may be productive of the worst consequences.

The question was now taken whether the bill which was the order of the day should be postponed, this being determined in the affirmative by a great majority.

Mr. *M'Lene* said he did not think it necessary to say much in stating the general principles of his bill: they were simply these, that all the power of the commissioners shall cease and determine until they are revived by some future house, and that all that had been done should remain suspended until that time.

The question was taken whether mr. M'Lene's bill should be read a second time, and there were for it 39—against it 27. whereupon it was read a second time.

Mr. *Clymer.* I wish the gentleman would satisfy us that any good is to arise from the bill he proposes, for though it is not a direct repeal of the former law, yet it amounts to the same thing, and it will immediately excite in those men a spirit of distrust and insurgency. It is objectionable also in another point of view: It says in the preamble that some doubts have arisen in the minds of the commissioners with respect to the grants intended to be made by the former act; this sir, is not founded in fact, for the commissioners at the bar of your house told you they had no such doubts, and reasons that are not well supported are always looked upon to be unjust; besides this management argues that this house may be governed by a principle of dis-

343

honesty; for if upon enquiry it should be found that the compensation will amount to any considerable sum, that then we do not mean to pay it, though our faith is already pledged both to the man from whom the land is taken and to whom it is given; this will not only tend to provoke the jealousy of those we mean to make our friends, but will tend to spirit up in their cause persons from every quarter, and they will have the best of pleas, namely, the breach of faith on the part of government; those people whose claims have been presented and adjusted will become your enemies, and will be ridiculed by those who have not submitted to your laws, which will make them more inveterate than if no attempt had been made to keep them quiet.

The general principles of the bill I wish to lay before you are two: first, to adjust and receive all the claims of the Connecticut people that have not yet been presented; and the second is, that when the commissioners have received and determined them, they shall lay before the house the amount, in order to enable them to take such measures as are just and politic to make compensation to those from whom the lands are taken: I submit to the house whether they will adopt the principles I lay down, or those that are advocated by the member from Franklin (mr. M'Lene.)

Mr. [William] *Lewis.* The public faith being once pledged mr. speaker, the gentlemen know it would be too disreputable that an open violation should take place; no member would come forward and offer a bill that should expressly have that object in view, but we are not to be amused by sounds and names whilst we ought to attend to the substance: If the bill shall in its nature and operation be a repealing law instead of a suspending one, we ought to decide against it in the same manner as we should if it avowed the intention. A repealing law is enacted for the purpose of anulling and destroying the operation of another law, and in this case the law destroys the other for ever, unless the repealing law should be repealed, in which case the former is revived. A suspending law has not this effect, but only prevents its operation for a limited time, after which its activity is restored: of which description is the bill before you? by its title it is a suspending law, but in its effect it is a repealing law, and it will require the interference of a future legislature to restore the quieting act to its operation; it ties up the hands of the commissioners, who can never proceed without another law. This petition is so plain that it requires but a moderate share of penetration to be fully convinced of its truth and validity. Let us

344

examine therefore into the consequences that will result from its adoption; will it tend to remove that confusion or obviate those difficulties to which we have long been exposed? I think it will not; it has appeared in evidence to this house, that a considerable part of the Connecticut settlers have exhibited their claims, and that the commissioners have gone forward in some instances to pass judgment on them; there are others who have not yet come forward conformably to the indulgence held out by the quieting act: the commissioners will be precluded from all power to receive those claims, or power to proceed in the decision of those already exhibited: they will not have power to examine the claim of even the Pennsylvania land-holder, nor to decide upon his right. A future legislature will therefore be as much in the dark as we are this moment on the amount of the compensation which it will be necessary to make, for how can this information be obtained? not by public rumour and news-paper publications; not by unsupported demands, but by commissioners vested with authority to receive, examine and decide upon them. Information is said to be the object of this law, but how can information be obtained: it will be impossible to know whether a claim is well or ill-founded. It is certainly a novel method to obtain information by taking away the means; it is like closing the shutter in order to let light into the room. It was mentioned by the honourable gentleman from Cumberland (mr. Kennedy) that commissioners should go so far as to hear the evidence without establishing or confirming the claim, but surely this is not the object of the bill, for nothing of the kind is mentioned in it, on the contrary, all the operations under the former law are totally done away; I observe also a reason assigned in the preamble of the bill that this measure is necessary, because the former law stands in need of explanation. Where in God's name is it to receive explanation? it is to receive explanation by the common rules of construction, by the laws of the land and the judges appointed under them. If this was not the case, every law would have to be explained by a subsequent one, and its operation be destroyed nine times out of ten, to satisfy one party or another: would not every man come forward and say, that I am entitled to either this or that, according to his own construction of the law, and call upon you to remove an ambiguity of expression, and by this *ex post facto* declaration, which is abhorrent to the constitution of our country, involve us in all the labyrinths and mazes of an eternal round of indecision. Let us examine whether there is a necessity of repealing the quieting act or not, for I insist upon it, that this bill if it is passed will have that effect. It is only in cases of the last necessity that the legislature have the right to sacrifice the property of individuals, but it is true the legislature are the only judges that can determine whether such necessity exists; in doing this they take into consideration the situations of the country, and examine whether so great a good will be acquired as to compensate fully for the injury. The house that passed the law which this bill is intended to repeal did this, and found that the finances of their country were exhausted, and themselves on the eve of a civil war: they found persons claiming the lands under Connecticut, and persons claiming the same under Pennsylvania; neither would recede from their demand: they were unable to raise an army to support the latter, or to march one into that country, and they knew that unless the others were reduced by force of arms the dispute could not be terminated; they knew the state possessed a brave and gallant militia, who had often bravely faced and driven from their coasts an invading enemy, but in a case of this kind they knew they would not be led on to the attack by the same motives: they considered the Connecticut people intrenched in their strong holds, and secured by almost impassable mountains: they knew if they were driven back they could return when the militia retired, and if the militia returned again to the attack they might as easily retreat; they considered that they were supported by the Susquehannah company and the state of Connecticut: they knew that the legislature of that state were highly inflamed when they learned that we were sending troops against them; they considered that the state of Vermont was ready with all its strength to support their allies. It was well known that general Parsons was about to lead a considerable force into that country,[3] and it was well known that the state of Massachusetts contained numbers of persons ripe for rebellion; and when all these circumstances are considered, can we doubt the propriety of the measure, which though it struck at the rights of some individuals, prevented a civil war from being kindled in the heart of our country. A like necessity for the repeal does not now exist: it has been alledged that some of those claimants who had applied to the commissioners had withdrawn their support and suffered an outrage to be committed against those persons, but this does not appear in evidence before us, on the contrary, it is said to be

---

[3] Samuel Holden Parsons. No documents have been found to substantiate this charge.

done by another class of men, I mean the half-share men; and it is in evidence before you, that so far from commiting a single act of violence, they have proceeded to perform the duties of good citizens? they have elected justices of the peace, members of assembly and council, they have chosen their militia officers, all of whom except four or five are in the number of those who submitted, and wish to support the government, and have opposed in every instance in their power the combination and designs of the half-share men.

By repealing this law which has hitherto had the best of consequences, you throw every thing back into a state of confusion; the Susquehanna company will again join them in their exertions in opposition to the state; the inhabitants of the state of Vermont will give them succour, and we shall shortly be exposed to all the horrors and calamities of a civil war; with this disagreeable reflection, that it is a consequence of our injustice and a violation of the public faith; for which reason I should be in favor of postponing the bill introduced by the gentleman from Franklin (mr. M'Lene) if the house are not determined to throw it out altogether.

Mr. [William] *Findley.* Was the law which is termed the quieting act a complete existing and operating law; could it be executed to answer those purposes for which it was intended, then let it be as bad as it may, I would say nothing in opposition to it. I think it has been discoursed enough of upon this floor, and it has hitherto answered no purpose; the operation of this law has been partial, and if partial it will have a mischievous tendency: one half of the claims have been given in, for I think it was about half that the commissioners informed us of. Those whose claims were not received, though within the design of the law, and equally interested, must be displeased at its operation, therefore the end which was to reconcile them to the government of this state has not been answered, for at this stage of the business it will only promote disgust, and the idea of injustice in the minds of the Connecticut claimants. I think it is nearly two years ago since I had the honor of being a member of a committee to convene with commissioners that came from Wyoming on this business,[4] and the committee I recollect recommended to the people that each man should bring in the amount of his claim, and lay it before the house, as they had it then in contemplation to make them compensation: this was brought before a late

---

[4] See Vol. VIII, no. 250, note 9.

house, but the amount was not ascertained; the house went into the mode of ascertaining it; happy would it have been for us had it been ascertained and determined before they ventured upon that law; a law that was not practicable, because it limited the powers of the commissioners, and directed that in such a time all the claims should be ascertained. But what definitive time could they be able to determine all those claims in? had the legislature granted a greater length of time to the operation of the act, we should not now be so much embarrassed; we find also another part of this law which does not answer the purpose for which it was intended: It does not direct such mode of compensation as will satisfy the Pennsylvania land-holder, and we shall have in this case to take another leap in the dark, therefore I think mr. speaker, that it is a time to look for information in order to found our conduct upon, but at the same time I own I do not like the bill offered by the gentleman from Franklin (mr. M'Lene) but much worse is the gentleman's from the city (mr. Clymer.) Though I look upon these as imperfect, yet I cannot suggest any method by which they may be made unexceptionable, but I believe there is less injury to be expected from the suspending law than any other, and the necessity of the case may justify it. I wish much that a mode should be fallen upon to ascertain the claims of both parties, and on this information a law could be made that we should know might be executed: I had it in contemplation but I could not effect it, to produce a bill to institute a board for examining those claims but without the power of determining thereon, so that another legislature might have it in their power to do something effective in this business, but I know there are objections to a measure of this kind, though I believe it would be less objectionable than to continue the former law without full information.[5] * * *

Mr. *M'Lene.* The honorable gentleman who represents the city of Philadelphia (mr. Lewis) has come forward and been at some pains to prove that this is a repealing law, and for fear of its being one he is determined to give it his negative, though there appears nothing like a repealing law on the face of it; and it is alledged that nothing more can be done in this business in consequence of the law, until another act is passed by the legislature. I admit sir, that this business is very embarrassed, and I know that this house has been tormented with it a long time, but it is necessary that something should be done, and the object

---

[5] Remarks by Schott, Clymer, and Findley are here omitted.

of this bill is to give time for procuring better information than we have hitherto had; for during the time the quieting act is suspended, the house may take such measures as they think proper for procuring information. I have no other thing in view than merely to procure quiet to the house until they can provide a proper mode for determining the business.

Mr. [George] *Logan.* I think it the duty of the gentlemen that support this bill, to be certain how far it will produce quiet in the county of Luzerne, rather than in the minds of the members of this house, and I think it their duty to be prepared with testimony in support of that position, before the house assent to this bill. I believe sir, the difficulties which the gentlemen mention have arisen from two causes, first that the private interests of individuals has been attended to rather than the public good, in the case of the Pennsylvania land-holders; and the other is, that they consider the claims of the Connecticut people in too light a manner: I shall beg leave to read from the minutes of a few extracts in the year 1773, [1783?] in order to shew the idea that was entertained of these persons claims at that time, from which it appeared that the legislature was disposed to allow their claims in some degree, but since that time they have been in continual uncertainty, and the improvement of that country almost totally suspended. If lenient and salutary measures had then been pursued, the state of Pennsylvania would have been at this time perfectly quiet; her improvements would have gone on and the interest of the state greatly advantaged, and though mr. speaker, the bill now offered by the gentleman from Franklin may produce tranquility in the house, yet I am afraid it will not have that effect in the county of Luzerne: I should therefore wish that it be postponed in order to make way for that prepared by the gentleman from the city.

Mr. *Peters.* A great part of the house have got such a set against this quieting act, that I have but small hopes of their agreeing to continue its operation, but whichever way the majority think proper to decide, they will do it in the best manner they can, as it must effect the character of the state, and either give the world reason to believe we are actuated by consistent principles, or those of dishonesty. I hope it is now understood that no act of explanation can be justified, and that therefore the amendment to this effect offered at the last session, by the gentleman (Mr. Findley) from Westmoreland, is improper.[6] I wish

---

6 No. 182, *ante.*

the house may not precipitate themselves into another measure, which they will have time enough to repent of hereafter. As this law is not a suspending but a repealing law, and as a repealing law is contrary to every principle of equity, I hope the members of this house will not agree to it without the fullest deliberation, for which reason it must be evident that postponing will be more eligible than an immediate decision; though I am not for procrastinating the business, if the members have made up their mind, as I am heartily tried [tired?] of the many fruitless attempts that have been made to obtain unanimity in deciding on the proper measures.

Mr. [Thomas] *Fitzsimons* thought it a bad reason that the house should adopt improper measures because the members were tired out with the subject. If any difficulties had been encountered by the house in pursuing this business, it was because they did not walk on the straight line of rectitude: the last assembly had passed a law to quiet the Connecticut claimants, and it must be considered that it was done on good grounds, though in operation it may be unpleasant to some. Now if from an unforseen accident the law has not been fully executed before it expired, what more have we to do than to revive and continue its operation; this would have been the straight road, and by continuing in this, we should have arrived without impediment at the object to which we aimed; but as we are affraid that our travelling in this road may be expensive, and cost something more than (as is pretended) we first supposed it would, we must deviate therefore either to the right or to the left and entangle ourselves in all the labyrinths of evasion.

We are told that gentlemen are willing to proceed, but first they must have better information; but of what do they want information? of the extent of the claims, and are the extent of the claims to govern the decisions of this house? certainly if it was right and justifiable in the first instance, to pledge ourselves for confirming their claims, then be their extent what they may it is our duty to confirm them: and what is meant by all this concern for knowing their amount? If it is a small sum we are disposed to pay it; but if it should be a large one, we do not mean to agree to it, certainly it must come to this at last, or the anxiety expressed on the subject is needless: and if this is the intention of the house, we are only creating trouble, and deceiving the people. And if the bill presented by the member from Franklin (Mr. M'Lene) is agreed to, the Connecticut Claimants, if they consider at all, will judge they have little to expect from the equity and justice of Pennsylvania: and in what situation will the Pennsylvania Claimants then be? (who have stirred up this uneasiness in the house) will they be able to obtain the property they claim, from those who are in possession of it, or is the state ready and willing to exert the ultima regio regnum, in their behalf, and drive off their opponents. One of these two things must be done, either satisfy the Connecticut people, by quieting them in their possessions, and thereby acquire an additional number of citizens, or support the Pennsylvanians, and drive off the others by force of arms, and embroil the state in an expensive and predatory civil war; which may eventually cost ten times the sum necessary now, to restore tranquillity and happiness to both parties. But cost what it may, to satisfy the Connecticut claims, it ought to be done; the state has promised, and the performance must follow, unless we are disposed to violate our engagements; if such is the disposition of the house, they had better avow it, than attempt it by concealed and covert designs, and openly declare that we repeal the law, and not suspend it, because the suspension upon the terms of that bill are in fact a total repeal.

Mr. *Findley.* By the quieting act, the legislature only promised to confirm the claims of such as complied with the terms of the law, and those who did not, have no cause to complain of a breach of faith; because the state is not bound to make a new law, to accommodate their convenience. The gift made the Connecticut Claimants was a very valuable gift, and it strongly shewed the lenient disposition of the legislature, when we took away the property of our own citizens, to give it to them; but how did they receive it? When the commissioners went up to accommodate them, they prevented the execution of the law: and what is the disposition of this house? why, sir, we are willing to grant, even to those who have acted in this untoward manner. The lands which they have pretentions to, as soon as we are informed of what they are: it is not merely keeping our faith with them, but going further and performing what we never stipulated to perform.

Mr. [William] *Robinson*, [Jr.] hoped Mr. M'Lene's bill might be postponed whether the house agreed to Mr. Clymer's, or not, because it was a repealing law, and hence a direct breach of the public faith. Those gentlemen who are disposed to vote in favour of this bill, will lay it down as a certain truth that their next step will be to vote for decisive and effectual measures to drive off the Connecticut setlers, or coerce them into obedience to our government, and before they declare in favour of the first, they ought to be well ascertained of the practicability of the latter.

The gentleman from Westmoreland (Mr. Findley) supposes that if the time, to which the former law was limited, is now extended by the legislature, we do more for the Connecticut Claimants than was stipulated. In this he draws a distinction without a difference, for undoubtedly the former house meant to confirm all such as could be properly supported, and they considered a definitive time sufficient to ascertain them in; but if on experience it is found insufficient, certainly it ought to be extended, in order to complete the primary intention of the law, for it was never in contemplation, to grant to some and refuse to others whose claims were equally valid; hence it becomes necessary for the state to perform its promise in fact, without studying to avoid it by chicane or dissimulation, which appears to be the object of the bill now under consideration.

Mr. *M'Lene*. The difference between the two bills is simply this, to continue the opperation of the former law, or to suspend it until we know what we are about. It is well known to the house that tho' the powers of the commission have ceased, with respect to receiving and hearing claims, yet they have not ceased in respect to deciding upon those that have been presented, and confirming such as they deem well supported; the object of the bill I presented it [is?] to prevent any thing further from being done, until we learn what is proper; the house can easily judge between them: If I had been in that house which passed the quieting law, I should have said it was a law founded on unjust and inequitable principles, and that it was a promise made in the dark and without a just cause, and I leave it to any one to say, whether it would not be unjust to proceed and allow the commissioners to confirm the claims of such as have applied, whilst there are many who cannot be benefited by the law; when as the gentleman who was up last, says it was intended to grant the same to all who could equally support the claims.

Mr. *Fitzsimons*. The house now understand the gentleman —He says we have made a promise in the dark and from hence infers that we ougt to be released from it. I shall not quarrel with the gentleman about the morality of such an opinion, tho' upon the same principle if an individual makes a promise, and does not find it convenient to keep it, he shall be at liberty to break it. This doctrine may be very convenient for the doctrine of to-day, but I question if any advantage will eventually result

352

to the state from it, for gentlemen will recollect that the state has made some other promises, and I fancy that upon the ground of justice and equity, the one is not much better than the other, and let them take care that while they refuse in this case, they do not lay a foundation for belief that they mean to do the same in the other, if it shall be deemed convenient; and perhaps a measure of that kind will be equally popular with the measure they now are bringing forward.

Mr. *Lewis* expressed his astonishment that gentlemen should deal thus lightly with the public faith; when once it was pledged it was too late to judge of its expediency: and he therefore hoped a majority of the house would join in voting for the postponement.

Mr. *Clymer* never met with any precedent for the two gentlemens (mess. M'Lene and Kennedy) opinion, but in the epic poem of M'Fingal, who holds it just that you may

> *Turn out a promise that is base,*
> *And put a better in its place.*

Sentiments like these are to be treated only in the manner in which they are ridiculed in that work.[7]

[213] Samuel Hodgdon to Timothy Pickering.[1]

Philadelphia 20th March 1788

Dear Sir

* * * Today the Wioming business has again been before the Assembly, and is decided on.[2] The Confirming Law is suspended until some Future Assembly with more light, information & knowledge on the subject, shall think proper to resume it—then the suspending Law may be repealed, and the Confirming Law revived, or new modeled as may suit the parties of the day, otherways (as is in truth intended) the suspending law may operate *ad infinitum.* The policy of this Law cannot be positively comprehended, but from the corner from whence it was ushered in (by the hand of McLane) it is thought the design

---

[7] At this point the Assembly took a vote on whether to postpone McLene's motion in order to introduce Clymer's; see no. 211, *ante.*

[213] [1] M. H. S., Pickering Papers, LVIII, 18-20, in Hodgdon's hand.

[2] See no. 211, *ante.* Final enactment was not completed until March 29; no. 220, *post.*

is to cheat the Pennsylvania claimants out of every species of compensation, though for the present it seems leveled at the Peace and good Order of the County, meaning to excite jealousies and suspicions, that may be fanned to overt acts of rebellion and thereby sanction attainde[d] and confiscation.[3] A Jessuit may have all these, and worse motives under specious appearances in view. Schott is chagrined, but thinks the Law is better as it is, than if kept in existence with its proposed supplementary aids, and I don't know but he is right, for now it is the interest of all Parties to unite to obtain what fear, fraud and design have hitherto prevented their attaining; I mean common justice.

I hope the people will remain quiet and let the Laws of the State operate freely in the County. Such a Conduct under reiterated injuries will procure the confidence and support of all good Men on the day of trial that must eventually come, and thereby defeat the Machinations of theirs and the States enemies. Steady boys Steady—should be their Motto. * * *

The road business goes on swimmingly, we shall get £1000-0-0 of the state, and the subscriptions are numerous and generous. The river is open and Allebone with a Number of other vessels have come up. George is hearty and well, but I think will seek an easier way of living. I am however determined he shall not be idle a day—will thank you to present my best respects to M[rs] Pickering and the family—and tell them I am to be sent forward in the Spring to examine the routs for the intended new road, then I shall assuredly visit Wioming. * * *

[214] Debate on the Third Reading of the Suspending Act.[1]

Mr. [James] *M'Lene* called for the third reading of the suspending bill which he had introduced last Thursday.[2]

Mr. [George] *Clymer.* I am much averse to proceeding in this business, unless some special reason can be given why we should rush rashly on to its completion without consideration or

---

[3] Compare George Clymer's judgment in no. 209, *ante.*
[214] [1] *Proceedings and Debates of the General Assembly,* III, 204-08, March 25, 1788.
[2] See no. 211, *ante.*

time for deliberation; beside, for my part I look upon this bill to be the signal for a civil war, and gentlemen ought to be satisfied that the circumstances of the state are such that they will be able to terminate it justly and honorably.

Mr. [Richard] *Peters*. It has been frequently acknowledged by the members of this house, that they never had more difficulty in making up their minds on any subject, than this relative to the Wyoming business; and yet it appears from the precipitation with which the suspending bill is urged forward, that nothing is more easy to them. I do not see mr. speaker, that there is any sudden necessity for passing this law during the present session. If gentlemen are apprehensive that the commissioners will go on to confirm the claims they have received, and do the other business of their appointment, I think I may venture to assure them that such fears are not well founded; for though I admit they will have the power to do these things, yet I conceive they will not have the inclination, especially as they will be informed of the measures that are depending before the legislature, and of the great majority by which the suspending bill has passed its second reading. The vast importance of this measure in every point of view in which it has been placed, seems to claim deliberation; but as there appears such a majority in favor of it, I shall not add more to induce them to wave it for the present, but shall content myself with giving it my negative.

Mr. *M'Lene*. The gentleman who was last up tells you sir, that the commissioners ought not to do any thing under the old law: if that is the case, I would ask him what harm then can this bill do? but I am well satisfied by the respectable majority with which this bill has been so far agreed to, that it is a rational and useful one, and it will be readily allowed me, that if it is ever proper to be adopted the present time is most suitable, delay can only add to our embarrassment if the commissioners should go on and execute the remainder of their business.

Mr. [Samuel] *Maclay* had long been a silent witness to the temper and embarrassments of the house on this subject, and it gave him great pain that nothing effectual could be done to give satisfaction to all parties: under these sensations he had essayed to draft a bill which he hoped might be more successful, and with the leave of the house he would state its general principles, and then lay it on the table for consideration, if he was seconded.

The title of it is, "an act for quieting the disturbances at Wyoming, and for confirming to certain persons called Connecticut claimants, the lands by them claimed in the county of

Luzerne :" ³ and from this may be discovered the ultimate object which he had in view.

It is no doubt in the recollection of the house, that the petition of those people had reference to seventeen townships, and they pray that that quantity of land may be confirmed to them, which will satisfy all their demands. In this bill the seventeen townships are to be given to them, whereby the house will be ascertained of the quantity, and they are to be left to themselves to divide it agreeable to the rules and regulations of the Susquehanna company. Upon their complying with the terms of the bill all this is to be given up, but upon their refusal they are to be forever debarred from any expectation of a like gratuity.

Mr. *M'Lene* did not discover how far this bill interfered with the other, he therefore wished it to lie on the table, and moved that the suspending bill be made the order of the day for tomorrow.

Whereupon mr. Maclay's bill was ordered to lie on the table.⁴ * * *

Mr. [Thomas] *Kennedy* hoped the house would agree to make this bill the order of the day, and enact it this session; because he believed the commissioners would go on, and were even now going forward with this speculation job; and it is well known to the house, that it is only in such cases as this that we are justified in passing laws, in the same session in which they originate; but the opposition does not arise from its being unconstitutional, but merely because they are opposed to the principles of the bill, and as the house have already agreed that they are proper ones, there can be no reason for delay.

Mr. *Clymer.* That member is right in saying that we are opposed to the principles of the bill, and he might have gone further, and assured you that there are men in this house who will always be found to oppose principles so inconsistent with honesty or good policy; for the object of the bill is not only to prevent the commissioners from completing their business, but also to destroy the little that has been done; if they confine themselves to the first, it would be sufficient to order them not to proceed, or if they did, to make their actions ineffectual: if their measures only aimed at this, it could be done without sacrificing justice and decency to rashness and indiscretion.

Mr. [Alexander] *Lowry* wished that as much caution had

---

³ No. 218, *post.*
⁴ Brief remarks by Clymer and Peters are omitted here.

been used in passing the quieting act, as was now recommended to the friends of the suspending bill, and then perhaps the house would not have been so much embarrassed.

Mr. *Peters* thought we ought to learn wisdom from their indiscretion, and if the former house erred for want of due deliberation, it was a good reason for this to be more considerate.

Mr. [Thomas] *Fitzsimons* thought something reprehensible had fallen from one gentleman (mr. Kennedy) during the debate, and he should be glad to know what he meant by the words *speculating job.*

Mr. *Clymer.* I believe sir, it is no matter what the gentlemen meant, because he does not understand the subject, nor never did.

Mr. *Kennedy* did not rate his abilities very high, and might not have a very great share of understanding, but it was well known that the house had been hurried into the quieting law, and that the step taken to surprise the house into that measure could not be justified on the principles of equity.

He further observed that gentleman who hurried a business on one occasion, acted inconsistently in urging the necessity of deliberation on another that was similar.

The question on making the suspending bill, the order of the day for to-morrow was put and carried.

[215] Extract from the Minutes of the Pennsylvania General Assembly.[1]

Agreeably to the order of the day, the bill, entitled *"An Act to suspend an act, entituled* * * * [The Confirming Act]*,"* was read the third time.

And in debating the following paragraph, viz.[2] * * *

On the question, *"Will the House adopt the same?"* the Yeas and Nays were called by Mr. [John Paul] *Schott* and Mr. [James] *McLene,* and were as follow, viz.[3] * * *

---

[215] [1] *Minutes of the Second Session of the Twelfth General Assembly,* 166-68 (microfilm copy), dated March 26, 1788.

[2] Section 2 of the law suspending the Confirming Act; see no. 220, *post.*

[3] The vote in favor of the motion to adopt this section of the Suspending Act was 42 to 21. With the exception of John Paul Schott's vote and one vote from Westmoreland County, all the nay votes were from the east— from the city and county of Philadelphia and from Bucks, Chester, Lancaster, and York counties. A probable explanation is that eastern repre-

So it was determined in the affirmative; and the bill having
been fully debated by paragraphs,

On the question, *"Shall the same be engrossed, for the purpose of being enacted into a law?"* the Yeas and Nays were
called by Mr. [George] *Clymer* and Mr. [William] *Robinson,*
[Jr.], and were as follow, *viz.*[4] * * *

So it was determined in the affirmative.

On motion of Mr. [William] *Findley,* seconded by Mr.
[Samuel] *Maclay,*

Ordered, That to-morrow be assigned for the second reading
of the bill, entitled *"A further Act for quieting the disturbances
at Wyoming, and for confirming to certain persons, called* Connecticut Claimants, *the lands by them claimed within the county
of* Luzerne,"[5] and that it be the order for the day.

[216] Final Debate on the Suspending Act.[1]

Mr. [Thomas] *Fitzsimons.* Although the house must be
heartily tired of this subject, yet I think it my duty to declare
again my sentiments on this last occasion. If the advocates of
this bill are serious in what they say is their desire of only suspending the operation of the quieting act, let the suspension be
for a limited time, and let that be a period long enough to obtain
that information which they seem so desirous of. If this will
satisfy the members I shall not oppose enacting the bill this session, and it will shew the world that our object is ultimately to
do what is just and proper, and it will also tend to prevent those
consequences which I fear will otherwise be felt in the destruction of the peace and tranquility of the state.

Mr. [George] *Clymer* considered an alteration of this kind
necessary to make it correspond with the title; because as the
bill now stood it was a repealing law. As it was necessary that
another act of assembly should be passed to revive the operation
of the quieting act: beside this, the bill is essentially wrong, as
appears upon the face of it. It bears evident marks of indiges-

---

sentatives reflected the desire of speculators to keep the Connecticut claimants quiet so that speculators might profitably dispose of lands bordering
the Connecticut settlements.

[4] The division was the same as on the preceding vote, 42 to 21.

[5] No. 218, *post.*

[216] [1] *Proceedings and Debates of the General Assembly,* III, 209-11,
March 26, 1788.

tion and error. It is here said that the execution of the former law was prevented by those who were to be benefited by it: pray is this the fact? and are gentlemen ready to put their hands to a falshood? Is it not known to every person that the people who prevented the execution of the law are those who cannot be benefited from it, but on the contrary, must suffer a total loss of their claims? Is not this the case with respect to the half-share men, who were the people that drove off the commissioners in a tumultuous manner.

In another part of the bill I find it set forth, that the former act contains an ambiguous clause, and therefore it ought to be explained.

This, sir, is a very dangerous doctrine, and such as all good politicians are ever guarded against; but where property is concerned, or to be affected by legislative explanations of laws, too much caution cannot be exercised, otherwise a precedent may be established to wrest the possessions from any person, let them be held under whatever title they may; since none can be more secure than such as have been confirmed by the express act of the representatives of the state.

The alteration proposed by my colleague, will tend to make the bill something better, for which reason I shall vote for the amendment though I am against the bill altogether, with a view, that if the bill does pass, it may do as little mischief as possible.

Mr. [James] *M'Lene* observed, that the opposition was still the same, though varied into the shape of an amendment, for the moment the limitation expired, the commissioners would go on with the business, which would only be delayed a few months, this he did not think to be the wish of the house; as the bill now stood nothing could be done until the legislature was satisfied of the extent and nature of the claims, and the quantity of compensation that would be requisite to make to the Pennsylvania landholders—and if he was not mistaken, the house would reject such amendment, because it was their opinion that nothing more in the business ought to be done without the direction of some future house of assembly.

Mr. *Fitzsimons* would consent to extend the period of limitation to a further session, but would leave it to the gentleman to propose the term, because he would have nothing to do with a measure that appeared to him so inimical to the true interest of the state.

Mr. [John Paul] *Schott* did not believe the bill would have any good effect, even if such amendment was agreed to; but this

359

subject had been spoken to so fully on former occasions, that it was useless to repeat, yet he could not help declaring again his apprehensions of the bad consequences which would ensue, and before he sat down he would just ask gentlemen how they expected to obtain that information which they seemed so anxious to procure, when this law suspends every operation by which the quantity of land claimed could be ascertained, and leaves the business just as it is now situated until a future house shall resume it and they will of consequence find it, without other or better information than what has been already acquired.

Mr. [Thomas] *Kennedy,* would not agree to any amendments of the kind, because the legislature might not be prepared to do any thing more at the end of six months than at present.[2]

[217] Debate on the Proposed New Confirming Act.[1]

Agreeably to the order of the day the bill for quieting the disturbances at Wyoming, after confirming to certain persons called Connecticut claimants the lands by them claimed within the county of Luzerne, was read the second time.[2]

Mr. [William] *Findley* had paid a good deal of attention to this subject, but from having been deceived on a former occasion he should be on his guard; not that he was suspicious of any intention of this nature being entertained by the gentlemen who approve of the bill. The act called the quieting act gave to the Connecticut claimants not only the seventeen townships mentioned in this bill, but even the lines of the county did not seem to circumscribe their claims: of two evils he would therefore choose the least, and as this law would bring to the knowledge of the house the quantity which was given up, a very considerable expence to the state would be saved in the articles of wages and contingences to the commissioners and clerks who might be a long time in determining on the claims, for although the law limited the time in which the claims were to be made, yet it affixed no period in which they should make their decision, there-

---

[2] At this point a vote was taken on section 2 of the Suspending Act; see no. 215, *ante,* note 3.

[217] [1] *Proceedings and Debates of the General Assembly,* III, 213-15, March 27, 1788.

[2] This was the measure proposed by Samuel Maclay; no. 218, *post.*

fore there was no saying how long the state might be subjected to this charge.

He was willing that the bill should be published for consideration, and was in hopes by the next session the house would have better information, when if it was proper to pass the bill it would be in train for that purpose.

Mr. [George] *Clymer* was of opinion that the seventeen townships would equal the grants made by the quieting act (as it is called) because they contained many lots which were not located. If he was not mistaken col. Pickering said on his examination before the house at the last session, that one third of the whole claims would revert to the state for want of sufficient evidence to support them, which would reduce them to a quantity equal to the seventeen townships.

Mr. [Richard] *Peters* was glad that the gentlemen were willing to advance this bill, because he hoped it would prevent many of the ill consequences which he apprehended from the suspending law, and hoped it might be the means of preserving the quiet and honor of the state.

Mr. [Samuel] *Maclay* could not speak with decision as to the difference between the quantity contained in the seventeen townships, and what would be given under the quieting act, but he thought it would not exceed it, and as was observed by the gentleman from Westmoreland (mr. Findley) it would have a great deal of contingent expence; besides, the good land that was passed under this bill could not exceed what was granted by the former, because all the good land in this district was taken up, and would have to be confirmed.

Mr. [John Paul] *Schott* approved of the bill, and thought the Connecticut claimants would receive it well, and be satisfied with it, because it was conformably to what they had all along in their petitions prayed for, and he therefore hoped for the honor and equity of the state that the house would agree to the bill.

Mr. *Findley* conceived himself at liberty to oppose this bill if he deemed it proper at the next session, by which time the house would be better informed on the subject, but for the present he was satisfied to vote in favor of it in order to have it published, and get the sentiments of the people.

Mr. [Thomas] *Kennedy* wished that the house would direct the compensation to be made to the Pennsylvania claimants at the time they took away their lands, and until he was satisfied in this respect he should oppose any bill of this nature.

Mr. *Clymer* thought it best to divide this subject, because it was impossible to tell what would be the requisite compensation, until the extent of the claims was ascertained. The Pennsylvania claimants are not placed in a worse situation by this law, than they are already, for he apprehended it was not the intention of the house to give them money, and the faith of the state had been already pledged to give them lands, and this is all they can expect or obtain; and this the house all along have agreed to give them when they were informed of the quantity.

Mr. *Maclay* had an intention to add a clause, directing the compensation; but he did not know any possible means of knowing what that was, until some previous measures were taken to come at the amount of the claims, therefore had omitted it.

Mr. *M'Lene,* as the compensation depends upon the information which the house is to receive, I think it proper before we agree to this bill, that some steps should be taken to acquire that knowledge, wherefore, sir, I shall move you to postpone this bill in order to decide upon the resolution which I have in my hand. Mr. M'Lene having read this for the information of the house; the bill was postponed, and the resolution read and agreed to as follows, viz.[3]

[218] Proposed Bill for Confirming Lands to Connecticut Claimants.[1]

State of Pennsylvania, In General Assembly,
Thursday, March 27, A. M., 1788.
The Bill, entitled *"A further act for quieting the disturbances at* Wyoming, *and for confirming to certain persons called* Connecticut Claimants, *the Lands by them claimed within the County*

---

[3] See no. 219, *post.*
[218] [1] *P. A.,* XI, 260-62. This measure was first introduced by Samuel Maclay on March 25; *Minutes of the Second Session of the Twelfth General Assembly,* 164 (microfilm copy).
The effect of this law, of course, would limit the Connecticut settlers to claiming rights only within the original seventeen towns and thus the law would not please the Franklin faction which sought validation of the whole Susquehannah Company claim. It probably would not even please many of the more moderate Connecticut claimants, for it would not include Athens and other areas. See no. 16, *ante,* note 2, and Pickering's proposals for a confirming law, nos. 189, *ante,* and 310, *post.* Pickering would have included areas assigned but not occupied because of the Indian danger and certain "pitches" outside the seventeen towns.

of Luzerne," was read the second time and debated by paragraphs.

Ordered, That it be transcribed, and in the mean time printed for public consideration.

Extract from the Minutes,

Peter Z. Lloyd,

Clerk of the General Assembly,

A further act for quieting the disturbances at Wyoming, *and for confirming to certain persons called Connecticut claimants, the lands by them claimed within the County of Luzerne.*

SECT. I. Whereas in attempting to execute the act of the General Assembly of this Commonwealth, entitled, "An act for ascertaining and confirming to certain persons called Connecticut claimants, the lands by them claimed within the county of Luzerne and for other purposes therein mentioned," it has been found much more expensive than was at first expected, as well as extremely difficult to ascertain the different interfering claims, as well of the Pennsylvania landholders, as those of the Connecticut claimants.

And whereas the commissioners appointed for adjusting and settling the claims aforesaid, have not been supported in the execution of their commission, but have been interrupted, insulted, and personally abused in the presence of those people whose duty and interest it was to support them; And whereas it is but just and reasonable that the said Connecticut claimants should at least be at the expence of settling and adjusting their own claims; therefore,

SECT. II. *Be it enacted, and it is hereby enacted by the Representatives of the Freemen of the Commonwealth of Pennsylvania in General Assembly met, and by the authority of the same,* That all and every of the seventeen townships, which were petitioned for by said Connecticut claimants, by the name of Salem, Newport, Hanover, Wilksborough, Pitstown, Northumberland,[2] Putnam, Mushhoppin, Springfield, Claverick, Ulster, Exeter, Kingston, Plymouth, Huntington, Bedford and Providence, agreeable to their original butts and bounds, be and they are hereby confirmed to such of them as were actual settlers there, at or before the termination of the claim of the State of Connecticut by the decree of the congressional court at Trenton to be by them settled, according to their original holdings in any way, which they may judge most convenient to them.

---

[2] This should be Northmoreland.

SECT. III. *And be it further enacted by the authority aforesaid,* That the Sheriff of the said county of Luzerne shall within [   ] days after the passing of this act, notify the Connecticut claimants, in one or more of the news-papers published in the city of Philadelphia and in Connecticut, as well as by handbills set up in the most public places in the respective townships, to meet at such time and place or places as he shall appoint, to elect by ballot, one suitable person, he being a freeholder within the said county, for a patentee for such township; and the claimants so assembled, shall within five days after such election, make return of the persons names and places of abode, who shall be highest in votes, to the said Sheriff who shall within ten days after such return or returns come into his hands, transmit the same to the Supreme Executive Council of this State, who are hereby directed and required to direct the Secretary of the Land Office, to issue a warrant in the name of each of the persons who shall be so elected and returned to them for each respective township, for which he shall be so as aforesaid elected, which warrant shall be directed to the Surveyor General, commanding him to cause a resurvey to be made forthwith, of such township, agreeable to their original butts and bounds and to make return thereof without delay, into the Surveyor General's Office in Philadelphia, and upon every such return a patent shall issue in the name of such patentee who was so as aforesaid, elected and returned in trust and for the use of the said Connecticut claimants in that township, clear of expense except for making out the patent, for which they shall pay the usual fees of office. And every Deputy Surveyor in whose district the township shall happen to be, shall for each and every survey by him made and returned as aforesaid, receive the usual fees and no more.

SECT. IV. *And be it further enacted by the authority aforesaid,* That in case of the death, neglect or refusal to serve, of any or either of the said patentees, then and in every such case, all the powers which was so as aforesaid conveyed to them, shall immediately be in the Prothonotary, Sheriff and Coroner of the said county of Luzerne for the time being, in trust as aforesaid, which Prothonotary, Sheriff and Coroner or any two of them, shall from time to time have full power and authority to transfer, convey and make over, all or any part of such township which shall so fall under their direction as fully and as amply as the original patentee could have done agreeable to the original intent and meaning of this act.

SECT. V. *And be it further enacted by the authority afore-said,* That when the Connecticut claimants by their proper representative, do neglect or refuse to make application for counsel for confirmation of their respective townships, as aforesaid, within [   ] months after the publication of this act, then and in every such case, the claimants to such township, which shall not be applied for, as is herein before directed, shall be forever after barred from any right or claim to the same.

Philadelphia: From handbill, printed by Thomas Bradford.

Endorsed: Wioming Bill, published for consideration, but never enacted.

[219] Extract from the Minutes of the Pennsylvania General Assembly.[1]

Agreeably to the order of the day, the bill, entitled *"A further Act for quieting the disturbances at* Wyoming, *and for confirming to certain persons, called* Connecticut Claimants, *the lands by them claimed within the county of* Luzerne," [2] was read the second time: Whereupon

It was moved by Mr. [James] *McLene* and Mr. [Thomas] *Kennedy,*

To postpone the consideration of said bill, in order to introduce a resolution which Mr. *McLene* read in his place,

And on the question, *"Will the House agree to the postponement for the aforesaid purpose?"*

It was carried in the affirmative, and the resolution adopted, as follows, *viz.*

"Resolved, That the Supreme Executive Council be, and they are hereby authorised and directed to devise and take the most proper and effectual measures to ascertain the quantity and quality of each particular tract of land, included within the townships of *Salem, Newport, Hanover, Wilksbarre, Pittstown, Northmoreland, Putnam, Misshoppen, Springfield, Claverick, Ulster, Exeter, Kingstown, Plymouth, Huntingdon, Bedford* and *Providence,* in the county of *Luzerne,* and claimed by *Pennsylvania* owners, and report to this House at their next sitting, that the

[219] [1] *Minutes of the Second Session of the Twelfth General Assembly,* 170-71 (microfilm copy), dated March 27, 1788.
[2] No. 216, *ante.*

365

House may the better be enabled to decide upon the compensation to be made to them." [3]

The House then resumed the consideration of the aforesaid bill, and having fully debated the same by paragraphs,

On the question, *"Shall the same be transcribed, and in the mean time printed for public consideration?"* the Yeas and Nays were called by Mr. *Kennedy* and Mr. [John Paul] *Schott,* and were as follow, viz.[4] * * *

So it was carried in the affirmative.

[220] Act Suspending Operation of the Confirming Act of 1787.[1]

An Act to suspend an act, entitled "an Act for ascertaining and confirming to certain persons called Connecticut claimants, the lands by them claimed within the County of Luzerne, and for other purposes therein mentioned."

SECTION 1. Whereas, By an act entitled "An act for ascertaining and confirming certain persons, called Connecticut claimants, the lands by them claimed, within the county of Luzerne, and for other purposes therein mentioned," it is, among other things, enacted, that certain commissioners therein named, or thereafter to be appointed, should, within a limited time, meet together with the said county, for the purpose of receiving and examining the claims of the said claimants, and ascertaining and confirming the same. *And whereas,* When these commissioners had met, in pursuance of the said law, they were interrupted in their proceedings by the combinations, threatening and outrageous violence of certain lawless people in the said county of Luzerne, and obliged to fly for the preservation of their lives. *And*

---

[3] On May 6 the Council requested the Surveyor General to supply "a copy of all the drafts of lands held in the aforesaid townships and county of Luzerne by Pennsylvania claimants, and which have been returned into this office"; *Pa. C. R.,* XV, 450. See no. 224, *post.*

[4] The bill was passed by a vote of 36 to 27. As would be expected, all 21 of those who had opposed suspending the Confirming Act voted for this new confirming law. The additional 15 votes came from a scattering of counties, western as well as eastern ones. The law, of course, never underwent final enactment. See Pickering's proposed amendments; no. 310, *post.*

[220] [1] *P. A.,* 2nd ser., XVIII, 675-76. This act was passed by a vote of 42 to 21. It was introduced in the General Assembly by James McLene. For analysis of the vote, see no. 215, *ante,* note 3.

whereas, Doubts have also arisen concerning the construction, true intent and meaning of said law, for which, and other causes, it hath become very difficult to determine the same, and to adjust the compensation to be made to those persons who will be divested of their property by the operation of the said law, if the same shall be carried into effect. *And whereas,* The time in which these commissioners were to receive their claims has expired, but their other powers still remain, which, if immediately executed, without further provisions and regulations being previously made, will tend to embarrassment and confusion."

SECTION 2. *Be it therefore enacted, and it is hereby enacted by the Representatives of the Freeman of the Commonwealth of Pennsylvania in General Assembly met, and by the authority of the same,* That so much of the said law as impowers the said commissioners to ascertain and confirm the claims of the said people, called Connecticut claimants, and all and every part of the said act, which gives any power and authority to the said commissioners, be and the same is hereby suspended, until the Legislature of this Commonwealth shall, by a law for that purpose to be enacted, make further provisions and regulations in the premises, and shall direct and require the said commissioners to proceed in the exercise of their said powers.

Signed by order of the House

THOMAS MIFFLIN, *Speaker*

Enacted at Philadelphia, Saturday the 29th day of March, 1788,

PETER ZACHARY LLOYD.
Clerk of the General Assembly.

[221] Tench Coxe to Timothy Pickering.[1]

Dear Sir

The house having adjourned, I take the opty by Captain Shotts to drop you a few lines. The bill for the roads is enacted precisely as we requested it, & a warrant is contained in it of £1000, so that we have succeeded to our utmost wishes.[2] I really think few events of more Consequence to the Agriculture, domestic & foreign trade of Penns[a] have taken place since the peace. Our Subscriptions are £525, & we shall now open them again,

---

[221] [1] M. H. S., Pickering Papers, LVIII, 20-22, in Coxe's hand.

[2] The roads bill was passed on March 28; *Minutes of the Second Session of the Twelfth General Assembly,* 177 (microfilm copy).

as we wish to lay out a cross road from the Bend to the forks of the Delaware at the carrying place, & another Road from the Ararat road to such Road as may now be open to the E. Side of Delaware.

I have made a proposition in behalf of yourself Major H & myself to the Penns, subject to your Approbation, to make a common interest of the Two Town-seats, ours at the Bend [3] & theirs at the forks of Delaware. By having the two & acting in concert we might make it of Consequence. Will you turn it in your mind. It seems likely that Michael Ross will be employed to lay out the Road from Tioga to Mount Ararat.[4] Do you know of any better man? We shall be glad of *early* information if you do. M^r or Dr Sprague [5] has applied for the Business. Do you know any thing of him. My optys with him have been small, but I think he does not appear equal to it. If we should want provisions, workmen, a waggon & a superintending hand to conduct the workmen after the Road is open'd could we get such supplies & aid in Wilkesbarre, & at what Rates. What do You think of the Idea of beginning at Tioga in making the road from Ararat thither. We shall have a good surveyor & superintendent to begin at Pocona & work up to Ararat, & another set to come down from the York line to Ararat. All three got going at a time will turn off the work we hope by the middle of August. Can you give us any hints upon the Subject that may be useful.

A law has been passed to suspend the powers of the Wyoming Comm^{rs} for which I am very sorry. Pains were taken to get the old law renewed, but it failed from the introduction of the other by McClane [6] &c^a. Another bill was then introduced to grant the 17 Townships & went thro at [the?] 2^d Reading 36 to 27. It is published for consideration;[7] but I fear it will be considerably narrowed or thrown out, tho I hope not the latter. I wish a petition from the owners of the lots in the pitches could be got signifying their desire to remove off the pitches & take their Share in the Townships, and some declaration of those in & out of the 17 Townships that they would be disposed to relinquish all pretensions *without* the Townships, if the lands *within* the Townships should be given them. The Objections to the depending

---

[3] A reference to lands in the Great Bend in the Susquehanna River, where it enters Pennsylvania from New York State and then returns to New York.

[4] Major James Smith of Cumberland got the contract; see no. 227, *post.*

[5] Dr. Joseph Sprague. See his comment about northern lands in no. 22, *ante.*

[6] James McLene introduced the bill to suspend the Confirming Act.

[7] No. 218, *ante.*

bill were that the State was asked to grant the 17 Townships & it could not be known, if the people would quit claim to every thing else.

I have some hope of having secured a body of Coal within 25 Miles of Philadᵃ on the Banks of Delaware and am very anxious for a little information from You of the Nature of the soil, the Nature of the Stone & strata, the external appearances of the earth, the symptoms of Metals or ores and other matters peculiar or uncommon to those tracts on which Coal is to be found in your County. If you could favor me with a line of accurate information I should be obliged to you. While you are making an Inspection into the Matter I shall thank you to consider & enquire into the Matter, as you would do if you meditated a coal purchase near Wilkesbarre, or on the Susquehanna. I have some particular Reasons, which will apply to *our joint benefit,* that induce me to wish you would be particular. I am, dear Sir, yʳ respectf h Servᵗ

Tench Coxe

Philadᵃ March 29ᵗʰ 1788

[222] Performance Bond for Construction of the Pennsylvania Landholders' Road.[1]

KNOW all Men by these Presents, That We John Nicholson Henry Drinker Tench Coxe Mark Wilcox and Tench Francis all of the City of Philadelphia are held and firmly bound unto His Excellency Benjamin Franklin Esquire, President of the Supreme Executive Council of the Commonwealth of *Pennsylvania,* Captain General and Commander in Chief in and over the same, in the Sum of two thousand Pounds, to be paid to the said Benjamin Franklin Esquire, or to his Successor in the said Office: To the which Payment well and truly to be made, we bind ourselves jointly and severally for and in the Whole, our Heirs, Executors and Administrators, firmly by these Presents, Sealed with our Seals. Dated the twenty-fifth Day of April in the Year of our Lord One Thousand Seven Hundred and eighty eight. The Condition of this Obligation is such That if the above bounden John Nicholson Henry Drinker Tench Coxe Mark Wilcox and Tench Francis shall well and faithfully execute and perform the duties required of them as Commissioners under an Act of the General Assembly passed the 28ᵗʰ day of March last inti-

---

[222] [1] P. H. M. C., Div. of Arch. and MSS., Record Group 27, Series: Exec. Corr., 1777-90, signed by each individual.

tuled "An Act for opening and establishing certain Roads in the Counties of Northampton and Luzerne" [2] and shall well and truly account for the monies which they shall receive from the State for the purpose of carrying the said Act of Assembly into exectetion—then the above obligation to be void, otherwise to be and remain in full force and virtue.

Henry Drinker

Jn° Nicholson
Tench Francis
Tench Coxe
Mark Willcox

Sealed and Delivered⎫
in the presence of us ⎭
   John Wagner
   James Duncan

[223] Petition of John Franklin to the Pennsylvania Council.[1]

His Excellency the President of the Hon[ble] the Supreme Executive Council of the Commonwealth of Pennsylvania

The Petition of John Franklin of the County of Luzerne and State of Pennsylvania now a State Prisoner confined in Goal at Philadelphia—humbly sheweth

That your Petitioner has been confined in Prison since the 5th of October 1787 where he has been near seven months, limited to a single room in a wing of the Goal, and is still languishing under his lonesome confinement; though by the Clemency of your Hon[ble] Body he has been released from his Irons in which he was at first confined, which demands his grateful acknowledgements.[2]

That the Hon[ble] Justices of the Suprem Court of this State on his Petition exhibited to them on the 16th Ins[t] agreed to admit him to Bail upon his entering into a Recognisance in the Sum of 2000 Pounds with his good securities for his appearance at the next Court of Oyer and Terminer &c to be holden for the County

---

[2] Mitchell and Flanders, *Statutes at Large*, XIII, 48-50, Chapter MCCCXLII.

[223] [1] Wyoming Historical and Geological Society, in Franklin's hand. I am indebted to Luke A. Sarsfield for calling this petition to my attention.

[2] Council had ordered the removal of Franklin's irons on February 8, 1788; no. 200, *ante*.

of Luzerne, and to keep the Peace and be of good behaviour in the mean while.[3]

That being remote from his friends and closely confined to a single Room where he is deprived of the advantage of social society he has not yet been able to obtain the security required

That so retired a Confinement is not only prejudicial to his bodily health (which is already much impaired) but lays him under many disadvantages of procuring security which he might otherwise do if he was liberated more largely to the Prison.

That he expects to procure the security required as speedy as he can Possebly apply to his friends, but their remote distance from him, the difficulty of Passing to and from that County at this season of the year and the many disadvantages under which he labours it will consequently be considerable length of time before he can be liberated at large.

Your Petitioner relying on your Clemency for his further relief Therefore Prays your Excellency and Hon[ble] Body to take his case aforesaid under your wise and Equitable Consideration and Grant (if consistent with the nature of his cause, the Honour of your Persons, and the Dignity of the State) that he may be permitted to a Room in the front of the Goal and have the liberty of the yard appertaining thereto. And he as in Duty bound will ever Pray

April 28, 1788   John Franklin

[224] John Lukens to Peter Muhlenberg.[1]

Surv[r] Gen[l] Office 8 May 1788

Hon[d] Sir

as requested I have Taken into Consideration the Extract of the minutes of Assembly left with me, in Order to sugest the best method of answering the Expectation of the house on the s[d] Resolve.[2] To set out properly will tend much to Shorten the Whole plan.

1st let the Surv Gen[l] & Each Deputy, be provided with the last Law describing the Bounds of Luzerne County

---

[3] See no. 225, *post.*

[224] [1] P. H. M. C., Div. of Arch. and MSS., Record Group 27, Series: Exec. Corr., 1777-90, signed by Lukens. This letter was read in the Council on May 9; *Pa. C. R.,* XV, 452.

[2] See no. 219, *ante.*

2dly Let a Deputy Surv^r of that part of s^d County lying East-ward of the East Branch of Susquehanna be appointed & that he have Free Access to the Record of the County Court to Asscertain the Boundaries of the Several Townships mentioned in s^d Resolve.

3dly that Mr Charles Stewart Late Deputy Surveyor of all s^d Luzerne County be Requested to furnish Council (or the Surv Gen^1) with all the Names Quantities & Quality of all Land by him Surveyed & Returned in his District on Applications & Warrants before or since the Revolution.

4thly That Wm Montgomery Esqr & Wm Gray be Requested to furnish The Like Documents in s^d Counties during their times

5thly That the Deputy Sur^r of said County shall lay down as soon as possible a plan of s^d County, & the several Townships therein from the County Record as nearly as he can, & from the best information of the Inhabitants, or owners of Land in the several Townships.

6thly When the foregoing, or any other method of Investigating the matters Required by the s^d Resolve may [occur?] to Council, in assisting the Deputy Surveyors & Such persons as may be appointed to Report on the Quality of the land they may be assured of all the Assistance in my Power.[3] I remain Sir your Most Obed^{nt} Humble Servant

Jno Lukens

[225] Thomas McKean and Jacob Rush to Timothy Pickering.[1]

Chester May 10th 1788

Sir,

At the last Supreme court the Judges agreed to admit John Franklin to Bail, on account of the peculiar circumstances of his

---

[3] On May 14, the Council named Stephen Balliet and Major William Armstrong as commissioners to proceed to Wyoming "to view and describe the lands . . . agreeably to the purport" of the Assembly's resolution. On June 12 they were provided with funds for the purpose; *Pa. C. R.*, XV, 455, 471. See also no. 240, *post.*

On September 11, 1788, the commissioners reported that the lands claimed by Pennsylvanians totaled 110,785 acres of four grades of quality-bottom lands, first-rate uplands, and two inferior grades; see Vol. X, William Rawle's "Background Notes."

[225] [1] M. H. S., Pickering Papers, LVIII, 31, signed by the two men.

case, tho' accused of treason. To save expence and trouble we would request the favor of you to take a Recognizance from his sureties, that is from as many freeholders as you shall be satisfied are worth two thousand pounds altogether, in that sum, for his appearance at the next court of Oyer & terminer and General goal delivery to be holden for the county of Luzerne, to take his trial for the above offence, and to keep the peace and be of the good behavior to all the liege people of Pennsylvania in the mean time. The Recognizance must be taken before two Justices of the peace of the county, and afterwards transmitted to the Prothonotary of the Supreme court.[2] We are, Sir, with esteem & regard, Your Most obedient servants.

Thos McKean
Jacob Rush

[226] Timothy Pickering to Samuel Hodgdon.[1]

Wilkesborough, May 18th, 1788

Dear Sir,

I received your favours by Mr Fell & Mr Oehmig. I am not myself discouraged about our northern lands, because of Capt. Jackson's abandoning Doctor Spragues discoveries:[2] A few miles very commonly make a wide difference in the quality of lands: tho' ours is generally (like his) heavily timbered, and a great part of the timber is hemlock. Capt. Jackson & his men were not properly qualified for subduing such lands, The New-Englandmen who have cleared the *Green Woods,* would be the

---

[2] A copy of the recognizance, taken before justices James Nisbitt and Benjamin Carpenter on May 24, is in *ibid.,* 33. Those giving surety for Franklin were Jonathan Corey, John Hurlbut, Solomon Avery, James Bidlack, Samuel Ayers, George Palmer Ransom, Stephen Barnes, Parshall Terry, Peleg Comstock, and John Jenkins. Corey was put down for £400, and Ransom and Barnes for £100 each. The rest were put down for £200 each.

For Pickering's reply to McKean and Rush, see *P. A.,* XI, 295.

On June 20 Samuel Hodgdon wrote to Pickering that some members of the Council felt that Franklin's bail was insufficient and that he would not be released; Pickering Papers, LVIII, 43. See also no. 307, *post.*

[226] [1] M. H. S., Pickering Papers, VI, 1-2, a draft in Pickering's hand.

[2] See no. 22, *ante.*

proper cultivators.[3] And as the projected roads will I presume, open passages thro' them, their settlement will be greatly facilitated: Yet while the fair flats on the Susquehannah & its branches remain any where vacant, people will not be fond of clearing hilly grounds heavily timbered: we must therefore have a *little* patience. Vast numbers of people are flocking in about Tioga, from all quarters, & the half-share-men taking possession of their rights at that place. The two surveys there belonging to our company will of course be covered. Schott, I am told, has been giving them assurances of their holding them, under the proposed law for granting the New Eng^d people the 17 entire towns.[4] The indecision of government on the Wyoming business seems now to be what it has been [5] these 18 years past; the settlements of the half share men, in the mean time, may become so strong, that the quieting *them* will be a matter of *expediency,* as the confirming law was with the old settlers. Thus more individual Pennsylvania purchasers will be wronged; or the state incumbered with a greater debt.

In one of your letters lately you told me that Mr Francis declined taking a share in our New-Purchase-lands; but would buy *my* share in the Old purchase, at two shillings an acre.[6] This is surely too low. I understood you that Mr Drinker gave Wallis 4/. or 3/9. At the latter prices I would sell *one half* of my share (or about six thousand acres) the surveys which are appropriated to me, to be divided by lot, and the purchaser to be interested to the amount of one half of my share now lying in common with you & Mr Cox. I have two reasons for selling half my lands in the old purchase, one because I have a higher opinion of the *quality* of our lands westward surveyed by Genl Potter; [7] the other, that I *want money* and I must make a sacrifice of some lands, to pay for those I have here at Wilkesborough, & to stock them. The indispensable necessity of supporting my family with bread, & of furnishing corn to the families of some poor labourers who are working for me, and keeping my horses fit for labour, has compelled me to run in debt

---

[3] The phrase "the proper cultivators" is interlined over the following, which is lined out: "fittest for bringing to such lands."

[4] No. 218, *ante.*

[5] The phrase "now to be what it has been" is interlined over the following, which is lined out: "To have been uniform."

[6] No. 208, *ante.*

[7] The following words are lined out here: "& that they will speedily get settled."

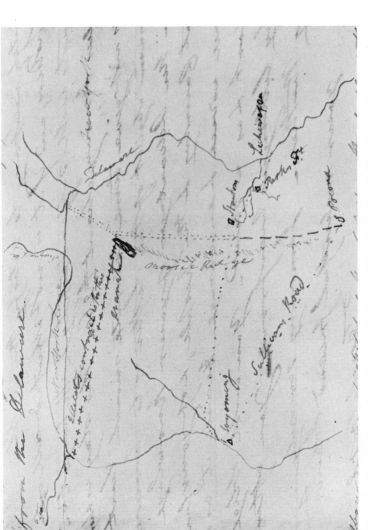

Sketch by Tench Coxe of roads proposed by the Pennsylvania Landholders Association; in a letter to Timothy Pickering, May 22, 1788, and reproduced through the courtesy of the Massachusetts Historical Society.

here to the amount of about sixty dollars, on a promise to draw on you for the same, payable either in 30 days, or at ten days sight. * * *

[227] Tench Coxe to Timothy Pickering.[1]

Dear Sir

I wrote you some time ago about the Roads, in which I mentioned our Contract with M[r] Ellicott &c.[2] We contracted with Major James Smith of Cumberland for that part of the road which lies between the upper Wyoming road to the New York line. It begins about 2 Miles from Stantons Tavern (about 22 or 24 miles from Wyoming) & runs thence under the East side of the Moosic Ridge by Mount Ararat thence up to the line at y[e] 1, 2 or 3 milestone from the Delaware.

Above is a rough sketch of the Country. The *double* dotted line is that to be done by Major Smith.[3] That by Stockus, from Pocona to Stantons, on the Wyoming road is to be done by John Hilborn, who we have no doubt, will go on well; but Smith has got discouraged. He is now in Town & takes up this to send it to you, and all the Comm[rs] ask as a particular favor that you will take a ride to him and endeavour to encourage & assist him, by your advice and direction. His contract is for £500 for the double dotted piece to be made 33 feet wide, but we think he had best open it well first for one perch throughout and then he can finish it. But the road of one perch this Season appears absolutely necessary to satisfy the public & the Landholders, and if it is not effected all our Interests will suffer deeply. He has got in supplies & money about £260. His stay is short & does not give time to write much but the main object of this letter is to procure to him the Advantages of your knowledge of that Country & the people, & of your fourtenance advice & encourage. He will it as a comfort & as a spur. You will oblige us by letting us hear from you after going thither I am very sinicirely your respectful friend & Serv[t]

Tench Coxe

Philad[a] May 22[d] 1788

---

[227] [1] M. H. S., Pickering Papers, XIX, 132, in Coxe's hand.

[2] Probably no. 221, *ante,* although no mention is made of the Ellicott contract.   [3] See accompanying sketch.

[228] Timothy Pickering to Peter Muhlenberg.[1]

Wilkesborough, May 27, 1788.

Dear Sir,

The inclosed letters to the Chief Justice & Mr. Burd[2] I should have transmitted directly to them had I not just been informed that the Supreme Court were sitting now at Carlisle, & both those gentlemen might be absent. The letter to the Chief Justice is in answer to one rec'd from him & Mr. Rush, desiring me to take a recognizance of so many freeholders here as were worth £2000.[3] The letter to Mr. Burd incloses the recognizance I have taken.[4] Should those gentlemen be absent, you will take what order is necessary in the matter.

The half Sharemen are taking possession of the lands assigned them by Franklin, particularly at Tioga. John Swift, Elisha Satterly, Wm. Slocum & [Elisha] Matthewson[5] (all I believe late officers of Franklin,) are among them. These four persons (I am just informed,) have taken possession of the lands they claim there, turning off by force the former occupants. Whether the latter had any *right* to their possessions I know not: but *Force* is the mode generally adopted in that part of the county to gain possession of lands; and this morning John Jenkins (usually called Major Jenkins, & Franklin's compeer,) avowed to me explicitly that there was no other mode by which any man in the county claiming land under the Susquehannah Company could get possession of them. "There is, said he, no law in this county for trying the titles of land: For the only rules by which they should be tried are the regulations of the Susquehanna Company; and those regulations are not, nor can be admitted to govern the courts of law in their decisions, until declared to be laws by an act of the General Assembly." I answered, That such of those regulations as were made prior to the decree of Trenton, would govern the courts of law in all disputes about the titles of land among the *Connecticut Claimants,* and that a positive declaratory act was not necessary for

---

[228] [1] *P. A.,* XI, 296-97. This letter was read in the Council on May 30; *Pa. C. R.,* XV, 465.
 [2] *P. A.,* XI, 295, gives the letter to McKean; a copy of Pickering's letter to the prothonotary Burd is in M. H. S., Pickering Papers, LVIII, 34.   [3] No. 225, *ante.*   [4] See *ibid.,* note 2.
 [5] A blank space is left for Matthewson's first name.

that purpose. But he persisted in his former assertion. Then (said I) your meaning is, that there being no law as you say, to try the title of your lands, when any one claims a particular tract, he is to take possession by force? "It is," said he.

I will make no comments on these transactions and opinions.

I beg the favour of you to deliver the inclosed letter to Mr. Hodgdon as speedily as may be, and remain, with respect & affection your most h'ble servant,

Timothy Pickering.

[229] Lawrence Myers to Timothy Pickering.[1]

Sir,

I received information last evening by Capt'n Hartsoff that one of Franklin's best friends told a person in Wilkesbor'g that all that party wanted was to Git Franklin out of Confinement and if as much again bail had been required they would have Given it but as soon as Franklin was at liberty; Bail Law and all should go together for they did not regard those bonds Given. I shall be at Wilkesburgh to-morrow. I think enquiry ought to be made before somebody goes to Philadelphia. I am, Sir, yours,

Law. Myers.

May 27th, 1788.

[230] Tench Coxe to Timothy Pickering.[1]

Dear Sir

I wrote you by Maj. Smith, who is to open the road from the upper Wyoming road to Ararat & the line.[2] He is to begin about 25 miles from Wyoming on the East Side of the Moosic Ridge or Mountain near to Stantons Tavern. I hope it has been in your power to visit him and give him encouragement and push him on. The accounts, which M'r Hilborn writes us of the road above Stantons is favorable & Smith really need not be discouraged.

M'r Drinker's Son who takes this is going up to view & sur-

---

[229] [1] P. A., XI, 296. Pickering sent this letter on to Peter Muhlenberg; see no. 233, post.

[230] [1] M. H. S., Pickering Papers, XIX, 134-35, in Coxe's hand, dated May 28, 1788.

[2] Probably no. 227, ante. See accompanying sketch of the proposed roads drawn by Coxe.

vey his fathers lands bought of S. Wallis. I write Ellicot [3] by him to this Effect. That the opening of a passage from Tioga to Ararat with absolute certainty & with the utmost dispatch is so much an object with us that we wish him to push on the width of one perch as quickly as possible. The extension of it to the width of 33 feet can be done after the passage is open. As letters and optys are uncertain in your Country the com[m] wish you would write by some other Conveyance to M[r] Elicot to the same purport.* * *

[231] John Paul Schott to Peter Muhlenberg.[1]

Wilksbarre, May 29th, 1788.

Sir,

I have undertaken to raise a Troop of Light Dragoons and have got forty-two the very best young gentlemen in this county [2] and true suporters of the Law, I had 37 of them together last Monday the 26 Inst., and proper Inspectors appointed to Elect their officers where they chose your Humble Servant for their Commander, Lord Butler for first Leu't, Roswell Wells for second Leu't and Ebenezer Bowman for Cornet, the whole troop is to equip themselves. I have the Honour to send you a Copy of their Ingadgement and the return of the Election. I hope the Honorable Counsel will send us the Commissions as your Honours will find this Troop very servisable in this County, there is no news here at present only there is more than one thousand people gone throw this settlement to Niagara within two weeks. I have the Honour to subscribe my self, Sir, your Most obe't and Most Humble Servant,

John P. Schott.

[232] John Paul Schott to Peter Muhlenberg.[1]

Wilksbarre, May 30th, 1788.

Sir,

I just remember a thing I for got in my letter from yesterday.[2] I should wish you would send me about six of those Bills

[3] Andrew Ellicott, contractor for the road from Tioga to Mount Ararat. [231] [1] *P. A.*, XI, 297.

[2] The agreement to serve lists the names of forty-one men, including Schott; *ibid.*, 299-300. [232] [1] *P. A.*, XI, 298. [2] No. 231, *ante.*

ordered to be printed for consideration in regard to the seventeen Townships, which should be confirmed to us,[3] as I find some of the unruly People doubt it; the Bearer is a save hand to bring them and the Commissions too, if Counsel should see fit, which will give great Satisfaction to to your Humble Serv',

John P. Schott.

[233] Timothy Pickering to Samuel Hodgdon.[1]

Wilkesboro' May 30. 1788.

Dear Sir,

I wrote you lately a long letter, containing three dates, & finally sent it by a youth named Perkins who was procured by Jenkins to carry to Philadelphia my letters to the Vice President &c. together with the recognizance for bailing Franklin.[2] As Jenkins, I find, suspected I might write something which might prevent Franklins liberation, so I should not be surprized to learn that he had gone on the road some way & opened the letters, & then sent forward only the naked recognizance.[3] I therefore beg the favour of you to call on General Muhlenberg (or if out of the way, on some member of council) and enquire whether he has rec⁴ from me a letter dated the 27th inst.[4] in which I mentioned a report of Franklin's officers, viz. Swift, Satterly, Matthewson & Slocum, having forceably taken possession of their half share rights at Tioga, & disregarded the process of law against them; and also a conversation which that same morning passed between me & Jenkins, in which Jenkins justified the using of force in such case, and declared, that there was no law in the county for trying Connecticut titles, and that any man claiming land in the County under Connecticut had no other way to get possession of it but by force. And this opinion he said he had given to every one who fell in his way when speaking on

³ No. 218, *ante.*

[233] ¹ M. H. S., Pickering Papers, LVIII, 22-24, in Pickering's hand.

² See no. 225, *ante,* note 2. The messenger was David Perkins.

³ Pickering's communications apparently arrived safely. On May 31 Hodgdon wrote to Pickering as follows: "I happened accidentally to be waiting on Council when your Packet arrived. A full Board was summon'd the door was locked, and the communication entered on privately, the result I have not heard, but am inclined to believe that Franklin will not for some time be liberated." * * * ⁴ No. 228, *ante.*

the subject. In the letter to the Vice President I inclosed a short letter from Major Myers [5] rec[d] & dated the 27th mentioning that one of Franklins best friends had said, they did not care how much bail was required; for as soon as Franklin was at liberty, there would be an end of bail law & all law together. I also inclosed to the Vice president one letter to the Chief Justice & Judge Rush, and one to M[r] Burd prothonotary of the supreme Court,[6] the latter inclosing the recognizance, and my letter to you. I wish to know as soon as possible whether all these letters were delivered. In mine to you I requested many things to be done more than I can now enumerate. A principal object was to raise money by the sale of *half* my lands in company with Francis, Coxe &c. I desired you particularly to pay five dollars to John Sparhawk, for two volumes I bought of him for M[r] Bowman, & which I promised to pay this present month. I also earnestly requested a small sum of money by the first safe conveyance, enough to buy me two or three cows, & answer contingences, say forty or fifty dollars. M[r] Frazier who will deliver you this belongs here. He is a tall straight scotsman, an old soldier, & I believe an honest man, who might be entrusted with such a sum, if in gold; for as he is on foot silver would be inconvenient. It is said since I wrote that the conduct of Swift &c. was not quite so bad. That they submitted to become prisoners on the warrants of Esq[rs] Gore & Hollenback, who were at the Point: But this be assured of, That tis the wish of the best men here that Franklin might still be kept in jail, or at any rate not suffered to come into this county or its neighourhood even *Col[o] Butler* thinks the bailing of him of dangerous consequence.* * *

[234] Jesse Cook to Timothy Pickering.[1]

Torrington June 2[d] 1788

Kind Sir

M[r] Watson how a Rived hear from Shorney [2] Last week informes me that your State has Repeled that Act that Secured the Land to y[e] Setleres in the County of Luzarn;[3] I am Sartin No man feles Destressed for the Setlers more then myself. I own in part it is Selfishness but y[e] gratest part for y[e] poor Inhabatents

---

⁵ No. 229, *ante.*   ⁶ See no. 228, *ante,* note 2.
[234] ¹ M. H. S., Pickering Papers, LVIII, 37-38, in Cook's hand.
² Shawney.
³ The Confirming Act was suspended on March 29, 1788; no. 220, *ante.*

how has ben thare So maney years in a State of Confusion and anachy; When I heard of the grate benevolence of the State of pensylvania in granting the Land to y° poore and very unhappy Setlers of Susquhanah how head ben thare so Long a time with out order and Reglation it gave me the gratest Sattifaction posable toward that State, which is Easer to fele then to Describe; I amed to be Came a Setlor by purchasing a Setling Right and y° Last Somer went Down and tuck a vew of my Land and found it better than my Exspacttion and Com home and one of my boys went Down to tack a vew of the Same and he was pleased with the Same; and this spring I prepd a teeme and all things was maed Redey for him to do Down and Settle thare; Just before he Set out I head word that it was Detarmed by your State Not to Grand the Land and Mʳ Watson Confarms the Desagreable News: I Do Not fele more Destrest for mySelf then for thos poore Setlers how has ben Desapinted So maney times: Mʳ Watson told me that there was Report that your Asembley ment to grant 17 town Shipes [4] to y° Setlors and half Share men but I fear that: but Sopos they Shold I Can Not See that that will be for y° peice of the inhabitunts more then the others act. in my opinyon it will be fixing things So as thare will be an Evelasting Despute betwen the forst Setlors and the half Share men how got thare Land by the way of franklin and the other Despottick commit how head mad a grand Living by Selling y° Land, of y° old Setlor wich y° Law of god and Commen Sence Could Not Justify; I wish to have a few Lines from your honor. what you think will be the state of y° Case for as thing are Now I Do Not know what to Do; I head it in vew to boght part of Tripes farm and Com Down and Lived with you; but thing are too pacareus to ventor apon; Sʳ give my Complyments to Colo Butler and Esq Hollingback and Esq Wells and tell them that my family is well and hearty as I hope these Lines will find all of yours &c &c.

Jesse Cook

[235] Jesse Cook to Zebulon Butler.[1]

Torrington June 2 1788

Sir I head fixed my Son with a Tem and was all Ready to Set of for youre Cuntry when I heard that your Asemble was about

---

[4] No. 218, *ante.*
[235] [1] Wyoming Historical and Geological Society, Butler Papers.

Repeling the act that gave the Setlors there Land; and then I postponed his going Down this Spring for fear what would tack place: Mr Watson aRived from your part of the world Last week and broght word that the Asembly head Repeled that Grate and benevolent act wich was the aplase of all men of understanding;[2] he told me that they was about Giving 17 townShips to ye Setlors and half Sharemen but I fear that and am afrad they will not secure the Land to Nobody but ye Land Jobbers how would be glad to Spread blood and Carnagee througe youre Settlement. But Sopose they Should grant the Land to the old Setlors and to the half Sharemen. I havnt the Least Idea that that will Settle pece amongst you for thare will be Nothing but Lawsuts betwen the old Setlors and the half Sharemen; the unjustifiable proseding of franklin and the Dispotick committy that Granted away muc[h] Land to ye half Sharemen wich Nither the Law of God Nor man could justifye has fixed things So that it will tack one Age to Right and Settle the afare; if franklin Should Return (wich without Dout he will) he will allways have the half Sharemen on his Sid and he will Due all that he can to tack away the Land from the old forst Setlors and plase them in the hand of the half Sharemen.

Sir I head it in my vew all Last winter to have boght part of that farm of Tripps and come Down and tack up my abod with you the Remanders of my Short Life but Sence things are Not Settled yeat I have posponed all Shuch thoughts at present; I wish to have youre Jugment apon the afare and wish you would send me a Letter the forst oppertunity that you have; and if you Should See Landlord Tripp Ask him what he will Ask for his house and about 40 or 50 Acres of his land betwixt his house and ye River and 40 or 50 Acres of Land up by his house. if I could get that and thing Should turn well with ye Setlors I would com and Live thare as I would wish to have as good Land in ye medow as he has got. I would Not be aganst giving a good prise for it: I have heard that he is in Det and must Sell part of the farm. if that is the case I would be glad to know what is the Lowest that he will tack for one hundred Acres and his hous. altho his hous is Not worth much yet it would answer untill I could Build me one; &c &c &c

Sir give my Complments to Colo pickron [Pickering] and Esq Hollingback and Esq Wells and Esq Catling together with your family and inform them that I and my family are all well.

Jesse Cook

---

[2] The Confirming Act was suspended March 29, 1788; no. 220, *ante.*

To Colo. Butler at Wilksbury State of pensylvania

I must Just inform you that y° Last Electtion we Left out of y° upperhous Gen [1] Wadwirth of Durham: that Grate Enimy to the Army and have put in Colo. Chestor of Wetherfield. the house of Asemble has Not Dun anything that is worth Relating to you. they Rose Last week. the Lore house Left out Colo. Dier from being a Juge of y° Suprem Corte but y° uper hous would Not Exept of it. all that they alage is that he is a party in Evry case.

[236] Proposed Division of Luzerne County for Election Purposes.[1]

Luzerne County ss.   At a Court of General Quarter Sessions of the Peace held at Wilkesbarre in & for the county of Luzerne on the third day of June in the year of our Lord 1788, before Obadiah Gore, William Hooker Smith, Benjamin Carpenter & Nathan Kingsly esquires, Justices of the same Court.

The Court agree in the expediency & propriety of the following divisions of the said county into districts, for the purpose of electing Justices of the Peace, viz. one for each district.[2]

1. From the upper line of the county to the place at which the road crosses Rosewell Franklin's mill creek, by an east & west line, comprehending both sides of the river Susquehannah.
2. From the line last mentioned to the mouth of Wyalusing creek, by an east & west line, comprehending both sides of the Susquehannah.
3. From the line last mentioned to the mouth of Tague's creek by an east and west line, comprehending both sides of the Susquehannah.
4. From the last mentioned line to the north line of Pittstown, on the east side of the river Susquehannah.
5. From the northline of Pittstown, & including Providence, to the lower line of Wilkesbarre, on the east side of the Susquehannah.

---

[236] [1] P. H. M. C., Div. of Arch. and MSS., Record Group 27, Series: Exec. Corr., 1777-90, in Pickering's hand.   [2] *Cf.* no. 191, *ante.*

6. From the lower line of Wilkesbarre to Nescopeck Creek, or lower line of the county, on the east side of the river Susquehannah.
7. From the east & west line at the mouth of Tague's creek to the lower line of Exeter, on the West side of the Susquehannah.
8. From the lower line of Exeter to the lower line of Plymouth, on the west side of the river Susquehannah.
9. From the lower line of Plymouth to the county line of Northumberland, on the west side of the Susquehannah.

Attest[r]

Timothy Pickering

Clerk

Endorsed: Read in Council October 2nd 1788.

[237] Timothy Pickering to Peter Muhlenberg.[1]

Wilkesborough June 14, 1788

Sir,

Just before I left Philadelphia in January last, a letter from Council, dated the 31st of December,[2] was put into my hands, desiring, among other things, that I, in conjunction with the county lieutenant & others would make inquiry relative to the conduct of those elected militia officers whose commissions were withheld. The inquiry was for a good while omitted: but this spring, the County lieutenant,[3] Col° Hollenback & myself, met together, and those persons, M. Fitch Alden, William Hyde, Abraham Nesbitt & Prince Alden attended. It did not appear that M. Fitch Alden & William Hyde were concerned in the disorders consequent on Franklin's capture; particularly they were not in arms. Nesbitt owned he was in arms, and Prince Alden had early crossed the river & was coming up the bank (alone I believe) with his musket, but was disarmed by M[r] Evans & Major M°Cormick. All of them, however, gave positive assurances of their future good behaviour and determination to support the laws of Pennsylvania. Upon the whole, it was our joint opinion that it would be expedient to commissionate them. Prince

---

[237] [1] M. H. S., Pickering Papers, LVIII, 40-41, a draft in Pickering's hand; *P. A.*, XI, 312-13.   [2] Not found.   [3] Zebulon Butler.

Alden has since moved up the river to Tioga, & a commission for him would be useless. Since the above mentioned examination, this battalion has had a field day. The officers elect appeared under arms as privates; and the whole battalion behaved very well.

By George Smithers I rec[d] a letter dated May 6th from the Secretary of Council,[4] mentioning that a petition had been presented to Council by Smithers, complaining of James Nesbitt & B. Carpenter Esq[rs] Justices of this county; and desiring me to enquire particularly into their proceedings in the matter which was the ground of Smithers's complaint. I gave notice to those gentlemen of this request of Council. M[r] Carpenter, a worthy man & possessed of feeling, was, as I expected, much hurt. I am entirely satisfied that he meant to act uprightly: but the prejudices against Pennsylvanians (or Pennamites) amongst whom Smithers is ranked, are so extreme, that men of the best intentions are thereby too apt to be warped in their judgements. The law is clear, that if Smithers had been in quiet possession for three years, the process for forcible entry & detainer could not apply: but because Smithers came into possession in the summer of 1784, when the N. England people were violently driven from their possessions here, it was concluded that he was of the party, & therefore that he got possession, not peacably but by force. Parks was the complainant against Smithers, & one of his witnesses deposed "That he heard Smithers say that if any came to possess themselves of the land in dispute, he would defend the same by force and arms, & they might depend the consequence." *When* this threat was uttered, is not mentioned in the Justices' proceedings. The notes of Smithers's counsel state this evidence differently. That Smithers said, if Parks comes, and comes *without law,* to takake possession he would keep him off with force & arms. This threat however, as stated by the Justices, seemed strongly to have influenced M[r] Carpenter & he turned to the Conductor Generalis, where 1, Hawkins 145. is quoted in which an *entry* or *detainer* is considered as forceable, if threats only of bodily harm are used.[5] Major Myers was foreman of the Jury, and he thinks there was evidence to warrant their verdict: but

---

[4] Charles Biddle's letter to Pickering is in *ibid.,* 27. An identical letter signed by Peter Muhlenberg is in *P. A.,* XI, 287.

[5] *Conductor Generalis: or, The Office, Duty, and Authority of Justices of the Peace, High-Sheriffs, Under-Sheriffs, Goalers, Coroners, Constables, Jury-Men, and Overseers of the Poor* (numerous editions with varying titles and places of publication).

people here have adopted the unwarrantable opinion that jurors may be determine by their private knowledge of facts never made known to the court and parties—an opinion indeed which once was conformable with the law. For farther information on this subject I beg leave to *refer* you to Mr Bowman, the bearer of this letter & who was counsel *for Smithers.* I will only remark, that without minutely enquiring into the proceedings, there was one irregularity which I presume is sufficient to set them aside— *Esquire Nesbitt was father-in-law to Parks the Complainant.* Of this impropriety Esqr Carpenter was aware, & therefore when pltfs counsel demurred to the defts plea, he urged that the plea sh^d be withdrawn, that the *decision* might not rest with the *Justices,* but be made on the merits of the cause by the *Jury.* As I said before, I am persuaded he acted with upright intentions, and I should be sorry to have him censured. Esquire Nesbitt who is old and very infirm, made a formal resignation of his office of Justice of the peace, immediately after the examination was over.

[238] Timothy Pickering to Shadrach Sill.[1]

Mr Shadrach Sill of Lewisburgh, State of New York
    Wilkesborough County of Luzerne June 18, 1788.
Sir,
  On the second of October last John Franklin of this place was apprehended by a warrant from the Chief Justice of Pennsylvania, for treasonable practices against the state, and carried away for philadelphia, where he now remains on a charge of high treason against said state. The same afternoon one Asa Starkweather * (who had resided here for some months before, & at Franklins house, as Secretary to a board of Commissioners appointed by the Susquehannah Company, of which board Franklin was the chief agent) [2] was met by William Hooker Smith esquire, who with a few men was coming to Wilkesborough, by whom said Starkweather was taken, & secured, on a supposition that, as he was now returning from Hudson, he would have letters & papers of consequence about him relative to the conspiracy

---

[238] [1] M. H. S., Pickering Papers, LVIII, 42-43, a draft in Pickering's hand.
 * Starkweather is a short man, with a squint eye, or some other blemish in one or both eyes.
 [2] See no. 68, *ante* for the entry signed by Starkwather.

of Franklin & others against the state of Pennsylvania. And the supposition was just. He had such letters and papers, particularly a number from Doctor Joseph Hamilton of Hudson to Franklin, in consequence of which, the said letters having been sent by the Council of Penn* to the Governour of New-York, said Hamilton was apprehended & his other papers seized, which as I have been informed, contained full evidence of the wicked plot of the conspirators to overturn the government of Pennsylvania in this part of the state. Starkweather was brought by Doctor Smith to the house of Matthias Hollenback Esq. in Wilkesboro where my family then dwelt, while I was absent, and secured by a constable and other keepers, until he was rescued the night following by a body of men in arms who assembled on the report of Franklin's being taken. These men or some of them with Starkweather finally got into the house & ransacked every part of it, to find me & the intercepted letters. Starkweather embraced this opportunity, favoured by the night & the confusion of the time, to steal my Great Coat & watch, which I have particularly described in the deposition herewith handed you.[3] In November last he advertised my great coat in the Hudson paper,[4] *pretending* it was taken in the dark by mistake, & said the owner might have it by calling at the house of James Bryan Esq. in Nobletown in the State of New York. But the villain took this step merely from the hope of saving himself from a charge of theft; for as he wore the coat day after day and was seen with it by divers people in this county he reflected that he could not escape detection; But while In the county, he pretended the coat was his own, and when it was remarked that it was much too large for him, he answered, that he had it made so on purpose. He was also seen by divers persons with a watch during the few days he remained in the county after Franklin was taken; and tho' it might not be known that it was my watch, yet it was well known that *before,* he had neither watch nor great coat, nor the means of purchasing either. Even the Great Coat he wore on his journey, when he was apprehended, was Franklin's, as Starkweather himself says in his advertisement; a copy of which I now hand you.

I have given you this circumstantial detail to show the high probability, and indeed the violent presumption, that the same dirty rascal who has confessed he took my Great Coat, stole my watch also. I have now to request you will take the earliest op-

---

[3] Pickering Papers, LVIII, 41-42.   [4] No. 172, *ante.*

portunity of enquiring where Starkweather is to be found, and upon the deposition I have given you, getting him apprehended & secured in some jail in your State, or whereever he may be found; until the Government of Pennsylvania shall be informed thereof, and demand his delivery to be brought to this county to be tried for his theft above mentioned.

I should not have let this matter rest so long, had not capt. Strong [5] taken with him an advertisement of the watch and coat last fall, & promised to secure & bring in the thief; & I have been expecting Strong in all the Spring; but have heard nothing from him. Possibly he may have applied for & received my Great Coat. Please to enquire. When Capt. Satterly was out in your state last spring he saw Starkweather, who was then keeping school at Nobletown. Upon your application to the watchmakers in Hudson, you will probably learn whether the watch described has ever been in their hands. Be so good as to write me how you proceed in the business, & with what success. If you can get hold of the watch and coat or either of them, I wish you to send them by a safe conveyance to Mr Peter Aupack in New York.

[239] Samuel Hodgdon to Timothy Pickering.[1]

Philadelphia 26th June 1788.

Dear Sir

* * *The New road Mr Bowman informs me is considerd among you as a Landjobbers accomodation without advantage to the Public. surely it was not so understood in the Assembly when they so liberally countenancd it by their grant.[2] They God knows are suspicious and jealous enough usually, but perhaps the people at large more suspicious may have conceived most of the Members are interested. This will account for their generosity. Bowman tells me that Mr Ellicot says that a road to Tioga by the way of Wyoming might have been made which would have been twenty Miles Nearer. If that be true let the people who own the lands on the route subscribe as we have

---

[5] Probably Solomon Strong, who had incurred the ire of Joseph Hamilton for being willing to cooperate with the commission engaged in settling land claims; see no. 113, *ante*.

[239] [1] M. H. S., Pickering Papers, XL, 254, in Hodgdon's hand.

[2] See no. 203, *ante*, note 3.

done and I doubt not they also may meet with Goverments assistance to open it, for I suppose the more the Country is intersected with communications the better. I never heard of any Country having too many roads. In our case we candidly gave out, and wished to have it understood, that we meant by the road now running to accomodate ourselves and raise the value of our lands to be effected by them, and I hope we shall reap a full harvest in its proper season, from our exertions. I have not found a favorable Opportunity to propose the sale of your Lands to Francis, or any One else, we are about a final adjustment of our accounts for those Lands, at, or before the close of which I shall propose it to him. * * *

[240] Peter Muhlenberg to Stephen Balliet and William Armstrong.[1]

In Council, Philad'a, June, 1788.

Gentlemen,

The General Assembly by their resolution of the 27th of March last, having directed the S. E. Council in the following words to wit:[2]

And Council considering it their duty to carry into effect the measures contained in the said resolution by the appointment of two discreet persons, whose business it sh^d be to view the lands comprehended therein, and make a true report. They hereby commission you for those purposes; requesting you wou'd proceed without delay to the County of Luzern and consult Messrs Montgomery & Gray deputy Surveyors of that Country, who are instructed to assist you with all draughts of surveys and any useful information or advice in their power. Col. Pickering also, the Clerk of the Court of Sessions, will furnish you with descriptions of the townships comprehended in the resolution of the House of Assembly. In full expectation that you will compass the business with all necessary care and dispatch, so as that the Board may be enabled, by your report principally, to comply with the intention of the Legislature. I heartily wish you health and success, &c. I am, Gentlemen, with great Respect, your most obedient & very humble Servant,

Peter Muhlenberg.

[240] [1] *P. A.*, XI, 304.

[2] For the language of the resolution omitted from this letterbook copy of Muhlenberg's letter, see no. 219, *ante*.

[241]   Extract from the Minutes of the Pennsylvania Council.[1]

Philadelphia, Tuesday, July 1st, 1788.
A letter from Wioming, dated the twenty-seventh day of June,[2] and signed by Messieurs Nathan Dennisen, Zebulun Butler, William Hookes,[3] and Nathan Carey, was read, from which it appears that on the night between the twenty-sixth and twenty-seventh ultimo, Colonel Pickering was, by a lawless banditte, made prisoner, and forcibly carried off from his dwelling in Wilkesbarre; that the officers of Government are exerting themselves to recover Colonel Pickering, and to bring the perpetrators of this daring outrage to condign punishment.

Resolved, That the officers of Government in Luzerne be informed that Council are much pleased with their spirited exertions on this occasion, and that every aid and assistance shall be given by the supreme executive, as far as the laws of the State will warrant.

Resolved, That the President is requested to give official information of this transaction to their Excellencys the Governors of New York and New Jersey, and request their assistance in securing the perpetrators of this daring villainy, if they should enter those States.

[242]   Samuel Hodgdon to Rebecca Pickering.[1]

Philadelphia 1ˢᵗ July 12 oClock
Madam
By Letters received this Morning from Mʳ Horton and Betsy I am made acquainted with your distress'd situation. At such a time I have to lament that I am not my Own Man, for with wing'd swiftness would I, if that was the case, come to your releif. The Marching a Company of Men from this City to the Ohio lays entirely on me, and I am directed to accomplish it by the 12ᵗʰ instant at farthest, after which, if I am not informed of

---

[241] [1] *Pa. C. R.,* XV, 484.   [2] Not found.
[3] This name should probably be that of William Hooker Smith, one of the justices of the peace in Luzerne County.
[242] [1] M. H. S., Pickering Papers, LVIII, 49-50, in Hodgdon's hand.

390

Mr Pickerings return, you may expect to see me. I have just seen Council on this business. They have done everything that was possible to vindicate the honour of Goverment, and procure Mr Pickering's release [2] and the authors of this violation of the peace of the County, will repent their rashness and intemperance. The thing they aimed at, (if they had anything particular in view) will not be accomplished. if I judge right it will strengthen their leaders chain.[3] Your friends are all exceeding apprehensive for your health under these reiterated distresses. your known firmness I depend on to preserve you, though I know your frame is delicate. bear up I beseech you—better times await you. I am very happy that Mr Ellicot and Horton were present, from their sage advice you will derive peace and information. I hope they will not leave you until Mr Pickering returns, or I come to your releif. * * *

[243] Timothy Pickering to Rebecca Pickering.[1]

July 3^d 1788.

My Dear Beckey

I hoped ere this to have relieved your anxiety in some degree by informing you that I was alive and well. We marched all the night & the next day after I was taken; & as one half the time it was thro' pathless woods, you may suppose I was not a little fatigued: but in this way I have since had no reason to complain. I have constantly lodged in the woods, sometimes in the open air, but generally under a shelter of bushes; at one time covered with bark which kept us from the rain. I know not how long I may be in such a situation, I shall therefore mention a few articles necessary to render it more tolerable; but send nothing else, as more would be burthensome in my movable condition. Tho' excepting two days when we had venison, my constant food has been fried salt pork & bread, with water for my drink, yet I am in perfect health; and as I eat this food with appetite, I desire you to send no article of diet except one pound of chocolate & a pound of sugar.

You must certainly understand that I was taken & am de-

---

[2] See no. 241, *ante.*

[3] Hodgdon is referring, of course, to the imprisonment of John Franklin.

[243] [1] M. H. S., Pickering Papers, II, 39-40.

tained, for the purpose of redeeming Franklin from goal. Had he been liberated lately on bail, they say this difficulty would not have arisen. Some would be satisfied with less; some with more: While one would be contented if he were bailed on condition of his residing in Connecticut or elsewhere out of this state, another desires he may be bailed at large. at the same time it is suggested that his leading friends here did not intend he should reside in this county, had he been liberated when Perkins [2] went with the bail bond to Phila*. What steps the government will take I know not: but in considering the means of my redemption, they will doubtless consult the dignity & safety of the state: this may prolong my confinement, & consequently add to your distress and mine: but, my dear, we cannot expect that the dignity & safety of the state should be sacrificed to the interests of an individual family. I beg you therefore to resume that patience & fortitude which you have so often manifested, & trust to that kind & wise Providence, under which we have hitherto been preserved, for my deliverance from my present confinement. For my own part, I feel resigned to my fate, as it was undeserved from the hands of men, especially of the people of this county, whom, as a body, I have uniformly striven to serve in everything consistent with justice and with prudence. —My captors & keepers have repeatedly said I should be well used, but used as Franklin has been. Accordingly this day my fetters were put on. My keepers discovered some feeling on this occasion, & apologized for putting me in chains, by saying *such were their orders.* In other respects I live as they do: they are civil, and take pains to make me as comfortable as my situation will admit.

The following articles I wish to have sent me as early as may be, viz: my old camlet cloak—2 pairs of my strongest worsted stockings—one shirt, one coarse pocket handkerchief, one coarse towel, $\frac{1}{2}^{lb}$ soap, $\frac{1}{2}$ quire paper, two quils, my penknife, my leathern gloves, needle thread & worsted yarn (the thread to dearn my fustian trousers) 1^{lb} chocolate & 1^{lb} sugar. To these add Dr. Prices sermons which I was lately sending to you and Betsy. All these may be put in a strong bag, which will make a pack convenient to carry at the back; and to sling it send me four yards of the strong yellow binding. I forgot shoes, send my strongest pair. Send also a small toothed comb.

Our friend M^r. Hodgdon will be anxious to learn what is my condition: for his information send him such extracts from this letter as you think proper.

---

[2] David Perkins. See no. 287, *post,* note 6.

If I had time, I should send some particular directions about my farming business:[3] but I must wait another conveyance lest I lose the present. God preserve you! Give my love to your sister, & kiss our dear boys for me.

Ever yours
Timothy Pickering

[244] Testimony Concerning the Capture of Timothy Pickering.[1]

Examinations of sundry persons before Nathan Denison & Wm H. Smith esquires, July 5, 1788

Joel Whitcomb sworn.

Que. Who sent you up to Kinny's?

Ans. It was that little Aaron Kilborn sent me up to Garret Smith & Thos Kinney, to tell them to come down to Dudley's, & if the boys were not there, for them to go down to Tunkhannock: That he went up. That Smith had hurt himself, & would not come without a canoe, & Kinney was not at home. That he had Gid^n Dudley's horse to ride up. That he saw a number 10 or 12 boys at Dudleys, Nathan Abbot, Gidon Dudley, Daniel Earl, Benj^a Earl, John Whitcomb, David Woodward, Noah Phelps, Benj^a Abbot, Joseph Dudley, & others. He saw at other times under arms in the company Timothy Kilbourn. That Dudley's boys took a bag of meal from the canoe & meant to take it to Joseph Kilburns to be baked for their company. That he saw Thos Kinney under arms in company with his brother (meaning Jno Whitcomb) going down the river.

Committed. Thos Kinney saith he was there under arms Sunday, and that he had been after cabbage plants & tobacco plants & hunting & that he was at Dudleys on Friday there he first heard of Col^o Pickering being taken & saw a number of men at Dudley's, & the men mentioned by Whitcomb at Joseph Kilborn's. That John Hyde offered him a paper of association to sign.

Discharged. Elijah Reynolds examined saith That he had no hand in taking Col^o Pickering & knew nothing of it. That the party had been at his house. That he saw Kilborn's boys

---

[3] Pickering added a long postscript containing directions for tending to his farm.

[244] [1] M. H. S., Pickering Papers, LVIII, 51-52, a copy in Pickering's hand.

carry wheat from Tylers That the two Earls and Gideon Dudley under arms & others were at his house.

Committed & Discharged July 19th. Joseph Earl examined saith That on wednesday he returned home, & when he arrived there he found his wife crying & told him that his sons with others had gone to take Col° Pickering. That on Friday Night the party, Dan¹ Earl, Ben. Earl, Zeb. Cady, Gideon Dudley, Joseph Dudley, brought Col° Pickering to his house, & that he eat in his house. That they took him out and the next morning brought him in to breakfast. Afterward they crossed the river with the Col°. That in the morning when they bro't the Col° in he was tied with a cord. That he released him. That it was his three sons with John Hyde & the two Dudleys, That he saw the company since in number 10. That Fred Budd was one of the party.

Committed. Ephraim Tyler (issuing commissary to the party) examined. That the party frequently had been at his house & that they had taken 18¹ᵇ meat.

Committed. Martin Dudley examined, Saith that he afforded the rioters relief as they passed back & forward & that he was forced to do it. That Ephraim Lewis had come from the government party, & told the rioters that a party was coming to attack Meshoppen, but supposed they had got lots.

Committed. Joseph Kilborn examined saith That his two sons left his house the night before the riot was committed, That there was bread baked at his house. That he understood that John Jenkins was their counsellor. That col° M°Kinstry & Major Beach have advised to suppress government.

[245] Deposition of Andrew Ellicott.[1]

June 8th, 1788.

This day I arrived at Tyoga. I found the inhabitants up the river above Wyoming, (with few exceptions,) disaffected to the Jurisdiction of Pennsylvania, and anxious for the liberation of Mr. John Franklin. At Tunchannock I found a number of people assembled in a riotous manner about the House of a Mr. Marcey,[2] they had taken off the Roof of his House, and were preparing to level it with the ground, which they effected before

---

[245] [1] P. H. M. C., Div. of Arch. and MSS., Record Group 27, Series: Exec. Corr., 1777-90, in Ellicott's hand; *P. A.*, XI, 327-29.

[2] Zebulon Marcy.

night. From my appearance they supposed me to be a Traveler, and enquired from what part of the Country I came, I informed them from Philadelphia; they then requested information relative to the liberation of Col. Franklin, as they were pleased to call him, I gave them all the satisfaction I could, and closed my relation with observing that I believe they gave him a military Title to which he had no claim. They answered that a free people had a right to appoint their own commandant. I advised them to submit to the Jurisdiction of Pennsylvania, but they treated the advice with contempt.

At Mishopping[3] I found one Mr. Dudley and his sons violently opposed to the Laws and Jurisdiction of this State.

At Tyoga I could plainly perceive the disposition of the people in favour of Franklin and the half Share rights.

On the 17th I was informed that a plan was just ready for execution that would throw the County into confusion, and was desired to put Col. Pickering on his guard. On the 19th I set out by water for Wyoming, in the afternoon I stopped at Obediah Gores, Esq'; while I was there we received information by a person who was a stranger to me, that on a day which he named, a meeting (in which John Jenkins presided) had been held down the River by the leaders in opposition to the Jurisdiction of Pennsylvania, in which it was resolved to take Col. Pickering, and retaliate for the captivity of Mr. John Franklin; he likewise informed us that the day preceding this meeting, John Jenkins passed chiefly at Col. Butlers. On the 22 I arrived at Col. Pickerings, and gave him all the information I could relative to the state of affairs up the River, and the general disposition of the People. he would not give any credit to that part of the information respecting the determination to take, and retaliate on him for the imprisonment of Franklin. On the 26th, in the evening, between the hours of 11 and 12 o'clock, M[rs] Pickering sent a person to inform me that a number of armed men, painted like Indians, had a few minutes before entered their House, made her Husband prisoner, pinnioned him and carried him off; immediately after receiving this information I went and alarmed Col. Butler and Cap. Schott. On the 27th, about 10 o'clock in the afternoon, Capt. Schott followed the Insurgents with 18 Horse Men; by 10 o'clock in the morning about 140 of the Militia were collected at Wilkesborough; and on the 28th, about 9 o'clock in the morning, 28 of the Militia were sent off. In the

---

[3] Meshoppen.

evening Capt. Schott returned with the Horse Men, after advancing within 7 miles of 7 of the Insurgents. the same evening, 10 of the Militia also returned. On the 29th, in the evening, the remaining 18 Militia returned, after taking two suspicious characters. On the first of July 50 of the Militia, under the Command of Major Mires and Capt. Ross, set out from Mr. John Hollenback's up the river after the Insurgents.

The following persons compose part of the body of Insurgents, Viz., John Hyde, Capt. Daniel Earle, Benjamin Earle, Cady, Wilkes Jenkins, Joseph Dudley, Gideon Dudley, David Woodward, John Whitcomb, Timothy Kilbourn and Thomas Kinney.

And. Ellicott.

In Council, July 7th, 1788.

Personally appeared Andrew Ellicot, Esq., and declareth on his solemn affirmation the foregoing narrative to be true.

Affirmed & subscribed in presence of [   ].

[246] Nathan Denison to Charles Biddle.[1]

Kington, the 8th of July, 1788.

Dear Sir,

I have to inform you that I received your letter of the first of this instant,[2] and give my harty thanks for your attention to the affairs of this Settlement. I have only to inform you that I do not think so much of the plan of the insurgent Now as I did at the time that Mr. Elicut left us, as there is but Eighteen that have been active in that party as yet, that we Can find out. Would not trouble you With a long account of affairs, but for particulars must refer you to a general letter to Council for the information of What has turned up with us Since We rote last. Pleas to give my compliments to Col. Reddick and Col. Deen, and except the same your Self. From your frind and Humble Servent,

Nathan Denison.

---

[246] [1] *P. A.,* XI, 327.

[2] Not found. Undoubtedly it was the result of a council resolution of July 1, calling for congratulations to be sent officers of the county for their zeal and promising help to them.

[247] Proclamation of the Pennsylvania Council.[1]

Pennsylvania, ss.

By the Vice-President *and the* Supreme Executive Council *of the Commonwealth of Pennsylvania,*

A PROCLAMATION.

Whereas by depositions taken according to law, it appears that several evil disposed persons have conspired to obstruct the execution of the laws in the county of Luzerne, and have violently seized and carried off the person of Timothy Pickering, esquire, an officer of government, whom they still retain as a prisoner: AND WHEREAS it is of great importance to the good people of this Commonwealth that such heinous offenders should be brought to condign punishment: WE have thought fit to offer, and do hereby offer, a Public Reward of THREE HUNDRED DOLLARS for apprehending and securing *John Jenkins,* THREE HUNDRED DOLLARS for apprehending and securing *John Hyde,* and the sum of ONE HUNDRED DOLLARS for apprehending and securing each and every of the following named persons, viz. *Daniel Earl, Benjamin Earl,   Cady,*[2] *Wilkes Jenkins, Joseph Dudley, Gideon Dudley, David Woodward, John Whitcomb, Timothy Kilburne,* and *Thomas Kinney,* or for apprehending and securing any other persons who shall be convicted of aiding and assisting in taking off the said Timothy Pickering—the reward for apprehending and securing any of the above named persons will be paid on their being delivered to the jail of the county of Northampton: And all Judges, Justices, Sheriffs, and Constables are hereby strictly enjoined and required to make diligent search and enquiry after, and to use their utmost endeavours to appre-

---

[247] [1] M. H. S., Pickering Papers, LVIII, 53; *P. A.,* XI, 329. The proclamation was printed in both English and German. The Council ordered its publication in the *Freeman's Journal* as well as in newspapers printed in York, Carlisle, and Pittsburgh. It was occasioned not only by the information sent to the Council by the Luzerne magistrates but also by Ellicott's deposition; *Pa. C. R.,* XV, 489.

[2] Ellicott's deposition had omitted Cady's first name. The list is in the order given in the deposition; no. 245, *ante. Cf.* the names given in no. 244, *ante,* where Cady's first name is given as Zebulon.

hend and secure the said offenders, so that they may be dealt with according to law.

GIVEN *in Council, under the Hand of the Honorable* PETER MUHLENBERG, *Esquire, Vice-President, and the Seal of the State, at Philadelphia, this eighth day of July, in the year of our Lord one thousand seven hundred and eighty-eight.*

PETER MUHLENBERG.

Attest. CHARLES BIDDLE, Secretary.

[248] Extract from the Minutes of the Pennsylvania Council.[1]

PHILADELPHIA, Wednesday, July 9th, 1788.

* * * On motion,

Resolved, That Mr. [David] Redick, Member of this Board, be requested to go to the States of New Jersey and New York, in order to communicate to the Executives of those States the intelligence which Council has lately received of farther outrages committed in the county of Luzerne, and to request their aid in apprehending and securing the persons concerned in seizing and carrying off Timothy Pickering, Esquire, Prothonotary of Luzerne county, if they should enter either of the States aforesaid.

Mr. Redick assured Council of his readiness to comply with this resolution.

The following draft of instructions to Mr. Redick was read and approved, vizt:

In Council, Philadelphia, July 9th, 1788.

Dear Sir:—The Board this morning re-assumed the consideration of the letters and other intelligence received from Wyoming, and are unanimously of opinion that the most vigorous and determined measures are necessary to restore order and good government in that distracted country. In consequence of this determination, a proclamation [2] is directed to issue offering ample rewards for apprehending the principals concerned in the late outrage against the person of Colonel Pickering; and in all probability an armed force will be speedily employed to reduce the insurgents to reason. But previous to this step being taken, the Board wish to communicate their intentions to their Excellencies the Governors of New York and New Jersey, to request that

---

[248] [1] *Pa. C. R.,* XV, 490-91.   [2] No. 247, *ante.*

those Governments would take such steps as may best conduce to facilitate our endeavours to prevent, if possible, the inhabitants of those States from giving aid and assistance to the insurgents, while acting in open opposition and defiance to our laws, and to prevent their finding an asylum or protection within those States. Council now request that you, as a Member of the Board, and fully acquainted with every thing that relates to this business, would be pleased to proceed immediately to New Jersey and New York, to carry their intentions into execution.[3] Your own discretion will govern you in transacting this important business; and the friendly disposition the States of New Jersey and New York have ever evinced toward this State, prevent the Board from entertaining the least doubt that those States will readily concurr in every prudent and necessary measures. With respect and esteem I am, dear sir, Your most obedient servant,

Peter Muhlenberg.

[249] Zebulon Butler and Others to Benjamin Franklin.[1]

Wilkesbarre, July 9th, 1788.

Sir,

As the Bearer, Mr. [Thomas] Wigton, goes this day to Philadelphia on his own private business, we think it highly expedient by him, to inform your Excellency & Council of the present situation of this County.[2]

In our last, we informed that the People in general, were spirited and seem'd determined to do all in their power to silence the lawless Banditti who committed the Riot of taking Col. Pickering. In this we have to inform that we were not deceived. The Militia under the Command of the Sheriff repaired near to

[3] Benjamin Franklin's letter introducing Redick to Gov. George Clinton of New York is in *P. A.*, XI, 335. New Jersey's governor, William Livingston, promised the fullest cooperation; *ibid.*, 336-37. Livingston's letter was read in Council on July 18; *Pa. C. R.*, XV, 493-94.

A warrant issued by Richard Morris, Chief Justice of New York, and forwarded by Governor Clinton to all civil and military officers in New York, and particularly to those at Chemung in Montgomery County, is printed in *P. A.*, XI, 340-41. On July 22, copies of these documents were brought to the Council by Redick; *Pa. C. R.*, XV, 495-96.

[249] [1] *P. A.*, XI, 330-31.

[2] Wigton was voted £15 by the Council on July 18 for his expenses; *Pa. C. R.*, XV, 493.

the place where the Rioters were posted, and after the scheme was agreed upon in which they were to be attacked, Capt. Ross with a party of twelve or fourteen began his march & just after day light appeared the next morning, met the Rioters, gave them Battle and oblig'd them to leave the ground. In the attack Capt. Ross behaved with much intrepidity and Calmness, but had the misfortune of receiving a wound through his arm and another through his body. However we are happy to find them not mortal. By appearances we have much assurance that he will soon recover, as yet we have no certain intelligence that more than one of the Rioters are wounded, However it is to be believed that there are more, how many we cannot tell.

After this small engagement the Militia soon returned. The places of the Rioters resort is so situated, that after mature deliberation it was concluded a smaller body of Men would much better effect their reduction. Their number does not exceed eighteen and it is generally thought and indeed reported that many of them are much disatisfied with the imprudence of their conduct, and some of them have left the County. Col. Pickering, by the remainder of them is still detained, but we have some expectation that he will be released by them in the course of the week. The fathers of most of the Rioters we have in close custody. Some or all of them have advis'd to the nefarious plan, and afforded comfort to the Rioters since their appearance in arms, for which proceeding we think their liberty ought to be restrained. They appear to be much affected with their confinement, and seem willing to acknowledge that they have been embarked in a most glaring enterpize. All possible pains are taken to transmit intelligence to their Children to release Col. Pickering, But whether they will do it or not immediately we cannot say. Measures to oblige them to it are now concerting, and will, the latter end of this week be carried into execution. A number of Men are preparing themselves to steal a march upon them and should the Rioters get no information of it (which we imagine they will not[)] no doubt but they will fall into our hands.

Whatever accounts may be given your Excellency & Council of the *inactivity* of the People of the County we are confident they will gain no ground of belief, when we inform every thing practicable to be done has not been omitted. The militia have done their duty with chearfulness and stand ready for the second Toure. On the whole, it is probable, and almost morally certain, that we shall disperse the Rioters if not captivate them in a very short time. In the fullest belief of this, we beg leave to subscribe ourselves your Excellency's most obedt and very humble servants,[3]

> Zebn. Butler,
> Wm. Hooker Smith,
> Lord Butler.

[250] Stephen Balliet and William Armstrong to Benjamin Franklin.[1]

Wilksbarre, July 9th, 1788.

Gentlemen,

We have the Honor to Inform You we arived at this place on the first Instant, & found the whole settlement in motion, on acc't of Col. Pickerings being carried off a few days before, by a Bandity here called Halfshear men or wild Boys, a Detachment of the Militia accompanied the Sheriff up the river, & several small parties were sent on in Quest of the Insurgents, on the 3d, a few random shotts ware fired across the river, & on the 4th, the Detachment Commanded by Cap't Ross, consisting of 18 men, who had six suspected persons under his Caire, fell in with the Insurgents in number 13, the letter we are Informed had several wounded & ware Obliged to retire, Cap't Ross was wounded, but it is Expected not Mortal. Nothing has happened since. Mrs. Pickering rec'd a letter from the Col., Dated the 3d Inst.,[2] Informing hir that he is well & that his Keepers Expected to Exchange him for Franklin, which Idea he Treats with contempt, aledging the State would act Consisting to their Dignity. We Rec'd a hint that a partie is raising secreatly, who are to take the woods in Quest of him. The Bearer waits at the dore, You will excuse hast. We remain with much Esteem Your Honors most Obedient & very Humble Servants,

> Stephen Balliet,
> Wm. Armstrong.[3]

---

[3] For the Council's answer, see no. 264, *post.*

[250] [1] *P. A.,* XI, 332.   [2] No. 243, *ante.*

[3] It will be recalled that Balliet and Armstrong had been recently named commissioners to determine the holdings of Pennsylvania claimants in the seventeen townships; no. 240, *ante.*

[251] Report of John Paul Schott's Trial.[1]

At a Court of Enquiry holden July the 12th 1788, by order of Zebulon Butler Esquire Lieut of the County of Luzerne, & pursuant to the request of Cap[t] John P Schott; for the purpose of examing into the conduct of the said Schott while up the River on the late expedition

Cap[t] William Hibbert Presd[t]   Lieut George Cooper
Cap[t] Daniel Gore   Lieut Philip Myers
Cap[t] G. P. Ransom   Lieut Thomas Drake
Lieut Shubal Bidlack   Members

Cap[t] Schott States that, altho a Company of Troop was raised & he appointed Cap[t] yet none of the officers had Commission.[2] But twas thought the late Insurrection would Justify his calling out his proposed company. he went with the troop the next morning. he expected & party of foot after him found many inconviniences on the march, Rain, false reports &c. staid at Jone's the 1st night next morning went on to Tankhannock. then all thought best to return.

2[d] time he march[d] on after a party of foot met them at Justus Jone's. an agreement was made that Cap[t] Ross[3] shou'd strike at black walnut bottom & come down to Meshoppin where the main body was to meet Cap[t] Ross, that he with his troop that night march'd on, and lodged at Ousterhoudts. Z Mercy then came and informed that the whole body of the Insurgents were at Tankhannock about 3 miles above us. a council was call[d], Mess[rs] Cary & Mercy went through the woods to meet Cap[t] Ross & call him back. could not find Cap[t] Ross. the main body march[d] at two A. M. to surround a house where the insurgents were, at break of day. the Insurgents were gone & the seige in vain. then march[d] to the *narrows* about 2 miles above, to learn what was become of Cap[t] Hartseph. heard nothing of him, or his party. there a young Lad came & informed that the insurgents would way-lay our party at Jaques hill (which M[r] Cary afterwards found true). then the main body march'd back to Mercy's house: the next morning between break of day & sunrise was the time to meet Cap[t] Ross at Meshoppin. A Consultation was held what time to march from Mercy's house, for his

---

[251] [1] Wilkes College Library, Wilkes-Barre, Pa., McClintock Papers, in two different hands, both unknown.

[2] See no. 231, *ante*.   [3] William Ross.

402

part he had no Commission, but was merely a Volunteer; he thought proper to march at ½ past 2 oClock; Maj^r Myers was present & the Sheriff who were authorized. the Sheriff &c ordered the march to begin at *one* oClock. The Centinel neglected, he, Capt Schott did not Countermand any orders given; he was not the highest in Command, and did but give his opinion. a gun was fired by one of the Centinels the party rous^d & found it was then three oClock. he ordered the troop to march on then as fast as possible. Arrived at Meshoppin as soon as possible—with the troop—the infantry did not go.

Mr Catlin,[4] says that Capt Schott with his troop came up with the foot at Justin Jones, & found that Maj^r Myers had Called Capt Ross party over the River, the Sh:ff & Coroner went over to them, & part came over, after we Join^d there was a Consultation & agreed that Capt Ross should take a party & go thro the woods & come in on the River at Black walnut Bottom & Maj^r Myers & Capt Schott, & the party was to meet Ross the next Morning after day Light at Masshoppin. we proceed^d and Lay^d at Ousterhouts, & in the Night March^d to Tunkannock in order to Surroun^d the house of Dan. Earl, but when we came to Tunk^k found the Insurgents were not there, then march^d to the Narrows in order to meet Capt Hartsiff. found him not there march^d back to Tunk^k, & there tarried untill Evening then agr^d to go on with the [hors?] to Miss^n the time being proposs^d Capt Shott said half after two the Sh:ff said they Must go sooner, and added that if the Officers would not go he would go with what men he could get, & turn^d to the Serj^t & told him to rouse them up so as to start at one oClock but it was not done untill break of day. they Immediately pursued & came to Messh^n when they came to Widgons the women told them that the Insurgents had gone up the hill about Three Q^{rs} of an hour.

Mr Staples says that he heard Capt Shott say he was of the Oppinion that it was soon enough to Start at three oClock but Mr Butler give me orders to wake up the people a soon as one by all means, he says that he was verry Sleapy and tired and not verry well after our Relief he told the Sentry to waik him up at the time if he goot him asleep Viz by one oClock. he then Lean^d down and fell Asleep & the Centry did not obey his orders but never waiked me untill the Centry fire^d which was about day break.

---

[4] All that follows is in a different hand from that for the testimony of Schott.

Saturday July 12ᵗʰ 1788 at a court of Enquiry held this day by order of the County Lᵗ whereby Capᵗ Hibbard is president.

Reporteth that upon after examining the Witness, & according to the present evidence are of Oppinion that Capᵗ Shott be acquitted with honor.

William Heberd President.

[252] Petition of John Van Campen and Others to the Pennsylvania Council.[1]

To His Excellency Benjamin Franklin Esquire President of the State of Pennsylvania and To the Honorable the Executive Council.

The Petition of the Subscribers, Inhabitants of the County of Northampton, Owners of Land at Wyoming and elsewhere on the River Susquehanna, claiming under Titles derived from this State, in Behalf of themselves and their Associates most humbly represent:

That your Petitioners from their present Places of Residence, North of the Blue Mountain, have not the Means of early Information on any Subject, we reside far from the Seat of Government and unfortunately for us, are often uninformed of the Measures pursuing by the State at Times when our Interest is essentially concerned. We Knew not of the Resolve of the Assembly passed the 27 day of March last,[2] before the Publication thereof in Dunlap and Claypoole's Paper, reached us by Accident on the 10ᵗʰ instant. We observe that the Commissioners require That the Claimants under This State do send "Such Papers and other Information as will enable the Commissioners to ascertain the Situation and Quantity of such Lands respectively claimed by them to Colonel Pickering at Wilksbarre, by the 25ᵗʰ Day of this Month." A Period so near at Hand and at a Season of the year with us the Height and Hurry of Harvest as renders the Absence of every Man among us, that has a Sheaf of Grain of their own to reap or depends on getting Bread for his Labour from his friend or Neighbour, impossible: We therefore, beg Council to consider the Embarrassments that present to defeat the Accomplishment of the Duty of the Commissioners. We Con-

[252] [1] P. H. M. C., Div. of Arch. and MSS., Record Group 27, Series: Exec. Corr., 1777-90, signed by each individually.

[2] See no. 219, *ante.*

ceive their Business is to view and Value every Tract of Land claimed by Us and our Associates, to have the fullest Information of the Improvements made on the Lands by the Claimants under Pennsylvania before their Expulsion, in Order that they might form a Judgment of the Value of our Property and the Amount of the Compensation to be made for our Losses. It appears to Us that to effect this with any Degree of Certainty the personal Attendance of the former Settlers will be absolutely needful, and if we set out on this Business now, We turn our Backs on our Crops and throw ourselves defenceless and unarmed in the Way of a Set of lawless Banditti who having formerly robbed and ruined many of us, are now quarrelling and destroying One another about the Division of our Possessions and Property and amongst whom at any Time, especially the present, neither our Papers or Persons would be safe; they have even suspected and seized upon their friend, Counsellor, and Advocate, Timothy Pickering, to whose extraordinary abilities many of our associates owe their Ruin and whose Machinations produced the Act of 27th of March 1787, which has entangled the State in Perplexity heretofore unknown in Pennsylvania.[3]

With the most perfect Respect for your Excellency and Council we pray for Leave to call to your Remembrance the Proceedings of April, 1783 Mess[rs] Joseph and William Montgomery and Moses M[c]Clean were appointed Commissioners by the Legislature, before whome the Claimants under Pennsylvania met at Wyoming and presented a State of their respective Claims,[4] at which Time the Surveyor of the District Col. Stewart, was call'd upon to produce the original Survey and General Drafts of that Country from Fort Augusta to the Bounds of the State, by which at one View the several Owners could shew the Spot he claimed and his Order or Warrant therefor. We can with Truth and Boldness affirm that the Commissioners were fully satisfied with our Conduct and that Demonstration beyond the Power of Contradiction, shone forth then on the Side of Justice, And that we and our Associates rested from that Time in full Confidence and on the most solemn Assurances of the State, pledged to us by their Commissioners for Support and Protection in our Property against all Invaders. How far and fataly we have been disappointed the Act of the 27st Day of March 1787 will shew. We,

---

[3] The reference is to Pickering's part in securing the Confirming Act; see no. 184, *ante*, for Pickering's own account of his role.

[4] For the exchanges between the commissioners and the Pennsylvania and Connecticut claimants, see Vol. VII, nos. 147-54 and 157.

therefore, beseech Your Excellency and the Honorable the Executive Council to take our Case under your Consideration, to bring in Review before You the Hardships we labour under and the Uncertainty and Hazard of either attending in Person or transmitting our Deeds, Drafts or Contracts to Timothy Pickering who we hear is at present in Duress, indeed it seems doubtful to us whether the Commissioners can proceed in the Business during those Times of Confusion. But if they may, it must be evident that without a View of the Premisses and General Draught of the Country now called Luzerne from Nescopeck to Tioga, they cannot neither ascertain whose the Lands of Right belong unto nor affix a Value so as to do Justice to the lawful Owners in Estimating the Compensation to be made them. Trusting therefor that your Excellency and Council will justify us in a perfect Neutrality in the present State of Riot and Quarrels at Wyoming, and that no Interference of Ours at present would tend to any good Purpose, but on the Contrary rather involve our worthy Citizens, the Original Owners in Feuds with the Banditti at Wyoming. We committ Ourselves and Associates to the Direction of Council on this Occasion, and as in Duty bound shall ever pray
Lower Smithfield Northampton County
July 14, 1788.

John van Campen. ⎫
John Chambers   ⎪
William Clark   ⎬ Agents for the Owners
John Smyth   ⎪ of Land at Wyoming
                ⎭ who reside in North-
ampton County

[253] Journal Kept by Timothy Pickering during His Captivity.[1]

Jovis 26 June 88. travelling all night & frid^y late P. M. reach^d Earls above Tunkhannock. Fri. nt in the woods. Satur^y travelled 2½ hours, & pitched in the woods. Sunday 29th, 30th & July 1. (T) march^d 2 or 3 hours, lay in the woods, open air. Wed^y 2^d marched 1 hour & pitch^d in woods. 3^d ibid. rec^d pen, ink, paper to write to my wife. Keepers said they had *orders* to supply me for that purpose, or to write to Phila^a if I chose.

[253] [1] M. H. S., Pickering Papers, LVIII, 45-46, in Pickering's hand. Copies in other hands are in *ibid.*, 46-48 and in LIII, 203-04. Words in brackets are supplied from the copies.

Wrote to my wife for camlet cloak, 2 pairs worsted hose, 1 shirt, 1 pocket handkerchief, 1 towel, needle; thread, yarn, leather gloves, 4 y^{ds} yellow binding, a bag, [1 lb chocolate], ½ lb soap, [1 lb sugar], ½ quire paper, shoes, 2 quils, penknife, Dr Price's Sermons, fine comb.[2]

4th July ibid. The anniversary of the declaration of independence! The birthday of American Freedom! All America rejoicing—but *I* am in chains!!! It began to rain this morning & is likely to continue all day. Covered our bush roof with bark wh. kept dry. P. M. fair. B Earl about noon went to get provisions, & returned without any. He informs that he called at E. Tylers, where Mrs Tyler told him the High Sheriff with D^y Shff Ross, & about 18 men had met with 3 of the boys & exch^d some shot, in wh. Gid. Dudley was wounded in the hand, & had his rifle stock split in pieces, & Wm Ross was shot thro' the body & fell & was carried into Wigtons. The engagement at Mesh[oppen] Creek, with Gid Dudley, Jno Whitcomb & Wm Phe[lps?]

Saturday July 5. fair morn. T. Kilborn returned from Tylers says Mr Ross was taken down in a canoe for Wilkesboro', but was not expected to live to reach that place.

☞ D. Taylor says that sows should be very moderately fed after pigging the first weeks, or y^y will get cloyed & not eat well & their pigs will never be fat. Oxen continue to grow till 6 & 7 years old—often worked in Connecticut till 12 years old. They plow among corn with oxen, but with a long yoke, & the staple not in the middle, so as better to avoid hurting the corn with the chain. No driver necessary, when oxen well broken. Price of an ox cart compleat in Con^t £5. LM^y. He says heifers often have their first calves at 2 years old—but then go farrow the next year.

July 5. P. [M.] small showers: left our camp, & marched near Tylers across the river & lay in the woods.
Sunday July 6. This morning wrote to Mrs P. dating it July 3^d the other of that date having been detained by the party, some of whom excepted to some expressions in it. Had plenty of milk bro't me for by breakfast. Then marched into the woods 4 or 5 miles & encamped near by a fine spring near [Little] Mahoopenny [creek & not] far from the middle one of [3?] wild

---

[2] In the original these items are in a list separated from the text with a brace. For his letter to his wife see no. 243, *ante*.

meadows. A. M. fair. P. M. towards evening thunder with considerable rain.

Monday July 7. Fair. moved our camp a mile no^{erly}. P. M. towards evening thunder with showers.

Tuesday July 8. Fair. P. M. Thunder with some rain. Shifted our quarters, & marched back near to the river, within a mile of Kilburns. rec^d thence milk for supper.

Wednesday July 9. Cloudy. (Sent a large wooden spoon & butter spoon to Kilburns, to be sent thence to my wife.) rain in ye forenoon. P. M. fair. & then rain. Milk for supper. No meat to-day.

Thursday July 10. rain before day-light. Gave Woodward a letter dated yesterday to forward to my wife. Desired her to send me a small tin kettle with a cover. Woodward returned— says my things are at Marcys with a letter for me. After the morning, fair & pleasant. T. Kilburn showed me the twig of a [tree] whose bark is a very agreeable bitter. He says there are many large trees of it on the flat by his fathers, & that they have used it in timber for part of Sills house frame—a soft wood. Tis called *Winter bark*. No meat—but butter to eat with bread. Ginseng at our encampment in the deep shades of hemlock woods. Que. if cultivated, whether it might not be under the shade of trees in an orchard or garden. The flowers come out of the stem, at the center of 3 branches—as the mayapple does where the stem branches. The buds now just opening. Each branch has 5 leaves, 3 of them of a size, the other 2 not half as large. Evening Woodward brought me a letter dated the 8th from Mr Bowman, informing of the health of the family & that the articles I requested are sent to March's.

Friday July 11th fair, moved our camp about 4 miles from the river, west of Kilburns, & about a mile over Mahoopenny Creek. Pork to-day, & what the guard called *coffee;* i. e. a crust of wheat bread toasted very brown or burnt, & then boiled in water, which is then sweetened; Tis very tolerable drink. Woodward has been in Vermont & western parts of Mass^{tts} where are beech & hemlock woods. He says they find the hemlock land the strongest. That in Mass^{tts} such land produces flax 15 inches taller than any he has seen on the flats of Wyoming; but that the same land was too cold for Indian corn: but excellent for grass and wheat. That in Vermont the practice is, when you hire, to get an acre cut down (except 10 trees, which being largest are only girdled) and cut into lengths, biggest 16 the smaller ones 18 or 20 feet lengths, and the limbs all loped off, for 4 & 5 dollars. That is done as soon as may be after planting. That the whole lies in this condition a year, and then in time for sowing winter wheat, fire is put to it, which consumes all the limbs, and then the logs are halled into heaps with one yoke of oxen, & burnt: then the wheat is sowed & harrowed in. The crop 20 to 25 bushels an acre. Hemlock (he says) after laying thus to dry one year, burns up much cleaner than beech & maple. Fences made with logs, or the young hemlocks cut into lengths & piled into a worm (Que. if these round rails would not last much longer if stripped of their bark?)

Saturday July 12. Fair with wind. Winter green tea last evening with supper & this morn[ing] with breakfast. P. M. thunder with rain—then fair. 2 meals to-day.
Sunday July 13. cloudy, with intervening sunshine. P. M. rainy. No bread or meal & of course eat nothing till bread arrived about one or two P. M. Learn that Mr Kilburn stays at Wyoming, & the Sills house frame & timber are [rafted] down for him to finish there. Tis said a day or two since that he heard his Dad had turned State's evidence.

Monday July 14. Fair.

Tuesday July 15. Fair.

[254] John Hyde, Jr., and Others to Timothy Pickering.[1]

County of Luzerne July 15, 1788.

Sir,

As you have generously declared your willingness to forgive us for the great injury we have done you, in seizing and keeping you a prisoner in the manner we have done, from the 26th of June last to this day on the single condition that in future we pay a due obedience to the laws & government of the state of Pennsylvania in which we live: We hereby express our thankfulness for your kindness in this matter, & solemnly engage that we will never hereafter disturb the peace of said state, nor of the county of Luzerne which is a part thereof, but, while we dwell therein,

---

[254] [1] M. H. S., Pickering Papers, LVIII, 54-55, in an unknown hand but signed by each individually, although every signature may not be genuine. Whitcomb's, for example, is not like that in no. 294, *post*.

will in all respects conduct ourselves as peaceable & faithful citizens. To be more particular. In case any writ or warrant be issued under the authority of said state, or of any lawful officer thereof, against us or any of us, or against any other persons whomsoever, we will not by any kind of force or threats oppose the lawful execution thereof; on the contrary, we will give every assistance to carry such writs and warrants into execution which by law it is our duty to render; and if any one or more of us shall fail of a faithful performance of this engagement you are then at liberty to prosecute us to recover damages for the injury done you as above mentioned: Only if any of the rest of us seize and deliver up to the proper authority of the county, or give to any lawful officer effectual assistance in apprehending & securing such offender or offenders, then we trust you will prosecute none of us, except such offender or offenders. This engagement to be binding upon us severally in respect to the recovery of damages, only while we severally continue citizens of or reside in said state.[2]

> Ira Manvill
> Benedick Satterlee
> John Tuttle [3]
> Timothy Kilbourn
> Benjamin Earll
> Daniel Earll
> Solomon Earl
> John S. Whitcomb
> Nathan Abet
> Benjamin Abet
> David Woodard
> John Hyde Jn[r]

[255] Petition of John Hyde, Jr., and Others to the Pennsylvania Council.[1]

To the Honarable Supreeme Executive Counsal of the State of Pensylvany, the Petition of the subscri[bers] inhabitants of the County of Luzerne, in s[d] State, most humbly sheweth. That a

---

[2] Two and a half lines of text that follow have been lined out and are illegible.   [3] See no. 255, *post,* note 5.
[255] [1] M. H. S., Pickering Papers, LVIII, 55-56, in an unknown hand but signed by each individually, although every signature may not be genuine.

number of your Petitoners in the Evning of the 26th of June
last being collected together, and in Arms, Entred the dwelling
house of Co^{ll} Pickring, at Wilkesbury in S^d County, and with
forse took and Caryed him away, and have detaind him a pris-
oner, Untill this day: that the motive of the party to ingage in
this unlawfull Undertakeing, Was to obtain the Releas of their
friend John Franklin, from the Jail of Philadelpia, Where he
had long ben confind. Upon the bail given for that end or such
other bail the Govrnment should require, that your petitioners
expected his release when the bail taken persuent to the direction
of the chief Justice Was forwarded to Philadelphia; [2] But ware
informed that Co^{ll} Pickring, Wrote a letter at the same time
With a Vew to prevent Mr Franklin being set at liberty and
that in consiquence of that letter he was continued in Jail.[3] that
excited the resentment of his friends Against Co^{ll} Pickring,
Which was increased by informa[tion] that Mr Franklin was in
bad helth, and if not soon released Would probably die in Jail, and
in the Rath of that resentment your petitioners was drawn into
the rash and violent measures above mentioned. That your petitioners are now Sensable of their error, of their part and agri-
vated Offence against government and the Wholsom Laws of
the State Made to preserve order and peas in surety, as Well as
of the deep injury they have done to Co^{ll} Pickring, that however Upon the pennatence mannafested by your petitioners, has
ben pleased to declare that he forgives their [personal?]
off[ence] Against him, Upon condition that they no more violate the laws of this state, and they have given him assurences
a[nd] an ingagement that their future conduct shall be such as
becomes good cityzens of Pensylvania on the failure of which
by any one of the party he is liable to his suit for the sore injury done him.[4] Your petitioners now most humbly besich your
honnerable board to pass by their publick offence. They repeat
With sorrow that it is a great offence against the state by violent seasing and unlawfully keeping prison[er] an innosent man,
and an officer commissioned by governme[nt] nevertheless, your
petitioners humbly hope they may be forgiv[en] on the deep and
hartfelt repentance which they now profes[s] Assuring and assuring your honours that they have ben misi[nformed] and mis-

---

[2] See no. 225, *ante,* note 2.

[3] Pickering's letter to Vice President Muhlenberg did not explicitly
urge denial of bail to Franklin, but Pickering did underscore the continued hostility of Franklin's supporters; see no. 228, *ante.*

[4] No. 254, *ante.*

led by men in whose Judgment and advise they have ben want to place an entire confidence; on this further assuren[ce] also of their future fidelity to the state, and of their redi[ness] to enter into such engagement for that end as your honours shall require. And as in duty bound shall ever pray &c
County of Luzerne July 15ᵗʰ 1788

> John Hyde Jnʳ
> Daniel Taylor
> Ira Manvill
> Daniel Earll
> David Woodard
> Benedick Satterlee
> Gideon Dudley
> Joseph Dudley
> John Whitcomb
> Benjamin Earll
> Timothy Kilbourn
> Nathan Abit
> Benjamin Abit
> Soloman Erl
> Friadreek Budd
> Wils Jinkens
> Aaron Kilbon
> Wᵐ Carny
> Zebulon Cady
> Noah Phelps⁵

[256] David Redick to Benjamin Franklin.¹

New York, July.

Sir and Gentlemen,

I arrived at this place on Saturday at night, Genˡ Irvin² took opportunities yesterday of conversing with divers members of Congress respecting the wishes of Council to have Zieglers Compʸ for the Wioming service, every Gentlemen he spoke to

---

⁵ The last signature, that of John Tuttle, has been lined out. See no. 258, *post*.

[256] ¹ P. H. M. C., Div. of Arch. and MSS., Record Group 27, Exec. Corr., 1777-90, in Redick's hand; *P. A.*, XI, 338-39. This letter was read in Council on July 18, 1788; *Pa. C. R.*, XV, 493. The endorsement given in *P. A.* as June 18 is an obvious error.

² William Irvine, one of Pennsylvania's delegates to the Continental Congress.

countenanced it. This morning the Gen¹ Coll. Reed and myself waited on the minister at war who appears well disposed:³ but says, that Ziegler has surely marched ere now, that nothing can have prevented; but at the same time says, that there are about 45 Jersey troops who will march within a few days to the westward by the way of Easton and that a further number of troops from one of the eastern States will march by the same route from west point, where they are now stationed, all which troops he is disposed should be ordered to take directions from some Gen¹ officer appointed by our government to command them.⁴

It will therefore be necessary, if Council will think proper to apply for these troops & that they do it Instantly.⁵ I am now sorry that a provisional application was not sent by me inasmuch as the whole of the members who have been spoken with appear, at this juncture, to be well disposed to serve us: and which may not happen to be the case at a future day, perhaps three days hence it may be otherwise, for as there will be a great question taken soon for the place in which the new Congress shall convene, minds may be soured and especially with Pennsylvania if Philadelphia should happen to be the place: for if that should so happen the eastern members might oppose us in the business; experience tells us that great men some times do little things on little reasons; it may therefore be necessary that a moment be not lost until the application be made through our Delegates; and at the same time it will be necessary to appoint some person to be in readiness to supply the troops with provisions, at, and from eastown. A Gen¹ Officer may also be thought necessary, agreeably to Gen¹ Knoxes Ideas; in that case permit me to suggest my Ideas on that subject. I hope my zeal will be my apology for taking that liberty.

It will in my oppinion be necessary that an officer of reputation and military abillities be appointed. The name of an old

---

³ Col. James Randolph Reid, another of Pennsylvania's delegates. The minister at war was Henry Knox.

⁴ On October 3, 1787, the Continental Congress had requisitioned from four states 700 troops for duty on the western frontier. On June 16, 1788, General Knox reported that 250 recruits would have to be obtained from Connecticut, New Jersey, and Pennsylvania to replace those men whose enlistment terms were due to expire in 1788. He expected these recruits to move westward during July and August; Ford *et al., Journals of Cont. Cong.,* XXXIII, 602-04; XXXIV, 236-38. Capt. David Ziegler commanded one of the Pennsylvania companies; *Pa. C. R.,* XV, 437.

⁵ See no. 257, *post.*

officer and a great man at the head of the Continental troops will tend at once to discourage every Idea of success in the minds of the Insurgents and at the same time they will crush those who may appear in rebellion. The Union will by this means appear as a principal party and not merely Pennsylvania and at the same time the Gen¹ officer being appointed by our Government will tend to keep up our own State dignity; Majʳ Reed in Conversation has said that as he thirsts for fame he would Serve the State without pay. I have no doubt but Gen¹ Irvine will, as he always has, be ready to do anything the State will request, the Council all know him, therefore I need not say a word more, however, I will just say further that the Commander being a member of Congress will have its proper Influence with such of the disafected as are capable of reasoning.

I purpose seting out for Pokepsey to-morrow to meet Govʳ Clinton he is not expected this week at N. York. No stage goes before Thursday, but I hope for a passage in an Albany sloop.

Council may rest assured that I will leave nothing undone which I may have in my power, it is now after 12 of yᵉ Clock and the mail will be made up in a few minutes therefore I must conclude with saying I have, &c., the honour to be Sir & Gentlemen, your most obt. humble Sᵗ.

David Redick.

[257] Peter Muhlenberg to the Pennsylvania Delegates in the Continental Congress.[1]

In Council

Philadelphia July 18ᵗʰ 1788

Gentlemen

From the late disturbances in the County of Luzerne Council are of Opinion that there will be a necessity of sending Troops there. We are informed that some Continental Troops are to march from Connecticut and New Jersey to the Westward,[2] and in that rout will be at Easton in this State. We request you will apply to Congress, that if it should be found necessary by this Government, those Men may have orders to

---

[257] [1] National Archives, Cont. Cong. Papers, 69, II, 561. The decision of Council to write the letter had been made on the same day; *Pa. C. R.*, XV, 493.   [2] See no. 256, *ante*, note 4.

proceed from Easton to Luzerne, and remain there untill relieved by Troops sent by the State, or untill the disturbances in the County are settled.[3]

I have the honor to be Gentlemen with great respect Your obedient and very humble Servant

Peter Muhlenberg

[258] Timothy Pickering to Benjamin Franklin.[1]

Wilkesbarre, July 19, 1788.

Sir,

I have the pleasure to inform you and the honourable Council that I am restored to my liberty. The band of ruffians who took me, finding themselves unsupported, even by the men who advised and directed them in the affair, came to me last Monday[2] with proposals to set me at liberty, saying they had been advisd by their friends & one of the magistrates whom they had seen, to make their peace with me, & petition Council for a pardon. With respect to myself I told them, that the injury was very great & that I was entitled to heavy damages, that nevertheless I would forgive the personal injury on the single condition of their strict obedience to the laws in future. This they said they were willing to comply with, and become engaged, the whole for each one of the party; and on failure by any one the whole to be still liable to my action. They then pressed me to intercede with Council for the pardon they should petition for, but I refused. However, as they continued their importunities, I at length told them, that on one condition I would intercede for them, this was, that they should give me the names of all their head men (as they called them) and advisers. They took time to consider of it, 'til the next day, when

<hr />

[3] On July 22 the Council promised to furnish supplies to the troops while they were at Easton and in the employ of the state; *Pa. C. R.,* XV, 496. Muhlenberg wrote again to the Pennsylvania delegates on this same day specifically requesting the use of the troops, promising supplies, and urging prompt action so that a commanding officer might be named; *P. A.,* XI, 350.

For the action of Congress, see nos. 265 and 266, *post.*

[258] [1] P. H. M. C., Div. of Arch. and MSS., Record Group 27, Series: Exec. Corr., 1777-90, in Pickering's hand; *P. A.,* XI, 346-47. This letter was read in Council on July 31 and answered August 5; *Pa. C. R.,* XV, 502, 505.   [2] That is, July 14.

they finally declined it. They then begged me to forward their petition to Council, as they should not have an opportunity of doing it. This I told them I would do, and I now inclose it.[3] The last name of the petitioners I have dashed out;[4] the young man having joined the party but a few days before I was released, for the sole purpose of discovering their lurking places, that he might conduct a party to relieve me. This young man has since collected three or four of his acquaintances, and with them lain in wait for two of the party, whose intended movements he was informed of while with them, and just before day yesterday morning, took both of them, and last night those two were sent off to be lodged in Easton goal.[5] The party were also very urgent with me to intercede for Franklin's being admitted to bail as soon as possible, but this I utterly refused to do. They expressed their fears that if not soon released he would die in goal, and wished me to believe, that it was not for the sake of getting him into the county again that they were so anxious for his enlargement; for if bailed on condition of his residing with his father in Connecticut they should be perfectly satisfed. They added That Major Jenkins had said that if Franklin had been released on the bail sent to Philadelphia, it was his intention that he should remain here not more than a month, just to settle his affairs & get new cloaths, when he would leave it. Altho' no reliance is generally to be put on what Jenkins says in such cases, yet it is probable he spoke the truth in this instance, for both he and several others of Franklins principal adherents are closely connected with Livingston, McKinstry & others, now usually called the York Lessees, *who have a plan to execute,* as I have heretofore taken the liberty of suggesting to Council.[6] Jenkins and Swift, by the last accounts, were both with the lessees at Canadesago lake, where they expect to hold a treaty with the Indians. From the testimony of the young

---

[3] No. 255, *ante.*   [4] The name of John Tuttle; *ibid.,* note 5.

[5] The two men captured were Ira Manvil and Benedick Satterlee. The names of the captors are given in no. 306, *post.*

On July 21, Henry Bush, jailer at Easton, certified that Manvil and Satterlee were delivered to him by one Thomas Drake; *P. A.,* XI, 347.

Although both Manvil and Satterlee had signed the petition on July 15 begging for pardon (no. 255, *ante*), there was nothing inconsistent about seizing and jailing them. In fact, Pickering himself took the initiative in trying to get his captors arrested; see no. 268, *post.* See also nos. 261 and 262, *post.*

[6] See no. 100, *ante,* note 5. For John McKinstry, see no. 105, *ante,* note 2.

416

man who has turned States evidence,[7] there is room to believe that Livingston & McKinstry encouraged the party to detain me as a hostage for Franklin's release. The reason is obvious, But there is another of the party which took me, who knows more, & the Justices have sent him a passport to come down & give his evidence. To this and the other the Justices have given the usual assurances of pardon on condition of their making full discoveries of the whole scene of villainy. These two persons, after I was released, and was on my way home, sent me a message declaring their readiness to turn States evidence if they could be pardoned. Council, I trust, will eventually cause the expectations of pardon to these two witnesses to be fulfilled, agreeably to the encouragement held up to them by the magistrates & me. I have honor to be, very respectfully Sir, your most obedient Servant,

Timothy Pickering.

[259] Warrant for the Arrest of Ezekiel Williams.[1]

To Asa Chadwick
Luzern County ss
Wharas upon the Oath and Inforamation made this Day It appears That Ezekel williams has ben privy too and Comfederat in a plot upon which the Late Insurection Aroase in the said County. These are therfore in the Name and by the athority of this commonweth of of Pensylvanya to Authrorse and Require you forthwith to apprehend the s^d Ezekel williams and him forthwith Caus to appeare Before us (the Subscriber two of the justices assinged to keep the peas in s^d County) at wilks barry to answer to the aforesaid Complaint given under our hands and sealls this 19th Day of July 1788.

Wm Hooker Smith
Justice of the Peace

Benjn Carpenter
Justice of the Peace

---

[7] Apparently Daniel Earll first offered to turn state's evidence but fled when his brother Benjamin was seized. The brother did offer testimony and escaped indictment; nos. 260, 270, and 299, *post*, note 2.
[259] [1] M. H. S., Pickering Papers, LVIII, 63, in Smith's hand but signed by both men.

[260] Deposition of Benjamin Earll.[1]

I Benjamin Earl of the township of Putnam in the county of Luzerne, do testify and declare, That on Thursday evening, the twenty sixth day of June last, John Hyde jun. David Woodward, Daniel Earl, Gideon Dudley, Joseph Dudley, Solomon Earl, John Whitcomb, Daniel Taylor, Timothy Kilborn, Frederick Budd, Wilkes Jenkins, Benedict Satterlee, Ira Manvil, Zebulon Cady, & myself, being armed with guns and tomahawks and having our faces painted & disfigured (excepting that John Hyde jun[r], David Woodward, Ira Manvil & Benedict Satterlee were not painted) surrounded, & the greater part of us entered the dwelling house of Colonel Pickering in Wilkesbarre in said county, where finding him in bed, we ordered him to get up & dress himself, & being dressed, we tied his arms & forced him out of his house, & compelled him to go with us up the river, and kept him a prisoner in different places in the woods about Meshoppin Creek, and in that neighbourhood, on both sides of the river, until Tuesday the fifteenth day of July instant, part of us constituting his guard, while the rest of us were ranging about to discover and oppose any parties of militia who might be sent against us. That on or about the second day of July, Timothy Kilborn, Daniel Taylor and I were the keepers of Colonel Pickering, and then Taylor & Kilborn put a chain about one of his legs, & with a staple fastened the other end of the chain to a tree, pursuant to the orders of said John Hyde, who had been appointed the head of the party. That this chain was kept on Colonel Pickering, whilst I remained on his guard, which was until Saturday the 6th of July instant, when we crossed the river. I further testify that John Jenkins & Stephen Jenkins, both of said county, repeatedly advised us to make up a party & seize Col° Pickering, as the only way to get Col° John Franklin out of goal. Particularly on the day, & the day before David Perkins was sent off to Philadelphia with the bail bond to bail Franklin,[2] I saw John Jenkins, & in conversation on the subject, he said, if Franklin did not come out on the bond given, the only way to get him out would be to seize

---

[260] [1] M. H. S., Pickering Papers, LVIII, 61-63, in Pickering's hand but signed by Earll. Forwarded to the Council by Pickering with his letter of July 29; no. 270, *post*. [2] See no. 225, *ante*, note 2.

Colonel Pickering: and my brother Daniel Earl informed me that the night before colonel Pickering was taken, those of the party with my said brother stopped at John Jenkins's house & there received a supply of powder. That living in the neighbourhood of Stephen Jenkins, & having frequently been with him in the course of two or three months before colonel Pickering was taken, he often talked about taking him as the only way to get Franklin released from goal, & he talked of it is such manner as made me understand & expect that he would be of the party to take him; & said col° Pickering must be kept in the woods, moving from place to place, tied or chained to a tree, until Franklin should be released; and his talk was always to the purport I have here mentioned until the plan was ready to be executed, the day the party marched from Meshhoppin, down the river, in order to proceed & take colonel Pickering, when he said it would not do, for the party would not be supported in it, and that it would undo the settlement if it was undertaken. Upon which I asked him to take his mare and ride up & stop the boys, or send up a boy, or I would go myself, for that purpose: but he would do neither; and said, let the Dudleys and the rest of the boys there come down & take col° Pickering, if they will, for as yet they have done nothing.

I farther testify That on Thursday (on the evening of which day col° Pickering was taken) while the party lay at the mouth of Toby's creek, Gideon Church of Kingston in said county, came to us & remained with us about two or three hours, and was asked to go with us, & take the command of the party to take colonel Pickering; but he declined it, saying that he had two hands employed about a frame, & he could not leave them without great damage; but that he would support the party with provisions, so far as to send us up one or two barrels of flour & fifteen or twenty gallons of whiskey, & perhaps he might make it up a barrel, and that he would also send us up a barrel of pork, if we could not do without it. And I think he said That if we should be pursued, he would then turn out & come to our assistance.

I further testify That the last time Elisha Satterlee of Shawnee went up the river, my brother Daniel informed me that said Satterlee went into the field where my brother was at work, & asked him what should be done to get col° Franklin out of goal. Daniel said he did not know. Satterly then proposed the taking of colonel Pickering as the means of getting Franklin out of goal; and said that his business was such that he could

419

not undertake it himself, but would give five dollars to the man who would bring him the first information that col° Pickering was taken, & that such informant was of the party which took him. I farther testify That after col° Pickering was taken, & had been with us a number of days, eleven of the party, of which Benedict Satterlee & I were two, went up to Tioga & called on Elisha Satterlee: but he would then hardly speak to his brother Benedict, & expressed his disapprobation of what we had done. Then leaving his house, Elisha walked down the road, & Benedict, with Ira Manvil & Daniel Taylor, followed him; and these three of the party afterwards told me That Elisha said he would rather have given all he was worth in the world than that his brother Benedict should have been in the scrape.

I farther testify That John Hyde & Frederick Budd, before named, went off for Tioga some days after we had taken colonel Pickering, & returned about the time we carried him across the river, to confine him on the west side of it; the morning after which, I with others of the party, recrossed the river, & went up to Woodwards, where we found Hyde & Budd, & Hyde pulled out a letter, which he said was from John Swift. It was dated at Katharine's town, & directed to Elisha Satterlee at Tioga. I heard it read. What I remember of it was to this effect. After desiring Satterlee to forward on some cattle for the treaty, it mentioned That Major Jenkins had told him that col° Pickering was taken & kept in the woods, that he had turned mad, & was chained, and that mad dogs were dangerous. That he (Swift) had either seen col° M°Kinstry,[3] or col° M°Kinstry had written to him, telling him that if we could not conveniently keep col° Pickering, and would bring him up to him, he would provide for his being kept; and that if we wanted provisions, there was a quantity of corn at Bryant's mill, from which, by a token mentioned, we could obtain a supply; and that if the boys or persons who had taken col° Pickering, should be obliged to leave their lands here, and would go to him (M°Kinstry) they should all be provided for and made whole out of the leased lands. I farther testify that some of the boys also told me, that they were informed at Tioga that col° Livingston (one of the Lessees) very much encouraged the keeping col° Pickering prisoner.

Benjamin Earell

Delivered on oath before
Wm H. Smith Esqr
July 19, 1788.

---

[3] For John McKinstry see no. 105, *ante,* note 2.

[261] Deposition of Ira Manvil.[1]

Ira Manvil of Plymouth in the county of Luzerne, yeoman, charged with being one of the party who on the 26th of last month in the night being armed, entered the dwelling house of Colonel Pickering in Wilksbarre and with force took and carried him away, & detained him a prisoner, in open violation of the law, being brought before William Hooker Smith & Benjamin Carpenter Esq[s] Justices of the Peace for said County, and asked what he had to say to the charge, answered. That he was guilty. He the[n] made a relation of the circumstances under which he engaged and continued in the party, in order to shew that he was unwillingly drawn into it, and that after he had been at Tioga to enquire into the foundation of the proceeding, and did not get satisfaction, & had returned to the party, he used his endeavours with the party to get Colonel Pickering set at liberty.

The above examination & confession taken and made the 19th day of July 1788. Before us [2]

Wm Hooker Smith } Justices of
Benj^a Carpenter } the peace

[262] Deposition of Benedick Satterlee.[1]

County of Luzerne ss.   July 19. 1788.

Benedict Satterlee of Plymouth in the county of Luzerne, yeoman, charged with joining and being one of the party of armed men, who with force entered the house of Col. Pickering in Wilkesborough in said County on the 26th ultimo and took & carried him away and detained him prisoner, was brought before William Hooker Smith & Benjamin Carpenter Esq[s] Justices of the peace for said county, and being asked what he had to say to the charge aforesaid, answered That he was guilty.

---

[261] [1] Amer. Phil. Soc., Documents Relative to the Wyoming or Connecticut Controversy, I, 237-38, a copy made in the nineteenth century; P. A., XI, 344.

[2] Smith and Carpenter immediately issued a warrant for the incarceration of Manvil and Satterlee in the Easton jail; P. A., XI, 345.

[262] [1] Amer. Phil. Soc., Documents Relative to the Wyoming or Connecticut Controversy, I, 238-40, a copy made in the nineteenth century; P. A., XI, 344-45.

He further confesses, & says that he had not heard of the design to take Col. Pickering until the day on which he was taken. That Frederick Budd & Ira Manvil on that day came to him at his School house, and told him that a bond had been sent to Philad* to bail Colonel Franklin according to directions from the Chief Justices, that he was not bailed, and that the bond was kept. That he Budd had come with a party to take Colonel Pickering as a hostage to redeem Colonel Franklin, and asked the confessor to join the party, which he declined, but at length said he would go and see them; which he did, but without joining them, and came and attended his school that afternoon. That he and Manvil afterwards went down to the river to see the party, where he was strongly urged, for full three quarters of an hour to join them, they saying that they had a good foundation for their proceeding, that they were to have rewards, or to be made good for their trouble; and and when he still declined John Hyde jun. one of the party said full two thirds of the settlement were with them, and that if he, the confessor, did not join them, he would not be able to live in the Settlement, and he consented to join them.

Taken & made before us [2]

Wm Hooker Smith } Justices of
Benj^a Carpenter } the Peace

[263] Motion of the Pennsylvania Delegates in the Continental Congress.[1]

Whereas Some alarming Disturbances have taken place in one of the Frontier Counties of the State of Pennsylvania, from a Number of lawless factious Persons, having armed and embodied themselves for the purpose of opposing the Authority of the established Government, and whereas the Articles of Confederation provide for the Interposition of the Arms of the Union in favor of any State whenever such assistance may be required to repel any force offered to, or attacks made upon Such State on any pretence whatsoever, and whereas a Number of Troops in the Service of the United States will Soon be on their March towards the Western Country, and be in the Vicin-

[2] See no. 261, *ante*, note 2.
[263] [1] Ford *et al., Journals of Cont. Cong.*, XXXIV, 350-51; National Archives, Cont. Cong. Papers, 20, II, 189 and 192.

ity of the County where the Insurrection has taken place, and whereas the Delegates of the State of Pennsylvania are instructed by the Supreme Executive Council, to request that Congress would permit these Troops to aid the authority of that State to Suppress the said Insurrection, Therefore

Resolved, that the Secretary at War take order to direct the Destination of those Troops in the most effectual Manner, to render Such Assistance as the State of Pennsylvania may require and Stand in Need of.[2]

[264] Peter Muhlenberg to Zebulon Butler.[1]

In Council, Philadelphia, July 23th, 1788.

Sir,

I am directed by Council to acknowledge the Receipt of your favor by Mr. Wigton[2] and at the same time to express to you, their entire approbation of the Conduct of the officers of government in Luzerne relative to the Rioters. Council are so well assur'd that every thing possible will be done by you, that they have hitherto postponed the raising, & marching troops to your assistance, until circumstances shall otherwise direct. You will be pleased to assure the officers of Government & the well affected Inhabitants, that if it is necessary they will on application be immediately supported by a sufficient number of troops, and in all probability a body of Continental Troops will be directed to assist in expelling the Rioters out of the Boundaries of this State; to effect this completely, proper measures have been concerted with the States of New York & Jersey.

Council further request you would be pleas'd to give them the earliest intelligence, if circumstances should take an unfavorable turn. That they may immediately take the necessary measures, as they are fully determined to enforce the Laws & to restore order & good government in Luzerne.

Peter Muhlenberg, V. P.

---

[2] The endorsement on the original reads as follows: "Motion of Pensylvania, 22 July 1788, Referred to Mr Clark, Mr Edwards, Mr Irvine. respecting aid of Continental troops. Acted on July 25th 1788."

[264] [1] *P. A.,* XI, 351.   [2] No. 249, *ante.*

[265] Report of the Congressional Committee on Pennsylvania's Request for Troops.[1]

The Committee consisting of [Mr. Abraham Clark, Mr. Pierpont Edwards and Mr. William Irvine] to whom was referred a Motion of the Hon the Delegates of Pennsylvania[2] pursuant to instructions by them rec^d from the Executive Council of said State to apply to Congress, that if it should be found necessary by that State Government, the Continental Troops under Marching orders from Connecticut and New Jersey to the Westward by the rout of Easton in Pennsylvania[3] may be ordered to proceed from thence to Luzerne County and remain there untill the disturbances now existing in that County are Settled.

Your Com^e having enquired into the grounds on which the motion to them referred is founded, find, that a number of the Inhabitants of the County of Luzerne, contrary to their Allegiance to, and in defiance of the authority of the State, have Assembled in Arms and Committed An Act of Outrage upon an Officer of the State residing in that county. The reasons inducing those rioters to this violation of the Laws are unknown to your committee; [But whatever they may be][4] as the number of the rioters does not appear to be great, or [such as State are incompetent][5] to Suppress in a constitutional way by calling out a small part of [its] Militia, the interference of the United States cannot with propriety be requested. Notwithstanding which, as a body of Continental Troops are soon to March to the Westward by the way of Easton, and as the State of Pennsylvania have not at present any troops in readiness to Suppress the riots in Luzerne, it may not be improper for the said Continental troops to halt a short time at Easton to be employed if necessary in quelling the disturbances in

---

[265] [1] Ford *et al., Journals of Cont. Cong.,* XXXIV, 353-54; National Archives, Cont. Cong. Papers, 20, II, 187-88.

[2] No. 263, *ante.*   [3] See no. 256, *ante,* note 4.

[4] The phrase in brackets is interlined over the following phrase, which is lined out: "be these what they may."

[5] The phrase in brackets is interlined over the following phrase, which is lined out: "their power any way formidable beyond the power of the State."

Luzerne untill the State can Provide troops for that purpose. Whereupon the following resolution is Submitted.

That the Secretary at War direct the detachment of Troops marching to the Westward to Rendezvous at Easton in Pennsylv[a] and from thence march into the County of Luzerne for quelling the disturbances in that county, provided the Executive Council of Pennsylv[a] shall find the assistance of those troops necessary; provided also that the said troops shall not be delayed in their march to the Ohio more than two weeks.[6]

[266] Extract from the Journals of the Continental Congress.[1]

The com[ee] consisting of M[r] [Abraham] Clark M[r] [Pierpont] Edwards and M[r] [William] Irvine to whom was referred a motion of the delegates of Pensylvania, in pursuance of Instructions from the Supreme executive council of the said state having reported thereon and the following proposition being under debate viz That the sec[y] at war direct the detachment of troops marching to the westward to rendezvous at Easton in Pensylvania and from thence march into the county of Luzerne for quelling the disturbances in that county provided the executive council of Pensylvania shall find the assistance of those troops necessary, provided also that the said troops shall not be delayed in the march to the Ohio more than two weeks.

The previous question was moved by the State of Virginia seconded by the State Massachusetts, that the main question be not put and on the question to agree to the previous question the yeas and nays being required by M[r] [William] Irvine [2] * * *

So the question was lost.

---

[6] The endorsement states that the report was entered and read on July 24.

[266] [1] Ford et al., Journals of Cont. Cong., XXXIV, 354-56.

[2] The vote was 5 to 5, with Massachusetts, Connecticut, New York, Maryland, and Virginia favoring the motion; that is, these states, according to the rules of Congress, voted for the previous question in the belief that the committee's motion could not properly be decided upon at that time. In the Connecticut delegation Benjamin Huntington and Jeremiah Wadsworth formed the majority against Pierpont Edwards.

The five states voting *no* were New Hampshire, New Jersey, Pennsylvania, Delaware, and Georgia. Because Rhode Island and North Carolina each had only one delegate present, their votes were not counted.

On the question to agree to the main question the yeas and nays being required by M^r [William] Irvine³ * * *

So it was

Resolved That the Secretary at War direct the detachment of troops marching to the westward to rendezvous at Easton in Pensylvania and from hence march into the county of Luzerne for quelling the disturbances in that county, provided the executive council of Pensylvania shall find the assistance of those troops necessary provided also that the said troops shall not be delayed in their march to the Ohio more than two weeks.⁴

[267] Zebulon Butler to Nathan Denison and Others.¹

Gentlemen.

I have A Favour to Ask of you and would Urge it as far as is consistant with decency that is that in the Examination of Evidences Relative to the Late Riot in Takeing and Abusing Co¹ Pickering you would be very strict in the Examination and Especially about my Self. the Reasons for my Requests are as follows. 1st that Mrs Pickering told Mr Catling² (Some days after Co¹ Pickering was taken) that She was informed that the plan for takeing him was formed in my House and that John Jenkins was in my House Secreted 24 Hours some Days before Co¹ Pickering was Take. 2dly that Esqr Smith told Co¹ Denison that they did not Like to Examine the evidences too close for fear it would Tuch Characters, and was asked who. He said Co¹ Butler & Co¹ Schott as Co¹ Denison and Mr Catling

---

³ Only Massachusetts and New York opposed the resolution of the committee. The vote of South Carolina was divided, and as before, the votes of Rhode Island and North Carolina were not counted. In the Connecticut delegation Huntington and Edwards formed the majority against Wadsworth. In short, Wadsworth consistently opposed sending troops to Wyoming and Edwards consistently favored sending the troops. Huntington changed his vote from opposing to favoring the use of troops.

⁴ The resolution of Congress was transmitted to Pennsylvania by its delegates on July 28. Their letter acknowledged receipt of the two requests from Council of July 18 and 22 (see no. 257, *ante,* note 3); *P. A.,* XI, 352.

[267] ¹ Wilkes College Library, Wilkes-Barre, Pa., McClintock Papers, in Butler's hand.

² Putnam Catlin. See no. 169, *ante,* note 4.

will Likely be present at the Examination. I need Not add only would not wish to be present my Self. I could wish the examination Respecting me mite be publish if consistant, but must Submit it to your Wisdom and Am Gente¹ your Most Ob' most Humb¹ Serv'

Zebⁿ Butler

Wilks Barre 28. July 1788
Honᵇ Co¹ Denison and the Rest of the Majistrates County Luzer

[268] Timothy Pickering to Benjamin Franklin.¹

Wilkesbarre July. 28. 1788.

Sir,

In my last² I mentioned the petition of the ruffians who lately made me their prisoner, & that I enclosed it to Council; but forgot to do it, being hurried by the bearer of it, when I sealed that & the other letters transmitted with it. I beg leave now to enclose that petition.³ It may be worth preserving as *evidence against the petitioners,* if it answers no other purpose.

By Mʳ Hodgdon I received several advertisements, in which Council offer rewards for apprehending the villains concerned in that act of violence. I sent immediately for two active young men in whom I could confide, & engaged them to make up a party to go in quest of the offender; and I have reason to think they might have succeeded, could the enterprize have been a secret: but the villains have too many abettors⁴ among those who are, or pretend to be, friends to law and regular government; and unfortunately also, the offer of the rewards was announced in the newspapers printed as early as the 14th instant; & Mʳ Hodgdon did not arrive till the 20th: and thus an expedition, the success of which depended on secresy, has in the first attempt⁵ has failed. The majority of the party, however, yet persevere, and mean to pursue the offenders as long as any chance of apprehending them remains. I have pretty certain

---

[268] ¹ M. H. S., Pickering Papers, LVIII, 64-65, a draft in Pickering's hand; *P. A.,* XI, 353-56.
² No. 258, *ante.* ³ No. 255, *ante.*
⁴ "Abettors" is substituted for "friends," which is lined out.
⁵ The phrase "in the first attempt" is substituted for "hitherto," which is lined out.

intelligence that five[6] of them fled by the upper road thro' the great swamp; & these will doubtless take refuge[7] in the states of New York and Connecticut. Their names, as far as I can learn them, are Daniel Earl, (the other person who offered to turn State's evidence),[8] Solomon Earl, Daniel Taylor & Zebulon Cady.

The County Lieutenant has shown me a letter from Council which was brought up by M[r] Hodgdon.[9] I read it with pain—because it indicated a continuance of that extreme forbearance & indecision of government which have been the bane of every public measure to introduce the regular & full operation of law into this county. I hope Council will pardon this freedom of expression. My exertio[ns] to establish the authority of the State in this settlement have been constant and open—they have consequently exposed me to the resentments of an ungrateful people: but expecting a due support from government, I have perserver[ed.] Even my late ignominious imprisonment[10] did not discourage me. Distressing as it was to me & my family, I did not repine: For I consoled myself with the idea, that much public good would result from the evil: I persuaded myself that Government would now take decisive measures to produce a due submission to the laws; one[11] is to send and station here a permanent military force, under a brave, sensible and *prudent* officer. Nothing else will [still the murmurs] and][12] prevent or crush the plots and conspiracies, or restrain the open violence of a turbulent unreasonably jealous people. Even among the old settlers, th[ere] appear to be few who do not anxiously wish for Franklin's liberation. This violent attachment I have often wondered at. It cannot be merely the effect of friendship, affection & gratitude. The consideration of *interest* will alone solve the problem. The

---

[6] *P. A.* has "four."

[7] Before "refuge" the words "up temporary residence" are lined out.

[8] The parenthetical phrase is omitted in *P. A.,* and the passage continues as follows: "This Daniel Earl is the man who first offered to turn States evidence; and as he was probably possessed of more information than any other of the party, the Justices sent up a passport for him to come down; but his brother Benjamin having been taken, he fled before the passport could reach his usual residence."

[9] Not found, but dated July 18. A copy of this letter was sent to Pickering by the Council on August 5; *Pa. C. R.,* XV, 505.

[10] "Imprisonment" is substituted for "treatment," which is lined out.

[11] "One" is substituted for "and this," which is lined out.

[12] The brackets are in the original; these bracketed words are omitted in *P. A.*

half-share-men have derived their imaginary property thro' Franklin, and by him only, released from prison, & placed at their head, they expect to maintain it. But besides these, who are called half-share-men in the strictest sense of the phrase, there is a multitude of the *old settlers* to whom Franklin had the policy to grant half-share rights to interest them in the support of his [plan] [13] of opposition to Pennsylvania. But independently of the influence these grants of half-share-rights, the old settlers, habitually jealous [of] the Government, and doubting whether their old rights of possession will ever be confirmed, ardently wish for Frankl[in's] enlargement; because, with him at their head; they may hope yet to maintain, by craft and violence, what cannot otherwise be secured. However, whether I have hit on the real cause of this people's attachment to Franklin or not, that it is strong to an astonishing degree and almost as general as it is strong, are serious truths.

The other measure is the confirmation of the *old settlers* in their rights & possessions regularly acquired before the decree of Trenton, according to the tenour of the confirming law, now suspended; [14] or in some other way at least equally comprehensive.[15] This confirming law, whether revived or not, added to their other grounds of claim,[16] it is supposed will effectually operate in a federal court to assure to this people all the lands therein expressed to be given or confirmed: and there can be no question, which will be most for the honour of the state voluntarily to establish its own grants, or to let them be established by a federal court.[17] That their old *possessions* should be confirmed seems to be the general voice of all [18] who have any knowledge of the subject. The very commissioners who passed a decree in favour of Pennsylvania, at the same time strongly recommended this confirmation.[19] And such confirmation alone *at that time,* it is morally certain, would have given satisfaction —not a man would have lifted his voice, much less his arm, against government—peace would have been restored—the laws introduced—and with these blessings, some thousands of orderly settlers, who would now have been good citizens, enriching

[13] "Plan" is lined out, as is a following illegible word.
[14] No. 220, *ante.*
[15] This phrase after the semicolon is interlined.
[16] The phrase beginning "added" is interlined.
[17] Lined out here is the phrase "be obliged to submit to the decisions of a federal court."
[18] In *P. A.* "all" is followed by "disinterested persons."
[19] Vol. VII, no. 129.

the state with the surplus of their produce, and by the payment of taxes, contributing to its support. The opportunity of taking this measure so prudent & so expedient, having been lost, and such various proceedings & events [20] as are within the knowledge of council having since taken place, something more seems [21] necessary now to secure the quiet of the county; and I may venture to say that nothing short of the measures above mentioned will produce that salutary effect.

I have dared, sir, thus freely to express my sentiments from a consideration of the duty I owe to the state, & a feeling sense of the duty I owe to myself and family. My coming hither was not originally an affair of my own seeking:—It was *proposed* to me—it was *urged* upon me—on the ground of probability that I might be the instrument [22] of giving peace & satisfaction to this settlement, & save the State from the expence of blood & money in a civil war. On this ground I applied for the offices Government have been pleased to confer upon me: expecting, it is true, that those offices, joined to the convenience of managing to more advantage the lands I had taken up in [23] the county under the State, would ultimately compensate for the difficulties I should have to encounter in effecting [24] so desirable an issue of this inveterate dispute.[25] I have now too much reason to repent the confidence with which I engaged in the undertaking. What have been the repeated distresses of myself & family, & what losses I must have sustained, Government can easily imagine: Whether those distresses shall be renewed—and whether I shall finally be ruined—God knows. The measures which Government shall now adopt will probably determine my fate—and the fate of the county. I have the honour to be &c.

T. P.

The President of the State

Endorsed in Pickering's hand: Substance of Letter to Council July 28, 1788. Wrote another [26] the 29th giving an account of

---

[20] The phrase "& events" is interlined and two illegible words are lined out.

[21] After "seems," which is interlined, several illegible words are lined out.

[22] Before "instrument" the phrase "able to effect" is lined out.

[23] For "in" *P. A.* has "within or adjoining."

[24] Before "effecting," a number of illegible words are lined out.

[25] *Cf.* Pickering's emphasis on his motives here with that in Vol. VIII, nos. 252 and 258.

[26] No. 270, *post.*

the taking of Joseph Dudley, & stating the cases of the prisoners generally.

[269] Deposition of William Carney.[1]

The examination of William Carney, before William Hooker Smith esquire one of the Justices assigned to keep the Peace in the County of Luzerne.

The said William being examined, made the following declaration.

That on Sunday, June 29th, a number of the party who had taken colonel Pickering, came to his Grandfather Parks's where he lived, and asked him if he would not join them. That he answered, he could not, that his corn wanted hoeing, & he could not leave home. That they continued to press him to join them, and finally threatened him if he did not join them, that he should not live on the place; by which he understood them to mean that he, his grandfather & the whole family should be driven off. That they declared to him that the greater part of the settlement below was in arms, that there should be no neutrals & that such as would not join them should be driven off immediately. That he then consented to join them; & took his arms, as they required, & went with them down to Tunkhannock; whence they sent him back with the canoe in which they had sailed down to Tunkhannock, & directed him to go afterwards up to Dudleys, at Meshoppen, which he did, reaching Dudley's, on Tuesday. That Captain Dudley was at home, & supplied the party with victuals, freely & cheerfully, as it appeared to him the said William. That colonel Pickering was sometimes the subject of conversation, in which captain Dudley joined, & appeared as well pleased as any of the party. That he knows not whether captain Dudley advised or directed them in the affair, as the leaders of the party kept the declarant at a distance, not admitting him into their councils; that however, he heard them (particularly Daniel Earl) say that John Jenkins was "knowing" to the affair of taking colonel Pickering, & that they called on him, said Jenkins, on their way down for advice and direction. That he also heard some of the party say That (after colonel Pickering was taken) Stephen Jenkins was gone

[269] [1] M. H. S., Pickering Papers, LVIII, 68-69, in Pickering's hand but signed by Smith.

down to Kingston for provisions for them. That he also heard some of the party say that Gideon Church was to bring them up some flour, whiskey and pork. That he also heard them say that old Mr Harvey was to send them up some flour. That they said that captain Swift & captain Satterlee were to come down from Tioga to join them, & that they expected them every day. That when they were in the bushes near David Woodwards, John Hyde jun. pulled out a letter which he said was from Col^o McKinstry, & read it. That he remembers it contained information that there was at Bryant's Mill a parcel of corn, which the party might have, and advice or direction that they should take colonel Pickering up to the Lakes. That he also understood from the party that colonel Livingston (one of the Lessees) was "knowing" to the taking & keeping colonel Pickering, and approved of it. That he saw colonel Pickering on Tuesday evening after they went from Dudley's, and some days afterward, when he had been carried across the river, & kept about a mile back of Joseph Kilborn's, he was one day on guard over him, & the next morning being relieved, he the declarant left the party, & went home, & never joined them again. That he left them because he was then convinced their proceedings were wrong.

The mark of
William   X   Carney

Luzerne County ss.   Taken the 29th of July, 1788.   Before Wm Hooker Smith

[270] Timothy Pickering to Benjamin Franklin.[1]

Wilkesbarre, July 29th, 1788.

Sir,

This morning was brought hither Joseph Dudley, one of the persons who took me off, & for apprehending whom Council have offered a reward. He is badly wounded, it is apprehended mortally. The party mentioned in my letter of yesterday, worn out with continual watching & fatigue, had dropped their pursuit, save one, whose name is John Tuttle. He went farther up the river & informed a captain Rosewell Franklin[2]

---

[270] [1] P. H. M. C., Div. of Arch., and MSS., Record Group 27, Series: Exec. Corr., 1777-90, in Pickering's hand; *P. A.*, 359-62.

[2] Rosewell Franklin, interestingly, was one of those who had months before signed a power of agency in favor of John Franklin; no. 69, *ante.*

that a number of the offenders were making their escape up the river. Capt. Franklin immediately collected a party of about fourteen, and on further information from one or two other persons, well attached to Government, that the offenders were at a certain time at Standing Stone, on their way up the river, he concluded to lie in wait for them at Wysock's creek. The offenders advanced according to the information. But it was expected, as the creek was much swoln with rains, that they would have called to the house on the other side for a canoe; when it was intended that one of capt. Franklin's party should go over for them, but on his return, overset the canoe; and by thus wetting all their arms & ammunition, render the capture of them easy, without hazard of shedding blood, on either side. But three of the offenders, Joseph Dudley, Nathan Abbot & Benjamin Abbot, came first to the creek, and forded it. Capt. Franklin ordered them to surrender: when Dudley called out *Don't fire* yet immediately raised his rifle to his face, on which several of Capt. Franklin's men fired, and wounded Dudley and one of the Abbots. But they all attempted to make their escape. Dudley ran four hundred yards & dropped, & while Tuttle & another pursued him, the Abbots did escape. The rest of the offenders took to the woods, doubtless with an intention to cross the creek two or three miles above its mouth.[3] Capt. Franklin however, rode forward, intending to go as far up as Sheshequenunk, (within four miles of Tioga,) or higher, to prepare the people to watch for the coming of the offenders & to seize them.

This day a woman whose son lives with John Jenkins, informed me that he had sent down to his wife to prepare to move with her family immediately to the Lakes. By the last accounts it appeared that Jenkins was engaged to survey lands in that country for the York Lessees.[4] The enclosed memorandum[5] shows the present situation of the party who took and kept me prisoner, according to the latest information I have received. Concerning some of these, the Justices, as well as myself, wish to receive some direction from Council & the Chief Justice or Judges of the Supreme Court.

I believe that in my former letter of the 19th or 20th instant,[6] (I took no copy of it,) I informed Council that Daniel Earl was the first of the party who offered to turn State's Evidence, and discover all concerned; and that he & his brother Benjamin the next day sent me a message that they both would

---

[3] See the account in no. 274, *post.*   [4] See no. 258, *ante,* note 6.
[5] No. 271, *post.*   [6] July 19; no. 258, *ante.*

turn State's evidence, if they could be pardoned. Benjamin was afterwards taken; and his information on oath I now enclose.[7] The father, Joseph Earl, who had been committed, but was discharged for want of evidence against him, was entrusted with the Justices passport, a letter from me, for his son Daniel: but on hearing that Benjamin was taken, Daniel fled, & the letter & passport probably have not yet overtaken him.

The father of William Carney came down last week to enquire whether lenity could not be shown him, as he was not of the party when I was taken, & left it some time before I was released. I advised his surrendering himself, as a further recommendation to mercy. This day he appeared and gave the information contained in the enclosed paper, which I believe is true, to the best of his knowledge.[8] The young man I find has sustained a good character; and I had formed so favourable an opinion of him during the day he was on my guard, that I had concluded voluntarily to recommend him to mercy, after he had quitted the party, & some days before I was released, he sent a message to Esquire Smith, informing that he was ready to deliver himself up.

Noah Phelps, by his wife, has this day prayed Esq. Smith that her husband might be admitted to bail; and he would forthwith surrender himself. She said they had a family of small children to provide for, a harvest of hay & grain to get in, and none to help them: That her husband joined the party unwillingly, at the same time that Carney joined them, and under similar circumstances of false information & threats. It appeared, however, that Phelps was with the party as late as the 15th of July (the day before I was released) and that he has not sustained a clear character; therefore Esq. Smith did not think proper to show him the indulgence he gave to Carney, whom he discharged on condition of his appearing when called, to do whatever shall be directed by the Chief Justice or the Judges of the Supreme Court, several of his friends also verbally engaging for him.

Joseph Dudley being so dangerously wounded, it is impossible for his captors to take him to Easton jail; Nevertheless I presume they will be deemed entitled to the reward as if they had delivered him there. Tuttle, in particular, has very great merit, for his zeal & perseverance. Council will observe one name to the petition is erased; It is Tuttles.[9] Having made the

---

[7] No. 260, *ante.*   [8] See no. 269, *ante.*

[9] See no. 255, *ante,* note 5.

party believe that he had joined them in heart, as well as person, it was necessary for him to sign it with them. He proposed the stratagem to some well affected persons, for the purpose of discovering my place of confinement, that he might then lead a party to deliver me & seize my keepers. He came accordingly to my retreat, but the party released me before there was an opportunity to execute the plan. He also made me a tender of his services to go to the Lakes and bring off John Jenkins, *before it was known that Government had offered a reward for apprehending him.* And this was a principal object of this last expedition; which Tuttle says he would have pursued, had not his companions given out.

In the expedition in which captain Ross was wounded, divers elderly men, fathers of families, were made prisoners, and brought down to Wilkesbarre, on suspicion that they were abettors of the party who took me. Of these one Reynolds was immediately discharged for want of evidence; and Joseph Earl (who had been committed) was, for the same reason, discharged on the 19th instant. Martin Dudley, (father of Gideon & Joseph Dudley,) Joseph Kilborn (father of Timothy & Aaron Kilborn,) Nathan Abbot (father of Nathan and Benjamin Abbot,) Ephraim Tyler, and Thomas Kinney, who is named in the proclamation of Council, still remain in the jail at this place. These men have applied to the magistrates to admit them to bail; but as they have been committed on evidence which the Justices deemed sufficient to warrant the measure their authority *now* to admit them to bail is doubted. As the evidence against them does not appear very clear, and all of them have families in distress, some of them miserably poor, perhaps the Justices may be prevailed on to bail them: Nevertheless, I am very desirous that particular directions may be speedily sent up concerning them, and all others whose cases I have particularly described. And I pray Council to take order in the matter as early as possible; and that when any directions are to come from the Chief Justice or Judges of the Supreme Court, that they may be requested to forward them as soon as may be.

Stephen Jenkins (brother of John) has been apprehended (& is now in jail at this place) in consequence of the evidence against him in B. Earl's deposition. Daniel Earl also told me that Stephen Jenkins was as deeply concerned in the plot as any one.

Gideon Church has not been apprehended; because good policy seemed to require that a door should be left open for repenting sinners. He went out with the three first parties to apprehend the offenders and rescue me. By the last company of volunteers he was chosen their captain, and conducted with such spirit and judgement as [10] pleased the whole of them; and they acknowledge that if they had fallen in with his advice they should doubtless have taken nine of the offenders: whereas they took but one, B. Earl.

Old Benjamin Harvey (who lived at the lower end of the Shawnee flat) fled a few days after I was taken, and said (as I have heard) that some others would be obliged to follow him: yet the hint in Wm. Carney's examination is the only evidence which has yet appeared against him. His flying, joined with his former conduct, affords a strong presumption of his guilt.

Evening, 11 o'clock. This moment the jailer here applies for a winding sheet, informing that Joseph Dudley is dead. I am sir, with great respect, Your most obedient servant,

T. Pickering.

P. S. There has just been handed me a transcript of the examination of Thomas Kinney & other prisoners, heads of families, in the jail of this County, which I enclose.[11] I have seen another account of their examination somewhat different; and from what I have heard, I conclude that enclosed is imperfect. Abbot's examination, I am informed, was private, at his own request, and the Justices did not commit it to paper. It is expected that further, and stronger evidence will appear against all or most of them.

[271] Timothy Pickering's Memorandum on His Abductors.[1]

Memorandum.

Daniel Earl }
Solomon Earl }
Daniel Taylor }   4. Fled thro' the Great-Swamp.
Zebulon Cady }

---

[10] The rest of the original is missing; what follows is supplied from *P. A.*

[11] Copies of statements by Joel Whitcomb, "Mr Keeney," Elijah Reynolds, Joseph Earll, Ephraim Tyler, Martin Dudley, and Joseph Kilbourn are in *P. A.*, XI, 358-59. Joel Whitcomb is not mentioned by Pickering. All the statements are uniform in denying that the deponent had any knowledge of the plan to abduct Pickering.

[271] [1] M. H. S., Pickering Papers, LVIII, 66-67, in Pickering's hand. The probable date of this memorandum is July 29, for it was enclosed on that date with Pickering's letter to Benjamin Franklin, and it does not indicate that Joseph Dudley had died.

Ira Manvil
Benedict Satterlee   } 2. In Easton jail.

Benjamin Earl   1. States Evidence, in the unfinished jail at Wilkesbarre.

Joseph Dudley   1. prisoner, wounded, at a private house in Wilkesbarre.

Nathan Abbot
Benjamin Abbot
John Whitcomb
David Woodward
John Hyde jun.   } 8. Flying towards Tioga.
Gideon Dudley
Timothy Kilborn
Aaron Kilborn

Wilkes Jenkins
  (brother of John)   } 2. Fled to the Lakes.
Frederick Budd

Wm Carney   1. Surrendered.

Noah Phelps   1. Desiring to surrender, & be bailed.
    $\overline{20.}$

John Hyde jun.
Daniel Earl
Benj Earl
Solomon Earl
Gideon Dudley
Joseph Dudley
Zebulon Cady   } 13 with their faces painted like Savages
John Whitcomb
David Woodward
Timothy Kilborn
Frederick Budd
Wilkes Jenkins
Daniel Taylor

Ira Manvil
Benedict Satterlee   } 2 not painted
    $\overline{15}$ surrounded the house, and took of T. P.

Noah Phelps	s.	
Wm Carney	s.	5 with the party afterwards
Nathan Abbot	s	$\overline{20}$
Benj Abbot	s	
Aaron Kilborn	s.	

* * *[2]

Endorsed: Read in Council August 7th 1788 and referred to the Attorney General to proceed against the offenders by Indictment for a Riot.[3] Extract from the Minutes

Cha" Biddle Sec^r [4]

[272] Zebulon Butler to Peter Muhlenberg.[1]

Wilkesbarre July 29, 1788.

Sir,

Your favour by Mr Wigton was handed me in five days after its date.[2] Am very happy to find by it that Council are satisfied with the conduct of those in office in using their endeavours to quell the tumult lately made in our County by those who made Col° Pickering a Prisoner. Every possible exertion has been made that could be to retake Col° Pickering and restore again peace and regularity among us—And our efforts have been so far successful as to oblige the rioters to release their Prisoner & meditate their escape from our County. Since the letter by the express to Council[3] was carried, the Sheriffs Posse, who at that time marched up the River, returned without doing much. The situation of those places to which the Rioters usually re-

---

[2] An additional page attached to the memorandum, here omitted, lists the names of fourteen of the men who participated in the actual seizure of Pickering. There is a check after each name and an additional notation after several—"killed" after Joseph Dudley's name, for example. The name of Benjamin Earll, who turned state's evidence, is omitted. This list is in an unknown hand and probably served as the basis for the indictment later drawn up; see no. 299, *post*.

[3] Also referred to the attorney general at this time were documents mentioned in no. 270, *ante*, notes 7, 8, and 10, as well as no. 282, *post; Pa. C. R.*, XV, 507.

[4] Biddle signed the endorsement.

[272] [1] P. H. M. C., Div. of Arch. and MSS., Record Group 27, Series: Exec. Corr., 1777-90; Amer. Phil. Soc., Documents Relative to the Wyoming or Connecticut Controversy, I, 241-44; *P. A.*, XI, 356-57.

[2] No. 264, *ante*, which Butler received on July 28.

[3] Butler's letter of July 9, which occasioned the reply Butler was now acknowledging; no. 249, *ante*.

sorted, was so very peculiar that it was found impracticable to meet them with any kind of advantage—if to meet with them at all. Finding this to be the case a number of Volunteers soon after the return of the Posse stole a march upon the Rioters and made of them Prisoners to the number of three but then I ought to remark the night before their capture, Col. Pickering was released and sent Down the River to his family. Since which time another Party has been up, and some of whom have this day returned with Joseph Dudley one of the Rioters dangerously wounded. He was taken yesterday, at a Creek called Yosocks—in company with him, were eight more who unfortunately made their escape. A very few shots, if any, were exchanged in the attack—By their route, and what information we can get they were on their march from this State to the Lakes. Their situation is very precarious. The People at Tioga point are mostly under arms and are now in pursuit of the remainder of the Rioters, and in all probability have before this either drove them from this county or made them Prisoners. A full determination seems to be in everyone's mind—to crush & disperse all those who have been active in the riot. It gives me singular satisfaction to find that an attachment to government very universally prevails among the People. Any force necessary to the free circulation of Law, or to quell similar disturbances to the one lately taken place, we can raise at any hour.

Council encourages that if any assistance should be necessary, that it shall be granted us. We return them our most hearty thanks for their assurances, but have every reason to conclude that the People of the County (by a very great majority) are so strongly attached to government, as to be able and willing to baffle and defeat all the machinations of the few, who are disaffected, without any assistance from the state.

Never before this, could I determine with much precition what defence, for the support of the Law would be made by the People of the county, if necessary. But I now may with propriety I believe assert, the advocates for government are so numerous that we never shall again be disturbed with such tumults and dissentions as we have been in times past.[4]

By the concession of all those whom we have now in custody, they have been most grossly deluded by a very few designing Characters, in whom by woful experience they find no kind of

---

[4] Butler's optimism is in glaring contrast to the feelings of Pickering in no. 268, *ante*.

confidence ought to be placed. Indeed not only they but others, on whom we have ever looked with a jealous eye are now of the same opinion. Very generally the People seem now bent on peace, and will if necessary, to obtain it hazard their lives with much readiness and freedom, and the late rupture instead of diminishing, has increased the friends of government. With this opinion I set myself down promising to the Inhabitants as well as to myself order and regularity for the future. I am with esteem your most obedient & very humble servant

Zebⁿ Butler

N. B. By Capt. Schotts I am informd that in consequence of representations respecting his conduct on the expedition up the River his character suffers much in the view of Council. I have only to inform that he was censured here, and on his own request, I summoned from the Battalion a number of Company Officers, who composed a regular Court of inquiry, and after hearing the complaint and the defence of Capt. Schotts, the Court acquitted him with honour.[5]

Yours as above
Z. B.

[273] Obadiah Gore to Timothy Pickering.[1]

S^r

I rejoice to hear that you are released from the hands of those woods Chaps. I am sure your Confinement with them must have been very Disagreeable. the first Information I had of your being taken was from Jn° Jenkins and the manner he Express^d himself Gave me such a Jealousy that he was in some measure at the bottom of it that I then Challenged him upon it. he went to the point,[2] and in a few days I was Informed by Capt Roswell Franklin that Jn° Hyde & Fred^k Budd had passed up to the point. he and I Called on John Spalding & we went in pursuit of them. we Called on Capt Bennet (who is appointed to the Command of the upper Company). he and his Lieu^t Shew themselves very Alert in assisting the Constable with about 20 men in Apprehending them who I had furnish^d with a warrant for that purpose. but they Stole a Canoe and

---

[5] No. 251, *ante*.
[273] [1] M. H. S., Pickering Papers, LVIII, 70-71, in Gore's hand.
[2] Tioga Point, now Athens.

made their Escape a little before Evening. however these movements made Jenkins retreat to Newtown and he is yet at the
Lake. It has been said by some that a number of them people
were avertise⁴. Others Contradicted the report. and I never
Could Learn that it was a fact untill last Evening. I wish some
of those Procklamations were posted up in these parts. on
monday last Capᵗ R. Franklin Exchanged a few shot with the
Insurgents in which I Expect Dudlys son recv⁴ a mortal wound.
from your⁸ &c

Obadʰ Gore

July 30 1788
I wish to hear the particulars of your Captivety the first Convenient opportunity. Mʳ Ellicott Will have cutt 30 miles on
their road.³

[274] Deposition of John Tuttle.¹

John Tuttle's information.
Captain Rosewell Franklin with a party of men collected in
his neighbourhood, & I, were lying in wait near the mouth of
Wysocks creek, expecting that John Hyde jun. Gideon & Joseph Dudley, & others of the party who lately took & kept
prisoner colonel Pickering, would cross there on their way to
Tioga. We had not posted ourselves more than five minutes,
before we saw three of the party who had crossed the creek.
On which I cocked my rifle and ran behind Strope's house;
captain Franklin & a few others of his party did the same.
Capt. Franklin first hailed the three men, ordering them to lay
down their arms & surrender themselves. One of the three
then called out, *don't fire.* Then captain Franklin & I both
called to them to lay down their arms & surrender themselves:
but they did not; and one of them cried out. "We'll see you
damned first." And immediately Joseph Dudley and one other
of the three raised their pieces as if to present & fire upon us;
upon which five of captain Franklin's party fired.² I pulled
tricker twice, but my Rifle missed fire. We saw that Dudley

---

³ The reference is to the road being built by the Pennsylvania Landholders.
[274] ¹ M. H. S., Pickering Papers, LVIII, 71-72, in Pickering's hand but
signed by Tuttle.
² Depositions given on August 4 by Benjamin and Nathan Abbot generally corroborate Tuttle's account of this exchange; *ibid.,* 79 and 80.

was wounded, and one other we supposed was wounded. The other two, Dudley afterwards told us, were Nathan & Benjamin Abbot. Dudley ran about four hundred yards after he was wounded, before he fell, or lay down. The two Abbots were pursued but escaped. When this event happened, six others of Hyde's party (including himself) were at the Creek, and nearer than the other three who had forded it a little way above; but we did not see them, as they stood in the bushes; and when Joseph Dudley was wounded, & ran, he cried out, *run boys! run like thunder!* This took place on Monday the 28th of July, in the afternoon. We put Dudley into a canoe as quick as possible, and brought him down to Wilkesbarre, where we arrived the next day about seven o'clock in the morning, as we rowed all night, and the river being raised the current was quick.

John Tuttle

Wilkesbarre July 30, 1788.

[275] Daniel Earll and Others to Timothy Pickering.[1]

to Cornel piCrien

[?] We humblely beg your Parden for what we have don and am determed to Inform Aginst Avry man that have brot us In the onhapy durty Afair but we hope that your will hav marcy on us for we humbley beg forgivness And I am no [piresiner?] and am in the bush In a frit for the Resen that I have this moment had word that my brother[2] Is taken a presner by Captain Gidden Church for which we think hard of him for he has bin always very forred to have it don and when the party ware Liing In the woods on Rossis hill he Came to us and said he wold fain gin the party but he said he Cold help us more to stay there he wold suply us with pervisions and Liker as much as we shold stan in need of not Long after we arived at hed quarters he sent us word he had a quanty of pervission Ready but he Cold not have aprtunity to send it, but we mit depend that he wold do all that Lay in his power and many more be-

---

[275] [1] M. H. S., Pickering Papers, LVIII, 57, probably in Daniel Earll's hand. The signatures of the two Earlls are in the same hand, but Cady's signature is his own. Daniel's signature looks like that in no. 121, *ante;* Solomon's does not.

[2] Benjamin Earll.

442

sides that we Can inform your onners [3] but we are in a grat
herry so no more at present but we will inform agin the hol
as soon as we Can have word from your onner what will be
don with my brother and our selves for we are afraid we will
be taken avery moment we remain humble sarvents

Daniel Earll
solomon Earll
Zeblon Cady

[276] Deposition of Elizabeth Wigton. [1]

I Elizabeth Wigton, wife of Thomas Wigton,[2] declare, That
the day after colonel Pickering was taken, Thomas Kinney &
Joseph Kilborn came from captain Martin Dudleys, to the
mouth of Meshoppin Creek, where I was, having just brought
Minor York across the river.   both Kinney & Kilborn appeared well pleased with something—I concluded they had
heard that the colonel was taken.   They staid & talked with
Minor York about an hour.   Kinney had with him a tomahawk,
a powder horn & pouch.   When I got to my house I found John
Jenkins there.   I charged him with being the head of the affair
of taking colonel Pickering, & that he was now going to raise
a party.   But he swore an oath and declared he knew nothing
of it till he came to Jone's at Wyalutinunk, where Mr Jones gave
him an account of it;[3] and if he had known it, he would not
for a hundred pounds have left home; for (says he) my enemies
will say that I am the head of the party.   My husband then
asked who commanded the party and Jenkins answered.   They
say Hyde commands it.   He then asked for some whiskey, for
he said the boys (meaning Hyde & his party) had emptied his
jug, & told him he could fill it again at Wigtons for he had a
barrel & they intended to sink it.   My husband fearing the boys
might do him an injury, asked him to stay, to protect him: but
as he could not stay, my husband asked him for a few lines to

---

[3] Benjamin Earll's deposition also names Church as a supplier of provisions; see no. 260, *ante*.

[276] [1] M. H. S., Pickering Papers, LVIII, 77-78, in Pickering's hand but
signed by Elizabeth Wigton and the justices. Pickering did not forward
this deposition to the Council because it contained "much hearsay"; no.
285, *post*.

[2] Thomas Wigton carried to Philadelphia Zebulon Butler's letter of
July 9 and carried back the Council's reply of July 23.

[3] *Cf.* here the testimony of Carney (no. 269, *ante*), Benjamin Earll (no.
260, *ante*), and Daniel Earll (no. 304, *post*).

capt. Hyde. Jenkins gave my husband a line to Hyde, recommending to him to suffer no harm to be done to him: but, says Jenkins, it will do you no good; for when I advised him to hurt nobody, because it would be easier to make twenty friends now, than one after he had misused them, Hyde replied—go along, I'll do as I please. My husband asked Jenkins if he did not think this would be a bad affair, & lead to fighting. I don't know, says Jenkins; but I swear (adds he) we must fight in order to have peace. The evening of this day I went with my husband down to Mʳ Parks's[4] and the next morning Thomas Kinney came there. Says Mʳ Parks, They say col° Pickering is taken: Yes, says Kinney, they say so, & added that he had the information from Major Jenkins. What (said Mʳ Parks) will be the consequence? Kinney answered, he did not know; and asked Mʳ Parks his opinion; who replied, that he thought it would stop the law; for as the prothonotary was taken, there would be nobody to issue any writs. Kinney said he thought so too. Mʳ Parks asked Kinney if he thought the militia would rise? Kinney said he believed not; for, says he, what can they do? how can they find the boys in the woods? & added, I reckon it will be as it was when Franklin was taken. they will gather together, & then go home, or go back again. Noah Phelps came in, and Kinney asked him if he would go with him to hunt up Mahoopenny creek. Phelps said he could not, for he had no shoes and there were no deer there, & Kinney appeared very indifferent whether he went a hunting or not. On Monday June 30. Benjamin Earl was at my house, & I asked him what they intended to do with col° Pickering. He said we mean to keep him till we get Franklin; and if this did not get him that they meant to kill col° Pickering. I told him the colonel was their prisoner, & if they did kill him, they all would be guilty of murder. He said no, they would not; & if they did kill him says he it will not be worse than their keeping Franklin in jail, for he is almost dead; and if Franklin dies Pickering shall die; and we'll run the risque of it.[5] I forgot to mention that Joseph Kilborn, met Minor York on Thursday June 26th, & said to him (as Minor told me) that he had better not go on the land he was going to improve, for he would not be suffered to hold it; for says he Hyde will be up in two or three days, & you will be driven off & hurt. This land, as

---

[4] Darius Parks.

[5] A deposition of the same date given by Isaac Blackmer of New Marlborough, Massachusetts, also testified to the willingness of Pickering's captors to kill him if Franklin died in jail; Pickering Papers, LVIII, 75-76.

I have understood, was an old Connecticut right taken up by Minor's father; but Martin Dudley & John Hyde claimed the same under their half-share rights. Kilborn added, If Pickering is something, then I am nothing; but if he is nothing, then I am something. Joseph Wheeler told me there was a man at work at Mr Tylers (this man I take to be Uriah Parsons) to whom Tyler said "I am as grand a man as Pickering, I have a guard round my house every night" "These fellows who have taken colonel Pickering are to have a dollar a day." The man asked "Who is to pay them?" Tyler answered "We are to pay them." Who are We? (says the man) I am not one. Tyler replies, "Not Wigton, nor James Smith, nor Wheeler; but I for one, & the rest of Whitehaven."⁶ Said Wheeler also told me, that Garret Smith informed him, that the Boys (of whom Gideon Dudley was one) told him if he would join them, they would give him James Smith's field of wheat, and told Parsons if he would join them, they would drive Wheeler off his place & put him (Parsons) in possession of it. Whilst I was at Parks's as before mentioned, Thomas Kinney asked for some tobacco plants; & bargained for a parcel with the girl to whom they belonged. Parks asked him if he had got the tobacco plants. Kinney answered that he did not want them then; for he had some leisure time, & meant to hunt about a little, & should not go home till the next day. I have since learnt from William Carney, that Kinney sent the plants home by two boys, & went himself down to Tunkhannock with *the boys*, that is Hydes party. Kinney said further, while at Parks's "If any body who has a better right to the land I live on than I have, will come and pay me for what I have done on it, I will quit it; but if not, I will fight for it till I die."

Elizabeth wigton

Luzerne County ss. August 1 1788. Sworn before Nathan Denison Benj^a Carpenter Wm Hooker Smith, Justices of the Peace

[277] Timothy Pickering to John Pickering.¹

Wilkesbarre, county of Luzerne Augt 4. 1788.

Dear Brother,

I have now made you a deed (which should have been done long ago) of my half of the middle and upper pastures & third

---

⁶ The substance of this conversation is corroborated in Parson's deposition; Pickering Papers, LVIII, 105-06.

[277] ¹ M. H. S., Pickering Papers, XXXV, 45-46A, in Pickering's hand.

of the lower pasture, which were our fathers, and of Osgoods lot. If it should be convenient to you to remit the balance on these sales & the small balance on the account between us, as stated by you, I wish it may be done. The remittance may be made to Mr Hodgdon at Philadelphia, who will therewith make some payments for me in September.

The public papers, and perhaps a letter from Mr Hodgdon to Mr Williams, will have informed you of the seizure & detainer of my person by a small band of ruffians in this county. Their pretence was, to compel the government of Pennsylvania to release from jail at Philadelphia, one John Franklin, of this county, who stands committed for high treason. He is an unprincipled fellow, and therefore a proper agent for a set of unprincipled men, members of a company called the Susquehannah Company, belonging chiefly to Connecticut, who formerly sent settlers to this place, as lying within the charter boundary of Connecticut. The dispute between Connecticut & Pennsylvania, both as to soil & jurisdiction, was finally, & irreversably settled, by the decree of a federal court of commissioners at Trenton, in December 1782. However, this decision only respected the two *States:* the question of *property* between *grantees under* the two states, severally, was yet open to trial, by the articles of confederation, in a like federal court. But the Susquehannah company, altho' they were always trumpeting the validity of their claim, were never willing to submit it to such trial.[2] The reason is apparent. The Federal Court aforementioned determined the great question in the following words. "We are unanimously of opinion that the state of Connecticut has no right to the lands in controversy. We are also unanimously of opinion that the Jursidiction and Right of Preemption [3] of all the territory lying within the charter boundary of Pennsylvania, and now claimed by the State of Connecticut, do of right belong to the State of Pennsylvania." The consequence is plain: If Connecticut had no right, she could grant none to the Susquehannah Company; nor the company to any subordinate assignees. Nevertheless, a number of the company, men generally as desperate in their fortunes as abandoned in their

---

[2] The Company failed to send representatives to a hearing scheduled for June 1784 for setting a trial, mainly because violence had broken out again in the Wyoming Valley. In the fall of 1785 Congress repealed its resolution calling for a trial; see Vol. VIII, Introduction, Section III.

[3] The official Trenton decision reads "Jurisdiction and Pre-emption," not "right of Preemption"; Vol. VII, 245-46. Pickering is copying the wording sent to him by James Wilson; no. 8, *ante.*

principles, still kept up their claim. And as Pennsylvania, influenced by narrow views, & the arts of the landjobbers who had located the best of these lands, had not the good policy & prudence to quiet the old settlers in the possession of their farms (a measure recommended too by the very court which had decided the great question in her favour) [4] those bad men, aided by a few like them who lived in the settlement, inflamed and exasperated the minds of the inhabitants against Pennsylvania, & thus prevented their submission to her jurisdiction. It was easy to work up the people to the highest pitch of violent opposition: because they had from their first settlement here in 1769 been engaged in perpetual war with Pennsylvania, until 1775, when the war with Britain demanding all the attention & resources of all the colonies, Congress recommended to the two states to cease all hostilities.[5] Pennsylvania too, from first to last, has acted without a particle of wisdom or prudence. She refused to confirm the Connecticut settlers in their possessions: yet did not send a sufficient military force to compel their submission: but only enough to produce skirmishes, in which a few lives on both sides were lost, and the minds of both were imbittered against each other. There existed mutual & extreme jealousies, & mutual complaints of breaches of faith. In this state of things I was urged to accept of the principal civil offices in this county just then erected, as the person most likely, for various reasons, to reconcile the people here to the government of Pennsylvania, the state at the same time manifesting a disposition to quiet the old settlers in their possessions. This I accomplished in such manner, that but for the lies and artifices of John Franklin, before mentioned, this county would now have enjoyed perfect peace. The people become habitually jealous of Pennsylvania, were seduced by the grossest lies & the weakest sophistry. Franklin is possessed of some art, & of bravery to desperation. He had signalized himself in defending the country against the incursions of the Indians in the late war, & had taken the lead of the settlement since the peace. And the dangerous insurrections in Massachusetts under Shays, will convince you how much mischief may be done by one desperate man & a few assistants in a united & well ordered government, as was that of Massachusetts: and that it must be infinitely easier for a similar character to raise a tumult in this county. A few days before Franklin was apprehended, he had

---

[4] Vol. VII, no. 129.   [5] Vol. VI, no. 241.

the desperate boldness to send orders in writing (in which he stiled himself Colonel Commandant) to his adherents, to assemble on the ninth of October last, with arms & ammunition, at a certain place; for then, says he, "the Pennsylvania Loyalists are to hold an election of militia officers, *which we are determined to prevent.*"[6]

The ruffians who lately seized me, were 15 in number, 13 of them painted like savages. Five others joined them after they had carried me thirty miles up the river. But they found themselves deserted by their principals, the men who had drawn them into the commission of this act of violence. They held me a prisoner from June 26. till July 15th; when they set me at liberty, being as they said, advised to it by their friends. Several parties of the county militia, & some scouts of volunteers, turned out successively, & ranged about near where I was kept, in order to discover & rescue me: but they kept me always in the woods, & frequently shifted from place to place, to prevent discovery. In one of these excursions, a captain of militia with a party, & the high sheriff, fell in with a few of the ruffians, when some shots were exchanged, in which the captain was badly wounded in the body, and one of the ruffians in the hand; both however are nearly well.[7] The Council also, on the 8th of July, issued a proclamation,[8] offering generous rewards for apprehending the offenders: These proclamations did not arrive till after I was released. I immediately engaged two young men to make up a small party to pursue & take the offenders. One of the two got a party of militia to assist him; when they fell in with three of them, who refusing to surrender, were fired upon, and one of them (a desperate villain) was mortally wounded.[9] The other two escaped, tho' one was thought to be badly wounded. The first was bro't hither & died last Tuesday of his wound. Three others of the party were before apprehended by the scouts, & are now in jail, together with five or six other men, who advised & assisted in the execution of the plot, three of them fathers to some of the young men who executed it. The rewards I expect will bring in some more. But notwithstanding these exertions to suppress this violence, there yet remains too much disaffection in the county; & unless the State raises & stations here a small body of good troops, under a brave & prudent officer, the quiet of the county cannot be insured: Such is the attachment of many to Franklin, & such their

---

[6] No. 133, *ante*.   [7] See the narrative in no. 249, *ante*.
[8] No. 247, *ante*.   [9] Joseph Dudley.

expectations that he will establish them in the possession of their lands, altho' Pennsylvania should not confirm them—such their inveterate jealousy & hatred of Pennsylvania. Besides the old Settlers, there is a considerable number of men known by the title of "half-share-men," to each of whom the Members of the Susquehannah Company & Franklin their agent, have since the Trenton decree granted two or three hundred acres of land, on this single condition, that they provided themselves with arms to defend the country against Pennsylvania. 'Tis on the aid of these men that Franklin & the Company have principally depended; and these men have been the instruments of all the outrages which have been committed since I have been here. The late act of violence upon me, however, seems to have sickened them. Those of the party actually engaged, who have not been taken or killed, are dispersed, & have fled & are flying in different directions, out of the State.

My friend Mr Hodgdon is now here; tomorrow he is to set off for Philadelphia, accompanied by my wife, who will probably remain there two months. The repeated disturbances here have strongly affected her, as you may imagine; and this relaxation of a visit among her Phila^a friends will probably be of much service to her. The Assembly will sit the latter half of September, when I mean to attend it, & endeavour to procure those decisive measures to be adopted, which, at the same time that they confirm the claims of the old settlers, shall provide an effectual guard against future insurrections.

Our children are all well: the youngest, Edward, is the fattest and stoutest boy we ever had. My wife & I bear our eastern friends in the most affectionate remembrance. That God may prolong your life, & give you health to enjoy it, is the ardent prayer of your brother

T. Pickering

[278] Peter Muhlenberg to Timothy Pickering.[1]

In Council   Philadelphia, August 5th, 1788.

Sir,

I am directed by the Board to inform you that your Letter of the 19th of July[2] did not reach them until Thursday last, and

[278] [1] *P. A.*, XI, 363-64.   [2] No. 258, *ante.*

tho' it was generally reported that the Insurgents had liberated & permitted your return to your Family, yet your Letter was the first Authentic Account the Board rec⁴ on that Head. I wrote a Letter to the Lieut. of the County on the 23d of last month, (a Copy whereof I enclose) ³ informing him that the Board would render every Assistance the Laws of the State would warrant to the Friends of Government—and that they were determined to enforce Obedience to the Laws—requesting at the same time the Lieut. would give Council the earliest information if any change should take place, favorable or unfavorable.

The intelligence your Letter contains is however every thing we have heard from Luzerne that can be depended on, and as it is impossible for Council to proceed with any degree of certainty to enforce the plan in view, They have thought it necessary to send an Express, and request you will be pleased to give them full information how matters are situated. They request likewise your Opinion—with the reasons annexed—whether an Armed Force is necessary to restore Order and good Government; and whether it will be necessary for the restoration & establishment of peace to the County to fix a post at Tioga! The Board direct me to inform you, That tho' they wish that this desirable end of restoring order & Good Governm⁴ in Luzerne may be obtained by lenient Measures, yet that they are now prepared to act with energy, and compel obedience to the Laws. Upon application of this Board to the United States in Congress, we have obtained their permission to employ the Troops of the Union ag⁴ the Insurgents.⁴ They are now marching to Rendevouz at Easton, where they will wait the Orders of the Board. This circumstance alone will convince you how necessary it is that Council should have the earliest & fullest information. I am, Sir, with great Respect, Your most obedient, and very humble Servant

Peter Muhlenberg, Vice President

---

³ According to minutes of the Council the enclosed copy of the letter to Zebulon Butler was that dated July 18, not July 23; *Pa. C. R.,* XV, 505. Butler was written to on both dates; the letter of July 18 has not been found.

⁴ No. 266, *ante.* Letters received on August 6 from Pickering and Butler together with depositions enclosed made it apparent that the crisis had passed, and the request for troops was withdrawn; *Pa. C. R.,* XV, 505. See no. 279, *post.*

[279] Peter Muhlenberg to the Pennsylvania Delegates in the Continental Congress.[1]

Philada., Aug't 6th, 1788.

Gentlemen,

By direction of the Board, I have the Honor to inform you That we have this morning, by express, rec'd Letters from Colo. Pickering and other Officers of Government in the County of Luzerne.[2] From these it appears that matters have taken a more favorable turn than was at first apprehended. Colo. Pickering was liberated by the insurgents on the 16th of July, & the men who carried him off are now by their petition, praying Council to grant them pardon.[3] The proclamation issued by the Board has produced the desired effect—two of the rioters are now confined in Easton Jail—and some others in that of Luzerne—several have been Wounded, & Dudley, one of the most notorious, died in Luzerne Jail of the Wounds he rec'd. Those of the rioters who still remain, are dispersed, and seeking refuge on the Lakes. From this change of affairs, and the Accounts from the Western Waters, which seem to indicate that the Troops of the Union will be wanted in that Quarter, as well as from the shortness of the time limited for which the Troops can possibly be spared, & the consideration that the chief end for which the application was made is already answer'd—The Board are induced to request you would be pleased to inform The Honble. The Congress of the United States, that we gratefully acknowledge the favor conferred on this State by so readily granting the assistance requested—but as the emergency has ceas'd, & as the State will now have time to act deliberately, and as circumstances shall in future direct, we furrther request that the troops of the Union may *now* be directed to continue their route agreeably to their first destination. The Board have in the mean time directed a Commissary to proceed to Easton to pro-

[279] [1] *P. A.,* XI, 364-65.
[2] Nos. 268, 270, and 272, *ante.*
[3] No. 255, *ante.*

vide for the subsistance of the Troops until further orders.[4]   I
am, Gent., your most obedient, and very humble servant,

Peter Muhlenberg.

[280] Deposition of Garret Smith.[1]

I Garret Smith of the township of Braintram, in the county
of Luzerne, & of lawful age, testify & declare That on Sunday
evening, on the twenty second day of June last, I was at
Meshoppin, and between the houses of Thomas Wigton & Martin
Dudley, met Gideon Dudley, said Martin's son, when Gideon
said he had a great secret to reveal to me, at the request of
Major Jenkins, colonel M°Kinstry,[2] & John Hyde (the son of
John Hyde of Wilkesbarre, as I took it), and asked me if I
would keep the secret.   I answered That I would, if it was not
to injure myself or my neighbours.   He then said it was to take
colonel Pickering, and carry him into the woods, and there keep
him, until colonel Franklin was returned to the county, or released (such like expression he made use of.)   I told him I
would think of it till the morning.   The next morning I called
at captain Dudley's (having lodged at said Wigton's) and told
Gideon I would go home and talk with my wife, but rather
thought I should go with them.   I then went down into the mill,
to captain Dudley, and asked him if [he] knew any thing about
the affair of taking colonel Pickering.   He answered yes—but
that he was unwilling that both of his sons should go.   I asked
him why.   He answered, for fear they should be found out, for
if one was at home, people would think the other was some-
where at work.   I then asked him which was going.   He answered, Gideon, and that he (captain Dudley) was willing he
should go, & support the cause; but wished his son Joseph might

[4] The delegates answered on August 11 that they had informed the Secretary at War of the changed conditions; Burnett, *Letters of Members,*
VIII, 777; *P. A.,* XI, 373-74. *P. A.* gives the date as August 18, however.

On August 13, as Commissary of Military Stores, Samuel Hodgdon
forwarded marching orders from the Secretary at War to the troops waiting in Easton. The orders were sent by express "to prevent further deten-
tion and expence"; *ibid.,* 374.

[280] [1] M. H. S., Pickering Papers, LVIII, 84-85, in Pickering's hand but
signed by William Hooker Smith; *P. A.,* XI, 371-73. A copy was forwarded to Council by Pickering, enclosed in his letter of August 9; no.
285, *post* and *Pa. C. R.,* XV, 514.

[2] John McKinstry; see no. 105, *ante,* note 2.

not go, lest it should be found out that his sons were in the Scrape. I then said, captain Dudley, I am a poor man—if I go, who is to support my family, while I am gone? He answered, I will. I have enough. After this I left Meshoppin to go home, in a canoe. When I had pushed up as far as Ephraim Tylers, I landed, & went to his house, where I found Joseph Dudley above mentioned, who immediately said to me—you are my prisoner for a while (he had a tomahawk in his hand). Then Ephraim Tyler asked me if I was willing to go and take colonel Pickering? Then Joseph Dudley added, speaking to me, you have promised to go, and must either do that, or go down to lieutenant Kilborn's (that is Joseph Kilborn's) and there lay confined till I return (meaning, as I understood, till he & the party returned from the taking of colonel Pickering). I then said I had not promised, but only that I would go home & talk with my wife; & if she is against it I will not go. I then set off to go to my canoe, but was followed by said Tyler & Joseph Dudley, who took hold of me, & by force brought me back to Tyler's house. I then said to Tyler, If I go, what shall I do for provisions in going, & to support my family while I am gone? Tyler answered, I have sent the flour of two bushels of wheat, and fifty weight of pork, to lieutenant Kilborn's, out of which you can be supplied; and I will see that your family has provisions in your absence; and I will get a man, or go myself to work on your land, and we will also allow you a dollar a day for every day you are gone. To whom (said I) shall I look for the pay? He answered, you may look to me for it. I then turned about, and said to him, I cannot go. Then Tyler's wife said, She had dreamed last night, that the boys went to take an Elk, and that a person had been there & told the Elk, & that he was gone. Then her husband Ephraim Tyler said. If Garret Smith will give me his word and honour that he will go, or that he will not reveal the secret in three weeks, then he may go home. He brought me a bible and asked me to lay my hand on it and swear: but I told him it was against my principles; He then asked me to hold up my hand which I did, when he spoke to this effect—You declare that you will keep this secret for three weeks. I answered, I will. After Tyler said if I would give my promise, I might go home, Elijah Reynolds who was by, said—Garret Smith has lived with colonel Hay, & knows what he is about. I rather guess it is best to have him sworn. And then Tyler offered me the bible, as above mentioned. I then left them, & went home. The same day I thought of my neighbour Thomas Kinney, and as he was a

453

half-share man, I suspected he might be concerned in the affair. In the evening he came to my house, and we set out together & went up Little Tuscorora Creek to hunt. On our way I said to him Mʳ Kinney, do you know anything of this affair of the boys going to Wyoming? He answered, Yes, and added, The Pennamites have drove the Connecticut (or New England) people and plundered them, and now we mean to have revenge, & plunder, and if you will go along, you shall have part. I forgot to mention, That while at Tylers, as abovesaid, Tyler told me, that if I would go along with the boys, I should have, besides what he had before promised, the place I lived on (part of which I supposed belonged to Doctor Smith) and the half of ten acres of good wheat which James Smith then had on the ground, for the other half must go to support the boys in the woods. When Gideon Dudley proposed the matter to me I asked him where we were to get support from? He answered, Out of the settlement. I then asked him, who was going to vindicate this cause. He answered That colonel McKinstry was coming with five hundred men, in order to support the settlement—That he (McKinstry) was to take possession of John Hollenback's mill & place, and John Hyde of Doctor Smith's place. I asked, What are you going to do with John Hollenback? He answered, tomahawk him as soon as we can see him. I also asked him (before this) if Doctor Smith was concerned in the affair. He answered, No, and that he (the Doctor) was a damned rascal. I also asked if colᵒ Butler was concerned. He answered, No, not that I know of.

The mark of
Garret X Smith

Luzerne ss. August 7. 1788. Then Garret Smith who has subscribed the aforewritten deposition, being duly sworn, did declare, That the same deposition contains the truth, the whole truth, & nothing but the truth, to the best of his present recollection. before

Wᵐ Hooker Smith
Justice of The Peace

I the said Garret Smith farther recollect & declare That about a week before colonel Pickering was taken, I saw Nathan Abbot, the elder, at his own house (which is in the township of Braintram) & He then swore, That he would support his place where he then lived, & that he would kill any damned Pennamite that should ever set his foot on it. Said Abbot holds his place, as I have always understood, by a half-share right.

The mark of
Garret X Smith

Sworn as above August 7th 1788. Before

Wᵐ Hooker Smith
Justice of The Peace

[281] Charles Biddle to Timothy Pickering.[1]

Secretary's Office, Philadelphia, August 7th, 1788.

Sir,
    Inclosed you have the opinion of the Judges on the late disturbances in Luzerne.[2] Council agree with the Judges that the best method that can be taken with the Prisoners will be to have them prosecuted for a riot—the Att'y General will take the first opp'y to forward on the papers necessary for this purpose.[3] I am Sir, your obedient and very humble servant,

Charles Biddle, Sec'y

[282] The Legal Opinion of Thomas McKean and George Bryan.[1]

To His Excellency the President and the Honorable the Supreme Executive Council of the State of Pennsylvania,

    We the Justices of the Supreme Court, whose names are under-written, Report that we have read and considered the letter from Colonel Timothy Pickering to Council together with the

---

[281] ¹ P. A., XI, 365.

² No. 282, post. On August 6 the Council had requested an opinion from Thomas McKean and George Bryan on the propriety of granting bail to those imprisoned for the abduction of Pickering; Pa. C. R., XV, 505.

³ This curt note with its enclosure was all the reply Pickering got to his embittered letter of July 28 (no. 268, ante), which accused the government of indecisiveness and weakness.

[282] ¹ M. H. S., Pickering Papers, LVIII, 87, a copy sent by the Council to Pickering; Pa. C. R., XV, 507. The opinion, along with documents sent by Pickering and mentioned in notes 5, 7, 8, and 10 of no. 270, ante, was transmitted to the Attorney General; ibid.

several papers accompanying it and thereupon beg leave to recommend that the outrageous Assault battery and imprisonment of Colonel Pickering, be prosecuted as a Riot. it is certainly one of a most audacious and atrocious nature but as the punishment for such an offence will not extend to life or member, a conviction of the Offenders in the present unsettled condition of the County of Luzerne may be attained with more facility and thereby the honor of Government preserved and Justice in a degree obtained. To accomplish this end it may be most proper for the Attorney General to prepare a Bill of Indictment himself inserting all the riotous Acts and aggravating circumstances of the case, and to have it presented to the Grand Jury for Luzerne County at the next Court of General Quarter Sessions of the peace. If it shall be found by them a true Bill, of which we conceive there can be little doubt, we would advise the Indictment to be removed by Certiorari into the Supreme Court and to be tried at the next Court of Nisi Prius for that County. By this mode of procedure the Justices of the peace of the County will have cognizance of the offence and will be authorized to bail such of the offenders as they may think proper; such as ought not be let at Large without giving the best Security and which they may not be able to procure may be committed to Easton Jail until they shall be brought to trial.

Thomas McKean
George Bryan

Philadelphia   August 7ᵗʰ 1788

copy

[283] Andrew Ellicott to Timothy Pickering.[1]

Philadelphia Augsᵗ 8ᵗʰ 1788

Dear Sir

Yours of the 19ᵗʰ of July came safe to hand. It was with the greatest pleasure that I observed it dated from Wilkesbarre, and I now congratulate you on your safe return to your family. It was my opinion when at Wyoming that if proper exertions had been immediately made upon your being taken prisoner, that you might have been released before the next night. I am yet of the same mind.

We were much perplexed in all our Councils at Wilkesbarre

---

[283] [1] M. H. S., Pickering Papers, XIX, 70.

by the admittance of the Luke-warm, (erroniously called prudent,) and the disaffected; they threw a damp on all our measures, and prevented the spirited execution of any one plan. Beware of C. Holbert![2] Mr John Franklin has been ill of a Dysentery, and is yet in a weak condition. the Physicians dispaired of his life, and proposed his being taken out of prison for the advantage of the Air, I joined with them in the application to Council; but it was to no purpose. Col. Oswald, (who is in Jail for a Contempt of Court,) sent him a present of Claret, and I furnished him with some Pine Apples, and Oranges; he is now out of danger. Eleven States have adopted the new General Government, and we are hourly in expectation of hearing of the ratification by the State of N. Carolina. For the kind treatment I met with in your Family, and the attention shewn me by yourself. you have my friendship and best wishes. I am Dr Sir Your Hb^l Servt

And^w Ellicott [3]

[284] Information from John Allen.[1]

Meeting of Susquehannah Company in June 1787.

Major Judd & Doctor Hosmer (Osmer) [2] told Mr John Allen of Plymouth that Judd had formed a constitution for a New State, to be erected in this county. That McKinstry [3] came on to aid in the setting it forward, & that they expected Genl Allen from Vermont would also come in for the same purpose. That the Constitution was sent on by Asa Starkweather & Mr Allen told Judd he supposed was taken on him, as a packet had been found with him which had fallen into the hands of Gov^t upon which Judd exclaimed Oh Hell! Hell! Hell! They have now got the whole of it.[4]

Endorsed: Information of Mr John Allen Noted Augt 9. 1788.

---

[2] Probably Christopher Hurlbut; see no. 25, ante.

[3] Ellicott had contracted with the landholders' association to build the road running from Tioga Point to Mt. Ararat.

[284] [1] M. H. S., Pickering Papers, LVII, 226, in Pickering's hand.

[2] See no. 14, ante, note 1.

[3] See no. 105, ante, note 2.

[4] There is a discrepancy here, for if the conversation with Judd took place in June, 1787, Allen could not have known about the seizure of Starkwather, who was taken on October 2, 1787; see no. 238, ante.

[285] Timothy Pickering to Peter Muhlenberg.[1]

Wilkesbarré August 9. 1788.

Sir,

Last evening I was honoured with your letter of the 5th with sundry enclosures by express.[2] The two requests of the board therein mentioned, I believe I have in a great measure anticipated by my letters of the 28th & 29th ult° sent by a Mr Morris.[3]

With respect to the first for full information "how matters are situated" here, I have to observe, That the whole county is at present in peace; all the insurgents who have not surrendered themselves or been taken, having fled into the neighbouring states. On the 4th instant the two young Abbots (Nathan & Benjamin) were conducted to this place, having surrendered themselves to N. Kingsley Esq; at Wyalusing: Their examination discovered nothing new.[4] They joined the insurgents after they had taken me up the river; they are simple fellows and appear not to have been intrusted with the secrets of their party. One of them is but about 17 years old. Their misconduct is probably chargeable to their father Nathan, the old man, now in Luzerne jail, who with an understanding not much better, has it is said a heart very depraved. He (as well as each of his sons) is a half share man, and his disposition in regard to the government may be learnt from the deposition of Garret Smith, a copy of which I now inclose.[5] By the same deposition the guilt of Martin Dudley and Ephraim Tyler is very clearly proved & the guilt of Thomas Kinney put past a doubt. Joseph Kilborn's own confession on his examination showed that he was guilty.[6] But several other depositions of their neighbours remain to be taken, when further proofs of their guilt will appear; & perhaps

[285] [1] M. H. S., Pickering Papers, LVIII, 91-92, a draft in Pickering's hand; P. A., XI, 366-71. This letter was read in Council on August 15; Pa. C. R., XV, 514.

[2] No. 278, ante.   [3] Nos. 268 and 270, ante.

[4] The depositions of Benjamin and Nathan Abbot are in Pickering Papers, LVIII, 79 and 80.

[5] No. 280, ante.

[6] P. A., XI, 359. Kilbourn contradicted himself, saying that he knew nothing about the scheme to seize Pickering yet admitting that he advised his son against joining in the plan.

some others may be criminated. These other witnesses are to appear here & give their evidence on the 18th instant.[7] I have also the deposition of the wife of Thomas Wigton, which contains some original information, with a relation of many small circumstances, & much hearsay & therefore I have not thought it necessary to send a copy to council.[8] One passage only I will here transcribe. After relating that John Jenkins called at her husbands house at Meshoppen, the day after I was taken off she says, "My husband asked Jenkins if he did not think this would be a bad affair, & lead to fighting? I don't know (says Jenkins) *but I swear* (adds he) *we must fight, in order to have peace.*"

A few days after young Dudley was buried, some people were for digging up the body, to expose it to a coroners inquest; for they said he was *murdered* by the party that took him: and I am informed that in the beginning of this week (while I was absent, accompanying my wife on her way to Philadelphia) a number of old settlers from Nantikoke & Shawnee, as many as eight or ten in all, came to Wilkesbarre, warmed with the same zeal for digging up the body of Dudley: but the sheriff & some other gentlemen talked with them, & partly by reasoning, & partly by threats, checked their zeal, & sent them home cool, & tolerably well satisfied. In fact a disposition to murmur at every correcting measure of government & act of the magistrate, tho' necessary for the establishment of good order, & strictly legal, prevails among great numbers of the people. Without referring to particular characters whose conduct & declarations would nevertheless mark not their own only but the disposition of a party, I beg leave to notice the late election of militia officers in the upper battalion. John Jenkins & John Swift were chosen Lieut. Col° & Major by a great majority.[9] And Martin Dudley Joseph Kilborn & David Woodward all names now familiar to Council,[10] were chosen captain lieutenant & ensign of one of the companies! Divers other similar elections of disaffected characters took place in the same battalion. In a word it would seem that such men were chosen, not to support, but, in proper time,[11] to oppose, the government of Pennsylvania.

---

[7] See no. 291, *post,* note 3.   [8] No. 276, *ante.*

[9] See no. 298, *post.*

[10] The phrase beginning "David Woodward" is interlined, and the words lined out are illegible.

[11] The phrase "in proper time" is interlined, and the words lined out are illegible. The wording of this sentence differs slightly in *P. A.*

In my letter of the 28th ult° I remarked that a multitude of the old settlers were half-share-men.[12] Within a few days past some of my neighbours have told me that they think *one half* of the old settlers & their sons are half-share-men; & I recollect that in Jan^r 1787, John Jenkins, at a town meeting called at my request, said that of the half-share-men then in the county, not more than 30, were *New-Comers*. E. Marcy Esq. of Pittstown (Lackawanock) a sedate, observing man, says there are now fewer well affected inhabitants in that town than there were 16 months ago.[13] In one word, altho' the measures taken by Council, and the officers & well affected people of this county, in consequence of the violent outrage on my person, have given the disaffected a severe shock, yet their disposition to murmur & to excite disorders [14] remains. They were as much shocked after their insurrection last October, when they had had time to reflect on their unwarrantable proceedings, & expected the vengeance of Government to overtake them: But they soon recovered their spirits, and began to meditate retaliation [15] for the imprisonment of John Franklin: & this was to seize & make prisoner of me. As instead of good officers & old soldiers, there was [16] sent hither only an ordinary company of militia, this served to heighten their confidence in their own party, & increase their contempt for the force of the state.

The foundation of all the disorders in this county was laid by John Franklin, as an inhabitant, and the prime agent of a junto of the Susquehannah Company. John Franklin was a principal assistant. The people universally think that in times past they have been ill-used, & deceived by Pennsylvania; and these men, by lies & sophistry, have found it easy to persuade great numbers that, notwithstanding all appearances to the contrary, they will still be ill-used & deceived; and therefore that they have no security for holding their lands but in their tomahawks & rifles. Their credulity [17] is truly astonishing. On one side the most improbable lie & the weakest sophistry have the effect of plain truth & the strongest reasoning. Their incredulity on the other hand, is not less extraordinary. For instance should the federal troops now rendezvousing at Easton,

---

[12] No. 268, *ante*.   [13] An illegible phrase is lined out here.

[14] The phrase "in the county" is lined out here.

[15] "Retaliation" is substituted for "revenge."

[16] "There was" is substituted for "Council," probably to make his criticism less direct.

[17] Two illegible words are lined out here.

not march into this county (& I do not think it at all necessary that they should) this class of the people will not believe they were intended to be marched hither; but will say the story was raised only to alarm their fears.

My former accounts of the state of this county, & what I have now said of its inhabitants, amounts to this—That the people, generally,[18] having, during a long course of years, been bickering with Pennsylvania—having, at sundry times, greatly suffered by her attempts to subdue or expel them—having, during the same period, entertained jealousies of her, lest one day she should crush them—these jealousies being (as is natural to the weaker party) in the greatest extreme, & have become habitual —these jealousies also, being still kept alive, by the artifices & lies of a few designing men—Many being willing to hazard every thing, rather than trust to the honour, the faith & generosity of the State—Many (like the men who resorted to David) having fled hither from other states, to escape from Justice, or their creditors—The mere half-share-men, having no other chance of holding any land but by overturning [19] the authority of the State in this settlement—Many others having old possessions [20] & by themselves or sons also holding half-share-rights, and wishing to secure the latter (in many cases the more valuable lands) as well as the former; and thinking they have a very good chance to secure both, by temporizing, by making a partial submission to the Government, & keeping themselves in readiness to resist when occasions call; and concluding from past uniform experience that they may do this with impunity: The junto of the Susquehannah Company (Major Judd, Doctor Hamilton, Doctor Benton, Zerah Beach &c.) and their head men in the settlement, being also closely connected with the New-York Lessees,[21] with whom, it is past doubt, this settlement was to act in concert, & from whom they expected to derive effectual support. From all these causes, many of the inhabitants have an utter hatred of Pennsylvania & many more have a greater or less degree of disaffection. And this disaffection has been confirmed by a ridiculous confidence that they were able to resist all the force the state could send against them. Not that the Militia of Pennsylvania were unable if disposed to destroy

---

[18] "The people, generally" is substituted for "a large portion of the people."

[19] "Overturning" is substituted for "opposing."

[20] "Having old possessions" is substituted for "holding old rights."

[21] See no. 100, *ante,* note 5.

them: but Franklin has made them believe that [22] a body of militia equal to this effect, and disposed to produce it, could not be raised; and that from the divisions in the state no other effectual force would ever come against them. Council know that Franklin himself, tho' far better informed than the mass of the people, had the madness & folly to attempt an open resistance to the state in arms. It was for this purpose he sent his written orders to his adherents particularly the half-share-men, to assembly, in arms, in October last, to prevent the election of militia officers; signing himself Col° Commandant. I suppose Council is now possessed of two of his orders,[23] in his own hand writing —M' Ellicot took them with him to Phila'. On that day (had not Franklin fortunately been previously carried off) the authority of the state in this county would doubtless have been utterly subverted, & every officer of Government banished, or compelled to swear obedience to this New Commander. At this moment great numbers of half-share-men are in actual possession of lands allotted them by Franklin & Jenkins from Tunkannock to Tioga.[24] I cannot believe that other claimants (either Pennsylvanians or old Connecticut Settlers) would be able to get possession of those lands in the ordinary course of law. Tho' many of these half-share-men have taken the benefit of the law to recover debts, & others, being debtors, have so far submitted to its operation, yet (like old Abbot, in Garret Smith's deposition) [25] swear vengeance against any One who shall attempt to dispossess them of their half-share-rights.

I therefore continue of the opinion *That in order to establish the peace of the county of Luzerne, it is necessary to fix a military post at Tioga.* This appears to me to be the dictate of *humanity* and *sound policy,* as well as of *necessity.* If a regular force sufficient to overawe the turbulent be there stationed, the laws will have their free & natural operation, & the *exercise* of force will perhaps never be requisite; thus the shedding of blood will be prevented; and a much less force will be adequate to overawe the disaffected, than to crush their rebellion when once they have flown to arms. I suppose, however, that *very few* of the people, even among the old settlers, deem it at all necessary

---

[22] The words "insufficient" and "incompetent" are lined out here.

[23] No. 133, *ante,* note 3.

[24] The following words are crossed out here: "and no longer ago than last Spring Some half-share-men at Tioga *by force* turned a number of other settlers out of possession, & hold the land."

[25] No. 280, *ante.*

to send troops hither, altho' it were only to fix a post at Tioga. They were of the same opinion after the tumults of last autumn subsided. Yet it is a truth that the Civil Officers have not been able to fully execute the laws more than 30 miles up the river from this place. At Tunkhannock & upwards, as well criminal as civil process (so far as the latter respected lands) has been [26] set at defiance. The coming of troops would hurt the pride of some, who would say it would be a reflection on the county: that troops alway plunder & do mischief & they & others fear that measure would operate in the Assembly against their claims & petitions for a confirmation of their lands. Of the latter tendency I am not insensible: but tho' interested myself, to obtain such confirmation, I feel no disposition to conceal my sentiments on this subject, or keep Government in ignorance of a single fact that may contribute to the forming a just idea of the state of this county. I confess that the exertions of the people here against the late insurgents [27] seem to have had a very good effect; and the folly of attempting by small numbers so to violate the laws, has been manifested: so that now there will be need of fewer troops than if the late disturbance had not happened. I must add another reason for fixing a post at Tioga. There are great numbers of orderly people farmers & tradesmen, who would come & settle in this county. divers such have to my knowledge been waiting for the establishment of peace, in order to remove hith[er] but they will not come, until the authority of government is indubita[bly] established. The present calm like the former they will justly suppose to be deceitful. But surely it is of vast importance that good citizens here should be increased.[28] Such would strengthen the hand of Government; and after no long period, the laws having had their full operation the troops might be disbanded. Whatever number should be raised it will be expedient that a part should consist of some faithful young men of the county, who are handy, & brave, who are woodsmen, & who know the inhabit[ants] & particularly the most noted disaffected charaters[, and the country.

The letter to the Sheriff, with the warrant, &c., from New York,[29] I delivered to him yesterday, and requested him to concert measures particularly for seizing John Jenkins. The

---

[26] Several illegible words are lined out here.

[27] An illegible phrase is interlined and lined out here.

[28] Nine or ten illegible words are lined out here.

[29] See no. 248, *ante,* note 3. The letter to the sheriff, dated July 18, has not been found.

Sheriff is now going to Tioga, and I hope his endeavours, with those of others who may be tempted by the offered reward, will be successful in seizing that atrocious offender.] [30]

[286] Timothy Pickering to Samuel Hodgdon.[1]

Wilkesbarre August 10. 1788.

Dear Sir,

You may recollect that I last year left in your hands some locations of Ebenezer Marcy Esq. of a body of from three to five thousand acres of land in this county, that you might find gentlemen to take it upon the usual shares. You did not succeed & returned the paper. He now tells me the new road goes thro part of it—that tis really valuable, and will soon be located by others. He is therefore very anxious to know whether the location can or cannot be so disposed of. I know not now where to find the Paper, perhaps tis among those my wife sent to Philaᵃ if not, I will search for it here & forward it by the first conveyance; In the mean time pray enquire if any one of our landed friends or others will take it up. Nothing new, except the deposition of one Garret Smith clearly proving the guilt of the old man in jail here.[2] In great haste. Affectionately farewell.

T. Pickering

[287] Samuel Hodgdon to Timothy Pickering.[1]

Philadelphia 14ᵗʰ Augᵗ 1788

Dear Sir

* * * I have repeatedly been with Council since my return, and among other things I mentioned your disapprobation of the Letter sent to Colonel Butler.[2] They informed me they had ex-

---

[30] The words in brackets are missing from the draft and are supplied from *P. A.*

[286] [1] M. H. S., Pickering Papers, LVIII, 93, in Pickering's hand.
    [2] No. 280, *ante.*

[287] [1] M. H. S., Pickering Papers, LVIII, 94, in Hodgdon's hand.
    [2] See no. 268, *ante*, note 9.

plained that matter to you,[3] perfectly agreeably to my apprehension express'd to you (a mere amusement). The troops at Easton by authority derived from the War Office, I have by express ordered to March to their first destination, (the Ohio) and to day I doubt not they are on their way.[4] All accounts hitherto agree that you are to have Troops yet, as the time of the sitting of the Assembly is so Near, I much doubt whether anything will be done until they come togath[er]. M^r C[5] and others have been with me to know what discoveries have been made relative to the origin of the late riot in your County—they believe that it originated *here,* and were in hopes detection would have followed disappointment and chagrin. I express'd to him the general suspicion that *Perkins*[6] brought or suggested the plan, but lamented that no evidence yet taken had thrown any light in this respect on the affair. On the whole all parties seem so much interested in this business that I cannot doubt but that it will be taken up in the early part of the session, and finally decided on. Decission from appearances I deprecate, as my friends may be involved—but I will not anticipate—sufficient to the day is the evil. I find I neither Misunderstood Council nor am deceived by them—their minds I know. * * *

Mr Drinkers[7] friends have agreed on a certain day to leave this City for a settlement on his Lands. They are about twenty in Number and bear the character of honest industrious Men. This will help to raise the value of those Lands. I have not yet looked to see whether Mercys [Marcys] papers returned with your papers,[8] but I will this evening and if they did, they shall again accompany this. I think if he can give an account of those lands that they are good from his *own knowledge* he had better come to Penn and dispose of them himself. They will readily sell if known or beleived to be good. Nothing further at this time from your friend and very humble servant

Samuel Hodgdon

---

[3] No. 278, *ante,* but see note 3.   [4] No. 279, *ante,* note 3.

[5] Probably George Clymer.

[6] For David Perkins, see no. 233, *ante.* Perkins visited John Franklin in jail on May 31; no. 307, *post.* Since Perkins was used by Pickering as a messenger on the recommendation of John Jenkins, some believed that Perkins had either told Franklin of the plot to capture Pickering or had brought back from Franklin to Jenkins the suggestion for such a move. Franklin, however, apparently denied any foreknowledge of the scheme in a letter to Governor Samuel Huntington of Connecticut; no. 312, *post.*

[7] Henry Drinker, one of the associated landholders; see no. 203, *ante.*

[8] See no. 286, *ante.*

[288] Henry Drinker to Timothy Pickering.[1]

Philad. 14ᵗʰ 8 mo. 1788.

Esteemed Friend

As I felt much sympathy & real concern on hearing of thy being so cruelly torn & separated from thy family & tender connections, so I may with much sincerity congratulate thee and them on thy safe return after a time of such severe tryal, thy delivery and releasement having been to myself and I believe to many others occasion of much rejoicing. Our Friend Andrew Ellicot is now absent on a journey to Baltimore. before he left this City he express'd an earnest desire that some money might be sent to Wilksborough, to be lodged there subject to the orders of his brothers Joseph & Benjamin now employ'd in opening the new road from Tioga Point Eastward to unite with the road already opened to the north end of Mount Ararat.[2] This money being intended to pay the wages of Labourers employ'd on that road. Major Hodgdon was kind enough to advise me of the present conveyance William George by whom have sent £62 5 11 to be delʳ to thyself as per copy of recᵗ inclosed. Be kind enough to hold this money in readiness for the purpose above-mentioned, which will oblige our said Friend A Ellicot, as also the Commissioners appointed to that business, on whose behalf I am, thy assured Friend

Henry Drinker

[289] Timothy Pickering to Samuel Hodgdon.[1]

Wilkesbarre August 17. 1788.

Dear Sir,

I am informed that Colº Denison sets off for the City tomorrow, & by him I intend to send this.

It is as I told you, that the Council were undetermined about troops to be stationed in this county. You met Mʳ White the express. He was sent by Council with a letter & some in-

---

[288] [1] M. H. S., Pickering Papers, XIX, 138-39, signed by Drinker.
 [2] See Coxe's sketch, reproduced facing p. 374.
[289] [1] M. H. S., Pickering Papers, LVIII, 98-99, in Pickering's hand.

closures.[2] The letter informed That some Continental troops were on their March to Easton, to proceed hither if needed. Council requested my opinion whether it was necessary that they should come in to quell the insurgents and whether it was necessary to raise troops & fix a military post at Tioga, with my reasons to be annexed. To the first question I answered in the negative: for none of the insurgents remained in the county— those who were prisoners excepted. To the second That there ought to be a post fixed at Tioga; and my reasons I gave at large. Should Council think my reasons valid; yet I imagine they will take no measures for raising troops, till the Assembly meets, as the session is so near. *Then,* perhaps, they may think of *laying my letters* [3] *before the House,* but I believe it would be much more proper that they should be inspected only by a *Committee of the House.* For the sentiments I have expressed cannot be pleasing to the people of this county; and if publicly read, besides the effect they might have here, would be made a handle of by the *Pennamites.* However, I do not feel very solicitous to have my letters kept from the house; for Denison & Schott will doubtless see them; [4] and what they see, they will probably report to the people here. Nevertheless, if kept back from the House, they will not appear *in print,* and consequently will be less public. I will write a letter to the Speaker of the House on this subject, & desire that a *prudent use may be made of them.* Before I was taken, I thought 100 men requisite: Now I believe a company of 60 or 70 may do as well as 100 would have done before. But if ever done, the measure should be executed with promptitude or its effect will be lessened; and the people, after an interval of quiet, will grumble the more at the sending of the troops.

Esqr Hollenback & one Harris set off from Tioga, went about 40 miles above, up the Susquehanna, & in the night took John Hyde. He requested to have time to send for his cloaths. Hollenback unfortunately indulged him. The boy who went, (or pretended to go for them) alarmed his comrades, who waylaid the road, & rescued him. One of them fired at Hollenback, & killed his horse. From the account come to hand of this af-

---

[2] No. 278, *ante* and see no. 285, *ante,* note 29.

[3] Those of July 28 and 29 and August 9; nos. 268, 270, and 285, *ante.* These and other documents were forwarded to the Assembly on September 6; *Pa. C. R.,* XV, 528.

[4] Nathan Denison and John Paul Schott, the former a member of the Council, the latter of the House.

fair, Hollenback appears to have behaved very gallantly.⁵ Young Aaron Kilborn was returning home, & being seen, was apprehended, & I suppose will soon be brought down prisoner.

Neighbour Fell's inmate, Morris, has come back: by him Council inclosed the opinion of the Chief Justice & Judge Bryan,⁶ That the ruffians should be indicted for a riot only, tho' (as they say) a riot of the most audacious & atrocious nature. They advise that the Attʸ Genˡ prepare a bill of indictment, & send it to the Court of Sessions here (this court sits Sept. 2ᵈ) & if the Grand Jury find the bill, then the Justices will have cognizance of the affair, & bail such of the offenders as they may think proper. Then the indictment to be removed by *Certiorari* to the Supreme Court. * * *

I understand the Assembly will sit Sept. 2ᵈ. If so, I must be down as soon as possible after our court is over. Till then I bid you an affectionate adieu.

T. Pickering

P. S. We neither see nor hear any thing of Wᵐ George

Endorsed: Recᵈ 23

[290] Deposition of William Griffith.¹

I William Griffith of lawful age testify, That a little time before colonel Pickering was taken, I was at the house of Darius Parks, when he said, he had told Jenkins (meaning, as I took it, Major Jenkins) they were put to it for want of a leading man that Jenkins answered, it was not so much for the want of a leading man, as for the want of provisions, that he (Parks) told him, he would give five pounds towards furnishing provisions, & if every one would do as much, there would be no want. This was said by Parks, in consequence of my remarking, That I looked upon it that Yankee was dead now, and that if I had an opportunity I would send to colᵒ Charles Stewart ² & get a confirmation of the land where I lived. Upon which Mʳ Parks said I could not then live there. Why, said I, They have

---

⁵ Hollenback wrote to Pickering a long narrative account of the episode; Pickering Papers, LVIII, 96.

⁶ No. 282, *ante*.

[290] ¹ M. H. S., Pickering Papers, LVIII, 101-02, in Pickering's hand but signed by Griffith and the justices.

² Stewart had long been a leader of the Pennamite faction; see Vol. VI, Index.

now no leading man; Franklin is in jail, & Jenkins has mov'd away (for I then thought he had moved) Afterwards, on the day that captain Ross was wounded, I again saw said Parks, when we conversed together, & the tenor of the conversation on the part of Mr Parks was of a nature like that above related; plainly expressing his approbation of the conduct of the party who took colonel Pickering; and of an opposition to the government of Pennsylvania; particularly by *fighting to defend the Half-Share-Rights.*

On the day I saw colonel pickering at Tunkhannock on his return home, I fell in company with John Hyde jun^r when I told him I wanted to ask him one question—that was whether colonel Butler had any concern in the affair of taking colonel Pickering. Hyde answered, to this effect. It has been hinted by some of our party, who knew no better, that he was concerned: but remember what I now tell you, (if it should be called in question) upon my honour that to the best of my knowledge, he had no concern in it, nor knew any thing of it. But Stephen Jenkins! Dam that Villain! If it had not been for him I should never have gone into this scrape. He sent to me once and again, to go and take colonel Pickering, but I refused. And that night he met me at Joseph Earl's, (being the time the party were about setting off to take colonel Pickering) he equivocated and said he could not go—he did not see how it could do for them to go—he did not see how they could get provisions. Then said I I will go home again—I won't go. But, Oh, Damn it (says Jenkins) I would not go back again. I would go, as I had set out to go. Then I got mad as a bear, & I swore I did not care what I did, & I went. Hyde added (still speaking of Stephen Jenkins) Damn him! It will never do for him to show his head again where I am, for I [would] cudgel him. He said further I shall bear the blame of this affair, but I am not so knowing in it as some of the rest of the company.[3]

About the Monday or Tuesday after colonel Pickering was taken, I saw Thomas Kinney, with his gun, at captain Dudley's, in company with John Hyde jun. & Noah Phelps.

---

[3] A deposition given by Elijah Oakley on this same day asserted that Jenkins supplied the abductors with powder, but depositions given by Calvin Adams and Jepthah Earll on August 19 declared that Jenkins looked upon the capture of Pickering as a foolish scheme; Pickering Papers, LVIII, 106, 109, 110. In his examination before the court on August 19, Stephen Jenkins denied having any part in Pickering's abduction or knowing anyone who did; *ibid.,* 108. But see nos. 297 and 305, *post.*

As soon as the party returned from taking of colonel Pickering I saw some of them at captain Dudley's at Meshoppen, when captain Dudley said He thought it strange that Kinney, S[tephen] Jenkins & Garret Smith had not joined them.
Luzerne County ss. Sworn August 18, 1788.

William Griffith

Before
Wm Hooker Smith } Justices of the
Benjamin Carpenter } Peace for said county.

[291] Deposition of Minor York.[1]

I Minor York of lawful age testify That on Thursday June 26th (the day on which col° Pickering was taken) being on my way down from Wyalusing to the upper end of Mehoopenny flat, with tools to go to work on a tract of land which had formerly been laid out to my father Amos York deceased, before the decree of Trenton, I met Joseph Kilborn, about two miles above Meshoppen. He asked me where I was going. I said, to a lot we pretend to own at Mehoopenny. Kilborn said it would not answer, for that the lot did not belong to me: it belonged to Mr Hyde (meaning John Hyde jun^r) and he would have it; & I, said Kilborn, advise you as a friend not to go on to it: for if you are found there within five days from this time, you will have a threshing. I made answer It would take a man to whip me. He replied We have men enough amongst us here; and I would advise you, as a friend, to go back with me, & tarry at my house, & go home to-morrow. No, said I, I shall certainly pursue, & see the fate of it. We parted. I went forward, to Meshoppen; and the next day crossed the river, & went to work on the lot. Here Thomas Kinney came to me, and said he heard somebody at work there, & came up the bank to see who it was. I asked him where he was going. He answered, To Mr Parks's[2] after some tobacco plants; adding, I have my rifle along (in his canoe, as I took it) and mean to go up Mehoopenny to hunt. He then went off, down the river. I kept at my work, till sun about an hour or two high, when Thomas Wigton's wife came over, & told me colonel Pickering was taken —that the boys had been out hunting four or five days, & this

[291] [1] M. H. S., Pickering Papers, LVIII, 103-04, in Pickering's hand but signed by York and the justices.
[2] Darius Parks; see no. 293, *post*.

was what they had been after : 'Tis supposed said she John Hyde is one of them; they are expected up to-night or tomorrow; and you had better not be found upon the lot. I then said This is what Mʳ Kilborn referred to, in what he said to me yesterday. I then crossed the river with her; and as we landed, I saw Joseph Kilborn & Thomas Kinney on the bank. Mʳˢ Wigton went home. I staid to take my tools out of the canoe, and Kilborn & Kinney came to me. Well (said Mʳ Kilborn) have you heard the news? Major Jenkin's has come up, & says the boys have taken colonel Pickering, & that they will be here tonight or to-morrow; & John Hyde is one of them; & it won't do for you to be found here at work; for John Hyde owns the lot, & he will take you off of it; & if he wanted help, I would turn out myself to take you off. Well (said I) if Mʳ Hyde can get it by law, he shall have it : otherwise I will hold it. You have no right to it (said Kilborn) you drew no right in the town of Whitehaven; & that is the way in which we hold our lands. I then told him that colonel Pickering had accepted my mother's writings about that lot as well [as] our other lands that we lived on. Mʳ Kilborn then said If Pickering & his laws are any thing, I am nothing, and hold no lands : but if I am any thing, & hold land, then Pickering & his laws are nothing; and we shall know in a few days how the matter will turn. Why, said I, you don't think there will be blood-shed? Mʳ Kinney answered If it must come to it, the sooner the better; but I don't want any lives lost, I want the matter should be settled. The next morning I saw Mʳ Kinney going down the river in a canoe. In the forenoon James Smith came down to Meshoppen to the mill. I told him what had passed, as above related. He then proposed that we should go down to Mʳ Parks's, where it was probable the boys would cross the river. I told him Mʳ Kinney was gone down : Smith a[n]swered He is waiting for them. We went to Mʳ Parks's, & found Kinney there. James Smith then began to talk to Kinney about col° Pickering's being taken, & told him that he (Kinney) was there waiting for the boys, & that he wondered he was not with them. For the other morning (said Smith) I saw Woodward running up thro' my wheat field, to get you to go with them : but you was rather afraid it would not turn out well. And the next morning one of Dudley's boys went up to Tom Kinneys, to get him to go along : but he was rather afraid, and concluded to meet them down here at Mʳ Parks's; and here you are, waiting for them. On which Mʳ Kinney said "I must confess you guess about half right." Smith asked Kinney how they expected to keep colonel Pickering? Kinney answered Two of the boys will keep him in the woods the whole season.[3]

Minor York

Luzerne County ss. Sworn August 18. 1788

Before us Wm Hooker Smith } Justices of the
Benjamin Carpenter } Peace for said
county

[292] Timothy Pickering to Samuel Hodgdon.[1]

Wilkesboro', Aug⁺ 19. 1788.

* * * The justices are bailing the prisoners. More evidence has appeared against the old men.[2] I believe you made a memorandum for some blank letters of administration & bonds: I want them. The family in perfect health. No Wm George yet appears.[3] Col° Montgomery, Col° Balliet[4] & I have been on the line of the two counties, N°umberland & Luzerne with a surveyor: as it now runs, pursuant to the last law, it cuts off five eights of Huntington, one of the Connecticut settlers towns. In great haste Adieu!

T. Pickering

[293] Deposition of Anna Dudley.[1]

I Anna Dudley of lawful age testify That in the month of April last or beginning of May, Darius Parks came to the house of

---

[3] On this same day depositions were also taken from Joseph Wheeler, Uriah Parsons, and Elijah Oakley, implicating Ephraim Tyler, Joseph Kilbourn, and Stephen Jenkins; Pickering Papers, LVIII, 100, 105-06, 106. On the last named, see no. 290, *ante*, note 3. See also Tyler's deposition, no. 300, *post*.

[292] [1] M. H. S., Pickering Papers, LVIII, 107, in Pickering's hand.

[2] That is, against the fathers of the young men who seized Pickering—Martin Dudley, Joseph Kilbourn, Thomas Kinney, and the like. See Pickering to Hodgdon for an account of the outcome of their trials; no. 321, *post*.

[3] Henry Drinker was sending money by George; no. 288, *ante*.

[4] William Montgomery and Stephen Balliet, who had served with Pickering as commissioners under the Confirming Act.

[293] [1] M. H. S., Pickering Papers, LVIII, 114, in Pickering's hand but signed by Mrs. Dudley and Gore.

my husband Martin Dudley at Meshoppen, and related a conversation which he said had passed the same day between him and John Jenkins. The old man (Parks) said he had been reprimanding Jenkins, for his neglect; as he was the only head man now Franklin was taken; & told him they might, if they pleased put a stop to all these affairs: for that thirty or forty men posted upon the roads would prevent troops coming in. That Jenkins answered to this effect—If we had men, what end would it answer? Where should we get provisions? That he, Mr Parks, told Jenkins, that he would give five pounds; and if every one would do as much, they would have enough, that he would turn out a young creature; & grain after harvest. Also that he (Parks) would turn out one man; for Billy should go at any time; and if needed, his servant boy also should go: for he could not go himself, as he was old & blind; and the young people should undertake it; & he could give counsel, which they wanted. Mr Parks then said, my husband must turn out provisions: but I told him he would not. He (Parks) said I must talk to my husband about it: but I answered that I should not; & that if any body should attempt to persuade him to it, I should speak against it. After colonel Pickering was taken, I had taken him went to Mr Parks's; and that the old man ordered Billy (meaning William Carney [2] his wife's grandson, understood from Thomas Harris, that some of the party who who lived with him) to join them: That the party wanted Noah Phelps [3] to join them: but he said he had no gun: That Mr Parks then said, he had a gun, & ammunition, & that Phelps should have them. Afterwards Mr Parks was at our house (the day after my husband was taken prisoner) and gave me the same account which I had before received from Thomas Harris, respecting his ordering Billy to join the party, & the offering his gun & amunition to Phelps; & added, When Phelps comes up here look of his gun, tis a nice one. A few days after this, Phelps was at our house, & I said to him Why you have got Daddy Parks's gun. Yes, answered Phelps I have.

Anna Dudley

Luzerne County ss. Sworn Augt 20. 1788. Before Obad^h Gore [4] Justice of ye peace

---

[2] See no. 269, *ante*.   [3] See no. 297, *post*.

[4] Also taken before Gore this same day was the deposition of Aaron Kilbourn, implicating Ephraim Lewis as one who gave information to the abductors; Pickering Papers, LVIII, 112. On Lewis see also no. 297, *post*.

[294] John Skinner Whitcomb and David Woodard to Timothy Pickering.[1]

August 20th 1788   Cor Pickrin Sir
       you may remember when we was trying to make a settle-
ment with you at mr kilborns you was not only so good as to
forgive us your one [own] parsonal Damage but also to advocate for us tords a settlement with the state for which you have
merreted our regards forever. we Acknoleg sir we gave you
Just reason to Expect that we would send Down a wrighting
which was left withus us [2] and persue a settlement with the
State Imediately but sur we are able to asighn a reason for this
our Delingsigve [delinquency?]. we made an atempt to so
secure kingsle in order to imploy him on this business but being
betraid by one whome some of the parte thought thay might
trust, we was abloigd to retire back into the wods use it as a
covert from the persueer and we should have sent the paper but
the parson that hath it refued to send it or let others have it
for that purpus. You may remember sir you gave us orders not
to fire upon or resist any parte that was out after us which
Charge we have puntuly cept, and when we was waylaid and
and fired upon where one of our parte was mortely wounded, we
could have rewarded them as they had served us by fireing before our retreet but would not brake our obligations to you but
pesable retired into the wods and made our ascape. thus we
have Done what we could to keep up to our agrement, we having
this opertunity to wright a line for our selves: since we could
not Do anithing toards a pasifycation of the State in compani
with the parte in Ginneral [3] we hope it wont be thought im-
propper to write a line for our selves both to let you know the
impediments we have met with in persuing this business and to
pentishon further favours for our selves. and what shall we say,
for if the breach wide like the sea that cant be heald our crime
to grate to admit of a pardon sir althow we have appeared enemi-
cal in times past we come true friends to the State and Could
we obtain a pardon you would find us loial Subgects true friends

---

[294] [1] M. H. S., Pickering Papers, LVIII, 113, in Whitcomb's hand.
     [2] An acknowledgment of their guilt for them to sign?
     [3] Pickering's agreement with his captors was that they would assist in
implementing warrants issued by the state against any of their party; no.
254, *ante*.

474

and valyant in Solgers for the state of penselvani. we are willing to bind ourselves large bonds for our good behavour for the
futer if our one bonds are insuffishent we git others to be bound
with us. we would ask your forgivenes and the forgivnes of
the athority of the State and all persons whom we have ofended
by our conduct. so no more at present but we remain your
abloiged friends and humble Sarvants

John Skinner Whitcomb
David Woodard

[295] Samuel Hodgdon to Timothy Pickering.[1]

Philadelphia 20ᵗʰ August 1788

Dear Sir
* * * The Cheif Justice [2] assured me he should visit your County
in November next. he also informed me he had been called on
by Council to consult on the best mode for bringing the Prisoners confined under the late Proclamation to trial.[3] he has advised
to prosecute all concerned *alike* for a high handed riot, for reasons which he gave me, but which from the Multiplicety of business in which I am at present engaged I have lost, but it was in
some way to pass before the quarter sessions, and to be committed
to your Management, the Council he said had concurred with
him in the mode of prosecution advised, and it would be pursued
accordingly. He will freely communicate to you when you come
to Town. He further informed me that Council expected to
derive their information from you, and from the information so
obtained to lay the Matter before the Assembly. And he doubts
not but that both branches will be unanimously disposed to follow in the Measures you may propose for effectually quieting the
disturbances in your County. he added, should they not do it, it
would be wise in you to retire and let them experience the consequences; thus he. I wrote fully by Mʳ George which you must
have received.[4] I have found Mʳ Mercys papers but despair of
finding a Locator,[5] I will however try.* * *

---

[295] [1] M. H. S., Pickering Papers, LVIII, 115-17, in Hodgdon's hand.
[2] Thomas McKean.
[3] No. 282, *ante.*
[4] See no. 292, *ante,* note 3.
[5] See no. 286, *ante.*

[296] William Bradford, Jr., to Timothy Pickering.[1]

Philad" Aug' 23. 1788.

Dear Sir,

It has been thought advisable to proceed against the persons who committed the late outrages against your person, for a riot instead of indicting them for the higher offence of treason. It has also been deemed proper to present the bill in the quarter Sessions to discover the temper of your juries and what prospect there is of a steady administration of Justice. I accordingly enclose you a rough draught of a bill which I beg you will have copied, inserting the names of all those who were directly or indirectly concerned in that business, in the blank, and correcting any mistake of facts that may be in the bill.[2] If this should be found, such of y° def" as are with you should be called on to plead: & then the proceedings removed by a certiorari which I enclose for that purpose, the record made up & sent down as soon as possible. The def" must either be bound with good secuties to appear at the Supreme Court, or kept in confinement. The Courts of Nisi Prius & Oyer & Terminer will be held in November.

It may be necessary to remark to the Jury that all *accomplices* are *principals* in a riot whether present or absent: & that all who knew of & *consented* to it, or in any measure approved of it, are as guilty as those who actually perpetrated it.

I am inclined to believe that a new bill will be presented at the court of Oyer & Terminer, when the offences may be more specifically laid: but the bill now sent will be sufficient to discover how far your juries respect the laws of this State. I am sir with great Esteem Your most Obed' Serv.

W" Bradford Jun Att' Gen'

[297] Deposition of Noah Phelps.[1]

I Noah Phelps of lawful age declare, That on Sunday the 29ᵗʰ of June last, John Hyde jun. and about fourteen or fifteen others

---

[296] [1] M. H. S., Pickering Papers, LVIII, 118-19, in Bradford's hand.
    [2] See the indictment, no. 299, *post*.

[297] [1] M. H. S., Pickering Papers, LVIII, 120-21, in Pickering's hand but signed by Phelps and the justices.

came to my house, & told me they had taken colonel Pickering. They were all armed with guns (John Hyde and one other excepted). They told me I must go down to Tunkhannock with them, without saying for what. I told them I could not go because my corn wanted hoeing. But they insisted upon my going with them, & threatened that I should be dispossessed if I did not go. That they had colonel Pickering in the woods, & a hundred men with him; and that two thirds of the settlement were ready to turn out & join them, with the chief part of the head men. Hence I was induced to go with them to Tunkhannock, where I staid with them one night, and the next day went home again, overtaking on my way, said Hyde & Thomas Kinney. Hyde told me he was going up to the Point (meaning Tioga) to see col° McKinstry[2] & John Jenkins, to see whether Jenkins would back them as he had promised; & to see what col° McKinstry said on the affair. I saw said Kinney on the Sunday above mentioned; and both then, & now that he was with Hyde, expressed his approbation of the taking of col° Pickering; and appeared by his discourse as forward in prosecuting the affair as any of the boys. I went home to my business. On or about Tuesday July first, William Carney & Benjamin Abbot came to me & said that Daniel Earl & Gideon Dudley would be at Meshoppen that day, & I must go up there. After this we went again to Tunkhannock, staid one night, & returned again to Meshoppen, on Wednesday. That evening Ephraim Lewis came to us, & told us that capt. Ross was out in the woods with about twenty five men. The next morning, Gideon Dudley John Whitcomb & I went upwards, and just after we crossed Meshoppen Creek we met captain Ross & his party, when a skirmish ensued, & captain Ross was wounded. About the Tuesday following, Daniel Earl, Frederick Budd, & others with myself, to the number of eleven in all, set off & went to Tioga, for the purpose of seeing major Jenkins & col° McKinstry, for if they would not support them as Jenkins had promised, the party determined to return & set col° Pickering at liberty. This party went to the Point, because we were not satisfied with Hyde's report, which was, That McKinstry & Jenkins were gone to the Lakes, but had sent word to John Swift, & he had written to Elisha Satterly, that they were well pleased with our having taken col° Pickering, and desired he might be kept, that there were thirty bushels of corn in Shaws Mill (the same that had been Bryant's) which the party might get by this token, That it was in a bin. The letter also men-

---

[2] Col. John McKinstry of Hudson, N. Y.; see no. 105, *ante*, note 2.

tioned that the Lessees [3] were likely to succeed with the Indians. As soon as Hyde had read the letter he tore it in pieces. This was at David Woodward's house. Hyde then said he had heard col° Butler had sent up a letter (to the party or some of them as I took it) with an expression in it to this effect, to keep close what we had got. Afterwards (and after col° Pickering had been released) I saw Hyde at Joseph Kilborns, & getting into discourse with Hyde, I reminded him that he had said col° Butler had sent up a letter; but Hyde now said that such a letter was never sent by Col° Butler, that he had sent no letter at all. I then told him, the man who would tell such a grand lie must be a villain: upon which Hyde & Gideon Dudley laughed. Pretty early after I joined the party, they said Gideon Church had promised them a barrel of pork, a barrel of flour, & a barrel of whiskey, & that Stephen Jenkins was gone for them. And when Ira Manvil & Benedict Satterlee came up to us (just before the party of us went up to the Point) they said Old Harvey had promised to put some provisions (as I recollect pork & flour) on board Lampher's boat & send up to them. The first time I was with the party at Tunkhannock, we were supplied with powder which was then brought out, in a keg, from Stephen Jenkin's house; & Daniel Earl said it had been sent up by John Jenkins. The principal advisers and directors of our proceeding, while I was with the party, were John Hyde jun. Daniel Earl & Gideon Dudley. As soon as I returned from the Point, I went home; it being my determination, before I left the Point, to quit the party.

Noah Phelps

Luzerne County ss. Sworn the 26th of August 1788,

Before   Obad^h Gore   } Justices of the
             Wm Hooker Smith } Peace for said County

[298] Zebulon Butler to Benjamin Franklin.[1]

Wilkesbarre, August 26, 1788.

Sir:

This may inform your Excellency and Council, that agreeable to request, I held the election of officers for the upper Bat-

---

[3] See no. 100, *ante*, note 5.   [298] [1] *P. A.*, XI, 381-82.

talion, and the enclosed [2] are the persons who were chosen to command the Battalion and the several Companies, which compose said Battalion. John Jenkins and John Swift, by Esquire Gore, I am informed are out of the State; and it is pretty generally known, that they are making all possible preparations to remove their families. This circumstance, I thought necessary to mention that Council might give further directions for a new election. I would likewise Inform Council, that by the advice of authority, I held the last election in different places. The reasons why I adopted this method, were the inconveniency of the people's assembling at one place. This I suppose was not altogether conformable to the law regulating elections; but when I inform that the district is exceedingly lengthy; perhaps the method by Council, may not altogether be deem'd inproper or ineligible. If it should be, your Excellency's and Council's pleasure will be, (I trust,) signified in the directions for holding another election. Also is enclosed the choice of Officers made by the light Draggoons and Infantry Companies.[3] That election of the light Draggoons, was once before held; but as it was not perfectly consistant with law; I thought proper to assemble them again; which being done, they proceeded and ratified their former choice, by the uplifting of hands. If this shall be deem'd illegal, when directions are given, I shall summon the company to another election. In the meantime I have the honour to be, your Excellency's most obedient and very humble servant.

Zeb'n Butler.

P. S. Vacancies in the Companies of the lower Battalion are filled up, which are on the return; I would just mention those whose Commission were not sent on. Whether I shall proceed to call other election or not? [4]

Z. B.

---

[2] *Ibid.*, 384-85. Butler's innocent-sounding statement about Jenkins and Swift is laughable. The Meshoppen company chose Martin Dudley, captain; Joseph Kilbourn, lieutenant; and David Woodard, ensign. Dudley and Kilbourn were in jail and Woodard was a fugitive—all of them implicated in the abduction of Pickering.

[3] The return has not been found, but the reference is probably to the dragoons raised by John Paul Schott; no. 231, *ante,* and note.

[4] Council declared null and void the election for the Upper Battalion, but accepted the officers chosen by the dragoons; *Pa. C. R.,* XV, 525.

[299] Indictment of Ira Manvil and Thirteen Others.[1]

Luzerne ss. At a Court of General Quarter Sessions of the Peace and Goal Delivery held at Wilkesborough in & for the county of Luzerne on the Second day of September in the year of our Lord one thousand seven hundred and eighty eight, before Obadiah Gore, Matthias Hollenback, William Hooker Smith, Benjamin Carpenter & Nathan Kingsley esquires, Justices of the same Court, assigned to keep the Peace in the said county, and divers felonies, trespasses & other offences therein committed, to hear & determine: By the oath of Lawrence Meyers, William Trucks, Benjamin Bailey, Jabez Fish, Solomon Avery, Elisha Blackman, Daniel Downing, Jacob Patrick, Thomas Bennett, John Dorrance, Philip Myers, Samuel Daly, Stephen Harding, Isaac Allen, Elijah Silsby, Samuel Miller, John Scott, Benjamin Jones, Joseph Wheeler, Leonard Westbrook, Justus Gaylord, and Joseph Elliot, good and lawful men of the county aforesaid, then & there impanelled, sworn, & charged to inquire for the Commonwealth of Pennsylvania and for the body of the said county, it is presented, That Ira Manvil of Plymouth in the county aforesaid yeoman, Benedict Satterlee of the same place yeoman, John Hyde junior, David Woodward, Daniel Earl, Gideon Dudley, Joseph Dudley, Solomon Earl, John Whitcomb, Daniel Taylor, Timothy Kilborn, Frederick Budd, Wilkes Jenkins, & Zebulon Cady,[2] all of the same county of Luzerne yeomen, the twenty sixth day of June, in the night time, in the year of our Lord one thousand seven hundred and eighty eight, with force and arms, viz. with guns, knives and tomahawks, riotously, routously and unlawfully to disturb the peace of the Commonwealth of s⁴ Pennsylvania in the county of Luzerne aforesaid, & within the jurisdiction of this court, did assemble themselves & meet together, and so being assembled, having their faces painted and disfigured, the mansion house of Timothy Pickering, in the town of Wilkesborough, & county of Luzerne aforesaid, and within the said Jurisdiction, then & there, with force and arms, to wit, with guns, knives, & tomahawks, did break and enter, & in & upon the said Timothy Pickering, then holding, by commission, under

[299] [1] H. S. P., Conn. Claims in Pennsylvania, I, 30, in Pickering's hand but signed by the justices.

[2] Omitted here is the name of Benjamin Earll, who turned state's evidence and thus escaped indictment.

the government of this Commonwealth, divers important offices, and in the peace of God & the Commonwealth, in the same house then being, with force & arms as aforesaid, an assault did make, and the said Timothy Pickering then & there did beat, wound and evilly treat, and him the said Timothy Pickering, having first bound him with cords, to distant parts of this country did carry and there cruelly and ignominiously put him in chains and kept him a prisoner for the space of nineteen days, exposed to their insults and the inclemency of the weather, so that of his life it was greatly despaired; and other harms to the said Timothy Pickering, then and there did, with the avowed purpose of compelling the government to release an offender charged on oath, and then confined, by due process of law, in a public Goal, for the heinous crime of High Treason, in exchange, for the said Timothy Pickering, an officer of government as aforesaid, & accused of no crime; to the great damage of the said Timothy, to the great terror of the people, and against the peace and dignity of the Commonwealth of Pennsylvania. Whereupon, the said Ira Manvil & Benedict Satterlee, being present here in court, in the custody of Lord Butler, esquire Sheriff of said county, for the cause aforesaid, are severally asked what they have to say to the said indictment, whether they are guilty or not guilty; and they severally say they are *not guilty*. Afterwards, with the leave of the court, they withdraw their plea, and say, severally, that they are *guilty*. And THEREUPON, John Cook esquire who now prosecutes for the Commonwealth of Pennsylvania, produces here in court a writ of the said Commonwealth closed in these words; Pennsylvania ss. The Commonwealth of Pennsylvania, to the Justices of the Court of General Quarter Sessions of the Peace & Goal Delivery for the county of Luzerne, GREETING: We being willing, for certain cause, to be certified of the indictment & conviction of Ira Manvil and Benedict Satterlee, of a riot & assault before you, or some of you, depending, DO command you that the conviction aforesaid, with all things touching the same, before the Justices of the Supreme Court of the State of Pennsylvania, at the said Supreme Court, to be held at Philadelphia, for the said State, the twenty fourth day of September next, so full and entire as in our Court before you they remain, you certify and send together with this writ, that we may further cause to be done thereupon, that which of right and according to the laws of the said State ought.

WITNESS the honorable Thomas M⸰Kean esquire, Doctor of Laws, Chief Justice of our said Supreme Court, at Philadelphia, the fifteenth day of July, in the year of our Lord one thousand seven hundred and eighty eight. Which writ being read & allowed, it is demanded of the said Ira Manvil & Benedict Satterlee that they find surities for their appearance before the Justice of the said Supreme Court at their next Sessions of oyer and terminer and general goal delivery to be held in this county. And they accordingly become bound by recognizance, to the Commonwealth of Pennsylvania, in the following sums, to wit, the said Ira Manvil in three hundred pounds and Jeremiah Coleman his surety in three hundred pounds, and the said Benedict Satterlee in three hundred pounds, and Nathaniel Landon & Ira Stevens his sureties, each in one hundred and fifty pounds, on this *Condition:* That the said Ira Manvil & Benedict Satterlee, respectively, shall personally appear before the Justices of the Supreme Court of the Commonwealth of Pennsylvania, at their next Session of oyer & terminer & general goal delivery to be holden at Wilkesborough in and for the county of Luzerne, then & there to receive & perform the Sentence of that court, and not depart without license; and that in the meantime they shall keep the peace and be of good behaviour towards all the liege citizens of Pennsylvania.

Which indictment & conviction and all things touching the same, WE Obadiah Gore, Matthias Hollenback, William Hooker Smith, & Benjamin Carpenter, esquires, Justices aforenamed of the said Court of General Quarter Sessions of the Peace and Goal Delivery for the county aforesaid, in obedience to the Writ aforesaid, do certify and send, together with the said writ, unto the Judges of the said Supreme Court, under our hands and the seal of the said county of Luzerne. Given at Wilkesborough aforesaid this fourth day of September in the year of our Lord one thousand seven hundred and eighty eight.

Obad^h Gore
Mathais Hollenback
Benj Carpenter
Wm Hooker Smith

[300] Deposition of Ephraim Tyler.[1]

I Ephraim Tyler of lawful age testify That early last Spring John Hyde jun^r came to me and said, one of the lots in my possession at Black Walnut Bottom belonged to him. Afterwards I found he had no writing to show for it. Hyde came

[300] [1] M. H. S., Pickering Papers, LVIII, 127, in Pickering's hand but signed by Tyler and the justices.

again to me after this, & said the lot belonged to him. I scrupled it, and asked him for his authority. He answered that he had not his writings with him. At the last June Court I was down at the Court House, & saw major Jenkins, & told him of Hyde's claim; and that I thought I had the best right to the lot, as I had it under improvement, & it lay between my other two lots. From what passed between us at this time I was led to conclude that Jenkins (who was one of the Committee for granting half share rights) would not give a certificate to Hyde till he Jenkins should have come up the river to my house. Notwithstanding which, such certificate was given to Hyde very soon after, as Hyde informed me. And after colonel Pickering was taken, major Jenkins came up the river to my house; and on my complaining to him for assigning that lot as a half share right to Hyde, he (Jenkins) answered That he had given it to Hyde for undertaking the job of taking colonel Pickering; and he added That he had also given them (meaning Hydes party), his own half share right at Tioga which he could have sold for fifty pounds. Ephraim Lewis had about twenty bushels of wheat at Joseph Wheelers, which he had desired me to sell for him, in such manner as to enable him to pay a debt he owed to Esqr Hollenback. Soon after col° Pickering was taken & brought up the river, Joseph Kilborn came up and agreed with me for ten bushels of the wheat, for which he said he would pay esq^r Hollenback as soon as he got his frame down; and I delivered the ten bushels to his son Aaron Kilborn and Joel Whitcomb. Before this three bushels of the wheat had been delivered to two other boys of Whitcomb's and Kilborns.

Ephraim Tyler

Luzerne County ss. Sworn the
fourth day of September 1788.
Before   Obad^h Gore
          Wm Hooker Smith

[301] Petition of Samuel Allen and Others to the Pennsylvania General Assembly.[1]

To the Honorable the Representatives of the Freemen of the Commonwealth of Pennsylvania in General assembly met.

[301] [1] P. H. M. C., Div. of Arch. and MSS., Record Group 7, Series: General Assembly File, 1785-88. The signatures do not look genuine. *P. A.*, XI, 386-87.

The Memorial & address of the inhabitants of the county of Luzerne,

most respectfully sheweth,

That with the most honest intention we uniformly present our respectful Thanks to your honorable House for publishing a Bill confirming to us those seventeen townships which are Named in the Bill.[2]

We now look up to your honors as our fathers Guardians and Protectors, to Pass said Bill into a Law and grant us the Priviledge to Devide said Lands among our self, agreeable to our Connecticut holding, which will not only save Cost to the State, but will give us the greatest Satisfaction and enable us, if there Should be any vacant rights to Distribute the same to our fellow sufferers who are not comprehended in this Bill.

Thus will you increase the Inhabitants of this Great and Flourishing State, and will give Joy and Comfort to the Widow & Fatherless.

And we as in duty bound will ever pray

Samuel Allen	Jonathan Rogers, Jun[r]
Nathaniel Chapman	Samuel Ayres
Josiah Kellogg	John Doll
Josiah Eves	Benj. Davis
Joel Holkomb	Joel Atherton
Daniel Ross	Eleanor ————
Josiah Eves Junior	James Bidlack
John Knickerbacker	Hezekiah Roberts
Benja. Roberts	Thos. Bennet
Samuel Bennet	———— Alden
Hezekiah Roberts, Jun[r]	———— Alden
Jacob Roberts	Mary Cornstock [3]

Endorsed: Petitions from about 300 inhabitants of Luzerne County [4]

---

[2] No. 218, *ante,* and note. This proposed law was anathema to the Franklin faction and probably not even wholly satisfying to the more moderate Connecticut settlers.

[3] Samuel Allen was from Shawnee, as were probably nine other of the identifiable signers. Eight names have not been found on any other list in this period. Curiously, four names—Joel Atherton, Samuel Ayres, Joel Holcomb, and Josiah Kellogg—are found either on the power of agency for John Franklin or on the petition demanding the removal of William Montgomery; nos. 69 and 121, *ante.* These two documents were pro-Franklin or at least anti-Pickering, of course.

[4] Although the endorsement refers to "about 300 inhabitants," as do the printed minutes of the Assembly, this figure was probably a mistake for 30. There was ample room on the sheet for additional names, and no other such

[302] Timothy Pickering to John S. Whitcomb and David Woodard.[1]

Wilkesbarre Septr 5. 1788.

To John Skinner Whitcomb & David Woodward

Richard Vaughan has just handed me your letter of the 20th of August,[2] in which you express your penitence for your late atrocious offence against Government, and the deep injury you did to me. I forgave you on a condition which has not been performed by the party:[3] but of that breach of engagement I shall take no advantage against penitents who surrender themselves to Justice. You are mistaken in supposing that I agreed to be your advocate to obtain a settlement or pardon for you from the State: You must recollect that several of the party repeatedly requested me to intercede for them with Council, to procure a pardon: but that I constantly refused to make such intercession, unless you would give me up the names of all your leaders and advisers which you would not do. I therefore undertook nothing for you, except this, to forward your petition to the Council, which I did, altho' your written engagement to me had not arrived; nor has it yet come to hand. I have now told your neighbour, Mr Vaughan, that 'tis in vain for any of the party, excepting such as have become States Evidences, to expect pardons, before they have surrendered themselves to justice nor even then. I will not deceive you by holding out too easy terms. Government are exasperated by the repeated violences committed by a few turbulent men in this county, and, by the information I have received from Philadelphia, is determined to punish in an examplary manner the persons who shall be convicted of the late audacious & flagrant violation of the laws of the rights of peaceable citizens. Government had determined on its measures many days before you set me at liberty: for the proclamation for apprehending you is dated the 8th of July. Nevertheless, by a late determination of Council, on the advice of the Judges of the supreme court,[4] the offenders are to be prosecuted for a

---

petition has been found. *Minutes of the Third Session of the Twelfth General Assembly,* 202 (microfilm copy).

[302] [1] M. H. S., Pickering Papers, LVIII, 128-29, in Pickering's hand. [2] No. 294, *ante.* [3] See *ibid.,* note 3. [4] No. 282, *ante.*

riot only; whereas the crime of which you & the rest of the party have been guilty, is clearly *high treason*. Of this I am satisfied by the examination I have made of the law since my return, and also by the opinion of gentlemen learned in the law. Government therefore have manifested great lenity & mercy towards the offenders in directing that they be prosecuted only for a riot, when they might be charged with high treason, &, on conviction, be punished with death. If you therefore wish to live again in Pennsylvania, you have no choice but to surrender yourselves to Justice, & trust to the mercy of the government & the Court. If you think it best to give yourselves up, you can do it before any justice of the peace. Esqʳ Kingsley lives near you, & can give you a certificate that you have surrendered yourselves prisoners to him, & a pasport to come down here to be examined, & give bonds for your appearance at the next court of Oyer & Terminer which will be the 4th of Novʳ next, at this place. Or perhaps one of the Justices may send you a passport now by Mʳ Vaughan.

T. Pickering

[303] Samuel Miles and Others to Timothy Pickering.[1]

Philadᵃ Septʳ 11ᵗʰ. 1788.

Sir

The present important crisis in the affairs of Pennsylvania having induced a considerable number of respectable Inhabitants of this City & neighbourhood to meet & consider of such measures as would be most likely to secure to the State a Representation of men in the next Assembly, equally known for their firm attachment to the federal Government, & real interests of this State, as well as for their candour, integrity & good sense, a Committee, to communicate their sentiments to, & correspond with their friends in the different Counties was thought essentially necessary.

We therefore as the Committee of correspondence, take the liberty to address you on this important subject, being not only well assured of your zeal & regard for the new Government, but that you will, on all occasions use your influence with your friends to promote its true interests.

To have persons of the best qualifications elected to repre-

---

[303] [1] M. H. S., Pickering Papers, XIX, 142-43, in an unknown hand but signed by individuals.

sent us in the general Assembly, is at all times an object of very great consequence, but at the present moment, when the new federal Constitution is to be carried into effect, it is a matter of the utmost importance. The ensuing Legislature will not only have the ordinary objects of our State affairs before them, but they will have in charge to complete the arrangements of the general Government, so far as the present House shall leave them unfinished. It is probable also that the great subject of amendments may form a part of their deliberations: All those points will require Representatives of undoubted integrity, & sound judgment: But to revise the new Constitution if that should be brought before them, they should be men of great candour free from prejudices against & well disposed to the continuance of an energetic power in our federal head.

The late meeting of the opponents of the new Constitution in the town of Harrisburg [2] must have given serious alarm to its friends, & the Election purposes, both with regard to the federal & state Representatives, which w[e] conceive it was calculated to promote, should excite our most active exertions, & vigilance, & awaken all our caution: You will see at once that as this measure was confessedly intended, so it may seriously affect the Election of the eight federal Representatives, as well as of the State Legislature. Their circular letter plainly recommends the nomination of eight persons for that purpose: [3] You will permit us therefore to put you on your guard concerning that Election also, & to recommend it equally to your attention in due time, according as the same may be ordered by the present or future Assembly.

As we shall on all occasions be happy to communicate to you every necessary information which we may obtain in this business, so we are desirous to receive the same from you. We remain with great regard & esteem Sir Your very hble. Servants

> Sam¹ Miles
> Walter Stewart
> Franˢ Gurney
> Tench Coxe
> John Nixon
> Benjⁿ Rush
> Hilary Baker

---

[2] On September 3, when representatives from fourteen counties, but not Luzerne, gathered, they adopted moderate resolutions, urging acceptance of the Constitution of the United States but calling for amendments through a national convention. See Brunhouse, *Counter-Revolution in Pennsylvania*, 213-15.

[3] On the Radical ticket see *ibid.*, 217 and note 80.

[304] Deposition of Daniel Earll and Statement of Solomon Earll.[1]

I Daniel Earl of lawful age confess and declare, that I was one of the fifteen men who on the twenty sixth of June last entered the house of Timothy Pickering in Wilkesbarre and seized & carried him away by force, and kept him a prisoner until the fifteenth day of July last: that on the same day on which David Perkins set off for Philadelphia, to carry the recognizance which had been taken here for the purpose of bailing John Franklin from the jail of Philadelphia, John Jenkins of Exeter (usually called major Jenkins) came to me (then at Kingston) and told me that the bond (or recognizance) had been sent; but that if Franklin should not be released upon that, some other way to release him must be undertaken; and proposed to me the taking of colonel Pickering as the way to get Franklin out of jail; and said he would give lands to the boys who should do it, and particurly promised to give me a right at Tioga if I would undertake it; and he afterwards sent up a certificate to me to entitle me to a right there. He also said he could sell his own right at Tioga for fifty dollars and that he would sell it, & the boys should have the money among them to make a frolic and that he would stand by us. During the time that Perkins was gone to Philadelphia, it was the general talk (among those who are called Wild Yankies) that if Franklin were not set at Liberty, colonel Pickering must be taken. Soon after Perkins returned from Philadelphia, Stephen Jenkins sent a message to me requesting me to go with him up to captain Dudley's, to see what we should do about taking colonel Pickering, and when the boys would be ready; and he and I were to have gone up the next day: but that evening Gideon Dudley came up the river, and called at my house, & told me that he had seen John Jenkins who advised that colonel Pickering should now be taken. The next morning Gideon & I went over to Stephen Jenkins's, where he & Gideon talked together, by themselves, a long time, perhaps an hour; and when they came into the house, said Stephen delivered Gideon a quantity of gunpowder to take up to the boys; and it was concluded by us all that the boys should get ready and be

---

[304] [1] M. H. S., Pickering Papers, LVIII, 134-35, in Pickering's hand but signed by Daniel Earll and Hollenback.

down in a day or two. Gideon told me that Stephen Jenkins or John Hyde was to head the party, & this was to be settled when the boys should come down. I then went home, & Gideon Dudley went up the river, to go to his fathers. In two or three days Gideon Dudley, Joseph Dudley, John Hy[de] jun^r John Whitcomb, David Woodward, Timothy Kilborn, Benjamin Earl & Zebulon Cady, came to Tunkhannock, where Frederick Bu[dd] Solomon Earl & I joined the party. I went down to Stephen Jenkins & told him the boys were come. We all expected he would join the par[ty] for he had often promised to join the party whenever they should go to take colonel Pickering. Stephen Jenkins went up & met the boys on the hill back of my father Joseph Earls. He (said Stephen) then told us he would not go with us: The next morning David Woodward & I took a canoe & came down the river, stopping against Asahel Atherton's to take in Wilkes Jenkins, and again at the three Islands, to take in Daniel Taylor. We four came down by water; the rest of the party went thro' the woods. The four of us who came by water; stopped over against Baldwins at Lackawanock, & Wilkes Jenkins & I went to his brother's, John Jenkins house, in Exeter, where we saw and conversed with him (John Jenkins[)] about the taking of colonel Pickering; in which undertaking he promised to stand by us, and said he would meet us on our return (which he did, at Justus Jones's) and after delivering a quantity of gunpowder (as I judge about three or four pounds to his brother Wilkes) for the use of the party, we seperated. W[ilkes] & I came down to *forty fort*,[2] & there got again into our canoe, which Woodward & Taylor had brought down from Lackawanock. We four then proceeded down the river (this was on wednesday evening, June 25th) & landed at Ross's hill, by the mouth of Toby's creek. It was at this place, on the next day, that Ira Manvil & Benedict Satterlee joined us, making up the number of fifteen, who went over in the evening to Wilkesbarre, & were present and concerned in the taking of colonel Pickering. While we lay at Ross's hill, June 26th Gideon Church came to us, & said he would go with us if we wanted him; if not, he would supply us with provisions, & join us whenever we did want him.

After David Perkins returned from Philadelphia, Elisha Satterly passing up the river stopped at Tunkhannock, & came to me where I was at work in the field, and we conversed about

---

2 In Kingston.

Franklin. Satterlee said he was not likely to come out of jail on the bond which Perkins had carried down, & something must be done. I told him what was talked of (to wit, the taking of colonel Pickering[)] which he said he knew, and that he would give five dollars upon hearing that he was taken, & support them (meaning those who should take colonel Pickering) as long as he could. Last Spring (after planting time) Constant Searl of Lachawanock came up to Tunkhannock. He came to me & asked me whether I would join him in taking colonel Pickering, and whether a party for that purpose could be made up at Tunkhannock. He said he was ready to take the woods at any time—that he had nothing to do, and had as lief be in the woods as any where else.

Said Stephen Jenkins at sundry times talked with me about taking colonel Pickering, & urged it, as the way to get Franklin out of jail; and by way of encouragement said he could support a hundred men in the woods during the summer; and he constantly encouraged the plan of taking colonel Pickering, until it was ready for execution, when the boys had assembled, & were on their way down; at which time he refused to join us, as is before mentioned.

The first time we went up to Joseph Kilborns, after col° Pickering was taken, we saw Thomas Kinney there with his gun, and he joined us right away, and came down with us to Tunkhannock, and appeared as well pleased with the measure, and as ready to support it as any of the party.

William Carney was encouraged to join us by Darius Parks his grandfather who fixed him out for the purpose, and appeared well pleased that we had taken colonel Pickering. Martin Dudley also, & Joseph Kilborn manifested great satisfaction for the same cause, and furnished us with victuals with signs of pleasure and hearty good will, as persons would naturally do who were pleased with any measure which they were willing and desiring to support.[3]

Daniel Earll

Taken on oath and subscribed, the 13th of September 1788. Before me Mathias Hollenback, a Justice of the Peace for the county of Luzerne

Solomon Earl, accused of being one of the party who took colonel Pickering on the night of the 26th of June last, volun-

---

[3] Here was further damning evidence against the fathers of the "boys" who had taken Pickering.

tarily surrendered himself; and being asked what he had to say, answered That at present he had nothing to say.

Luzerne County ss. September 13, 1788.

Examined before
Mathias Hollenback
Justice of the Peace

[305] Deposition of William Smith.[1]

September 13th, 1788.

Luzerne County, ss.

Personally appeared before me, Mathias Hollenback, one of the Justices of the Peace for the said County, The person of William Smith, and being duly Sworn, Deposeth and saith, That he, this Deponant, on the 27th of June Last, that he, this Deponant, Being one of Capt. John Paul Schoots company of Light Dragoons, on an Expedition up the River Susquehannah in order to retake Colo. Timothy Pickering from the Insurgents, He, this Deponant, often Urged said Capt. Schoots to be more Expeditious on his March, or else this deponant feared they would not come up with the Insurgents. Schoots replyed to this Deponant that he had no inclination to be in too much of a hurry, for he feared the insurgents would be too Strong for them, He chose to delay his March untill the Company of foot came forward. Captain Schoots went no further than Jones that night, which was about Sixteen miles from Wilkesborrogh, and this Deponant further saith that the could have easy went 30 miles where the party lay that Night that took Col. Pickering. This Deponant and many others of the Company, urged said Schoots to push on to Tanckhannock, where the insurgents lay that night, which he expressly refused to do; and this Deponant further saith that said Schoots delayeth the March untill nine or Ten o'Clock the next day, (which was the 28th of June) Then, on the said day, Capt. Schoots Delayed the March as before, (the foot not Coming up) and this Deponant continued to urge Capt. Schoots to be more expeditious, Then Schoots reply'd to this Deponant that they must do something and make a bluster, In order to satisfy Government, if they went but a few miles after them it would be sufficient, for Government would not know but they had done their Endeavours to take them, and that they're

---

[305] [1] *P. A.*, XI, 393-94.

turning out and making a Bluster would gain the Company a great name; and further this Deponant saith not.[2]

Wm. Smith.

Sworn to and subscribed this 13th day of September, 1788. Before me,

Mathias Hollenback.

[306] Petition of William Smith and Others to the Pennsylvania General Assembly.[1]

To the Honorable, the Supreme Executive Council of the Commonwealth of Pennsylvania, in Council met.

The memorial of William Smith, John Gore, Benjamin Dorrance, & John Tuttle, & Daniel Ross, Inhabitants of Wioming, in the county of Luzern, in the State of Pennsylvania.

Humbly sheweth,

That your petitioners were the only Persons that took & made Prisoners of Benedict Satterly and Irey Mandwell, two men who were of the Party which took Coronal Pickering Prisoner. The said Sattely & Mandwell we Brought before William Hooker Smith, Esqr., & Timothey Pickering, Esqr., for Examenation & Commitment, where they Confessed Gilty[2] & ware by a mitemas Committed to the Gaol at Wilksbury under the hand & Seale of Esqr. Smith. Some time after thare commitment the Goal in this County was by the athorety thought to be Insufficient. The athorety then ordered the Prisoners to be Removed to Easton Gole, In Northampton, from whence they have since been Braught to our Last Court in this County, where Bills of Indictment have bin found against them by the Grand

---

[2] On September 13 John Hollenback testified to the same effect before Justice William Hooker Smith; *ibid.,* 394. *Cf.* no. 251, *ante.*

On September 15 Schott wrote Council thanking them for his commission as commander of light dragoons, and asking for arms in anticipation of trouble when John Franklin and others went on trial in November. His request was granted; *P. A.,* XI, 397.

[306] [1] *P. A.,* XI, 400-01. This petition was carried to Philadelphia by Capt. William Ross and was supported by Pickering. Muhlenberg transmitted it to the Assembly on September 25; *ibid.,* 402. On September 23 the Council voted to present a sword to Capt. Ross in appreciation for his services; *Pa. C. R.,* XV, 543-44.

[2] Nos. 261 and 262, *ante.*

Jury,[3] which we Expect will more fully appear by copies of the Records from this Cort.

We your morilests humbly conceive that your Honors will be convinsd when you come to hear Captn Ross's Reports Concearning this matter, & our Conduct in this Struggle, that we are only Intitled to the Rewards offered by Government for the said Satterly & Mandwell, & we Do Expect Coronal Pickering will be in Town with Captin Ross, & will be able to Testefye In Regard to our Conduct, & we as in Duty Bound shall Pray

Captn. Ross Receipt shall be Excepted by

> Wm. Smith,
> John Gore,
> John Tuttle,
> Benjamin Dorance.[4]

Wioming, Septr. 13th, 1788.

This ma Certefye That Wm. Smith, John Gore, Benjamin Dorrance, & John Tuttle, Have to the Best of my Knoledge Turned out on Every Scout (to oppose & persue the Insurgents) as Loyal Subjects.

> Wm. Hooker Smith.

Wioming, Septr. 13th, 1788.

[307] John Franklin to a Committee of the Pennsylvania General Assembly.[1]

Prison Philadelphia Sep^t 17, 1788

Gentlemen

You will Please to pardon me while I address you upon a subject that most nearly concerns me, the subject to which I relate is stated in my Petition lately presented to your Honble House, and which is refer^d to you to enquire into and report there[on].[2]

---

[3] No. 299, *ante.*   [4] Why Daniel Ross did not sign is not known.

[307] [1] Tioga Point Museum, Athens, Pennsylvania, in Franklin's hand; Harvey-Smith, *Wilkes-Barré*, III, 1614-15. Material in brackets is taken from the printed copy.

[2] Franklin's petition was first presented to the Assembly on September 8. After a second reading, it was referred to a committee composed of George Logan, Peter Burkhalter, and John Paul Schott. This committee reported on October 2, but no action was taken upon its report, nor was it included among those matters recommended for consideration by the next Assembly; *Minutes of the Third Session of the Twelfth General Assembly,* 218, 227, 265, 273. The petition itself has not been found.

The notice taken of me in this my unhappy situation, and the opportunity I had yesterday with Doctor Logan, who was pleased to honour me with a visit on the subject of my Petition [deserve] my grateful acknowledgements. But as some matters have since occurred more fully to my memory, you will Permit me to lay before you a State of facts, which I would wish to do only for information.

The Hon[ble] Justices of the Supreme Court on the 16th of April agreed to admit me to Bail upon my entering into a recognisance with two good securities in a Sum therein required, as Stated more fully in my Petition. I obtained a Certificate accordingly from the Clerk of the S[d] Court, after which I addressed his Honour the Cheif Justice in a Letter stating the difficulty which would probably take place in procuring any two Persons at Luzerne to be my Bail, who would be adjudged equal to the Sum Required, and Requested that four or more Persons might be taken as security and that some such Person within the S[d] County as his Honour thought Proper might be Directed to take the Recognisance, he was pleased to grant my request: However not any thing was done to effect until the 9th of May when a friend of mine was permitted to see me, he being accompined with an Hon[ble] Member of Council, by whom I was informed that the Cheif Justice had agreed to Direct the Prothonotary of Luzerne to take four Persons as security for my appearance at Court &c. But would have me Nominate them. I accordingly Nominated Mess[rs] Josiah Rogers, Jonah Rogers, Christ[o] Hurlbut, John Hurlbut, Nathan Cary, John Jenkins, Hez[kh] Roberts, Benj[n] Harvey, Daniel Gore, Sam[ll] Ayres, Jonat[h] Carey, that the number required might be taken from those nominated as the Cheif Justice should think Proper. before the Business was compleat the Cheif Justice had set off on the Western Circuits. my friend went on as far as Chester, and return[ed] on the 10th when I was informed that he had a Letter from the Cheif Justice, to send forward to the Prothonotary at Luzerne to take the security at that Place,[3] and that whenever the Recognisance was sent, that Justice Bryan would take my own Recognisance. this Letter together with a Letter which I was Permitted to write to my friends at Luzerne,[4] on that subject was Immediately sent forward. May 31st I had Information that security was taken and the Recognisance came to hand by a young man sent for that Purpose.[5] I expected to be Liberated the same Day, But heard nothing farther until the 4th of

---

[3] No. 225, ante.   [4] Not found.
[5] David Perkins; see no. 287, ante, note 6.

June, when the young Man was Permitted to see me, he being in Company with a Member of Council. I was then informed that nothing could be done until the Chief Justice Returned, who accordingly Returned soon after. application was made to him by my friends in my behalf to obtain my Discharge on the Bail. I Did all in my Power to obtain my Discharge from Prison or to know what Prevented me from being liberated. I was Inform'd that the Chief Justice gave for Answer that he had nothing to do with it. that it lay entirely in the breast of Council. application was made to that Board in my behalf. it rested until about the 8th of June when an Honble Member of Council came to see me. I stated the matter fully to him and urged to know whither I was to be liberated on the Bail or not, or whither any of my securities were Judged insufficient, or what Prevented my Discharge. I Proposed to him that in Case the security was not sufficient I would obtain others and if no security whatever was to be taken I wished to be informed that I could provide accordingly. in Answer to this he informed me that M^r M Kean [McKean] had the Recognisance, that it rested entirely with him and that Council had nothing to do in the affair, but finally gave it as his own opinion that the security was judged insufficent. [His] reasons were that not any ten of the Wyoming settlers were worth 200£ much more 2000£ that the Whole of the settlers were a pack of thieves from Connecticut who had Robbed others of their Property and now presumed to call it their own, and that the whole of the Connecticut settlers were not sufficent to Bail me in the Sum of 2000£. after receiving this Answer, the young man who was present at that time, returned to Wyoming after Waiting 9 Days in this City at my expence. I was still kept in close Confinement, Deprived of the Advantages of social society as I before had been, and could not be informed of any reason why I was not liberated, except as before Represented, neither did I ever by any Authority know what other Reasons were assign'd until Doctor Logan informed me yesterday that the security was Deemed insufficient, that some of those who were taken as security had at the same time mad threatning language &c which Probably Prevented me from being liberated. I have not heard the Names of all those who are my security, but have been informed that some of those I Nominated were absent and others accepted by the Prothonotary in Lieu thereof, ten Persons being Required to enter Bail.[6]

---

[6] For the names of the men who entered into security for Franklin, see no. 225, *ante,* note 2. One of them, John Jenkins, was accused by several, of course, of being involved in the seizure of Pickering.

If any Person who has been accepted as security for me has been so imprudent as to use threatning language on that subject I hope that their Misconduct will not Prejudice those equitable rights to which I may be Judged entiteled to. I wish if the Honble Com^tee think Proper that the Matter may be fairly investigated whither the Persons who entered Bail for Me, are the Identical Persons who made use of threatning Language &c (I do not Pretend to know to the Contrary but I have enemies who would Perhaps wish to injure me and be fond to have me wear out the last remains of life in prison[)]. I therefore only wish that such enquiries may be made as to Prevent any undue measures operating to my hurt, that equal Justice in that, as well is in every other case may be done me.

I must Confess that I earnestly expected to be Liberated on Bail Conformably to the encouragement given me, and really thought that I had right so to expect. and I most solemnly Declare that in case I had been Liberated, I was fully Determined to *return* to Wyoming and to use my influence in quelling the Disturbances at that Place if any there should be, and to Prepare myself to take my tryal when called therefor before a Jury of my Country, as the Constitution Directs, but as I was not Liberated I made my appeal to the Legislative Body the guardians of the People from whose Justice and humanity I am Induced to Believe I shall in some way obtain relief. As to the Circumstances of my Confinement that is fully set forth in my Petition. I have lately been very sick with a fever but am now recovered from the Disorder, though my sickness togather with a long Confinement has reduced me to a feeble State, which is hard to be recovered in a Place of confinement.

I was Destitute of Money at the time of my Commitment but agreed with a friend to support me with Provisions and never knew that any Provision was made for me by Government until I was Liberated to the front of the Goal the 24th of June since which I learn that the Person who supported me has had his Bill allowed by Council for my weekly subsistance though Paid in Depreciated currency which I shall be under obligation to make good unless the sum he has receiv'd is made equal to my Weekly subsistance which I am not able to Determine. my Retired situation has prevented me from doing any thing for myself to any advantage whic[h] I might otherwise have done.

If after a full Investigation it should be thought Proper to admit me to Bail on the security already taken it would Prevent a Pecuniary expence which would take Place in procuring other

496

security if req[uired] but in case I am Liberated in any other way I shall make myself satisfied, and if Continued in Prison I am Resolved to be submissive to whatever Providence has assign'd me. I have only wrote you informal[ly]. I earnestly hope that whatever may be alledged against me will not Prejudice any equatable rights to which your Com^{tee} and the Honble Assembly may adjudge me Entiteled, as equal Justice is all that I Demand. I am Gentlemen with every sentiment of respect your obedient servant

John Franklin

[308] Timothy Pickering to Benjamin Franklin.[1]

Philadelphia, Sept. 24, 1788.

Sir,

Captain William Ross is in town, & has been waiting since Friday last for an opportunity of presenting to Council several orders for the rewards offered for apprehending the ruffians who seized & kept me a prisoner;[2] and for the information of Council, I beg leave to state the cases in which the rewards are now claimed.

Ira Manvil & Benedict Satterlee were two of the fifteen men present at the taking me off. They have been indicted, & pleaded guilty. They were apprehended by the five persons named in Doctor Smith's certificate.[3] Manvil & Satterlee were the only persons who in consequence of the proclamation of Council were committed to Easton Jail. That others, however, were not alike committed, was not the fault of their captors. The majority of the Justices did not think it necessary or expedient; and as the object of Council must have been only *to secure the persons of the offenders,* it was supposed by a candid construction of the proclamation, that the captors would be equally entitled to the rewards as if the offenders were actually committed to Easton Goal.

Benjamin Earl was apprehended by a party of about twenty men who chose Gideon Church for their captain. This Earl was also of the party that took me. He offered to turn State's

[308] [1] P. H. M. C., Div. of Arch. and MSS., Record Group 27, Series: Exec. Corr., 1777-90; *P. A.,* XI, 399-400.

[2] See no. 306, *ante,* note 1. *P. A.* has "Congress" for "Council."

[3] *Ibid.*

evidence: & being admitted as such by the Justices, was not conveyed by his captors to Easton Goal.

Thomas Kinney was apprehended by the party commanded by Captain Ross; but was not present with the party that took me; but there is evidence of his joining them in arms: However, he has pleaded not guilty, & is to be tried.

The four culprits above named were apprehended before it was known that reward were offered.

Stephen Jenkins was apprehended by the last party, formed after the proclamation of Council was issued. Of this party were Christian G. Oehring, Willm. Smith, James Litton, John Tuttle, & others. But Stephen Jenkins has pleaded *not guilty*, & for him the reward does not appear to be due before conviction.

Joseph Dudley also was apprehended after the proclamation of Council was published. Captain Rosewell Franklin (captain elect of a company of militia about Wysocks) raised a part of his company, & joined by John Tuttle, lay in wait for a party of the offenders, but all save Dudley, effected their escape. He refusing surrender, Captain Franklin & some of his men fired & mortally wounded him. He was brought to Wilksbarre, & died a day or two after.

Aaron Kilborn is a lad of about 15 years old. He joined the armed party after I was taken, has been indicted, & pleaded guilty. The manner of his being apprehended (which was about the 15th of August,) is certified by Doctor Smith.[4]

As some disputes may arise about the persons entitled to shares of rewards, I beg leave to suggest whether it may not be expedient to order the monies to be paid to Captain Ross, *for the use of the persons to whom the same are due;* and to advise, that in case of dispute, the claims be heard & adjusted by any three of the Justices of the peace of the county.[5]

I beg leave to add That captain Ross, since the first introduction of the laws of this State into the county of Luzerne, has manifested a uniform zeal to support the government of Pennsylvania, and a readiness to expose himself to any hazards which the welfare of the state could demand of a spirited & faithful citizen. Besides the loss of time occasioned by the wounds he received in pursuing the offenders now referred to, he has incurred an expence of upwards of eleven pounds, which his

---

[4] Not found.

[5] Council followed this recommendation; *Pa. C. R.,* XV, 546-47, 548. For further documents on rewards claimed and the report of Council's committee on these claims see *P. A.,* XI, 551-55.

surgeons have charged for their attendance on him. But what is most unfortunate, he, by these wounds, is probably rendered *an invalid for life*. It would seem to merit the consideration of council Whether a reward should not be given him not only as due for his exertions & consequent sufferings; but as an exemplary encouragement to other spirited & faithful citizens to engage in hazardous enterprizes when the peace & welfare of the State shall demand it. I have the honor to be Sir, very respectfully, your most obedt. servant,

T. Pickering.

[309] Samuel H. Parsons to Timothy Pickering.[1]

Marietta 25 Sep' 1788

Sir

In October 1785 I laid in my Claim to Lands at Wioming agreeably to the Act of the General Assembly of Pensylvania;[2] by which I suppose myself intitled to three Hundred Acres of Land at that Place. Since which I have not had Opportunity to see you or gain any Information respecting my Claim. General Muhlingburg one of the Commissioners[3] told me, that a Claim laid in at that Time would avail me Notwithstanding the Repeal of the Law, that he had no particular Rememberance of my Claim but thought it probable it had been allowed. The Bearer M' Colt, will call on you, and I shall esteem it a favor to be informd of the Decision of the Commissioners on my Claim. The Settlement of this City[4] proceeds with as much Rapidity as we can reasonably expect, I think we shall soon be in a State of respectability in point of Defence & Number of Inhabitants. the Treaty is expected to commence in about three weeks.[5] we

---

[309] [1] M. H. S., Pickering Papers, LVIII, 137, in Parsons' hand.

[2] Parsons is probably referring to the Assembly resolution of September 7, 1784, which authorized the appointment of commissioners to examine into Connecticut claims; see Vol. VIII, no. 43. No rights to claims within the Susquehannah Company purchase were ever actually authorized until the Confirming Act of March 28, 1787; no. 38, *ante*.

[3] Peter Muhlenberg was an original commissioner under the Confirming Act.

[4] Marietta, Ohio. Parsons was one of the judges of the newly created Northwest Territory.

[5] The Treaty of Fort Harmar.

have hitherto injoyed perfect peace with the Natives. I am S^r
with Esteem & Respect y^r Obed^t Servt

Sam. H. Parsons.

[310] Timothy Pickering's Draft Bill for Confirming Lands to Connecticut Claimants.[1]

A further act for quieting the disturbances at Wyoming & for
confirming to certain persons called Connecticut Claimants the
lands by them claimed within the county of Luzerne.

Whereas by the act of the General Assembly of this Commonwealth, entitled "An Act for ascertaining and confirming to
certain persons called Connecticut Claimants, the lands by them
claimed within the county of Luzerne, & for other purposes
therein mentioned," a time was limited within which their claims
should be exhibited to the Commissioners appointed in pursuance
of that act: And whereas the said Commissioners were interrupted in the execution of their commission by a number of
the inhabitants of the said county, rising in arms;[2] and the time
limited as aforesaid has expired: And whereas some general expressions in the above mentioned act of the General Assembly
open a door for the admission of claims beyond the cases stated
in its preamble & in the petition[3] of the said Claimants on which
the said act was grounded, and contrary to the apparent intention of the said General Assembly: And whereas it is expedient
that further time be given for the admission and adjustment of
the claims of the said Connecticut Claimants, and to make provision for the payment of the expences which shall arise about the
same: Therefore Be it enacted &c. That such rights or lots in
the seventeen townships, situated in the county of Luzerne, and
referred to in the petition aforesaid, by the names of Salem,
Newport, Hanover, Wilkesbarre, Pittstown, Northmoreland,
Putnam, Meshoppen (or Braintrim) Springfield, Claverack,
Ulster, Exeter, Kingston, Plymouth, Huntington, Bedford and

---

[310] [1] M. H. S., Pickering Papers, LVIII, 138, in Pickering's hand. This
bill was designed to correct shortcomings in the bill before the Assembly;
no. 218, *ante.* In January 1789, Pickering sent it to Philadelphia for George
Clymer's use; *Susquehannah Company Papers,* X, no. 3.

[2] The following words are lined out here: "who rose in arms, and
obliged three to leave by the violence threatened and committed induced
obliged them from a regard to their personal safety, to leave the county."

[3] No. 16, *ante.*

Providence,[4] agreeably to their original buts & bounds to be ascertained by sufficient vouchers, as were actually settled upon, occupied and improved at or before the termination of the claim of the state of Connecticut by the decree of the federal court held at Trenton in December 1782, either by the present settlers or those under whom they hold agreeably to the regulations of the company usually called & known by the name of the Susquehanna Company, be and they are hereby confirmed to such of the said Connecticut Claimants who shall exhibit and support their claims to the same respectively, by showing that the same rights or lots were so settled upon occupied, and improved and that they have regularly acquired a title[5] to the same under the said company; to be held by them their heirs and assigns, according to the original allotments and holdings of the same.

And whereas several of the said Claimants or their parents or other ancestors, had rights or lots of land granted to them under the said company within some of the said townships, but in situations so exposed to the depredations of the Savages during the late war, that they could not with safety settle upon and improve the same; and altho' actual & personal settlers and sufferers within that part of Pennsylvania now called the county of Luzerne, at or before the passing of the decree aforesaid, yet by the above enacted clause will be left destitute: Therefore

Be it Enacted &c. That the claimants last described shall each of them be entitled to one such right or lot by them acquired pursuant to the regulations aforesaid at or before the passing of the said decree altho' such right or lot was not occupied & improved at or before the same period; Provided that such right or lot do not exceed three hundred acres; and that the children or other legal representatives of any one such settler shall hold only the single right or lot to which such settler if living would hereby be entitled; and provided also that such claimants had not at the time of passing the said decree, nor have at the time of passing this act, any land which is or will be confirmed by any other clause thereof.[6]

---

[4] The list omits Athens; see *ibid.*, note 2.

[5] The word "Connecticut" is lined out before "title."

[6] This whole paragraph is crossed out. Even as it stood it would have made more limited provision than Pickering's earlier proposal (no. 189, *ante*) for claims to lands lying in exposed areas. In the margin substitute wording appears as follows: "Amendment proposed Jan[y] 26, 1789. 'But as the number of these rights is unknown, & an unlimited confirmation of such undefined claims would be improper: Be it therefore enacted &c. That the claimants of these said unoccupied rights shall have the same time

And whereas several others of the said Connecticut Claimants, or those under whom they hold, had, at or before the passing of the decree aforesaid, settled upon and improved certain parcels of land, now within the county aforesaid, & by them called Pitches, & which are not included within the townships aforesaid; and it is alike expedient that the same should be confirmed as if they were comprehended within the said townships; Therefore

Be it enacted &c. That the said pitches be and they are hereby confirmed to the claimants thereof & to their heirs and assigns; provided they do exhibit and support their claims to the same by showing that those pitches were respectively located, settled upon and improved at or before the passing of the decree aforesaid, agreeably to the regulations of the Susquehannah Company, and that they the claimants thereof respectively have regularly acquired Connecticut titles to the same.

Provided Always, & be it further enacted &c. That nothing in this act contained shall be construed to extend to any lands in the present actual possession of any settler holding under a title originally derived from this state or the late proprietaries thereof; but that every such Pennsylvania settler shall remain undisturbed in his possession to the full extent of the tract so settled upon & possessed, according to the original survey thereof; any thing in this act to the contrary notwithstanding.[7]

And whereas sundry persons residing in Connecticut and elsewhere became adventurers in or un[der] the Susquehanna Company in the project of holding an extensive tract of country within the boundaries of Pennsylvania, & comprehending the lands now lying within the county of Luzerne, but never became personal settlers th[ere] altho they now set up large[8] claims to lands under said company, some parcels of which they may have possessed and improved by their age[nts] sent on for the purpose of taking and maintaining such possession in opposition to the

---

allowed them to make & support their claims before the Commissioners hereinafter mentioned as is provided for the claimants of occupied rights and immediately after the expiration of that time, the said Commissioners shall make report of the said unoccupied rights so claimed, the title to which under grants from the said Susquehannah Company shall be satisfactorily supported, to the General Assembly, that with a full knowledge of the subject a suitable provision for such personal settlers & sufferers may be made, by a confirmation of the same unoccupied rights, or such of them as shall be reasonable & proper to confirm.[']" This amendment would, of course, leave more discretion in the hands of the Assembly.

[7] The whole paragraph is crossed out. For provision for Pennsylvania claimants, see the final enacting clauses.

[8] Several illegible words are crossed out before "large."

Government of Pennsylvania; and as it would be highly improper to reward or countenance such adventurers Therefore Be it enacted &c. That the claims of all such adventurers and of their heirs and assigns, shall be and they are hereby declared to be null and void; excepting only the claims of such of the heirs or assigns of the said adventurers as became personal [9] settlers on the rights, lots or pitches by them respectively claimed at or before the passing of the decree aforesaid.

And be it further enacted, &c. That for the purpose of ascertaining the Claims to the lands by the act confirmed,[10] to the said Connecticut Claimants, the Supreme Executive Council shall appoint three Commissioners, who or any two of them, shall recceive & examine the same, and allow such of them as shall be supported in the manner by this act directed and required: and that the said Commissioners shall be allowed each   shillings & their clerk   shillings a day for every day they shall be necessarily employed in the execution of this act.

And that full opportunity may be given to the said claimants to make and support their aforesaid claims, and at the same time, that all unnecessary delays and expences may be prevented:

Be it further enacted &c. That the said Commissioners to be appointed as aforesaid shall meet and open their office at Wilkesbarre in the said county of Luzerne at such times during the course of one year from the passing of this act [11] as they shall judge will be most convenient to the said claimants to exhibit and support their claims, and shall sit for the space of   days in the whole, during the said year, if they find the duties incumbent on them by this act cannot in a less number of days be executed;[12] and every claim not made and supported as aforesaid within one year next after the passing of this act shall be deemed inadmissible and void

And be it further enacted &c. That the Sheriff of the said county of Luzerne [&c. as in the second enacting clause of the bill, until you shall have read the words 'and upon every such return a patent shall issue in the name of such patentee who was

---

[9] "Personal" is substituted for "actual."

[10] Several illegible words are here crossed out.

[11] The phrase beginning "during" is interlined.

[12] Here clauses written in the margin were to be inserted: "and that the claimants may have due notice of this act, the said Commissioners shall cause the same to be published in one or more of the news papers printed in Pennsylvania and Connecticut, with advertisements subjoined of the time and place of their first meeting; & also to be posted up at divers of the most public places within the said county of Luzerne."

so as aforesaid elected and returned'—after which continue the paragraph thus] [13] And such patentee shall stand seized of such township for the following Uses, to wit, for the use of the Connecticut claimants aforesaid for such parts thereof the claims to which shall be allowed by the said Commissioners, & for which such claimants shall within fifteen months next after the passing of this act produce to the said patentees respectively certificates under the hands of the said Commissioners declaring & ascertaining the claims so allowed; and for the residue of the lands in such township, to and for the use of this state. And it shall be the duty of the said Patentees respectively to make, on the back of each of the said certificates which shall be produced to them as aforesaid, a conveyance of the land therein described, to the claimant or claimants therein named; and such certificate and conveyance being recorded at length by the recorder of deeds in said county, shall vest in the claimant or claimants therein named a title to the land therein described in like manner as if a particular patent were issued for the same.

PROVIDED, And be it further enacted &c. That it shall not be necessary to resurvey such of the said townships as have been already duly surveyed by the sworn surveyors appointed by the Commissioners under the law mentioned in the preamble of this act; but as soon as the returns of such surveys shall be made into the Surveyor General's Office in Philadelphia patents shall be issued in the names of the persons who shall be elected the patentees of such townships respectively.

And be it further enacted &c. That the several claimants of the pitches aforesaid shall on their demand receive from the land office warrants for surveying their respective pitches; and on the returns of the surveys thereof together with certificates under the hands of the Commissioners who shall be appointed in pursuance of this act ascertaining by definite descriptions the extent of such pitches, as by them allowed, patents shall be issued, as usual in other cases, in conformity with such certificates and for the said warrants, surveys & patents, the claima[nts] respectively shall pay the usual fees, and no more.

---

[13] The reference to "the second enacting clause of the bill" is to Section III of Samuel Maclay's proposed bill, no. 218, *ante*. After the brackets Pickering intended that clauses in the margin be inserted: "clear of expence, except the patent, for which he will pay the usual fees of office. And every deputy surveyor in whose district the township shall happen to be, shall for every survey by him made and returned as aforesaid, receive the usual fees and no more."

And be it further enacted &c. That if any deputy surveyor as aforesaid shall refuse or neglect for the space [of]   days next after demand made by any pat[entee] or claimant aforesaid, to commence the surveys by this act required to be made, or to prosecute and complete the same in a reasonable time, of which the Commissioners in pursuance of this act to be appointed shall judge, in every such case they the said Commissioners shall appoint a competent surveyor who shall be sworn faithfully to make & return every such survey; for which the usual fees shall be paid him; & no more.

[Here introduce the 3ᵈ enacting clause of the bill.] [14]

And be it further enacted &c. That if any of the said Connecticut claimants shall refuse or neglect to make application to the Supreme Executive Council for warrants and patents [15] and to exhibit and support their claims, as by this act is required, before the Commissioners to be appointed in pursuance there, within [16] the space of one year next after the passing of this Act, the said claimants so refusing or neglecting, shall derive no benefit from this act; but every claim afterwards made under the same shall be forever barred & excluded. [17]

And be it further enacted &c. That the wages of the Commissioners who shall be appointed in pursuance of this act, [18] and of their clerk shall be paid out of the treasury of this state, by orders from the Supreme Executive Council; but the whole amount thereof so paid shall be charged to the said county of Luzerne, & be assessed & levied with the first state taxes which shall be there assessed and levied after such amount shall be ascertained, & repaid into the treasury of the state.

And be it further enacted &c. That all the lands now claimed by the persons called Pennsylvania claimants, and which have been duly surveyed for them or those under whom they hold, pursuant to warrants from the Land office, and which shall not be covered by the claims of the said Connecticut claimants allowed & confirmed as by this act is directed, shall be the property of this State, & hereafter be disposed of as the legislature thereof shall direct; and all locations and surveys there

---

[14] Pickering meant to have inserted here Section IV of Maclay's proposed bill; no. 218, *ante.*

[15] Two illegible lines are crossed out after "patents."

[16] Several illegible words are crossed out after "within."

[17] This whole paragraph is crossed out.

[18] After "act" interlined and illegible words are crossed out.

made in the mean time shall be void. PROVIDED nevertheless, That if any tracts now claimed by Pennsylvania Claimants shall remain entire and be in no part covered by the Connecticut claims which shall be allowed & confirmed in pursuance of this act; and that such Pennsylvania Claimants shall not in the mean time have received compensation for the same, then such entire tracts shall revest in such Pennsylvania Claimants, who shall have the same estate therein as they had before the passing of this act.

And whereas Justice requires that the said Pennsylvania claimants should receive compensation for the lands of which by this act they will be devested: Be it enacted &c. That the faith of this Justice, & it is hereby pledged to make such compensation within a reasonable time, as the legislature thereof shall hereafter direct.[19]

Endorsed: Bill for confirming Wyoming Lands draughted Septr 1788.

[311] Extract from the Minutes of the Pennsylvania General Assembly.[1]

A motion was made by Mr. [George] *Clymer*, seconded by Mr. [John Paul] *Schott*, and adopted, as follows, *viz*.

"Whereas the various provisions necessary to the prudent and equitable settlement of the contested *Pennsylvania* and *Connecticut* claims to lands within the county of *Luzerne* have demanded greater consideration than this House have had it in their power to bestow, yet, highly sensible of the importance to the state of a speedy termination of those disputes:

---

[19] Pickering's proposed bill went beyond anything yet enacted by making more specific what lands the Connecticut people might and might not get confirmed. He would have allowed claims to occupied lands within "pitches" outside the seventeen towns, and he would have made possible, at the discretion of the Assembly, confirmation to settlers in Luzerne County of unoccupied lands that before the Trenton decree were too exposed to danger to be settled. He would have specifically denied any claims of adventurers in the Company who had never become settlers in the county. Finally, he would have permitted confirmation of claims under a Pennsylvania title if such whole tracts were entirely free of conflicting Connecticut claims. None of these provisions would have been pleasing to the John Franklin faction, which sought confirmation of the entire Susquehannah Company purchase.

[311] [1] *Minutes of the Third Session of the Twelfth General Assembly,* 268 (microfilm copy), dated October 3, 1788.

Resolved, That this subject be recommended to the early and serious consideration of the succeeding House of Assembly." [2]

[312] Samuel Huntington to Benjamin Franklin.[1]

New Haven, Oct. 14th, 1788.

Sir,

I did myself the honour some time past, to address your Excellency on the subject of Imprisonment of John Franklin in Philadelphia, and afterwards received with much satisfaction information of the kind and humane proceedings of your Excellency & Council, relative to the prisoner in consequence of my letter on that subject.[2]

I have now before me a letter from the same prisoner,[3] wherein he acknowledgeth his situation hath been made as comfortable as close confinement could admit, both in sickness and health, except he is unable to procure comfortable clothing; but he complains grieviously that he is still held in close confinement without being admitted to bail, or the liberty of a trial for the offence wherewith he is accused.

I am also informed that the Legislature of Pennsylvania have suspended their act, which had been passed for quieting the

---

[2] The meaning of the resolution was that no action would be taken in this session on the proposed new confirming act; no. 217, *ante.* Early in the session in response to a message from the Council on Pickering's abduction and the measures pursued by the Council in the Assembly's recess (*Pa. C. R.,* XV, 528), the Assembly had appointed a large committee to consider what more might be done about Wyoming. Both Clymer and Schott were members of that committee, which had never made formal report; *Minutes, Third Session,* 219.

In the first session of the Thirteenth General Assembly, a new committee, composed of Clymer, Gerardus Wynkoop, John McDowell, Richard Downing, Jonathan Hoge, John Nevil, James Johnson, and later Obadiah Gore, reported a bill on November 19 to confirm the lands of the Connecticut claimants, but the *Minutes* give no particulars. See, however, no. 324, *post,* note 5. When Clymer sought on November 21 to have a second reading of the bill, a motion for postponement offered by James McLene and seconded by Adam Orth was successful. That move killed any further consideration of a confirming law; *Minutes of the First Session of the Thirteenth General Assembly,* 9, 19, 24, 36, 46.

[312] [1] *P. A.,* XI, 409-10. For the Council's reply, see no. 315, *post.*

[2] Huntington's letter has not been found, but for Muhlenberg's reply, see no. 201, *ante.*

[3] Not found.

settlers at Wyoming,[4] and their consternation and uneasiness in consequence of the suspension.

It is presumed those transactions are well known to your Excellency & need not further explanation.

As the people first settled at Wyoming, under countenance of this Legislature,[5] and for a time lived under the exercise of the Government of this State; Government have always thought themselves under some kind of obligation to take notice of their complaints and distresses; which is my apology for troubling Your Excellency at this time.

But considering the Irritable nature of the Susquehannah Controversy the powerful connections, which the settlers there have with a numerous class of Citizens in this State in both the ties of interest and consanguinity, and the disagreeable consequences of wounding an old fracture when apparently almost healed; I have thought it expedient to address your Excellency on this subject, without laying the complaints above refer'd to, before the Legislature.

Let me then suggest to your Excellency, whether it be consistent with the free constitution of the Commonwealth of Pennsylvania to hold any person a close prisoner from year to year mere upon accusation, without admitting him to bail, or the liberty of a trial, when Government is in profound peace and full exercise.

And doth not the dignity of Government, and the dictates of sound Policy require that the act in nature of a grant which was passed for quieting the settlers at Wyoming, and securing to them their land, done with so much deliberation and notoriety, should be held sacred and inviolate, and that future disturbances, disputes and disagreeable consequences should be prevented if possible.

The prisoner above mentioned is apprehensive that the lawless & outrageous proceedings of the Banditti, who carried off that worthy Gentleman, Col. Pickering, may operate to his disadvantage, although as I am informed it was done without his knowledge or apprehension.

I have only to add that I am perfectly satisfied, your sentiments and inclinations will fully concide in all proper exertions, to alleviate the distresses & miseries of the wretched, among individuals and is promoting harmony, mutual conciliation and

---

[4] No. 220, *ante.*

[5] Huntington's statement is, of course, inaccurate. The settlements under the Susquehannah Company did not receive the sanction of Connecticut until well after their beginning—not until 1771.

good neighborhood, between States and societies, so far as may be consistent with the principles of Justice and the honour and safety of Civil Government. With the highest sentiments of Esteem and Respect, I have the honor to be, your Exc'ys hble. Servt.,

James Huntington.[6]

[313] David Redick to George Clinton.[1]

In Council, Philadelphia, October 21st, 1788.

Sir,

Our Justices of the Supreme Court set out in a few days for Luzerne, where the noted John Franklin will be put for trial, and as Council wish to furnish the Att'y General with all the Testimony they can procure, I am directed to request your Excellency will order the Letters written by Franklin to Doctor Hamilton of your State, and any other papers you may have that respect this business, to be transmitted here.[2] Should your Excellency wish them returned you may depend upon their being sent to you.[3] I have the honor to be, With great Respect, Your Excellency's most obedient, And very humble servant,

David Redick, V. President.

[314] Zebulon Butler to Charles Biddle.[1]

Wilks-Barre, Luzern County, October 24th, 1788.

Sir,

I received your Letter (circular) of the 22d August last,[2] I am sorry to inform you that my best exertions have as yet failed to procure legal Returns of the Persons subject to militia Duty in this County, among the first elected Officers of the first Battalion. Capt. Ross, Capt. Alden, Lieut. Nezbit, Ensign Hide,

---

[6] Obviously an error for Samuel Huntington.

[313] [1] *P. A.,* XI, 412.

[2] When Joseph Hamilton was arrested by New York in October, 1787, his papers were seized; no. 161, *ante.*

[3] On October 24, Richard Morris, Chief Justice of New York, forwarded several letters "purporting to be written by John Franklin to Doctor Hamilton," which he wanted returned; *P. A.,* XI, 413. No copies have been found, but see the opinion of the attorney general on them; no. 317, *post.*

[314] [1] *P. A.,* XI, 414.

[2] *Ibid.,* 379. The circular letter called for a list of those subject by law to militia service and of those who actually attended musters in 1785, 1786, and 1787.

& Ensign Alden, were not immediately Commissioned. Since
Capt. Ross has received his commission, Col. Pickering, with
myself and others, were appointed to examine the others and report to Council. Col. Pickering informed me he made report,
but I have not received their Commissions. Ensign Alden has
left the State, Ensign Hyde has engaged in the Horse.[3]

The elected officers in the second Battalion I have been informed are not to be commissioned.[4] As soon as I receive
Orders from Council for holding a new Election, I shall proceed
in the Business & use my best endeavours to organize the Militia
and make Returns; I have no returns for the years 1785, 1786,
and 1787. I am Sir, your obedient and very humble servant,

Zeb'n Butler, County Lieutenant.

[315] David Redick to Samuel Huntington.[1]

Sir,

Your letter of the 14th instant, directed to the late President
of Pennsylvania, Dr. Franklin, has been read in Council,[2] and
in answer thereto I have the Honor of observing that in the
case of the prisoner, Mr. Franklin, the peace and tranquillity of
Luzerne depended, in the opinion of Gov[t], in a great measure
on the confinement of this man untill he could be brought to
trial, which will now take place within a very few days, and
which is as early as the Supreme Judges have had it in their
power, agreeably with their established order of doing the duties
of their offices, to go to Luzerne, and we presume that the
charge against Mr. Franklin, and that not merely such unsupported by affidavits, as your Excellency's letter would seem to
imply,[3] together with the well known spirit and uniform conduct
of this person, & the disturbances which have subsisted in the
settlement of Wioming almost ever since his detection, will fully
justify the measures pursued by the Gov[t]. The people of both
the Gov[t] that over which you preside, as well as of Pennsy'a,
have at least the scars remaining of the wounds they have received in the unhappy dispute which formerly subsisted, and

[3] That is, in the light dragoons led by John Paul Schott.

[4] See no. 298, ante, note 4.

[315] [1] P. A., XI, 414-15, written October 25; Pa. C. R., XV, 575.

[2] No. 312, ante. Franklin had been succeeded by Thomas Mifflin as
president.

[3] Huntington had implied that Franklin was being kept in jail on the
basis of mere accusation. For the evidence against Franklin aside from
depositions, see no. 319, post, note 2.

which we have now no doubt of having quite healed up, unless some unhappy interposition should prevent, we hope, sir, that the wisdom and justice of the legislature of Pennsylva, will lead to such measures as will Justify the Gov' to the unprejudiced, and be assured that nothing will afford a higher gratification to this State than to find that Connecticut should be so happy as to view it in the same point of light.

Be assured, Sir, that it will be the care of Pennsylvania to cultivate a good understanding with your State, and we shall be happy in pursuing such measures as will have a real tendency to ease the feelings of our Citizens of the County of Luzerne as well as those of their friends and connections in the State of Connecticut. I have the Honor to be Sir, with great respect your most obedient & very humble servt.,

David Redick, Vice President.

[316] William Bradford, Jr., to Timothy Pickering.[1]

Easton, Oct' 31. [1788]

Dear Sir,

It will oblige me exceedingly if you will take the earliest steps to procure the attendance of such witness as may be able to prove any overt act of Treason in J. Franklin. Particularly to subpoena the person to whom the Letters which I put into your hands were directed.[2] If it be possible to form an abstract of testimony before I arrive it will contribu' much to expediting the business of the Court. I am Dear sir Your Most Obed' ser'

W. Bradford Ju'

[317] William Bradford, Jr., to Charles Biddle.[1]

Easton, Nov. 1, 1788.

Sir,

I have received the papers which you forwarded by Laud [Lord] Butler Esquire, Sheriff of Luzerne,[2] but upon examina-

---

[316] [1] M. H. S., Pickering Papers, LVIII, 145, in Bradford's hand.
[2] The reference remains obscure.   [317] [1] P. A., XI, 419.
[2] The papers were those that had been forwarded by Richard Morris, Chief Justice of New York; ibid., 415 and no. 313, ante, note 3. They were

tion, I do not find that they will be of any essential service in the prosecution.

Be pleased to inform Council that the Commonwealth has been successful in both the suits brought by James Delancy & Margaret his wife, to recover certain lands sold by the State to J. McNair & others, as forfeited by the attainder of Andrew Allen. The property immediately in dispute was about 300 acres, that which was involved in the question was about a thousand acres.

The Judges set out for Luzerne to morrow, J. Franklin went forward this day under the Custody of Sheriff Butler. I am sir, with great Esteem, your most obedt Servt,

Wm. Bradford, Jur.

[318] Grand Jurors of Luzerne County, 1788.[1]

A Return of Grand Jurors summon^d for the Supreme court, to attend on the 4th Novr 1788

Name	Place of Abode	Occupation
Zebulon Butler	Wilksborough	Farmer
Matthias Hollenback	Ditto	Merchant
William Hooker Smith	Ditto	Farmer
Benjamin Carpenter	Kingston	Ditto
Nathan Kingsley	Wyalusing	Ditto
Lawrence Myers	Kingston	Inkeeper
Abel Peirce	Ditto	Farmer
John Hagemen	Ditto	Inkeeper
William Trucks	Ditto	Farmer
James Sutton	Ditto	Miller
Thomas Bennet	Ditto	Farmer
John Allen	Ditto	Ditto
John Dorrance	Ditto	Ditto
John Hollenback	Wilksborough	Inkeeper
Jesse Fell	Ditto	Ditto
John Paul Schott	Ditto	Ditto
Jabez Fish	Ditto	Farmer

letters written by John Franklin to Joseph Hamilton; that they were not incriminating suggests that Franklin's activities may not have been treasonable in so far as planning a separate state goes. Presumably he was making such plans with Hamilton and others, but Beach had vigorously denied the charge in the public prints (no. 171, *ante*), and all the evidence for a separate state is found in letters and depositions of Franklin's enemies.
[318] [1] H. S. P., Conn. Claims in Pennsylvania, I, 32.

John Staples	Ditto	Ditto
Abraham Westbrook	Ditto	Ditto
Benjamin Bailey	Ditto	Blacksmith
Christopher Hurlbut	Hanover	Farmer
Jonah Rogers	Plymouth	Ditto
Samuel Allen	Ditto	Ditto
Robert Faulkner	Ditto	Miller

[319] Presentment of John Franklin and Others.[1]

County of Luzerne ss.

The Grand Inquest for the Commonwealth of Pennsylvania upon their oaths & affirmations do present That John Franklin late of Wilkesborough in the county of Luzerne yeoman, and Zerah Beach, John McInstry & John Jenkins all late of said county yeomen, being inhabitants of & residing within the state of Pennsylvania & owing allegiance to the same state, not having the fear of God before their eyes, but being moved & seduced by the instigation of the Devil, the fidelity which to the same state they owed wholly withdrawing, on the twenty ninth day of September in the year of our Lord 1787 with force & arms &c. at the said county maliciously & traiterously did endeavour to erect & form a new & independent Government within the boundaries of this Commonwealth,[2] as described in the Charter granted by Charles the Second King of Great Britain France & Ireland &c. to William Penn & settled between this state & the state of Virginia, to wit in the said county of Luzerne & in Parts thereto adjacent & then & there in pursuance of such their wicked & traiterous purposes & endeavours, together with other persons to the inquest unknown, maliciously & traiterously did combine conspire & agree together to raise & levy war insurrection & rebellion against this state & the Government thereof and to depose, overthrow, expel & destroy by hostile force the said Government & the administration thereof within the said county & parts adjacent & then & there maliciously & traitereously in

---

[319] [1] M. H. S., Pickering Papers, LVIII, 146-46A, a copy in Pickering's hand.

[2] See no. 133, *ante,* which was the sole piece of evidence aside from hearsay testimony that Franklin and his associates planned to erect an independent state. *Cf.* nos. 105, 109, and 284, *ante* and 320 and 326, *post.*

pursuance of their traiterous purposes and endeavours aforesaid did summon invite and endeavour to persuade one Gideon
Church & Jehiel Franklin and a great multitude of other persons
whose names are as yet unknown, amounting to the number of
two hundred & more, residing in the said county, to assemble &
join themselves together against this Commonwealth, armed &
arrayed in a hostile and warlike manner against the duty of
their allegiance contrary to the form of the act of assembly in
such case made and provided, & against the peace & dignity
of the Commonwealth of Pennsylvania.

Wm Bradford jun.
Att^y Gen[1]

John Franklin ⎫
Zerah Beach ⎬ True Bill
John McKinstry ⎭
John Jenkins, Ignoramus.

Zebⁿ Butler foreman
John Franklin being arraigned pleads non cul. & de hoc po
se &c.

[320] Deposition of John Shepard.[1]

John Shepherd of lawful age, examined by Matthias Hollenback
esquire. The said John deposes That about the beginning of
September in the year 1787, John Franklin, John McKinstry &
Zerah Beach met together at Tioga. One Benjamin Allen (usually called captain Allen) came in with McKinstry. The two
latter brought with them three or four half casks (each containing about fifty pounds) of gunpowder with them, which they
lodged for a while in the store of Matthias Hollenback esquire,
at Tioga, then under the deponent's care; but in a few days it
was removed, and deposited with James Fanning at Tioga.
Soon after their arrival, an advertisement, signed by John
Franklin, was set up, calling on the people or proprietors of
the town of Athens to assemble for the purpose of choosing
a Committee to regulate the prudential affairs of the town.
After this committee had been appointed, they (to wit, Joel
Thomas, Eldad Kellog, Joseph Thomas & perhaps one or two
others) put up a notification, requiring all persons dwelling on
lands in the town which they did not own, to move off by a

---

[320] [1] M. H. S., Pickering Papers, LVIII, 147-48, in Pickering's hand
but signed by Shepard and Hollenback.

certain time, the deponent thinks in November following, & declaring if they did not remove by that time that the Committee would compel them to remove.

While Franklin, Beach, MᶜKinstry & Allen remained at Tioga (which was during ten days or a fortnight, as well as the deponent recollects) they had several meetings and consultations. At one time Elisha Satterlee[2] & Phinehas Stevens were present with them, when they were in a bed room next the store (a board partition only seperating them) the deponent[3] heard them reading something for a considerable length of time; and by what Stevens said to the deponent afterwards, he concluded it was a new constitution for the county of Luzerne, or the country claimed by Members of the Susquehanna Company, which,[4] was, as the deponent took it, intended by Franklin, Beach, MᶜKinstry & their leading associates, to be formed into a New-State, independent of Pennsylvania, Captain Allen, having mentioned their design of forming a new state, if the country was not otherwise to be obtained.[5] the deponent asked him where they would get men to support it? He answered That they could get as many as a thousand men up and down the river, and he could bring a thousand more from Rhode Island, who would rise at a minutes warning.[6] It was also mentioned in company by Beach MᶜKinstry or Allen, that they would have assistance from Vermont. Phinehas Stevens, after being in the consultation aforementioned, said that the deponent would soon see an alteration of times—that the men then in civil authority would not stand long, and that a new mode of government would be introduced—or words to that effect.

After John Franklin had been taken, last year, and the people assembled in arms, the party from Tioga[7] took off with them two or three casks of gunpowder which the deponent saw in a canoe, and asked Fanning if it was not the same which had been in the deponents custody; to which he answered in the affirmative, & that they were going to carry it down to Wyoming; MᶜKinstry followed the same or the next day.

Beach had left Tioga last fall, to go to Wyoming, but re-

---

[2] Elisha Satterlee's name is substituted for that of John Swift.

[3] "The deponent" is substituted for "I" in several places.

[4] Lined out here is the phrase "if not otherwise to be obtained."

[5] The hearsay character of this testimony is obvious.

[6] Two illegible words are lined out here.

[7] "The party from Tioga" is interlined over "McKinstry," which is lined out.

turned with one Jasper Parish, who came express & informed that Franklin was taken. Immediately Beach wrote a number of billets (the deponent saw him write them) to call together the men who expected to hold Lands under the Susquehannah Company, to meet together at Tioga with arms and amunition, either to march to Wyoming, or to take further orders when assembled; the purpose, as the deponent clearly understood, being to march to Wyoming in consequence of Franklin's being taken. And w[hen] the men had assembled in arms (perhaps to the number of twenty) McKinstry took the command of them and set off with them for Wyoming.

County of Luzerne to wit, Novr 9, 1788.   Jno Shepard

Taken & sworn before Matthias Hollenback Justice of the Pace.

[321] Timothy Pickering to Samuel Hodgdon.[1]

Wilkesbarre Novr 9. 1788.

Dear Sir

I arrived here with my wife this day week, in the morning, from Kellys, without any accident, & without much fatigue. On Monday the Judges arrived, & the next day opened the court of Oyer & Terminer.[2] Of the rioters, the young men, who had been in arms, were on account of their poverty, & because misled by the old men, mildly dealt with. Young Kilborn who had particularly insulted me, was sentenced to one months imprisonment, & to remain confined till he should pay the costs, upwards of £7.—the rest of the young men were fined 20/. each, to pay costs from £7. to £9.—& stand committed till the fine & costs are paid. Zeb. Cady, an atrocious villain, was taken whilst the court was sitting by Oehmig & Dr Smiths sons & brought into court. He pleaded guilty: The court in compassion to his poor wife & children did not fine him, but sentenced him to suffer 3 months imprisonment & to pay costs. Of the old men, Captain Dudley, Ephraim Tyler & Nathan Abbot were acquitted by the Jury: for the pointed evidence of the principal witness against them was laid aside by the Jury, sundry other witnesses produced by Dudley Tyler & Abbot having deposed that that witness had for many years been publicly reputed a

---

[321] [1] M. H. S., Pickering Papers, LVIII, 149, in Pickering's hand.
   [2] The court opened on November 4.

516

liar. Yet nobody doubted of the guilt of these three men, & the examinations of some of the convicts on oath, read afterwards, confirmed to the court the truth of the evidence given in this case by the Witness of bad fame; and the Judges obliged Dudley Tyler & Abbot to enter into recognizance (without securities) in £500. cash to keep the peace and be of good behaviour for three years. Old Parks (a blind man of 90 years of age, but as full of fire and the devil as any man amongst them) was sentenced to pay a fine of 50 dollars & costs & stand committed till paid. Thomas Kinney Joseph Kilborn & Stephen Jenkins were each sentenced to pay a fine of 100 dollars & costs, and be imprisoned six months. The sentence of the latter gave particular satisfaction at my house; he was the unfeeling rascal who ordered my wife to prepare herself & children to move in one hour for Tioga. The Chief Justice animadverted on their conduct, told them that they had been guilty of High treason, and that in any country in Europe they would all be hanged, and it was to the mildness of the government of Pennsylvania they were indebted for the light punishment now ordered.

John Franklin, Zerah Beach & John M\ucKinstry were indicted for High Treason. Franklin was brought into court, arraigned, & pleaded not guilty: but was not ready to go to trial, & prayed further time: So the trial is postponed: which happens just as one would wish: for he is in consequence recommitted, & will be taken off, perhaps to-morrow, for Philadelphia jail. The Court ended their session on friday Evening highly pleased with the conduct of the Juries & the People who attended their proceedings. The Chief Justice says he shall think it his duty to make a particular representation thereof to the Assembly. My family are well, and join me in love to our particular friends in the city. Farewell

T. Pickering

[322] Timothy Pickering to Thomas Mifflin.[1]

Wilkesbarre, Nov. 15th, 1788.

Sir

This will be presented to your Excellency by Captain Ross. He takes with him John Franklin, to deliver to the Sheriff of

---

[322] [1] *P. A.,* XI, 424-25.

Northampton; after which he proposes to go to Philadelphia, where, among other business, he will make application to Council for the reward due for some of the convicted Rioters of this county.[2]

At the Court of Oyer & Terminer held here last week, Stephen Jenkins, Joseph Kilborn, Thomas Kinney and Darius Parkes, were tried and convicted of the riot committed here in June last, when I was taken & kept a prisoner in the woods. For Kinney, I believe the reward has already been paid, and Parkes was apprehended by a constable on a warrant from a Justice of the Peace, in the ordinary course of law; for him therefore no reward is due. The captors of Stephen Jenkins & Joseph Kilborn I suppose are entitled to a hundred dollars for each of them. A claim will be presented for 100 dollars for the taking of Aaron Kilborn by Gideon Osterhout a constable.[3] I doubted the propriety of this claim; for I recollected that Esq. Smith told me he happened to be up the river in the neighbourhood of Kilborn's father's house, & hearing that the lad had come home, he issued his warrant for apprehending him, which was executed by Osterhout the Constable: but the latter says he took him on the proclamation of Council. Young Kilborn is but about fifteen years old, and on his examination, I remember he said he had come home with a view to give himself up, but was seized before he had time to set off for Wilkesboro' for that purpose. He was brought to this place about the 20th of August last, at which time the party with whom he fled remained within the State of New-York, where he also might have continued, his brother (of full age) being one of them, had he not come home with a design of surrendering himself. These circumstances I thought it my duty to mention for the consideration of Council. I wish well to Osterhout for his steady attachment to Government, and because he has formerly suffered for it, from some of the gang who took me; and had he pursued young Kilborn when fleeing, or incurred any hazard in the act of taking him, I should have thought he merited the reward.

Zebulon Cady, another of the rioters, & a notorious villain, was seized by two sons of esquire Smith and Mr. Ochmig, during the sitting of the Court of Oyer & Terminer, before which he was brought; and being arraigned, pleaded guilty, & received

---

[2] Cf. no. 308, ante.   [3] P. A., XI, 553-54.

his sentence. His captors richly deserve the reward; they broke open his house in the night, & took him with his arms in his hands, standing upon his defence.

The Attorney General said he should write to Council to propose the revocation of the proclamation:[4] I wish it may have been done, & that the revocation may be soon published here: for I am apprehensive of collusion between the remainder of the rioters and their friends, for the purpose of getting the rewards; seeing the Court, commisserating the culprits for their poverty, & because misled by the Jenkinses & other men in years, have inflicted very light punishments. But I beg leave to suggest, whether with the revocation it will not be expedient to require all the officers & ministers of justice to apprehend the remaining rioters. It would also seem to me expedient to except John Jenkins from the revocation, but to reduce the reward to 100 or even to 50 dollars. This man was the prime instigator of the plot, and has gone hand in hand with Franklin, altho' the Grand Jury did not find evidence to indict him of high treason. He has been indicted for the riot, on the clearest evidence; and the continuance of the offer of a reward will either insure the taking of him, or keep him in York State, whither he went as soon as I was taken & where he still remains; and where, for the good of this settlement, it might be well if he should ever remain; for tho' deficient in courage to execute, yet he has a heart base & wicked enough to contrive any mischief whatever. I have the honour to be, Very respectfully, Sir, Your most obed't servant.

Timothy Pickering.

P. S. On my return hither I found the enclosed return of the election of Justices of the peace had been lodged in my office;[5] I now transmit the same, that Council may commissionate one of them; and beg leave to observe, that there will be a convenience in its being done immediately, lest there should be a defect of Justices at our next term, which commences the second of December, and at present there are but four Justices in commission in the county.[6]

---

[4] Council revoked the proclamation on November 20; *Pa. C. R.*, XV, 602-03.

[5] Not found, but see no. 323, *post*.

[6] Mathias Hollenback, William Hooker Smith, Benjamin Carpenter, and Nathan Kingsley.

[323] Timothy Pickering to Samuel Miles.[1]

Wilkesbarre Nov.r 15. 1788.

Dear Sir,

Herewith I transmit to Council the return of the election of Justices of the Peace[2] to supply the vacancy in the 2.d district of this county occasioned by the Resignation of James Nesbitt esquire. You will see that Lawrence Myers has the greatest number of votes: but I am satisfactorily informed that this happened rather from the superiour knowledge of electioneering of himself & his brother[3] (who have been conversant in the practice in N°umberland county) than a preference in the minds of the freeholders. The next highest in votes is Noah Murray, whose friends admitted M.r Myers in *their* ticket, while those of the latter carefully excluded the former & so obtained a majority. [Myers also (who was the inspector) has noted against Murrays name "No Freeholder." but this is a mistake: he has a connecticut right in one of the seventeen towns.][4] But, without regarding this circumstance, there is in my mind no doubt which of the two ought to be commissioned; M.r Murray being a man of sense,[5] of an inquisitive turn, accustomed to public speaking, having been a lay preacher of the Gospel, and in morals also unexceptionable.[6] Such a person is greatly wanted on the bench of Justices in this county, especially since the resignation of esq.r Gore,[7] who is now in the Assembly. Major Myers, on the contrary, is a man of small talents, to whose judgement I should be very loth to submit the decision of matters of any consequence. I speak from my own knowledge.[8] At the same time, as a neighbour and honest citizen, & one who has ever manifested a friendship for me, I esteem him:[9] With

---

[323] [1] M. H. S., Pickering Papers, LVIII, 151, a draft in Pickering's hand. Miles was a councilor from the city of Philadelphia.

[2] Not found.   [3] Philip Myers.

[4] The words in brackets are interlined.

[5] Above the phrase "a man of sense" interlined words have been crossed out and are illegible.

[6] The phrase "and in morals also unexceptionable" is interlined; words crossed out below are illegible.

[7] Obadiah Gore, who replaced John Paul Schott.

[8] This sentence is interlined.

[9] A clause is lined out here. Its substance is that the writer would be sorry to see Myers in the post of justice.

Mr Murray, indeed I have no personal acquaintance; and the character I have given of him is grounded on the information of others; but 'tis the information of gentlemen on whose discernment & integrity I can rely, & whose object in the present case is obviously no other than the public good, by providing for the more certain and equal administration of Justice. There is another reason for preferring Mr Murray: He lives in Plymouth about 8 miles from Justice Carpenter in the adjoining township of Kingston; whereas Major Myers lives in Kingston, & within about 4 miles of Justice Carpenter: but Plymouth is as populous as Kingston, and Mr Murray's situation will accommodate the inhabitants of Huntington & Salem & of the rest of the county down to the Northumberland line. For these reasons it is my earnest wish that Mr Murry may be commissioned.[10] It is a plain case in which the right [11] of council to prefer the second in votes to the highest ought to be exercised. It is a delicate matter to describe characters, and no man wishes to give offence to a good neighbour; and therefore I do not wish this letter to be made public, without a real necessity. If col^o Denison's [12] opinion should be asked, he will say that Mr Murray is a new-comer: but he has lived in the county above a year, has a family, & has fixed his residence here for life. As Esqr Gore has lived up the river 80 miles above Plymouth, ever since Mr Murray has lived in the settlement, he probably is quite unacquainted with him: I think however he will say little in favour of Major Myers' abilities altho' he married esq^r Gore's sister. I am &c

T. P.

[324] Samuel Hodgdon to Timothy Pickering.[1]

Philadelphia 17th November 1788

Dear Sir

* * * The business of Wyoming is not yet come on, but it is expected it will shortly, at present it wears a favour[able] complexion, all sides agree that the Conferming Law w[ill] be re-

---

[10] Murray was commissioned a justice of common pleas; Pickering Papers, LVIII, 153. See also *Pa. C. R.,* XV, 606 and no. 325, *post.*

[11] "Right" is substituted for "power," which is lined out.

[12] Nathan Denison, member of the Council.

[324] [1] M. H. S., Pickering Papers, LVIII, 152-53.

vived, but the making compensation to the Pennsylvanians that will be deprived of their lands frigh[tens] many of the Members. Your Merchandize must be with you before this, as it went by a very safe hand from hence two days after you left us. Mr Drinker [2] is returned from the interior parts of your County, He likes the Land quite as well as he expected, but complains loudly of the conduct of Smith and Ellicot relative to the roads cut by them therein, neither judgment or honesty appear in anything they have done.[3] His report will subject both to censure and expence. Tench Coxe is appointed a Delegate in Congress to serve until March next. Finley was his Competitor— Coxe 32 Votes Finley 24—the representation is Armstrong, Read, & Coxe only three being sent. 19th November. Mr Tench Coxe has just called on me to inform that a certain Mr Comstock who has for some time past occupied our land in the *Bend,* now asks for an improving lease. As you have been on the spot, you can tell whether it is proper to lease it to *him* at all, or if leased for how long, and what conditions he should have. will thank you for early information on the subject. Another Matter he Mentioned which *I* wish your advice on. He thinks in York [4] (whither as a Delegate he is shortly going) he can sell some of our lands as high as five shillings per acre (not those in the bend) and he wishes to have liberty to do it, as he can purchase other lands more valuable from situation with less than half the Money. if authorized to act for us as for himself I think we shall reap an advantage from his speculations. On this matter be particular in your next * * *

Nothing conclusive is done relative to the Wyoming business, **nor** will there this session. A Bill is reported and under consideration, the purport of which is, as Near as I can learn to confirm *One* right to each *actual* occup[ant] previous to the decree, to be surveyed as *other* lands in the Old or New purchase, and subject to the same charges for surveying & patenting.[5] A board of Commissioners appointed by Council to determine on the claims handed in, and certify that the claims are such as comes within the strict letter of this last Law. I am

---

[2] Henry Drinker, one of the associated Pennsylvania landholders.

[3] Major James Smith and Andrew Ellicott. Smith was to open the road from Mount Ararat to the New York line; Ellicott from Tioga to Mount Ararat. See no. 227, *ante.*

[4] That is, Tench Coxe is going to New York.

[5] Compensation in other lands would, of course, be a sticking point with the Connecticut claimants. Most of them wanted to keep their homes and had steadfastly refused earlier attempts at such compensation. The Old and New purchases refer to the purchases from the Indians in 1768 and 1784.

sensible many objections will arise to this mode of adjustment, but a[s] the bill will be published, objections will naturally be made to the objectional parts, previous to its being pass'd into a Law. Inclosed you have the Ticket agreed on at Lancaster.* * *

[325] Samuel Miles to Timothy Pickering.[1]

Philad[a] November 22[d] 1788.

Sir,

I Received your favor of the 15[h] Inst[t] respecting the two Gentlemen elected for Justices of the peace.[2] I conversed with M[r] Denison on the Subject, and he agrees with you, that M[r] Murry would be the most suitable person to be commissioned: but as the return was incomplete, Council did not chuse to act upon the return as it stood, & have therefore order'd the Secretary to send it back to you. If the Necessary papers which ought to have accompanied this return, should be wanting: I suppose there will be a new election ordered. In that case the people will have an oppertunity of placing M[r] Murry the highest, if they think him best qualified. I thought, however, that giving M[r] Murry the Commission of the plea's, might influence the people in his favor, and, (as it seemed to be your wish that he should be prefered to M[r] Myres) be usefull to the County. He is according Commissioned as a Justice of the Court of Common Pleas.

I am Happy to find, from the Attorney Gen[ls] letter to Council, that there is the greatest reason to hope that pleace & good order will remain & be fully established in your County. This prospect must afford much Satisfaction to yourself & good family, whose comfort & happiness is the sincere wish of, D[r] Sir Your Obed[t] Serv[t]

Sam[l] Miles

[326] Deposition of John J. AcModer.[1]

I John J. Acmodrey testify That in the Fall of the year 1786,[2] I was in company with D[r] Joseph Hamilton of Hudson & Ethan

---

[325] [1] M. H. S., Pickering Papers, LVIII, 154, in Miles' hand.
[2] No. 323, ante.
[326] [1] M. H. S., Pickering Papers, LVIII, 160-61, in Pickering's hand but signed by AcModer and Hollenback.
[2] "Fall of the year 1786" is interlined above "month of March 1787," which is lined out.

Allen, when they conversed about the affairs of Wyoming; & they both explicitly declared it was the design of them & their associates to hold the lands comprehended within the Susquehannah Purchase; & for that purpose to take up arms against the State of Pennsylvania to defend them. They also explicitly declared it was the design of them & their associates to erect a new State, which should comprehend not only the lands within the Susquehannah Purchase, but other [3] territory west of it,[4] and the lands claimed by the State of New-York northward of Pennsylvania as far as the British lines.[5] In the Spring of 1787, I heard Dr Hamilton avow the same sentiments. Afterwards I was at Hillsdale & heard Doctor Caleb Benton avow explicitly the same design. Afterwards I was at Farmington in Connecticut & heard Major William Judd express similar sentiments, but not so fully as the others above named had done. Through the persuasion of said Doctor Hamilton, who pretended that the Susquehannah Purchase would be established, so that titles to lands therein under the Susquehannah Company would be valid, I had bought of him & others Thirty two whole share rights therein. In consequence of which I was admitted into the secrets of the company, as above related.[6] In April 1787 I came to Wyoming, and brought letters from Doctor Hamilton to John Franklin, at whose house I lodged during my stay at Wilkesbarre, which was four or five days. In that time I repeatedly conversed with said Franklin, who likewise explicitly [7] avowed it to be the design of the company, of which he was one, to erect a new state as above mentioned. He particularly [8] spoke to this effect, "We (said he) must endeavour to stop the election here (meaning the election of Justices) and if we cannot, then we must sweep in settlers, to make ourselves strong; then if a writ of ejectment under Pennsylvania is served, we will rise & beat off the Sheriff; and if Pennsylvania sends

---

[3] "Other" is substituted for "all the."

[4] A following phrase, "within the boundaries of Pennsylvania," is lined out.

[5] The phrase "as far as the British lines" is interlined.

[6] That AcModer was privy to the plans of Franklin and others is apparent from Franklin himself; see no. 65, *ante*. But Franklin in mentioning AcModer gives not even a hint of separate statehood. He writes solely in terms of organized resistance to the state so long as it fails to confirm the entire Susquehannah Company purchase. See also no. 89, *ante*.

[7] An illegible word is lined out after "explicitly."

[8] Lined out here is "said That they." This change and others makes one wonder how much coaching AcModer got.

a party against us, we will embody and drive them out; & then we will openly proclaim a new state, comprehending the Susquehannah Purchase, the lands east of it as far as the Delaware, & westward & northward as far as the British lines. The York Lessees,[9] as they have been called, were in this scheme, and to do their parts towards carrying it into Execution. In the year 1787 I was at Sharon in Connecticut, at Joseph Gallo's, where I saw Zerah Beach, who also explicitly avowed the same design of holding the Susquehannah lands, and of erecting a new state; and said, if they could not otherwise accomplish it, He would be damned if they would not employ the Indians & Tories for the purpose. In 1787, before John Franklin was apprehended, Col° John McKinstry (who was closely connected with Dr Hamilton, Beach & Franklin) told me it was their design to declare a New State in the fall of that year. This, M^c-Kinstry declared at Roger Conants, at Newtown.

Jn° J. AcModer

Sworn Decr 22^d 1788. at Wilkesbarre, County of Luzerne Before Matthias Hollenback Justice of the Peace

---

[9] See no. 100, *ante,* note 5.

Appendix

EDITORIAL NOTE

In the two documents that follow, Timothy Pickering and John Franklin, the two protagonists of Volume IX, set forth their views on the validity of the Connecticut settlers' claim to the soil. This was a subject much on the minds of both men in 1787, when Pickering was trying to get the settlers to accept the Confirming Act and the laws of Pennsylvania, and Franklin was trying to maintain the Company's right to the whole Susquehannah purchase. It will be recalled that Pickering received from James Wilson in January, 1787, answers to his questions about the Trenton trial and he probably wrote his statement after reflecting upon Wilson's words. Internal evidence makes it almost certain that Franklin wrote his piece in 1787.

Because the Trenton decision on jurisdiction necessarily depended, in Pickering's eyes, upon a prior determination that Pennsylvania had pre-emption right to the soil, he concluded that the Connecticut claimants could have no legal right to their lands; theirs was only an equitable right. Franklin, on the other hand, stressed the priority of the Connecticut charter and the stipulation in the Articles of Confederation that disputes over private right of soil when grants from two different states were involved had to be settled by a special court established for the purpose by Congress. As an interested party, Pennsylvania could not possibly rule, even through a jury, on private rights of soil.

[327] Case of the Wyoming Lands Considered.[1]

Question 1. Did the Federal Court at Trenton determine the *private right of soil,* or only the *jurisdiction* of the Wioming Lands.

---

[327] [1] M. H. S., Pickering Papers, LVII, 34-37A, an undated draft in Pickering's hand. None of the changes made in wording seem to be substantive ones.

Question 2. If their decree decided both, had they a right to comprehend both? ought they not to have confined their judgment to the point of jurisdiction?

Answers. 1. As to the 1st question, tis admitted That they declare, in their decree, that the right of *preemption* was in Penn*; which consequently determines the right of soil to be in that state: for if she had the pre-emption right, then any purchase of the natives, made by Connecticut, must have been a nullity; and consequently all her grants must be void in law.

2. Whether the Court could legally decide on the private right of soil, or ought to have confined themselves to the matter of jurisdiction, cannot be positively determined, without knowing what was the petition of Connecticut (or Penn*) to Congress, stating the matter in question, and the order of Congress thereon, for constituting the court. But as both of these documents are wanting, we can only *reason* from the nature of the case.[2]

State of Facts.

1. Charles the 2ᵈ granted to the governour & company of Connecticut a patent (or charter) of a certain tract of country, bounded by Massachusetts on the north, Narraganset Bay & River on the east, by the sound on the south, to a certain point, and running westward to the south sea. The great object of this charter was evidently to secure the title to their lands as bounded *westerly by the state of New-York*. They accordingly remained satisfied within that limit, for above 90 years after they received *their* charter and above 70 years after the same king's grant (or charter) to William Penn comprehending the lands westward of the province of New York from the Delaware river thro' 5 degrees of Longitude and within the latitude of Connecticut.

2. At length, a company of adventurers, chiefly inhabitants of Connecticut, took upon themselves to

---

[2] For Pennsylvania's petition and the action of Congress upon it, see Vol. VII, nos. 74 and 80.

purchase of the Indians a large tract of land within the boundaries of Penn's patent in breadth lying between the end of the 41st & beginning of the 43^d degree of latitude, & in length, from 10 miles east of the Susquehanna running westward thro' 2 degrees of longitude, *or 120 miles.* This purchase was made in the year—1754. In 1759 the first settlers under the Susquehanna company began to cultivate the land.

3. From the time of the purchase (real or pretended) of the Indians, & thro' the whole period of settling, to this day Pennsylvania has asserted the pretensions of the Susquehanna Comp^y & of Connecticut to those lands to be unwarranted and without right, & the whole country claimed under Connecticut to be the property of Pennsylvania; and the claimants under Connecticut have maintained their possessions *only by force of arms.*

Argument.

1. The word *Charter,* which is the name given to a paper by which the Kings of England have granted to companies or individuals of their subjects divers tracts of land in N. America is but another name for what among those subjects and the citizens of the U. S. has been & now is called *Deed.* Such deed was in truth in the ancient laws of England called a *Charter.*[3] Now these charters of the Crown, being of the nature of deeds, they have the like effects; and the companies or individuals to whom they have been given, were thereby constituted bodies corporated, & made capable of holding lands. The property in such lands was of course to be subject to regulations founded on the general principles of the laws of England. In consequence hereof, the disputes between these corporations relative to their rights to particular tracts of land, were submitted to the judgement & determination of the King & Council, or of special Courts or Commissioners appointed by the Crown.

---

[3] The language used here suggests that Pickering was addressing himself to a general audience, probably the Connecticut settlers.

This mode of decision was necessary. Had the property of these corporations lain in *England,* their mutual claims would have been heard & determined by a jury of the county in which the lands lay. But the lands in question lay *without the realm;* and consequently could not be judged of by an *English* jury. And no *jury* could be constituted in America, because the people of the *vicinage* were parties in the dispute; and because the principles and rules of the laws of England had their operation only by the acts of the several corporations, which made no provision for terminating disputes between them by the intervention of juries.

2. One rule of the law of England, which has been in force during the whole existence of the charters in question, is, that uninterrupted possession, for 60 years, gives an *absolute right.* Neither charters (or deeds) nor any other evidence to prove the *property* can be admitted against such long & continued possession. But Mʳ Penn took possession of the lands granted him by the King of England, in 1681, and held the same quietly & uninterruptedly until the year 1759, a period of 78 years. Or if the supposed purchase of the Susquehanna Compʸ be considered as a claim on the part of Connecticut, still this was not made till 1754, 73 years after Penn took possession. Consequently, even admitting that the Connecticut Charter was really intended by the Crown to skip over the provinces of N York & New Jersey, & to extend to the South Sea, & therefore to cover the land in dispute; yet the right thereto has been lost by Connecticut, for want of taking possession, or making & continuing her claim to it.

If it shᵈ be said, That Connecticut having taken possession of part of her chartered lands, thereby acquired possession of the whole: To this it may be answered That the part of her lands included in Penn's charter was as a *seperate field,* of which Penn also took actual possession, & maintained the same upwards of 60 years, & consequently, by the laws of England acquired the *property* as he before had the possession of the land. If you call Penn an *intruder*—no matter—Connecticut took no steps to remove the intruder—not even by complaining of the wrong: till by neglect she lost the right to complain or at least the right of enforcing that complaint in law.

As to the truth of Penn's possession, it cannot be disputed for if Connecticut by taking possession of her present territory can in contemplation of law be deemed to have also taken possession of the lands in dispute, altho' she must thereby be imagined to skip over the intervening provinces; much more must Penn's possession be admitted, when he & his tenants were actually settled on the field in which the disputed land is comprehended.

3. If it sh^d still be contended that the disputed land was within the charter of Connecticut; that under the charter, the Susquehanna Company had a right to purchase the soil of the Indians: and that the decree of the Court at Trenton could determine nothing but the *jurisdiction;* because nothing more was submitted to them, I would ask On what principles they could determine the jurisdiction to be in Pennsylvania, unless they, as a foundation of such jurisdiction, determined the *right of soil* to be hers. It is true, the land is disjoined from Connecticut: but a joining of lands is not necessary to give a jurisdiction. Most of the European states have their lands seperated by other states or by mighty seas and to come near home, Massachusetts extends its jurisdiction over what is called the province of Maine, altho' seperated by the state of New Hampshire lying between. In the same manner could Connecticut exercise her jurisdiction over the Wyoming lands, tho seperated from her by N. York & New Jersey. Such seperation, therefore, could not have induced the court to strip her of the jurisdiction. Neither could they have done it because Penn's charter included those lands: for if the Connecticut charter was valid to comprehend them, then Penns charter, so far as it

interfered with it was void; & consequently could not furnish foundation on which to decree the jurisdiction to Pennsylvania. On what principle then could the jurisdiction have been so decided? Truly on nothing but the right of soil. Accordingly we find the court declaring That the right of preemption of the disputed lands was in Pennsylvania; & consequently the right of soil; and if the right of soil, then the right of jurisdiction; which they decreed accordingly.[4]

4. But 'tis said That when a tract of inhabited country is ceeded by one sovereign state to another, or acquired by Conquest, the private right of soil remains unviolated. Granted. The policy of nations has *generally* confirmed it; for a country without inhabitants is of no value. Its value commences with its population. The sovereigns of the old world have been more solicitous to acquire *subjects* than *naked lands*. But let us put the case That the subjects of one state had dispossessed the subjects of another or taken possession of lands which the latter had granted or was about to grant to its own subjects, and that the state whose subjects gained this wrongful possession, had annexed the territory to her own dominions; and that at length the state which lost such territory should again acquire possession of it, either by cession or conquest? What then would be its conduct, towards the individual who had been the disseisors? Why doubtless to turn them out of possession, & restore the lands to its own subjects; but if the land had never been so appropriated, good policy would certainly confirm the intruders in their possessions; *provided they consented to hold them on the like terms on which such lands were held by the other subjects of the state.* If, indeed, any state acquires an inhabited territory either by cession or conquest, to which before it had no pre-

---

[4] For some time after writing this argument, Pickering was unaware that the judges at Trenton had written privately to John Dickinson about the private right of soil, implying that the determination of it would have to be made as prescribed by the Confederation, that is, in a separate trial for the purpose; Vol. VII, no. 129.

tension, common justice demands that the property of the inhabitants be held sacred. Tho' to say the truth, such Conquest being an act of *violence* no rules can be prescribed to it but the pleasure or policy of the conqueror; & that policy leads him to quiet the inhabitants (who now become his subjects) in their possessions. And in the case of cessions, the state which makes it, usually stipulates for certain conditions, particularly that the inhabitants of the ceded country may either hold their possessions, or sell them & remove out of it. So that neither of these cases will apply to the dispute about Wyoming: For here there has been neither conquest nor cession; but a *recovery in a trial of law.* This dispute did not originate between two sovereign states, but between two corporate members of the British empire; and the decree at Trenton was made for the purpose of putting an end to it.

5. There is one case in which the individuals of a ceded territory may with perfect justice hold their possessions. Such a case has happened between the two states of Penn^a & Virginia. Both states, for a great many years back, supposed the boundary line between them ran a certain course, & each granted away the lands up to that line. But about 2 years ago they mutually appointed commissioners to run the line with the greatest exactness, by astronomical observations. The event shewed, That the former line was erroneous & that Virginia had granted a multitude of farms which really lay within the bounds of Pennsylvania. What does Pennsylvania do on this discovery? Did she attempt to turn the Virginians out of possession? By no means. She knew that these people had fairly purchased their farms at a time when she supposed & admitted that Virginia had a right to sell them; not a man therefore suffered the least molestation. But how different is the case of the Wyoming lands? Penn^a far from admitting, always *denied* the right of Connecticut to one foot

of them; and the determination of the Court at Trenton justifies them in the denial; for if Connecticut had at that time no right to the lands, then she *never* had a right; consequently could never legally convey them, and all grants made by her are therefore void in law.[5] And not only the Susquehanna Comp^y but the first actual settlers, knew that they settled on a doubtful title; and therefore rec^d their first grants—not for valuable considerations paid in money or other property, but *on condition of taking & keeping possession for five years*.[6] They knew that, Penn^a claimed the same lands; & that their holding them or not must depend on the decision of that claim. On this doubtful title they were willing to settle & hazard their improvements. In *strict law* therefore they have no right to complain, if turned out of possession. But

6. They have during many years been in actual possession of the lands, and in general were the first occupants. They spent much of their time & property in building houses barns & in other improvements: they have been a frontier against the Indians during the late War, in which a large proportion of them lost their lives, & all of them their houses & barns & moveable property: they have also suffered the most cruel usage from persons pretending to act under, but grossly abusing the authority of Pennsylvania. A great number of the people too, may charitably be presumed to have believed that Connecticut had a just right to the lands, & these are considered as innocent but mistaken men. On all these grounds the Connecticut settlers prior to the Trenton decree, & their heirs & assigns, are deemed to have an *equitable* claim to the lands by them actually occupied & improved; and every at-

---

[5] Strictly speaking, of course, Connecticut had never made any grants. The state merely recorded the Indian deed in 1782 just before the Trenton trial.

[6] See Vol. II, Introduction, xxv. The first actual attempt to settle at Wyoming was not made until 1762.

tempt to dispossess them, would be pronounced ungenerous, unkind, & even cruel. But on the other hand, If they are entitled to be considered in equity, the Pennsylvania claimants, on honest purchases, are entitled to equal consideration. They believed the Connecticut people to be intruders, & that Penn[a] had the sole & exclusive right to the lands. These claimants certainly ought to be reimbursed the monies they paid for the land, with interest. And if the Connecticut settlers are allowed to hold the lands, they should pay to the others their money. If those claimants should make further demands, on account of the present increased value of the lands, 'tis presumed the state will undertake to satisfy them, by grants of some of her wild lands.

7. The validity of the Indian deed to the Susquehannah Company, which is made a corner stone to support the claim of the Connecticut settlers, may well be questioned. It was in fact refused by the court at Trenton to be admitted in evidence because of its palpable forgeries.[7] Such alterations had been made in the essential parts of the deed, after the execution of it, as rendered it void in law.

8. Treaty of Peace said to be governed by the N. England charters [8]

9. Cession by Connecticut accepted by Congress said to prove her right of soil.[9]

---

[7] The court at Trenton did not refuse to admit the Indian deed; rather, it even admitted sworn depositions taken in 1760 and 1761 in support of the deed. Two of Connecticut's agents, Root and Johnson, however, chose to base their case finally on charter grounds, denigrating the value of Indian deeds. See Vol. VII, Introduction, xxv, xxvii, and xxix.

[8] This and the next point Pickering left undeveloped. At the Trenton trial Johnson made the plea that the sea-to-sea clauses in colonial charters would help establish the claim of the United States to lands as far west as the Mississippi despite the Quebec Act and the Proclamation Line of 1763; Vol. VII, Introduction, xxxi and p. 451.

[9] This was a claim made by both John Franklin and Ethan Allen and one that members of the Continental Congress feared would be made as a consequence of accepting the Connecticut cession; Vol. VIII, Introduction, xxxvii-xxxviii and nos. 220, 226, 205, note 3, and 206, note 2.

[328] Queries Concerning the Trenton Decree.[1]

1 Query—Whither the Decree of the Congressional Court at Trenton the 30th of December 1782 giving to the State of Pennsylvania the right of Jurisdiction and Preemption of the Territory of Country then in controversy between the s[d] State of Pennsylvania and the State of Connecticut Does in any manner affect the private right of soil of those Lands within s[d] Territory purchased of the Native Proprietors by Individuals, with the consent, and under the Authority of the s[d] State of Connecticut[2] and which had become Individual property Prior to the settlement of the Jurisdictional Territories

2 Query Whither the right of *Preemption* given to the State of Pennsy[a] by the afores[d] Decree does or could extend further then to the Lands then claim'd to be the Property of the State of Connecticut

3 Query—Whither the Purchace made within s[d] Territory by the Susq[h] Company, under the Authority of the State of Connecticut Antecedent to the settlement of Jurisdictional Territories is not valid until otherwise Determined by a legal tribunal

4 Query Whither Possession in part is not a possession of the whole and whether the Possession and settlements made on s[d] Lands by the Proprietors and owners thereof Prior to the afores[d] Decree is not a legal and lawful Possession of the whole tract of Land Purchased and Claimed by the s[d] Proprietors

5 Query Whither any other tribunal Except a Federal Court have a legal right to hear and finally determine controversies regulating the private right of soil within the Purchace afore-

---

[328] [1] Tioga Point Museum, Athens, Pennsylvania, in Franklin's hand and undated.

[2] The Susquehannah purchase was not made with the consent and under the authority of Connecticut; indeed, failure to get the prior consent of the colony was one of the arguments made at Trenton against the validity of the claim. Connecticut did not acknowledge the Indian deed until 1782; Vol. VII, nos. 121 and 128, note 83 (p. 191).

said which controversies arise between Persons Claiming the same s⁴ Lands under grants of different States [3] or whither the party aggrieved in such case by the judgement of a Court of Comon Law held by and under the sole Authority of the State in which the same is found to be may not legally appeal to a Federal Court for a final Decision of such Controversy and whither the Congress are not authorized by the articles of Confederation to Constitute a federal Court to hear and finally Determine all such controversies or Whither the Congress will not be vested with like authority under the new Constitution proposed for the United States of America, whenever the s⁴ Constitution shall be ratified by the Conventions of Nine States [4]

Ans⁵ to the 1ˢᵗ Query—The Court of Commissioners appointed for the purpose of deciding the controversy between the States of Pennsylvania and Connecticut were appointed agreeable to the articles of Confederation in that case provided for the sole purpose of hearing and determining the right of Jurisdiction over the Territory of Country then in controversy between the two States—the Private right of soil was by no means a matter in controversy between the contending States [5]—

The Articles of Confederation having Prescribed the mode for Constituting a federal Court for the sole purpose of hearing and Determining controversies respecting the private right of soil in any State claimed by persons under grants of different States, which claims originated antecedent to the settlement of Jurisdictional territories—a trial to be had by itself, distinct and seperate from a Tryal for Jurisdiction—which trial could by no means be necessary or proper previous to the settlement of Jurisdictional territory—hence we may infer that the Court appointed for the Purpose of hearing and determining the right of Jurisdiction between the contending States, were not authorized by such appointment to Interfere with private property—Conse-

---

[3] It was the contention of Pennsylvania that grants of lands made by different states were not at issue, for the grants at Wyoming had not been made by Connecticut but by the Susquehannah Company; *ibid.,* no. 214, note 4 and Vol. VIII, nos. 149 and 152.

[4] Obviously this passage dates Franklin's argument in the fall of 1787 or the spring of 1788. Since he was kept in very close confinement after his arrest on October 2, 1787, he probably wrote it just before he was seized.

[5] Franklin's judgment here agrees with the tenor of the judges' letter to John Dickinson; Vol. VII, no. 129.

quently the Decree of the Court of Commissioners at Trenton the 30th Day of December 1782 does not, nor could not in any manner affect the Private right of soil within said territory which had been Purchased under the authority of the State of Connecticut, and became Individual property antecedent to s^d Decree

Answ^r to 2^d Query—the Court of Commissioners being appointed for the sole purpose of hearing and determining the controversy between the two contending States, were not nor could not be authorized by such appointment to make any Decree that should in any manner Interfere with or change any Property of Lands within the Controverted territory which was not then claimed to be the property of either of the Contending States— any lands within the s^d territory purchised by individuals or Proprietors tenants in commen—by consent and under the Authority of the State of Connecticut could not be said to be the property of the s^d State—The Decree of s^d Court is in express words that the Jurisdiction and Preemption of the territory of Country in controversy and Claim'd by the State of Connecticut does of right belong to the State of Pennsy^a they did not by s^d Decree Determine that any private property or Individual Claims should be and belong to the State of Pennsy^a but the Preemption rights of Such Lands only as were then Claimed to be the property of the State of Connecticut

The Susq^a Purchace made by Individuals in 1754 under the Authority of the State of Connecticut had by *Consent of the State* and by repeated Acts of the Legislature thereof became Individual property to all intents and Purposes—and therefore ceasd to be the prope[rty] of the State, so that it was not in the Power of the State or Legislature thereof (Without the consent of the Individual proprietor and owners of such Lands) to dispose of any such property or to agree to or ratify and confirm the appointment or Decree of any Congressional Court Interfearing with private Property or Individual claims—The Court of Commissioners might as as well have determined that all property both real and Personal that should be found within the disputed Territory should be and belong to the State of Pennsylvania, as to have Determined that any Lands the Property of Individuals should belong to s^d State which in either case would be a nullity—Consequently the Decree of the s^d Court at Trenton giving the right of Preemption to the State of Pennsylvania, does not, neither could it extend further in that case then to the right of Preemption of such Lands as were then Claimd to be the property of the s^d State of Connecticut

Ans^r to 3^d Query The Territory of Country had in Controversy between the States of Pennsyl^a and Connecticut is fully and amply included within the Royal Charter of the Late Colony, now State of Connecticut granted by King Charles the Second in 1662—Eighteen years Prior to the Charter of the Late Provence now State of Pennsyl^a granted to Sir Willm Penn the Lands West of the River Delaware are as amply included within the limits of the Charter of the Colony now State of Connecticut as the Lands East of Connect^t River—their Charter Being previous to any other grant of s^d Territory—the grant to s^d Wm Penn being 18 years after could not reasonably be supposd to have right to Interfere with a legal and prior grant of the same territory—The Purchace made of the Natives in 1754 by the Susq^h Company with the consent and under the Authority of the State (then Colony) of Connecticut is not only fairly Included within their Charter but was amply made of the natives previous to any other Purchase made of s^d Lands under any other authority whatsoever—thus the State of Connecticut having a Compleat grant of the s^d Territory prior to any other grant of the same had an undoubted right to Dispose of the whole or any part thereof as might have commenced their first settlement there or previous to the grant of pennsylvania their Charter being the oldest and legally granted must be considered a Valid to all intents and Purposes untill it was otherwise Determined by a tribunal having right to take Cognizance thereof—Therefore the purchase made of the Natives original owners of the soil, by the Susq^h Company under the Authority of the Colony now State of Connecticut Antecedent to the settlement of Jurisdictional territory between the Contending States had became Individual Property prior to s^d settlement, and is of Consequence Valid to all Intents and Purposes until otherwise Determined by a legal tribunal

Ans^r to 4th Query—If not necessary in order to make a Possession on a Particul^r farm (and the same may be applied to a large tract or territory of Country) that the whole of such Lands should be actually occupied and Improved neither is that ever supposd to be the case in making a Possession—an individual purchasing a single farm of wild and uncultivated Lands cannot be supposd to occupy and Improve every foot of Land containd in the whole farm, at the Instant of taking possession—a house being purchased may be taken into possession and occupied at

538

the same time—but to suppose that an uncultivated farm taken in a state of Nature must all be cleared, fenced occupied and Improved at the same Instant of taking Possession is not Possible neither is it expected—A person purchasing a single farm of wild and uncultivated Lands 100 Acres or more it is not material as to the quantity, a house erected or any Improvements made by the purchaser on any part of such Lands is suposed in Law to be a legal and lawful possession of the whole farm or tract of Land.

Any number of Individuals have an undoubted right to make a purchase of a tract of Land in Company, to be conveyed to them in Company Jointly and severally from the owner or owners of such Lands, and such Conveyance would be Valid in Law and equity—either of the grantees so purchasing in Company, taking Possession of such Lands, in the name and under the authority of the Company would be considered a legal Possession for the whole Company, and of the whole tract of Land—though such Possession being made by by an individual and though he be a Proprietor and owner of such lands in company it does not Deprive the other owners or either of them of their equal proportion of such Lands, for quantity and quality—suppose for instance five men in Company purchace 5000 Acres of Land and obtain a legal and ample conveyance of such Lands from the original Proprietors or Legal owners thereof, conveyed to the Purchasers in company jointly and severally—it is not supposed that the whole of the Purchasers are obliged to settle on such Lands and have the whole Immediately occupied or Improved in order to obtain a legal Possession of the same—Neither is it necessary that any one of the owners should ever settle thereon in his own Person—such Lands being conveyd to them in Company they have an undoubted right to dispose of the whole tract or any part or parcel thereof or in case of making a Possession may Convey a certain part to other individuals for the Purpose of making Possessions on s^d tract for the whole Company—on Supposition they convey to five Persons (on Certain conditions) 100 Acres to each Person (or more or less it is not material) to be taken out of the general tract for the purpose of making Possession thereon—Such Persons Proceed to survey to themselves 100 acres each whether in a body together or seperate from each other it matters not if the Company of Grantors are agreed. the Company of settlers proceed to occupy and make settlements on their respective farms for themselves though in the name and under the Authority of the Company of Proprietors—Such Possession and settlements would be considered in law and equity to be a legal and lawful possession of the whole tract of Land, for the whole Company of Proprietors. The same may be applied to a large tract or to a Territory of Country it is not material as to the quantity of Lands. an Individual or a Number of Individuals in Company have an undoubted right to purchase any quantity of Land that they can pay for; a Deed of Conveyance of 1000 Acres to an Individual or to a Company of Purchasers from the original Proprietor or Lawful owner of such Lands at the time of executing the Deed is as equally Valid as a Deed of one Acre only and the same will apply to a greater or smaller quantity The purchase made of the Natives in 1754 by the Company, known by the name of the Susq^h Company was made not only with the Consent and under the Authority of the State then Colony of Connecticut, then Claiming the right of Jurisdiction, but by a good and ample Deed of Conveyance well executed from the Aboriginal Proprietors of the soil [6] granting and conveying to a number of Individuals expressd by name in Company a Certain tract of Land, bounded East ten Miles East of the N East Branch of the Susqh River and Extending west 120 miles, and Including the whole breadth of the 42^d Degree of Northen Latitude, the Particular boundaries being expressed in s^d Deed Conveying said tract to s^d Company to them their heirs and Assigns forever, by which Conveyance it became the Property of said Company as Proproprietors and Joint tenants in common with each other—it could not be supposed necessary that every proprietor should settle on s^d Purchase in his own person or that the whole tract should be actually occupied and improv'd in every part thereof by the Company in order to make a legal Possession [7]—the Company had an undoubted right to substitute other Persons to take possession of settle occupy and improve such Lands for them and in their Name behalf and Stead or to Convey such part thereof as they Judg'd proper to individuals for the purpose of making settlements thereon—they did so; they undoubtedly had a legal right. in 1755 they proceed to locate and survey Lands on the N East Branch of the Susq^h River, within s^d Purchace—in 1762 a part of the Proprietors to the number of

---

[6] Franklin slides over the inadequacies in the deed; Vol. VII, Introduction, xxv.

[7] Franklin has in mind interpretations of the Confirming Act which made confirmation of titles possible only for actual settlers. Franklin, of course, was the leader of those who claimed the right to the whole purchase whether it had been assigned to individuals or not.

540

119 proceed to take Possession of occupy and Improve on s^d Lands in the name, and under the authority of the whole company, but being drove off by the Savages in Oct 1763 no further settlements could be made at that time. early in the year 1769 the Company reassume their Possessions 400 settlers were Actually sent on the same year most of which were proprietors—the Company grant five townships of five miles square each to 240 Persons on Certain Conditions that the grantees should take Possession of and make settlements on the general tract such townships to be laid out on the N East branch of the Susq^h River, and to be taken out of the general tract of Country, the 240 Persons Actually went on to the Lands and took Possession, five townships were Actually surveyed and settled, one of which was granted to 40 settlers the other four to the other 200 a township to each 50, one other township of six miles Square was granted at the same time to fifty other settlers on the same conditions to be laid out on the West branch, and taken out of the general tract, these settlers also went on to the Lands, a township was Actually surveyed near Munsey Creek by these settlers, the settlers on the general tract though not on that Particular township this body of settlers Consisting of 290 in the whole were part of the 400 that went on the same year, these were mostly or all proprietors in the general tract, they took actual Possession of the whole tract not only for themselves but under the Authority and in the Name behalf and stead of the whole Company of Proprietors—the remaining part of the 400 took Possession the same year, several other townships were surveyd and settlements made thereon—tho the settlers were molested in the year 1770 and 1777 by Persons Claiming said lands under grants from Pennsylvania which put a stop to the Progress of the settlements for a short time. however the settlers soon surmounted those Difficulties and were rapidly Increasing for a number of successive years and until the Month of July 1778 at which time the whole of the Inhabitants then Consisting of upwards of 1000 families were either Massacreed or Drove of by the Savages and tories and the greatest part of their effects eitherd being carried off or otherwise Destroyed by the enemy—previous to this a great number of townships as well as single farms had been surveyed and settled so that the settlers had extended their settlement upwards of 100 miles in length up and down the River and within the original tract and made large Improvements thereon and enjoyd a complete Civil and Milatary establishment under the Authority of the state of Connecticut

all of which settlement and Possessions were made more than four years prior to the settlement of Jurisdictional territories— these settlers were mostly proprietories in the general tract, they settled not only for themselves but for the whole Company of Proprietors, they were part of the Company substituted by and in the name and under the Authority of the whole Company and took Possession of the whole tract for the whole Company

Consequently the Possessions and settlements made on the Susqʰ Purchase by the Proprietors settlers and owners thereof and their substitutes for and in the Name behalf and stead of the Company and under the authority of the State of Connecticut Antecedent to the settlement of Jurisdictional territories cannot be Construed in other way than to be in ample Compleat and Legal Possession of the whole of the Purchase, and for the whole Company of Proprietors

Ansʳ to 5 query—It is ever considered to be the right of all freemen in all Free Countries to have the priveledge of tryal by Jury in Causes where the title of Lands is in question a Priveledge which the Citizens of the several American Colonies had right to enjoy while subjects of and under the Realm of England—the same priveledge is still reservd and secured in each of the American States, either by Charter bill of Rights or by the Constitution of each and every particular State tho different modes may be prescribed in different states—In all causes between parties where trial is to be had by Jury, whether the title of land is in question or not it is necessary and also agreeable to the Laws of the Land that the Jury be Impartial and Disinterested. no persons have right to sit as a Judge or Jury in his own cause, or in any cause where he will be Interested for the event with either party. It is often the case that whole town or Incorporated society are Interested in the same cause—Lands appropriated to the use of a particular town or Incorporated society becomes the property and Interest of all the Legal Inhabitants of such town or society. a suit may be commenced between an individual and such town or society respecting such appropriations though such suit may be commenced against an Individual as a Trustee yet the whole town or Society would be Considered as Interested in the Suit. Consequently no person being thus Interested would have Right to be a Judge or Juror in such cause the same may be applied to a larger body, a County or even a whole State may be Interested in the same suit—Lands Claimed to be the Property of a State are Considered as being the Property of every Citizen of the State, no such Lands can be desposed of by the Consent of the Citizens or their legal Representatives, any Revenue Raised by the sale or rent of any such Lands is Considered as a benefit to every Individual in the State more or less—a Number of Individuals may Purchase a farm or tract of Country, to be Conveyd to them in Company, in such case the whole Company becomes Interested—Instance the Susq^h Purchase contains a large tract of Country and Claimd by a number of Individuals in Company by a purchase from the Native Proprietors and under grants from the State of Connecticut this tract being Conveyd to a number of Persons in Company they became joint tenants in Common each Individual became Interested in every part of the whole tract, the Company of Proprietors had undoubtedly a legal right to make a Division of the whole of such Lands so purchased in Company or of such part thereof as they should think proper. a Certain part of the whole tract has been Divided, each Individual Proprietor having been legally Authorized by the Whole Company, to Locate and Survey to himself a Certain number of Acres to be laid out agreeable to Certain Rules and regulations to become the Property of such Individual and as a part of his whole right or share in the general tract. such Lands so surveyd and taken up by any Individual ceased to be the property of the whole Company— though such Individuals are still Interested in the undivided part of the general tract with the Company one with the other—The State of Pennsylvania by Virtue of Sundry Purchases Subsequent to the Purchase made by the Susq^h Company under the Authority of Connecticut, Claim the same Lands their purchases being made by the State, Consequently the whole State becomes Interested. the State have Conveyd part of such Lands to Individuals warranting and Defending the same to the Grantees against all Claims whatsoever, these Claims so conveyd by the State to Individuals Interfere with the Claims of Individuals under grants of another State originating antecedent to the settlement of Jurisdictional Territories or supposition a suit of Ejectment is Commenced against a Connecticut Claimant, an Impartial and Disinterested Jury is necessary to be had, a Certain number of freeholders in the Vicinity Claiming Lands under the same title are summoned for that purpose, the question will arise are such persons Disinterested in the Suit, it may be said they really are in one respect, they have no Claim to, or Interest in the particul[ar] Lot or farm in Controversy but still the title to their own Lands is equally the same, originated from and under the same Authority, and must Consequently share the same fate, they are Interested in Common in the general tract with the Defendant though not in that Particular controverted term yet they must and will be considered as Interested in the final event of such suit which is equally the same and will consequently be rejected from Determining such suit—The same objections will arise against Persons Claiming any such Controverted Lands under grants from Pennsylvania, the same event may happen to all under the same Claim, they would Consequently be Considered as Interested in the final event, and would therefore with Propriety be rejected, but suppose a Jury are summoned that are not owners of or Particularly Interested in any such Controverted Lands under either Claim yet it is necessary that they be Inhabitants of the same County and holders of lands therein and Consequently Citizens of the state, the question will arise are such persons Disinterested. it may perhaps be said with Propriety that they are not particular owners of any such Disputed Lands nor Interested with either party in such Particular suit but still are they not Interested in the final event. the general tract of Country in Controversy is claimed to be held under the State by Virtue of Purchases made by the State, they have also as a state disposed of such Lands by giving ample Deeds of Convyance warranting and Defending the same to such Individual grantees. Judgment rendered against such grantees would be against the Whole State, they are Responsible as a State to such Individual Grantees, Money paid to the State for any such Lands must be refunded, every Citizen of the State must bear his proportion of the loss. it is not only a single farm but a large and Valuable tract of Country that must share the same equal lot—Consequently every Person in the State who has obtaind the right of Citizenship sufficient to entitle him to the right and Priveledge of being a Juror—is Interested in the final event of every such suit, and may therefore with propriety be rejected—

The Convention of the several American States in the framing the Confederation for the United States of America foreseeing that such Controversies would probably arise between persons Claiming Lands under grants of Different States made provision therefore, wisely calculated in the Articles of Confederation that in all controversies respecting the private right of soil in any State Claimed under grants of different States and which Claims have originated Antecedent to the settlement of Jurisdictional Territories the same shall be heard and finally Determined by a

Federal Court Constituted for that purpose and in the same manner as near as may be as Jurisdictional territories—the Articles of Confederation being Ratified by the Legislatures of the several States became the supreme Law of the Land—The Congress still retains that Power altho the Confederation may be inadequate to the exigencies of the national affair of the Union yet such deficiencies are not supposed to revoke or even to lessen any powers vested in the government of the United States by the Articles of Confederation, and all such Powers so vested in the Congress by the Confederation must be Esteemed Valid until revoked by the people of the United States, either by Alterations and Amendments as by the adoption of a New Constitution in lieu of the Confederation—hence we may infer that a Federal Court is the only Tribunal who have legal right to hear and finally determine controversies respecting the private right of soil in any State Claimed under grants of different States originating previous to the final settlement of Jurisdictional Territory —any Person or number of Individuals Claiming or Possessing any such Lands and being molested therein in any manner either by forceable entry and detainer made by opposing Claimants under grants of a different State or by being dispossessed by a Verdict or order of Court of common Law, held by and under the sole Authority of the State Claiming the Jurisdiction over the Territory have an undoubted right to an appeal to a federal Court for a hearing and final decision of any such controversies

Consequently the Proprietors settlers and owners of Lands in the Susqʰ Purchace under the Connecticut Claim, in case of being molested in occupying and Improving in any manner dispossessed of any such Lands by opposing claimants in consequence of interfering claims under grants of the state of Pennsylvania; have a legal right at their option to apply for, or appeal to a Federal Court for a hearing and decision of such controversies who are the sole Legal Tribunal having right to take Cognisance thereof, and who have a Legal right to hear and finally Determine the same.

INDEX

Baker, Jeremiah: 16, 109, 198.
Baker, William: 16.
Baldwin, Isaac: 197, 209.
Baldwin, Isaac, Jr.: 197.
Baldwin, Thomas: 197, 308.
Baldwin, Waterman: 43, 198, 216, 223 and n, 224 and n, 226, 232.
Balliet, Stephen: 92 n, 93 n, 95, 149 and n, 150, 152, 153, 168, 372 n, 401 and n, 472 and n; and Wyoming roads, 181; appointed commissioner, 389.
Barlow, Joel: 74, 132 and n, 133 and n.
Barnes, Stephen: 373 n.
Bartlett, Eben: 311.
Bates, Caleb: 26, 108.
Bayard, John: 133.
Beach, Abner: 26.
Beach, Alexander: 26.
Beach, Zerah: xxv, xxvii, xxviii, xxxii, 38 and n, 116 and n, 169 and n, 180, 192, 216, 233, 242, 243, 249 n, 252, 255, 259, 260 n, 264 n, 272, 304, 309, 394, 461, 512 n, 514, 515; and independent state, 179; and half-share men, 182; arrest of, sought, 205, 207; defends Susquehannah Company, 260 ff.; arraigned, 513; indicted for high treason, 517.
Bear Creek: 235.
Bedford: 24 n.
Bennet, Capt. ———: 440.
Bennet, Amos: 107.
Bennet, Andrew: 108.
Bennet (Bennett), Asa: 19, 106, 114, 123, 300.
Bennet, Charles: 107, 114.
Bennet, Elijah: 106, 198.
Bennet (Benett), Elisha: 107, 110.
Bennet, Ezra: 198.
Bennet, Isaac: 16, 107.
Bennet, Ishmael: 127, 197.
Bennet, Ishmael, Jr.: 108, 123, 198.
Bennet (Benett), Joshua: 110.
Bennet, Oliver: 16, 107.
Bennet, Rufus: 106, 114, 123.
Bennet (Benit), Solomon: 217, 316.
Bennet (Bennett), Thomas: 34, 39, 108, 123, 252, 480, 484, 512.
Benton, Caleb: xxiii, xxvi, xxix, xxx, xxxiv, 147, 157 and n, 187, 192, 193, 230 and n, 234, 236 n, 246, 461, 524; and York Lessee Company conspiracy, 171 n.
Bentonsborough: 193.
Bethlehem: 59.

Bewelman, Samuel: 217.
Biddle, Charles: 124, 166 n, 171 n, 177, 205, 225 n, 230 and n, 250, 385, 396, 398, 438, 455, 506.
Bidlack, Benjamin: 107, 197.
Bidlack, James: 109, 124, 250, 373 n, 484.
Bidlack, Shubal: 402.
Bidwell, Barnabas: and Cyrus Griffin letter, 133 and n.
Bigelow, John: 110.
Bigelow, Oliver: 123, 197.
Billings, Increase: 13, 14, 23, 107.
Billings, Increase, Jr.: 27, 107.
Billings, Ransler: 27.
Bingham, [Charles?]: 53.
Bingham, Charles: 106.
Bingham, Chester: 15, 123, 216.
Birney, Henry: 15.
Blackman, Eleazar: 15, 107.
Blackman, Elisha: 15, 107, 123, 480.
Blackman, Elisha, Jr.: 15, 107.
Blackman, Ichabod: 107, 123.
Blackmer, Isaac: 444 n.
Blackstone, Sir William: *Commentaries on the Laws of England*, 80 and n.
Blakeley, ———: 150.
Blanchard, Jeremiah: 15, 27, 108.
Blanchard, John: 287.
Blancher [Blanchard?], Leban: 109.
Board of property (of Pennsylvania): 86 and n, 103.
Boundaries: of Pennsylvania, 1, 528; between Luzerne and Northumberland counties, 202 n; New York and Pennsylvania, 203, 240 n; of Luzerne County, 308 and n; of Connecticut, 527.
Bowman, Ebenezer: xxix, 168, 224, 231, 242 f., 247 f., 268 f., 286, 335, 378, 380, 386, 388; requests certain books and forms, 271.
Boyce, James: 108.
Boyd, John: 42 and n, 43, 52, 99 n.
Boyd, Julian P.: xxv n.
Bradford, Thomas: xxxii, 60, 476, 511 f., 514.
Bradford, William, Jr.: terms Franklin-Hamilton letters not essential to trial, 511 and n.
Braintrim: 240; *see also* Meshoppen.
Brearley (Brearly), David: 51, 59.
Breed, John M.: 238 and n.
Brink, Benjamin B.: 14, 27.
Brink, Nicholas: 14 and n, 37.

Brink, Thomas: 109.
Broadhead, Garret: 306 n.
Brockway, Richard: 108, 123.
Brokaw (Brohaw), Abraham: 217.
Brown, Benjamin: 107, 114.
Brown, David: 108, 114.
Brown, Enos: 107.
Brown, Enos, Jr.: 107.
Brown, Humphrey: 123.
Brown, James: 15, 27, 108.
Brown, James, Jr.: 15, 27, 108.
Brown, Moses: 123.
Brown, Robert: 26 n, 73, 87.
Brown, Thomas: 123, 217.
Bryan, George: 175 n, 455 n, 468.
Bryan, James: 264, 387.
Bryant, Prince: 217.
Buck, ———: 312.
Buck, Elijah: 105 n, 106, 110, 111, 125, 179.
Buck, Henry: 12, 14.
Budd, Frederick: 123, 197, 394, 412, 418, 420, 437, 440, 477, 489; indicted, 480.
Budd, John: 15, 27, 108.
Buffalo Creek: 241.
Bullock's tavern: 59.
Bunell, Jonathan: 198.
Burble, ———: 104.
Burd, Edward: 376 and n.
Burkhalter, Peter: 493 n.
Burn, Richard: *The Justice of the Peace and Parish Officer,* 80 and n, 271 n.
Burrite (Burrity), Peleg: 197.
Burrite (Burrity), Stephen: 197.
Burvilt, Stephen: 16.
Bush, Henry: 416 n.
Butler, John: 171 and n.
Butler, Lord: xxi, 18 and n, 91, 108, 117 n, 149, 174, 222 and n, 239, 378, 401, 481, 511; elected sheriff, 20, 57, 243 and n; secretary of Susquehannah Company commissioners, 119, 122; criticized, 270 and n.
Butler, Zebulon: xvii, xviii, xx, xxiv, xxviii, xli, xliii n, xliv, 2 and n, 5, 6 and n, 8, 12, 13, 18 and n, 19, 31, 33, 38, 39, 44, 46, 48, 50, 51 n, 52, 56, 58, 62, 66, 70, 71, 73, 76, 88 and n, 90, 95, 97, 106, 113, 119, 125, 129 n, 174, 189, 190, 209, 210, 226, 238 n, 241, 252, 255 n, 266, 300, 308 and n, 381, 384 n, 390, 395, 402, 403, 423, 450 n, 512; berated, 75; John Franklin on, 117; commissioned lieutenant of Luzerne

County, 171 and n, 176, 180 and n; and bail for John Franklin, 227, 380; implicated in new state conspiracy, 254; on Luzerne militia, 265, 479 and n, 509 *f.;* accusations against, 265, 312 *ff.,* 454, 469, 478; and pamphlet on Constitution, 270; reports on rioters, 399 *f.,* 438 *ff.;* wants "examination" of his conduct made public, 426.
Butler, Mrs. Zebulon: 6, 190.

— C —

Cady, ———: 156.
Cady, Zebulon: 26, 198, 394, 396, 397 and n, 412, 418, 428, 437, 443, 489; indicted, 480; pleads guilty, 516; convicted, 518.
Caler, Thomas P.: 109.
Campbell, Daniel (Othniel): 26, 27, 198, 217.
Campbell, John: 107.
Canadesago Lake: 416.
Capouse (Capows): 62, 67.
Carey, [Barnabas?]: 49, 66.
Carey (Cary), Barnabas: 16, 27, 108, 111.
Carllinghouse, John: 107.
Carney, William: 412, 431, 432, 434, 436, 437, 438, 443, 445, 473, 477, 490.
Carpenter, Benjamin: 16, 19, 109, 124 and n, 127 n, 373 n, 383, 385, 417, 421 and n, 422, 445, 470, 472, 480, 512, 519 n, 521; elected justice of the peace, 116 n.
Carpenter, Gilbert: 16.
Carver, Jonathan: 109.
Cary, Benjamin: 16, 106.
Cary, Comfort (Cofort): 107.
Cary (Carey, Caray), John: 106, 108, 114.
Cary, Nathan: 19, 21, 106, 494; elected coroner, 57.
Cary (Carey), Seth: 27, 108.
Catlin, Putnam: 255 and n, 426 and n.
Chadwick, Asa: 417.
Chambers, John: 406.
Chambery, Peter: 109.
Chapman, ———: 117.
Chapman, Nathaniel: 484.
Charles, George: 14, 57.
Charters: Pickering defines, 528; and law of "uninterrupted possession," 529; New England, and treaty of peace, 534 and n; *see also separate entries.*

Edwards, Pierpont: 423 n, **424**, 425, 426 n.
Egelson, Amos: 26, 108.
Ejectments: 3, 35, 130, 544.
Elections (Luzerne County): xvii, xx and n, xxi, xxxiii, 2 and n, 9, 13, 37, 62, 106 n, 110, 149, 196, 235; Pickering on, 3, 7, 32, 34, 38, 45, 76, 192, 297, 510; William Judd warns settlers against, 6 and n; William Hooker Smith on, 11 n, 12, 111, 112; officials for, listed, 17, 18; results of, 18 and n, 19, 20, 57; John Van Campen on, 22; John Jenkins on, 40; acceptance of, 50, 53, 56, 104 and n, 106, 109, 224, 227, 239, 243, 245; John Paul Schott on, 54; and violence, 57; of justices of the peace, 58, 95, 96, 97, 102, 113, 127, 140, 196, 519, 520; Benjamin Franklin on, 68; John Franklin on, 103; Nathan Denison on, 115, 125; bill on, 201 and n; Lord Butler on, 222; of military officers, 243, 248, 253 n, 254, 268, 308 and n, 459, 479.
Ellicott, Andrew: xli, 375 and n, 378 and n, 388, 391, 395, 441, 456, 457 n, 466, 522 and n; deposition of, 394 *ff.*, 398 n.
Elliot, Joseph: 123, 209, 480.
Ellis (Eliss), Christopher: 107.
Ellis, Ebenezer: 17.
Ellis, Ebenezer, Jr.: 17.
Ellsworth, ———: 206.
Ellsworth, Oliver: 142.
Elster, Casper: 12, 17 n, 26, 108.
Enos, [Ebenezer?]: 39.
Enos (Ennos), Ebenezer: 15, 108.
Enos, Job (Joab): 16, 110.
Erwin, ——— : 141.
Esland, James: 16.
Evans, ———: 384.
Evans, Edward: 330.
Evans, Griffith: xxiv and n, 162, 188, 228, 246.
Evans (Evens), Luke: 109.
Evans (Evens), Nathaniel: 109.
Evans, Samuel: 252 n, 303, 306, 334.
Eves, Josiah: 484.
Eves, Josiah, Jr.: 484.
Ewing, John: 37.
Exeter: 24 n, 34, 109, 122 n, 233.

— F —

Fanning, James: 197, 217 and n, 514, 515.

Farman, ———: 330.
Farmers, Col. ———: 192.
Faulkner, Robert: juror, 513.
Fell, Jesse: 373, 512.
Finch, John: 197.
Finch, Samuel: 109, 114.
Findley, William: 26 n, 73, 82, 87, 183 and n, 279 n, 281, 292 n, 295 n, 297 n, 301 n, 307 n, 328 n, 334, 337 n, 358; and Confirming Act, xxxv, xxxvii, 275, 287 and n, 288 *ff.*, 289, 290, 292, 293, 296 n, 347, 348, 351; and half-share men, 293 and n, 302, 303 n; and proposed new confirming act, 360, 361.
Finn, Rev. James: 44, 108.
Fish, Jabez: 19, 106, 300, 480, 512.
Fishing Creek: 179.
Fitch [Fish?], Jabez: 20.
Fitzsimons, Thomas: xxxiv, 204, 281 n, 287 n, 301 n, 304, 306, 357; and Pennsylvania landholders in Wyoming, xxxvi, 201 and n; and Confirming Act, 200, 277, 290, 293, 295, 350, 351, 352; on compensation to Pennamites, 201; and military measures, 278; on half-share men, 294; and suspending bill, 358, 359.
Flenniken, John: 87.
Follet, ———: 116.
Fort Allen: 273 n.
Fort Augusta: 405.
Fort Harmar: treaty of, 499 and n.
Forty Fort: xx, 48 and n, 53, 58, 104 n, 219, 232, 489; John Franklin's speech at, 102.
Foster, Isaac: 197.
Francis, Tench: 150 and n, 151 and n, 165, 176, 302, 328, 330, 333, 336 and n, 369, 374.
Franklin, Benjamin: xxviii, xxxiii n, xlv, 91, 126, 127, 133, 147, 148, 162, 180, 226, 231 n, 236, 238, 369, 399 and n, 404, 412, 415, 427, 432, 436 n, 479, 497, 507, 510 and n; on Luzerne County elections, 68; on arrearages due on state lands, 68; forwards Confirming Act to governor of Connecticut, 101; requests Governor Clinton's co-operation, 202, 229 and n; wants warrants held up, 235; on arrest of Joseph Hamilton, 247; instructs militia regarding treatment of Luzerne settlers, 273.
Franklin, Jehiel: 197, 209 and n, 514.

553

Gore, Obadiah (*cont.*)
  state issue, xxvi; and county
  elections, 101, 102 n, 104, 223;
  loyalties of, 186 n; wants to be
  deputy surveyor for Luzerne,
  271; on maintaining troops in
  Luzerne, 311.
Gore, Samuel: 27, 216.
Gorsburgh (Goresborough, Goresburg) : 186 n, 193.
Government: inhabitants of Luzerne County support, 106 *ff.*; introduction of, in Luzerne County,
  126 *f.*; Pennamite view of functions of, 134 *ff.*; Pickering sees
  need for, 154.
Grand jury (of Luzerne County) :
  Pickering's charge to, 177 *f.*; in-
  dicts John Franklin, 192; and
  Pickering's abduction, 468, 480;
  for Franklin's trial, named, 512,
  513; conduct of, praised, 517;
  and Jenkins' conviction, 519.
Gray, Ebenezer: xxiv, xxx, 190 n;
  and confirmation of his claim,
  189 and n, 266.
Gray, Samuel: xxiv, 190 n.
Gray, William: 372, 379.
Great Bend: holdings at, 150 and
  n, 165, 173, 176, 214, 232, 336 n,
  368 and n.
Great Britain: and York Lessee
  conspiracy, xxvi, 171, 241; op-
  pressiveness of, compared to that
  of Confirming Act, 136; and Sus-
  quehannah Company, 260, 305.
Great Swamp (in Wyoming) : 30,
  93, 94, 126 n, 252, 436.
Green, ———: 179.
Gridley, Daniel: 16, 106.
Griffin, Cyrus: 59, 133 and n.
Griffith, William: 27, 468, 469.
Griste, John: 109.
Griswold, Elijah: 197.
Griswold, Gov. Matthew: 133.
Grove, Avery: 216.
Gurney, Francis: 487.

— H —

Hageman, John: 15, 106, 113, 124
  and n, 512.
Hageman, Joseph: 15, 107.
Haines, Reuben: 302, 330.
Half-share men: xxiii n., xxvii,
  154, 156, 182, 347, 359, 374, 381,
  449, 454, 458, 469, 483; and John
  Franklin, xxxii; and old settlers,
  xxxvii, 240, 382, 460, 461, 462
  and n; summoned to meet, 209;

Pickering on, 245, 258, 376, 429;
  Obadiah Gore on, 267, 311; and
  William Findley, 293 and n, 303;
  Thomas Fitzsimons on, 294; and
  election of military officers, 308;
  and Assembly, 309; and Picker-
  ing's abduction, 401.
Half-share rights: 379, 395, 429,
  445, 455, 461, 462.
Hall, John: 156.
Hall, William: 26, 108.
Haller's tavern: 8, 29, 59, 246.
Hallsted (Halsted), Joseph: 108.
Hallsted (Hallstead), Richard: 17,
  19, 26, 108.
Hallsted (Halsted), Richard, Jr.:
  27, 108.
Hallsted (Halsted, Holsted), Samuel: 108, 311.
Halsted, Isaiah: 27, 310.
Hamilton, Joseph: xxi, xxviii,
  xxix, xxx, xxxii, xxxiv, 5 n, 116,
  169 n, 187, 230 and n, 234, 236 n,
  246, 251 n, 258 n, 264 n, 266, 338 n,
  387, 388 n, 412 n, 461, 509 and n,
  523; Susquehannah Company
  commissioner, xxiii; and separa-
  rate state issue, 52 and n; on
  Susquehannah Company towns,
  184 and n; berates Franklin for
  nonaction, 185, 186, 188; arrest
  of, 247, 250.
Hamilton (town) : xxiii, 147 n,
  193.
Hammond, Lebeus: 16, 216.
Hanover: 24 n, 120, 209, 298.
Harbeson, ———: 156.
Harding (Hardin), Abraham: 26,
  108 and n, 114.
Harding, Amos: 27, 108.
Harding, Daniel: 108.
Harding, Elisha: 26, 198.
Harding, Henry: 108.
Harding, John: 110, 311.
Harding, Joseph: 26.
Harding, Stephen: 16, 480.
Harding, Thomas: 20, 26, 108, 197.
Harris, Charles: 198.
Harris, Elijah: 198.
Harris, Jonathan: 216.
Harris, Jonathan, Jr.: 217.
Harris, Thomas: 467, 473.
Hartseph (Hartsoff), Capt.
  ———: 377, 402.
Hartsouf (Heartsouf), Lewis:
  109.
Hartsouf, Zacharias: 109.
Harvey, Benjamin: 52, 56, 110,
  123, 432, 436, 494.

Harvey, Eleshar: 109.
Hawley, Daniel: 21.
Hazen, Nathan: 109.
Heath, Thomas: 197.
Heberd (Hibbert, Hibbard, Hybert), William: 107, 114, 123, 402, 404.
Heister, Gabriel: 252 and n, 303, 334.
Heller (Hellar), Stephen: 197.
Henry, ———: 173.
Herinton, Reubin: 315, 316 n.
Herrington (Herinton), Jacob: 217, 316.
Herrington, Nathan: 216.
Herrington, Nathan, Jr.: 217.
Hiester, Daniel: 83 n, 149 and n, 152, 153, 162; and resignation as Wyoming commissioner, xxii, 161, 163.
Hiester, Joseph: 87.
Higginson, Mrs. ———: 77.
Hilborn, John: 375, 377.
Hillman, Joseph: 109.
Hodgdon, Samuel: xxii, xxvi, xxviii, xl, xliii, 7, 10 and n, 37, 45, 77, 116, 140, 144 and n, 153, 158, 168, 170, 181, 193, 243, 319 n, 335 n, 337, 379 n, 390, 391 n, 392, 446, 449, 464, 466, 472, 475, 516; on Wyoming commissioners, 150, 152, 165; on Great Bend holdings, 150 and n, 151, 165, 176, 522; on transportation of Pickering's goods, 151, 152, 176; on opening a store in Wyoming, 152, 164, 176; on John Franklin, 163, 222, 223, 373 n; on York Lessees informer, 166 and n; on militia in Luzerne County, 175, 176; on Assembly's approval of Pickering's conduct, 183; and Confirming Act, 204, 353, 354, 521; on a "secession" from Assembly, 221; on discovery of a new tract, 221; briefs Pickering on Assembly membership, 250; on legislation for compensating Pennamites, 335, 522; on landholders' road program, 336, 388, 522; on ordering troops to march to Ohio, 452 n, 465.
Hoge, Jonathan: 507 n.
Holbrook, David: 193, 197.
Holcom, Stephen: 106.
Holcomb, Joel: 109, 123, 484 and n.
Hollenback (Holleback), John: 14, 19, 20, 31, 42, 56, 60 n, 106, 156,
217, 219, 396, 454, 467, 468 n, 492 n, 512.
Hollenback (Holleback), Mathias (Matthew): xvi, xxi, xxxi, 14, 18, 29, 30, 44, 59, 60, 107, 127 n, 149 and n, 153, 161, 168, 172, 179, 181, 192, 195, 223, 248, 263, 270, 272, 300, 380, 384, 387, 480, 490, 492, 512, 514, 519 n, 523 n, 525; elected justice of the peace, 116 and n; John Franklin on, 117; and Susquehannah Company, 120; reports on maintaining troops in Luzerne, 311.
Hollingsworth, Levi: 302, 330.
Holly (Holley), Daniel: 12, 14, 26, 107.
Hopkins, Timothy: 109.
Hopper, Cornelius (Cornel): 26, 198.
Horton, John: 197.
Horton, William: 151, 173, 244, 390.
Hosmer, Timothy: xvii, xxvi, 21 and n, 22.
Hosmer, Titus: and talk of a new state, 457.
Houston, William C.: 59.
Hover, John: 13, 26, 107.
Hover, Samuel: 1 and n, 12, 13, 19, 32, 56, 63, 107.
Howell, Isaiah: 16, 107.
Howell, Samuel: 330.
Hubley, Adam: 26 n, 73, 75.
Hudson (N.Y.): 5 and n, 101, 169 and n, 171, 182, 183, 184, 236 and n, 247, 338 and n, 386.
Hunt, Aaron: 107, 123.
Huntington, Benjamin: 426 n.
Huntington, Jedidiah: 143.
Huntington, Gov. Samuel: 82 n, 101, 118 n, 465 n, 510 and n; and Confirming Act, xlv, 126, 508; and John Franklin, xlv, 324 and n, 507 and n, 508.
Huntington (town): 24 n, 299, 308, 472, 521.
Hurlbut, Christopher: xx, 17, 18 and n, 19, 20, 32, 40, 53, 58, 59, 95 and n, 96, 97 n, 107, 108 n, 112, 113, 115, 269, 312, 457 and n, 494, 513; elected commissioner, 57; gives reason for not signing settlers' petition, 69; elected justice of the peace, 116 and n.
Hurlbut, John: 18, 19, 20, 197, 373 n, 494.
Hurlbut, William: 27, 107, 122, 198.

Hutchenson, James: 330.
Huydon, David: 198.
Hyde (Hide), Jedidiah: 77 and n.
Hyde, John: 18, 19, 20, 107, 114, 121, 394, 396, 397, 418, 509.
Hyde, John, Jr.: 198, 409 *f.*, 410 *ff.*, 420, 422, 432, 437, 440, 441, 445, 467, 469, 470, 471, 476, 482, 489; denies Zebulon Butler's complicity, 469, 478; indicted, 480.
Hyde, Peleg: 77 n, 90.
Hyde, William: 15, 107, 198, 384.

— I —

Independent state: *see* New state movement.
Indians: and York Lessee Company, xxvi, 171 n, 416, 478; and pre-emption issue, 10; and Susquehannah purchase, 35, 51, 100 and n, 141, 528, 533 n; and Pennsylvania purchases, 69 and n, 86 and n, 129, 158, 522 n; and half-share men, 241; 1783 uprising of, 317 n; 1784 Pennsylvania purchase from, 331 n; and road program, 332; and right of soil issue, 530; Pickering on Susquehannah Company deed from, 534 and n, 535.
Ingersoll, Daniel: 109.
Ingersoll, David: 198.
Inman, Edward: 15, 107.
Inman, Elijah: 107, 198.
Inman, John: 14, 20.
Inman, Richard: 123, 198.
Irvin, ———: 158, 161.
Irvin, Isaac: 27.
Irvine, ———: 236.
Irvine, William: 208, 247, 412 and n, 414, 423 n, 424, 425.
Ives, Benjamin: 198.
Ives, Timothy: 198.
Ives, Titus: 198.

— J —

Jacason [Jacobson?], Silv(a): 107.
Jackson, Capt. ———: 373.
Jackson, Asa: 108.
Jackson, Philip: 108.
Jackson, Samuel: 272.
Jackson, Silas: 12.
Jackson, William: 12, 14, 20, 27, 107.
Jackways (Jackays), William: 15, 123, 197.

Jacob's Plains: 20 n, 33, 37, 66, 122 n; inhabitants of, supporting Pennsylvania laws, listed, 108.
James, Alexander: 107, 197.
Jameson, [Abigail?]: 41.
Jameson, Joseph: 123.
Jenkins, Benjamin: 20.
Jenkins, John: xix, xxv, xxvii, 6, 9 n, 18, 19, 21, 32, 35 and n, 54, 55, 74 and n, 119 and n, 121, 122, 123, 158, 169, 180, 197, 205, 208, 224 and n, 249 n, 308, 376, 397, 416, 426, 435, 440, 460, 465, 468, 479 and n, 494; and half-share men, xxiii; and Pickering's abduction, xliii, 395, 418, 419, 420, 431, 443, 444, 463, 471, 473, 477, 478, 483, 488, 489; and oath of allegiance, 34, 212 n; and validity of Susquehannah purchase, 36; and Luzerne County elections, 40, 48, 53 and n, 104, 105, 112; calls law for erecting Luzerne County unconstitutional, 44; and new state issue, 179; continues to survey Susquehannah Company land, 191; ordered seized, 207; Pickering on, 258 and n, 379, 519; security for John Franklin, 373, 495 and n; and York Lessees, 433; elected lieutenant colonel, 459; arraigned, 513.
Jenkins, Stephen: 16, 54, 123, 198, 431, 472 n, 498; and Pickering's abduction, 418, 469 and n, 470, 478, 488, 490; jailed, 435; convicted and fined, 517, 518.
Jenkins, Steubin: 53 n.
Jenkins, Wilkes: 396, 397, 412, 418, 437, 489; indicted, 480.
Jenkins, William: 104, 117, 123, 197; and Pickering's abduction, 179.
Jennings, John: 317 n.
Johnson, Francis: 330.
Johnson, Rev. Jacob: 27 and n, 28, 29, 38 and n; favors the Susquehannah Company claim, 50, 51; and Luzerne elections, 54.
Johnson, Jacob, Jr.: 107.
Johnson, James: 507 n.
Johnson, Jehoiada P.: 15, 107.
Johnson, John: 15, 107.
Johnson, William Samuel: 35 n, 42, 60, 61 n, 89 n, 142, 219 and n, 534 n.

Lewis, William: 295 n, 296 n, 334, 353; debates changes in Confirming Act, 281 f., 355 ff.
Light Dragoons: 510 n.
Lincoln, Benjamin: 21, 89 and n.
Litton, James: 498.
Livingston, John: and York Lessees' conspiracy, 171 and n, 176, 304, 416, 420, 432.
Livingston, Gov. William: 399 n.
Lloyd, Peter Z.: 86, 363, 367.
Logan, George: 349, 493 n, 494, 495.
Lollar, Robert: 296 n, 334.
Lone, Nicholas: 124.
Loots, Conrad: 108.
Lord, Leonard: 110.
Lott, Leonard: 14, 21, 27.
Lowns, Joseph: 330.
Lowrey, Alexander: 252 and n, 303, 334, 356.
Loyes, Conrad: 107.
Lucas, Abraham: 108.
Luce, ———: 30.
Luce's tavern: 59.
Lukens, Jesse: 146 and n.
Lukens, John: 151, 225, 371, 372.
Lutz (Lutsee), John: 15.
Luzerne County: and Continental troops, xxxiii, 242; and oaths of allegiance, xxxv; and speculators, xxxviii; and elections, 2 and n, 6 n, 106 ff., 383, 384; and Confirming Act, 82; remonstrance of, against Joseph Montgomery, 139 f.; remonstrance of, against William Montgomery, 195 ff.; permanent military force in, debated, 273 ff.; records and surveys of, needed, 371; total land acreage of Pennamites in, 372 n; new commissioners appointed to report on, 389; see also Connecticut settlers, Elections, Government, and Militia.

— M —

McClean, Moses: 103 n, 405.
McCluer, John: 216.
McClure (McCluer), Thomas: 123, 179, 183, 197, 216 and n.
McConnell, Matthew: 151 and n.
McCormick, David: 15, 34, 108, 197, 384.
McCormick, Henry: 14, 108.
McDaniel, Cornelius: 216.

McDowell, John: 287, 302, 334, 507 n; and Confirming Act, 87.
McDowell (McDowel), Robert: 19, 108, 114.
McGeringer, Zachias: 114.
McKay, Ephraim: 198.
McKean, Thomas: 175 and n, 234 n, 376 n, 455 n, 475, 481, 495; on bail for John Franklin, 372, 373; recommends abductors be prosecuted for a riot, 455.
McKinstry (McInster), John: xxiii, xxv, xxvii, xxviii, 180 and n, 205, 216, 233, 236 n, 242, 249 n, 255, 259, 261, 272, 304, 309, 394, 416 and n, 420 and n, 432, 452 and n, 457, 477, 478 n, 515, 525; implicated in plotting a new state, 179; and half-share men, 182; ordered seized, 207; arraigned, 513; indicted, 517.
Maclay, Samuel: 358, 360 n, 362 n, 504 n, 505 n; proposes new confirming act, xxxviii, 355; and quantity of land in seventeen towns, 361; and compensation for Pennamites, 362.
Maclay, William: 331.
McLene, James: xl, 55, 250, 252 n, 275, 282 n, 289, 303, 304, 334, 337 n, 356, 357, 368 n, 507 n; and Confirming Act, xxxvii, xxxviii, 306, 338, 352, 355, 359, 362; on use of Continental troops, 273, 274; and compensation of Pennamites, 305; amendment of, to proposed new confirming act, 365.
McNair, J.: 512.
Mahoopenny Creek: 408.
Makem, James: 198.
Man, Adam: 106, 114.
Mangin, John, Jr.: 198.
Manvil (Manville), Ira: 15, 109, 198, 410, 412, 416 n, 418, 420, 421, 437, 478, 480, 489, 492, 497; warrant issued for, 421 n; pleads guilty, 481; admitted to bail, 482.
Manvil, John: 123.
Marchell, Joseph: 216.
Marcy (Mercy), Ebenezer: 19, 62, 66, 108, 111, 193, 221, 460, 475; elected justice of the peace, 116 and n; ouster of, 152 and n, 154 and n, 164, 464.
Marcy, John: 26.

Parks, Darius (*cont.*)
  n, 471, 472, 473, 490; fined and
  convicted, 517, 518.
Parks (Park), Thomas: 109.
Parshals, Israel: 108.
Parsons, Samuel Holden: 346 and
  n, 499 and n.
Parsons, Uriah: 445 and n, 472 n.
Patrick, Jacob: 480.
Patrick, Joseph: 109.
Patrick, Joshua: 123.
Patterson, Abijah: 27.
Patterson, Alexander: 37, 49 and
  n, 52, 57, 99, 302 n.
Patterson, William: 147.
Pease, Asa: 197.
Peirce (Pierce), Abel: 19, 108,
  119, 124.
Peirce, Daniel: 109.
Peirce, John: 109, 271.
Peirce (Pierce), Pelatiah: 109.
Peirce (Pearce, Perce), Timothy:
  12, 14, 26, 108.
Penn, John: 317.
Penn, William: 51, 513, 529;
  charter, 530, 538.
Pennamites: xvii, xxxix, 43, 44,
  154, 158, 302 n, 385, 454, 467,
  468 n; opposition to Confirming
  Act, xxxiv, xxxv, 133 *ff.;* and
  issue of compensation, xxxv,
  xxxvii, xxxviii, 284 n, 304 n, 334,
  337; at Luzerne County elections, 56; Pickering on, 210;
  see also Pennsylvania claimants
  and Pennsylvania settlers.
Pennsylvania claim: 10 *f.,* 527, 529,
  530, 532, 536-37, 538.
Pennsylvania claimants: xvi, xl,
  35, 139 n, 148 n, 161, 189, 195,
  196, 205, 238, 260 n, 295, 318 n,
  354, 366 n, 401 n, 405 and n; and
  Confirming Act, xix, 133 *ff.,* 351;
  and compensation issue, xxxviii,
  86, 304 n, 305, 334; ask Council
  to halt acceptance of claims in
  Luzerne and Northampton counties, 148; in seventeen towns, 502
  and n, 505; *see also* Pennsylvania
  settlers *and* Pennamites.
Pennsylvania Council: xxii, xxvi,
  xxx, xxxviii, 4, 76, 81, 87, 92,
  104, 118, 125, 139, 166 n, 170, 180
  and n, 199, 208, 225, 273 n, 324 n,
  364, 366 n, 371 n, 373 n, 379 n,
  387, 412 n, 416, 418 n, 423, 424,
  450, 452 n, 465, 468, 475, 497,
  498 n, 505, 510; and Confirming

Act, xix, 148, 265; and Pickering's abduction, xliii, 390, 397,
  410-12, 438, 455 and n, 519 and
  n; and justices for Luzerne
  County, 127 n, 310, 312 n; and
  petition from inhabitants of Easton, 134, 144, 145: and New
  York's cooperation, 202, 398,
  399; and John Franklin's arrest
  and bail, 205 n, 230, 323, 370 and
  n, 457; dispatches Nathan Denison to investigate Wyoming situation, 237; and state militia, 238,
  242, 251; and new state issue,
  251; on renewal of disturbances
  in Wyoming, 251; and Continental troops, 252, 253 n, 413, 415 n,
  450 n; on a permanent military
  post in Luzerne County, 264 and
  n, 274, 285; and Pennamites'
  compensation, 305, 404-06; and
  Butler censure, 312; and Luzerne
  County elections, 315, 479 and n;
  Pickering's criticism of, 428.
Pennsylvania General Assembly:
  xvi, xix, xxii, xxxv, xxxvii, xl,
  2, 3, 4, 40, 50, 72, 75 n, 76, 80, 88,
  104, 113, 133 n, 139, 140, 148 and
  n, 183, 192 n, 200 and n, 201 n,
  220, 250, 251, 253 n, 264, 273 n,
  287 and n, 318 n, 319 n, 353 n,
  389, 404, 449, 475, 484 n, 486, 499,
  500; and issue of compensating
  Pennamites, xxxiv, xxxviii,
  304 n, 305, 306 n; and roads, 46,
  328 n, 336; on Luzerne County
  elections, 68; committee of, favors confirming settlers' titles,
  73 *ff.;* appointment of commissioners by, called unconstitutional, 87; and "secession" in-
  cident, 221; committee of, on
  Wyoming disturbances, 251 n;
  committee of, favors retaining
  Confirming Act, 260 n; on raising troops, 273 *ff.;* and changes
  in Confirming Act, 283 *f.,* 288 *ff.,*
  302 *ff.,* 305 *f.,* 306 *ff.,* 333 *f.;* on
  half-share men, 303 n; and issue
  of bail for John Franklin, 324 n,
  493, 494; debates suspension of
  Confirming Act, 338 *ff.,* 354 *ff.;*
  enacts Suspending Act, 366 n;
  quashes consideration of new
  confirming act, 507 and n.
Pennsylvania landholders: xxxvi,
  339, 340, 345, 348, 349, 359, 363,
  369, 375, 441 n, 457 n, 465 n, 522;

Pickering, Timothy (*cont.*)
17, 34, 114; journals, 29 *ff.*,
406 *ff.;* on Susquehannah Company claim, 35 and n, 36, 51, 143,
446, 526-34; on Pennamites, 37,
210, 534; on taxes, 37, 45; on
Ethan Allen, 38; on John Jenkins,
44, 376, 379; on use of title of
"colonel," 46; on move to Wyoming, 47, 76, 77, 80, 172, 181; on
Trenton trial, 48, 446 and n. 526 *f.*,
530; on laws of Nature, 55; sells
Salem, Mass., property, 80, 445;
on roads, 92, 93, 94, 126; and
kidnap threats, 112, 169, 218,
233; on Luzerne County courts,
140, 141, 147, 335; on New York
State and law enforcement in
Luzerne, 154; on starting a country store in Wyoming, 155, 172,
194; considered for governorship
of Northwest Territory, 159 and
n; on domestic affairs, 160, 161,
174, 223, 224; on a permanent
military post in Wyoming, 171,
256, 258, 428, 462, 467; on his
land holdings in Wyoming, 173,
191 n, 214, 232, 300, 373, 374; instructs Luzerne County grand
jury, 177-78; on need for a jail,
192 and n; orders a volume by
Noah Webster, 194 and n; protests over threats to his wife,
217; sees Pennsylvania using
force if opposed, 219; on Continental troops, 245, 466; on William Judd's influence, 257; on
Pennsylvania's "impolitic measures," 286; outlines acreage allotment of early Wyoming townships, 299; on effect of new
boundaries of Luzerne County,
299; and issue of pitches, 307 n,
501 and n, 502; and loss of a
"Great Coat" and a watch, 386,
387; on trial and punishment of
abductors, 393, 394, 411 and n,
417 and n, 418, 421-22, 477, 480,
485, 488, 511, 516, 517, 518, 519;
and rewards, 397, 427, 497, 498,
518, 519; on farming practices,
407, 408; berates government for
its policies, 428 *ff.;* Council's curt
reply to, 455 and n; wants justices commissioned quickly, 519;
prefers Noah Murray for justice
of the peace, 520.
Pickering, Timothy, Jr.: 286.

Pickering, William: 286.
Picket, Thomas: 27.
Pickle, Perregreen: 63 and n.
Piper, John: 87, 252, 338, 339.
Pitches: xxxv, xxxix, 307 and n;
and proposed new confirming
act, 362 n; Tench Coxe on, 368;
Pickering on, 502, 503, 504, 506 n.
Pittstown: 24 n.
Platner, John: 17 n, 123.
Plymouth (Shawanese): 24 n, 122,
521.
Porter, Abijah: 107.
Porter, Andrew: 157, 164.
Potter, James: 374.
Pottman, John: 14, 57.
Powell, Samuel: 328, 330.
Pre-emption: and Trenton decree,
10 and n; as an issue in Wyoming controversy, 28, 51, 446 and
n, 527, 535.
Preston, Joseph: 123.
Price, Rev. Dr. Richard: xlii, 106,
392, 407.
Prices: of land, 78, 80, 336, 374; of
commodities, 152, 155, 164, 171-
72, 194; of road-building, 375.
Proclamations: 204, 391.
Prouty (Prowty), Edward: 13, 26,
107, 114.
Prouty, John: 13, 26.
Prouty, Stephen: 107.
Providence (Capous): 24 n, 122.
Putnam: 24 n, 310.
Pyke (Pike), Abraham: 17 n, 123,
198.

— Q —

Quebec Act: 534 n.
Queen Esther's Flats: 179.

— R —

Racer, Benjamin: 109.
Raillighport, Humphrey: 107.
Ransom, George Palmer: 109,
373 n, 402.
Rathbun, Joseph Avery: 123, 198.
Rawle, William: 372 n.
Rawson, Jonathan: 107.
Ray, James: 120.
Rea, Sampson: 7, 141, 151, 152,
159 and n, 162, 174, 176.
Read, Thomas: 26, 107, 124 and n.
Real Sufferer, A (pseudonym):
316 *ff.*
Redick, David: 229 and n, 230, 236,
396, 412 *ff.*, 510 *f.;* commissioned

565

567